THE FUNDAMENTALS
FOR THE
TWENTY-FIRST CENTURY

THE
FUNDAMENTALS
FOR THE
TWENTY-FIRST
CENTURY

Examining the Crucial Issues
of the Christian Faith

MAL COUCH
GENERAL EDITOR

kregel
PUBLICATIONS

Grand Rapids, MI 49501

The Fundamentals for the Twenty-First Century:
Examining the Crucial Issues of the Christian Faith

Published in 2000 by Kregel Publications, a division of Kregel, Inc., P.O. Box 2607, Grand Rapids, MI 49501. Kregel Publications provides trusted, biblical publications for Christian growth and service. Your comments and suggestions are valued.

Unless otherwise indicated, Scripture quotations are taken from the *New American Standard Bible.* © 1960, 1962, 1963, 1968, 1971, 1972, 1973, 1975, 1977, The Lockman Foundation. Used by permission.

Text marked KJV is from the King James Version of the Holy Bible.

Scripture quotations marked NIV are from the *Holy Bible, New International Version®.* © 1973, 1978, 1984 by International Bible Society. Used by permission of Zondervan Publishing House. All rights reserved.

Scripture quotations marked NKJV are from *The New King James Version.* © 1979, 1980, 1982, Thomas Nelson, Inc., Publishers.

For more information about Kregel Publications, visit our web site: www.kregel.com

Cover design: Frank Gutbrod

All views expressed in this work are solely those of the authors and do not represent or reflect the position or endorsement of any governmental agency or department, military or otherwise.

Library of Congress Cataloging-in-Publication Data
Couch, Mal.
  The fundamentals for the twenty-first century: examining the crucial issues of the Christian faith / by Mal Couch, general editor.
      p.   cm.
  Includes bibliographical references and index.
  1. Fundamentalism. 2. Theology, Doctrinal. I. Couch, Mal.
BT82.2. F865 1999 230'.04626 21—dc21 99-043086
ISBN 0-8254-2368-6

Printed in the United States of America

2 3 4 5 / 04 03 02 01 00

Contents

Contributors

Kerby Anderson, M.A., M.F.S., is president of Probe Ministries, based in Richardson, Texas. He is an author, lecturer, and radio commentator.

Paul N. Benware, Th.M., Th.D., is professor of Theology at Philadelphia College of Bible, Langhorne, Pennsylvania.

Mal Couch, M.A., Th.M., Th.D., Ph.D., D.D., is founder and president of Tyndale Theological Seminary and Biblical Institute in Fort Worth, Texas.

Timothy J. Demy, M.A., M.A., Th.M., Th.D., is a military chaplain, author, and Bible teacher who lives in Middletown, Rhode Island.

Thomas R. Edgar, Th.M., Th.D., is professor of New Testament Literature at Capital Bible Seminary, Lanham, Maryland.

Paul P. Enns, Th.M., Th.D., is a professor and director of extension for Southeastern Baptist Theological Seminary, Tampa, Florida.

Paul R. Fink, Th.M., Th.D., chairs the Department of Biblical Studies at Liberty Baptist University in Lynchburg, Virginia.

Harold D. Foos, Th.M., Th.D., is professor of Bible and Theology and chairman of the Department of Theology at Moody Bible Institute, Chicago, Illinois.

Arnold G. Fruchtenbaum, Th.M., Ph.D., is founder and director of Ariel Ministries, Tustin, California.

Robert G. Gromacki, Th.M., Th.D., is a pastor and distinguished professor of Bible and Greek at Cedarville College, Cedarville, Ohio.

Gary R. Habermas, M.A., Ph.D., D.D., is chairman of the Department of Philosophy and Theology at Liberty Baptist University, Lynchburg, Virginia.

Edward E. Hindson, M.A., Th.M., Th.D., D.Phil., is vice-president of There is Hope Ministry in Atlanta, Georgia, and an adjunct professor at Liberty Baptist University, Lynchburg, Virginia.

Henry Holloman, Th.D., is professor of Systematic Theology at Talbot School of Theology, LaMirada, California.

H. Wayne House, M.A., Th.M., M.Div., J.D., Th.D., is distinguished professor of Biblical Studies and Apologetics at Faith Seminary, Tacoma, Washington, and professor of Law at Trinity Law School, Santa Anna, California.

Thomas D. Ice, Th.M., Ph.D., directs the Pre-Trib Research Center in Arlington, Texas.

Beverly LaHaye is founder and chairman of Concerned Women for America. She lives in Rancho Mirage, California.

Tim LaHaye, D.Min., D.D., is an author and minister, president of Tim LaHaye Ministries, and chairman of the Pre-Trib Research Center. He lives in Rancho Mirage, California.

Robert P. Lightner, Th.M., Th.D., teaches theology at Tyndale Seminary in Fort Worth, Texas, and is professor emeritus of Systematic Theology at Dallas Theological Seminary in Dallas, Texas.

Erwin W. Lutzer, M.A., L.L.D., D.D., is an author, speaker, and pastor of the Moody Church in Chicago, Illinois.

Jobe R. Martin, Th.M., D.D.S., is an author and president of Bible Discipleship Ministries. He lives in Rockwall, Texas.

Steven L. McAvoy, Th.M., Th.D., is director of the Institute for Biblical Studies, Lake Oswego, Oregon.

Thomas S. McCall, Th.M., Th.D., is an author, conference speaker, and researcher for Levitt Ministries. He lives in Bullard, Texas.

John A. McLean, Th.M., M.A., Ph.D., is an author and educator living in Canton, Michigan, and past president of Michigan Theological Seminary.

George E. Meisinger, Th.M., D.Min., is president of Chafer Theological Seminary and pastor of Grace Church in Huntington Beach, California.

Henry M. Morris, Ph.D., is president emeritus of the Institute of Creation Research, El Cajon, California.

David A. Noebel, M.A., Ph.D. candidate, is cofounder of Summit Ministries in Manitou Springs, Colorado.

L. Paige Patterson, Th.M., Th.D., is president of Southeastern Baptist Seminary in Wake Forest, North Carolina. He has served as president of the Southern Baptist Convention.

Russell L. Penney, M.A., Th.D., is an author and missionary/theology teacher serving in Bolivia, South America.

Albert T. Platt, Th.M., Th.D., is president emeritus of Central American Mission. He lives in Dallas, Texas.

J. Randall Price, Th.M., Ph.D., is founder and president of World of the Bible Ministries, San Marcos, Texas.

Renald E. Showers, Th.M., Th.D., serves on the staff of the Friends of Israel Gospel Ministry. He lives in Willow Street, Pennsylvania.

Gary P. Stewart, M.A., M.Div., Th.M., D.Min., is a military chaplain, author, and speaker. He lives in Libertyville, Illinois.

John F. Walvoord, M.A., Th.M., Th.D., D.D., is chancellor of Dallas Theological Seminary. He lives in Dallas, Texas.

Harold L. Willmington, Th.M., D.Min., is dean of Liberty Bible Institute, Liberty Baptist University, Lynchburg, Virginia.

Abbreviations

BAGD   Walter Bauer, *A Greek-English Lexicon of the New Testament and Other Early Christian Literature,* 2d ed., rev. F. W. Gingrich and Frederick Danker, trans. William F. Arndt and F. W. Gingrich. Chicago: University of Chicago Press, 1979.

LXX   Septuagint, the Greek Old Testament.

TDNT   Gerhard Kittel and Gerhard Friedrich, eds., *Theological Dictionary of the New Testament,* 10 vols., trans. G. W. Bromiley. Grand Rapids: Eerdmans, 1973.

TWOT   R. Laird Harris et al., eds. *Theological Wordbook of the Old Testament.* Chicago: Moody, 1980.

Preface

From 1910 to 1915, a series of twelve book-length essays, *The Fundamentals: A Testimony to the Truth*, was sent to pastors, missionaries, and Christian workers in the United States and throughout the world. So effective were these popular defenses of core Christian doctrines that within a decade they had given a platform, a banner, and a name to the majority of North American conservative Christians: "fundamentalists." When apostasy continued to threaten the Western churches in the ecclesiastical struggles of the 1930s and 1940s, these books offered guiding principles to a second movement of world scope: "evangelicalism."

Generations of pastors and Bible teachers have been well served by these brief and remarkably clear books, which were written by some of the leading scholars of the late nineteenth and early twentieth centuries. These theologians wrote with a sense of urgency, for each saw how compromise was threatening doctrines indispensable to Christianity.

Nearly a century later, the authors of these chapters feel a similar urgency. The next generation of Bible teachers and pastors must understand which issues are not open to compromise.

This is not to say that every Bible-honoring Christian reader will agree with all the arguments presented here. There were honest interpretive disagreements among brothers and sisters after *The Fundamentals* was published. But it is hoped that this book will be a beacon for coming generations.

Contributors to *The Fundamentals* were responding to the classic liberal and spiritualist heresies that abounded before World War I. They could not foresee the neoorthodox, existentialist, modernist, nihilist, liberation, feminist, situation ethic, and New Age theologies that would lash the twentieth-century church. Nor can the writers of this volume see exactly how Satan will attack the church of Jesus Christ in the twenty-first century. He is a master at throwing a given generation into moral and doctrinal confusion, appearing as an angel of light who makes good seem evil and evil, good.

The scholars represented in this volume are proclaimers of the Word of God to a century in which many will be tempted to drift from key truths and principles that have been a stabilizing influence since the publication of *The*

Fundamentals. We sense that we are walking in giant footsteps; none of us has felt truly worthy of the mantle we have picked up. But all of us have been profoundly affected by these writings and so dedicate our spiritual insights, time, and scholarly training to see these truths reinterpreted in the language of a new generation.

In two aspects these writers have not followed exactly the pattern of the original documents. First, because of the cultural turmoil of the past fifty years, more energy has been directed toward applying fundamental biblical principles to social and cultural issues. Second, this volume takes a self-consciously premillennial and pretribulational rapture position. This seems appropriate since the majority of the writers of the first books held this position. The fundamentalist movement that grew from their work overwhelmingly adopted these doctrines about the return of the Lord. It is hoped that those not in agreement with this eschatological position will be able to appreciate and benefit from other portions of the work.

The contributors to this book do not believe themselves to be prophets who have received new revelations from God, as did Isaiah or Ezekiel. But as long as the Lord tarries, we trust that future generations will take seriously this call to a foundationally biblical faith. We believe in a coming apostasy of the church, but we also believe that by God's grace a remnant will not be part of it. May we not be a "rebellious people, false sons, sons who refuse to listen to the instruction of the LORD." Such faithless sons say, "Let us hear no more about the Holy One of Israel" (Isa. 30:9, 11b NASB).

How terrible for any generation to walk away from the truths that have been set forth by the God who saved us and who loves us even now!

MAL COUCH

The Historical Significance of *The Fundamentals*

Edward E. Hindson

Fundamentalist is the name that came to identify most conservative American Christians after 1920. Even Bible-believing Christians who have disavowed the label tend to find themselves in common cause and faith with most aspects of fundamentalism. Today fundamentalists still view themselves as the legitimate heirs of historic New Testament Christianity. They see themselves as the faithful defenders of biblical orthodoxy and hold strongly to the basic tenets they were debating a century ago. These defenders of the faith range from well-educated professors to country preachers. They wear a variety of other labels as well: "evangelical," "Bible-believing," "theologically conservative," "born again," or simply "Christians." During the tumultuous twentieth century, fundamentalists have dominated the dynamic conservative Christian impact on North American life and culture.

Fundamentalism takes its name from the publication of a series of volumes defending historic biblical Christianity. These were published originally in twelve volumes between 1910–1915 as *The Fundamentals: A Testimony to the Truth*. The project was financed by Lyman and Milton Stewart in response to a sermon preached by A. C. Dixon in 1909. The Stewart brothers invested two hundred thousand dollars to publish, promote, and distribute more than three hundred thousand volumes to pastors, missionaries, and Christian workers around the world.[1]

The Fundamentals were a collection of scholarly but popularly written articles defending the basic fundamentals, or essentials, of the Christian faith. The original volumes were edited by R. A. Torrey, A. C. Dixon, and others. They included contributors from America, Canada, England, Scotland, Ireland, and Germany. Contributors included such men as Robert Anderson,

W. J. Erdman, Arno Gaebelein, James M. Gray, W. H. Griffith Thomas, Melvin Grove Kyle, William Morehead, G. Campbell Morgan, H. G. C. Moule, James Orr, A. T. Pierson, C. I. Scofield, R. A. Torrey, and B. B. Warfield. Pierson wrote the most articles (five), and Orr wrote four.

The writers represented Princeton Theological Seminary, Oberlin College, Wycliffe College (University of Toronto), McCormick Theological Seminary, United Free Church College (Scotland), Southwestern Baptist Theological Seminary, Moody Bible Institute, and the Bible Institute of Los Angeles (now Biola). Bible Institute of Los Angeles published a four-volume edition of *The Fundamentals* in 1917, from which most current reprints are taken. An updated edition, produced by Charles L. Feinberg and Biola University in 1958, is presently in print with Kregel Publications.

Topics discussed in *The Fundamentals* included the inspiration of the Bible, the deity of Christ, the virgin birth, the resurrection, the atonement, the second coming, evangelism, missions, higher criticism, evolution, and archaeology. A series of articles critiqued the theologies of Roman Catholicism, Millennial Dawn (Jehovah's Witnesses), the Latter-Day Saints (Mormons), Christian Science, and the various forms of occult spiritualism. Also included were personal testimonies by the vicar of St. Paul's Cathedral in London, a lawyer in New York City, a medical doctor from Johns Hopkins University in Baltimore, and missionary C. T. Studd. The most unusual chapter was entitled "Tributes to Christ and the Bible by Brainy Men Not Known As Active Christians." Quotations were included from Benjamin Franklin, Daniel Webster, Ralph Waldo Emerson, Napoleon Bonaparte, William Shakespeare, Byron, and John Stuart Mill.

THE DEFINITION PROBLEM

Even in their native region of strength on the North American side of the Atlantic Ocean, fundamentalists have been described as backward, cultic, obscurantist—even Nazi.[2] Ernest Sandeen defines fundamentalism as nothing more than an offshoot of millenarianism.[3] D. B. Stevick more accurately observes that fundamentalism began as an "uneasy coalition" of divergent groups of conservative Christians who faced the common threat of classic theological liberalism.[4] No honest historian equates real fundamentalism with such extremist cults as Appalachian snake handlers. A careful study of the origins of the fundamentalist controversy show that the fundamentalist movement had dimensions far beyond those debated in the 1920s. In a chart analyzing the contents of *The Fundamentals*, Milton Rudnick demonstrates that twenty-seven articles dealt with the Bible, nine with apologetics, eight with the person of Christ, and only three with the second coming of Christ. The author concluded that "an examination of the contents of *The Fundamentals* reveals that their prime purpose was the defense and exaltation of traditional views of the Bible. Nearly a third of the articles (27 . . .) were devoted to this subject." Rudnick observes that in every article the infallible inspiration of Scripture for both doctrine and life was vigorously defended.[5]

George Marsden provides an excellent description of twentieth-century fundamentalism as a movement "closely tied to the revivalist tradition of mainstream evangelical Protestantism that militantly opposed modernist theology and the cultural change associated with it."[6] Fundamentalism shares certain traits with pietism, evangelicalism, revivalism, millenarianism, and Pentecostalism, but Marsden points out that fundamentalism must be clearly distinguished from these movements by its focal point—militant opposition to liberalism.

Part of the inaccurate perception is caused by the misunderstanding of church historians who come from theological traditions totally unlike that of the fundamentalists they study. Only a minority, such as Marsden, have personal roots in or near the movement. Also, as Marsden observes, the image of fundamentalism was forged in the furious and often sensationalistic battles of the 1920s, a war for the very soul of mainstream Christian denominations and the wider culture.

"When these efforts failed," Marsden concludes, "they became increasingly separatist, often leaving major denominations and flourishing in independent churches and agencies. . . . The phenomenon that I have defined as 'fundamentalism' was overwhelmingly American in the sense that almost nowhere else did this type of Protestant response to modernity have such a conspicuous and pervasive role both in the churches and in the national culture."[7]

EVANGELICAL CHRISTIANITY REAFFIRMED

The explosive impact of Darwinistic science, higher criticism in biblical scholarship, and liberal theology in general did not shake the fundamentalists' commitment to Christ and the Scriptures. They were confident in the truth of their message. They viewed themselves as affirming genuine historical faith against modernism's rationalism and militant secularism. The threat of a common enemy that opposed the gospel was strong motivation for Bible-believing theologians of every conceivable orthodox background to put aside other differences. They shared space in *The Fundamentals* because it was a mutual alliance of self-defense. Nothing else could have brought into one publication Episcopal bishops, Methodist evangelists, Baptist pastors, and Presbyterian theologians. The contributors were rectors, curates, Egyptologists, authors, editors, vicars, chancellors, moderators, and attorneys. The fundamentalist movement later became fragmented and polarized, but in its embryonic days it joined together a broad spectrum of conservative leaders.

These men can hardly be looked upon as a group of wild-eyed fanatics and obscurantists against scholarship and learning. They were against the sloppy scholarship, unsupported conclusions, and skeptical, even atheistic assumptions drawn by critical scholarship of the day.[8] Modernists exalted a "scientific" scholarship and looked with disdain on all other forms of biblical and theological studies. Fundamentalists likewise ridiculed their opponents' humanistic and man-made scholarship. Rhetorical war was declared.

One of the most thoughtful contributions to this war was by an unlikely warrior, a reticent Princeton scholar who never felt comfortable being called a fundamentalist, though he quipped that the name fit better than some other things he was called. J. Gresham Machen published his classic *Christianity and Liberalism* in 1923.[9] In this epic work Machen argued that the conclusions of liberal scholarship were utterly incompatible with Christian faith. What liberals proposed, he wrote, was nothing less than the replacement of Christianity by a new religion— one that denied the supernatural inspiration of the Bible; miracles; and the deity, atonement, and resurrection of Jesus Christ. This was unlike anything the Catholic or Protestant churches had ever held. Liberals waved a Bible they did not believe was from God. They proclaimed a Christ whom they doubted had lived and certainly had not died for the sins of humanity nor rose again! Machen wrote,

> At this point a fatal error lies in wait. It is one of the root errors of modern liberalism. Christian experience, we have just said, is useful as confirming the gospel message. But because it is necessary, many men have jumped to the conclusion that it is all that is necessary. . . . No matter what sort of man history may tell us Jesus of Nazareth actually was, no matter what the story of His alleged resurrection, may we not continue to experience the presence of Christ in our souls? The trouble is that the experience thus maintained is not Christian experience. Religious experience it may be, but Christian experience it certainly is not.[10]

TWENTIETH-CENTURY LIBERALISM

While it had many philosophical parents, religious liberalism most directly looks to the influence of the German theologian Friedrich Schleiermacher (1768-1834), who considered the ultimate authority in religion to be founded in the experience of the soul, rather than in the content of Scripture. Eventually liberal theologians transferred religious authority from the Bible to the psycho-spiritual experience of the individual. Coupled with the emerging influence of higher criticism, this movement ultimately led to wholesale rejection of absolute biblical authority.[11]

In America, liberalism turned humanistically outward in the "social gospel." This emphasis was founded mainly on the social activism of Walter Rauschenbusch (1861-1918) and the religious education theories of Horace Bushnell (1802-1876). Following Schleiermacher's lead, these men and others placed Christian "nurture" above confrontational evangelism and promoted an experience of Christianity that was not dependent upon any biblical verification. In his evaluation of liberalism and its stepchild, neoorthodoxy, Charles Ryrie observes, "Insofar as the Bible was true it was inspired, but it was the task of the liberal critic to determine at what points the Bible was true."[12] This attitude eventually undermined the last vestiges of a Christian foundation for liberalism. The resulting movement lacked any authoritative message. Classical liberalism died in the inhumanity of the trench warfare of World War I, but its successor liberal theologies flourished because their vague theologizing easily adapted to fit any radical or relativistic philosophy that came along. But by the century's end the entire structure of liberal theology had been seen for what it was—worse than no religion at all. Still influential, it began losing its grasp on Protestant northern Europe first, and finally was no longer so attractive to North Americans.

J. I. Packer identifies five basic characteristics of the worldview of classical liberalism at the turn of the century:

1. God is pure benevolence—benevolence without standards.
2. Every human being has a divine spark within.
3. Jesus Christ is Savior only in the sense that He is a perfect teacher and moral exemplar.
4. Christ differs only comparatively from other people, and Christianity differs from other religions merely as the best religion that has appeared.
5. The Bible is a human testament of religion, so Christian doctrine has no inherent God-associated authority over ethics or religious experience.[13]

The lack of absolute authority or truth, and a patently unrealistic optimism about humanity's social evolution, were the fatal flaws that led to the demise of liberalism and the dissolution of its impact on American society. Given the implications inherent in its foundation, the extreme left wing of liberalism was only being consistent when it drifted into what was called Christian atheism, the popularly labeled "God Is Dead Movement," in the 1960s. This movement was consistent enough to be a wakeup call even among many modernists, for it dropped the euphemistic speech and admitted what religious existentialism truly is.[14] A new direction was undertaken to reinstate some faith foundation. This "neo-liberalism," which identified with the "postmodern" philosophical bent of Western society, was only a pulling back into the masks. Unfortunately it had strong appeal to the more liberal sectors of the evangelical churches.[15]

At the end of the twentieth century, lack of authoritative direction had left much of the evangelical movement adrift to the left in a postmodern theology of experience. Even the historically orthodox church had returned to the birthplace of classical liberalism, the experiential subjectivity of Schleiermacher.

Carl F. H. Henry, a founder and guide of evangelicalism, states, "Evangelicals seem to be in a holding pattern, sometimes approaching a long-awaited landing, then circling 'round and 'round a cooperative objective, even at times moving exasperatingly away from it. We perform a series of maneuvers whose outcome is complicated by gathering storms that may divert us to an unforeseen and unintended destination."[16]

The evangelical movement must request an instrument flight rules (I.F.R.) flight plan that commits it to the doctrinal absolutes of Scripture without regard to the cultural milieu passing its windows. Otherwise, this "unforeseen and unintended destination" will be a landing field of polarization and disintegrating biblical distinctives. Evangelicalism is moving toward becoming yet another form of liberalism. This is why it is necessary to issue *The Fundamentals for the Twenty-First Century*.

THE EVANGELICAL IMPULSE

Fundamentalism and evangelicalism have become world movements, but to understand them it is necessary to travel to their native soil in the United States and Canada. Even now the North American fundamentalists and their sibling evangelicals have their own personalities and quirks. The framework that would become the Fundamentalist Movement was influenced by two nineteenth-century sources of thoughtfully reasoned conservatism.

First, the "Old-School" or more Bible-centered branch of the nineteenth-century Presbyterian churches was blessed with a cadre of godly and scholarly theologians who could speak clearly and persuasively to the average church member on subjects ranging from the new studies in archaeology to the human-centered revivalism of Charles Finney to the technical arguments of Darwinian evolution. The *Biblical Repertory and Princeton Review* was their eclectic theological pulpit, and it was read by a vast audience. Archibald Alexander, Charles Hodge, Alexander Hodge, and B. B. Warfield, among others, wrote on Scripture, defended orthodox doctrines with zest, and enthusiastically applied the Bible to every corner of life.

From its founding in 1812 until liberal theologians captured control a little over a century later, Princeton Seminary stood as a bastion of biblical orthodoxy in the Western world. Under Alexander, the Hodges (senior and junior), and Warfield, the cornerstone of Princeton theology was the unequivocal inspiration and authority of Scripture.[17] Warfield asserted three foundational postulates: (1) the inspiration of Scripture extends to the very words of the Bible itself; (2) Scripture witnesses to its own inerrancy; (3) inspiration applies literally only to the "original autographs," but God has protected the truth so far as the modern scholarly translations.

The second force was the Bible conference and Bible school movements that multiplied after the American Civil War. D. L. Moody was the architect of this influence with his Bible institute and Northfield Conference, but many others participated to put excellent Bible study resources and skills and Bible-based education within reach of the average layperson. One strategy that Moody and others took full advantage of was the Colportage Association, a publishing and sales network aimed at distributing inexpensive popular theology books to the most remote villages. Moody and his brother-in-law, Fleming H. Revell, founded the Revell Publishing Company to mass produce Colportage volumes and evangelistic pamphlets on cheap paper on a previously unimagined scale, selling at prices the most impoverished farmer could afford. Books were given to those who could not afford them at all.

This case for biblical inerrancy was widely accepted by the proto-evangelicals of the day and became the foundation of the fundamentalist view of the Bible. Machen was a covenant theologian who did not accept the premillennial aspect of the fundamentalist platform. Nevertheless, he was a flag-bearer for biblical inerrancy throughout the fundamentalist controversy. Unable to sway the board of Princeton to remain firm in its biblical heritage, Machen led a withdrawal of faculty and students to establish Westminster Theological Seminary in Philadelphia in 1929. He and other conservative Presbyterians then organized a world missions program to counter the liberal missionaries sent out by their denomination. In an ironic move, the Northern Presbyterian denomination tried and defrocked Machen and his colleagues as schismatic heretics. He died soon afterward while still a young man, a martyr to this stressful battle.

Since the amillennial Machen strongly supported fundamentalists in their campaign to defeat liberalism, the fundamentalist-modernist struggle obviously was not over eschatology. Rather, it was centered in the doctrine of biblical inspiration and authority.

This is not to say that premillennial theology was not important to most fundamentalists. A unique feature of American conservativism was the influence of premillennial eschatology in the late nineteenth century. The historical premillennial position of Bible commentators such as the German Lutheran F. J. Delitzsch (1813–1890), the Swiss Reformed scholar Frédéric Godet (1812–1900), and British Baptist preacher F. B. Meyer (1847–1929) encouraged a general expectation of Christ's future earthly reign. With the addition of the dispensational emphasis of John Darby (1800–1882) and C. I. Scofield's Bible annotations (1909), the distinctly American conservative church was complete. Historian Bruce Shelley considers that "if the theology of the fundamentalists was oversimplified, that of the liberals was oversecularized. If the liberals had a point in insisting that Christianity's survival depended upon its speaking to modern men, fundamentalists were right in demanding that it declare the public message."[18]

THE SHAPING OF A FUNDAMENTALISM

The increasing impetus of liberalism forced conservatives to react in an organized fashion. Two events particularly set this organization in motion and determined what path it would take. As stated above, a fundamentalist position was framed through the twelve booklets of *The Fundamentals: A Testimony to the Truth.*

These booklets were sent to pastors, evangelists, missionaries, professors, students, and personnel of the YMCA/YWCA organization throughout the world. As many as 3 million booklets were distributed in this first articulation of the movement. No other book aside from the Bible had ever been so widely distributed. Many identify the birth of fundamentalism with these calm, well-reasoned, and well-balanced testimonies.[19]

The second major publication of the early twentieth century was the *Scofield Reference Bible,* edited by Scofield (1843–1921), a former lawyer, Kansas state legislator, and Congregationalist minister. Scofield was pastor of the First Congregational Church of Dallas, Texas, from 1882 to 1895 and 1902 to 1907. Moody handpicked Scofield to lead his nondenominational ministry in Northfield, Massachusetts, from 1895 to 1902. Scofield retired to operate his Bible study correspondence course, built around study notes that he eventually published in the *Scofield Reference Bible* in 1909. These notes were edited and amplified in 1919 and revised in 1966. It would be difficult to overstate Scofield's impact on preachers, Bible teachers, and laity. The *Scofield Reference Bible* was "the Bible" of dispensational fundamentalism for most of the twentieth century.

The Issues in Fundamentalism

Fundamentalism was born in the conservative Christian doctrinal controversy with liberalism. From the beginning the ultimate issue has been whether historic Christian faith in a supernatural religion would be overpowered by Christians whose faith was centered in a naturalistic, humanistic philosophy. Fundamentalism affirms Christian belief and a distinctively Christian lifestyle in opposition to the surrounding secular society. It is the opposite of radical liberal Protestantism, which has secularized Christianity and Christianized secularism.

Viewed from the standpoint of supernaturalism versus secularism, the modernist Old Testament scholar James Barr is right when he observes that there is ultimately little difference between the theological frameworks of fundamentalists and those in the evangelical movement. While acknowledging that a difference of attitude does exist between the two, he nevertheless charges the evangelical movement with attempting to hide its fundamentalism behind the "conservative evangelical" label. He asks the searching question: "Has Evangelicalism succeeded in developing a conceptual framework recognizable, distinct from the Fundamentalist one?" Then he answers his own question: "It is not clear the modernized and updated Evangelicalism has yet attained to any conceptual framework that is intrinsically different from the fundamentalist one, or that it has even tried."[20] This point is exactly what contemporary evangelicalism needs to face—the fact that it is not intrinsically different from mainstream fundamentalism.

To an outsider such as Barr, evangelicalism and fundamentalism seem to be in fact one and the same. While those within the movements can more easily see the nuances and the extremities on both sides, we too must face the fact that we share a common heritage. Organizationally the two came into being in the same modernist controversy cauldron. Conservative Christians within the evangelical and fundamentalist circles, and even the Reformed, Episcopal, and Lutheran camps outside such labels, can present a unified stand for the truths of Scripture we all hold dear.

Most people trace the basics of fundamentalism back to the five fundamentals that became crucial in the fundamentalist-modernist controversy. These are usually expressed as

1. The inspiration and infallibility of Scripture.
2. The deity of Christ (implying as well His humanity and virgin birth).
3. The sufficiency of Christ's death to pay the penalty owed by fallen individuals to an infinitely holy God.
4. The literal resurrection of Christ from the dead.
5. The literal return of Christ in the Second Advent.

This list of Christian essentials has been expanded and amplified many times. Subsections under these categories include such issues as the deity and work of the Holy Spirit, the depravity before God of all humanity, the existence of a literal heaven and hell, the importance of being God's representatives to unbelievers in evangelism, the personal, spiritual existence of Satan, and the importance of the local church.[21] Nevertheless, it is more correct to limit the definition of doctrinal fundamentalism to those "fundamentals" that always have been at the heart of the movement.

Inspiration and Infallibility of Scripture

The fundamentalist position on the inspiration of Scripture is essentially that of the faithful wing of the evangelical movement.[22] Both groups recognize the plenary (complete and unconditional) and verbal (word meaning) inspiration of Scripture. Both groups have conditioned this understanding around the doctrine of Scripture defended at "Old Princeton" Seminary in the nineteenth century. This doctrine has been stated differently, but is the historical Christian understanding. Fundamentalists and faithful evangelicals hold to a basic belief that the Bible's documents are inerrant (without error) in their original autographs (documents first penned by the human authors). While errors have crept into the copied and recopied documents over thousands of years, study of available ancient documents has brought the modern Hebrew and Greek texts very close to the actual words of the autographs. We can have utter confidence that were the clay tablets of Moses and the parchments of Paul to suddenly appear, not one properly interpreted doctrine would be brought into question.

To fundamentalists, the inerrancy of Scripture is inextricably linked to its authority in all it teaches. In the words of Paul in 2 Timothy 3:16, it is "God-breathed" in its statements and affirmations. Robert Lightner asks, "How can an errant Bible be God's revelation? How can it be God-breathed? How can it possibly be authoritative and therefore trustworthy? How can Scripture possibly be inerrant in some parts and errant in others at the same time? In a book which claims God as its author, inspiration must extend to all its parts. If it does not, how does one go about determining what is and what is not God-breathed and therefore free from error?"[23] Lightner thus warns radicalizers of either evangelical or fundamentalist positions that anything less than total inerrancy is intellectual accommodation to rationalism and liberalism.

Christ as God

Without the deity of Christ, there is no Christianity to defend. Attention shifted in the mid-twentieth century to the inspiration of Scripture, since it is from Scripture that true Christians derive all of their beliefs. Nevertheless, the battlefield on which early fundamentalists bled was christological. Who is Jesus, the Christ? Most conservatives agreed with Scofield Bible editor William G. Moorehead (1836-1914), president of Xenia Theological Seminary, when he wrote his essay: "The Moral Glory of Jesus Christ, a Proof of Inspiration."[24] Fundamentalists have always felt that belief in the deity of Christ was impugned by any denial of the inspiration of Scripture, since Christ Himself quoted Old Testament Scripture as being inspired of God. Christ assumed the existence of "questionable" historical individuals, such as Adam (e.g., Matt. 19:4-6), Noah (e.g., Matt. 24:37-39), and Jonah (e.g., Matt. 12:39-41).

Warfield wrote the article on the deity of Christ for *The Fundamentals*. He argued that Christ Himself claimed to be God, accepted worship from others, and was viewed as divine by the apostles and the early church. A related issue is that of the virgin birth of Christ. This article in *The Fundamentals* was written by the Scottish theologian James Orr, who argued that it was essential to Christ's unique and sinless personality.

Substitutionary Atonement

The doctrine of the substitutionary atoning sacrifice of Christ's death is also intertwined with that of His deity. At the time of the fundamentalist controversy, several new theories regarding the atonement of Christ were advanced so that liberals could have a strictly human Christ and also some sort of salvation message. Christ's death was an extension of his life, said one popular argument. Its moral message saves and heals hurting people and influences society. To fundamentalists, this was the fairy tale Christ, a cancer that ate away at the core of Christianity. The message of the gospel centers around the death, burial, and resurrection of Christ. If humanity truly did not irretrievably die to God through sin, then the Cross was not needed. We can save ourselves. On the other hand, if humanity as a race did commit infinite treason against the perfect justice of a holy God who can abide no dirtiness in his sight, then no limited human Christ, whatever his moral attainments, can do a thing about it.

In the Bible teachings that have been described as the "substitutionary atonement," the gospel message surrounding the death of a divine and human Christ is the only possible answer for the problem identified. They fit one another as has no set of theories proposed by liberal, neoorthodox, or liberation theologian. This is precisely what the apostle Paul described as his own generation's response to the Cross (1 Cor. 1:17-31).

The Resurrection of Christ

If Jesus Christ did not die for sin as the only adequate substitute for a sinful human being, and if He was not literally raised from the dead, then there is no good news for the world. The entire evangelistic imperative can only be seen in light of the death and resurrection of Christ.[25] So the resurrection is closely aligned with the atoning sacrifice.

The atoning sacrifice has to do ultimately with "justification." Can an infinitely holy God accept human sinners and still be just? The resurrection is a confirmation of life. If God gives the believer a pat on the back but still sends him off to oblivion in the grave, the victory of the Cross is hollow.

Only if Christ defeated death can He share that victory with His brothers and sisters. Apart from the resurrection of Christ from the dead there is no good news to tell. Where modernism is content to proclaim a superficial, humanized version of the sermon on the mount, fundamentalists have a fully orbed evangel—and thus the only possible evangel. They have had a message to tell to the nations because they shared with the early church its overwhelming conviction that Jesus Christ is alive.

Through their evangelistic and missionary endeavors, fundamentalists offer no dead teacher of the past but a living Savior who transforms today and tomorrow. Fundamentalists/evangelicals view themselves as relevant to humanity's needs while superseding unworkable and hopeless philosophical trends.

Christ's Second Coming

Belief in the literal, bodily return of Christ is also essential to a consistent, biblical faith. Since Jesus promised to return, and the Scriptures indicated that He will return "in like manner as ye have seen him go into heaven" (Acts 1:11 KJV), the literal return of Christ is interrelated theologically with the literal resurrection of Christ. In their rejection of modern theology's doubts as to whether a historical Jesus ever lived or rose from the dead, those who ascribe to either the evangelical or fundamentalist banner believe that He will definitely and literally return to bring history to its ultimate culmination. While this doctrine is the most debated and divergent of all the fundamentals, it holds no matter how the conservative Christian interprets the eschatological texts. The return of Christ is the point of commonality among premillennialists, postmillennialists, amillennialists and among pre-, mid-, or posttribulationists in terms of a rapture of Christians. Likewise, all conservatives agree that Christ will judge the world and vindicate the righteous in Christ.[26]

There can be no doubt that this belief has left its impression on Western culture in general with our national insistence that a superhero will one day intervene in human history and save the world. That person will in fact be Jesus Christ Himself!

SUMMARY

Doctrinally, fundamentalism is nothing more or less than Christian orthodoxy. It arose as a defense of minimal doctrinal essentials, apart from which Christianity ceases to be Christian. Historically, fundamentalism owes its name to the publication of *The Fundamentals*. These amazing volumes had a major impact on the development of conservative American Protestantism in the twentieth century. Even theological liberal Kirsopp Lake admits, "It is a mistake, often made by educated persons who happen to have but little knowledge of historical theology, to suppose that Fundamentalism is a new and strange form of thought. It is nothing of the kind: it is the . . . survival of a theology which was once universally held by all Christians."[27]

In essence two religions had arisen within American Protestantism when *The Fundamentals* were published. On the one side stood liberalism, an attempt to speak religiously from stringently natural, rational, and social dimensions of life. Opposing it stood historical Christianity, centering upon faith in God as revealed in the spiritual, the supernatural, and the infallible Word of God. Out of this controversy was born the century's clearest and strongest expression of faithful commitment to the essential doctrines of biblical Christianity. Twentieth-century evangelicalism was one voice of that expression, an organizational means to confront the modern age with a renewed commitment to the fundamentals of Christian faith.

As the twenty-first century dawns, we again stand at a theological watershed.

The critical objections of liberalism have been tempered by existential/experiential approaches to theology. These have now turned to a "do-it-yourself" religion. Emotional subjectivism has replaced any fixed point of reference in defining liberal Christianity by objective standards of biblical truth. Whereas the classical liberals of the early 1900s were sure they alone were right, the new liberals believe that each individual can create a theology that is personally "right."

Such a religion refuses to face the logical consequences of a secular world that has turned from its God. Instead of repenting of rebellion against God, the new century's religious are opting for a scientific mysticism that combines minimal Christianity with transcendentalism, spiritualism, transpersonal psychology, and even occultism.[28]

The challenge to genuine Christianity has come full circle. Again we must reaffirm, define, and defend the "fundamentals" of faith to a new generation. Only now we face a generation that asks if there is anything "real" in a world of broken promises, video image, political spin, and media manipulation. The watching world still looks for the real thing. They will find it only turning to the unchanging reality of Jesus Christ as Lord.

CHAPTER 1

Can Truth Be Known?

Steven L. McAvoy

The concept of absolute, unchanging truth, is of first importance to Christians. Before Pilate, Jesus claimed to bear witness to the truth, and said "Everyone who is of the truth hears My voice." Pilate asked, "What is truth?" (John 18:37–38).[1] Pilate's question inquires not into the truth he was judging, but rather into the concept or nature of truth. Either he was convinced there was no answer or he did not care to hear it, for he did not wait to hear Jesus' response.

THE SEARCH FOR AN ANSWER

Many Pilates have questioned the nature and knowability of truth. Until the Enlightenment, truth was assumed to be absolute, objective, and propositional correspondence to reality. It was knowable.[2]

That changed dramatically with the philosophical speculations of Immanuel Kant (1724–1804).[3] Kant's epistemological doubt was so powerful and revolutionary that it indelibly marked the Western view of reality. We can never assume that knowable, absolute truth is part of the worldview of any partaker of Western culture. To the contrary, we can assume that most people we meet have a view of reality built upon relativism. They assume that truth is subjective, personal, and pragmatic. They consider belief in a transcendent reality or absolute truth to be the height of narrow-minded chutzpa. Without the possibility of a firm epistemology for discerning truth, Western thought is adrift in a sea of confusion. No intellectual or moral moorings are possible.

Ironically, Kantian anti-rationalism has dominated nonscientific thought processes in the rationalistic Enlightenment. Enlightenment thought prided itself on its pure, sophisticated logic, but Kant pulled away the mask. He showed rationalism to be compartmentalized and so internally inconsistent that it must inevitably collapse in upon itself.

The Enlightenment seemed to be gasping a death rattle through the last half of the twentieth century, falling prey to the new intellectual age of postmodernism. Postmodernism is the logical destination of Kantian thought. Within the postmodern mind, relativism underlies everything.

In the battle between modernism and Christianity that began about the time of Friedrich Schleiermacher in the 1830s, modernists have tended to abandon absolutes. Schleiermacher wanted to defend Christianity against the Kantian concept of truth, but he and his successors never got beyond the content and discernment of truth. Modernism has held that truth is determined by reason, that belief in the supernatural is irrational and anti-intellectual, and that all knowledge is determined by empiricism—through sensory experience. This rationalistic, "scientific" approach to the study of the transcendent is as fatally flawed as Kant's unknowable transcendent. In fact the two ideas are reverse sides of the same conception that human beings are the ultimate arbiters of the search for absolute truth.

RECENT DEVELOPMENTS IN THE SEARCH

Now the battle lines have shifted. The focus is no longer "What is true?" but "What is truth?" The nature of truth (rather than the epistemology for discerning it) is in question. Postmodernism holds that truth, and hence morality, is relative. Contrary to modernists, postmodernists teach that there "is no such thing as objective rationality (unbiased reason) in the sense that modernists use the term. Objective reason is a myth."[4] For the postmodernist, reality is in the mind of the beholder. Reality is what's real to me, for I construct my own reality in my mind. We cannot judge things in another culture or in another person's life, because our realities differ. Intuition and feelings might tell us more about reality than does reason.[5] Rationalism having failed, postmodernism is irrationalism. Modernists do not believe that the Bible is true. Postmodernists discard the very question of biblical truth as meaningless. Gene Edward Veith Jr. compares the rationalist and irrationalist views thus:

> In the premodern and modern eras, religion involved beliefs about reality. There either is a God, or there is not. Either Jesus was the incarnate Son of God, or He was just a man. Miracles happened, or they did not. Some Christians vehemently disagreed about realities: Is there such a place as Purgatory? Does Mary intercede for us in Heaven? Are some predestined to damnation? These were disagreements over questions of fact. Today religion is not seen as a set of beliefs about what is real. Rather, religion is a preference. We believe in what we like. We believe what we want to believe.[6]

Signs of this intellectual revolution appear everywhere—on university campuses and television screens. Relativism has gained its foothold in evangelical churches.

The Effect on the West

Western relativism struck with sledgehammer blows. Allan Bloom saw this phenomenon taking over his classrooms at the University of Chicago in the late 1980s: "There is one thing a professor can be absolutely certain of: almost every student entering the university believes, or says he believes, that truth is relative."[7] In 1991 the Barna Research Group reported that 28 percent of Americans agreed strongly with the statement that "there is no such thing as absolute truth; different people can define truth in conflicting ways and still be correct." Some level of agreement was expressed by 67 percent.[8] Most alarming, 53 percent of persons identifying themselves as "born again" Christians and 53 percent of adults associated with evangelical churches expressed some agreement with the statement. In 1994, 72 percent of American adults—almost three out of four—affirmed some kind of relativist understanding.[9]

The Enlightenment remained a relatively Western intellectual event, at least until world wars and global technologies spread its gospel. Postmodern relativism is also a Western phenomenon, developing in post-World War II Western Europe and spreading to North America. Americans received and developed it with an evangelistic passion. But in the global village, the traditional sociocultural distinctions blur. Veith has stated,

> Now the assumptions of modernism have fallen apart, from Moscow to San Francisco. The enlightenment is discredited. Reason is dethroned, even on university campuses. The Industrial Revolution is giving way to the Information Age. Society, technology, values, and basic categories of thought are shifting. A new way of looking at the world is emerging. . . . These views respond to the failure of the Enlightenment by jettisoning truth altogether. The intellect is replaced by the will. Reason is replaced by emotion. Morality is replaced by relativism.[10]

Ethicist Robert E. Fitch describes this as a pervasive loss of ethical foundation everywhere:

> Ours is an age where ethics has become obsolete. It is superseded by science, deleted by psychology, dismissed as emotive by philosophy. It is drowned in compassion, evaporates into aesthetics, and retreats before relativism. The usual moral distinctions between good and bad are simply drowned in a maudlin emotion in which we feel more

sympathy for the murderer than the murdered, for the adulterer than the betrayed, and in which we have actually begun to believe that the real guilty party, the one who somehow caused it all, is the victim and not the perpetrator of the crime.[11]

The Intolerant Tolerance

Carl F. H. Henry relates that "never has the question been more important whether our beliefs are simply scientific tentatives, speculative conjecture, private psychic certitudes, or universally valid truth."[12] For this reason a watchword of postmodernism is tolerance.

But this is tolerance with a difference. The concept no longer means that "everyone has a right to his or her own opinion," and that this right should be recognized and respected. Today's definition of tolerance means that every belief, value, lifestyle, and truth claim is equally true or equally valid. Any attempt to learn whether one truth claim is right while another is wrong is an invalid, intolerant enterprise. Everyone not only has an equal right to a belief, but no belief can be challenged. Never mind that this defies the laws of reason and logic; reason and logic are intolerant.

On the surface, this new "tolerance" appears to be a charitable worldview. It treats all opinions, ideologies, and moral viewpoints as equal. But herein lies a problem: The issue is no longer the truth of the message but the right to proclaim it. Truth has been abandoned.

No wonder such "tolerance" is so intolerant when a Christian speaks against homosexuality, pornography, or abortion. For the postmodernist, there is no transcendent, fixed mooring for morality. Exclusivistic truth claims, such as "there is no salvation apart from Jesus Christ" (John 14:6) sends the postmodern man into apoplexy: Such closed-minded, arrogant bigotry is not to be borne.

A Century Adrift

Postmodern civilization enters the twenty-first century without a fixed reference point outside of itself by which to determine what is true and false, right and wrong, important and trivial. Relevance is determined by feelings, intuition, and emotion. Right and wrong are determined by individual preference. Postmodernism, says Andrew Delbanco, has "sanctified the rights of the self and charged malice to any obstructor of those rights."[13] Perhaps the greatest challenge the church faces in the twenty-first century is relativism's denial of absolutes. Leith Anderson says that the issue is sometimes identified as pluralism, but that is a mistake. The issue is relativism:

Cultural pluralism is already a reality in North America, just as it was a reality in the first-century Roman Empire. While this is uncomfortable for many people, it is not necessarily a negative for the gospel of Jesus Christ. Christianity has often flourished when openly competing with contrary ideas.[14]

The greater crisis is in the growing acceptance of relativism, which denies the existence of absolutes. Anderson believes that there is a popular belief that "the only absolute is that there are no absolutes." Individualism and tolerance are elevated as the highest virtues. Where relativism prevails, there is no call to choose between competing claims for absolute truth. Instead the call is for isolation and acceptance that "you have your truth and I have my truth and let's just leave each other alone."[15]

What Is at Stake?

Relativism is a serious opponent to a Christian faith founded on a God of truth and His true Word (Isa. 65:16; Ps. 146:6; Jer. 10:10; 2 Sam. 7:28; Ps. 119:160; John 17:17).[16] If people are to be saved from sin and death; made heirs of the "spirit of wisdom and of revelation in the knowledge" of God (Eph. 1:17), and made "alive together with Christ" (Eph. 2:5), it matters a great deal what we believe and understand about the nature of truth.

While there are conflicting theories on the nature of truth, one can legitimately categorize all views other than the correspondence view as noncorrespondence views.[17] It is beyond the scope of this essay to look in depth at the different schools of thought. Only the correspondence view makes much sense when we approach the biblical and philosophical evidence.

EVIDENCE FOR A CHRISTIAN CONCEPT OF TRUTH

Objections have been raised against using philosophical proofs in a defense of absolute truth. Doesn't Colossians 2:8 warns us to avoid philosophy? A study of the context of Colossians 2 effectively shows that Paul is decidedly not opposed to philosophy. He frequently uses philosophical reasoning himself. Winfried Corduan shows that philosophical thinking "is an integral part of the way that we understand and disseminate revealed truth."[18]

Through philosophy we can be helped by the presuppositions of logic, which are vital to meaningful thought about God. God has revealed Himself in reasonable and logical forms, and he created humankind with the ability to use reason and logic so that we might know Him.[19] This reason and logic allows us in a very limited sense to be able to think God's thoughts after him. God built a universe that obeys the logical law of noncontradiction, in which "A" cannot be "non-A." To understand implications of that law is to understand something about how God works. Reason and logic are essential to knowing truth in Scripture or creation and in knowing the true God who is revealed. Moreover, it is a point of contact with other worldviews. It is undeniable that certain truths are self-evident, whatever one's view of truth or God. Philosophical arguments therefore, do have validity.

The Bible may not provide a systematic account of the nature of truth in either its theological or philosophical dimensions. It may be true that the writers did not teach or "assert as correct" any theory of truth. But this does not mean that Scripture does not recognize and teach a valid theory of truth. One can follow this coherent system through all the completed body of Scriptures, making it more important than the theology of any individual writer. After all, it is the Scripture that is inspired (2 Tim. 3:16–17)—not the human writers. The writers were "moved by the Holy Spirit" (2 Peter 1:21). Other things they said or wrote were probably very wise and true, but they were not inspired as are the words they penned in the supernatural power of the Spirit. It is therefore valid to draw doctrinal conclusions from the whole that no single writer had thought through. This development in a teaching, and the overall revelation of God concerning it is the task of biblical theology.

This is mainly how we arrive at the biblical concept of the triune or three-person nature of God, which is not fully developed in any one Scripture text, but is definitively presented by the whole. By induction we gather the evidence from which certain principles can be made. From these principles we may make logical deductions that should prove to be true so long as our premises are true and our logic sound. Because God is rational and has communicated to us rationally, we can follow the facts to determine what He has said and how He has said it. If God is the God of truth (and the Bible says He is), He has communicated to us truthfully (and the Bible says He has). If the Bible is God's inspired Word to us (as it claims to be), we should be able to determine truth.

We can make this confident determination, even though it seldom or never was a writer's single-minded intention to teach about the nature of truth. As John V. Dahms puts it, our knowledge of the truth implicit in Scripture need not have been a conscious understanding of the biblical writers.[20] These writers would have been amazed at the truth issues we face. They simply were telling the truth as God was revealing it to them and through them to us. One implication of the correspondence view of truth is that we can depend on the truth of whatever a writer of Scripture affirms by assumption.

We can set forth this principle of revelation: The Bible says what God intends it to say, which may be more than its human authors intended.[21] The human writers of Scripture, superintended as they were by the Holy Spirit, composed and recorded God's revelation, so that God can speak to our culture and times in ways that could never have occurred to those writing in those times and places (Isa. 59:21; Matt. 22:43; Acts 4:24–25; 1 Cor. 2:13; Heb. 1:1–2; 2 Peter 1:20–21).[22]

The Bible Teaches a Concept of Truth

A biblical theology of truth might begin with a look at the usage of Hebrew and Greek terms related to our English term, truth. In the New American Standard Bible, one of the most precisely worded English translations, *truth* occurs 201 times (92 times in the OT; 109 times in the NT). Of course there are related words to consider as well. *Truthful* occurs four times (2, OT; 2, NT); *truthfully* is a good translation only in Luke 9:27; *true* occurs eighty-seven times in the NASB (28, OT; 59, NT); and *truly*, which was one of Jesus' favorite words to introduce important statements, 141 times (31, OT; 110, NT).

The Old Testament

The most common Old Testament words for truth are *emet* and its cognate, or kindred term, *emûnâ*. Both are derived from the verb *āmēn*, (cf. English *amen*), which in its basic stem means "to confirm, support or uphold" and in its derived stems "to be established, be faithful, be certain," and "firmness, fidelity, and steadiness." The basic idea is firmness or certainty.[23]

The word *truth* in the English versions of the Old Testament almost always corresponds to the Hebrew *emet,* though it is not always translated that way. It is sometimes rendered "faithfulness." That meaning however, more properly and frequently belongs to *emûnâ*. The noun *emet,* (the most common form of the root *āmēn*), is frequently used of speaking the truth as opposed to lying (Josh. 9:15-16, 19; 1 Kings 17:24; Isa. 48:1; 59:13-14; Jer. 5:1, 3; 9:3, 5-6). Hence, *emet* is "what is true," or "that which corresponds to the facts."As Moberly says, "A fundamental principle of OT (indeed biblical) ethics is the imitation of God: as Yahweh is, likewise Israel is to be. This is most famously expressed in Leviticus 19:2, 'Be holy because I, the LORD your God, am holy' (for NT formulations of this principle, see, e.g., Matt 5:43-48; 1 Cor. 11:1). It is no surprise, therefore, that if Yahweh is faithful, it is expected of Israel that they should be faithful too."[24]

More important, *emet* is also used to depict the character of God (e.g., Exod. 34:6, by God's own testimony; Pss. 31:5; 40:10-11; 57:10; 86:15; 89:14; Isa. 65:16; Zech. 7:8). Often it occurs in couplets or combination with other words that ascribe attributes to God such as lovingkindness (Gen. 24:27; Exod. 34:6), righteousness (Ps. 85:10-11), living (1 Thess. 1:9; 1 Tim. 3:15), and justice (Ps. 111:7).

The major theological significance of the Old Testament word for "truth" (*emet*) is its frequent use to depict the character of God. The same may be said for its kindred word *emûnâ*, and in a more indirect way, its root word *āmēn* and its cognates. Jack B. Scott concludes his excellent study of *emet* with these words: "As we study its various contexts, it becomes manifestly clear that there is no truth in the biblical sense, i.e., valid truth, outside God. All truth comes from God and is truth because it is related to God."[25] Truth in the Old Testament then, is (1) a characteristic of God, also to be reflected by His people, and (2) facticity, or correspondence to reality. Truth is theocentric and corresponds to things as they really are.

The New Testament

In the New Testament, the primary word that can be translated "truth" is *alētheia*. It occurs 109 times in the Greek New Testament. With few exceptions, it is always translated "truth." Kindred words are *alēthēs*, "true, truthful"; *alēthinos*, "authentic, genuine"; and *alēthos*, "truly, really."

Too much is sometimes made of the etymology of *alētheia*. In secular Greek (e.g., Parmenides and esp. Plato) *alētheia* is sometimes used metaphysically to refer to "the notion of truth as against mere appearances and as that which belongs only to the realm of timelessness and immateriality."[26] But as Thiselton demonstrates, there is little evidence that the etymology of the word played any part in determining its meaning in later Greek of the Classical and Hellenistic periods.

Even within Greek philosophy *alētheia* is used to denote "truth" that "has a more positive relation to the material world."[27] Secular Greek also commonly used *alētheia* for (1) that which stands in opposition to falsehood, (2) that which corresponds to the facts, and (3) that which is real, authentic, or genuine. This conforms to the New Testament. There truth is used, in contrast to falsehood or falsity, to denote that which corresponds to reality or the facts (John 8:44–47; Acts 26:24–25; Rom. 1:25; 3:4–8; 9:1; 2 Cor. 13:8).

The New Testament does not present a fundamentally different concept of truth than that of the Old Testament. This is particularly apparent in the New Testament writers' importation of the Hebrew *āmēn*, to the Greek *amēn* (cf. English "amen"). This word occurs 129 times in the New Testament, most of which are found in Jesus' words, *"Amēn,* I say to you." This is perhaps best translated "truly." In Revelation 3:14, Christ is called "the *Amēn,* the faithful and true Witness." This clearly recalls Isaiah 65:16, where Yahweh is twice called "the God of *āmēn,"* i.e., the God of truth. "The maintenance of the Semitic 'amen' in the midst of a text written in Greek . . . manifests the impact of Hebraic concepts and language on the thought world and worship of the early church."[28]

In Matthew, Mark, and Luke, the Synoptic Gospels, *alētheia* occurs infrequently. It usually points to speech that is true, exactly correct, or trustworthy, as opposed to falsehood or deceit. Jesus' sayings often attack hypocrisy or discrepancy between word and deed, or between word and reality (as in Matthew 23 or Luke 11:46). Contradiction between word and deed is deceit. This reflects the Old Testament understanding of the moral nature of truth.

Paul has a lot to say about the concept of truth:

1. It is revealed in general revelation and the law (e.g., Rom. 1:18; 1:25; 2:8, 20).
2. It is embodied uniquely in the gospel (e.g., Col. 1:5; 2 Thess. 2:10-13).
3. It stands unalterably opposed to all lying or deception (Rom. 1:25; 2 Cor. 4:2; Gal. 4:16).
4. It is an attribute of God revealed in God the Son (Eph. 4:21; Titus 1:1-2).
5. In keeping with the Old Testament principle that we are to imitate God, truth is to characterize our relationship with God and one another (1 Cor. 5:8; 13:6; 2 Cor. 6:4-7; Gal. 5:7).

John uses *alētheia* forty-five times and related terms about forty-eight times. John does not use *alētheia* in the Book of Revelation at all, but he uses *alēthinos* ("true") ten times. Among other truth-centered words John uses are *alēthes* ("truthful, valid, true, genuine, real"), and *alēthos* ("truly, really, actually"). Also important in understanding John's concept of truth are his frequent references to falsehood. As other writers of Scripture, John often contrasts truth with lies and falsehood (John 8:44; 1 John 1:6-10; 2:21-24; 4:6; 2 John 1:2, 7).

John also sees truth as the revelation of God. Truth is revealed. In the prologue to his gospel, Jesus, the incarnate Logos, is described as "full of grace and truth" (1:14). It is widely acknowledged that Exodus 34:6 is the background to John 1:14 and 17.[29] In Exodus 34, God renews His covenant with Israel. In so doing, He reveals His glory to Moses on Mount Sinai. "Then the Lord passed by in front of him and proclaimed, 'The Lord, the Lord God, compassionate and gracious, slow to anger, and abounding in lovingkindness and truth" (Exod. 34:6).

In His own words Yahweh declares Himself to be abounding in "lovingkindness" (*ḥēsēd*) and "truth" (*emet*). This phrase occurs frequently in the Old Testament and expresses Yahweh's covenant loyalty and unchanging truth. John connects with Exodus 34 the incarnation of God in the Logos is presented as the supreme disclosure of the Lord who revealed himself to Moses in the giving of the law at Sinai (1:17). Jesus shows us God as he really is.[30] Jesus, the incarnate Logos then, is the truth of God revealed. His person, work, and word are a revelation of truth. Jesus is both the messenger and the message of truth (John 14:6).

Perhaps John's greatest contribution to the biblical concept of truth is that he forcefully roots all truth in God. As clearly as any author, he teaches that truth is absolute and theocentric. We have seen that John presents truth as an attribute of God revealed in the incarnate Logos or Word of God. God is truth. His ontological reality is ultimate reality. There are no standards outside God by which to evaluate His reality. As ultimate reality, God is the only absolute standard for evaluating the truth of anything in the world (John 5:33-40; 8:31-32, 42-47).

Moreover, both Jesus and the Holy Spirit are said to be "the truth" (John 14:6, 16–17; 15:26;1 John 5:7–10). So the Father is truth, the Son is truth, and the Holy Spirit is truth. The locus of truth is the Triune God. God is truth.

The Word Is Truth

Central to the Christian epistemology is that the Word of God is truth. This is the unequivocal claim of Jesus Christ: "Thy Word is truth" (John 17:17, cf., John 8:31–59). In the early church, John extends this to a declaration that the apostolic word is "the spirit of truth" by which "the spirit of error" can be exposed (1 John 4:6). The term translated "error" here, does not mean "mistake," but rather "deceit or a leading astray."[31] When God speaks, His words are true because He is truth itself. It is impossible for God to speak falsehoods (2 Sam. 7:28; Titus 1:2; Heb. 6:18). Whether He speaks directly, through Jesus (Deut. 18:18), or the prophets and apostles (1 Kings 17:24; Jer. 1:1–4; 2 Tim. 3:16; 1 Peter 1:11–12; 2 Peter 1:21), His Word is reliable because it is rooted in, and ruled by, the divine absolute. It corresponds to reality because reality is measured by God, the ultimate reality.

The Truth According to Scripture

Concerning the biblical concept of truth, we conclude,

First, God is truth. Truth is ontologically rooted in God. Truth is an unchanging, fixed, absolute attribute of God. Truth is thus unchanging, fixed, and absolute.

Second, truth corresponds to reality.[32] Truth is what is true as opposed to falsehood and lies.

Third, truth is propositional and verifiable.

Fourth, truth is revealed, and therefore objective, knowable, and systematizable. Because God's Word was spoken and written, it may be taught and learned.

Fifth, truth may be personally practiced inasmuch as truth determines what is right and wrong, moral and immoral, righteous and unrighteous, real and unreal. The person who is faithful to God is so because he or she is "true to God", i.e., ideologically and morally aligned to the true God, the God of truth.

The biblical concept of truth may be summarized by two over-arching propositions: (1) truth is theocentric and therefore absolute, and (2) truth corresponds to reality. From these two propositions we can deduce certain philosophical implications.[33]

Philosophical Implications

If truth is absolute and correspondence to reality, then the following implications must be true:

Truth Is Universal

Whatever is true at one time and in one place is true at all times and in all places. Relativists object, saying that a proposition like "it is raining" may be true in Portland but not Pittsburgh. But this merely demonstrates that meaning is relative to context. Once context is considered, meaning is understood, and truth is clearly absolute. It is true that it may be raining in Portland but not Pittsburgh. But the proposition "It is raining in Portland" is just as true in Pittsburgh as it is in Portland, so long as it is raining in Portland.

Other truth statements transcend context. The laws of gravity, mathematics, and physics are no less true in one nation than in another. The reality of God and the claims of Christ fit in this category. Belief is irrelevant. So far as objective truth is concerned, the reality of God is no less true for a Japanese Shintoist than for the evangelical believer standing next to him on the subway. Further, the Bible's truth claims are exclusive. If the evangelical's beliefs correspond with reality, then the Shintoist's beliefs cannot. That may seem harsh, but truth is, by definition, exclusive. Except where they may superficially agree, biblical truth claims are utterly incompatible with the truth claims of any other religion.

Truth Statements Are True for All Persons

Everyone is entitled to a personal opinion, but not personal "truth." Truth cannot be created in the metaphysical sense; it can only be discovered. Truths correspond to reality independent of religion or moral behavior or consensus or personal preference. If truth is relative, then Hitler's views, policies, and deeds have as much validity as Mother Teresa's. Absolute truth does not change. Whatever is true and right, is true and right for all people, in all places, under all conditions.

Infinite Epistemological Regress Is Impossible

Each truth statement has a foundational starting point. These starting points are first principles—self-evident, absolute truths. The implication of relativism is that every truth claim rests upon another, so that there is an infinite regression and so no absolute. If this is "true," then there is no truth (and so it is not true). It is logically impossible for the very reason that logic is possible.

How then do these first truths come to exist? There must be a resting place for them, as well, and that can only be in God.

Mutually Exclusive Truths Cannot Coexist

"A woman has the right to terminate her unwanted pregnancy, for the fetus inside her is not a living human being with God-derived rights." This kind of statement is made by relativists all the time, but it is an absolute truth claim. It is either true in all its parts, or it is not true. They recognize that it is not true and untrue at the same time and in the same sense. As our universe works, a fetus cannot be both a blob of tissue without God-derived rights and a preborn human being with God-derived rights.

Relativists in the end must accept the law of noncontradiction. Not to do so is self-defeating. The truth claim *"There are no absolutes"* is an absolute truth claim. The fact that truth is absolute forbids contradictory conditions or truths. Relativism would require that the universe be full of mutually contradictory truths.

Truth Claims May Be Made and Believed

The relativists who make the sorts of truth claim stated above are not consistent relativists. If truth were relative, it would be impossible to rationally believe or claim that anything is true or false. Nothing would be true; nothing would be false. Again, to affirm that "truth is relative" is to affirm an absolute statement. If one truth is absolute, then the entire thesis of relativism is disproved.

This is a serious dilemma for the relativist, as demonstrated by Josh McDowell and Norman Geisler from a "Winnie-the-Pooh" story:

> Winnie the lovable bear has a notorious appetite, which brings him to the door of Rabbit for something to eat. When Winnie-the-Pooh knocks, Rabbit, who has no intention of feeding the bear, calls out, "Nobody home." Wise Winnie responds, "There must be somebody home or else he could not say, 'Nobody home.'"
>
> Winnie is right, of course. Rabbit cannot deny his own presence unless he is present to deny it. Similarly, those who deny the existence of absolutes cannot hold that all things are relative unless there is some unchangeable ground on which their affirmation can stand. It's senseless to pronounce everything relative while not allowing that very position to be relative as well. In reality, the relativist stands on the pinnacle of his or her own absolute in order to pronounce everything else relative.[34]

As a child, I remember hearing my uncle call upstairs to my little cousin who was supposed to be asleep, saying, "Karen, are you asleep?" Much to our amusement, she answered "Yes." Her truth claim, of course, did not correspond to reality (unless she was talking in her sleep). If truth were not absolute, this incident would have been unremarkable, without humor, and meaningless. It was humorous because we saw the implication of her truth claim.

Truth Can Be Stated in Terms of Propositions

A proposition is simply a truth claim or statement. It follows from what has been said that only an absolute truth can be propositional. Only relative statements could be made about relative truth. The relativist cannot logically say that "There is no propositional truth," for that is a propositional truth claim. Attempts to deny propositions use propositions and so are self-defeating.[35]

Relativists are allergic to propositional statements, which makes much of what they say rather meaningless. A television talk-show hosted a forum consisting of a group of teenagers on one side, and their parents on the other. When asked what each considered "acceptable" behavior, either side frequently disagreed with the other. Much of what the teenagers considered "acceptable," the parents rejected as *un*acceptable.

"Why is the behavior unacceptable?" they were asked. The relativistic parents could only answer: "Well, we just feel it is." They could reach no solution with their teen children because they had no appeal to absolutes for the teens to consider. In fact, no solution to this dilemma *can* be achieved apart from absolutes. Parents who embrace relativism as their own criteria of ethics, cannot consistently deny their children the same criteria.

One Can Be Mistaken or Deceived

If truth were relative, no one could be mistaken or make a false statement. In the field of theology, for example, there would be no such thing as heresy in a relative universe, for heresy simply is an error—an incorrect or deceptive statement about God. In a relative universe, lies would be impossible. Rabbit lied to Pooh when he said he was not home. We can dismiss a deceptive statement like this, or Karen's "sleep-talking" with amusement. The ability to discern that some statements are true and some are false is often a life-or-death matter, however.

Learning Is Possible

Learning is a process of replacing uncertain agnosticism or beliefs that prove false with true propositions. Relativists, then, are being inconsistent when they send their children to school and help them learn their multiplication tables. If truth were relative, one could never learn. There would be no point in trying.

Truth Is Static

Truth is static in that it is unchanging and constant. The statement "It is raining in Portland" will no longer be true when the sun comes out, but it is locked into unchangeable reality for the moment when it was true. If it rained on July 21, 1881, at 2:00 P.M. that fact will not change through all eternity.

If a truth remains the same throughout all ages, then the idea of "process" or temporal truth is preposterous. "Truth," says Carl F. H. Henry, "is not subject to revision as are the airline schedules. . . . The good and the true cannot be reduced to whatever Hollywood and Madison Avenue momentarily approve, or to whatever culture-ridden sociologists and secular humanists command."[36]

It will be true forever, then, that 2 + 2 = 4. A conflicting truth claim will never *become* true. Truth will never *become* error as long as its context does not change. A corollary to this is that how we perceive or process truth can change, but the change is in us, not in the truth being processed. R. Scott Richards says this well: "Perspective, geography, or the time on the clock may change the way we view reality, but reality remains unchanged. When reality is described accurately, we encounter truth. Absolute truth."[37]

Truth Is Knowable

Education is possible, because truth is knowable. It is independent of us. But one can conceptualize, or *know* truth, and what one conceptualizes does radically affect how one lives or what one does. Knowledge of truth is cognitive and intellectual.

Relativists who will not admit this face the same kind of logical dilemma mentioned above. The denial that truth can be known is an assertion that a truth can be known.

For the Christian, all truth is conceptualized as revelation from God, knowable from examining creation or providence, or from God's revealed words in Scripture. God speaks in forms we can understand and *test* or *verify*. Jesus said, "You shall know the truth and the truth shall make you free" (John 8:32). One teaching to draw from this text is Jesus' affirmation that truth can be known.

Truth Is Rational, Rather Than Existential

Truth that is knowable is not something "wholly other" from our experience, which was a popular notion in twentieth-century existentialism-based theology. Knowable truth is attainable by understanding.

Truth Doesn't Come in Degrees

A major implication of relativistic truth has been that we can shade it in hues of gray. We can make a deceptive statement that in some sense technically is true, though the actual facts of the truth are being obscured. Rather, something that is said with a design to alter or deny access to descriptions of reality is a lie. Something can't be partly true and partly false.

Something Can Be True Only If It Affirms or Denies Something

Truth statements can be reduced to logically valid propositions. They must have content that is either self-evident or that can be tested and proven or rejected. The statement that begins this paragraph makes an affirmation: *Truth statements can be reduced to logically valid propositions.* It can be judged according to the definitions of the word symbols *truth* and of *logically valid propositions* and be shown to be foundational and undeniable.

This principle occasionally is brought up as a proof that the teachings of Christ were not always coherent. Jesus said, "I am the way, and the *truth* and the life" (John 14:6a). If Jesus "is" truth, then truth is not a statement but a person. Anyone who studies the gospel of John knows that Jesus' "I am. . . ." statements use parabolic, metaphorical language. Affirmation about Jesus is implied in Jesus' identification with truth. That affirmation is a recurring theme in John 1:14 and 8:31–32. The affirmative content here implied is "Jesus is God, the source of all truth." This is a valid proposition that invites itself to be tested and proven or disproved.

Truth Is Theocentric

As stated above, if truth is absolute, it must have a basis for its "absoluteness." The only sufficient basis is God. A significant corollary must be drawn from this principle: *All truth is God's truth; all truth is theocentric.*

Augustine wrote, "Every good and true Christian should understand that wherever he may find truth, it is his Lord's."[38] Gordon R. Lewis says, "Every story has three sides—your side, my side and God's. Our assertions are true insofar as they conform to God's mind. . . . All truth is God's truth, whether on your side or my side, or wherever it may be found."[39] The same thesis is argued by Frank E. Gaebelein in his notable book, *The Pattern of God's Truth.*[40]

Christian education (ideally all education) should present all subjects of study as parts of an integrated whole with Scripture at the center. Every truth, wherever found, is part of the "whole." Behind the "whole" is the divine absolute of God.

God Can Be Known

God is truth. Truth is absolute and objective, and can thus be known. God, therefore, can be known. This does not mean that we can have exhaustive, absolute knowledge of God or of truth in general. It does mean that the *basis* of our knowledge, or the *object* of our knowledge is absolute because it is the absolute God.

Theology Seeks to Understand an Unchanging God

All systems of theology are human efforts to understand and consider the implications of the person and character and attributes of God. Systematic theology assumes that there are rational, unchanging categories around which to build, so the very fact that we try to look at God systematically is a witness against relativism.

There is an aspect of relativity, for theologies are written to communicate to a specific cultural context, and the formulations are therefore relative to the people addressed. But to the extent that these theologies are honest attempts to understand the God who has revealed himself in Scripture, they look to absolute truth claims and fundamentally are based upon what is unchanging. The job of systematic theology is never done. There always are new applications to draw, new generations to reach, or interpretive errors to judge and correct.

While it is a fallible, human process, systematic theology's task of seeking to organize the knowledge of God in a systematic way that communicates to people in a particular context is a worthwhile endeavor. If truth were not absolute, we would have no goal to shoot for. Categories could not be related, and systematizing, by definition, would be impossible.

Everything That Is Not True Is False

We must be diligent to seek the truth. No one can say (truthfully) that the content of belief doesn't matter (if one is sincere). In the reality we experience, there is no middle ground between what is true and what is not true. Aristotle's definition of truth demonstrates this polarity of truth and falsehood: *"To say of what is, that it is not, or of what is not, that it is, is false; while to say of what is, that it is, and of what is not, that it is not, is true."*[41] It is by the facts of the matter—by their being so, or not so—that a statement is found to be true or false.

It Matters What You Believe

If Christian truth claims are absolutely true, my eternal salvation depends upon the content of what I believe and who I accept as the final authority in life. More immediately, my safety or well-being depends upon what I believe. It also depends upon what those around me believe. If the people standing about my house can justify lawlessness as their moral right, my family's well-being is in danger. That is precisely what has happened in times of civil unrest, with horrifying results.

Another implication, if Christian truth claims are true, is that there is only one meaning to life, and any attempt to establish human autonomy leads inevitably to meaninglessness. Meaning is contingent upon reality—what is true. When truth is diminished, knowledge disappears. If it doesn't matter what we think, then what we *feel* is our guide. It is easy to see why no stable society has ever been built upon relativism or stood apart from absolute truth. Each human being has both a moral responsibility and a practical motivation to know truth (Pss. 51:6; 119:51; Prov. 3:3; 23:23; Titus 1:1). Relativism's rejection of this reality robs humanity of meaning and worth.

There is no genuine caring in the absence of truth. Where there is no truth there is no human value nor a basis for showing love. A pastor said of his church, "we cannot be just a crowd; we must be a church where people care and truth matters."[42] He was right that the two are inextricable from one another. To be a church that really cares we must embrace the truth.

The understated summation of these points is that truth matters. And if truth matters, it matters what we believe. Dorothy L. Sayers said, "It is worse than useless for Christians to talk about the importance of Christian morality, unless they are prepared to take their stand upon the fundamentals of Christian theology. It is a lie to say that dogma does not matter; it matters enormously."[43]

Truth Is Objective, Rather Than Subjective

Truth is a matter of fact, not our feelings. Truth is objective because God exists outside of our feelings. It is universal because God stands outside of all that exists. Only his existence is independent. McDowell and Bob Hostetler discuss this needed understanding for the twenty-first century:

> It is impossible to arrive at an objective, universal, and constant standard of truth and morality without bringing God onto the stage. If an objective standard of truth and morality exists, it cannot be the product of the human mind (or it will not be objective); it must be the product of another Mind. If a constant and unchanging truth exists, it must reach beyond the human timelines (or it would not be constant); it must be eternal. If a universal rule of right and wrong exists, it must be above us all. Yet, absolute truth must be something—or Someone—that is common to all humanity, to all creation. . . . it is God's nature and character that defines truth. He defines what is right for all people, for all times, for all places. But truth is not something He decides; it is something He is.[44]

Christianity is predicated upon this "claim to absolute, objective *truth*," says R. Albert Mohler Jr. "To surrender this ground is to surrender the faith itself."[45]

Truths Can Be Related to Other Truths to Interpret Reality

We have said that if truth statements do not correspond to fact or reality, there can be no systematic understanding of them. We seek systematic knowledge in any discipline because it applies to the way something is or works, or might work. This relatedness interconnects all of life and truth.

Truth Can Be Tested

If truth corresponds to reality, it can be checked against reality. Most truths are verifiable, all or in part. Keep in mind in this verification process the difference between truth and our communication of it, which uses words or some other linguistic symbols. There must be translation from the actual "truth" to the comprehensible conception of it. The concept is limited by the limits of the human mind and the limitations of human language. Still, we should be able to test our mental conceptions and find a close correspondence to reality. There must be a real difference between things and the statements about the things. But this real difference between thought and things is precisely what is entailed in a correspondence view of truth.

An Error Need Not Be Intentionally Misleading to Be False

The biblical standard of revelation is that the truths in Scripture present God's communication about reality. This seems obvious, given the Bible's truth claims about itself, but it was the issue in the "inerrancy" debate of the 1970s and 1980s.

On one side were Bible scholars who believed the Bible is a book written by culture-bound human beings only, so it naturally has errors. However, we still can honor Scripture as God's truth in some subjectively mystical sense because the authors were telling what they believed to be true. They never intentionally misled, so their statements need not correspond that closely to reality.

This redefines the term *error* as an intent to mislead, and maintains the odd premise that whatever a writer intends to affirm is true, however it corresponds to the facts. This might be called an *intentionality view* of truth. It accomplished what the author intended it to accomplish.[46]

No wonder the opponents of these scholars, the "inerrantists," demanded more precision about what we mean when we say the Bible is "true." Inerrantists stand on the final authority of God-breathed Scripture. They believe the original texts (autographs) were without error and that modern translations have extremely close correspondence to the autographs—and to reality.

The Law of Noncontradiction Applies

If truth did not correspond to reality, then two mutually exclusive truth claims could both be true. As J. Oliver Buswell Jr., says:

> If we accept the sovereign Triune God as revealed in the Bible, it follows that we accept propositional truth, and the laws which are

inherent in the nature of propositional truth. These laws are not imposed upon our basic presupposition but are implicit in it and derived from it. The Bible is a book in human language. If we are not talking nonsense we must then believe in the rules of linguistic expression. The Bible as a book written in human language claims to speak the truth. If the word truth is not meaningless, it implies the laws of truth, that is, the laws of logic.[47]

Truth cannot be defined as "that which works." The pragmatic view of truth is false.

Truth is an *expression* of reality, not an existential *experience*. Geisler and Ronald Brooks illustrate the propositional nature of truth:

> Meaning is a disclosure of the author's intentions, but it can only be discovered by looking at what he actually said. Since we cannot read the author's mind when we want to know the meaning of a statement, we look at the statement itself. Only when we see the proper relation of all the words in the sentence, and the sentence to the paragraph, etc., do we understand the big meaning of the affirmation. Then we check it against reality to see if it is true or false.[48]

The Bible Is True

The ninth commandment is predicated on a correspondence view of truth. The law "You shall not bear false witness against your neighbor" (Exod. 20:16) depends for its very meaning and effectiveness on a correspondence view of truth. This command assumes that a true witness states what happened and that a false statement does not correspond to reality.[49]

Lies, Falsehood, and Heresies Are Possible

If truth did not correspond to reality, then it would be impossible to lie. If one's statement need not correspond to the facts in order to be true, then any statement is compatible with any given state of affairs. This would rob the Bible of its authority and make systematic theology impossible.

Communication Would Break Down Without Corresponding Truth

Factual communication depends on informative statements. But informative statements must be factually true in order to communicate meaningful information. Because the gospel and the Bible correspond so closely to truth, we can translate, interpret, and contextualize the Christian message with confidence. World and neighbor evangelism, biblical witness, and Christian education are worthy and necessary enterprises. Systematic theology becomes not only possible but essential. Disciplined reflection on biblical truth is essential for Christian living and ministry. If truth resides in God, every person must be a theologian.

THE KNOWLEDGE OF TRUTH

To this point, three principles have seemed interwoven in the discussion of the nature of truth:

1. Truth is absolute.
2. Truth corresponds to reality.
3. Logic applies to reality.

We easily can see that the third principle, logic, is a bridge between consideration of the nature of truth and understanding whether truth can be known, and the source of that knowledge. So it must also appear among the principles still to consider:

3. Logic applies to reality.
4. Creation resembles the Creator.
5. Religious language is analogous.

The Basis for Thought

The answer to the question posed in the title of this essay is, of course, affirmative. Truth can be known, so long as we have an adequate epistemology for knowing it. It was the epistemological question that so dogged Kant and his philosophical children.

We can know, first of all, because there are laws of thought as certainly as there are laws of physics. Three fundamental laws govern all rationality:

1. *Mutually contradictory statements cannot both be true.* This is called the *law of noncontradiction.* "A" is not "non-A," in the same sense, at the same time.
2. *A thing must be identical to itself.* If it were not identical to itself, then it wouldn't be itself. This is the *law of identity.*
3. *There is no middle ground between "being" something and "not being" something.* We may call a rude and selfish person a "pig," but we know that this unpleasant being still is a human being in its essence. *Pig* and *human being* are mutually exclusive categories. A human being is not, nor can he be, a pig, and a pig cannot be a human being. This is the *law of the excluded middle.*

All the rules of logical, rational thought relate ultimately to one or more of these three principles. We use them to know all that we know. The knowledge of God is no exception. For example, through logic we can argue for the being and attributes of God from what is observed. Through principles of logic, the principle of causality ("only being can cause being") helps us use naturalistic, cosmological, ontological, teleological, and anthropological arguments to validly argue that God exists, and to make meaningful fact statements about him.

Knowledge of Truth About God

Epistemologically, logic is the basis for all knowledge of God. Ontologically, God is the basis of all logic. Epistemologically, reason and logic are the starting point to the knowledge of truth. Ontologically, revelation is the starting point.

Logical deductions can be made. Argumentation can take place and be profitable. The law of rational inference applies, otherwise theological argumentation is implausible. By logical deduction we arrive at doctrines we would otherwise not know, such as the Trinity and inerrancy.

A momentously significant subpoint here is that *religious language, or "God-talk," is possible and it can be meaningful, despite God's transcendence.* We may not puzzle. Knowledge of all truth is intimately connected with knowledge about the source of truth, and the source of creation. We can make truth statements about reality, creation, and ourselves if we know truths about God. And we can logically discern truths about God if we know truths about reality, creation, and ourselves.

For example, our understanding of anthropology shows some correspondence to our understanding of theology as it is revealed in creation and Scripture. God shows every sign of thought and foresight, of being a moral being, and other attributes that fit what the Bible says about humankind as the image-bearer of God. The Scriptures logically extend this teaching to a revelation that God has those and other attributes in infinite and inexhaustible proportion.

The Bible makes the truth statement that this image in humanity is distorted by fallenness. However, this defacing of the similarity between humanity and God does not destroy the fact that it is there. Theology refers to the *via eminentiae* (the "way of eminence") as our derivation of the eminent attributes of God from the finite examples of those attributes found in human beings. This is an acceptable line of reasoning so long that it doesn't turn God into an anthropomorphic extension of ourselves. We can easily see that power seen in creation and human relations has strong correspondence to what the Bible teaches of God's omnipotence; likewise wisdom shows strong correspondence to a belief that God is all-wise and that he exhaustively knows every fact (omniscience).

If creation did not resemble the Creator we couldn't know anything about God through nature or even the Bible, since its writing is a creaturely manifestation. We could not even know in any meaningful, ultimate sense about the incarnation of Christ.

This correspondence makes logical arguments for God valid. It is legitimate and justifiable to reason toward God from that which He has created. By extension we can reason that there is a correspondence between reality and what is proposed about reality. We have a basis for analogical language, which in the end is the only possible way for finite beings to communicate truth about the transcendent and infinite. Using analogical language we can develop a systematic understanding of the Father, the Son, and the Holy Spirit. This would, of course, be impossible without Scripture's propositional statements about God and the relationship among his persons. With Scripture as our guide we also can draw pieces of this systematic understanding from nature.

If creation did not resemble the Creator, then we could not assume that being produces being.

More needs to be said about the importance of analogy to knowing. Kant was looking for a way beyond analogical thought, when none existed or was necessary. We use analogy continually in our thought processes. Something is like or unlike something else, so I will think and act about those things accordingly.

When it comes to thinking and speaking about God, analogy is indispensable. We only have three alternatives for descriptive God-talk: (1) *equivocal language* (totally different); (2) *univocal language* (totally the same); or (3) *analogical language* (both the same and different). Univocal language leads to skepticism—the philosophical dilemma of the Enlightenment. Equivocal language either reduces God to the mortal or elevates man to deity. That leaves us with analogy as the most helpful epistemological tack.

Only because religious language is analogous can we use the *via negativa* ("way of negation") arguments to deny any imperfections in God. Negation identifies and defines God's attributes by looking at the finite order and seeing that God is not the same as that. Creatures are measurable; the universe cannot contain the being of the divine, the earth and its creatures are mutable but God is unchangeable.

This preserves the transcendence of God, answering the charge of many modern theologians that no statements about God have validity, for he is totally "other." If language were not analogous, these theologians would be correct. Analogous language is possible for God-talk, if God is immanent as well as transcendent. Every evidence assures us that he is.

The Necessity of the Five Premises

There is an interdependence among the five premises: (1) Truth is absolute. (2) Truth corresponds to reality. (3) Logic applies to reality. (4) Creation resembles the Creator. (5) Religious language is analogous. If one of these premises were not true, none would be true, and there would be no epistemology for truth of any sort—either about God or about the reality of which God is author. There is a Creator-creature relationship in which all being of the creature derives from the Creator.

The Creator-creature relationship sets up a basis for analogy. Otherwise, there could be no correspondence between reality and what is proposed about reality. The fact that creation resembles the Creator allows language that is analogical. That religious language is analogous, is dependent upon the fact that logic applies to reality. The application of logic to reality is dependent upon truth, which is unchanging and absolute.

That logic applies to reality is a necessary presupposition to religious language, or God-talk. Ultimately, all these premises are necessary. In his inimitable way Ravi Zacharias says,

> As a sloganeering culture, we have unblushingly trivialized the serious and exalted the trivial because we have bypassed the rudimentary and necessary steps of logical argument. Reality can be lost when reason and language have been violated. . . . It is understandable why textbooks in logic do not hit the bestseller list, but the laws of logic must apply to reality else we may as well be living in a madhouse.[50]

REASON AND TRUTH

Resolving the Kantian dilemma is only part of the issue, however. If the Christian epistemology of Word/creation/systematic study of God is ultimately the only reliable way to truth, then Christians should be, of all humanity, the most incisive and reasonable thinkers. Certainly we should have no trouble following Peter's urging that we should be ready to give a reason for "the hope that is in you" (1 Peter 3:15b). In what Jesus declared as "the great commandment," He said, "You shall love the Lord your God with all . . . your *mind*" (Matt. 22:37). The apostle Paul urges, "Whatever is true . . . let your mind dwell [i.e., *think*] on these things" (Phil. 4:8). God Himself asks, "To whom will you compare me or count me equal? To whom will you liken me that we may be compared?" (Isa. 46:5 NIV). As Geisler and Brooks write, "Thinking is not an option for the Christian; it is an imperative."[51]

But how much can we count on reason? What are the limitations of reason? What is the relationship between reason and faith? In Christian apologetics, there are widely differing opinions about the relationship of faith to reason. Some argue for the priority of reason; others insist on the priority of faith. The best answer seems to be that both are important and we should strive for a proper balance.[52] In whatever way the fall affected the mind, it is the certain testimony of Scripture that we still *can* and *must* reason.[53]

I would suggest the following implications of what we "know" about reason, relating them to theology.[54]

What Reason Can Do

Reason Can Prove the Existence of God

The medieval philosopher theologian Thomas Aquinas (1224–1274) insisted that God's existence could be demonstrated by rational proofs. This does not mean that anyone can know God personally by reason alone, or that reason alone brings one to saving faith in God. It does mean what Paul says about general revelation in Romans 1:20, that the unregenerate can see God clearly enough through nature. They see at work "the eternal power and divine nature." As theologian Henry C. Thiessen says, "The revelation of God in nature reveals that there is a God and that he has such attributes as power, glory, divinity, and goodness."[55] Aquinas would add, "To know that God exists in a general way is implanted in us by nature."[56] Thomas C. Oden affirms, "A limited reasoning toward and about God . . . can proceed, without direct reference to Scripture or the history of revelation, on the basis of natural human intuition, moral insight, and reasoning."[57]

Reason Is a Means of Understanding Revelation

Revelation must be grasped by reason. Revelation presupposes reason.

Truths, to be received as objects of faith, must be intellectually apprehended. Faith must have knowledge content or it is not faith. In believing we affirm the truth of the proposition believed. If there is no proposition, we have nothing to affirm. The first and indispensable office of reason in matters of faith, therefore, is the cognition or intelligent apprehension of the truths proposed for our reception.[58]

Reason Tells Us What Is Reasonable to Believe

Reason processes the message of revelation and determines whether it is rational, coherent, or believable. Reason applies the law of noncontradiction.

Reason Verifies the Credibility of Revelation

"It is not enough to understand the revelation and declare it free of contradiction; reason must determine its credibility."[59]

Reason Argues for the Dependability of Revelation

By reason we know that God stands behind the revelations he has given to us. Once we correctly understand them, we can depend that the truth behind them will not change, for God does not change.

Reason Interprets the Content of Revelation

When we claim to recognize, acknowledge, or know God through His revelation, reason is by no means suspended. Without reason we could not interpret revelation. Faith needs reason, or else we could not gather the revelations into a coherent picture of the object of our belief.

This is not to say that reason takes priority over revelation. Once reason tells us what is revelation, and so worthy to be believed, reason subjects itself to the revelation. Once one has determined, by reason, that the Bible is the Word of God, it is absurd to sit in judgment on it.

Reason Helps Confirm Faith

Faith is not an "upper story" leap without evidence. On the contrary, faith rests on the certitude of objective truth, or facticity. The person with faith is willing to accept the evidence for what it really is (John 7:17). Faith, W. G. T. Shedd says, "is yet an intelligent act."[60]

What Reason Cannot Do

Reason Cannot Form the Basis for Faith

The basis for faith is revelation; what God has told us. Reason considers revelation, faith receives it. Revelation has to do with content and message; reason has to do with method. Reason learns, it never teaches.

Reason Cannot Take the Individual to Faith

If reason were the only way open to the knowledge of God, we would remain in miserable ignorance. Man must reason, but reason must be assisted by the Spirit of God as it considers the Word of God.

Unaided Reason Cannot Understand Revelation

Apart from the work of God in the human heart, reason cannot reach salvific knowledge of God.

Reason Alone Is Unable to Interpret Revelation

The Holy Spirit is the spirit of truth in the heart, illuminating revelation, helping reason see that it is revelation, and applying its implications. Reason without the Holy Spirit cannot comprehend the things of God.

Reason Is a Servant

Reason is the servant of God in understanding revelation and coming to faith. When reason becomes master we no longer have faith but rationalism.

CONCLUSION

Strong, reliable convictions concerning right and wrong cannot long remain afloat in a sea of relativism. Without absolute truth, we are not equipped to evaluate moral issues. Without a sound spiritual and moral standard we cannot hold the truth of the Christian faith. If we do not hold to truth as absolute, knowledge will disappear, tyranny will follow in the wake of moral anarchy, and all that is good, right, and just, will be engulfed in a tide of intellectual and moral nihilism.

What must we as Christians do? First, we must *pursue* truth. We must renew our conviction and enlarge our understanding that truth is rooted in God and recorded in His Word. Jesus said, "If you abide in My Word, then you are truly disciples of Mine; and you shall know the truth, and the truth shall make you free" (John 8:31–32). The pursuit of truth requires that we love the truth (2 Thess. 2:10), and embrace it (2 Chron. 15:2; John 7:17; 8:47; 18:37; 1 John 4:6). Blaise Pascal (1623–1662) might have been describing our own day when he remarked, "Truth is so obscure in these times and falsehood so established, that unless we love the truth, we cannot know it."[61]

Second, the Christian church must *proclaim* the truth. Truth must be taught in the home (Deut. 11:18–19) and around the world. Contributor to *The Fundamentals*, B. B. Warfield of Old Princeton (1851–1921), said, "Christianity is in its very nature an aggressive religion; it is in the world just in order to convince men; when it ceases to *reason*, it ceases to exist."[62]

Over one hundred and twenty years ago, J. C. Ryle (1816–1900) said, "If ever there was a time in the world when Churches were put upon their trial, whether they would hold fast the truth or not, that time is the present time."[63] One can only wonder what Ryle would think of today's church and its flirtation with relativism.

The cost of relativism is the loss of relevance. Truth that is relative is insignificant. Os Guinness has written, "Without truth, relevance is meaningless and dangerous."[64] As Alister McGrath says,

> To allow relevance to be given greater weight than truth is a mark of intellectual shallowness and moral irresponsibility. The first and most fundamental of all questions must be this: Is it true? . . . No one can build his personal life around a lie. Christian doctrine is concerned to declare that Christian morality rests upon a secure foundation.[65]

Third, we must *practice* the truth. We know so much, yet do so little of what we know. Again, McGrath is on target:

> An obedient response to truth is a mark of intellectual integrity. It marks a willingness to hear what purports to be the truth, to judge it, and—if it is found to be true—to accept it willingly. Truth demands to be accepted because it inherently deserves to be accepted and acted upon. Christianity recognizes a close link between faith and obedience—witness Paul's profound phrase "the obedience of faith" (Rom.

1:5)—making it imperative that the ideas underlying and giving rise to attitudes and actions should be judged and found to be right.[66]

In the end, we must accept one of two alternatives. Either truth is relative or truth is absolute. Either we live in a universe where truth and morality are relative and all is meaningless and irrelevant, or truth is absolute, and moral rules exist and we are accountable to a holy and righteous God.

CHAPTER 2

Through the Written Word, Spiritual Truth Can Be Known

Thomas R. Edgar

The church has always regarded the Bible as God's word. It is inspired and without error, the ultimate authority on all matters about which it speaks. It is the absolute and only authority on all spiritual matters. Some who wish to justify a weaker view of scriptural authority have claimed that the inerrant, authoritative view was not the historic view of the church. However, the supporting evidence advanced for this view is not only selective but often wholly inaccurate.[1]

There is little question that the orthodox church has always viewed the Bible as both inerrant and authoritative. The *Cambridge History of the Bible* asserts,

> At the end of the eighteenth century, as throughout it, the traditional conception of divine revelation was still everywhere accepted in western Christendom: Catholics and Protestants alike conceived of revelation as contained in inerrant propositions written down in the Bible by authors who were directly inspired by the Spirit of God.[2]

This historical study also states, "Before the nineteenth century it was almost universally assumed that the whole Bible was equally true, since the Holy Spirit of God was the real author of the Scriptures in every part." Also, until the end of the eighteenth century, "the Bible was thought of as a collection of revealed truths, the very oracles of God himself."[3] Belief that the Bible is inerrant and authoritative in all matters on which it speaks is not a product of Enlightenment rationalism, as has been charged. It has been the normal opinion of Christians throughout the history of the church.

The Bible is the authority from which the church derives its theology. It is the only objective standard by which we determine what is true.

REBUFFING SCRIPTURAL AUTHORITY

A continuing war has been waged over the Christian conception of authority between the church and unbelieving philosophers and theologians. In the later twentieth century, leaders in traditionally evangelical churches, particularly in academic circles, even joined the attack against the traditional view of Scripture This attack is not only against the inerrancy of Scripture but against Scripture's *objective* authority. An *objectively authoritative* Bible is not dependent for authority on anyone's recognition of that authority. It is God's Word; therefore, it is true, even if not one person accepts it.

There is another facet of authority: Does the individual submit to Scripture as the authority in personal life, as opposed to matters of faith. Alongside the defection of their colleges and seminaries and many pastors, a good many professing Christians have looked for ways around the full ethical and spiritual weight of biblical authority in their lives. In the late 1900s this was frequently demonstrated, as in the "lordship debate." Did one need to submit to Jesus as Lord to be saved? Movements placed subjective continuing revelation alongside or even over the Bible. In TV church personality cults, the teachings of individuals dominated their followers' thinking. Worship and Christian education models downplayed Bible teaching. There was much evidence of a widespread decline in submission to scriptural authority.

The general decline in submission to authority cannot be separated from the widespread assault on the church's traditional view of Scripture. Among evangelicals, this is more a matter of declining individual spirituality than a conscious rejection of the Bible. However, a weak view of the authority of Scripture was basic to that spirituality malaise. Any application of Scripture as the authority for one's life derives from one's view of the objective authority of Scripture.

FACING THE NONRATIONAL ASSAULT

Academic Assault

The modern assault on Scripture is apparently a result of the teachings of post-enlightenment philosophers who discoursed on the subject of knowledge, particularly "religious knowledge." Their thinking was followed by nonevangelical theologians. These theologians and philosophers spurned the idea that religious truth could be communicated through propositions, through literal, objective truth such as a written propositional communication from God. They argued that objective religious truth or cognitive knowledge about God is impossible; that any knowledge about God, particularly revealed knowledge, is impossible since faith is nonrational and has nothing in common with knowledge.[4]

The Christian epistemology of truth was discussed in the last chapter. It may seem very mystically spiritual to speak of experiencing or encountering the Ultimate, but this implies that we cannot rationally know God or fact content about God. Such mind-emptying spirituality denies that God reveals content to us in creation, the Word, the person of Christ, or communion with the Holy Spirit. Is it even possible for Him to communicate information to us? Such a view became pervasive over the twentieth century. No church escaped its ramifications. Its assumptions reject God in any objective, literal sense. It substitutes anything an individual wishes to manufacture by a nonrational process. This process is then sanctified under a newly redefined idea of "faith."

Belief that the Bible is the literally true and inerrant Word of God, which conveys propositional information about God, is regarded by many theologians as a development of the scientific spirit of the age. The concept that the Bible is literally true, said one critic, "reflects the spirit of the age in agreeing that there is only one kind of truth, namely the literal or scientific; if the Bible is true, it must be literally true, since there is no other kind of truth than the literal."[5] He adds that this is incorrect, since "religious truth is not primarily a matter of verifiable propositions about God and human destiny. It is rather an existential awareness of man's situation in relation to God and the world, which can be expressed and communicated only under the forms of imagination and symbol."[6] Thus, religious truth is different than literal, objective, scientific truth, and faith is not based on rational thinking.[7] This rejection of the Bible as God's inerrant word is grounded in unbelief.

The constant pressure on Christian scholars to gain academic acceptability in nonevangelical circles, and an infatuation with "academia," has resulted in a great deal of dialogue and increasing tolerance of nonevangelical worldviews by evangelical theologians. The nonevangelical attitude toward the Bible has influenced many evangelical scholars. Through their writings and teaching, they influence those studying to enter the ministry. They may not fully accept the nonevangelical views of Scripture to which they are exposed, but there is a subtle depreciation of emphasis on the authority of Scripture. This trickles down to the individual Christian through pastors for whom Scripture has taken a back seat to experiential aspects of the Christian life. Over time the cognitive aspects of Scripture become less important. The Bible is no longer the absolute authority for life.[8]

Cultural Assault

The nonpropositional, nonrational concept of religious truth fits well with the pervasive and growing New Age movement. As one scholar says,

> Because New Age teachers are prone to use Christian terminology which they have loaded down with different meanings from that of

Christian orthodoxy, some Christians and many who are merely "Christianized" will be led astray. . . . Some researchers have suggested that some Christian churches and leaders have become a party to New Age techniques. Mysticism, visualization, and positive mental imaging are common practice in some Christian groups. . . . The New Age stress on an experiential religion as opposed to an objective one, and to feeling over against rationality, will find a ready ear in the modern generation.[9]

There is a forbidding correspondence between the New Age movement and some of the basic thinking of the academic community, both of which affect the church. To this is added the overall relativism of our society, which denies any distinction between truth and error.

Assault on Logic

No one can know anything about God apart from revelation. By natural revelation people know that there is a God and that He has everlasting power. This is stated by the apostle Paul (Rom. 1:20). Although enough to make man responsible to honor and seek God, this is minimal knowledge to overcome the state of sin in which each unbeliever lives. By means of personal knowledge we know nothing about God. By natural revelation, we can only know that God exists.

Let us think logically about these assertions that humanity cannot know God by human knowledge and that God cannot communicate with people. Such errors are based on the presupposition that we must somehow make contact with God but that God has little or no interest in communicating back. They begin from the wrong perspective. Assuming there is a personal God, it is not a leap in logic to assume that He wishes to communicate. Whatever He desires, it is certain that an infinite being is *able* to communicate. Humans communicate propositions and information to other humans by linguistic symbols called words. If we cannot communicate well enough in our own set of words or language, we can learn another person's language to do so. Certainly God can do as much. He can manage to communicate through language and within the limitations of human intellect and thought categories.

Although humans cannot understand everything there is to know about God, and human language may not be a perfect vehicle to convey precise information about the depths of God, He can convey enough information—all that he wishes. We do not need exhaustive knowledge about God, nor could our minds process it if we had it.

Information or knowledge that is not complete can still be accurate. If I have at my disposal all the multiplication tables and I say that 2 x 2 = 4 and

2 x 4 = 8, the information is complete and accurate so far as it goes. There is simply more that could be said on the subject. Whether God *can convey* total information about Himself through human language is not the issue. Nor is the issue whether a human being *can achieve* exhaustive comprehension of some divine attribute. The issue is whether God can convey all that he wishes us to know via the Bible and whether we can comprehend it.

FINDING RATIONAL FAITH

Faith in God extends beyond mere acceptance of true facts about who he is. It includes total trust in the goodness and correctness of what he says. However, although the faith is not in facts, faith has no content apart from facts. To have a basis for faith one must have confidence that certain facts are true. The faith grows from the specifics that are known. It is essential that we have confidence in the truth of certain facts for us to have a genuine faith. Faith cannot exist solely in the subjective or nonrational sphere. It needs a propositional knowledge foundation if it is to survive.

This is not to say that everyone who has religious faith has put confidence in the right set of facts. Faith can be invalid or illogical or based on lies. But if it is faith, the person has come to accept fact statements as true and has put confidence in the object behind the facts. We cannot have faith in that of which we know nothing. To say that faith is noncognitive or nonrational is a nonrational assertion.

But this assertion has become a serious indictment of the way in which many Christians view faith at the end of the twentieth century. Faith is not feeling or a convenient explanation for nonrational thoughts. Existentialist faith—as a blind leap apart from any rational basis, which is somehow valuable in itself—is not faith. It is definitely a nonrational concept. Although this existential, nonrational concept of faith is influential in Christian circles, it is neither the biblical nor the traditional Christian meaning.

The Validity of Biblical Faith

The concept of faith presented in the Bible directly contradicts the existential, nonrational models advanced in contemporary theology and philosophy. Throughout the Bible we are told to have faith in God. What is proposed is not a blind irrational leap into existential space. Nor is it a "faith in faith," in which sincerity is all that matters. We are called to a narrow faith in a uniquely true God. The uniqueness of that necessary truth encompasses the gospel. We are to believe in Christ because of who He is. Faith in a tree is not significant nor valid nor even appropriate. Any significance, validity, or appropriateness to faith is due solely to the object of the faith. The Bible is saturated with this concept of faith.

The apostle Paul states that it is possible to believe in vain (1 Cor. 15:2). This does not refer to a problem with the individual, that he or she is somehow defective in believing, which is how many understand this verse. Paul's statement is connected by the word *for* to the immediately following testimonies for the resurrection (vv. 3–11). Paul uses the example that faith in a resurrected Christ would be vain faith if Christ has not in fact been raised. What would be worse than to believe in a gospel that is a lie. Paul states this most explicitly in verses 14 and 17: "And if Christ has not been raised, our message is empty and your faith is also empty. . . . If Christ has not been raised, your faith is in vain. You are still in your sins."[10] Faith without a valid object is empty. Similarly, an existential, nonrational faith is without basis and is pointless.

The familiar discussion of faith is found in Hebrews, chapter 11. The first verse describes faith as "the assurance of what is hoped for, the conviction regarding things that are not being seen" (NASB). The remainder of Hebrews 11 illustrates and supports the description. In 11:1, the word translated "things" refers to tangible objects. Since it is a conviction regarding things, it is about something known. It is cognitive—based on propositions. To hope for something requires cognitive, or propositional, information on which to base hope.[11] The text goes on to show that hope is based upon the acts and promises of God. It is explicit and propositional.

True, Rational Faith

God is able to overcome barriers of human language or the authors' imperfections and communicate propositional information to humans. We cannot know anything about God apart from his special revelation. There is no *different* knowledge or *secret path of* religious truth by which a fallen human being can attain sufficient knowledge of God to reach God. The initiative must be from God, and it must use cognitive propositions and the communicative symbols of language as the means. There is no true Christian faith apart from propositional content.

THE SOURCE OF PROPOSITIONAL REVELATION

The Historical Uniqueness of Scripture

Where do we find God's propositional revelation? Of all religious Scriptures of the various world religions, there is a remarkable dearth of factual evidence to back up any of the things said. One must rest solely on the word of the human writer in the Qur'an or *The Book of Mormon*, for example, or human tradition as in Eastern religions. The Bible alone is supported by credible evidence.[12] Further, unlike other books alleged to be from God, there is not a single human author but dozens, spread over fifteen or more centuries. Yet there is internal literary consistency and a continuity of testimony to the same theological precepts and, behind them, to the same God. Study shows that there is no difference in character or attribute or being between the God of Adam and the God praised by John in his revelation on Patmos.

Rather than mystical interactions, Scripture describes direct contacts with God that were sensibly witnessed by both believers and unbelievers. These were recorded and accepted as true at a time when witnesses or their children were alive to dispute the accounts. New Testament accounts of miracles in particular make direct appeal to the existence of living witnesses (for example, Luke 1:2-4; John 21:24; Acts 26:26; 1 John 1:1). They could have been refuted by enemies; instead, they were passed down with full acceptance of truth. In the Old Testament the miracles of the Exodus that were recorded during the lifetime of Moses are an example.[13]

A further proof of the Old Testament is the precision with which its fore-telling prophecies have been fulfilled. Some are quite specific, yet have been fulfilled in detail. The New Testament sometimes appeals to the Old Testament messianic prophecies to demonstrate that Jesus' birth, ministry, and passion fulfill those detailed and diverse predictions. The New Testament stands on its own credibility in proclaiming that Jesus Christ was confirmed by miracles, which frequently fulfilled prophecies.

That same Jesus staked his credibility as the Son of God on recognition of the Old Testament as God's absolutely true and authoritative revelation. The apostles testified directly to the divine origins of the Old Testament and parts of the New Testament. They were confirmed as God's messengers through supernatural manifestations, which in turn substantiated what they wrote.

It would be beyond the scope of this article to go into the considerable body of extrabiblical witness to events described in the New Testament.

Christians believe that there is another level of testimony to the God-breathed revelatory power of Scripture. That is the confidence instilled by the presence of the Holy Spirit in the heart of the individual Christian. This internal testimony helps confirm what writings are in God's Word and helps apply them to life.[14]

What Does the Bible Say?

Regarding Its Value and Authority

The Bible claims to be from God and to be inspired. It was confirmed as inspired by our Lord Jesus Christ and by the apostles.[15] It is absolutely true and inerrant.[16] Thus, it is the authority for all things it covers. God's revelation is authoritative for all human beings, but it is the special authority for believers.

Regarding Knowledge of Its Content

The very fact that God has revealed all the detailed information in the Bible is ample proof that He desires that Christians know it. The Bible is full of the concepts of knowing and teaching spiritual truth. The leaders of the church are to be "apt to teach" (1 Tim. 3:2) and are worthy of double honor (remuneration) if they rule well—"especially those who labor in the word and doctrine" (1 Tim. 5:17). All elders rule but there is a special emphasis on those who teach doctrine.[17] In the Pastoral Epistles, the young minister, Timothy, is warned to be careful regarding his teaching. Paul states that the scriptures, "the things written beforehand," were "written for our instruction" (Rom. 15:4). In 1 Corinthians 10:11 he asserts that the Old Testament was "written for our instruction [warning]."

Many theologians avoid the book of Revelation, since from their theological perspective it is difficult to understand or not material to their thinking. Some might expect this prophecy to be a possible candidate for nonpropositional information. However, not only is it a propositional record but the book itself comments on this very fact. It is explicitly stated to be a revelation from God, which He gave in order to show His servants specific events that will happen (Rev. 1:1). It is stated that those who read and hear and obey the words "of this prophecy" will be blessed (v. 3). When John received this revelation from God, he was told to "write what you see in a book and send it to the seven churches" (v. 11). The glorified Christ tells John to "write the things which you have seen and which are and which will be" (v. 19).

John also heard the revelation of the "seven thunders," but when he prepared to write them down for this written revelation, he was told not to write them (10:4). This shows that God has not recorded every possible revelation that we are capable of understanding but only that which He desires us to know. God has no problem communicating propositional truth to men. He is able to communicate much more if He so desires. However, He has communicated all that is necessary for us to know. In closing his book, John says "These words are faithful and true and the Lord, the God of the spirits of the prophets sent His angel to show to His servants the things which must soon come to pass and behold I come quickly. Blessed is the one who keeps the words of the prophecies of this book" (22:6–7). He ends by warning against adding to or subtracting from this book (22:18–19).

John states that this written word is a revelation from God to be read and observed in its propositional details by God's servants, that there is blessing for so doing, and that anyone changing the words (specific propositional details) of this revelation will be punished. Thus, even in this frequently neglected book of the Bible, we see that the truth is propositional, the details are specific, and they are to be revealed to and observed by God's people. It is directly stated that this is God's word. As such, no one should tamper with its words.

Propositional Understanding

Christians are to have deep propositional understanding of the things of God. In 1 Corinthians 2:1–5, the apostle Paul tells the Corinthians that he first came to bring them the gospel (vv. 1-2) in God's power rather than with wise and persuasive arguments. Although this was formerly true, Paul argues that it is no longer true now that they belong to Christ. Now he does speak wisdom to them or should be able to do so (v. 6). This wisdom is not the world's wisdom. It was hidden but now is revealed to believers (vv. 7-12). It concerns the things that God has prepared for the believers (v. 12). It concerns "the deep things of God"(v. 10), taught in words (v. 13). It is specific, knowable, and propositional and is grasped cognitively. Paul is not speaking of a religious, nonrational knowledge, grasped by existential experience. The necessary element for understanding the "deep things" of God is the personal presence of the Spirit of God in the believer (vv. 10-16). Since every Christian has the Spirit of God, all Christians can understand the "deep things" of God. We only know a limited amount about other individuals with whom we are in contact. But if we had their very spirit inside us, we would know more, including the deep things of the person (v. 11). We do have God's Spirit and, therefore, we can know the deep things of God (v. 12).

What interferes with the Christian's ability to receive information from God, allowing for a reasonable span of time to grow in knowledge, is not defective experience nor the imperfection of human language nor an improper approach to religious truth, but sin (1 Cor. 3:1-4). Unbelievers, although lacking the Spirit of God, can have cognitive knowledge of God's revelation. They can know enough to reject it and to regard it as foolish (v. 14). As both Scripture and experience verify, they can have a great deal of cognitive information. However, they cannot understand or evaluate it accurately, Paul says, because it is spiritually evaluated or discerned (vv. 14-15).[18] The necessary element for understanding God's truth is not a different kind of religious knowledge but the presence of God's Spirit.

The Bible is not only propositional, but there is a great stress on knowing and understanding its propositional concepts. To really understand and evaluate these concepts, to know the deep things, one must have God's Spirit. All believers have God's Spirit; thus they are potentially able to understand the deep things of God. As Hebrews 5:12-14 implies, this takes time and effort.

Typical Objections

Certain objections are commonly raised against these concepts. We would be naive to think that these always are genuine questions to which the objectors seriously desire answers. They are raised in the hope of silencing the voice that the Bible is the authoritative, propositional revelation from God. However, the issues still may genuinely bother some individuals. These objections are without merit and have been refuted by others in detail; a brief summary answer will suffice here.

First, it is argued that the Bible is so prone to misinterpretation that we do not really know what God says; thus the fact that the Bible is inspired means little. The original content may be infallible, but the fallibility of its interpreters makes the message itself fallible.[19]

If this were a logically valid argument, no communication could be certain. Every communication can be misinterpreted, so there would be no accurate communication and little reason to be concerned with the accuracy of any communication. The objection itself is pointless, for we cannot know that we are interpreting it correctly.

Fortunately, the fallibility of readers does not detract from the merits of the propositional nature of any writing. There is no logical correlation between the inspiration, infallibility, or propositional nature of a writing and its interpretations. Inspiration, infallibility, and authority do not depend on what the reader thinks it means.[20] The Bible possesses these factors apart from anyone's interpretation. It is the interpreter's responsibility to interpret accurately. The infallibility and authority of the Word of God makes this effort worthwhile.

Second, we say that only the original documents written by the biblical writers (the autographs) are infallibly inspired. Since we have only copies, what we read cannot be inspired.

The theological definition of inspiration has been carefully worded to refer only to the originals in order to exclude errors that have entered in copying. Over the centuries, copy errors and editorial glosses have crept into the Bible manuscripts. In order to have accurate copies we must compare the various documents. This is called textual. Most mistakes are similar to typographical errors and are easily discovered by comparing different "families" of text. We do something similar every day, for much of what we read in books or newspapers or over the internet is made up of copies of other written documents. When we read we take into account spelling mistakes, the omission or addition of words, or mixed word order. Usually there is no question what is in the original. Of the remaining differences, few bring into question the meaning of the text.

The important point is that we have an inspired, absolutely true word from God to copy. Therefore, the goal is to have copies that are as accurate as possible. If we had completely accurate copies of the originals, the copies would still not be inspired. However, they would be completely accurate copies of what the inspired original says. Thus, we would know just as certainly what the inspired original says and would have lost nothing in this process from that which we would have if the copies were inspired or we possessed the originals. Whether the copies are inspired or not makes no difference.

Third, human language is insufficient to communicate the infinite, so God must accommodate his thoughts for humans to comprehend and communicate. As a result of this accommodation, the communication is inadequate.

This misses the point. Human language is inadequate for what? Certainly there are eternal truths that would be difficult to communicate, but does God desire to communicate these? The problem is the inadequacy of the human intellect rather than language. There is no reason God cannot communicate all that He desires. The crucial fact is that He could communicate the limited portion of his knowledge he wanted us to have, and he framed this knowledge in the propositions stated in the Bible. We are confronted with this, not with hypothetical possibilities that do not exist.

The issue confronting us is not how many of all possible concepts God can communicate. The issue is our response to the concepts God has communicated.

SCRIPTURE ALONE

The Word, in Person and Word

Jesus Christ regarded the Bible as God's Word, thereby, recognizing it as absolutely true, as authoritative and as the only revelation from God. He also saw himself in its pages. The apostle Paul testifies that what he was writing was nothing less than a look at the wondrous mystery of the gospel of salvation in Christ—a mystery that had been given to no one before the Incarnation. (Eph. 3:5, 9–12). The gospel of Jesus Christ is the secret wisdom of God, which was not revealed to important rulers but to the weak and despised (1 Cor. 2:7–10). What had been hidden was now gloriously made clear to believers (Col. 1:26). And the ultimate way God proclaimed his incarnated *logos* was in Scripture, His true revelation of his revelation.

Scripture is intimately connected with the person and work of the Logos, the Son of God. John gets right to the point, calling Jesus "God" in John 1:1. This is an immense statement, particularly coming in Scripture, because the Bible everywhere makes clear that there is one true God. Thus Scripture stands in partnership with Jesus to tell the most fantastic story the world has ever heard. Jesus claimed God as His father in a way that implied equality (for example, John 5:19). The biblical witness will not allow us the option of passing this off as a misunderstanding of Jesus' words by the Jews. Jesus said that He is the (only) way, truth, and life (John 14:6). If we believe his words, then we must believe that all he said was divine revelation, a new, intimately personal level of revelation. In addition to relaying Jesus' claim to divinity, Scripture represents the evidence for the truth of that claim and examines all that this means to God, to creation, and to humanity. The only special verbal revelation reveals the most special incarnate revelation and explains how to come to God through Him alone. Such is the uniqueness of the Bible.[21]

This makes the self-description of the Bible that it is true an important matter, for only here is the only way to God revealed. And if it is God's Word, like the incarnated logos it is as unchangeable as its Author (see Heb. 6:17). Paul says that God will be true to His word even if every man is a liar (Rom.

3:3–4). The angel tells John that the words he is to write are "true and faithful" (Rev. 21:5; 22:6).

The Jews who heard Paul preach in Berea were quick to see the relationship between the Word of God and the claims of Paul that God had come to them as a living Word. "They examined the scriptures daily to see if these things were as Paul said" (Acts 17:11). The eloquent preacher Apollos is described as "powerful in the scriptures" (18:24), because he used them powerfully to show to the Jews that Jesus fulfilled the promises of a Christ (v. 28). Standing before the Roman official Felix, the apostle Paul says that he serves God according to the way that the Jews call a heresy (Christianity) "because I believe everything that is written in the law and the prophets" (24:14).

Modern "Revelations"

Prophecies, Dreams, and Visions

It is the uniqueness and sufficiency of the partnership of the Word of Incarnation and the Word of Scripture that Hebrews 1:1–2 so eloquently describes, and why Christians no longer have the option of looking beyond this partnership for God's directly revealed will. Any claim of personal, direct revelation beyond the ministry of the Holy Spirit in every believer to apply the Bible's truths is egregious error.

Even before the completion of the Scripture's writing, Christians were never told to expect dreams or visions from God. Nor were believers given any indication that these were normal experiences they were to seek. They are always presented as unexpected, unusual events, directly related in the New Testament to God's acts of salvation through Christ and the founding of the church.[22] The angelic appearances to Zacharias (Luke 1:11–22) and to Peter (Acts 12:1–16) were regarded as highly unusual. Peter had difficulty believing that he had seen an angel (vv. 9–11). The other disciples had the same difficulty (vv. 14–16).

The Lord instructs Paul in Acts 18:9–10 regarding ministry in Corinth. Paul is told that he is to go to Rome to minister (Acts 23:11; 27:23–24). However, there is no indication that the average believer saw visions. Those recorded seem to be special. They are usually ministry oriented for unusually significant aspects of ministry appropriate for the beginning church. They provide information that would otherwise be very difficult for the church at that time to know. The focus in the visions and communications recorded in the New Testament is on the practical content or information revealed. God's help in administering the new kingdom enterprise is the reason for the revelation. There is no emphasis on the amazement aspect. These communications were not signs to convince unbelievers as were the apostolic miracles and healings.

Though there are New Testament references to foretelling prophets and their visions, and even a prophetic gift, these are never looked to as God's revealed teachings. They encouraged the hearers by preparing them for what was about to happen. They usually concerned specific instruction for an immediate situation; they did not have general application.

Only the Old Testament was given the submission as universally applicable documents, along with most of the New Testament books as they came along. These were regarded as applicable to Christians over all the contemporary world and were preserved because they had universal future application as well. An interesting example is found in the book of Revelation, where God specifically states that the prophecy was heeded in heaven as well as on earth and was to be kept open before the whole church until all things would be fulfilled (22:9–10). From that moment it was intended to be regarded as Scripture.

The Historical View of the Church

Almost in direct proportion to the honor given to the Bible, the church has considered genuine only the prophecy from the apostolic age. Mystics were sometimes listened to, but usually on the basis of their personal godliness and insights into God, not because of direct revelation. Where prophets and prophecies emerged to supplement Scripture, error followed. This tendency was strongly proven during the twentieth century.

The opinion that genuine prophets and prophecies are present today has been thoroughly refuted in many historical theology and biblical theology studies, based on evidence from the Scriptures.[23] At the beginning of the twenty-first century we have just been treated to a series of century-ending and millennium-ending prophets and prophecies. All are so defective compared to the biblical prophets and so different from those in the New Testament that, in order to defend their validity, some scholars invented an entirely new order of prophet from those of the Bible. These sometimes are channels for God's new communications through extraordinary works of the Holy Spirit. Yet they are lesser prophets who sometimes make inaccurate prophecies. Such prophets are sometimes admitted to be no more reliable than anyone else, though they exercise a gift *from the Holy Spirit by the Holy Spirit's* control.[24] This is an expedient to defend the indefensible. God said that any prophet who makes even one inaccurate prophecy is not His (Deut. 18:22).

Other Forms of Divine Communication

In stark contrast to New Testament church prophecies, today's visions usually stress the amazement factor. The information is usually personal or without relevance to the ministry of the body of Christ as a whole. Some practitioners announce astonishing information of significance to one person out of an entire group. This does not fit with Scripture, and it inevitably damages the body's theology of Scripture. Such communications tend to lack any real information. They concern some secret or individual problem that might easily apply to several in the group.

The argument is advanced by continuing revelationists that Nathaniel's confrontation of David about his sin with Bathsheba used special revelation to expose a secret personal problem and that other prophets accused kings at the command of God. However, these messages spoke to a theocracy in which the king's personal conduct had significant ramifications for the entire nation's welfare and spiritual standing with God. It is doubtful that these communications uncovered personal sins that were not common knowledge. Instead these are "forthtelling" prophecies of judgment—condemning sermons that applied God's law to an individual. They are recorded to explain this part of the salvation story (see, for example, Romans 9–11). In no sense does this apply to current theologies of ongoing revelation, especially in an era when we have the ethical instruction of Old and New Testaments, the presence of the Holy Spirit, and a church in which that instruction is applied.

We conclude that the Bible is God's only revelation that functions as the absolute truth and authority for us. He has given natural revelation in creation; however, this communicates only the most basic facts of His existence and our obligations to honor Him. At special times God has communicated directly, and his ultimate communication was the Word made flesh in the Incarnation. All of these communications are preserved in the Bible because they continue to be relevant.

In neither the Old nor New Testaments did individuals receive personal communications or revelations as help for their personal lives, for solutions to problems, to make life easier, or to strengthen wavering faith.

THE PROSPECT

Until there is intervention by the Lord, the downhill slide away from a biblical emphasis and authority seems certain to pick up momentum. The basic problems that caused today's deficient attitudes toward scriptural authority will only grow worse. This is the latest chapter in an ancient rebellion. The Bible is absolutely true, absolutely authoritative, and discloses propositional truth. Fallen men and women do not like the propositions it reveals. Since the entire cultural outlook is increasingly opposed to propositional absolutes of any sort, there is little reason to expect the current authority crisis will improve, even in evangelical churches. As stated above, even evangelical scholars are under pressure to be intellectually acceptable to skeptical academia, so they provide a conduit for unsound ideas and attitudes. They may in a bland, intellectually inoffensive way argue for a *moderate* evangelical view, but moderate theology has demonstrated its negative effect on orthodox theology. Since this desire for the world's acceptance is on the increase in evangelical circles, we can anticipate further decline in orthodoxy.

The charismatic philosophy has likewise introduced disturbing influences that parallel the nonevangelical replacing of objective, rational truth for a feelings-based experiential religion. As Jack Deere, a leading charismatic theologian, stresses, experience is the charismatic's primary emphasis.[25] A main argument by charismatic theologians against those who do not believe that the "charismatic gifts" are present today, is that this is due to rationalistic thinking. By this, they really mean rational thinking. They argue that the gifts dropped out of use due to Western intellectual movement toward a stress on rational thinking that overtook the early church. This corresponds to the nonevangelical argument that modern scientific thinking caused the church to incorrectly believe that the Bible provides propositional information about God. One unfortunate charismatic answer to biblical arguments is that one must *by faith seek the experience.* Experience supercedes study to determine what is biblical. This is a new way of approaching the existentialist's blind leap of faith toward religious experience. There is an obvious similarity here to the modern nonevangelical idea of faith as nonrational, existential event. Participants often regard this experience as placing them in more direct contact with God than "merely reading the Bible."

Thus, a group of Christians that are in evangelical churches or who hold common cause with the evangelical movement connect philosophically in their views with the premises of existential modernists. At the end of the twentieth century, most charismatics are generally not sympathetic with nonevangelical religious thinking, yet their emphasis on experience and deemphasis on rational thinking and ultimate authority make them susceptible.

Due to this multifaceted assault, the outlook is not favorable for biblical authority and doctrine. Outside the most stringently conservative churches, the individual Christian will, in most cases, receive little help from leaders. Individual Christians increasingly are forced to stand alone until they can find a group of Christians who believe the Bible in all that it teaches.

CONCLUSION

The only revelation from God is the Bible. Without the propositional information in the Bible no one can evaluate any spiritual activity or teaching to determine if it is true. The Bible is the church's absolute authority. It is the basis and authority for every doctrine, all truth, and for the Christian life. It is the only way we know anything about God. Without it we can know nothing about God or hold a reasonable eternal hope.

The church, in the coming decades, must not give up the priority and the authority in Scripture that it has always recognized.

CHAPTER 3

The Importance of Hermeneutics

John A. McLean

The discipline to follow direction is important when one is using a roadmap, a cake recipe, a chemical formula, or the Bible. Of course one must have all the rules and know how to apply them. One of my son's high school teachers assigned a cooking project in which a set of ingredients was to be mixed according to specific instructions. My son and his partner mixed the ingredients precisely and placed the mix in the oven. They began to worry because the anticipated result was not occurring. They removed the pan and increased the amounts of the mix. Finally, in desperation, they experimented with the recipe. After about thirty minutes, the concoction at last began to rise and bubble. Suddenly, from inside the oven a loud BANG! was heard. The creation had exploded. Goo had been blown into every crevice of the oven. Hours were required to clean up the mess. Later their teacher profusely apologized. In duplicating the recipe the final ingredient had failed to copy.

The ingredient was flour.

We can have trouble doing or reading anything if we don't know the rules. That applies to a nation's constitution, a Shakespearean play, a contract, or the biblical book of Isaiah. Principles govern interpretation, and missing a rule of interpreting Scripture can also cause a frightful mess.

THE IMPORTANCE OF HERMENEUTICS

Bernard Ramm defines *hermeneutics* as "the science and art of biblical interpretation. It is a science because it is guided by rules within a system; and it is an art because the application of the rules is by skill, and not by mechanical imitation."[1] Hermeneutics can be called a *science* in that a system can be explored, with some variables, following rational guidelines. It can be called an *art* in that it involves proper, consistent application to the unique qualities of a text.

The science and the art are both necessary to the work of *exegesis*—the deriving of meaning from a text. Peter warns about properly interpreting the Scriptures.

> *Bear in mind that our Lord's patience means salvation, just as our dear brother Paul also wrote you with the wisdom that God gave him. He writes the same way in all his letters, speaking in them of these matters. His letters contain some things that are hard to understand, which ignorant and unstable people distort, as they do the other Scriptures, to their own destruction. Therefore, dear friends, since you already know this, be on your guard so that you may not be carried away by the error of lawless men and fall from your secure position.* (2 Peter 3:15–17 NIV)

Paul exhorts: "Do your best to present yourself to God as one approved, a workman who does not need to be ashamed and who correctly handles the word of truth. Avoid godless chatter, because those who indulge in it will become more and more ungodly" (2 Tim. 2:15-16 NIV).

Besides warning us to avoid rabbit trails of speculative, "godless chatter" concerning the Bible, Paul shows us by his own example that we should not substitute human wisdom for the wisdom of God in the gospel, which comes to us through Scripture.

> *When I came to you, brothers, I did not come with eloquence or superior wisdom as I proclaimed to you the testimony about God. For I resolved to know nothing while I was with you except Jesus Christ and him cruci-fied. I came to you in weakness and fear, and with much trembling. My message and my preaching were not with wise and persuasive words, but with a demonstration of the Spirit's power, so that your faith might not rest on men's wisdom, but on God's power.* (1 Cor. 2:1-3 NIV)

In the hands of the Holy Spirit, the Word of God is the most powerful tool for sanctifying (making holy) the believer (Col. 3:16; 1 Thess. 2:13). It also is the Holy Spirit's powerful weapon of discerning judgment (Heb. 4:12) and the witness of Christ that can bring the unbeliever to faith (Rom. 10:17). No wonder the people of God seem powerless when they substitute other sources of authority for Scripture in the pulpits and classrooms. Or, more to the point of this chapter, they put so little effort into hermeneutical development while they hone their fine homiletic structure that a beautiful facade covers dis-torted content—the words of man and not the words of God.

The dangers can be subtle. When the focus of the message is application driven, the preacher must be very careful that it also is derived from sound exegesis. Otherwise, people are doing for God without the power of knowing God's will. Another example is an illustration so memorable or evocative that the response generated in the reader overwhelms the real message of the text. However worthy the heartrending intention, the result is false spirituality because it is generated by feelings and ideas not derived from Scripture. It is not enough for a preacher to elicit a spiritual response. To be God's response it must flow from understanding of the biblical.

PREMISES IN HERMENEUTICS

The most important contribution that can be made in the spiritual life of an individual believer is to provide that person with the tools needed to confidently understand what the Bible is saying. It is more important that people be equipped to do accurate hermeneutics than that they listen attentively to a sermon. It is important to train people to think biblically so that they can accurately discern what is true in their church and denomination and what is not. Only as Christians are nurtured in personal Bible study can we be certain that they will know whether something said in the name of the Lord is what the Lord has said. In a world when unbiblical theology is readily available, only anchored people can work from an accurate view of the true God in their individual and family lives.

Beyond teaching hermeneutics in the church, the best way to teach a good interpretation of the Bible is to model it in all that is preached and taught. This places a heavy responsibility on the interpreter, and demands introspective self-judgment of attitude. It is easy to step off the hermeneutical path when the exegete is burdened with an agenda. The motive might be to deal with a problem that a text doesn't really speak to but could with a little help. The motive may be to find that astounding interpretive coup, a connection that few have put together before. Gordon Fee and Douglas Stewart note that "interpretation that aims at, or thrives on, uniqueness can usually be attributed to pride, a false understanding of spirituality or vested interests. Unique interpretations are usually wrong."[2]

So the interpreter needs to keep in mind an interpretational syllogism:

1. All I want to do is God's will.
2. I must accurately know God's Word in order to do God's will.
3. Therefore, all I want is to accurately interpret God's Word so I can know and do God's will.

A FORK IN THE ROAD

Any piece of communication has three distinct components: (1) the author; (2) the text; and (3) the reader. Those who have studied communications theory might remember these components as (1) the encoder, (2) the code, and (3) the decoder, or (1) the sender, (2) the message, and (3) the receiver. Whatever the terminology used, the basic concept is that the words must be transferred from one mind to another, preferably with minimal degradation of meaning. In common speech and writing we use words—verbal symbols—to make this transfer possible.

In written communication, the author composes and the reader interprets. Who determines the correct meaning of the verbal symbols attached to the text? Is authoritative meaning determined by authorial intent or reader response? What if the author is God? Should the reader singlemindedly strive to recreate the thoughts of the original author, or is there freedom to understand the text from a personal viewpoint that takes into account differing situations?

John Stewart calls the hermeneutic approach that stresses recreation of the authorial thoughts *reproductive*. Stewart contrasts this with a *productive* hermeneutic, which strives for relevance and context.

In the reproductive approach, meaning equals intent:

> This type of hermeneutic lies behind much contemporary theory concerning effective communication, which usually goes something like this: "If we want to reach some form of meaning or understanding between us, then I need to grasp as best I can what you are saying to me (the intention behind your words), and you need to grasp as best as you can what I am saying to you (the intention behind my words)."[3]

The productive approach works from the premise that correspondence between sent and received ideas may not be so important. Why recreate the thoughts and words. Why even be concerned with our conversation partner's intent for its own sake. Rather, sender and receiver should cooperate to produce "mutual meanings" that serve both.[4]

Friedrich Nietzsche (1844–1900) is recognized for his impact on this latter approach to hermeneutics. He asserted that factual knowledge of written documents cannot truly be known. We can only know interpretations of these documents.[5] The original meaning of a text is lost in history. Only today's interpretation by each reader is of value. Generally the priority of an authorial-intent interpretation has lost ground over the last two centuries to a reader-response hermeneutic. Immanuel Kant (1724–1804) argued through his enlightenment epistemology that the interpreter must have courage to use personal reason, rather than be blindly obedient to tradition's imposing tutelage.[6]

Christian parents have long known that the faith of their children would be challenged in the science classroom. What they have not realized so clearly is that a greater challenge to faith comes from the deconstruction and existential philosophies of Kantian hermeneutics. It is the English and literature teachers who often argue that a text has no absolute meaning. What is important is reader response. A text only means what it means to you. The meaning carries no absolute truth or authoritative accountability to anyone.

Those who disregard authorial priority for reader response have already deter-mined that they will be sovereign over the interpretation of the text and the intent of the original author. This has serious logical implications regarding any sort of writing, but it is disastrous when it concerns the Bible. The overall authorial intent of Scripture is to raise a sovereign authority over all of faith and life! An interpreter who does not submit to authorial intention is in es-sence rejecting accountability or responsibility to God.

A STEP IN THE RIGHT DIRECTION

Because they are exposed to this philosophy, Bible students need to con-sciously adopt a principle that at first glance seems ridiculously self-evident: *Always examine the text of Scripture to seek the accurate authorial intention.* Authorial intention must be the final judge over everything else that is con-sidered. The hermeneutical approach must appreciate the literal, grammatical, historical meaning, as well as the literary technique at work. A. Berkeley Mickelsen summarizes the focus of the exegetic: "The task of interpreters of the Bible is to find out the meaning of a statement (command, question) for the author and for the first hearers or readers, and thereupon transmit that meaning (and application) to modern readers."[7]

Interpretation involves an explanation of the original sense of a speaker or writer. Literal interpretation means to explain the original sense of the Bible according to the normal and customary usage of its language. One must consider the accepted rules of grammar and rhetoric. Where accurate infor-mation is available, the exegete should be aware of the historical, literary, and cultural context of the writing.

AUTHORIAL-INTENDED HERMENEUTICS: A SYSTEM

We can summarize all this as five areas that influence our understanding of the human and the divine writers' meaning: (1) literary context; (2) historical-cultural background; (3) word meanings; (4) grammatical relationships; and (5) literary genre.

1. Maintaining the big picture of literary context helps to control the direc-tion of exegesis so that the exegete does not get off on to hermeneutical rabbit trails that have little to do with the argument of the book.
2. The historical-cultural background must be investigated so that the cultural norms that are unknown to the interpreter are properly understood.

3. Word studies examine semantics—how words function within grammar and syntax.

4. Grammar examines, categorizes, and applies the ways in which a particular language uses linguistic symbols. This descriptive process includes the study of syntax, which seeks to understand how words interrelate in their phrases and sentences.

5. An appreciation for literary genre helps the exegete apply the special hermeneutical principles needed to understand a text's meaning as poetry, prophecy, historical narrative, legal prescription, parable, or some other literary form.

In this process the *art* of exegesis comes into action. To the best of his or her ability and using what resources are available, the person should examine, without bias, the exegetical issues that are unfamiliar. The hermeneutical adage is worth repeating: *When the plain sense of Scripture makes common sense, seek no other sense; therefore, take every word at its primary, ordinary, usual, literal, literary meaning unless the immediate context clearly indicates otherwise.*

For those who have at least a basic understanding of the original language, the ideal first step of hermeneutics is to make a personal translation of the book or section within a book, comparing and noting differences with another translation. The interpreter who does this will quickly see nuances that cannot be easily conveyed in translating. It will also become apparent that no translation should be allowed the final word. The interpreter without access to the original language, or whose exposure is too limited to be of much help, should invest in multiple translations, comparing the differences as areas needing further exploration.

The second step is to read the book enough times that it becomes a familiar friend. Get to know this friend as well by gathering information about its historical background, the circumstances that shaped the book. Keep as a reminder the list of questions that should be known about the text:

• Who was the human author?
• When was the book written?
• What (so far as is known without too much speculation) prompted the author to write?
• What problems, situations, or needs does the author address?
• What are the main subjects discussed in the book? Writing and memorizing a very brief content outline can be very helpful here.
• Who were the first readers or hearers of the book?

Answers to these questions can help establish the historical background for understanding the book.

The third step is the completion of a synthetic chart of the entire book (or major section) so that the exegete has the big picture of the context in mind at all times. An understanding of the larger context provides direction and controls to the entire process. Words and grammar have little meaning apart from context. The pattern of some exegetes is to dig into the details of a text that is difficult to interpret. It may be better at times to back off and see the text in its greater context.

The fourth step is to set in mind the purpose for the writing and how its points are developed, validated, and defended. This speaks to the overall purpose for writing. The argument may be explicitly stated by the author or implied and uncovered through an inductive study of the text. The gospel of John records John's argument in John 20:30–31: "Jesus did many other miraculous signs in the presence of the disciples, which are not recorded in this book; but these are written that you may believe that Jesus is the Christ, the Son of God, and that by believing you may have life in his name" (NIV). The main argument of John is that Jesus is the Christ, the Son of God. The exegete should keep these two statements about Jesus in mind as a governing principle by which to understand any text in the gospel and how it fits into the whole.

HERMENEUTICAL ERRORS

It is not enough to read a commentary or commentaries and allow others to do the work, even if they did their work very well. The biblical text must be revisited and affirmed personally by each interpreter and applied individually. Otherwise the Bible cannot speak personally and the interpreter cannot adequately internalize the message and its application. Although there is only one correct authorial interpretation, there may be multiple ways in which a text may be applied in keeping with what God intended.

Exegesis that properly interprets a passage but points to invalid application is in error. This was a weak point in the evangelical Christian culture of the late twentieth century. Christian communicators seem compelled to offer a chapter-and-verse prooftext for their every statement. In prooftexting the statement is made first and then a verse is sought to back it up. One has the impression of subordination to Scripture, but that may not be so at all, especially when the Scripture agrees with the prooftexter only because it has been yanked violently from its context.

Such prooftexting is seen everywhere in sermons, financial planning seminars, counseling sessions, and weight-loss workshops. Almost always these are well-intentioned people who are sure that Scripture supports the principles of their programs but do not really study the text to make sure. It is a subtle form of humanism, in which the Bible is subordinated to the personal agenda.

The following errant interpretive and applicational approaches are common mistakes of sincere Bible students. These interpretive errors usually come from carelessness or laziness in handling God's words. One may be committed to authorial-intended interpretation, but still take a reader-response path in practice. Therefore, these approaches must be avoided so that we communicate the Word of God and not the homilies of man. Bad interpretation leads to bad theology, which produces bad doxology and bad praxeology.

1. Allegorical Interpretation

Allegorical interpretation disregards the historical and contextual interpretation for a deeper, or mystical understanding. The message often presents good lessons but has little if anything to do with the authorial or historical purpose. The interpretation is left to the imagination of the expositor, with few linguistic controls. An example is when the historical narrative of Esther is interpreted as a theological story about the struggle of the Christian life. Esther represents the Christian, Haman represents the old, adamic nature and Mordecai represents the Holy Spirit or new, regenerated nature. Historical narrative describes what happened and proclaims the great acts of God in his plan of salvation. To give it mystical spiritualized significance is to fall into the modernist existential and liberation theology interpretive strategies.

2. Spiritualizing Interpretation

Spiritualized interpretation is similar to allegorical method. The interpreter acknowledges the descriptive nature of the historical narrative, until the application step is reached. Then the historical purpose is replaced in favor of a theological meaning. God wants us to conquer our sins or diet, just like the Israelites did when they conquered Jericho. Just as Jesus blessed the plain water and turned it into expensive wine, so God can bless your simple tithe and return it to you with great benefits.

3. Typological Interpretation

Typological interpretation is the excessive application of the literary form of *typology* to every aspect of the Bible. The typologist sees everything in the Bible as either an Old Testament foreshadowing or a New Testament fulfillment of the life and ministry of Christ. Every detail of the tabernacle symbolizes something in the life of Christ. Everything in the New Testament looks back to the Old Testament as a fulfillment of past shadows. The authorial-intent of the Old Testament text is neglected because New Testament theology is spread over it. The progressive revelation of God is lost to the typological understanding of Old Testament events through the Christian experience.

4. Cross-Reference Interpretation

In *cross-reference interpretation* the interpreter searches for uses of the same or similar passages, words, or phrases anywhere in Scripture. The problem is that assumptions are made from superficial similarities without regard for the immediate context. The person looks at the cross-reference margins or a computer program and jumbles together information from other authors and passages and pushes it into the context of the immediate passage. This method is particularly abused with the Gospels. For example, each of the four Gospels has its unique focus and goal, so the same stories, debates, or miracles are used to make substantively different points. Harmonies or reconstructions of the life of Christ from the four Gospels are helpful but are never intended to equate authorial intention in the passages placed together. A similar problem is that different authors (Paul and James are most explicit examples) may use the same words with different definitions or linguistic nuances.

5. Systematized Interpretation

Systematized interpretation approaches the text through an unbending theological grid. The interpreter demands that Scripture fit into the system. The theological system rules the principles of interpretation. Extremely systematized theologies, for example some highly developed treatments of Calvinism or Arminianism, are prone to this kind of abuse, trying to fit Scripture around their system, instead of subordinating the system to Scripture. A strong hermeneutical framework can move from being a help to being a hindrance when the overriding concern is to support church dogma or tradition. This is not to suggest that systematic theology has no place in interpretation, but the system must not rule the conclusions of exegesis rather than exegesis modifying the system.

6. Prophetic Interpretation

Just as errant systematic interpretation takes a legitimate tool to illegitimate lengths, so *predictive interpretation* takes the fact that Scripture does contain prophecies to an extreme in which prophecies are seen everywhere. Cryptic, symbolic codes are identified and seen to refer at some level to future events. The interpreter must get underneath the plain sense of Scripture and discover these secret messages relating to current and future events. Some interpreters push this to the extent that arrows become scud missiles and chariots symbolize motorized weapons. Computers have made this kind of false interpretation more prevalent, since searches can be arbitrarily programmed to identify any sort of construction.

7. Wooden-Literal Interpretation

Wooden-literal interpretation fails to appreciate the many literary genres and figures of speech that bring color and expression to the Scriptures. This approach is so "wooden" in the concrete, literal understanding of the words that the interpreter would have us "cut off a right arm" or "gouge out an eye" to fulfill the passage. This method fails to appreciate the figurative or nonliteral meaning of words.

8. Personalized or Devotional Interpretation

Devotional interpretation makes every passage relate directly to the reader's life. A promise to Abraham, David, or Paul becomes a direct promise to the reader. The motto of this method is "All the promises in the Bible are mine." Application that is not derived from authorial intent or based on the textual principles to the first audience is often misinformation and misapplication. This can result in unwise actions that the interpreter believes were given as personal messages. Do not interpret the Scriptures in light of experience but interpret experience in light of the Scriptures.

9. Prooftext or Dogmatic Issues Interpretation

Prooftext hermeneutics has already been used as an illustration of poor interpretive practice. In this procedure, the interpreter tries to find biblical support for everything he or she is saying, even if the supporting verses must be taken out of context to prove a doctrinal or contemporary teaching. In one form of this error, the interpreter takes one verse or phrase and builds an entire doctrine or sermon from it. This approach usually neglects the context and authorial intent. The resulting doctrine is almost always unbiblical, or true and solid textual support would be found for it. In one of the most dangerous examples of this error, some paramilitary groups use Old Testament passages about God destroying His enemies to justify arming themselves for battle against authorities.

10. Rationalistic Interpretation

Rationalistic interpretation is the negative extreme of the positive principle of rational interpretation. The rationalist seeks to maintain the understanding of the text within the realm of human reason or comprehension. Scripture is subordinate to reason. If something cannot be proven by scientific investigation or it seems to go against scientific theory, then it must be modified to be "believable." For example, the rationalist cannot understand how God can be three persons in one essence, so the triunity of God is replaced by a unitarian or modalistic model. The rationalist cannot understand how the sin of Adam degrades all human beings, so original sin and human culpability are traded for a moral influence view. The person does not understand the complex scientific questions involved, so creation is dismissed in favor of naturalistic or theistic evolution. It seems more in line with human "knowledge" or it is easier to understand than the clear revelation of God.

11. Demythological Interpretation

Demythological interpretation is a rationalistic approach, except that this system does not seek to comprehend the biblical story on any factual level. Any historical aspects or dogmatic assertions are dismissed as irrelevant. One must peel them away as the literary vehicle by which the truth is taught. The Bible doesn't contain actual history. The interpreter must remove the myth to understand the truth. The book of Jonah is a mythical story used to teach the spiritual lesson that God loves everyone, or it has nothing to do with God at all, and simply means the human family should get along.

12. Historical Interpretation

Historical interpretation is a nuanced misuse of the study of historical narrative to suggest that the historical narrative we have before us is an incorrect interpretation of what actually happened. The Bible contains an account of history from the perspective of a particular cultural setting and represents their biases and values and views of reality. *De facto* it is not true revelation about God or theology. The Israelites fallaciously perceived that God was with them when they were victorious in battle. When they were defeated by their enemies, they believed that God was angry and had caused them to lose the battle. In a polytheistic world milieu, the writers of the Bible were interpreting life through a mythology in which Yahweh was greater than Baal. This was superstition playing out in events and culture-bound theology.

13. Literary Interpretation

Literary interpretation understands the Bible to be magnificent literature (which it is as a side benefit) but they do not accept it as the Word of God. It is read as other great masterpieces with literary power and authority but no revelatory reality. The story of Esther is a masterful, tightly-woven story about the courage of a woman in a male-dominated world

FUTURE ISSUES

Today's hermeneutical debates will likely continue to dominate study of Scripture. The secular world will continue to espouse and practice reader-response hermeneutics, resulting in the claim that a text has no absolute meaning. Just as constitutions and laws are frequently given radically different spins in the high courts, and laws, community codes and legal contracts are manipulated in the lower courts, so reader-response hermeneutics will try to maneuver exegesis into a desired mold. People will continue to be taught that there is no absolute meaning, particularly involving religious or moral truth. The Word of God will continue to be misinterpreted by well-intentioned Bible students who bring improper practice or incomplete preparation to the work.

Christians must boldly proclaim the gospel of the death, burial, and resurrection of Jesus Christ for our sin so that people will be saved and learn by the power of the Holy Spirit to submit to the absolute authority of the Word of God. All Christians, and particularly teachers, must be trained to rightly interpret the Word of God. The study of hermeneutics cannot be only the domain of the Christian university, college, or seminary. The tools must be taught in churches, Christian day school classrooms, and households. Pastors and teachers must not only proclaim the Word of God; they must also model and directly instruct in the principles of a correct hermeneutical system.

The Revelation, Inspiration, and Inerrancy of the Bible

Harold D. Foos and
L. Paige Patterson

Foos (top left) and Patterson

In a monastery precariously perched on the side of a Himalayan mountain overlooking a narrow, snow-filled pass, priests seated on straw mats gather around a low table. In their saffron-colored robes they pour over documents for interminable hours until they arrive at the moment of truth. Armed with multicolored carved opium poppies, each monkish scholar casts a red poppy if he believes the saying being studied is authentic to Siddhartha Gautama, the Buddha (c. 563 B.C.–c. 483 B.C.). A gray poppy indicates that Gautama probably thought it, but never said it. A black poppy indicates that Gautama never said it.

Consider the drama unfolding at the University of Tehran. Leading Shi'ite Islamic scholars examine the Qur'an. They are certain that there lived at least two Zaid ibn Thabits. Zaid was the actual assumed author of the Qur'an. "Deutero-Zaid" gathered oral traditions attributed to Muhammad nearly one hundred years after the death of the first scribe.

Judged by whatever standard, the Hebrew Bible and the Greek New Testament, joined forever as the Bible, constitute the most remarkable religious book ever composed. The white hot passion of its advocates can perhaps be matched by the passion of some factions of Muslims for the Qur'an, but the latter book never elicited the level of hatred from adversaries that the Bible has aroused. The Bible has been both attacked and defended with a violence unique in history. Scholars who neither defend nor malign are so fascinated by these ancient texts as to commit their lifetimes to the investigation of minute questions. Their conclusions require countless pages of writing. "Biblical studies" in some form provides the platform for a multitude of academic careers. Enormous societies, from the Evangelical Theological Society to the Jesus

Seminar, exist to promote scholarly research on the Bible. The scholarly groups embrace conservative Bible colleges and radical university divinity schools. No similar energies are expanded on other sacred literature within any faith.

What creates this love-hate fascination with the Bible? Several possible explanations present themselves. Perhaps the extraordinary claims the Bible makes for its own authority account for this intensity. Whatever authoritative claims are made by the Vedas and the Bhagavad Gita, there is no sense in which this literature claims to speak for God as does the Bible. Even the Qur'an, which does claim to speak for God, doesn't have texts comparable to Matthew 5:18; 2 Timothy 3:15–17; or 2 Peter 1:20–21, which attempt to account for how fallible men spoke the very words of God.

Or perhaps the finality of the Scriptures regarding judgment and eternal destiny evokes such passion. Here, however, the Qur'an, dependent as it is on the Old Testament, boasts similar tenets. Even the concepts of reincarnation and nirvana carry certain finality. Once again, however, the clarity and consistency of the Bible statements about judgment and eternity make it a book with which to be reckoned.

The point at which the message of the Bible violently diverges from all other sacred books is its estimate of human failure and consequent inability, joined to a salvific motif that focuses alone on the grace of God. The tendency of the Scriptures to disallow human endeavor and merit in relating properly to God is at odds with the "human attainment" emphasis found in every other sacred book. This issue seems to occasion both the adoration and the hatred. The Bible teaches that man is hopeless to help himself. It reduces the possibilities to live in faith and to please God solely to His mercy. In a human-centered world this is reprehensible. The Bible's message must either be jettisoned or explained in some socially acceptable way.

THE STORY OF CHRISTIAN THOUGHT

The history of the church can be related to three doctrinal challenges during its 2,000 years. The first six centuries was the era of christological definition. To oversimplify the matter, the churches eventually declared that Scripture presents Jesus as "very God and very man." Challenges from those who wished to make Jesus either less than fully human or less than fully God were declared to be in error by such councils as Nicea in 325 and Chalcedon in 451.

Having established some measure of agreement about the identity of Jesus, the confrontation of the Reformation regarded how one can get to Jesus. Both Orthodoxy and the Roman Church were insistent that one must come to Christ through the church. Outside of the church there is no salvation. Luther, Calvin, Zwingli, and the radical reformers saw this view as heresy. The church was the lighthouse and not the lifeboat. Salvation was the result of the grace of God apprehended by faith alone.

The sixteenth-century Reformation debate yielded no consensus. Ecumenical efforts notwithstanding, the breech created by the Reformation remains. Contemporary forays into dialogue between Rome and various other bodies in the post-Vatican II milieu have given ecumenists some hope. Dialogues with such Bible-centered Protestants as the Southern Baptists, however, brought mutual understanding of one another—and demonstrated that the chasm is not bridgeable this side of eternity.

If the first great discussion of church history was *christological* and the second *soteriological*, the third controversy has been *epistemological*. Beginning with the Enlightenment thinkers, the question now became, "How do you know what you say you know about Jesus and salvation?" Traditionally, Christians believed that God had given a sure word of revelation in the Bible. Most Christians, Catholic or Protestant, assumed that the Scriptures were true and authoritative, although Roman Catholics set tradition and church as coauthorities with Scripture. This high view of Scripture was largely unchallenged, except by heretical groups such as the followers of Marcion (second century) and Porphyry (232-c. 305), until the Enlightenment.[1]

Enlightenment rationalists found it increasingly difficult to justify belief in the miraculous, which was prominent in many books of the Bible. At first, the tendency of Immanuel Kant (1724–1804) and others was simply to bifurcate knowledge. Scientifically verifiable truths were in a lower story of demonstrable truth, while religious experience resided in an upper story that lay out of the reach of rational inquiry. Faith was thus placed in a "safe zone," ostensibly to protect it, but actually to marginalize it. More scholars came to doubt significant portions of the biblical record. Nature miracles were the first to be scrutinized, and then the creation stories. Ultimately even the resurrection of Jesus was cast aside.

By this time the historical-critical method of reading biblical documents had exercised its full hegemony in the scholarly world. The world was assured that Adam, Job, and Jonah did not really live, although the existence of three Isaiahs made up for them. The search was on for the "real Jesus of history." A century and a quarter later the "Jesus Seminar" still searched for the historical Jesus. At this writing the select group is still publishing pseudo-scholarly papers out of their common perspective and agenda. They vote on what limited number of statements they will allow Jesus to have actually made. They assure a gullible and largely ignorant secular press and a mystified public that most of the words attributed to Jesus in the Bible were written by Christians much later.

A contemporary alternative opinion to Enlightenment rationalism appeared near the end of the twentieth century in the form of postmodernism. Postmodern thinkers remain skeptical about the certainty in which Enlightenment rationalism habitually cloaks itself. Some postmodernists even reject claims of science for which there are demonstrable proofs. Others confine their skepticism to the evaluation of literature. They favor the idea that objective meaning in literature is neither possible nor desirable and should be jettisoned in favor of reader–response hermeneutics. Postmodern biblical interpreters care little about authorial intent, which they doubt could ever be discovered anyway. Stanley Hauerwas, for example, warns,

> Once Paul's letters become so constructed canonically, Paul becomes one interpreter among others of his letters. If Paul could appear among us today to tell us what he "really meant" when he wrote, for example, 1 Corinthians 13, his view would not necessarily count more than Gregory's or Luther's account of Corinthians. There simply is no "real meaning" of Paul's letters to the Corinthians once we understand that they are no longer Paul's letters but rather the Church's Scripture.[2]

Evangelical Christians, on the other hand, have continued to insist that *the book called the Bible is a series of letters, prophecies, instruction, laws, and principles that owes its origin to a unique confluent process in which the eternal God imparted eternal truth through the medium of fallible humanity.* Superintended by the Holy Spirit, these fallible authors were empowered to write words that were infallible and inerrant. This process of inspiration extended not just to the thoughts revealed in the Bible but also to the very words chosen (verbal inspiration) and to every one of the sixty-six canonical books (plenary inspiration).[3] This being so, the Scriptures may have new specific applications, but the "meaning" of the text and the general application are established forever by God, for these are his words.

This position is unpalatable both to people informed by Enlightenment rationalism and to those enamored with postmodernism. To the first group, whatever meaningful religious experience there may be is outside the realm of verifiability and is ultimately only personal experience. To the latter, nothing can be verified, and religious truth is a matter of social convention. It is impossible to verify the text, or the process is unhelpful, for it can be no source for morality, theology, and meaningful truth.

What recent theologians say about the Bible has become a matter of paramount importance to evangelicals. Christians must acquaint themselves with the claims the Bible makes for itself in order to cast a vote for or against its trustworthiness and accuracy. In the process of making this decision, evangelicals must also decide for themselves whether there is such a thing as knowable truth.

RECENT THEOLOGY AND THE BIBLE

No theologian has exercised any greater influence on the twentieth century than Karl Barth (1886–1968). Evangelicals who delight in denigrating Barth need to remember that classical liberals of his day regarded Barth as a fundamentalist. Barth made a radical right turn in his commentary on Romans by suggesting that God indeed spoke in the Bible.[4] Barth's position was not that of the orthodox faith, but was, as it would became known, "neoorthodoxy," a new orthodoxy that was not biblical. Barth heard the voice of God *in* the Bible but not *in all* of the Bible and not because the Bible is propositional truth. Barth insists that the Bible is a *witness* to revelation. He said, "We have here an undoubted limitation: we distinguish the Bible as such from revelation. A witness is not absolutely identical with that to which it witnesses."[5] This means in turn that there can be (and are) egregious mistakes in the Bible while it still maintains some distinction as God's Word.

> The men whom we hear as witnesses speak as fallible, erring men like ourselves. What they say, and what we read as their word, can of itself lay claim to be the Word of God, but never sustain that claim. We can read and try to assess their word as a purely human word. It can be subjected to all kinds of immanent criticism, not only in respect of its philosophical, historical and ethical content, but even of its religious and theological. We can establish lacunæ, inconsistencies and overemphases.[6]

If anyone thinks that Barth only intended to recognize technical errors that were of little consequence, he makes himself abundantly clear by saying, that "the vulnerability of the Bible, i.e., its capacity for error, also extends to religious or theological content."[7]

The Bible claims much more than Barth admits, or perhaps even imagines. The Swiss theologian left no method for determining what may be judged the word of God and what must be dismissed as the intrusion of the human author. Emil Brunner explains the neoorthodox view of this intrusion by his analogy of a phonograph over which the needle reproduces beautiful music, along with minor distortion because of the scratching of the needle. Brunner, of course, failed to provide a way to distinguish the scratch from the melody.[8]

IS IT ONLY SEMANTICS?

There was a time when the word *inspiration* adequately conveyed the concept of a fully trustworthy Scripture. But to convey anywhere near the same idea today we must add more and more modifiers: *verbal* (down to individual words), *plenary* (fully in all parts), *infallible* (incapable of fault), *inerrant* (free from error), or even *fully inerrant*, a compelled redundancy. Also, when the original *Fundamentals* were issued, the word *evangelical* was adequate to identify one with an unquestioned commitment to the historic orthodox faith of the church, including a fully reliable word from God.[9]

In 1926, at the height of the Liberal-Fundamentalist controversy, Kirsopp Lake, a liberal New Testament scholar, openly acknowledged that fundamentalism wore the mantle of historical orthodoxy:

> It is a mistake often made by educated persons who happen to have but little knowledge of historical theology, to suppose that fundamentalism is a new and strange form of thought. It is nothing of the kind; it is the partial and uneducated survival of a theology which was once universally held by all Christians. How many were there, for instance in Christian churches in the eighteenth century, who doubted the infallible inspiration of all Scripture? A few, perhaps, but very few. No, the fundamentalist may be wrong; I think that he is. But it is we who have departed from the tradition, not he, and I am sorry for the fate of anyone who tries to argue with a fundamentalist on the basis of authority. The Bible and the *corpus theologicum* of the Church is on the fundamentalist side."[10]

For almost two thousand years the Christian church accepted a fully authoritative Scripture. Then in the late 1800s rationalism and destructive higher criticism began to blur the line between divine revelation and human words. In North America the line of demarcation was set in the fundamentalist-modernist controversy. Liberal theology chose to view Scripture as errant, while the orthodox insisted that a verbally inspired and inerrant Scripture was fundamental to the faith. The stage was set for 1942, when the Federal Council of Churches repudiated the full authority of Scripture, and a new organization, the National Association of Evangelicals, was established to defend biblical authority. The N. A. E. emphasized an *inerrant* Scripture. Both fundamentalism and those preferring to be called evangelicals understood how crucial it was to maintain a reliable Bible.

Departure Within Evangelicalism

Attacks on the authority and integrity of Scripture are nothing new. However, in the mid- to late-1900s the Christians who drifted from biblical authority were not the strict rationalists, the modernists, the existentialists, or the neoorthodox. The attack on the full integrity of the Bible came from the ranks of those who passionately called themselves evangelical. They did not always express themselves frankly, hiding their views of Scripture behind carefully-parsed terms. This departure was brought into the open at "The Seminar on the Authority of the Scripture," convened at Gordon College and Divinity School in Wenham, Massachusetts, on June 20–29, 1966.

At that conference it became clear that not all who called themselves evangelicals subscribed to biblical inerrancy. According to Lindsell, in the wide ranging discussions the same old story came to light. Some held to inerrancy as an essential biblical doctrine. Others did not. All of them agreed on the complete truthfulness of the Bible and its authoritativeness as the infallible rule of faith and practice. None of the participants affirmed the errancy of the Bible. They only refused to accept inerrancy. . . . The statement released by the group meant only those parts of Scripture are completely truthful that have to do with matters of faith and practice.[11]

This position was more widespread than suspected. Its various shades colored entire denominations, Christian colleges, seminaries, publishing houses, and learned societies. Understandably, the response to these defections was spirited. Some individuals and institutions responded that their theology was no less evangelical than before, and that charges to the contrary were erroneous.[12] Others counterattacked, charging that fellow evangelicals who insisted on inerrancy were spending needless time and effort on a debatable nonessential. Why did they not turn their attention to speaking prophetically on pressing social and political issues. An editorial in a widely read journal, *The Other Side*, made this point.

The Bible just slips through the net of people who are concerned mostly about its accuracy. It was not given to a scientific, mathematical age, and it will not yield its treasures to shallow questioning about correctness. Which isn't to say that the Bible is incorrect or inaccurate, just that it isn't hung up on such questions. Nor is it to say the Bible is unhistorical; historicity is vital to the biblical message. What the Bible offers is not science but a panorama of God and people which will make us worship God and love the people he has made. It shows us the wonderful way of life he offers and our own stupid, wicked rejection of it. But it tells us how to get back to the way. Which is the point.[13]

In the same commentary the author accuses those who believe in inerrancy of being regularly blind to justice. "The fruit of inerrancy has been a millstone," he contends.[14]

Others espoused Biblical inerrancy but feared that an internecine fight would fragment the evangelical cause, destroying its impact. They tried to pour oil on the troubled waters.[15] Inerrancy, it was said, should not be made into a theological weapon for driving evangelicals into a nonevangelical camp; nor should it be used to invalidate the contributions of those evangelicals. Some joined Clark Pinnock to suggest doing away with the use of the term *inerrancy* to disarm the issue.[16]

There were (and are) "evangelicals" who insisted on distinguishing be-tween *inspiration* and *inerrancy*. They did not object to saying the Bible is inspired, but they refused to believe it totally inerrant. The Bible can err and does err in some details. Some representatives of this view even use the word *inerrant*, omitting such modifiers as *totally* or *completely*. This makes for mis-leading use of language as words are invested with new meaning. Robert Lightner has said,

> Strangely, the battle is not being fought, as it once was, by evangelicals who embrace all the essentials of the historic Christian faith, including its full inerrancy, on one side and nonevangelicals on the other, though some aspects of that old battle continue. Instead, today there is a conflict within the camp of those who lay claim to the label *evangelical*. Some believe the Bible in its original documents is free from all error and omission—the total inerrancy of Scripture. . . . Others, who also view themselves as evangelical, believe there are errors in the Bible. They claim the errors are not in matters relating to the Bible's central theme, but only in the peripheral areas.[17]

In 1978 J. I. Packer observed that "when you encounter the current evan-gelical debate on Holy Scripture, you are encountering an awkwardly con-fused situation." The sides have

> "cross purposes," "divided values," "domino thinking," "subjectiv-ism," "interpretive techniques," "preferred ways of speaking in apologetics and dogmatics," "definitions." . . . The dim light of the discussion, allied to the heat that it generates, makes clarity hard to achieve, and debate is never easy when the state of the question is unclear. Also, because of the way in which academic faculties have lined up, it is hard to take any position in the debate without seeming to call into question someone else's competence or good name as an evangelical, and this is most unfortunate.[18]

Seeing something positive in all this Charles Ryrie has observed that the "debate has drawn lines among evangelicals that needed to be drawn" and "has also served to sharpen distinctions that surround the concept of inerrancy."[19]

THE IMPORTANCE OF INERRANCY

In a 1965 article on inerrancy, John Warwick Montgomery referred to a statement made by James Orr in his *Progress of Dogma*. Orr observed that in each great epoch of its history the Christian church has been forced to struggle with one aspect of the faith that has had a major impact on the ongoing direction of the church. In the early church it centered on the persons of the Godhead with particular attention to the deity and humanity of Christ. The medieval church wrestled with the atonement. In the Reformation era the struggle was over justification by faith alone; and these issues were faced and solved. Today the watershed issue has become the authority of Scripture. If it should be finally settled that Scripture can err, the church and its theologians will have no source and standard remaining by which further doctrinal problems can be ultimately settled.[20]

Clearly this issue has tremendous ramifications, for, as Packer comments, "When you encounter a present day view of Holy Scriptures, you encounter more than a view of Scripture. What you meet is a total view of God and the world, that is, a total theology, which is both an ontology, declaring what there is, and an epistemology, stating how we know what there is. . . . Every view of Scripture, in particular, proves on analysis to be bound up with an overall view of God and man."[21]

It has become increasingly clear that there are major differences in this area among those who would claim the label *evangelical.* Centering on the extent of the Bible's inspiration, the debate encompasses the related aspects of the reliability, sufficiency, finality, and ultimately the authority of the Bible. Do Protestants still accept the Reformation concept of *sola scriptura,* in which the Bible is accepted to be the sole and only fully reliable source for the knowledge of divine truth. The foundation of our knowledge of God and his workings are, therefore, only as secure as the Bible is trustworthy. And *sola scriptura* cannot be sustained apart from an inerrant Bible.

The absolute necessity of a totally reliable revelation is most clearly understood when the doctrine of *the incomprehensibility of God* is placed alongside the doctrine of *human depravity* from the fall. In such a context of contrasting truths it is absolutely essential that special revelation should be known authentically. Packer cogently observed that

> when you encounter the evangelical view of Holy Scripture, you are encountering the source, criterion, and control of all evangelical theology and religion. . . . Methodologically, evangelical theology stands apart from other positions by its insistence on the clarity and sufficiency of the canonical Scriptures, and evangelical religion is distinctive by reason of the theology and the method of application that determines it. . . . Evangelicalism characteristically says that Scripture is both clear and sufficient; that the God-given Scriptures are the self-interpreting, self-contained rule of Christian faith and life in every age.[22]

As Pinnock clearly saw in the period when he was more closely aligned with evangelicalism,

> An erring standard provides no sure measure of divine truth and human error. The assurance in which the believer knows and rejoices in his Lord's nature and purposes is threatened when the reliability of Scripture is questioned. . . . The surrender of Biblical infallibility would be a disastrous mistake, having deadly effects upon the Church of God and its theology. These results are even now highly visible in the tragic ambiguity of contemporary Christian thought.[23]

Lindsell was among the theologians to regard Biblical inerrancy as *the rallying point* for the last stand of evangelicalism. Francis Schaeffer called it "the watershed of the evangelical world." But it was seen as an important issue long before those evangelical leaders. John Wesley (1703–1791) asked, "Will not the allowing there is any error in Scripture, shake the authority of the whole?" He wrote further, "If there be one falsehood in that book, it did not come from the God of truth."[24]

As concern grew over the church's lack of confidence in the Bible's full reliability, a number of evangelical leaders founded the International Council on Biblical Inerrancy (ICBI) in 1977. This organization of pastors, professors, and Christian layman proposed "the defense and application of the doctrine of biblical inerrancy as an essential element for the authority of Scripture and a necessity for the health of the church." The organization was created, according to its statement of purpose, "to counter the drift from this important doctrinal foundation by significant segments of evangelicalism and the outright denial of it by other church movements."[25]

In October 1978, an international conference of nearly three hundred theologians and church leaders from all Protestant denominations met in Chicago, Illinois, under the auspices of the ICBI. This meeting produced the Chicago Statement on Biblical Inerrancy. Composed of a preface, a short statement of introduction, nineteen articles of affirmation and denial, and a brief exposition,[26] this document has shaped the debate since 1978 as a manifesto for churches and Christian organizations determined to understand and proclaim a fully authoritative Scripture.

The opening statement in the preface to the Chicago Statement on Biblical Inerrancy reads: "The *authority of Scripture* is a key issue for the Christian church in this and every age. . . . Recognition of the *total truth and trustworthiness* of Holy Scripture is essential to a full grasp and adequate confession of its *authority*" (emphasis added).[27] Follow-up conferences dealing with related issues (e.g., hermeneutics) followed, as did numerous publications expanding and clarifying the central theme and related issues.

At this writing, one ongoing battle is for accurate definition and use of terms. James Boice, a founder of the ICBI, has commented that some consider *infallibility* a better word than *inerrancy* for expressing the soundest evangelical position on Scripture. He wisely observes,

> As some use this word, the choice of infallible would probably be acceptable. They recognize that in order for the Bible to be infallible in its truest and fullest extent it must be inerrant. Unfortunately, the majority of those who choose *infallible* rather than *inerrant* do so because they want to affirm something less than total inerrancy, suggesting erroneously that the Bible is dependable in some areas (such as faith and morals) while not being fully dependable in others (such as matters of history and science). Because of this situation and because of its commitment to total inerrancy, the ICBI has chosen to name itself by the use of the stronger word.[28]

VIEWS OF BIBLICAL AUTHORITY

Biblical authority has always been the central epistemological concern of Protestant theology. There have been four alternative positions.

First, some affirm that the Holy Spirit uses the totally human material of the Bible to create real theological and spiritual responses within the heart. These may or may not have a direct link to what the human writer originally intended to convey. The groups holding this position have been varied as the Illuminists, Quaker theology's "inner light" theology, and contemporary liberal and existentialist theologies.

Second, others insist that, while the Bible is a fallible and sometimes fallacious human witness, God has endowed it with an unusual authority as a means for speaking persuasively to hearts and minds. By virtue of God's authority, human words in the Bible become the Word of God to us in a subjective, individual way. Barth, Brunner, and neoorthodox theologians have subscribed to some form of that approach.

A third view affirms that biblical authority resides in its divine origin, though the God-given text may contain technical errors in such matters as history, science, and geography. The errors are explained as divine accommodation to the mental and cultural limitations of either the messengers or recipients or both. This view is clearly dialectical in that it affirms that the Bible's content can at the same time be God's truth or not God's truth, depending on how *truth* is defined. Proponents include G. C. Berkouwer, Jack Rogers, Donald McKim, and Pinnock.

The fourth alternative believes that the Bible is God's own word and testimony, given through human words. It is inerrant by necessity because of its divine origin and character. Twentieth-century exponents have included a host of conservative theologians. Strong statements have been made by Lindsell, B. B. Warfield, A. H. Strong, Herman Bavinck, Louis Berkhof, Geoffrey Bromiley, Cornelius Van Til, Louis Sperry Chafer, and Carl F. H. Henry.

Infallible, but Not Inerrant?

It would appear that those who claim the name *evangelical* and wish to stand within the orthodox confessions must reject options one and two. But why have so many chosen option three? Why do some declare a belief in an inspired, even infallible Bible, but not in inerrant Scripture? Ryrie offers two possibilities.

> One cannot see motives, but for some it is the result of honest wrestling with problems which have shaken their faith. For others, one cannot help but feel that it is part of the current worship of intellectualism as a sacred cow and a necessary step in achieving the approbation of godless intellectuals so-called.[29]

Robert Lightner acknowledges the provocation of difficult challenges but makes the following contrast. Those who hold to inerrancy take as their theological starting point the claims that the Bible makes for itself. They honestly wrestle with the problems to find solutions in harmony with Scripture's self-testimony. Lightner says those who begin with the inspired-but-errant view see the difficult areas in Scripture "as evidences that the Bible cannot be totally inerrant. Even the claims of the Bible for itself and our Lord's view of it are adjusted to fit the view that is based on looking at the problems."[30] Pinnock states that what has happened is

> a result of the *collision* between the traditional belief in the infallibility of the Bible and the critical perspective on the Scriptures nurtured in the enlightenment which saw in it only a record of man's imperfect spiritual and moral evolution. . . . The result has been an unsettling ferment in which Christians have been forced to ask after the sense in which the Bible is the Word of God.[31]

Packer addresses this issue with less sympathy for Pinnock and his colleagues when he insists that

> the way in which they deal with the Bible is fundamentally un-Christian. They hold that what needs revision is our doctrine of biblical authority; but it seems that what really needs revision is their method of biblical scholarship. Instead of subjecting their own judgment wholly to Scripture, they subject Scripture in part to their own judgment. They

treat the question of the truth and authority of Scripture, which God has closed, as if it were still open; they assume the right and competence of the Christian student to decide for himself how much of the Bible's teaching should be received as authoritative. They accept what they do accept, not simply because it is Scripture, but because it satisfies some further criteria of credibility which they have set up; so that even when they believe the right thing, in so far as they are consistent subjectivists they do so for the wrong reason. Their whole approach to the Bible is fundamentally unbiblical.[32]

SO WHAT IS INERRANCY?

The word *inerrancy* is derived from the Latin *errare*, which means to wander; thus the concept implies a departing or going away from the truth. With the prefix *in* having the negative force, the word *inerrant* denotes freedom from error and is in this sense applied to the Scriptures.

> The inerrancy of the Scriptures, then, implies their freedom from any error of doctrine, fact or ethic. To state the matter in a slightly different way, every assertion of the Bible is true, whether the Bible speaks of what to believe (doctrine), or how to live (ethics), or whether it recounts historical events. On whatever subject the Scripture speaks, it speaks the truth, and one believes its utterances.[33]

Simply put, *inerrancy* means that Scripture in the original manuscripts (*autographs*) does not affirm anything that is contrary to fact, that the Bible *always* speaks the truth concerning *everything* it addresses.

Inerrancy does not demand that the human authors were mere automata, through whom the Scriptures were dictated. It does not mean that when the same events are recorded they must be in actual verbal agreement or recorded in identical order. Nor does it require that when two writers translate from another language that their translations must be in verbal agreement. It does not require that different writers give the same details from the same perspective when recording the same event.[34]

Further, when it is asserted that the entire Bible is true and God-inspired, allowance is made by inerrantists for the fact that the Bible sometimes records within the historical accounts the lies told by Satan (e.g., Gen. 3:4) or by others within the account. It may also recount inaccurate reasoning, as among Job's friends or by the writer of Ecclesiastes when he presents the worldly perspective. In such places the philosophizing does not go beyond human wisdom, nor was it intended to by the writers. What is recorded must be tested against the clear affirmations of truth elsewhere in Scripture. However, when the Bible states a fact as a fact it must be true, whether it involves God himself, or his moral standards, or whether it involves history, geography, or science. According to Edward J. Young,

> the Scriptures possess the quality of freedom from error. They are exempt from the liability to mistake, incapable of error. In all their teachings they are in perfect accord with truth. . . . All that it teaches is of unimpeachable, absolute authority, and cannot be contravened, contradicted, or gainsaid. Scripture is unfailing, incapable of proving false, erroneous, or mistaken. Though heaven and earth should pass away, its words of truth will stand forever. It cannot be changed nor destroyed.[35]

Continued Rejection

Yet some "evangelicals" continue to reject the position that Scripture is inerrant, arguing for a "modified inerrancy," insisting that the biblical writers "accommodated" their messages to false ideas current in their day, thus including factual errors in "nonsalvific" and "peripheral" matters.[36] They speak of the Bible as having an "inspired purpose." Despite its factual errors and insoluble discrepancies, it nonetheless retains a "doctrinal integrity" and so accomplishes perfectly the divine purpose. That makes the Bible fully reliable with regard to matters of "faith and practice."

Ray Summers, who represents this position, states it this way: "I confess the infallibility and inerrancy of the Scriptures in accomplishing God's purpose for them—to give man the revelation of God in his redemptive love through Jesus Christ."[37] What this understanding of *inerrant* and *infallible* means is that God's principal revelation—salvation—has been transmitted reliably by means of records that are quite fallible with "inconsequential errors."

A series of questions may help frame a response to this position.

BY WHOSE AUTHORITY?

Once the inerrancy of Scripture is given up, what will be the basis for deciding what is error and what is not? Why are some statements judged to be nonrevelatory, while other statements are revelatory? The question is—do we establish some other authority to be above the Scripture?

Old Testament Testimony

Many times the Old Testament claims to be the Word of God. Expressions equivalent to "the Lord said," "the Lord commanded," and "thus says the Lord" occur about 2,400 times. Jesus referred to the Old Testament Scriptures as the "commands of God" and "the word of God" (for example, Mark 7:10-13) and asserted that it would stand (Matt. 5:17-18; John 10:34-36). He used Deuteronomy three times as an authority over Satan (Matt. 4:1-11;

Luke 4:1–13). Regarding marriage, Jesus said to the Pharisees, "Have you not read, that He who created them from the beginning made them male and female, and said, 'for this cause a man shall leave his father and mother, and shall cleave to his wife and the two shall become one flesh'?" (Matt. 19:4–6 NASB; c.f. Gen. 2:24). There is no introductory "God said," yet Jesus did not hesitate to equate these unattributed words in Genesis with the utterance of "He who created them from the beginning." As far as our Lord was concerned, what the Old Testament Scripture says is what God says.[38]

New Testament Testimony

New Testament Scripture likewise claims divine authority (cf. Gal. 1:8–9; 1 Thess. 2:13; 4:8; 2 Tim. 3:16–17; 2 Peter 1:20–21, 3:15–17).[39] First Timothy 5:18 combines an Old Testament quotation and a New Testament quotation and calls them both "scripture."

Every argument from Scripture for inspiration is at the same time an argument for its inerrancy. The Bible claims to be from God literally hundreds of times.[40] Again, as the earlier Pinnock opened a section on "The Biblical Basis of Infallibility" he wrote, "Infallibility is a *necessary,* not merely an *optional,* inference from the Biblical teaching about inspiration. It is an intrinsic property and essential characteristic of the inspired text. This deduction from inspiration is proposed because it is one drawn by Jesus Christ and his Apostles."[41] He concludes: "If inerrancy be a necessary inference to be drawn from the Biblical teaching on inspiration, there is nothing to fear in defending it. It can be falsified only if God has lied to us concerning his Word. The danger is thus a highly artificial and hypothetical one."[42]

The Character of God as a Testimony

It is expected that error and at least partial falsehood would characterize the speech of every human being, but it is characteristic of God's words, even when spoken through imperfect and sinful human beings, that they should never be false or affirm error (Num. 23:19). It should be clear that to question the inerrancy of Scripture is to raise questions about the very character of God. Since he has spoken to us in his Word about his words (claiming them as his own) his veracity is at stake. God tells us by his word that he does not lie (Titus 1:2; Heb. 6:18; cf. John 17:17); is flawless (Ps. 12:6; Prov. 30:5), eternal (Ps. 119:89, 96; Matt. 24:35), and trustworthy (2 Sam. 7:28). Therefore, to disbelieve or disobey any word in Scripture (properly interpreted) is to disbelieve or disobey God.

Young gets to the heart of the matter when he writes,

> To assume that God could speak a Word that was contrary to fact is
> to assume that God Himself cannot operate without error. The very

nature of God therefore is at stake. If we assert that the *autographa* of Scripture contain error, we are saying that God is guilty of having told us something that is not true. It may be a matter which we ourselves would call minor, but in this case a minor error is no less an error than a major one. A person who continues to make so-called trifling mistakes is not one whom we can trust. And one who constantly slips up in lesser points is one whose words may well be brought into question when greater matters are involved. If God has communicated wrong information even in so-called unimportant matters, He is not a trustworthy God. It is therefore the question of Biblical theism which is at stake.[43]

Further, on what basis are we to trust anything that God says if we cannot trust him at this point. Lindsell identifies this crux issue:

For anyone who professes the Christian faith the root question is: From where do I get my knowledge on which my faith is based? The answers to this question are varied, of course, but for the Christian at least it always comes full circle to the Bible. When all has been said and done, the only true and dependable source for Christianity lies in the book we call the Bible. This is the presupposition from which I start this discussion. . . . Since Christianity is indubitably related to and rooted in the Bible, another question follows inexorably. . . . "Is the Bible a reliable guide to religious knowledge?"[44]

At the conclusion of an essay dealing with the alleged errors in the Bible Young adds this cautionary note:

The belief, however, that the Bible is the inerrant and infallible Word of God, does not depend upon human ability to show that the Bible is free from error. One does not believe that Scripture is God's Word on the basis of his ability to demonstrate that it does not contain errors. The Bible is the Word of God because God has Himself so declared. If the Bible is the Word of God, then it is true and perfect, for it has been issued by the mouth of Him that cannot lie. The Word is the expression of His thought, and it is impossible that His thought be other than pure and holy.[45]

HOW "HUMAN" A BOOK?

It is frequently argued by those who hold to an errant Scripture that inerrancy overemphasizes the divine aspect of Scripture and neglects the human. It is, they say, the "genuine humanness" of Scripture that causes nonrevelatory errors in history and science. God guaranteed the "infallibility" of Scripture in matters of faith and practice. The impression is given (by assumption if not explicit argument) that if the composition of the Scriptures genuinely involved human activity, and if the authors were more than "human typewriters" by which the Spirit "dictated," then we must allow for the possibility of error—perhaps even insist on it.

Are we then saying that God *could not, would not,* or that in fact he purposely *did not* preserve the human writers from error in composition? In this particular endeavor should we not expect that God would providentially guard their human personalities and abilities in such a fashion as to preserve them from error in the writing of His Word? Is that not what we would expect of an all powerful, all wise, loving God? Is this miracle impossible for God or a work not in keeping with his character? Just what precisely is 2 Peter 1:20–21 teaching?

Divinely Superintended

There is an assumption on the part of Pinnock and others that humanness must equal error. This forces them into a christological corner if they confess that within the human nature of Jesus Christ he was truly human. If they say that the divine nature made his human nature capable of perfection, they are claiming precisely what they refuse to claim for Scripture. A miraculous combination of the divine and the human was at work within the Living Word, and the same type of miracle is claimed in texts such as 1 Peter 1:20–21 for the written Word. If overemphasis on the humanness of Jesus has led to error, an analogous emphasis on the "humanness" of Scripture offers the same danger. This analogy between the natures of Jesus Christ and of Scripture was analyzed by Warfield:

> Between such diverse things there can exist only a remote analogy; and, in point of fact, the analogy in the present instance amounts to no more than that in both cases Divine and human factors are involved, though very differently. In the one they unite to constitute a Divine-human person, in the other they cooperate to perform a Divine-human work. Even so distant an analogy may enable us, however, to recognize that as, in the case of Our Lord's person, the human nature remains truly human while yet it can never fall into sin or error because it can never act out of relation with the Divine nature into conjunction with which it has been brought; so in the case of the production of Scripture by the conjoint action of human and Divine factors, the human factors have acted as human factors, and have left their mark on the product as such, and yet cannot have fallen into that error which we say it is human to fall into, because

they have not acted apart from the Divine factors, by themselves, but only under their unerring guidance.[46]

Another consideration the errantist theologians must face is how their view of Scripture relates to their view of God. Given the kind of God they claim to believe in as evangelicals, would it be in keeping with his nature to give us an errant Scripture. Such a view of God forces the assumption that he had the power and authority to give a completely true revelation, accommodating human intellect without untruths. So what flaw in his person caused him to fail? Is it further within the nature of God to leave his people puzzling over what parts of Scripture are from God—(thus without error) and what are only of the human writers (thus capable of error)? The Scripture itself calls us to interpret its words; it does not caution us to worry over a divine-human differentiation.

To insist upon inerrancy is not to close one's eyes to the human side of the Bible's composition, as some insist. Rather Bible students who believe the historic doctrine of Scripture continually note how David's life was reflected in his psalms or how Paul's personal perspective adds a dimension to the Epistles—personal but without error.

DIFFICULTIES WITH INERRANCY

Neither does the Bible student who believes in inerrancy ignore the "difficult texts," where there appear to be contradictions and factual errors. We must respond to the presence of such problems or our doctrine is found to be hollow. Fortunately there aren't as many of those issues as all the talk of them would indicate; there are far fewer than there were in the first half of the twentieth century.

One reason is that the evangelical movement has encouraged more, not less, in-depth biblical, historical, archaeological, and textual scholarship. Not coincidentally, over the era of the evangelical movement these studies have answered a great many questions to everyone's satisfaction. Without exception the definitive discoveries touching on historical or textual problems have explained and vindicated the text.

Given the number of issues solved during the twentieth century, the fact that we cannot address every difficulty hardly means that there are no solutions. One reason for our difficulty is the simple fact that we are unaware of all the factors involved—the big picture. With the further unfolding of the plan of salvation we may readily see solutions. Young advises,

> It is well, when we cannot explain, merely to allow the matter to stand. We have no right to declare that there is no answer. To say the least, such a conclusion involves considerable conceit. We cannot see

the explanation of a particular problem; does it therefore follow that there is no answer? Such a conclusion is certainly not consonant with the Biblical doctrine of inspiration.[47]

We must not make our own understanding a higher standard of truth than the Word of God itself. And we must be honest in our methodology, not resorting to strained or forced harmonization or explanations. Attempts at intellectual dishonesty or forced solutions have only heaped scorn on the standard of inerrancy in the past, further convincing the opposition that our case is weak. About a century ago, when there were considerably more quandaries than there are today, Warfield gave sound advice:

> Much as we might wish that we could explain all difficulties, we can console ourselves with the thought—and a true thought it is—that those who have rejected the Biblical doctrine of inspiration have far greater problems and difficulties to solve. . . . We could indeed wish that those who so constantly and confidently reject the Biblical doctrine of inspiration would give evidence that they realize somewhat the implications of what they are doing.[48]

But this great Bible scholar urged caution on both sides.

> If, however, it is rash to profess to solve all the problems which the study of the Bible brings upon us, it is yet more rash to make the dogmatic assertion that there are actual errors in the Bible. The proper method of dealing with difficulties is not to dismiss them as positive errors, for if the Bible is indeed God-breathed, it follows that it must be true and infallible. To assume that God could speak a Word that was contrary to fact is to assume that God Himself cannot operate without error.[49]

Judging Scripture

One continual problem in the writings of scholars who subscribe to a flawed Scripture is how certain they are, without much apparent justification, that some matters are "peripheral," "nonessential," and "inconsequential" with regard to the "primary intent" of divine revelation. Are "trivialities" of time and place unworthy of the Spirit's inspiration? Does the Bible recognize this dichotomy? In his 1967 defense of infallibility, Pinnock recognized the problem that he evidently fails to see three decades later. In 1967 he said,

> What is "essential" can indeed be discerned by grasping the sense of a passage, but this does not sanction our discarding that which we

deem "non-essential." The New Testament itself regards relatively minute details of the Old Testament history to be as true factually as the major events. For who, in the last analysis, is the judge able to differentiate between matters of great weight and those of none at all? The Bible is a unitary product. Any attempt to dissect out of the body of Scripture the trivial and errant minutiae is manifestly foolish and unwarranted. . . . The very idea of "trivialities" in Scripture suggests an irreverent attitude toward it. It calls into question the wisdom of God in willing the inspired Scripture to have this form that it does have. *All* Scripture was written for our learning (Rom. 15:4). It does not all aim at meticulous precision or a high degree of magnification in detail. But its content, the doctrine of inspiration assures us, is reliable in all matters the writers affirm.[50]

What confidence can we have to distinguish the essentials of "faith and practice" from the nonessentials? Can history be separated from doctrine? In Christ's life, for example, significant doctrines can have much to do with the accuracy of historical facts.

Young stated a corollary to this:

If the *autographa* of Scripture are not infallible, we can never be sure at what points they are trustworthy and at what they are not. We would then have no sure position for the defense of Christianity. If, as a matter of fact, the revelation of God is not free of error, the message of Christianity must ever remain in doubt.[51]

Elsewhere, Young summarizes a crucial reason why Scripture must be without error:

[The Christian] realizes that if the Bible has failed him at one point, he cannot be certain that it will not fail him at other points. If, for example, the New Testament is mistaken in referring to passages in Isaiah 40–66 as the work of the prophet Isaiah, by what warrant may one say that it is not mistaken in what it asserts concerning Jesus Christ? That irrepressible question is the reason why the Christian believer insists upon maintaining belief in the inerrancy of Scripture.[52]

DID JESUS QUESTION SCRIPTURE?

Those committed to Biblical inerrancy are often accused of placing the Bible above Christ, of making it an idol—the center of our worship. They remind us that the Christian's final authority is Christ, not the Scriptures. They insist that we must see him as apart from and above Scripture. He is its judge and his disciples are to judge Scripture by him, receiving only what is in harmony with his life and rejecting everything that is not. In response to such assertions Packer makes some penetrating observations:

> But who is this Christ, the Judge of Scripture? Not the Christ of the New Testament and of history. That Christ does not judge Scripture; He obeys it and fulfills it. By word and deed He endorses the authority of the whole of it. Certainly, He is the final authority for Christians; that is precisely why Christians are bound to acknowledge the authority of Scripture. Christ teaches them to do so. A Christ who permits His followers to set Him up as the Judge of Scripture, One by whom its authority must be confirmed before it becomes binding and by whose adverse sentence it is in places annulled, is a Christ of human imagination, made in the theologian's own image, One whose attitude to Scripture is the opposite to that of the Christ of history. If the construction of such a Christ is not a breach of the second commandment, it is hard to see what is. It is sometimes said that to treat the Bible as the infallible word of God is idolatry. If Christ was an idolater, and if following His teaching is idolatry, the accusation may stand; not, however, otherwise. But to worship a Christ who did not receive Scripture as God's unerring word, nor require His followers to do so, would seem to be idolatry in the strictest sense.[53]

Before believers attempt to deal with any of the critical issues of Scripture they must ask whether their general approach is that of Jesus himself. Where can we learn this but from the Scriptures themselves? Packer writes that those who would acknowledge the authority of Christ in other matters

> ought equally to acknowledge it in their approach to the Bible; they should receive Scripture as He did, accepting its claim to be divinely inspired and true and studying it as such. Those who pooh-pooh such an approach as obscurantist, unscientific and intellectually dishonest, should remember that they hereby stigmatize Jesus Christ, who taught his disciples this approach and thereby excluded any other.[54]

The Savior on Inerrancy

Jesus demonstrated the highest esteem for the Scriptures and always treated them as fully authoritative. He confessed his total confidence in all of Scripture. He said, "Do not think that I have come to abolish the law, or the Prophets; I have not come to abolish them but to fulfill them" (Matt. 5:17 NIV). The Savior could not have employed stronger words to declare his view.

His expression "the Law and the Prophets" was the normal way for rabbis to refer to the entire Old Testament. To say "the Law and the Prophets" was to mean every cranny of the Old Testament.

Jewish rabbis sometimes referred to the Scriptures in a threefold division that gave the first five books and the poetic books special notation. After his resurrection, Jesus used this standard terminology to declared that all things *must be fulfilled* that had been written of him "in the law of Moses, the prophets and the psalms" (Luke 24:44b). He also referred to the Pentateuchal laws as commandments of God as opposed to the traditions of men (Mark 7:8-9), and asserted that the Scriptures cannot be broken (John 10:35). He employed it authoritatively in responding to the temptations of Satan (Matt. 4:4, 7, 10). Christ frequently referred to historical narratives in the Old Testament and always treated them as records of fact.

Quotations of the Old Testament extend to every important section and are often from books that are most disputed by liberal critics, such a Deuteronomy, Jonah, and Daniel (Deut. 6:13, 16; 8:3; Dan. 9:27; 11:31; 12:11; cf. Matt. 4:4, 7, 10; 12:40; 24:15).

He confessed his confidence down to the very letters and the details that make up the letters (Matt. 5:18; cf. Luke 16:17). Lightner comments,

> If the Savior was teaching anything at all by the words jot and tittle, he was teaching that the most minute portions of the Old Testament as originally written, the very markings that gave meaning to words of Scripture, would not fail of fulfillment because they came from God and were thus without error.[55]

That Christ's view of inspiration extended to the word and letter level is indicated by his teachings that rest on one or two words of an Old Testament passage (for example, Matt. 22:23-33, 43-45; John 10:34-36). "If that word or those words did not have the authority which he claimed for them," notes Lightner, "his arguments would have been fruitless and would certainly have been recognized as such by his critics who knew the Scriptures so well."[56] This is not thought or concept inspiration. Christ based his teaching upon the linguistic symbol level, grammatical constructions, and nuances of word meanings. As Young has observed, "Scripture means writing (that which is written) and writing is composed of words and letters."[57] Regarding one theological problem on which he was questioned, Jesus replied to the religious leaders, "You are mistaken, not understanding the Scriptures, or the power of God" (Matt. 22:29). Everett F. Harrison notes, "How striking it is that the one allusion to error by our Lord in the days of his flesh was not to something in the Scriptures but to failure to know them and interpret them aright."[58] Lightner sets down the central issue for those who would try to set a weak view of Scripture alongside a strong view of the teachings of Christ.

> To construe Christ's teaching of Scripture as anything less than complete inerrancy and absolute infallibility is to accuse either Him, the Gospel writers, or both, of the crassest sort of ignorance and hypocrisy. He used the Scriptures for Himself and for others with complete reliance upon their absolute accuracy. This inerrancy He not only applied to matters of ethics and morals but to matters of history and geography as well. Too, His teaching of inerrancy and infallibility applies both to revelational and non-revelational matters, to that which the writer only knew through special divine revelation and to that which was already known as matters of history.[59]

In anticipation of the continuation of divine revelation, Jesus gave the disciples authority in their teaching (Luke 10:16; John 17:14, 18; Heb. 2:3–4) and promised the same inspiration for the New Testament by the Holy Spirit (John 14:26; 15:26–27). The disciples would receive truth from the Spirit (John 16:12–13) and would be witnesses to the truth (Matt. 28:19–20; Luke 10:22–23; John 15:27; Acts 1:8). There is ample evidence for this work of the Holy Spirit given by the New Testament writers themselves (1 Cor. 2:9–13; Rev. 1:1–2). Not only did they claim the authority of God for their own writings they also claimed this authority for the writings of their peers (1 Tim. 5:18; 2 Tim. 3:16; 2 Peter 3:16).

Against the objection that inerrancy is a moot point since we do not possess the originals, we would note that the Scriptures used by Jesus and the apostles were copies and translations. He did not qualify his complete confidence in what these Scriptures taught. In his 1967 essay on infallibility, Pinnock tied this confidence to the confidence that Jesus and the apostles had in God's providential concern for an accurate revelation:

> The respect for the extant Old Testament text which Jesus and the Apostles held expresses their confidence in the providence of God which assured them that these copies and translations *were indeed substantially identical to the inspired original.* There is a major difference between a reliable text with minor transcriptional errors, and a Bible with the texture of fallacy in copy and original.[60]

Can't We All Just Get Along?

But are these semantic differences over infallibility and inerrancy worth the disruption they have caused in the church? What about peace in the body of Christ and the progress of the Lord's work? This chapter has argued that the absolute purity of truth contained in Scripture is worth defending. In the near future evangelicals may be able to hold to historic Christianity despite waffling. But what about the consequences for the next generation? The lesson of history is that when God's people forsake the full reliability of Scripture, doctrinal deviations follow quickly. Despite protests against this "domino principle," the evidence is too weighty to be ignored. What Harold John Ockenga wrote decades ago, as noted earlier in this discussion, has only been further confirmed: "The evidence that those who surrender the doctrine of inerrancy inevitably move away from orthodoxy is indisputable."[61]

Francis Schaeffer warned against false security. The generation of those who forsake biblical inerrancy might maintain a warm relationship to Jesus Christ and a commitment to biblical evangelism so that they can "live theologically" on the basis of their limited inerrancy position. But what will happen to the next generation, as they try to build on that foundation? G. Aiken Taylor, who watched the Southern Presbyterians in the United States slide from a strong tradition of inerrancy, found the path to doctrinal deviation all too easy to trace: "The authority of Scripture cannot be *maintained* though it be initially affirmed, if authority is affirmed while inerrancy is denied."[62]

One wonders, too, about the ethical issue when individuals who do not personally subscribe to the doctrine of biblical inerrancy sign the doctrinal statements of schools and associations that affirm it. What measure of trust are we to put in institutions that knowingly retain faculty members who reject their doctrinal statements? How should we respond when doctrinal statements are reworded, often dropping the word *inerrant* from a statement on Scripture? Should we believe the accompanying insistence that the institution has in no way changed its doctrinal stand?

Granted, not all who assent to inerrancy follow that belief with perfect consistency. But the issue of holding to one view of Scripture and assenting publicly to a very different view is too specific and significant to be simply dismissed as imperfection. This issue centers specifically on the trustworthiness of Christian leaders and teachers and the institutions that would occupy positions of authority in the evangelical community. These of all people should carefully acknowledge their true positions, without resorting to semantic games. Those who believe *inerrant* is not a good word should make their case. They should let their constituents judge whether their arguments place them in agreement with the historic doctrines of the church.

If *infallible* doesn't mean "inerrant," what precisely does it mean? Just what falls under "faith and practice"? Credible theological leaders make distinctions openly and without ambiguity and let their arguments stand or fall in open forum on their own merits. Misrepresentation of the issues should be avoided, regardless of how noble the cause may seem to be.

The Battle for the Bible

Does the "battle for the Bible" still rage at the beginning of the twenty-first century? At this writing it is not being waged as openly as it was within the last generation. But the issues are fundamentally the same as at the beginning of this last century and at its midpoint. The fact that the struggle is more subtle makes the situation doubly perilous. An underground warring between worldviews is like an unseen cancer that eats away life. Lindsell's words of challenge are now two decades old, but they must be heeded in the twenty-first century.

> To ignore the battle is perilous. To come to grips with it is necessary. *To fail to speak is more than cowardice; it is sinful.* There comes a time when Christians must not keep silent, when to do so is far worse than to speak and risk being misunderstood or disagreed with. If we Christians do not learn from history, we are bound to repeat its mistakes. (emphasis mine)[63]

New battle lines are continually drawn, and Christians must determine the important hills on which to raise their banner of allegiance to God. May it be a response informed by the very Word of God itself, a choice and a commitment that will honor God and his eternal truth.

Sole deo gloria.

CHAPTER 5

The Reliability and Historicity of the Biblical Creation Account

Jobe R. Martin

For the invisible things of him from the creation of the world are clearly seen, being understood by the things that are made, even his eternal power and Godhead; so that they are without excuse: Because that, when they knew God, they glorified him not as God, neither were thankful; but became vain in their imaginations, and their foolish heart was darkened. Professing themselves to be wise, they became fools. (Rom. 1:20–22)[1]

Pius had grudgingly admitted evolution as a legitimate hypothesis that he regarded as only tentatively supported and potentially (as I suspect he hoped) untrue. John Paul, nearly fifty years later, reaffirms the legitimacy of evolution . . . but then adds that additional data and theory have placed the factuality of evolution beyond reasonable doubt. Sincere Christians must now accept evolution not merely as a plausible possibility but also as an effectively proven fact.[2]

—Stephen Jay Gould

THE VIEW OF MODERN SCIENCE

People as diverse as agnostic scientist-philosopher Stephen Jay Gould of Harvard University and Pope John Paul II now place evolution beyond the realm of doubt. Can we any longer have any credibility if we place faith in the reliability and historicity of the Bible's creation account? Professor Emeritus Ernst Mayr, also of Harvard, writes, "Since Darwin, every *knowing* person agrees man descended from the apes. Today, there is no such thing as the theory of evolution. It is the fact of evolution."[3]

The statements and teachings of the atheistic scientific community at the

111

end of the twentieth century strongly support a universe that began at the explosion (big bang) of a speck of infinitely dense matter between 7.3 billion and 20 billion years ago. Some gasses and dust of this big bang gradually collected into what was to be planet earth. Volcanic activity began to produce water. In an isolated pond of this planet, inorganic matter without design or Designer somehow developed organic structure. About 3.5 billion years ago the speck of life emerged. According to most evolutionists, reproducing cells appeared 600 million years ago, becoming human-like life within the last 5 million years.[4]

Given enough time, says the theory of evolution, and beginning with the explosion of the big bang billions of years ago, random chance processes could have produced everything that now exists.

Berkley professor David Berlinski candidly expresses the impossible magnitude of this theory as he writes in the Jewish intellectuals' magazine *Commentary*:

> The creation of the universe remains unexplained by any force, field, power, potency, influence, or instrumentality known to physics—or to man. The whole vast imposing structure organizes itself from absolutely nothing.
>
> This is not simply difficult to grasp. It is incomprehensible.[5]

If big bang cosmology is "incomprehensible," then it may be fanciful theory but it is not verifiable, reproducible science. Old universe cosmology does not qualify as empirical science. It falls under forensic science, in which conclusions are drawn as in police detective work from the available clues. It may be labeled "speculative philosophy." Most directly, the origin theories of the evolutionary community can be placed within the arena of faith. Their faith is in the eternality of matter. This means that *everyone believes by faith in something eternal*—either faith in eternal matter or faith in an eternal Creator. Of course, talk of faith generates screams of protest from the community of evolutionists. Internationally respected professor of law Phillip E. Johnson deals with the problem of faith in this manner:

> One of the illusions of scientific materialism is its insistence that materialists don't have faith commitments. Faith is not something some people have and others don't. Faith also isn't something opposed to reason. Faith is something that everybody needs to get started in any direction, and to keep going in the face of discouragement. Reason builds on a foundation of faith.
>
> For example, scientific materialists have faith that they will eventually find a materialistic theory to explain the origin of life, even though

the experimental evidence may be pretty discouraging for now. Because they have faith in their theory, Darwinists believe that common ancestors for the animal phyla once lived on the earth, even though those ancestors can't be found. Niles Eldredge calls himself a "knee-jerk neo-Darwinist" in spite of the invertebrate fossil record—because he is convinced, on philosophical grounds, that the theory must be true. That's every bit as much of a faith commitment as the belief of a young-earth creationist that all radiometric dating must be wrong because it contradicts the literal words of Genesis—and because it is a lot easier to deal with the problem of suffering if pain and death first entered the world after human beings had sinned.[6]

Evolutionists, then, cling to the illusion that they do not base their position on faith—in spite of the fact that their position is not supported by empirical science. Johnson goes on to say,

> Given that every position has its difficulties, where should we put our faith? To use the words that Jesus taught us, what is the foundation of solid rock, and what is the foundation of sand? The Christian says that the rock is God, and we should trust in the goodness of God all the more when the presence of evil and suffering inclines us to doubt. The materialist says that the rock is matter, and that we should never move from an unshakable faith in science and materialism even when we begin to be discouraged by the difficulties of explaining all the things that do exist without allowing a role to a Creator. . . .
>
> Whatever their faith commitments, good thinkers ought to be dissatisfied about the way things stand at the present time. The evidence that can survive baloney detecting isn't likely to satisfy either materialists or creationists. It seems for now as if new forms appeared mysteriously and by no known mechanism at various widely separated times in the earth's history. Maybe we'll be stuck with a mystery like that indefinitely, but I think it more likely that the twenty-first century will see a scientific revolution that will completely change our understanding of the history of life.[7]

Here is a convincing argument that evolutionists and creationists alike live within faith-based worldviews. He himself seems to give credence to an old-earth view, with "widely separated times" involved in the process.

THE VIEW OF AN EYEWITNESS

In truth, the Bible already sets forth a consistent history of life from its beginning to the end, one that satisfies the evidence accumulated by forensic science. The Bible sets out an eyewitness account for creation, a faith presupposition that underlies all Scripture. According to Romans 1:20, attributes of God are observed in what He has made. "For the invisible things of him from the creation of the world are clearly seen, being understood by the things that are made, even his eternal power and Godhead; so that they are without excuse."

"In the beginning God created the heaven and the earth." The first verse in the Bible announces that God *(Elohim)* made the universe. *Elohim* is a plural noun but its verb in the Hebrew is in the third person singular, "He created." A plural noun should not have a singular verb. In English this would be like saying, "They was." God is telling us in Genesis 1:1 that He is a plurality *(Elohim)* and a singularity (He created). This hints at one of God's primary attributes. The Godhead is the three in one: God the Father, God the Son, and God the Holy Spirit.

God's creation proclaims and displays His Trinitarian attribute. He created one universe in three aspects: time, space, and matter. "In the beginning" is time. "God created the heaven" is space. "And the earth" is matter. Time has a threefold nature: past, present, and future. The trio of space is width, depth, and height. Matter also has a "Trinitarian" aspect: solid, liquid, and gas, or, more fundamentally, energy, motion, and phenomena. Scientists have not yet discovered the "Trinitarian" aspects of a solid, liquid, or gas, but "plasma" may turn out to be a start in that direction. Plasma is not quite a solid, nor is it exactly a liquid or gas, but it may be one of the three parts of a solid, a liquid, or a gas.

CREATURES THAT DEFY EVOLUTION

God's attributes are displayed through His creation.[8] If we carefully study what God has made, we will either honor Him as God and give Him thanks or be reduced to vain imaginations and foolish speculations. *Macroevolution*, the idea that a big explosion created planet earth, and ultimately us, is a vain speculation among people who are grasping for a mechanism that doesn't require the intervention of a Creator.

But even the bombardier beetle, an insect one-half inch long, establishes the necessity of a Creator.

The Bombardier Beetle

If any creature on earth could not possibly have evolved, it is the bombardier beetle. It had to be created with all its systems present and fully functional. The bombardier beetle is an extreme example of what Lehigh University professor Michael Behe calls the "irreducible complexity" of life systematization."[9] A complex of interrelating systems had to function in order for the bombardier beetle to live long enough to reproduce and send its gene pool to the next generation. Evolution has no mechanism adequate for the development of such a system for which no intermediate stages are possible. Science writer Angelie Natier describes the defense system as

> extraordinarily intricate, a cross between tear gas and a tommy gun. When the beetle senses danger, it internally mixes enzymes contained in one body chamber with concentrated solutions of some rather harmless compounds, hydrogen peroxide and hydroquinones, confined to a second chamber. This generates a noxious spray of caustic benzoquinones, which explodes from its body at a boiling 212 degrees Fahrenheit. What is more, the fluid is pumped through twin rear nozzles, which can be rotated, like a B-17's gun turret, to hit a hungry ant or frog with bull's eye accuracy.[10]

For all this to work, microscopic chemical factories inside the beetle manufacture and mix chemicals that violently react to produce something similar to an explosion. Error in the mix would cause the beetle to explode. Researchers have studied the beetle's defense mechanism in slow motion and discovered that it is a series of rapid-fire, sequential mini-explosions. The sequential explosion is needed so that the insect does not blow itself out of the vicinity while it is shooting an enemy with the force of the "pop."

How could the beetle evolve such a means of defense? This problem has had evolutionists scratching their heads for over fifty years. Simplistically speaking, evolutionary theory says that you do not evolve something unless you need it. For example, evolution texts teach that fossil cockroaches and fossil turtles are several hundred million years old. Fossil roaches and turtles look exactly like living roaches and turtles, which means, the evolutionist say, that roaches and turtles are perfectly suited to their little niche and have never needed to change.

When would an early-stage bombardier beetle have known it needed to change? Not until after it had blown itself up.[11]

All irreducible complexity is general revelation. Through it human beings see the attributes of God as Master-designer and Creator. They should, as a result, praise Him.[12]

The Bull Giraffe

Another example of design complexity is found among giraffes. These long-necked marvels needed a system of highly specialized body parts from the first day.

A bull giraffe is about eighteen feet tall. In order to pump blood against gravity up his long slender neck he has a particularly powerful heart muscle. His heart, in fact, can be two and one-half feet long. This pump is so powerful that if the giraffe bent his head down to get a drink of water and his heart suddenly was pumping *with gravity* instead of against gravity, he would burst the blood vessels in his brain and die.

This is a problem, for dead giraffes do not evolve. What keeps the giraffe alive while he is drinking is a series of valves in the arteries of his neck that close to decrease the blood pressure. That, alone, would not be enough, however, for the shut-down valves do not stop that last pump at full throttle. Marvelously, this last pump of blood does not go into the brain. It is shunted into a sponge-like collection of vessels under the brain to reduce the pressure and spare the giraffe. As the spotted animal raises his head after drinking, the "sponge" gently squeezes the fresh blood into the brain, the arterial valves open, and valves in the veins that descend the neck close. Cranial blood pressure remains a healthy constant.

The Chuckwalla Lizard

Chuckwalla lizards should die of salt poisoning. These reptiles live in the desert and cannot find water much of the year. Enough salt builds up in their blood to kill them, but it does not. God designed a desalination factory in the nose of the chuckwalla. When the salt content becomes elevated, a valve automatically establishes a detour, so that blood is purified in the nasal desalination factory. Sneezes expel pure salt crystals.

The Beaver

The beaver has transparent eyelids for underwater sight. Fur-lined ear, nose, and throat flaps protect him from the icy winter water.

The Gecko Lizard

Some irreducible complexity is not a matter of survival but of special convenience for a particular animal. For example, gecko lizards can run upside-down across a ceiling without falling. At 2000x magnification, little tufts of hairs are observed on their feet. At 35,000x magnification, microscopic suction cups are discovered on the tiny hairs. These suction cups are so powerful that the gecko would be inextricably stuck to whatever his foot touched if he did not have specially designed feet. Evolution has no explanation for this design and function of the gecko.

The Green Woodpecker

The European green woodpecker has a tongue that goes down his throat, out the back of his neck, up over the top of his head (under the skin), out a little hole between his eyes, through the right nostril into his beak and then as much as ten inches out of his beak.

Other Woodpeckers

Woodpeckers open their eyes, focus, aim their beak and then close their eyes between each peck on the tree. The force of the beak pounding against the tree is so powerful that if the bird did not close its eyelids its eyes would pop out.

PUNCTUATED EVOLUTION

For another reason, Darwinian theory has lost credibility among scientists—even those in the international community of atheistic evolutionists. The primary reason is that the fossil record does not show the transitional forms that Darwinism demands. The transitional fossils simply do not exist. No less a champion of materialism than Stephen Jay Gould readily admits the problem:

> The absence of fossil evidence for intermediary stages between major transitions in organic design, indeed our inability, even in our imagination, to construct functional intermediates in many cases, has been a persistent and nagging problem for gradualistic accounts of evolution.[13]

Fellow evolutionist Mark Ridley summarizes the evolutionist answer—*punctuated equilibrium:*

> Some palaeontologists point out that the fossil record offers no firm evidence for such gradual change. What really happened, they suggest, is that any one animal species in the past survived more or less unchanged for a time, and then either died out or evolved rapidly into a new descendent form. . . . Thus, instead of gradual change, they posit the idea of "punctuated equilibrium. . . ."
>
> In any case, no real evolutionist whether gradualist or punctuationist, uses the fossil record as evidence in favor of the theory of evolution as opposed to special creation.[14]

Evolutionists Gould of Harvard and Ridley of Oxford and other evolutionists have moved toward punctuated equilibria as their only real alternative. This theory posits that, throughout the billions of years of evolutionary history, the normal situation has been equilibrium or stasis. Everything stayed the same. However, at certain intervals, because of doses of massive radiation or for other reasons that haven't been deciphered, the equilibrium was interrupted by a relatively frenetic period of change. Life forms rapidly evolved through genetic changes into new, radically different life forms. After this short period of rapid evolutionary change, equilibrium *(stasis)* was reestablished for more thousands or millions of years.

THEISTIC EVOLUTION OR PROGRESSIVE CREATION?

If macroevolution results in such speculations and assaults on logic, why do so many of God's people seem to accept it in its personae of *theistic evolution* or *progressive creation*? Theistic evolution is Darwinian evolution plus God.

Almost from the moment Darwin's *The Origin of Species* was in print, many Christians accepted it uncritically and scrambled to rewrite theology to take evolutionary processes into account. By the early days of the twentieth century slow, gradual, *theistic* Darwinian evolution already was welcomed into the academic Christian community. Late in the century a great many Christians had learned with everyone else of the bankruptcy of Darwinism. However, instead of catching the implication that the Bible was correct all along, most joined atheistic evolutionists in their flight toward the reformulated theory of punctuated equilibria. The new view, modified slightly to include God, tends to be called "progressive creationism." This view differs slightly from that of day-age creationists who do not accept macroevolutionary processes. Neither the slow (Darwinism) nor the fast (punctuated equilibria) theories of evolution are observable, for they both demand millions of years. There is no more evidence for punctuated than for gradual evolution. In fact, it introduces a whole new failure to account for the mechanism that triggered these sudden bursts of change. Its only virtue is that it takes away the necessity for a Creator—something Christian progressive creationists fail to notice.

In spite of the fact that the atheistic evolutionists, such as Gould, admit that there are no transitional forms in the fossil record, progressive creationist Hugh Ross finds it necessary to be more evolutionary than most evolutionists. He argues that God used transitional forms over millions of years as He created:

> The so-called "transitional" forms of dinosaurs and birds suggest that God performed more than just a few creative acts here and there, letting natural evolution fill in the rest. Rather, God was involved and active in creating all kinds and stages of dinosaur and bird life, not to mention all other life—the first, the last, and all the forms along the way to the advent of modern humans.[15]

Ross accepts "stages" between the first and the last. However, the Bible teaches that the first *is* the last. The Creator made each life form "after its kind."[16] Ross also teaches through lecture and writing the position that the universe is billions of years old.[17] This clearly violates a literal understanding of the text of Scripture.

THE BIBLE ON CREATION

The ideas of theistic evolutionists and especially progressive creationists will continue to penetrate the church of the twenty-first century. Christians must decide whether to trust scientific theory or God's revelation?

One essential question is whether the days of Genesis 1 can be stretched to the billion or more years necessary to accommodate evolutionary theory. Another is whether Christians should start from the assumption of an infallible science in which evolutionary theory is indisputable, and because of that assumption decide to believe that the Bible must accommodate an ancient universe. Those who start with science must bring the idea of aeons to the Bible and try their creative best to squeeze the billions into the text. One method is the *day-age theory*, which posits that the days of Genesis are each long periods of time.

How Long Is a Day?

If the biblical text is approached without any preconceived ideas about the age of the universe, the only conclusion possible is that the universe is very young. Genesis 1–2 uses the Hebrew term *yom* for day. The first mention of "day" is in Genesis 1:5, for which God defines day as light. For each of the days of the Genesis creation week, *yom* is used with the numerical qualifier: first through seventh. Throughout the Old Testament *yom* with the numerical qualifier consistently means a solar-length day. There are other Hebrew words that God could have used in Genesis 1 if He had wanted to convey the idea of long, indefinite periods.[18]

Adam lived 930 years.[19] Assuming that Adam lived at least one half of the sixth day, all of the night between the sixth and seventh days and all of the seventh day, how old was Adam when he died? If those days in Genesis are believed to be one billion years each then Adam would have been 1,500,000,930 years of age at his death. Or, as some progressive creationists teach, if the days were normal days but the time between each day was a long period, then again how old was Adam when he died? There can not be aeons of time between each creation-week day since Adam lived throughout the entire time of one of those nights (between the sixth and seventh days).

Also, each of those days was half light and half dark. One-half billion years of total darkness (one-half of a creation-week day) followed by one-half billion years of unrelenting light (the other half of the day) is not the way our solar system works. In the midst of the Ten Commandments, God defends His seven-day creation week. He writes, "Remember the Sabbath day, to keep it holy. Six days shalt thou labor, and do all thy work." There is no question of meaning here. Man works six days and rests on the seventh. Man does not work six billion years and rest for the seventh billion. God through the biblical author equates the human workweek with God's creation workweek: "For in six days the Lord made heaven and earth, the sea, and all that in them is, and rested on the seventh day." The God of the Bible made the heaven, earth, and sea, and "everything in" the heaven, earth, and sea within the same kind of week cycle of seven solar days by which people live. Then He ceased his labors on the same kind of day that people use for rest.[20]

If the days of Genesis 1 are anything but one rotation of planet earth in front of its light source, Genesis 1:14 makes no sense: "And God said, let there be lights in the firmament of the heaven to divide the day from the night; and let them be for signs, and for seasons, and for *days*, and *years*." If a day is stretched out to be one billion years to accommodate the time demands of evolutionary theory, then how long is a year? Is a 360-day biblical year equal to 360 billion years? Not even evolutionists claim that the universe is 360 billion years old.

Was There a Gap?

Another attempt to accommodate the evolutionary timetable and fossil record is called the gap theory. Gap theorists teach that there was a gap of millions of years between Genesis 1:1 and 1:2. This idea is untenable. The Creator writes in Exodus 20:11 that He not only made everything *in* the heaven, earth and sea, but that he made (not "refashioned") the heaven, earth, and sea *within* the six-day creation week. The gap theory demands that he did it before the first day of that week.

Gap theorists are forced to change the clear meaning of the Hebrew text. In Genesis 1:2 the phrase "And the earth was without form" is altered to read "And the earth *became* formless." In this grammatical construction, "became" is not within the acceptable range of meaning in Hebrew usage. For example, a similar construction is used in Genesis 2:25: "And they were both naked." Adam and Eve did not "become" naked, they were naked from the beginning. This verb and grammatical form is used in Genesis 3:1: "Now the serpent was more subtle than any beast of the field which the Lord God had made." The serpent did not "become" more subtle, he *was* more subtle from his beginning.

The fossil record displays life that requires sunlight. Genesis 1:2 states that "darkness was upon the face of the deep." How could darkness cover the earth if, as in the gap theory, the sun already existed? The literal words suggest that a light beam *created* by God with no sun behind it broke through the darkness to provide the light for the first three days of the creation week. God did not create the sun until the fourth day.[21] Hence, the sun, not yet being created, did not "appear" from behind the clouds on the fourth day as the gap assumes. The Creator could have used the word that means *appear* since He had already used it in Genesis 1:9, but, instead, He chose the word that is accurately translated *made*.

We do not know why God used a beam of light with no sun behind it for the first three days. Perhaps He knew that one day humans would worship the sun as the source of life, and he wanted to declare that it had no primacy.

The light beam, with no sun behind it, makes the statement, "Don't worship the sun. Worship the God who made the sun and does not even need the sun to illumine the earth!"

Much discussion has centered around the phrase "And the earth was without form, and void." The gap theory states that "without form and void" means chaos existed in Genesis 1:2 as a result of God's judgment on a pre-Adamic civilization. This cannot be a correct interpretation of the text since death came as a consequence of the sin of Adam.[22] There can be no death and destruction of a pre-Adamic wicked race of people before death existed.

The words "without form and void" in a literal interpretation simply means that, as God began His creative work, the earth was unformed and unfilled. This is corroborated in Isaiah 45:18: "For thus saith the Lord that created the heavens; God Himself that formed the earth and made it; he hath established it, he created it not in vain, he formed it to be inhabited." God took His unformed, unfilled earth; He formed it and filled it.

If God made the heavens, the earth, the seas, and *all* that is in them within the six-day creation week and not before the first day of that week, He, then, must have created Lucifer and the angels early in the week. Perhaps He created the angels first. Job declares that the angels shouted for joy as God accomplished His creation.[23] No angels fell during that week, since God tells us that everything he made during that week was "very good."[24]

Scripture has very little to say about the origins of the angels. If we assume that they were part of the creation sequence, we can speculate that Satan sinned immediately thereafter and almost immediately pulled Adam and Eve into his rebellion. Eve could not have borne children before the fall or such babies would have been born without the Adamic sin nature. Scripture seems to indicate that Adam and Eve were created fully mature and able to understand God's instructions. Their bodies were perfect in form and function. Part of the Creator's command was to fill the earth.[25] Eve would surely have conceived within the first month. This is biblically impossible if the fall had not happened quite soon.

God has done everything possible to the text of Genesis 1 to alert us to the fact that He created the earth, heavens, and seas and *everything* in them quickly and in six solar-length days. In order to believe this, one assumption must be made: God does not need time.

When the reliable and historical Genesis account is studied without any preconceived ideas derived from evolutionary "science" it is obvious that the Creator creates fully mature systems and organisms. Adam is made from dust into a grown man. The Creator made man from dust, not from reworked monkey genes, as a theistic view of evolution teaches. Adam appears to be perhaps twenty-five years of age, but he is only seconds old. God puts Adam to sleep, takes out one of his ribs and fashions Eve. Adam awakes to meet what apparently is his fully mature wife. Eve is mature, but not old. "And the rib, which the Lord God had taken from the man, made he a woman, and brought her unto the man."[26] The God of the Genesis account, as it appears in its most logical and literal sense, does not need time to create fully mature systems.

The statement that God made Eve from Adam's rib brings up a problem for those who say evolution and Genesis are complementary and compatible. *Is there even one evolutionist that believes that the female evolved from the male?*

The accusation has been made that if God creates fully mature systems with the outward appearance of age He is being deceptive. There is no deception here since the Creator has told us exactly what He did. We also have a model of God the Son doing just this kind of creative work in his first recorded miracle. Jesus, as described in John 2, worked an act of creation that formed something fully mature. He turned water into wine. This wine was of a quality that comes only as fruit juices are aged to perfection. After the ruler of the feast tasted the wine, which was water a few minutes before, he said, "Every man at the beginning doth set forth good wine; and when men have well drunk, then that which is worse: but thou hast kept the good wine until now."[27]

In Genesis God took six days and created the universe and everything in it with full maturity. In John 2 the Creator, the Lord Jesus Christ, took six water pots and created wine that apparently tasted like aged (fully mature) wine. The Creator stepped into His creation to become the Redeemer and His miracles prove who He is by manifesting His power and His glory.

A similar example of this miraculous power to create in maturity occurred in the miracles of the multiplied loaves and fishes. The Lord Jesus did not send disciples out to catch fish and others to bake bread. The bread Jesus produced must have looked and tasted as though it had gone through a process that required time, but God did not require time.

Yet again Jesus used this power in healing. An example is the healing of Malchus, the servant of the chief priest, after Peter sliced off his ear with a sword. From the text it would seem that Jesus put the damaged ear in its place, and it was restored. No prolonged healing time was required.[28] The Creator stepped into creation to manifest His glory and to die for Adam's sinful race. His miracles prove He is above time, for He created time. He is God!

THE CREATION OF MAN

As to the hard evidence for human evolution from a common ancestor with monkeys, there is none. Evolutionist Lyall Watson said it this way: "The fossils that decorate our family tree are so scarce that there are still more scientists than specimens. The remarkable fact is that all the physical evidence we have for human evolution can still be placed, with room to spare, inside a single coffin."[29]

Writer Richard Milton, a science journalist and a confirmed materialist without "any religious beliefs of any kind," still must write, "Paleontologists have continued to make finds of bones and teeth in Africa, Asia, and elsewhere. But despite more than a century of energetic excavation and intense debate the glass case reserved for mankind's hypothetical ancestor remains empty. The missing link is still missing."[30]

Milton challenges the evolutionary community to produce evidence to support their confidence that man evolved from monkey-like ancestors: "Strangely too, this modern confidence and apparent precision in reconstruction is not based on further discoveries of fact, but takes place *despite* the discoveries of recent decades—that the evidence for humankind's own evolution is actually nonexistent."[31]

If the evidence for humankind's evolution is nonexistent, where do the museums of natural history and such publications as *National Geographic* get their displays and photographs of apelike creatures gradually becoming people? The anti-creationist *Science Digest* was unusually candid in a 1981 article:

> Unfortunately, the vast majority of artists' conceptions are based more on imagination, than evidence. . . . Much of the reconstruction, however, is guesswork. Bones say nothing about the fleshy parts of the nose, lips or ears. Artists must create something between an ape and a human being: the older a specimen is said to be, the more ape-like they make it. . . . Hairiness is a matter of pure conjecture. . . . The guesswork approach often leads to errors.[32]

Museum displays and the sequential "monkey-to-man" illustrations are "artists' conceptions," "imagination," and "guesswork." Thus it seems that some Christians go out of their way to accept evolutionary dogma over the word of Jesus Christ that there were male and female people on earth from the beginning of creation.[33]

THE VEGETARIAN ANIMAL KINGDOM

The Bible teaches that the first people ate fruit and vegetables. Genesis 1:29 records the instruction of God to Adam: "Behold I have given you every herb bearing seed, which is upon the face of all the earth, and every tree, in which is the fruit of a tree yielding seed; to you it shall be for meat." Not until Genesis 9, after the global flood of the days of Noah, does God give permission to eat meat. "Every moving thing that liveth shall be meat for you; even as the green herb have I given you all things."[34]

Animals were commanded to eat only plant material before the flood. "And to every beast of the earth, and to every fowl of the air, and to every thing that creepeth upon the earth, wherein there is life, I have given every green herb for meat: and it was so."[35] If every beast of the earth was to eat plant life until after the global flood, then dinosaurs, including Tyrannosaurus Rex, must have been included.

A number of dinosaur species are consistently portrayed as ferocious predators. The problem with this assumption is clearly visible in skeletal remains of "T-Rex." The teeth of this monstrous animal have exceedingly long crowns and very short roots. The ratio of crown length to root length averages seven-to-one. If this giant dinosaur attempted to catch and devour a squirming, wrenching lizard, its teeth would have been ripped from their sockets. These are the teeth of a herbivore. Before the flood of Noah's day even Tyrannosaurus Rex ate green plants. His sharp teeth would have been ideal for stripping leaves from trees.

Ancient animals that have been found preserved in the permafrost of arctic tundra muck have undigested plants in their stomachs. Woolly mammoths had undigested buttercups in their mouths and stomachs.[36] These animals may have been caught and frozen at the time of the flood. Most evolutionary textbooks picture the woolly mammoth standing in a blizzard with a slowly creeping ice age pursuing him. This could not be further from the truth.

The freezing of the mammoths was rapid and thorough. A century ago, before much scientific study had been done and remains preserved, the meat of these ancient beasts was actually eaten by arctic people:

> In many instances, as is well known, entire carcasses of the mammoth have been found thus buried, with the hair, skin and flesh as fresh as in frozen New Zealand sheep in the hold of a steamer. And sleigh dogs as well as Yakuts themselves, have often made a hearty meal of mammoth flesh thousands of years old.[37]

Not only were they caught and frozen extremely quickly, rather than by a creeping ice age, but their skin and hair could only tolerate a hot climate. The woolly mammoth has no sebaceous (oil) glands in its skin.[38] Only animals with copious amounts of oil to lubricate their hair can survive frigid climates. Polar bears, seals, wolves, etc. have rich oil to waterproof their fur. The oil keeps the water away from their skin. Without oil in their skin and hair water would flow through to the porous skin and quickly freeze. The Siberian mammoths were warm temperature animals grazing on warm temperature plants. They were caught in a climactic event so catastrophic that many animals quick-froze. Not many events could account for such finds. One that could is a world flood cataclysm in which the insulating water canopy suddenly fell upon the earth and greenhouse warmth suddenly became polar cold.

THE WATER CANOPY

Evolutionists have no valid explanation for the rapidly frozen animals. An asteroid strike could not account for the rapidity indicated by the mammoth remains. Creationists have the only feasible explanation. The Bible records that the Creator placed water above the firmament: "And God made the firmament, and divided the waters which were under the firmament from the waters which were above the firmament: and it was so" (Gen. 1:7). God placed some kind of a water canopy above the atmospheric heaven. The firmament of Genesis 1:6–8 is the air in which the birds of Genesis 1:20 fly.

This water canopy was destroyed when "all the fountains of the great deep" were broken up and the "windows of heaven were opened."[39] As the protective water canopy was fractured, perhaps by volcanic activity of the fountains of the deep, the warm air surrounding planet earth shot out into space, creating frigid temperatures on earth's surface and quickly freezing millions of animals. Evidence that the "fountains of the deep" of Genesis 7:11 referred to intense volcanic activity is imbedded in the oldest polar ice. Deep Arctic and Antarctic ice and tundra muck are saturated with volcanic ash.[40]

Existence of a water canopy helps explain another problem unsolved by evolutionists. Fossil flying creatures have been discovered with wingspans of over fifty feet. These creatures could not fly in the atmosphere of planet earth as it exists today. But they could have flown in a more dense atmospheric pressure. A water canopy would provide the added weight to increase atmospheric pressure, enabling the flight of huge creatures. Again the biblical picture is reliable in contrast to the speculations of the theorists of the evolutionary community.

High atmospheric pressure, a warm earth that encouraged plant growth and vegetation-eating animals would have been an ideal climate to support long life and encourage large sizes. If nothing was eating them, and they had unlimited food, the dinosaurs could follow their genetic design for immense size in the pre-flood environment.

Another characteristic of the pre-flood ecosystem's water canopy was the absence of rain. Earth would have been a global terrarium. God states that there was no rain. A mist watered the whole earth.[41] So Noah had never seen a rainbow in the clouds. After the deluge God said to Noah, "I do set my bow in the cloud, and it shall be for a token of a covenant between me and the earth." [42]

THE GLOBAL FLOOD

If the flood of the days of Noah was regional, as Darwinism demands and many theistic evolutionists and progressive creationists believe, then the covenantal rainbow given by the Creator means nothing, for there have been many local river overflows in the Middle East since Noah's time. The implication is that the historical record of the Bible cannot be trusted. Does the Bible explain what happened to all the water after the flood? Creationist researchers Ken Ham, Andrew Snelling, and Carl Wieland state,

> There are a number of Scripture passages that identify the Floodwaters with the present-day seas (Amos 9:6 and Job 38:8–11, note "waves"). If the waters are still here, how is it that the highest mountains are not still covered with water, as they were in Noah's day? Psalm 104 gives us the answer. After the waters covered the mountains (verse 6), God rebuked them and they fled (verse 7); the mountains rose, the valleys sank down (verse 8) and God set a boundary so that they will never again cover the earth (verse 9). They are the same waters!
>
> Isaiah gives this same statement that the waters of Noah should never again cover the earth (Isaiah 54:9). Clearly, what the Bible is telling us is that God acted to alter the earth's topography. New continental land-masses bearing new mountain chains of folded rock strata were lifted from below the globe-encircling waters that had eroded and leveled the pre-Flood topography, while large deep ocean basins were formed to receive and accommodate the Flood waters that then drained off the emerging continents.
>
> That's why the oceans are so deep, and why there are folded mountain ranges.[43]

When the fountains of the deep shot their waters up into the sky they may have left large caverns in the earth. As the flood waters receded, they could, to some extent, have soaked back into the these caverns. This highly mineralized floodwater seeping back into the caverns in the earth would have provided the ideal conditions for the rapid formation of stalactites and stalagmites. Conventional geology teaches that stalactites require hundreds of thousands of years to form. The United States, for example, has great caverns where tours view large stalactites. Each may have one drop of water on the tip of the rock formation. Naturally, at that rate vast years would be needed to form a large mineral formation. Yet, in some of these caverns where there is more water flowing, the stalactites form so rapidly that the Park Service must frequently scrape them off the electrical lines. If they did not, their rapidly increasing weight would break the lines![44]

THE GEOLOGIC "TIME CLOCK"

Many such "time clocks" indicate a young universe or do not prove the passage of eons, as evolutionists suggest. Scientists know of more than seventy methods to measure the effects of the passage of time. If results are evaluated objectively, most indicate a relatively young earth. Only a few are publicized because they give incredibly long results.[45]

There is measurable scientific evidence that our solar system is less than ten thousand years old. The gravitational field of the sun pulls cosmic dust into itself—the Poynting-Robertson effect. Our sun is estimated to burn about one hundred thousand tons of cosmic dust every day. A sun as ancient as evolution demands should have "pulled in" and destroyed all the particles in our solar system. Yet, our solar system is full of particles.[46]

One can explore many such indications of a youthful creation: the relatively limited deltas for great river systems, bristle-cone pine trees,[47] the recession rate of the moon,[48] comets with a quite limited life span,[49] depletion of the magnetic field,[50] radio-halos in coalified wood and Precambrian granite,[51] planetary rings,[52] volcanic geology,[53] clastic dikes,[54] ocean salt content,[55] continental erosion,[56] ocean floor sediment,[57] and "instant petroleum."[58]

THE GENEALOGICAL TABLES

In spite of the preponderance of scientifically testable evidence for a young earth, some Christians believe that there are huge gaps in the biblical genealogical records. Some see this as a necessity because they believe Creation had to be far earlier than posited by the scientific creationist. But others use this as a justification for a theistic evolution model.

It is commonly accepted that a little more than four thousand years have elapsed since the days of Abraham. Any gaps in the record must be between Adam and Abraham. Jude 14 follows the genealogical counting in calling Enoch the seventh generation from Adam. Jude clearly states that there are no gaps between Adam and Enoch.

Enoch and his wife gave birth to the oldest man who ever lived, Methuselah.[59] Methuselah was the grandfather of Noah and undoubtedly knew his grandson well. No gaps are biblically defensible from Adam through Enoch to Noah. This only leaves the possibility of gaps between Noah and Abraham.

This reasoning that gaps exist in the genealogy developed during the twentieth century from the early postmodern conceptualization that words, as life itself, have no meaning. If the words of text have no inherent meaning, then billions of years of macroevolution can be crammed into the texts of the Bible that describe the creation events. However, the words of Genesis do have specific, inherent meaning.

CREATION OR EVOLUTION?

Life presents us with many either/or decisions. The "creation–evolution" controversy is a decision with profound implications for life. The early chapters of Genesis document the origin of the universe and of life itself, and they also are foundational to most New Testament doctrines. If the creation account cannot be trusted as historically reliable, the rest is cast into doubt as well.

It is obvious that creation and macroevolution as it is expounded at the end of the twentieth century cannot both be true. The primary objective of this chapter has been to show that there still is plenty of reason to believe that the biblical creation account is reliable and historically accurate. We do not have to throw out our brains or any true, scientifically testable and verifiable science to believe in a creator/designer God who made everything exactly as He reveals in the biblical account of six twenty-four-hour creation days that occurred approximately six thousand years ago.

Isaiah 48:11 states that God will not share His glory. Evolution robs God of His glory by offering an explanation for our existence apart from anything supernatural or miraculous. John explains to us that people love the approval of men much more than the approval of God (John 5:44, 12:43). The approval of men at the beginning of the twenty-first century involves "politically correct" thinking which has as its foundation atheistic evolution. It is a shame that even the evangelical Christian church has been contaminated and compromised with old universe beliefs, thus robbing the Lord of His glory and stealing His praise.

The general revelation of God's creation shouts of His existence and His attributes. His wisdom, power, and glory are displayed through the marvels of His creation, marvels such as bombardier beetles, giraffes, woodpeckers, and the stars of the heavens.

CHAPTER 6

The Fall, the Curse, and a Groaning World

Henry M. Morris

For we know that the whole creation groaneth and travaileth in pain together until now. (Rom. 8:22)[1]

Yes, our world is in pain. Wars, crime, pollution, persecution, poverty, drugs, corruption, disease, famine, and other evils abound, but the question is, "Why?" Why should a world created by an omnipotent and loving God be in such pain? As Michael Ruse, a philosopher of evolutionistic science, says, "The problem of evil is the most troubling of all."[2]

Any question beginning with "Why . . . ?" ultimately will have a theological answer. Science can deal with the "What . . . ?" "How . . . ?" "Where . . . ?"— and sometimes "When . . . ?"—questions, but not with the "Why . . . ?" The true theological answer to the problem of pain can be found only in Genesis, for of all the world's religious books only Genesis even *attempts* to answer the question of the ultimate origin of all things, including the universe itself.

"In the beginning ['time'] God created the heaven ['space'] and the earth ['matter']." Thus is answered the most basic of all questions in the very first verse of the Bible (Gen. 1:1). And when God completed His work of creating and making the time/space/matter universe, He pronounced it all to be "very good" (Gen. 1:31). There was nothing bad—no pain, no sorrow, no death— in all the creation. There was certainly no "struggle for existence," for all creatures—animal as well as human—had everything they would need. But "sin entered into the world, and death by sin" (Rom. 5:12); "by man came death" (1 Cor. 15:21). As a result of human rebellion against God's Word, God pronounced the great curse on human dominion.

129

THE GLOBAL CURSE OF SIN

Thus entered death into the world. The curse fell on Adam as head of the human race, and through him on Eve and all their descendants. "In Adam all die" (1 Cor. 15:22a). "By the offense of one judgment came upon all men to condemnation" (Rom. 5:18a). Nor is it solely Adam's sin that warrants such universal condemnation: "Death passed upon all men, for that all have sinned" (Rom. 5:12). By genetic inheritance from Adam and Eve, all men and women have an innate sin-nature, so that "there is not a just man upon earth, that doeth good, and sinneth not" (Eccl. 7:20). Therefore, "the scripture hath concluded all under sin" (Gal. 3:22a).

The biblical doctrine of the fall and its resulting curse is abhorrent to modern sophisticates, who cannot stomach the notion that suffering is the result of sin. There is unquestionably suffering and death in the animal kingdom, as in the human family. The atheist Richard Dawkins makes quite a point of this as a reason for not believing in God at all.

> The total amount of suffering per year in the natural world is beyond all decent contemplation. During the minute that it takes me to compose this sentence, thousands of animals are being eaten alive, many others are running for their lives, whimpering with fear, others are being slowly devoured from within by rasping parasites, thousands of all kinds are dying of starvation, thirst and disease. . . . The universe that we observe has precisely the properties we should expect if there is, at bottom, no design, no purpose, no evil and no good, nothing but pitiless indifference.[3]

Such atheistic evolutionists as Dawkins thus use this evil world as their excuse for not believing in God, substituting macroevolutionary processes, operating by the mechanism of natural selection, to explain all things. Dawkins is Britain's most articulate evolutionist, whereas Stephen Jay Gould—also an atheist—holds that distinction in America. Gould holds forth on this subject:

> Moreover, natural selection, expressed in inappropriate human terms, is a remarkably inefficient, even cruel process. Selection carves adaptation by eliminating masses of the less fit—imposing hecatombs of death as preconditions for limited increments of change. Natural selection is a theory of "trial and error externalism"—organisms propose via their storehouse of variation, and environments dispose of nearly all—not an efficient human "goal-directed internalism" (which would be fast and lovely, but nature does not know the way).[4]

Gould is at Harvard University, Dawkins at Oxford. They argue with each other about the mechanism of evolution, but they agree that evolution, however it works, is purely materialistic. No "god" could be involved in such a process. As another humanist says,

Nature makes everything in vain. After all, what is evolution? A mindless process built on evil; that's what it is.—So natural selection seems smart to those who see only the surviving products, but as a design process it is idiotic. And the raw brutality of the process is offensive.[5]

Yet many Christians believe that God used evolution as His method of creation! They call this belief "theistic evolution."

THEISTIC EVOLUTION AND THE FALL

It is really quite easy to understand why doctrinaire evolutionists would be atheists. If evolution really explains everything, as they assume, then God is redundant. Furthermore, if God does exist, they will say, He certainly would not have used evolution as His method of creation, for it is the most wasteful and cruel process that could ever be imagined by which to produce man. As the atheistic philosopher Bertrand Russell said,

Religion, in our day, has accommodated itself to the doctrine of evolution,—the unfolding of an idea which has been in the mind of God throughout. It appears that during those ages—when animals were torturing each other with ferocious horns and agonizing stings, Omnipotence was quietly waiting for the ultimate emergence of man, with his still more widely diffused cruelty. Why the Creator should have preferred to reach His goal by a process, instead of going straight to it, these modern theologians do not tell us.[6]

For the evolutionist, there was no "fall" at all. Evolution has been rising, not falling, from amoebae to humankind, and there has always been suffering and death. For Charles Darwin, in fact, that was the very essence of evolution:

Thus, from the war of nature, from famine and death, the most exalted object which we are capable of conceiving, namely, the production of the higher animals, directly follows.[7]

According to Darwin's concept, "by death came man," whereas the Bible says, "By man came death" (Rom. 5:12).

Nevertheless, the "theistic evolutionists," who desire to be both "scientific" and "religious," think of evolution as God's method of creation. Some would even claim to be *"Christian* evolutionists," but this is an oxymoron in the fullest sense, since Jesus Christ Himself stood solidly for creation. He not only was a creationist, He was the Creator! "For by Him were all things created" (Col. 1:16). The theistic evolutionist must either ignore the great Curse altogether, or else possibly try to argue that it applies to mankind only, since suffering and death were functioning long before man, if evolution was really happening. But that is a poor "cop-out," at best. It not only contradicts Scripture but also ignores the terrible sufferings in the animal world before man's coming. David Hull, professor of philosophy at Northwestern University, said,

> The evolutionary process is rife with happenstance, contingency, incredible waste, death, pain and horror.—[God is] not a loving God who cares about His productions. He is not even the awful God portrayed in the book of Job. [He] is careless, wasteful, indifferent, almost diabolical. He is certainly not the sort of God to whom anyone would be inclined to pray.[8]

If this awful cruelty among animals is not an outgrowth of sin and the curse, then the Creator (that is, Jesus Christ) instituted a process based on death, in which all creatures struggle for existence and only the "fittest" survive. In the words of another atheist, Carl Sagan,

> The secrets of evolution are death and time—the deaths of enormous numbers of life forms that were imperfectly adapted to the environment, and time for a long succession of small mutations that were by *accident*, adaptive, time for the slow accumulation of patterns of favorable mutations.[9]

It is recognized, of course, that sincere and intelligent Christian people *do* accept such compromise theories. This evaluation is not meant to be critical of anyone personally, but only of their unnecessary accommodations to the evolutionary age-system. For example, Pattle Pun, a progressive creationist, makes the admission, "It is apparent that the most straightforward understanding of the Genesis record is that God created heaven and earth in six solar days, that man was created in the sixth day, that death and chaos entered the world after the fall of Adam and Eve."[10]

PHYSICAL EFFECTS OF THE FALL

Certain progressive creationists have argued that the effects of Adam's sin were only spiritual in nature—specifically that Adam died spiritually, losing his fellowship with God. He eventually would have died anyhow, so they say, like all other creatures. But that idea would make a mockery of the atoning death of

Christ, which was an exceedingly painful *physical* death. Why should Christ have to suffer and die *physically* to atone for the *spiritual* death of Adam and his progeny? The fact is that Adam died spiritually the moment he sinned ald also *began* to die physically at the same time. And today each person begins to die as soon as he or she is born. Although gerontologists are busily trying to unravel its mystery and thereby to prolong life, all are agreed that death is somehow programmed into our very genes. Physical death (as well as spiritual death) is indeed "the wages of sin" (Rom. 6:23). In the new earth, with our then-incorruptible bodies, "there shall be no more death" (Rev. 21:4).

The curse of physical and spiritual death under the law (Rom. 8:2) now controls Adam and his descendants. Its physical corruption also affects the animals and vegetation and even the inorganic creation. Before God pronounced His curse upon Adam and Eve, He cursed the serpent (whose body Satan had used in the temptation) "above all cattle, and above every beast of the field" (Gen. 3:14). That is, the cattle and all other beasts were brought under the curse, the serpent most of all. Plant growth was included, "thorns also and thistles" now appearing (Gen. 3:18). People would have to wrest sustenance out of the inhospitable ground.

The very "ground" was cursed, the earth out of whose "dust" all life had been formed (Gen. 1:11, 24; 2:7; 3:17). As used in Genesis, this "dust" of the earth would encompass the atomic/molecular structure with which all things are knit together. This structure also was cursed. The Hebrew word for "ground" in Genesis 3:17 also can mean "earth" and one quickly sees from the context that this is precisely what is meant. In today's terminology the curse extends to the covalent bonds of atomic structure, where the ultimate "dust" comes together. The curse of decay and death pronounced on Adam extended to Adam's entire dominion. That dominion includes all the earth (Gen. 1:26). The "bondage of corruption" that Paul discusses in Romans 8:20-23 is pervasive.

This universal reign of decay and death is confirmed in Scripture:

> *Of old hast thou laid the foundation of the earth, and the heavens are the work of thy hands. They shall perish, but thou shalt endure; yea, all of them shall wax old like a garment; as a vesture shalt thou change them, and they shall be changed. (Ps. 102:25-26; quoted in Heb. 1:10-12)*

> *For He knoweth our frame; He remembereth that we are dust. As for man, his days are as grass: as a flower of the field, so he flourisheth. For the wind passeth over it, and it is gone. (Ps. 103:14-16a)*

> *Lift up your eyes to the heavens, and look upon the earth beneath; for the heavens shall vanish away like smoke, and the earth shall wax old like a*

garment, and they that dwell therein shall die in like manner. (Isa. 51:6)

Heaven and earth shall pass [literally "are passing"] away, but my words shall not pass away. (Matt. 24:35)

For all flesh is as grass, and all the glory of many as the flower of grass. The grass withereth, and the flower thereof falleth away. (1 Peter 1:24; cf. Isa. 40:6–8)

In this "present evil world" under the curse, "the earnest expectation of the [creation] waiteth for the manifestation of the sons of God" (Rom. 8:19). It is thus not only "the sons of God" who are earnestly awaiting their manifestation as such when Christ returns. The whole creation has this as its earnest expectation.

Christ defeated the power of death. That would have been unnecessary if death was not part of the curse. Unbelievers understand this:

It becomes clear now that the whole justification of Jesus' life and death is predicated on the existence of Adam and the forbidden fruit he and Eve ate. Without the original sin, who needs to be redeemed? Without Adam's fall into a life of constant sin terminated by death, what purpose is there to Christianity? None.[11]

The above evaluation was written by one who calls himself a "The Joyous Atheist." The following appeared in another atheistic journal.

Those liberal and neo-orthodox Christians who regard the creation stories as myths or allegories are undermining the rest of Scripture, for if there was no Adam, there was no fall; and if there was no fall there was no hell; and if there was no hell, there was no need of Jesus as Second Adam and Incarnate Savior, crucified and risen. As a result, the whole biblical system of salvation collapses.—Creationists rightly insist that evolution is inconsistent with a God of love.[12]

The prominent Darwinian philosopher-scientist Michael Ruse sums up his own evaluation of this state of affairs:

Either humankind is in a state of original sin or it is not. If it is, then there was reason for Jesus to die on the cross. If it is not, Calvary has as much relevance as a gladiator's death in the Coliseum.[13]

Ruse, as a convinced evolutionist, believes Christianity is a fraud. Once a thinking person rejects the Fall and the Curse, there is no other logical stopping point. In another article, Ruse rejects the atoning death of Christ in the following words:

> Some of the problems of Christianity strike me as being so blatantly rational-belief-destroying that there is almost a sense of farce in seeing its devotees trying to wriggle from under them. Chief among these is the problem of explaining how somebody's death two thousand years ago can wash away my sins. When you combine this with the doctrine of the Trinity and the implication that the sacrificial lamb is God Himself (or Itself) and that this therefore makes things all right with this self-same God, the rational mind boggles.[14]

Ruse illustrates 1 Corinthians 1:18. "For the preaching of the cross is to them that perish foolishness, but unto us which are saved, it is the power of God." His diatribe also relates to Colossians 2:8: "Beware lest any man spoil you through philosophy and vain deceit, after the tradition of men, after the rudiments of the world, and not after Christ."

The mystery is why so many evangelicals feel they must somehow accommodate the Genesis record of creation and the fall to the same unsubstantiated geologic age system on which unbelievers base their faith in evolution. There is no firm scientific evidence for evolution, nor can we see any sign of macroevolution taking place within all of human history. Even if one uses the utmost creativity, it is impossible to put together a single substantive transitional series from among the fossils that have been uncovered.

There is a much more cogent explanation for the fossils in the Bible than the geologic ages. So why compromise? Is it because "they loved the praise of men more than the praise of God?" (John 12:43).

THE LAW OF ENTROPY AND THE CURSE

In fact, the very laws of nature negate the possibility of macroevolution. The "bondage of decay" that the Creator has imposed upon the "groaning and travailing" creation is more than a theological idea. Its implications are recognized in science as a fact of natural order. Although most scientists will not acknowledge the biblical and theological aspects of this law, they do recognize that things universal move from order toward decay and disintegration. This is the law of "increasing entropy," the second law of thermodynamics.

This law must be taken into account by all scientists, in every field of research. Different branches of science phrase it according to its individual application to their particular fields. But they all recognize and apply it. It can be expressed in complex mathematical and statistical equations, but it can also be defined in terms of everyday experience, which is more germane to our purpose. An especially vivid expression of this law was framed by the prolific scientist Isaac Asimov.

> Another way of stating the Second Law, then, is "The universe is constantly getting more disorderly." Viewed that way, we can see the Second Law all about us. We have to work hard to straighten a room, but left to itself, it becomes a mess again very quickly and very easily. Even if we never enter it, it becomes dusty and musty. How difficult to maintain houses, and machinery, and our own bodies in perfect working order; how easy to let them deteriorate. In fact, all we have to do is nothing, and everything deteriorates, collapses, breaks down, wears out, all by itself—and that is what the Second Law is all about.[15]

It seems clear that this universal law of disintegration poses a serious problem for the theory that evolution has been an age-long process of growth in complexity, all the way from molecules to man. But evolutionists often try to sidestep this problem by arguing that the second law applies only to isolated systems, whereas the earth is an open system—open to ordering energy from the sun. Roger Lewin comments,

> One problem biologists have faced is the apparent contradiction by evolution of the second law of thermodynamics. Systems should decay through time, giving less, not more, order. One legitimate response to this challenge is that life on earth is an open system with respect to energy and therefore the process of evolution sidesteps the law's demands for increasing disorder with time.[16]

However, this is *not* a legitimate response. The second law applies to open systems as well as to closed systems, though the equations become a little more involved. The internal mechanics of the system still *tend* toward entropy (that is, disintegration). In certain special cases, where specific dynamics can be seen at work, entropy can be overcome or postponed by a greater influx of energy from outside the system (for example, the growth of a seed into a tree or a pile of construction materials into a building).[17]

The very fact of universal decay testifies to the fact of primeval creation. According to the Genesis record, when God finished His work of creating and making all things, He *rested* from calling things into existence and from organizing created entities into complex systems (Gen. 2:3). Whatever processes He may have used during the six days of creation, He stopped using. He is no longer *creating* things; He is now "upholding all things by the word of His power" (Heb. 1:3). He has completed His work of creation (except in rare miracles), and is now carrying out His work of *conservation*.

This principle of conservation is also a basic scientific law, called the Law of Conservation of Mass/Energy; or the first law of thermodynamics. It is considered the most certain, best-proved law of science, along with the second law. Matter and energy changes form, but nothing is either "created" by coming into existence from nothing or "annihilated" by going out of existence into nothing. Energy changes form in a given process (e.g., electrical energy becomes light energy in a light bulb). Energy can even become matter (as in thermonuclear fusion). But the total amount of matter and energy within the universe remains unchanged. God is *conserving* what He created. Asimov comments that "this law is considered the most powerful and most fundamental generalization about the universe that scientists have ever been able to make."[18]

Evolutionary speculators have impressed many evangelicals with their talk about black holes, oscillating universes, quantum fluctuations, and other ephemeral and ethereal notions that are used to explain the universe without God. The fact is, however, that these are all ideas that are backed up by no observational evidence. The scientific *laws* (not guesses) of thermodynamics, on the other hand, observably speak against the possibility of macroevolution and point to primeval special creation.

That, of course, explains why there is no real scientific evidence for evolution, either in the records of the past or the observations of today's natural processes. God's curse is on the earth, and things are going downhill, not uphill, under the *bondage* of decay. No doubt, in the original complete "very good" creation, the principle of conservation applied both to energy and entropy, so that every downhill process was balanced by an uphill process. That's the way it will be again when God renews His creation (Rev. 21:4-5; 22:3).

THE FLOOD AND THE FOSSILS

What about those billions of fossils resting in the great global cemetery in the earth's crust? If they don't represent the evolutionary history of life over the geological ages, what do they tell us? If the Genesis record is to be taken as literal history, as Christ Himself understood it (for example, Matt. 19:3-6; 24:37-39), then they must somehow have been buried in these sediments after the Fall. There was no death of conscious life before that.

The answer clearly is that most of them were buried by the waters of the flood. Unbelievers and neoevangelical Christians ridicule this fact, and the "flood geology" to which it leads, but there is really no other viable answer. If they were not buried at the flood, they must have suffered and died before Adam sinned, and this both contradicts Scripture and libels the omniscient, omnipotent, gracious character of God.

One thing fossils reveal is the global reign of death. There they are—dead things by the billions, buried in sedimentary rocks which once were sediments, eroded and transported and buried in water. Not only are fossils found all over the world, but so are sedimentary rocks, even in the highest mountains. At one time or another, every part of the world has been under water.

All of this seems *prima facie* evidence of a global flood, and the early geologists (such as Steno, Woodward, and Burnet) so interpreted it. This was before evolutionists developed the system of evolutionary geologic ages. Then rocks and fossils were categorized by the era in which they supposedly were laid down (from Cambrian to Pleistocene ages). Derek V. Ager writes that "Fossils have been and still are the most useful method for dating rocks to a particular age."[19] But that leads to circular reasoning, because new fossil finds are normally dated by the rock in which they are discovered. Niles Eldredge, a paleontologist at the American Museum of Natural History, is one researcher who is concerned about this:

> Paleontologists cannot operate this way. There is no way simply to look at a fossil and say how old it is unless you know the age of the rocks it comes from. And this poses something of a problem; if we date the rocks by their fossils, how can we then turn around and talk about patterns of evolutionary change through time in the fossil record?[20]

This is strikingly illustrated by two encyclopedia articles, written by the same author, Samuel Paul Welles, in the same encyclopedia—World Book. In his article, "Fossils," he said, "Scientists determine when fossils were formed by finding out the age of the rocks in which they lie"[21] And in his article, "paleontology," he said, "The age of rocks may be determined by the fossils found in them."[22]

So how did this circle of reasoning get established? The real answer is the assumption of evolution. The standard evolutionary progression of life was essentially established before many fossils were available. So early evolutionists drew by analogy from the order seen in embryonic development. This led them to develop a so-called "great chain of being," which drew on ideas that extended as far back as the ancient Greek philosophers.[23] Despite the ubiquitous gaps in the evolutionary record, evolutionists point to the sequence of changing life forms in the various "ages." But these sequences are determined by the assumption of evolution in the first place! Geologists themselves have long admitted that there is no truly objective way to determine the age of a rock:

> This book tells of the search that led to the development of a method for dividing prehistoric time based on the evolutionary development of organisms whose fossil record has been left in the rocks of the earth's crust.[24]

Merely in their role as distinctive rock constituents, fossils have furnished,—through their record of the evolution of life on this planet, an amazingly effective key to the relative positioning of strata in widely separated regions and from continent to continent.[25]

The rocks do date the fossils, but the fossils date the rocks more accurately. Stratigraphy cannot avoid this kind of reasoning,—because circularity is inherent in the development of time scales.[26]

The charge of circular reasoning in stratigraphy can be handled in several ways. It can be *ignored,* as not the concern of the public. It can be *denied,* by calling down the Law of Evolution. Fossils date rocks, not vice versa, and that's that. It can be *admitted,* as a common practice.[27]

The only chronometric scale applicable in geologic history for the stratigraphic classification of rocks and for dating geologic events exactly is furnished by the fossils. Owing to the irreversibility of evolution, they offer an unambiguous time scale for relative age determinations and for worldwide correlations of rocks.[28]

Historic geology relies chiefly on paleontology, the study of fossil organisms.—The geologist utilizes knowledge of organic evolution, as preserved in the fossil record, to identify and correlate the lithic records of ancient time.[29]

The method of dating rocks has not changed for almost a hundred years. Computers have speeded the process, but index fossils and fossil assemblages still are the standard means of determining geologic ages of rocks, and these are based ultimately on the false assumption of evolution.

The bottom line is that there is *no* reliable way to date fossils and therefore no way to determine the age of sedimentary rock. This means that it is not possible to prove that any rock system is older than any other. For all we can tell, they could all be essentially the *same* age! In general, it is reasonable that rocks at the bottom of any local geologic "column" would have been laid down earlier than those on the top, but the time involved need not have been longer than days or weeks. The possibility that all could have been deposited during the year of the great flood is not so farfetched after all.

In fact, physical evidence strongly supports this interpretation of the data. It is very significant that the total geologic column (the worldwide complex of sedimentary rocks, extending from the surface down to the crystalline basement rocks on the bottom) shows no worldwide time break. That is, although there is *local* "unconformity" in the rock columns, there are no *global* unconformities, except at the very bottom. An "unconformity" is a surface that has been eroded before more deposits were laid down upon it. That would indicate that the geological column never had time to erode before another level of rock was deposited. Sediment deposition was going on, somewhere at least, during the entire period of formation of the total geologic column. Consequently, the formation of the fossil-bearing part of the earth's crust, averaging about a mile in depth, was essentially one continuous event, from beginning to end, or bottom to top. The question then becomes one of duration. How long did it take for the deposition process? Was it one of slow action, stretched over almost a billion years, or of rapid deposition lasting a short time?

The geologic column holds serious problems for uniformitarianism, the standard geologic dogma for over 150 years. Uniformitarianism states that "the present is the key to the past," with all processes acting very slowly. The only exceptions are earthquakes, volcanic eruptions, and similar intermittent local catastrophes. Geologists in the late twentieth century tended to abandon, or at best greatly modify, uniformitarianism, in favor of neo-catastrophism. Ager has been a leader in this movement. Although Ager did not believe in the Genesis flood, nor in the Bible generally, his field studies led him to conclude that *all* geologic structures and formations formed rapidly and catastrophically.

> My thesis is that in all branches of geology there has been a return to ideas of rare violent happenings and episodicity.[30]

> To me, the whole record is catastrophic—in the sense that only the episodic events—the occasional ones—are preserved for us.[31]

> The history of any one part of the earth, like the life of a soldier, consists of long periods of boredom and short periods of terror.[32]

Ager has been very influential in gaining a review of the evidence. In a review of one of his books, Professor Allmon of the Paleontological Research Institution in New York, says,

> The volume is the summation of a lifetime of global geological work by one of the most influential stratigrapher-paleontologists of his generation. Yet by the eminence of its author and the straightforwardness of its tone, this volume may mark the arrival of catastrophism as the status quo.[33]

Another reviewer of the same book says,

> Now all is change. We are rewriting geohistory. Even the most staid
> of modern geologists are invoking sedimentary surges, explosive phases
> of organic evolution, volcanic blackouts, continental collisions and
> terrifying meteoroid impacts. We live in an age of neocatastrophism.[34]

In his presidential address to the Society of Economic Paleontologists and
Meteorologists, Robert Dott said,

> I hope I have convinced you that the sedimentary record is largely a
> record of episodic events rather than being uniformly continuous. My
> message is that episodicity is the rule, not the exception.[35]

In explaining why he used the word "episodicity" rather than
"catastrophism" Dott said that the latter tended to "feed the neo-catastrophical-
creation cause," and so "should be purged from our vocabulary,"[36] even though
his term means the same thing.

Clearly these and other geologists are looking at the evidence and seeing
that its best reading is quick placement—catastrophic—not slowly over great
ages. Although many, possibly most, geologists recognize this fact, only a
relative minority accept the biblical flood as the cause of rapid deposition.
Ager's opinion is typical: "I am coming more and more to the view that the
evolution of life, like the evolution of continents and the stratigraphical column in general, has been a very episodic affair, with short 'happenings' inter-
rupting long ages of nothing much in particular."[37]

Thus, he tends to equate the periods of "punctuation" in evolutionary
biology with the regional catastrophes in evolutionary geology, and the long
times of "stasis" in evolution with the long ages of quiescence in geologic
history. However, this concept does not deal with the lack of worldwide
"unconformity," which argues loudly against any sort of time gap.

The best explanation for the available evidence is that fossil-bearing sedimentary rocks of the earth's crust were formed by regional catastrophes, mostly
hydraulic, and that the whole series was interconnected and continuous, com-
prising finally a worldwide hydraulic cataclysm, associated with volcanic and
tectonic activities. Or, as Peter put it, "The world that then was, being over-
flowed with water, perished" (2 Peter 3:6). Evidence for the Genesis flood is
seen everywhere one looks in the earth's crust!

It is good to remind ourselves why the Flood is important theologically as
well as scientifically. With probably millions of antediluvian human inhabitants drowned in the flood, along with billions of animals killed and preserved
as fossils, it is evident that the flood involved the greatest visitation of death

on the earth. But death is "the wages of sin" (Rom. 6:23), and the flood was sent by God because, in the antediluvian world "the wickedness of man was great in the earth, and that every imagination of the thoughts of his heart was only evil continually" (Gen. 6:5).

The doctrinal truth that God must and will eventually judge sin appears not only in the Bible, but everywhere one looks on the earth. The flood really occurred, just as the Bible recorded, and it is "willing ignorance" (2 Peter 3:5) to explain it away, as do even many evangelical Christians.[38]

Christ referred to the flood as a prophetic type of His second coming and the future judgment by fire (Luke 17:26–30; 2 Peter 3:6–7). Sin, which entered the world so innocuously when Adam and Eve questioned and then disobeyed the word of God, soon bore bitter fruit in Cain's murder of Abel. It culminated in a world so "filled with violence" (Gen. 6:13) that the only remedy was a global drowning and a new beginning.

Unfortunately, it is necessary to show that the Bible itself teaches a global flood. This seems obvious from the account of Genesis 6 through 9, but many argue that the flood was *local*, inundating only a portion of the Middle East. Others say that it was global but so *tranquil* that it didn't leave a trace. These equivocations fall far short of the account. The flood was said to cover all the mountains, including the mountains of Ararat, which now range to 17,000 feet . The length of time of this full coverage was five months (Gen. 7:19–8:4). A five-month-long, 17,000-foot-high "local flood" is a hydraulic impossibility. Further, the project of building the gigantic ark and maintaining two of every kind of land animal inside for a whole year was absurdly unnecessary if the Flood was a local phenomenon.[39]

An even more serious objection to the local flood idea is that God promised never to send such a flood again (Gen. 9:11, 15). If this was only a local flood, God lied! There have been numerous devastating local floods since *that* local flood, all over the world, every year.

And these are only three of the numerous objections to the local flood compromise.[40]

The tranquil flood theory is, if anything, even more futile. Even local floods produce extensive devastation and sedimentation. A worldwide tranquil flood would be about as reasonable as a worldwide tranquil earthquake or a worldwide tranquil volcanic explosion. The reason so many otherwise sound Bible teachers reject the clear biblical teaching of the global cataclysmic is a commitment to the geological ages. They also believe there must have been animal death and suffering previously. Since they have at least some understanding of geology and hydrology, they realize that the geological ages are incompatible with a global flood. Such a flood would have completely eroded and redeposited whatever previous formations existed. The resulting geologic column would inevitably be a record of the flood, not of the supposed ages before the flood. Consequently, those who hold to either the gap theory or the day-age theory in order to retain the geological ages necessarily must also reject the worldwide cataclysmic flood.

Biblically, the fall of Adam and God's curse on human dominion explain the very existence of sin and pain and death. The flood of Genesis 6–9 also explains the geological and paleontological data that have, until now, been misapplied to support evolution and the geologic ages.

SUMMARY

The fall of Adam was a profoundly important historical event. Adam, of course, was a real person, not just a generic term for a population of evolving hominids. In fact, he was the "first man" (1 Cor. 15:45) and Eve was the "mother of all living" (Gen. 3:20). The Bible never hints of a "pre-Adamite" people, as some theories have postulated.

Adam and Eve were both "created in the image of God" (Gen. 1:27), unlike the animals, which were placed under their dominion, along with "all the earth" (Gen. 1:26). Adam and Eve were in perfect fellowship with God. Everything was "very good" (Gen. 1:31). There was no death, no suffering, no struggle for existence.

But Satan, perhaps the highest of God's angels, the "anointed cherub" at God's throne, rebelled against God's Word and was "cast to the ground," out of heaven (Ezek. 28:14, 17). God allowed him to test Adam and Eve. Possessing the body of the serpent that God had created, He led the two innocent humans into doubt, then infinite rebellion, and eternal death if not for hope of an infinitely valuable sacrifice.

God, therefore, removed Adam and Eve from His presence, and (as God had warned) they began to die. The very elements of which all things had been made ("the dust of the ground," presumably the basic elements of matter), were brought under "the bondage of corruption" (or "decay"—Rom. 8:21). This was the great curse on the ground, which extended to Adam's entire dominion, so that "the whole creation groaneth and travaileth in pain together until now" (Rom. 8:22).

This bondage of decay affects all men and women, for "in Adam all die" (1 Cor. 15:22). Because of the inherited sin-nature, each person is both born a sinner and continually in rebellion against God, so that all stand twice judged— by nature and by practice—for "the wages of sin is death" (Rom. 6:23). This death does not just mean banishment from Paradise, but eternal separation from the fellowship with God for which we were created.

The fall and curse affected the whole creation. The principle of decay and death is so pervasive in all God's created systems and processes that it has come to be recognized as the Law of Increasing Entropy, the second law of thermodynamics. This universal scientific law refutes Satan's evolutionary religion, by which He seeks to persuade people to reject God as Creator. All of nature points inexorably to the necessary truth of a created primeval perfection, from which all things are now deteriorating.

Pervasive human wickedness became so flagrant that God cleansed the world with the great flood, which destroyed all people and all land animals except those in Noah's Ark (Gen. 7:21–23; cf. Job 12:15; 2 Peter 3:6).

The entire topography of the earth was altered, and thick sediment layers were deposited. Animals drowned and settling in these layers sometimes became fossils, the silent testimony of the antediluvian world. This fossil graveyard has been transmuted by evolutionists into a billion-year record of evolutionary history. Its real message, however, is not that life evolved over many ages, but that it was destroyed in a single cataclysm.

There is no need or justification, therefore, for evangelicals to distort the Genesis record to accommodate evolutionary geologic ages. The latter never existed, and needs to be refuted, not appropriated.

In the meantime, the curse remains and death reigns in a society that is separated from God and living in spiritual death. But God had already prepared His plan of redemption: "For as in Adam all die, even so in Christ shall all be made alive" (1 Cor. 15:22). God in Christ was "the Lamb slain from the foundation of the world" (Rev. 13:8), paying the awful price for the redemption of lost men and women.

"Christ hath redeemed us from the curse of the law, being made a curse for us" (Gal. 3:13). The redemptive work of Christ has both delivered believers from the curse on all creation and the specific curse imposed in the Mosaic law on lawbreakers (Deut. 27:26).

In that glorious age to come, when the new heaven and new earth replace these that are passing away (Matt. 24:35), "there shall in no wise enter into it any thing that defileth, . . . but they which are written in the Lamb's book of life" (Rev. 21:27).

All of God's primeval purposes in creation will be accomplished. "And there shall be no more curse, . . . and they shall reign for ever and ever" (Rev. 22:3a, 5c).

CHAPTER 7

Holy Angels, Satan, and Demons

Robert P. Lightner

A NEW FASCINATION

The resurgence of interest in the spiritual world, especially in angels—both holy and wicked—is everywhere evident. God's Word, especially the New Testament, has much to say about angels and demons. *Young's Analytical Concordance* lists 284 references to the word *angels* in the Bible. There was much angelic and demonic activity on earth when our Lord Jesus Christ graced this planet. From the close of the canon of Scripture until the mid-1970s, however, Western culture paid scant attention to them. Only Bible-believing Christians spoke and wrote about these spirit beings with genuine belief in, and respect toward, them.

Now that has changed. Throughout the 1990s there was widespread interest in "holy angels" that often translated into worship of them and prayer to them. Demons and Satan, their leader, shared much of this attention. A large, well-lit billboard along the highway between Fort Worth and Dallas, Texas, illustrates how deeply the current angelphilia and demonphilia has dug its way into popular culture. The sign reads

ANGEL TERMITE COMPANY
We get those little devils.

The Source of the Angelic Craze

What, we might ask, has brought about the angel-demon-Satan craze? Why are they the subject of so much attention?

Interest in demons and Satan has always been strong in some world societies, for example among animists, Haitian voodooism, and the Roman

Catholic-related Santeria cult. Astrology, witchcraft, spiritualism, and the other occult arts, of course, always have been practiced in Western society, always just under the surface. Except for Ouija boards, ghost stories, "horror films," and newspaper horoscopes, they seldom found popular expression. Certainly no one was going off-Broadway to a briefly-successful rock musical called *The Satanic Bible* until 1971. Near the end of his long career as a religion writer and observer, Louis Cassels was right-on when he described the upsurge of public interest in such things as one of the most curious phenomena of American life.

Regardless of where the resurgence has occurred in once-Christian societies, a basic reason has been the corresponding rejection of the Bible as God's inspired, authoritative message. With the rejection of this message from God, there has naturally come a denial of the God who is revealed in Scripture.

In place of God's Word, existential humanism's "modern man" became the dominant source for authority. But a humanistic philosophy is inadequate to answer life's perplexing questions. Disappointed humanists could not find the answers in themselves, so they looked elsewhere for an authority base and inevitably found themselves in a world of spiritism, whether through the old nature religions or Eastern pantheism in all its manifestations. The spirit world gave strange but authoritative answers to the most bewildering questions:

> Who am I, really?
> Why am I here?
> How did I get here?
> Where do I go from here?

Whether the current craze leads one to worship Satan and demons or pray to holy angels, the result is the same. The God of the Bible and the Bible itself have been replaced by persons from the world of unseen spirits.

HISTORICAL OVERVIEW

The Early Church

Early in the Christian era, the church fathers wrote with an apparently universal assumption that both good and evil angels existed. They taught that angels were created by God in a perfect state. Some of these holy creatures had followed Satan in his rebellion and had fallen from their state of perfection.[1]

Through roughly the first five hundred years of church history, theologians were kept busy wrestling with the doctrines of sin, salvation, and the triunity and attributes of God. There was little energy to delve into the doctrines of angels and demons.

As indicated in New Testament references to errors involving angels, there were problems. Second-century Gnostics worshiped them as part of a pantheon in which Christ was the highest among many "aeons" or spiritual emanations from the Source. Jesus, thus, was half angel and half divine.[2]

In about 500, *Celestial Hierarchy* discussed the angelic world from the assumption that the current three-level structure of church authority followed the angelic pattern. In the highest rank of angels were Thrones, Cherubim, and Seraphim. In the second were Mights, Dominions, and Powers. In the third and lowest rank were Principalities, Archangels, and Angels. The work's author was an anonymous fifth/early-sixth-century theologian who wrote under the name Dionysius the Areopagite. Dionysius was a Neo-Platonist, possibly a Syrian mystic, who claimed apostolic authority; he had considerable influence in the church. Since he claimed to be Dionysius the Areopagite of Acts 17:34, he came to be known as Pseudo-Dionysius or Dionysius the Pseudo-Areopagite.

The Middle Ages

During the Middle Ages the doctrines of angels and demons suffered, as did other important doctrines. The theologian, philosopher, and rational apologist Thomas Aquinas (1224–1274) made the greatest contribution to the doctrine of angels of this period. In *Summa Theologica*, Aquinas answered 118 pointed questions about angels. He set forth eight specific proofs for their existence.[3]

The Period of the Reformation

Likewise, the Protestant Reformation period (c. 1500–1648) saw little development in the doctrines of angels and demons. Both Reformers and Counter-Reformers stressed the power of Satan and demons as wicked and powerful enemies of God and His children. Holy angels were said to minister continually to God's people. Some believed in guardian angels while others denied their existence.

Article twelve of the Belgic Confession (1561) presents a succinct statement of the generally accepted Reformed view, as it was formulated within the Geneva Academy that was begun by John Calvin (1509–1564).

> He also created the angels good, to be his messengers and to serve his elect: some of whom are fallen from that excellency, in which God created them, into everlasting perdition; and the others have, by the grace of God, remained steadfast and continued in their primitive state. The devils and evil spirits are so depraved that they are enemies of God and every good thing to the utmost of their power, as murderers watching to ruin the Church and every member thereof, and by their wicked

stratagems to destroy all; and are therefore, by their own wickedness, adjudged to eternal damnation, daily expecting their horrible torments.[4]

Calvin stated all that he thought could be said without undue speculation in Book 3 of *Institutes of the Christian Religion*. Where Scripture was silent or even brief in its teaching, Calvin remained less than dogmatic in his beliefs. The Puritan poet John Milton (1608–1674) put his own spin on angels and demons in *Paradise Lost* and *Paradise Regained*.

Scholars argue the theological merits of Milton's writings, but their popular influence was immense and lasted for many generations of readers. In *Paradise Lost* Milton fantasizes a great deal about God the Father, God the Son, and Satan. He does the same with angels. His is an artist speculating, without much concern about what Scripture teaches.

Some have adamantly opposed Milton's presentation of angels and demons. Duane Garrett observes that *Paradise Lost* is no more a story of real angels than Ovid's *Metamorphoses* is about real gods:

> Simply put, these very human spirits have little relation to the angels and demons of the Bible. As humans, we cannot tell a story that is anything other than a human story. In the very act of imagining spirits and inventing stories about them, we humanize them and so construct idols. These angels look less than angelic and these demons look better than demonic. We create spirits in our own image: this is the very essence of myth. As we are mixtures of good and evil, so are they.[5]

The Modern Era

Truly the rationalism of the eighteenth century affected the doctrines of angels—good and bad—just as it has all other doctrines of the historic Christian faith. Side by side with the denial of the Bible as the inspired Word of God in the modern era (from 1648) has come a denial of the existence of angels.

Liberal theologians speak and write of angels as symbolic representations of a caring and concerned God. Neoorthodox thinkers speak of angels as "ontological functionaries possessing half-divine powers."[6] This means that they do not have objective existence.

With the rise and invasion of the occult has come the revived interest in the spirit world. Books and articles have flooded the market with material both for and against each conception of angels and demons.

The Secular View

Three individuals have decisively shaped the secular view of angels and demons in the modern period. Their views have spilled into religious circles.

Karl Barth (1886-1968), the father of neoorthodoxy, was insistent that the Bible must be our base for what we believe about angels and demons. He tried to relate his view of angels to Christ. This all seems a bit inconsistent in view of Barth's weak beliefs about the Bible and Christ. In neither case did he hold to the historic faith.

John Geddes Macgregor (b 1909), in his book, *Angels: Ministers of Grace*, advocates that angels are a super race of evolved extraterrestrials. This modernist Scottish Presbyterian has beliefs about angels related to his views about evolution and reincarnation. Macgregor's popular book has had wide circulation and has many supporters in the new age community.

Emanuel Swedenborg (1688-1772) wrote about thirty books in which he was, he insisted, guided by angels. This scientist-turned-mystic said he talked with angels and they with him. Angels, in his view, have virtually all the human characteristics—they eat, breathe, read, and enjoy marriage and sex. Swedenborg had a large body of followers during the nineteenth century, because his thought meshed with the subjective romanticism and transcendental philosophy that was current. Swedenborgian beliefs have found renewed expression in New Age thinking.

New Age Beliefs

New Age beliefs have much to do with the "angelology" in the late twentieth century. To understand the implications of these beliefs, a brief description of what is meant by "New Age" thinking is in order. The essence of this philosophy-religion arises from ancient Hinduism. The belief that everything is a part of God—part of a divine oneness—is called monism, and is central to both of these religions. Since we are all part of "god," we need only look within ourselves to answer all of our problems. Philip Lochhaas put it bluntly, and correctly, when he said,

> It is the most anti-God philosophy to come on the scene in recent years, a blatant repetition of Satan's first and most successful temptation: to be as God. Yet its various expressions have attracted students, laborers, housewives, clergymen and teachers, and a host of businessmen and captains of industry.[7]

New agers have written a library full of books on angels.[8] There is no pretense that they build their beliefs on facts found in the Bible. The authors draw with uniform appeal upon the Qur'an, pseudepigraphical early Christian books, the Bible, and the writings of Swedenborg. The authors make frequent claims that their information comes from personal angelic instruction. Some claim to be on a first-name basis with their contact angels.

Anyone can contact and communicate with angels, according to New Age thinking. The way to do it is to get rid of all negative feelings, surrender your mind to the spirit within, and meditate. When you see a light appearing before you, you are approaching an angel. When the angel actually appears before you, you can ask for whatever you want. In this way you can reach your higher self. When a negative thought enters your mind, you must concentrate on angels. When an angel is visualized, it will cleanse the mind. Angels come to your aid when you are discouraged and despondent.

New Age thinking is a way to replace God and the authority of His Word. God's people desperately need to know what God's Word says about angels and demons so they will know how to evaluate all anti-biblical views.

BIBLICAL DESCRIPTIONS OF ANGELS

Similar to Man

There are a number of comparisons and contrasts that can be made between humans and angels. God created both and did so perfectly. Both are creatures with personality. Humans and angels were both placed under times of probation, and both sinned during those times. God created both to serve and worship Him. The Bible teaches that neither humans nor angels are to be worshiped.

Different from Man

Contrasts also exist between humans and demons. The outstanding difference between them is that, while God extended grace to the fallen human race, He did not extend that same grace to angels when they sinned. They were confirmed in their wickedness, with no hope of deliverance. On some ontological level, God established angels as a "higher" order than human beings. Hebrews 2:9 says that Christ was made "lower" than the angels in the Incarnation, so that He could "taste death for every one" (Heb. 2:9). In the eternal state, believers will "judge" angels (1 Cor. 6:3). Man, we are told, was made in the image and after the likeness of God. This is not said of angels. People propagate as God told our first parents to do, but angels do not reproduce among themselves (Mark 12:25).

Angels Are Spirit Beings

They do not have physical bodies that die. The Bible teaches that angels are spirit beings, both holy angels and wicked angels, including Satan. Though they do not have physical or material bodies, they appear on earth sometimes in human form. Their appearance is sometimes described in Scripture as bright and gleaming, as when they appeared at Christ's empty tomb (Luke 24:4; cf. Acts 10:30; 2 Cor. 11:14; Rev. 18:1).

The Bible also presents angels as spirit beings possessing personality. They are not mere figments of human imagination, nor personifications of good and evil. The pronoun it cannot be used for them; they are not disembodied powers, or forces. They possess intellect, emotion, and will—the essentials of personality. They "long to look" (1 Peter 1:12) into man's salvation and everywhere Scripture mentions them the holy angels are working toward God's honor or actively giving praise to Him. They are described as wise to the extreme (2 Sam. 14:20), yet God alone possesses omniscience.

Angels Are Creations of God

That God created angels is clear from Scripture. When He created them is not clear. All we know for sure is that they were present when earth's foundation was laid (Job 38:4, 7). But both Old and New Testaments affirm that God did create them (Ps. 148:2, 5; John 1:3; Col. 1:15-16). We are never told the precise reason angels were created, but they live to serve Him and His sovereign plan. Clearly, the chief responsibility of holy angels is to bring honor and glory to God. They have from their creation worshiped and served their Creator (Ps. 103:20-21; Heb. 1:6; Rev. 5:11-12).

We also know that angels were created innumerable. They are described as "the host of heaven" (1 Kings 22:19), "thousands upon thousands" and "myriads upon myriads" (Ps. 68:17; Dan. 7:10). The New Testament gives the same descriptions of their numbers in Luke 2:13; Hebrews 12:22; and Revelation 5:11. These heavenly creatures have their abode, it would appear, in the "second heaven." We know from the apostle Paul's message to the Corinthian Christians that there are at least three heavens (2 Cor. 12:2). Christ "passed through the heavens" (Heb. 4:14) as He returned to the Father. Here then is strong implication that angels dwell in the second heaven although they also have access to the third heaven, which is the very presence of God. The first heaven would refer to the atmospheric or stellar heaven.

THE ANGELIC MINISTRIES

Just what are the functions of angels, according to the Bible? Many believe that angels are necessarily doing now whatever they did in biblical times. This is an untenable position (see the argument of Hebrews 1). Since the canon of Scripture is completed, angels are no longer being used to reveal God's will to humans. Angels are not known to be opening prison doors today, as they did at least once in New Testament times (Acts 12:6-10). We do not know which specific ministries of angels might continue. The Bible does not tell us.

Satan delights in getting God's people to take their eyes off of Jesus to focus on anything else, including angels. Why would special visitations by angels be important or even beneficial? It is significant that those who see or hear angels are usually at odds with historic Christian teachings that are found in Scripture. The Bible is our sufficient revelation to show us how to live effectively for God and all that He has promised. We need to keep our eyes on Him, not on angels—even holy ones.

We know from God's Word that holy angels are His ministering spirits sent to those who are heirs of salvation (Heb. 1:14). The important thing is that God uses them for His glory. They serve Him, but our attention needs to be on Him, not them.

One definite witness of Scripture is that angels were deeply involved with the work of Christ on earth. Angels announced the birth of His forerunner, John the Baptist (Luke 1:13). Gabriel told Mary that she would give birth to the Messiah (Luke 1:32). Twice, angels gave specific instruction to Joseph (Matt. 1:20; 2:2). The birth of Israel's Messiah was heralded to shepherds on the Judean hills (Luke 2:9-13).

As the Savior faced the devil in the great temptation, angels ministered to Him (Matt. 4:11). In Gethsemane as Jesus prayed and the disciples slept, an angel from heaven ministered to Him (Matt. 22:43). At His tomb, after He had risen from the dead, an angel rolled away the stone and encouraged those who came to find Him (Matt. 28:1-7; Luke 24:1-9). As Jesus ascended to His Father, angels spoke words of promise to the disciples (Acts 1:1-11). Angels in heaven magnify and worship the Son of God (Rev. 5:2-7). It was Christ's angel who ministered to the apostle John so he could see and record the vision recorded in the book of Revelation (Rev. 1:1; 22:16). Finally, when Jesus returns both in the rapture and to establish His kingdom on earth, holy angels will be involved (1 Thess. 4:16; Matt. 25:31).

THE "ANGEL OF LIGHT"

The apostle Paul described Satan as "an angel of light" as he warned the Corinthian Christians about false teachers (2 Cor. 11:14). The point of his warning was that since Satan is deceitful, it is not surprising that false teachers, who are his servants, are deceitful.

Where did Satan come from? The Bible uses a number of names, each of which describes his perverse and perverting nature. Since Satan is a member of the angelic order, he was created by God like all other angels, both those who are holy and those who are wicked. This means Satan is not eternal. There was a time when he was not. God and Satan are not opposing equals who are in some sort of cosmic struggle to control the world. The sovereign God has control of the world. Satan, along with all other angelic beings, is a limited being, though he has personhood, just as the other angels and God Himself have personhood.

Satan's original sin was his desire to be like God. He exercised his will in defiance of God. He acted independently of God. There are two extended passages of Scripture which seem to clearly describe Satan before his fall and the fall itself. Ezekiel 28:11-19 does not name Satan but describes his prefallen state as "the king of Tyre" (v. 12).[9] Before his fall, Satan was the greatest of all God's creatures. Ezekiel states clearly that at one time Satan was in Eden (vv. 12-13). Brief mention is also made in the passage of Satan's sin (vv. 16-17). This passage seems to describe the same person as Isaiah described in Isaiah 14:12-19.

Writing about eight hundred years before Christ was born, Isaiah ministered to God's people who, it appeared, were about to be overtaken by Assyria. God used Babylon to overpower Assyria but promised through the prophet to use Babylon to punish Israel for her persistent rebellion. Later, Babylon would also be judged by God (Isa. 14:1-11). There is little doubt that the historic king of Babylon is in view in these verses. It is highly unlikely, however, that the same person is described in verses 12-19.[10]

THE DEMONS OF HELL

In the first world countries it used to be true that only Bible-believing Christians believed in the existence of demons, just as only they believed in angels and Satan. By the late 1900s that was no longer true. Westerners joined the rest of the world. Those outside the European sphere had, for the most part, always admitted the existence of a dark spiritual reality. There is still wide-scale confusion as to how demons exist, but pollsters can find a relatively high incidence of belief that they are here, there, or somewhere.

Very little is said directly about demons in the Old Testament. In the New Testament they appear often, especially in the Synoptic Gospels.

There is biblical evidence that demons are wicked angels. They are the once-holy angels who followed Satan in his rebellion against God. These sinning angels are described as the Devil's angels (Matt. 25:41) and Beelzebub's demons (Matt. 12:24). Both holy and wicked angels are called "spirits" (Matt. 8:16). The holy and wicked angels carry out analogous work for their respective masters (compare the work of holy angels with what demons are doing, for example, in Matt. 17:14-18; Mark 9:17; Luke 22:3).

Demons are limited, created beings, but they also are supernatural beings. As noted regarding holy angels, demons have personalities. Jesus spoke of demons as "spirits" (Luke 10:17, 20). He engaged in conversation with them (for example, in Matt. 8:16). He rebuked them (Mark 1:25-27); James said they fear and tremble (James 2:19); Paul said they spread errant beliefs (1 Tim. 4:1-3).

It is most important to recognize that demons are supernatural servants of the Devil himself (Eph. 6:12). In the Gospels they are said to be unclean or evil, which describes their being ethically (e.g., Matt. 10:1; Luke 7:21). It is frequently asked, How much do these corrupt emissaries of Satan know? is a frequently-asked question. The Bible does not tell us, but we know by analogy to holy angels and from descriptions of their subtle actions that they possess far greater intellectual ability than human beings, though their knowledge is incomparably less than the omniscience of God (Mark 1:34; 5:7; 1 John 4:1–4).

During the tribulation, the demons of hell will be allowed by God to control elements of nature so as to bring God's judgments upon the world (Rev. 9:1–11, 13–19; 16:14). As agents of Satan, demons oppose God and His people continually. They, like Satan, answer to God and can do nothing without his permission. In view of the wickedness and strength of these spirit creatures, it behooves the children of God to walk closely to their Lord. Anyone who is out of fellowship with Him for even the shortest period of time is vulnerable to attacks.

There are no clear descriptions in Scripture of a believer who was possessed by demons. Those who believe Christians can be demon possessed believe they have heard credible personal testimony of it. Or they base it upon their interpretation of such texts as 1 Samuel 16:14; Luke 13:11–16; Acts 5:3; 1 Corinthians 5:5, or 2 Corinthians 12:7.

In none of these texts is there certainty that (1) the individuals were believers or (2) that they were indwelled by demons. Certainly believers are buffeted by demons, but it is inconceivable that the Holy Spirit would share his abode in a believer with the demons of hell.

What of the current practice of demon exorcism? The Greek word from which the English word exorcist is derived is used only in Matthew 26:63 and the LXX version of Genesis 24:3.[11] Our Lord certainly exorcised or cast out demons who had been operating destructively within individuals' minds and bodies (for example, Matt. 8:28–34; 15:21–28; 17:14–21; Mark 1:23–28). At specific times, Christ gave the apostles authority to exorcise demons as he did (Matt. 10:1, 8; Mark 6:13; Luke 9:1). Having been given power to do this, the apostles cast out demons by a command in the name of Jesus (Mark 16:17).

Has God given special power to some Christians, that they can cast out demons today? I do not believe so. The ability to exorcise demons and the practice of it paralleled that limited time period when temporary gifts had particular purpose to authenticate the message and messenger and when demons were prevalent (for example, Matt. 15:30–31; Luke 9:42–43; Acts 10:38; 19:10–17; 28:3–9; 1 Cor. 12:7, 9). Scripture makes virtually no distinction between the ability to heal physical maladies miraculously and the authority to cast out demons (e.g., Matt. 10:1, 8; Acts 5:12; 8:6–7; 19:11–12). Therefore, because the New Testament gift of healings, along with the other temporary gifts, has ceased, I believe the ability to exorcise demons has also ceased.[12]

We are on much safer ground spiritually if we ask God to deliver those we think might have a demonic presence inside their bodies than if we try to contact the demons. God can and does deliver from demon oppression and indwelling through the finished work of His Son. No human has the power or ability to do this.

SPIRITUAL WARFARE

There can be no doubt: The child of God is involved in spiritual warfare and is the target of Satan and his demons. We are in a gigantic struggle against spiritual wickedness—supernatural evil of the highest level. God's people are, however, already on the victorious side. Though spiritual skirmishes and battles ensue, the real war is over. Satan and his hosts were defeated at Calvary. The empty tomb is ample proof that the Lord Jesus Christ was victorious over Satan at the Cross. God is sovereign; Satan is always subject to Him. Satan can do nothing to any of God's people, or anyone else for that matter, without God's consent.

Why does God allow Satan, demons, and sin in His world? The Bible does not say. It is enough to know that we can go on through the darkness in that world by His strength. Ours already is the victory He achieved at Calvary.

What does the twenty-first century hold for the child of God? Will satanic and demonic activity increase? There certainly seems to be Scriptural warrant for answering that it will. Current interest in angels and demons may very well be one of a number of indicators that our Lord's return is near. His coming is imminent; that is, He could come at any time. All around us, however, we see precursors of the great evil that will reach full-flower in the coming Great Tribulation. So it builds confidence to know that God has triumphed at Calvary. His glorious sovereign plan will be consummated in His time and way, regardless of what Satan and his hordes of demons do.

Paul the apostle warned Timothy that "in latter times some will fall away from the faith, paying attention to deceitful spirits and doctrines of demons" (1 Tim. 4:1). False teaching about the Bible and its doctrines is not only inspired by demons; it is promulgated by them. In His Sermon on the Mount, Jesus warned that many will say to Him on the day of judgment, "Lord, Lord, did we not prophesy in Your name, and in Your name cast out demons, and in Your name perform many miracles?" The Lord's answer on that day will be, "Depart from Me, you who practice lawlessness" (Matt. 7:22–23).[13]

In preview of the sixth-bowl judgment that will be poured out on planet earth, John was led by the Spirit to see "unclean spirits like frogs" (Rev. 16:13) coming out of Satan, the Antichrist, and the False Prophet. These, he said, were "spirits of demons, performing signs" (v. 14). Their task was to gather the nations of Satan's world program for the campaign of "Har-Magedon" (v. 16).

Regardless of how satanic and demonic activity increase in the twenty-first century, we have the promise from the Lord Himself that the gates of Hades shall not prevail against or stand before the church (Matt. 16:18).

CHAPTER 8

Where Are We Now?
The Prophetic Plan of
the Abrahamic Covenant

Arnold G. Fruchtenbaum

THE UNCONDITIONAL COVENANTS

Intertwined with Israel's election are four unconditional covenants God made with the nation. An unconditional covenant can be defined as a sovereign act of God, whereby God unconditionally obligates Himself to bring to pass definite promises, blessings, and conditions for the covenanted people. It is a unilateral covenant.

This type of covenant is characterized by the formula *I will*, which declares God's determination to do exactly as He promised. The blessings are secured by the grace of God. This is not to say that there are no expectations of behavior or obedience, but even the most egregious rebellion will not vacate the covenant itself. A covenant is "unconditional" when God will fulfill His promises without regard to acts of obedience among those with whom the covenant is made. He will accomplish all promises stated in the covenants, no matter what happens. The conditions stated are not the bases upon which the covenants will be fulfilled. God intends to keep his promises; they are dependent upon Him alone.

Five things should be noted concerning the nature of the unconditional covenants. First, they are literal covenants, and their contents must be interpreted literally. Second, the covenants God made with Israel are not abrogated with time. Third, since these *unconditional* covenants were not dependent on obedience, their ultimate fulfillment is a certainty.

Fourth, the covenants in view were made with a specific people: Israel. Paul relates in Romans 9:4 that to the Israelites belong "the adoption, and the glory, and the covenants, and the giving of the law, and the service of God, and the promises."[1] Paul stresses that these covenants were made with

Israel and are Israel's possession. Paul uses the present tense, even after the foundation of the church. He says something similar in Ephesians 2:11-12:

> *Wherefore remember, that ye being in time past Gentiles in the flesh, who are called Uncircumcision by that which is called Circumcision, in the flesh, made by hands; that at that time ye were separate without Christ, being aliens from the commonwealth of Israel, and strangers from the covenants of the promise, having no hope and without God in the world.*

The unconditional covenants belong to the people of Israel and, as this passage notes, gentiles are not included in these particular promises.

Fifth, while a covenant is made at a specific moment in time, the provisions may be for a far distant future. At the time the covenant was established or sealed, three things happen: (1) The recipients immediately owned the promises. Benefits relating to their identity as people of promise were immediate. (2) Some went into effect in the near future. (3) Some were far-off blessings that could be apprehended only by faith in the generations that received the promises.

This chapter will focus on one set of unconditional promises, the Abrahamic covenant.

THE ABRAHAMIC COVENANT

Six texts in Genesis flesh out the provisions of the covenant: 12:1-3; 12:7; 13:14-17; 15:1-21; 17:1-21 and 22:17-18. In all six passages, God and Abraham were involved. Abraham did not stand for all humanity, as was the case in the Edenic and Adamic and Noahic covenants. He stood as father of the Jewish nation—the representative head of that people. A list gleaned from these Genesis passages shows a total of fourteen provisions in this covenant:

1. A great nation (Israel) was to come out of Abram (12:2a; 13:16; 15:5; 17:2b; 22:17b).
2. A land (Canaan) was promised (12:1, 7; 13:14-15, 17; 15:18-21; 17:8).
3. Abram himself would be blessed (12:2b; 22:17a).
4. Abram's name would become great (12:2c).
5. Abram would be a blessing to others (12:2d).
6. Those who blessed him would be blessed (12:3a).
7. Those who cursed him would be cursed (12:3b).
8. In Abram all the nations would ultimately be blessed (12:3c; 22:18).
9. Sarai would bear a son to Abram (15:2-4; 17:16-21).
10. Their descendants would become slaves in Egypt (15:13-14).
11. Other nations also would come from Abraham (17:4-6).

12. His name would be changed from *Abram* to *Abraham* (17:5).
13. Sarai's name would be changed to Sarah (17:15).
14. Circumcision would be the visible token of the covenant (17:9–14), and so a sign of Jewishness.

These provisions can be categorized in three areas: to Abraham, to Israel, and to the gentiles.

Concerning Abraham

Promises were made to Abraham individually:

1. He was to be the father of a great nation (Israel).
2. His bequest to that nation was land that was for them alone. It would come to be called the "Promised Land."
3. He also would be the father of other nations (including the Arab states).
4. Among his descendants would be kings.
5. He would personally prosper in material blessings.
6. He would be a blessing to others.
7. His name would be great—as it is among Jews, Moslems, and Christians.

Some of these individual promises were fulfilled in his lifetime, but some (such as ownership of the land) awaited a future fulfillment at his death.

Concerning Israel

When the term *seed* was used as a collective singular to refer to Abraham's offspring, the reference was to racial Israel. Promises made to the Jewish people were:

1. The nation founded among the Jews (Israel) was to become great.
2. Israel would become an innumerable people.
3. Ultimately Israel would possess all of Canaan.
4. Israel would have ultimate victory over its enemies.

Concerning the Gentiles

Promises also were made to the gentiles in the Abrahamic covenant:

1. Those who blessed racial Israel would themselves be blessed.
2. A negative promise was made that if they cursed the people of promise they would be cursed.
3. Spiritual blessing would come through one specific Seed of Abraham, the Messiah.

When the term *seed* was used as an absolute singular, it referred to the Messiah. At this point, the Abrahamic covenant contained physical and spiritual promises. The physical promises were limited to Israel; the spiritual blessings were to all of the human race.

DYNAMICS OF THE COVENANT

At its most elementary level the covenant contains three aspects: the land, the seed, and the blessing. The land aspect is developed in a land covenant that many have called the "Palestinian covenant." The seed aspect is covered in what is usually referred to as the "Davidic covenant." The blessing aspect is presented in a "new covenant."

Abraham had eight sons by three different women. The question is: through which son(s) would the covenant be passed? From the start, God revealed that it was to be through Sarah's son only. He confirmed this to Isaac (Gen. 26:2–5, 24).

In confirming the covenant to Isaac, five provisions were stated:

1. Isaac would be blessed (26:3a, 24c).
2. The land was promised to Isaac's lineage in perpetuity (26:3b, 4b).
3. His descendants would multiply to become a great people (26:4a, 24c).
4. Gentiles would be blessed through the Seed (26:4c).
5. The basis of the confirmation was God's covenant with Abraham (26:3c, 5, 24c).

Isaac had two sons and God chose to confirm the covenant with Jacob only, as seen in Genesis 28:13–15.

In the confirmation of the covenant to Jacob, three specific provisions were made: (1) the Land is promised to both Jacob and Jacob's seed (28:13, 15); (2) the seed will be multiplied (28:14a); and, (3) the gentiles will someday be blessed through the seed (28:14b).

It was confirmed through all of Jacob's twelve sons, who fathered the twelve tribes of Israel (Genesis 49). Thus, the Abrahamic covenant provides the biblical definition of Jewishness: a descendant of Abraham, Isaac, and Jacob by race or adoption into their relationship with God.

The Continuity of the Covenant

The Abrahamic covenant became the basis for the dispensation of promise. Because the Abrahamic covenant is unconditional, it is still very much in effect, though it remains largely unfulfilled. The ultimate fulfillment will come during the kingdom age. The unconditional nature of the covenant is affirmed and often reaffirmed. For example, God rescued the children of Israel during their wilderness wanderings and brought them into the land of promise. This mercy was given on the basis of the Abrahamic covenant, according to Exodus 2:24 and 6:2-8, despite their unrighteousness, rebellion, and murmurings. This is further reaffirmed in Nehemiah 9:7-8; 1 Chronicles 16:15-19; 2 Chronicles 20:7-8; and Psalm 105:7-12.

In conjunction with the choosing of Moses to lead Israel out of Egypt, he was almost disqualified because of his failure to circumcise his son in Exodus 4:24-26:

> *And it came to pass on the way at the lodging-place, that Jehovah met him, and sought to kill him. Then Zipporah took a flint, and cut off the foreskin of her son, and cast it at his feet; and she said, Surely a bridegroom of blood art thou to me. So he let him alone. Then she said, A bridegroom of blood art thou, because of the circumcision.*

Moses endangered his life by failing to circumcise his son in keeping with the penalty of the Abrahamic covenant contained in Genesis 17:14 for failure to circumcise meant being cut off from among his people.

It was on the basis of the Abrahamic covenant that God finally brought Israel into the Promised Land as God's last words to Moses made clear in Deuteronomy 34:4. Although Israel in the land had a long history of disobedience and idolatry, and although God frequently disciplined the nation, yet He promised the nation would always survive on the basis of the Abrahamic covenant. On that basis, Moses pleaded with God to spare Israel from His divine wrath in Exodus 32:11-14. Another example of this is 2 Kings 13:22-23. While God used the Syrians to punish Israel, Syrian damage could only go so far because of this covenant. Certainly God expected Israel to be obedient, but Israel's obedience did not condition God's fulfillment of His promises. This is exactly what dispensationalism means by an unconditional covenant.

It was on the basis of this covenant that the Messiah came to bring redemption to Israel, according to Luke 1:54-55 and 68-73. It was on the basis of this covenant that Jesus taught the fact of the Resurrection when confronted by Sadducees who did not believe in it (Matt. 22:23-33). Paul made the same point in Acts 26:6-8. In Galatians 3:15-18, Paul drew a contrast between the Abrahamic and the Mosaic covenants, pointing out that the Mosaic was temporary, while the Abrahamic was eternal. The author of Hebrews 6:13-20 derived his assurance of salvation on the basis of this covenant.

Finally, it is on the basis of this covenant that the final restoration will occur, according to Leviticus 26:40-42:

> *And they shall confess their iniquity, and the iniquity of their fathers, in their trespass which they trespassed against me, and also that, because*

they walked contrary unto me, I also walked contrary unto them, and brought them into the land of their enemies: if then their uncircumcised heart be humbled, and they then accept of the punishment of their iniquity; then will I remember my covenant with Jacob; and also my covenant with Isaac, and also my covenant with Abraham will I remember; and I will remember the land.

Just as God fulfilled His promises to Israel in the past, He will do so again in the future because of the unconditional nature of the Abrahamic covenant. The Abrahamic covenant, being an unconditional covenant, is still very much in effect.

The Token of the Covenant

The token or sign of the Abrahamic covenant was circumcision, to be performed on males only and only on the eighth day of birth. Circumcision on the eighth day would distinguish Jewish circumcision from all other circumcisions practiced in that day. It would also serve as a reminder that this covenant was a blood covenant. It served as a sign of their Jewishness. Failure to do so would mean that the father would be "cut off" or executed. For this reason Moses almost died for failing to circumcise his second son and only when the act was done was the life of Moses spared (Exod. 4:24–26).

THE PRESENT OUTWORKING OF THE ABRAHAMIC COVENANT

Covenant theologians of all schools insist that in a lesser or greater degree the biblical covenants are now being fulfilled in the church. Some believe that these covenants were made with the church from the very beginning. Others admit that they were made with Israel, but have now been transferred to the church. As for Israel, all that was promised either has already been fulfilled or has been forfeited through Jewish unbelief. Even covenant premillennialists, who do see a future for ethnic Israel, still insist that Israel is amalgamated into the church.

Dispensationalists, though very clear as to how the unconditional covenants work out in relationship to Israel past and Israel future, have been far less clear with Israel present. Some took the view that the Jewish covenants are now in "abeyance," and others failed to recognize the existence of the remnant today. No such view of the covenants is necessary or defensible. The fact is that all four unconditional covenants are not only still in effect, but also still operative at the present time. The church does, indeed, have a relationship to these covenants, but it is not that described by covenant theology.

A point of observation is in order. It must again be stressed that, although a covenant may be made at a specific point of time, it does not mean that all provisions of the covenant go immediately into effect. Some do, but some may not for centuries. The Abrahamic covenant is a good example. Some of God's promises did go immediately into effect, such as providing for Abraham's physical needs in the land, his change of name, and circumcision. Others were fulfilled only in the near future. For example, Abraham was promised a son through Sarah, but had to wait twenty-five years before that promise was fulfilled. Other provisions were fulfilled only later in Jewish history, such as the Egyptian sojourn, enslavement, and the Exodus (400 years later), which was also part of the covenant. Finally, other provisions are still future, never having been fulfilled, such as Abraham's ownership of the land and Israel's settlement in all of the Promised Land.

It is important to note that although a covenant is made, signed, and sealed at a certain point of history, this does not mean that all the promises or provisions go immediately into effect. It should come as no surprise that not all of the provisions of the unconditional Jewish covenants are presently being fulfilled to, in, or by Israel today. This is not necessary for the covenants to still be in force. Nor is this a valid reason to teach that the church has taken over these covenants or that they are now being fulfilled to, in, or by the church.

The Seed

The Abrahamic covenant promised a seed, land, and blessings among its many provisions. The seed was to develop into a nation, and so it did at the foot of Mount Sinai. Today, Israel is a scattered nation but still a nation. Just as Israel remained distinct in Egypt, the Jewish people have remained distinct throughout the church age. No other nation that lost its national homeland and was dispersed for centuries survived as a distinct entity. On the contrary, where they scattered they intermarried and disappeared into a melting pot. Not so the Jews, whose distinctive history is easily traceable throughout the years of Jewish history. The fact that Jews have continued to survive as a people in spite of so many attempts to destroy them shows that this covenant has continued to operate.

The Land

As for the land, within the confines of the church age there has been no real independent government in the land since A.D. 70. The land has been overrun many times and ruled by many people, but always ruled from somewhere else. It has been controlled by Romans, Byzantines, Arabs, Turks, and Britons. Even under Arab control, no independent Arab government was ever set up; it was ruled from somewhere else: Baghdad, Cairo, Damascus, Amman, etc. Though renamed "Palestine" by Hadrian, there never was a Palestinian state with a Palestinian government or a Palestinian flag. The first time an independent government was set up in the land since A.D. 70 was in 1948 with the State of Israel. The history of the land also shows that the Abrahamic covenant continues to be fulfilled with the people of Israel.

The Spiritual Blessings

As for the blessings, history shows that those who blessed the Jews were blessed just as those who cursed them were cursed. Furthermore, the spiritual blessings have now been extended to the gentiles through the new covenant.

Circumcision

The seal of the Abrahamic covenant was circumcision and this is still mandatory upon all Jews, both believers and unbelievers. However, does not the book of Galatians argue against the practice of circumcision? Yes and no. Circumcision for gentiles, circumcision on the basis of the Mosaic Law, and circumcision for justification or sanctification are all wrong. Galatians condemns circumcision as a means for justification. Except perhaps for health and medical reasons, there is no requirement for gentile circumcision. Furthermore, Jewish believers who circumcise on the basis of the Law of Moses are also wrong, since the law ended with Christ. This same book clearly states that the Abrahamic covenant is still very much in effect with all its features, and this includes circumcision (Gal. 3:15–18).

Circumcision on the basis of the Abrahamic covenant is right and proper; it is still very much in effect for Jewish believers. Paul, who taught the gentiles not to circumcise, did not do so with Jews; this is clear from Acts 21:17-26 and from Acts 16:1-3 when he had Timothy circumcised. It was not circumcision *per se* that was ruled out, but rather circumcision on the basis of the Mosaic Law. Since Jewish believers still fall under the physical and spiritual provisions of the Abrahamic covenant, they also fall under the rule of circumcision as a sign and seal of this same covenant. Dispensationalists have been inconsistent on this point insisting on the continuity of the Abrahamic covenant but then denying the continuity of circumcision. This has largely been due to a failure to distinguish circumcision under the Abrahamic covenant and circumcision under the Law of Moses. A careful distinction between the two will clear up this confusion and make dispensationalism more consistent when speaking of and about the Abrahamic covenant.

THE OUTWORKING OF THE ABRAHAMIC COVENANT IN THE FUTURE: THE POSSESSION OF THE LAND

The Covenantal Base

One facet of the final restoration of Israel is the possession of the land encompassing two aspects: its total boundaries and its productivity. The basis for this facet is the Abrahamic covenant as found in various passages of the book of Genesis. The first passage to deal with the land aspect is Genesis 12:1-3. At the time the covenant was initially made, Abram was simply told to leave for a land that God would show him. When he arrived in the land, God again revealed Himself to Abram in Genesis 12:7. In this verse, the promise is stated in such a way that it is Abram's seed that is to possess the land. From this passage alone, it might be concluded that Abram himself was never to possess the land. That is not the case, however, as another passage on the Abrahamic covenant makes clear, Genesis 13:14-17.

The Prophetic Development

This facet of Israel's final restoration, the possession of the land, was further developed in both the Law and the Prophets. As far as the Law is concerned, it is found in Leviticus 26:40-45. Following the regeneration of Israel (vv. 40-41), God will fully carry out the promises of the Abrahamic covenant concerning the land (v. 42). On the basis of the Abrahamic covenant, He will restore to them the land that has laid desolate for so long (vv. 43-45). In another part of the Law, the possession of the land is also part of the (Palestinian) covenant in Deuteronomy 30:5.

The prophets of Israel developed this facet even further in both the Major and Minor Prophets. One passage is Isaiah 27:12. In this passage, the first aspect (the borders of the land) is brought out. The northern (Euphrates River) and the southern (the Brook of Egypt) boundaries are possessed for the first time in all of Israel's history. Israel will be able to settle in all of the Promised Land. In another passage, Isaiah 30:23-26, the second aspect (increased productivity of the land) of the third facet is stressed. The land will be well watered and will produce abundant food both for men and animals (vv. 23-25). Furthermore, there will be a tremendous increase of light with the moon shining as brightly as the sun, while the light of the sun will be increased seven times what it is today. As for the deserts of Israel, Isaiah 35:1-2 states,

> *The wilderness and the dry land shall be glad; and the desert shall rejoice, and blossom as the rose. It shall blossom abundantly, and rejoice even with joy and singing; the glory of Lebanon shall be given unto it, the excellency of Carmel and Sharon: they shall see the glory of Jehovah, the excellency of our God.*

Isaiah later brought out the productivity aspect again in 65:21-24. With the possession of the land of Israel, not only will the Jews be able to build houses and plant vineyards and crops (v. 21), but they will also enjoy the work of their hands, for no enemy will take it from them (vv. 22-23). They will enjoy it until a ripe old age (v. 24).

Another major prophet, Jeremiah, also stressed the greater productivity of the land in the final restoration. According to Jeremiah 31:1-6, because of God's everlasting love for His people (vv. 1-3), He intends to restore and build them again (v. 4). Once again for Israel there will be a time of plenty (v. 5), and the hills of Ephraim will echo with the call to come and worship God in Jerusalem (v. 6). Later, in the same passage, Jeremiah returned to the theme in 31:11-14. After the redemption of Israel (v. 11), they will be restored to the land, which will produce an abundance (v. 12), giving joy to all the inhabitants of the land (vv. 13-14).

After Jeremiah, the next major prophet, Ezekiel, picked up the motif of the possession of the land in Ezekiel 20:42-44. Israel is to be brought back into their land in accordance with the promises of God to the forefathers in the Abrahamic covenant (v. 42). Israel will turn away from her sins of the past and will detest them (v. 43) and now serve God alone (v. 44). Later, in Ezekiel 28:25-26, following her regeneration and regathering, Israel will then possess the land in accordance with the Abrahamic covenant (v. 25). The security in which Israel will live and enjoy the works of her hands is then emphasized (v. 26). The security aspect, along with the element of increased productivity, is the theme of Ezekiel 34:25-31. Since there will no longer be any wild beasts in the land, Israel will be able to enjoy the land in total security (v. 25). The rains will come in their proper time and in proper amounts (v. 26) increasing the productivity (v. 27a). Not only is Israel to be secure from the wild beasts, but also from all her enemies of the past (vv. 27b-28). None will come to destroy the crops (v. 29). In every way Israel will be rightly related to God and will be His peculiar possession (vv. 30-31).

Nor is this the end of the subject as the prophet continued in Ezekiel 36:8-15. In spite of years of desolation, the land is to be tilled again (vv. 8-9) and populated; that is, the inhabitants of the land will be greatly increased (vv. 10-11). Israel will again possess the land (v. 12), and the production of the land will be tremendous (vv. 13-15). Later in this passage, the prophet further elaborated in Ezekiel 36:28-38. Ezekiel declared that Israel will again possess the land (v. 28) as a result of her regeneration (v. 29). The reproach of Israel will be removed (v. 30), and Israel will detest her past sins (v. 31). It is not for Israel's glory (v. 32) that the regeneration (v. 33), possession (v. 34), and the rebuilding of the land (v. 35) will occur, but it is for God's own glory among the nations (v. 36). As for Israel, the population will increase and the desolate places will be rebuilt (vv. 37-38).

The possession of the land is also promised in the Minor Prophets, such as in Joel 2:18-27. God will be jealous for His land (v. 18), and this burning jealousy will bring about a great productivity in the land (v. 19). The land will be secure from any further invasions (v. 20), and it will produce abundantly (vv. 21-22). The rains will come at the proper seasons and in proper amounts

(v. 23), causing a tremendous amount of surplus in their storage (v. 24), recuperating all previous losses due to pestilence (v. 25). Israel will never again be shamed (v. 26), but will have a special relationship to God (v. 27). Later, in Joel 3:18, the prophet declared that there will be an abundance of water in the land. The increased productivity of the land is again pointed out in Amos 9:13.

For the first time in Israel's history, she will possess all of the Promised Land while the land itself will greatly increase in its productivity and be well watered, all on the basis of the Abrahamic covenant.

CHAPTER 9

Rock Witness to a Written Word

J. Randall Price

The ancient Greeks used the word *archaeology* to describe their discussion of ancient legends or traditions. The word first reached print in the English language in 1607. At first *archaeology* referred to the study of ancient Israel from literary sources, including the Bible. Joseph Callaway recaptures this early understanding when he observes that "the real business of archaeology is to establish factual benchmarks in the world of the Bible to guide interpreters."[1] Some archaeologists would agree with him; more would disagree. Near the end of the twentieth century, an article in the Archaeological Institute of America's publication, *Archaeology*, asserts that "archaeological evidence in some cases flatly contradicts biblical assertions."[2] With the opening of the new millennium this discussion divided the archaeological community. Is archaeology the handmaiden or the assassin of biblical studies?

Fortunately, it is not the Christian who needs to worry that discoveries will destroy faith. Archaeological evidence has been "flatly contradicting" the Bible since the beginning of the discipline. The discoveries and objective analysis of evidence do not contradict the Bible; rather a pervasive antisupernatural skepticism forces data into a preconceived mold. Continually, developments on the field have forced a change in the preconceptions—but never in the accurately interpreted Bible record.

Through most of the Enlightenment higher critical assumptions have been militantly skeptical. Generations of secular and liberal church scholars have loathed those who interpreted the Bible, as Harvard professor of biblical studies Frank Cross, put it, "literally and fundamentalistically."[3] In response, conservative scholars have spent much energy answering the critics and their interpretations, when they could have done more to "establish factual benchmarks."

In general, it is easy to define attitudes behind the assertions that archaeology disproves the claim of a literally-true Bible narrative. They arise from (1) antisupernatural presuppositions, (2) faulty interpretation of Scripture, (3) faulty interpretation and application of archaeological data. Usually a combination of these factors is at work. Despite the biases, archaeology has made some remarkable finds that solidly support the biblical text. However, we must be careful to make a valid integration of archaeological and biblical studies, understanding the nature of this material evidence and its limitations.

ARCHAEOLOGY AND ANTIQUITY

In the infancy of archaeological studies in the late eighteenth century, no one foresaw the wonders that would be revealed. The ancient Middle Eastern world was a dreamland. It was mostly lost, except for the Bible's parade of names and places. Meager was the surviving testimony that corroborated the Bible narrative. The reader was blessed by its truths, yet often baffled by references to geographical sites and unknown subjects. Archaeology has reclaimed much of that lost heritage, chasing away the spiders of time, whose webs have obscured the view. Future generations will have more certain facts upon which to found faith than have any other since the accounts were written. Archaeology has been of special importance to those who seek to capture the original context of Scripture.

THE PURPOSES OF ARCHAEOLOGY

Archaeology has revealed the cities, the palaces, the temples, and the houses of those who lived shoulder to shoulder with those whose stories are recorded in Scripture. Tangible artifacts and writings assist faith in its growth toward God. Occasionally evidence brings us tantalizingly close to being able to proclaim, with the apostle John, "what was from the beginning, what we have heard, what we have seen with our eyes, what we have beheld and our hands handled, concerning the Word of Life" (1 John 1:1).[4]

Archaeology uncovers tangible history, developing a context of reason to accompany faith. It ought to help us strike a balance between faith and fact, confirming the reality of the people and events of the Bible. Skeptics and saints alike can perceive the spiritual message within an historical context.

This is not to say that the purpose of archaeology is to "prove" the Bible. The Bible describes itself as the Word of God, which places its spiritual teaching outside the realm of what can be proven by archaeology. The proper use of archaeology in relation to the Bible is to confirm, correct, clarify the historical context, complementing the theological message.

Confirming the Word of the Bible

To "confirm" is to give new assurance of the validity of something. Archaeology provides assurance from the stones to accompany the assurance from the Spirit.

Only a little over a century ago critical scholars scoffed at the historical existence of a people called the Hittites. Yet Hittites are mentioned forty-seven times in the Old Testament. Ephron the Hittite sold Abraham his burial cave (Gen. 23:10-20), and Uriah the Hittite was the husband of Bathsheba. In 1876 the ruins of the Hittite capital were uncovered at Boghaz-Koy, including archives of more than ten thousand clay tablets—the chronicles of their history.

Excavations frequently come up with confirming finds, though seldom is the contribution quite so extensive. Field investigations have taught us about the historical sites of Ninevah, Babylon, and lost cities throughout Israel and Jordan. Amihai Mazar, director of the Hebrew University of Jerusalem's Institute of Archaeology, notes,

> In certain cases, we can even throw light on certain events or even on certain buildings which are mentioned in the Bible. We can enumerate many, many subjects like this where the relationship between the archaeological finds and the Biblical narrative can be established. The earlier we go, the more problems [we encounter] and the questions are more difficult to answer. With the later periods of time [the time of the Monarchy] things become more secure and better established.[5]

Until recently there was no material evidence to confirm the existence of King David. That changed in 1993-1994 when Professor Avraham Biran unearthed a monumental inscription in the northern Israelite city of Dan. The inscription, written by one of Israel's ancient enemies (so no Israelite can be accused of fabricating it) recorded the name of one of Judah's kings "of the house of David." Since there had to be a David to have a house of David, the inscription attests to the existence of Scripture's most famous warrior and psalmist.

Correcting Our Text of the Bible

One of the first steps toward understanding Scripture is to discern the precise wording of the original text. It is unlikely that archaeologists will ever discover actual "autographs," the original document in the pen strokes of the author. However, the ancient copies that have come to us have been preserved and passed down in such a manner as to give us confidence that we have the very "Word of God" in our hands. From Egypt to the caves of Qumran, archaeology has unearthed hundreds of whole or fragmentary Old Testament books and thousands of pieces of the New Testament books.

The oldest copy of a biblical text now available for study comes from an inscription discovered in 1979 by Israeli archaeologist Gabriel Barcay in a tomb in Jerusalem's Hinnom Valley. Among more than one thousand objects taken from the tomb were several tiny silver scrolls dating from before the Judean exile of 586 B.C. One contained the complete text of the Aaronic benediction in Numbers 6:24–26. This text showed scholars how well our later versions of the Bible preserved this blessing. It embarrassed higher critical claims that most of the Pentateuch was written after the exile.

Twenty miles southwest of Jerusalem lies the Dead Sea at a record level of thirteen hundred feet *below* sea level. Coming down from bleak, rugged limestone cliffs, one meets the sun-parched desert. The Dead Sea itself is forty-five miles long and nine miles wide. In its water is a chemical stew of 26 percent solid matter in the form of dissolved salts. From the beginning of biblical history, patriarchs and prophets came to this desert region to seek God's revelation and to prepare themselves for coming judgment. Perhaps this heritage led an orthodox, but breakaway, community of Jews to settle at a site known today by its Arabic name, Khirbet Qumran (lit. "ruins of Qumran").

These Jews represented the priestly line from Zadok, high priest under Solomon, whose line officiated in the first temple. They lived out their days in a strictly ritual lifestyle atop a chalky plateau beside the Dead Sea, studying Scripture and awaiting the fulfillment of the biblical prophecies concerning the Messiah, the judgment of the nations, and the restoration of the Jewish nation. Their study of Scripture required numerous copies of the books of the Bible, preserved in scrolls. They produced numerous commentaries on biblical books. Most scrolls were written in columns in Hebrew, Aramaic, and Greek on papyrus of leather parchment, which was made from goat or sheep skins. One, the *Copper Scroll,* was written on pure copper. Before the community was destroyed by the Roman army in 68, members of this sect hid their texts and sectarian writings in jars, deposited in caves high above the Dead Sea. It is these documents that we today refer to as the Dead Sea Scrolls.

The pieces that survive are from eleven hundred ancient documents. There are several intact scrolls, plus more than one hundred thousand fragments. Between 223 and 233 of the total manuscripts are copies of biblical books. So far a representative of every book of the Old Testament except Esther has been found.[6] These constitute our oldest known copies of the Scriptures. They also contain commentaries on biblical books, apocryphal and pseudepigraphical works, and sectarian documents (some written by a leader known as "the Teacher of Righteousness").

Numerous versions of the books of the Old Testament preserved among the scrolls enable us to compare texts that pre-date the traditional Massoretic text that serves as the basis for most translations into modern languages. Such a comparison allows us to see how well the scribes who preserved this Hebrew text did their job. Until the Qumran discoveries, the oldest version of the Hebrew text was only a thousand years old. Bible students could never be sure how well the Hebrew text had fared through about 1400 years of scribal copying. How many of their mistakes had found their way into Bible translations? The Hebrew scrolls closed this gap and let scholars compare texts behind our translations with those that were in some cases only a few hundred years from the originals.

This comparison revealed an extremely careful textual transmission. No substantive changes to the Old Testament were needed because of Dead Sea Scroll studies.

Also important are discoveries of nonbiblical manuscripts. One of the finds more interesting and helpful to scholars was a library of Gnostic texts at Nag Hammadi in Egypt. Thousands of long-lost manuscripts were discovered in the late 1900s at Saint Catherine's monastery, located at the base of the traditional site of Mount Sinai. Such ancient manuscripts show the precise form, grammar, and syntax of the Hebrew, Aramaic, and Greek words used in the Bible, as well as isolating their exact meaning at the time. Such literary treasures have given a far more accurate Greek and Hebrew text than that possessed by the church in previous centuries. From this improved text, better translations can be made.

Clarifying the World of the Bible

Archaeology continually fills in details of daily life, society, culture, and religion of people living in the Bible's world. This again helps reconstruct this context in which the theological truth appeared. Excavations in Egypt, Mesopotamia, and Israel have revealed much of the shape and substance of these societies. From Egyptian tomb art and relief carvings on temples we know what the biblical patriarchs may have looked like. There are records and depictions of wars in which foreign armies attacked both Egypt and ancient Israel.

Complementing the Witness of the Bible

The sixty-six books of the Bible were written over fifteen hundred years by prophets, poets, peasants, shepherds, and statesmen. While a vast and diverse witness, the Scriptures is not a comprehensive chronicle, even for the era of the kingdoms covered from 1 Samuel through 2 Chronicles. Certain people are mentioned and specific events recorded because they are necessary to the larger theological purpose. Much of historical significance is deliberately excluded from the narrative so that the truths can be developed.

Those who expect Scripture to be a historical chronicle look upon the deletions as failure and so question the historical accuracy of the authors. Archaeology, through its revelation of context, culture, and recorded events, adds a complementary witness. It fills in the outline drawn by the biblical authors and verifies particulars they present.

A notable example is King Omri who made Samaria capital of the Northern Kingdom of Israel. Although he was one of the region's most important rulers between 885 B.C. and 874 B.C., the biblical text gives him only a passing reference (1 Kings 16:16–29). This was most likely because he was a wicked Israelite king, whose prideful accomplishments did not deserve recognition. Archaeology provides background information about his exploits from the recovered records of his foreign foes. It agrees with the biblical assessment of the man and his character.

All over the ancient world texts have been uncovered that give individual perspective accounts of creation and the flood. Some tell stories parallel to Scripture accounts, yet different enough to show that the Bible is not dependent upon them. Studies of these texts raise controversies on occasion but have all tended to show the trustworthiness of Bible. As Gonzalo Báez-Camargo has noted: "No longer do we see two different worlds, one the world of 'sacred history' and the other the world of 'profane history.' All of history is one history, and it is God's history, for God is the God of all history."[7]

The complementary nature of these textual studies is that they reveal the Bible's historical character, and they emphasize its uniqueness when compared with other ancient Near Eastern documents. Discoveries of the religious literatures of the Sumerians, Egyptians, Hittites, Assyrians, Babylonians, and Canaanites all highlight the originality and theological singularity of the Bible.

THE LIMITATIONS OF ARCHAEOLOGY

While archaeology is of great help, the biblical evidence in the text must be given priority over the archaeological evidence from the field. The reason is that there are inherent limitations within archaeology. Findings are both incomplete and liable to conflicting or mistaken interpretation.

The primary limitation of archaeology is the extremely fragmentary nature of the evidence. A small fraction of what was made or written is available for study. Most Eastern archives were destroyed through war, looters, natural disasters, or the ravages of time. The archives at Alexandria, Egypt, the greatest known to have existed, held almost one million volumes, including the original manuscript of the Septuagint (LXX), the Greek translation of the Old Testament. All of these works were lost when the city was burned in an Arab invasion in the seventh century A.D. In other cases fire can be the historian's friend. Unless an archive was burned by fire clay tablets stored there would not be baked and thereby hardened and preserved. Otherwise, almost all writing material in clay, leather, or papyrus turned to dust over the centuries. Hundreds of sites also have been destroyed in recent years through building projects and military maneuvers. Modern Bedouins and others make a living by dealing in black market antiquities.

Only a fraction of the thousands of known ancient sites have been surveyed, much less excavated. Only 2 percent of the Israel sites have been studied. When excavated, only a fraction of the site is actually examined, and only a fraction of what is excavated is ever described in publication. Kathleen Kenyon's final reports from Jericho took thirty years to be published. There was a forty-year delay in releasing even photographs of the Qumran material from Cave 4. Of the half million cuneiform texts discovered over the past hundred years, 10 percent have been published.

THE BIBLE—AN ARCHAEOLOGICAL DOCUMENT

Because of the limitations of archaeology, the Bible must be given priority in the final determination of accuracy of the history it records. Beyond consideration of God's direct revelation through its pages, Scripture has been shown even by secular scholars to adhere to a higher standard of accuracy than any other ancient source, and its text has been far more carefully preserved.

It must be remembered that the Bible itself is an archaeological document. While we have only a limited number of archaeological artifacts from the biblical period, the Bible represents the most complete literary record we possess of these times. Having survived in one form or another since it was first committed to writing by Moses, it remains the most accurate and trustworthy account of antiquity in the archaeological record.

So it is improper and unnecessary to elevate other archaeological inscriptions above the biblical text in order to challenge the latter's integrity. Frequently the information needed to resolve a historical or chronological question is lacking. Just as frequently the popular press has trumpeted a discovery that "disproves" the Bible's account, only to learn that the findings were in error or misleading. It is naïve and prejudiced for secularists to assume that material evidence taken from the more limited content of archaeological excavations is stronger than the archaeological witness found in the canonical Scriptures.

However, despite its limitations, when regarded as a handmaiden to the Bible, archaeology can clarify and enlarge the scope of its statements. While the Bible is a complete revelation, it is not exhaustive. Though its message can be readily understood in any age, it is still selective and was written in a particular culture and time. Therefore, archaeology has added its rock witness to the written word.

THE OLD TESTAMENT WITNESS

"It is today a truism to say that archaeological investigation in Palestine and in surrounding lands, . . . has transformed our attitude towards, and our understanding of, ancient Israel and the Old Testament," D. Winton Thomas declares.[8] Mazar explains the value of these discoveries:

> We can calculate even the population size in places like Jerusalem or the entire area of Judah, or the kingdom of Israel. We can imagine how many people lived, in what type of settlements they lived, what type of town plan there was, what kind of vessels they used in every day life, what kind of enemies they had and what kind of weapons they used against these enemies—everything related to the material aspect of life in the Old Testament period can be described by archeological finds from this particular period.[9]

Witness to Genesis

In addition, discoveries from other cultures, older than those of Old Testament Israel, have also brought their own significant witness. Parallels between early Mesopotamian literature and the Genesis accounts of the creation and flood were established late in the nineteenth century. The *Enuma Elish* Mesopotamian creation account was studied by George Smith of the British Museum in 1875. Some fragments of this account could be read on tablets from Ashurbanipal's (669–626) library at Ninevah. Other fragments of the same story were later found in Assyria, Uruk, and Kish.

The strange name of the text was taken from the Assyrian words that introduce it. *Enuma elish* means "when above." The text itself recounts the story that the component parts of the universe originated with principal gods representing forces of nature. Final assembly was completed by Marduk, who became the head of the Babylonian pantheon (assembly of gods). As in the Genesis account, there is mention of a watery chaos that was separated into heaven and earth (cf. Gen. 1:1–2, 6–10). Light existed before the creation of sun, moon, and stars (cf. Gen. 1:3–5, 14–18). The number seven also is prominent (cf. Gen. 2:2–3).

The *Atrahasis Epic* is a cuneiform tablet inscribed with accounts of creation and the flood. The tablet is from about the seventeenth century B.C., but the story dates to the third millennium. Named for its principal character, Atrahasis, the story presents the theological perspective of the Babylonians, but it contains details that make for interesting comparison to the biblical account. In the Babylonian tale, the gods rule the heavens and earth (see Gen. 1:1). They make man from the clay of the earth mixed with blood (cf. Gen. 2:7, 3:19; Lev. 17:11) to take over the lesser gods' chores of tending the land (see Gen. 2:15). When men multiply on the earth and become too noisy, a flood is sent (after a series of plagues) to destroy mankind (cf. Gen. 6:13). Atrahasis alone is given advance warning of the flood and told to build a boat (cf. Gen. 6:14). He builds a boat and loads it with food and animals and birds. Through this means he is saved while the rest of the world perishes (cf. Gen. 6:17-22). Much of the text is destroyed at this point so there is no record of the landing of the boat. Nevertheless, as in the conclusion of the biblical account, the story ends with Atrahasis offering a sacrifice to the gods and the chief god accepting humanity's continued existence (cf. Gen. 8:20-22).

Another account of the flood was discovered in an Old Babylonian cuneiform tablet, the *Gilgamesh Epic*. Its principal character, King Gilgamesh, allegedly ruled the Mesopotamian city of Uruk around 2600 B.C. Dated in its earliest fragments to 1750 B.C., its flood story seems to have been borrowed directly from the *Atrahasis Epic*.

The *Gilgamesh Epic* caused a sensation rivaling Darwin's *Origin of Species* when it was published in Europe in 1872. Some claimed that it was historical proof of the Genesis flood, the Mesopotamian variation on the biblical text. Others argued that it diminished the Bible's claim to uniqueness, since the biblical author obviously borrowed his account from Mesopotamian sources.

As scholars studied the significant differences and omissions between the accounts, they concluded that neither the Mesopotamian nor the biblical author borrowed from the other. The biblical account is strictly monotheistic and its characters ethically moral, while the Mesopotamian stories are polytheistic and its characters ethically capricious. There were differences in such significant details as the size of the boat, the duration of the flood, and the sending out of the birds. If the biblical text had borrowed these ideas from the Mesopotamian account there was large-scale revision and reinterpretation, which is highly unlikely. Such literary alteration cannot be demonstrated in any other Hebrew or ancient Near Eastern composition. From a literary standpoint the most likely and normal interpretation would be that the Mesopotamian and Israelite versions record a common knowledge of antediluvian history. Each was told from its culture's distinct religious perspective. Based on comparative analysis, the biblical account appears to preserve the original history of events. The Mesopotamian deviations are the kind of departures from the facts that might be anticipated after the disintegration of the original culture that recorded them (see Genesis 10-11). Memories of the essential events remain, yet they are adapted to fit the new culture's mythology.

Witnesses to Early History

Books are continually being written to update the survey of archaeological corroboration for Old Testament history. This does not include the flow of studies on each significant excavation.[10] Here we will briefly relate some of these discoveries to the biblical text.

The Patriarchs

The era of the patriarchs is the biblical period for which the details are most contested in modern archaeology. Those in the *minimalist school* (so-called because they minimize the biblical data) believe there were no patriarchs. The patriarchal mythology was wishful thinking by nationalistic Jews who wanted a glorified, if mythical, past. This backward projection supposedly was written during the mid-first millennium (600 B.C.–400 B.C.). While minimalists and some less radical skeptics leave no piece of evidence undisputed, the period is attested in the archaeological record.

The biblical account of the patriarchs from Abraham to Joseph (Genesis 12–50) indicates a Middle Bronze Period date from the late third millennium to the mid-second millennium before the Christian era (2166–1805). Archaeological evidence relating to this period includes the Code of Hammurabi, Egyptian and Hittite texts, and thousands of clay tablets from the Amorite cities of Mari (Tel Hariri), Nuzi (city of the biblical Horites), Tel Leilan, and Alalakh. At this writing the reports of the Syrian site of Ebla (Tel Mardikh) still are being prepared, but this site offers law codes, legal and social contracts, and religious and other types of texts.

Comparisons between the ancient law texts and the Bible have shown that the laws that governed the patriarch's social behavior were based on local laws and customs of that era. For example, in Genesis 49 Jacob blesses his twelve sons (by two wives and their concubines) and gives each an equal share of the inheritance. Mosaic Law, given later at Mount Sinai, stipulates that the eldest son should receive a double-inheritance (Deut. 21:15–17).

The obvious explanation for this legal contradiction is that Abraham lived earlier than did Moses, in a culture with differing rules. This is supported by the studies comparing ancient Near Eastern inheritance laws. The law code of Lipit-Ishtar (twentieth century B.C., the time of Abraham) gives equal inheritance rights to all sons. However, 200 years later in Hammurabi's Code (eighteenth century) a distinction is made between the sons of a man's first wife (who get first choice) and his secondary sons. In the texts from Mari and Nuzi (eighteenth to fifteenth centuries) inheritance law stipulates that a natural first-born son was to receive a double share, while an adopted son would not, even if he was the eldest. Neo-Babylonian laws of the first millennium B.C. also have the sons of a first wife receiving a double portion and secondary sons only a single portion. The changing social customs reflected by these laws indicate that Abraham observed laws specific to his time and place.[11]

David and Solomon

The tenth century B.C., the height of the united kingdom of Israel, remains a period for which archaeological evidence is sparse. Identification of the "City of David" in Jerusalem's southern Kidron Valley, is suspect. The structures found at that site, including Warren's Shaft, which has been considered the structure mentioned in relation to David's conquest of the city (2 Sam. 5:8; cf., 1 Chron. 11:5–6), may be earlier Canaanite construction, rather than Israelite occupation. Until recently, no extrabiblical inscription containing a reference to Israel of that time had been found, either on land of the kingdom or in any neighboring country. Nevertheless, based solely on the ceramic evidence, Kathleen Kenyon once observed,

> At present this phase [of Israelite domination of Ammon, Moab, and Edom, cf. 2 Sam. 8–12] is only documented archaeologically by scattered pottery finds in Transjordan. However, some of them reflect cultural links westwards into Phoenicia and Cyprus, complementary to the widely ranging contacts of Solomon's realm. Material remains of his ascendancy may everywhere remain meagre, but at no point does what survives invalidate the record of the Old Testament.[12]

There are Hebrew inscriptions from the tenth century, such as the Gezer Calendar, but the most significant find relating to the Davidic dynasty comes from the northern site of Tel Dan in a wall constructed in the ninth or eighth century. Several Aramaic fragments of a monumental stele were discovered in 1993 and 1994. The stele apparently was erected as a war memorial by Ben Hadad, king of Damascus, who gained a victory over the Israelis about 150 years after the time of King David. What was especially exciting was the mention in this inscription that he had defeated Jehoram, the son of Ahab (2 Kings 8:7–15; 9:6–10). There was a reference in this inscription to the "House of David." Based on the revelation of this Aramaic text, the French scholar André LeMaire was able to identify the reading of the name "David" in a formerly unreadable line, "House of D . . ." on the ninth century B.C. Mesha Stele from Moab. If there was a "house of David" there must have been a "David" to have the house.

Major archaeological sites in Jerusalem and elsewhere are associated with Solomon, directly or indirectly. In particular, the sites of Gezer, Hazor, and Megiddo are stated in the Bible to have been chariot cities fortified by Solomon (1 Kings 9:15, 19). Excavations at these sites (some still in progress) have uncovered massive walls, gate systems, water-tunnels, silos, and storehouses, all bearing the style of royal monumental architecture. Originally these structures were attributed to Solomon, but they may belong to the period of the later Northern Kingdom's King Ahab. Yet, even if these sites are not direct evidence for Solomon, they fit into the plan he started and so indirectly confirm his accomplishments.

Archaeological remains from the first temple complex are attributed to Solomon. While structural remains of the temple itself may never be found due to the extensive nature of King Herod's rebuilding of the second temple on the same site, buildings from the first temple period have been discovered south of the temple platform known as the Ophel. The particular design of the Solomon temple, as given in the Bible (1 Kings 6:2–17), is a style reminiscent of the long-room temples common in Syria during the second millennium.[13] The best archaeological examples yet discovered are long-room tripartite temples from Tel Tainat in the Amuq Valley on the northern Orontes River and Ain Dara in Syria excavated in the 1930s by the University of Chicago's Oriental Institute. This confirms that the biblical description of the first temple agrees with historical models of the time. In particular it fits the architectural design expected for a building engineered by Phoenician artisans (2 Chron. 2:13–14).

The Gospels

Archaeology is of immense help in establishing the New Testament and reconstructing its world. Evidence uncovered has been very damaging to higher critical theories meant to undermine the historicity of the text in a first-century milieu. Discoveries have uncovered references to persons and places prominent in the New Testament. The physical remains agree to an extraordinary degree with New Testament details.

The accuracy of the accounts has been under attack since the mid-1800s search for the "historical Jesus." The campaign to discredit the accounts was continual through the twentieth century. Bultmannian demythologizing of the text gave way to the Jesus Seminar of the 1980s and 1990s. Rather than debate the evidence, the latter group of biblical scholars actually voted to see what Scripture portions were to be regarded as genuine.

Typical of the cynicism beyond the century's scholarship is a statement by Marcus Borg, Oregon State University professor and chairman of the Jesus Seminar: "The truth of Easter does not depend on whether there really was an empty tomb. . . . It is because Jesus is known as a living reality that we take Easter stories seriously, not the other way around." Taking the resurrection stories "seriously" does not mean taking them literally. According to this school of thought, Bible students need not concern themselves about what actual historical events are associated with Jesus' life. "Truth" is a subjective, individual experience; therefore faith can exist in spite of the facts, and truth can exist in the context of error.

All archaeological finds that show "truth" to be associated directly with what really happened are bad news for the demythologists. And nowhere more than in the Gospels and Acts is the theological message set amid so much historical context. The writers offer plenty of facts for archaeologists to check out and verify or disprove. So it is no small matter that the historical context so carefully set out can be readily identified from both extrabiblical textual evidence and the archaeological record.

As to individuals connected with Jesus in the Gospels, the name of King Herod is associated with one of the greatest building programs in history. Herodian architecture is a distinct style. In addition to all the written historical accounts of Herod and his family, there can be seen an ostracon from Masada.[14] An ossuary has been discovered that evidently contains the bones of Joseph Caiaphas, the high priest who presided over Jesus' trial (Matt. 26:57, 63–66; Mark 14:53; Luke 22:54; John 18:13, 24, 28).[15] The name of Pontius Pilate, who sentenced Jesus to the cross (Matt. 27:11–26; Mark 15:1–15; Luke 23:1–25; John 18:28–19:16), is seen on a dedicatory stele he erected at Caesarea in honor of the Roman emperor Tiberias.[16]

Roman censuses were frequent in the years surrounding Jesus' birth. Two later census decrees order the same compulsory return to the family city (Luke 2:3–5). Oxyrhynchus papyrus 255 is from about A.D. 48 and British Museum papyrus 904 is from 104.

The Roman manner of capital punishment—crucifixion—had often appeared in extra-biblical literature, but until recently no evidence of the act had ever been discovered in Israel. Then in 1968 the remains of a crucified man from Giv'at ha-Mivtar, a northern suburb of Jerusalem, was discovered in an ossuary from near the time of Jesus.[17] The name of the man, from an Aramaic inscription on the ossuary, was Yohanan ("John") ben Ha'galgol,[18] and from an analysis of the skeletal remains indicated he was in his thirties, about the same age as Jesus when He was crucified.[19] The significant evidence of crucifixion was an ankle bone, still pierced with a seven-inch-long crucifixion nail and attached to a piece of wood from a cross. When the man was crucified, the nail had apparently hit a knot in the olive wood *patibulum* and become so lodged that the victim could not be removed without retaining the nail and a fragment of the cross. Based on studies of the position of the nail in the bone of the ankle, it can now be determined with some accuracy how the body of a crucified victim was hung on the cross.

Among the monumental building projects of Herod the Great, the Gospels are most concerned with his reconstruction work on the Jerusalem temple. During His last days on earth, Jesus, while walking through the ongoing Herodian construction, spoke to his disciples of the future disaster of the Jews (Matt. 24:1–2; Mark 13:1–2; Luke 21:5–6). According to the extra-biblical sources, Herod began the building project in 19 B.C., and dedicated it ten years later. His dynastic successors continued embellishing the project until shortly before the Roman destruction of the city. The Gospels document that as Jesus' disciples pointed out the grandeur of the temple He made a prophetic pronouncement to them: "Truly I say to you, not one stone here shall be left upon another, which shall not be torn down" (Matt. 24:2; Mark 13:2; Luke 19:44).

Jesus' words were fulfilled when the Roman army, under the command of the emperor's son, Titus, stormed the precincts and burned the temple in 70. The archaeological excavations at the foot of the temple mount, especially that directed by Benjamin Mazar at the western and southern corners, have vividly revealed the massive destruction wrought by the Romans. On a section of ancient street that lined the outside western wall of the mount, excavated by Ronny Reich in 1995–1996, heaps of the rubble pushed from the temple area above were uncovered. They give dramatic evidence of the fulfillment of Jesus' words that "not one stone shall be left upon another."

ARCHAEOLOGY AND THE FUTURE

We live in a technological age that is exponentially increasing in its knowledge and ability to retrieve and preserve data. We have unparalleled access to a storehouse of information unavailable to other ages. It is certain that more information about the Bible is available than at any other time. On some subjects we can know more than those living during biblical times. Archaeology is one reason such a bold statement can be made. At this writing, the Israeli Antiquities Authority data base is in process of cataloging one hundred thousand archaeological relics discovered in Israel since 1948. Internet access agreements makes all that data readily available.

OTHER NEW TECHNOLOGY

Technological advances at the turn of the millennium enable archaeologists to make more finds without digging. Rather than having to choose what portions of a site to excavate by educated guess, archaeologists can take readings of masses beneath the ground of a promising site. They can determine exactly where to begin. Remote satellite imaging, ground penetrating radar, seismic resistivity, infrared scanning, and digitally-enhanced photography and other computer-assisted techniques have produced startling results, revealing long lost buried cities or restoring the obscured writing on an ancient scroll.

Recent examples have been the discovery of traces of the Pishon River, one of the ancient water sources of the Garden of Eden (Gen. 2:11) and the computerized scanning processes that may bring to light sections of Qumran manuscripts that until now have been unreadable. On the horizon, breakthroughs in imbedded chip design and miniaturization promise significant enhancements to existing technologies and the opportunity for greater access to knowledge of the ancient world. Not many years ago archaeologists said that it would take over a thousand years (at current rates of excavation) to study just the sites then known. But with new technology we could see an explosion of archaeological data and, consequently, in biblical knowledge.

CHAPTER 10

The Past, Present, and Future of Israel

Thomas S. McCall

For four thousand years, since the time of Abraham, Israel has been an enigma to the world. Israel has been an enigma to generations of Christians for almost two thousand years, since the church came into being. Throughout the history of anti-Semitism the institutional church has tried in turn to ignore the Jews, assuming that Israel is no longer a factor in the plans of the Almighty, or to convert them by force or wipe them out. The true church through the centuries, even among early Protestant Reformers, sometimes has been infected with this unbiblical ambivalence.

The miraculous continuing existence of the Jewish people through all of this, and particularly since the modern state of Israel came into being, are mysteries to the world and to much of the church. The only way to discover the meaning of Israel is in the Scriptures, and the key to that discovery is in Romans 9–11. In this remarkable section of the New Testament, which is frequently ignored, the Lord has revealed to those who will believe His Word the amazing chronicles of Israel's past, present, and future.

What seems astonishing, and unbelievable to many Christians and to most Jews, is that *two chosen peoples of God* live in the world today, side by side. These two chosen peoples are Israel and the church. Each has its own purpose and one destiny. They are like two sisters with the same father, but neither one wants to recognize the status of the other. Those Jews who care about God look upon the church as an idolatrous religion that worships three gods, deifies a human being (Jesus), and causes all kinds of persecution, especially against them. Nondispensationalist Christians, on the other hand, look upon Israel as though it were some kind of vestigial organ, like an appendix or tonsils. The learned clerics say that at one time in the past, Israel had a purpose,

183

but it has served the purpose God had for the nation, and it has no further usefulness.

There are even a few extremists who still use a Christian identity as a cover for anti-Semitism. Because they do not have a clue as to what the atonement was about, they see Israel as the people responsible for the death of Christ. Therefore, they believe, Jewish people are doomed to ignominy and perpetual punishment.

Behind much of this sad history has been a Christian teaching that the church is the new Israel in every sense and old Israel is rejected forever. Some of this has not been from outright prejudice so much as a failure to correctly interpret such texts as Romans 9–11. This extreme discontinuity between ethnic Israel and the church sometimes is called "replacement theology." Others look at these texts from a similar hermeneutic and take a more lenient, but still unscriptural, view: Ethnic Israel had a purpose in the past and will have a purpose in the prophetic future. But in between, God's plan is being carried out through the church, and only ethnic Jews in Christ are the remnant of old Israel in God's chosen people. The Jewish people today and the modern State of Israel have no special meaning and no covenantal relationship with God. Thus, Israel means no more to them than any other nation—and some would say even less. A simple reading of the Word of God, however, will show that God has a continuing covenantal relationship with both Israel and the church in this age. Each group has its distinct function and purpose in the plan of God as follows:

1. God has a *continuing* covenantal relationship with Israel. He wants to show to the world that He keeps His promises by protecting, throughout history, the Jews' role. They have provided the vehicle for preserving the Old Testament. He has worked in them a saved remnant in every generation and set aside their unique land and Holy City. Theirs is the ultimate prophetic destiny as the "head of the nations" under the rule of the Messiah of Israel, the Lord Jesus Christ.
2. God has a *new* covenantal relationship with the church, with the soteriological (salvation) purpose of calling out a people for Christ's name from among the Jews and Gentiles. Those who now believe in and accept the Lord Jesus Christ are baptized into the body of Christ. The church is a testimony of the death, burial, resurrection, and ascension of the Lord to a lost and dying world, to the Jew first and also to the Gentiles.

ROMANS, THE CHURCH, AND ISRAEL

The epistle to the Romans has been called the Cathedral of the Faith. It is placed at the beginning of the Pauline epistles, not because it is the earliest of his letters, but because it is foundational for all the rest. Romans is very nearly a complete systematic theology. It lays out in logical order, the themes of sin, salvation, and sanctification of the believer in Christ in the church age. Thrown into the heart of this powerful theological treatise in the ninth through eleventh chapters is a somewhat unexpected revelation concerning Israel.

At first glance this discussion seems out of place, and some commentaries refer to the entire section as parenthetical. Some studies of Romans tend to skip over this section, and I have not heard of many sermons being preached on these chapters, except as touching tangentially the themes of missionary work or predestination. The theme of the section concerning Israel still seems to be, for the most part, ignored in church circles. It may be that gentile believers are disobeying the major admonition of the apostle in this section of Romans which states, "Boast not against the branches. But if thou boast, thou bearest not the root, but the root thee" (Rom. 11:18).[1] Nevertheless, in these three chapters resides the key to the understanding of the enigma of Israel in the church age.

It appears that Paul is wrestling with a few primary questions: First, what has happened to Israel? The Messiah has come and was not received nationally. He died and rose from the dead and returned to heaven, and now that He has created a new entity, the church, has God rejected Israel? Second, is Israel significant to the church? Do gentiles who believe bear special responsibility to the nation that largely does not believe? Third, is the covenant God had with Israel in the Old Testament still in effect?

In Romans 9–11, Paul develops answers to these questions by affirming that even though Israel did not receive Christ at His first coming, His faithfulness to Israel remains steadfast. In this age a remnant of Israel is receiving Christ and is part of the church. Gentile believers are grafted into Israel's olive tree as a temporary administration of the plan of redemption. They must not boast about their salvation and the lost status of the Jewish unbelievers, for ultimately God will save the living nation of Israel at the second coming of Christ. All of this is brought out in the arguments from the Old Testament that Paul marshals in this unusual section. He speaks to the glorious past, the tragic current situation, and the magnificent future for the children by blood of Abraham, Isaac, and Jacob.

THE GLORIOUS PAST OF ISRAEL

To this point in the tight development of Romans, Paul has traced the progress of an individual from the depths of sin to the point of salvation by grace through faith in Christ and His redemptive death and resurrection. He has observed the struggle of the believer over the conflict between his old and new natures and shown the believer's victory over the old nature through the power of the Holy Spirit in Christ. The eighth chapter rings with victorious exultation that the curse of the law may still affect our lives, but ultimately it is powerless. Nothing can separate the believer from the love of God in Christ. As the ninth chapter opens, there is a decided change in attitude. Paul writes:

> *I say the truth in Christ, I lie not, my conscience also bearing me witness in the Holy Ghost, That I have great heaviness and continual sorrow in my heart. For I could wish that myself were accursed from Christ for my brethren, my kinsmen according to the flesh: Who are Israelites. (Rom. 9:1–4a)*

The apostle now turns and says, "I am carrying a terrific sorrow perpetually in my heart. I cannot shake it, I cannot get rid of it." Is this the same writer? Yes, but his perspective is no longer Paul the victorious believer but Paul the child of Abraham. He does not look at himself nor within the body of Christ, with all of our prerogatives and privileges. For the next three chapters Paul looks outside to a lost and dying world, and particularly to Israel's sad circumstances. This caused Paul a great and continual burden of grief and sorrow. His grief was so great that if he could give his salvation to the Jewish nation, he would be willing to be separated from Christ. James Luther Mays in *Harper's Bible Commentary* states that Paul's offer is hypothetical, but it still is genuine and strong, as was the self-sacrificing appeal of Moses:

> Yet, in a manner reminiscent of Moses's impossible offer of his own life to atone for the worshipers of the golden calf (Exod. 32:31–32), Paul entertains the fleeting thought of being accursed and cut off from Christ, something just declared impossible (8:35, 39), in their place, as if they are under a ban or spell.[2]

In other words, though he cannot be separated from Christ, he would be willing to go to hell if it would mean the salvation of Israel. Paul has just said that no power can separate him from Christ. But if it were possible, and if it would make a difference, he would be willing for that to happen. This is not just the human Paul sharing his burden with us. Through Paul, the Spirit of God is bearing God's compassion for His people, the Israelites. He lists the eight remarkable prerogatives of the nation of Israel so we will not mistake that he is speaking about his own brethren. The prerogatives listed in 9:4–5 are uniquely Israel's.

"to whom pertaineth the adoption"

God has adopted Israel as His son. God told Moses that Israel was His firstborn son among the nations (Exod. 4:22–23). That adoptive love was so strong that if Pharaoh would not release God's son, Israel, God would slay Pharaoh's son. God has adopted Israel and has never disowned His son.

"and the glory"

When Israel came out of Egypt the *Shekinah* glory of God, the pillar of cloud by day and fire by night, preceded them through forty years of wilderness journey. When the people entered into the land of promise the *Shekinah* glory went with them. Finally, when the Solomonic temple was built, the cloud of God filled the *Kôdāsh Kādāshîm*, the Holy of Holies. The glory of the Almighty was in their midst. No other nation can make that claim.

"and the covenants"

God has made some covenants with all of mankind after the Fall, such as what some call the Adamic covenant (Gen. 3:14–19). This covenant doesn't promise much for the short term. Man is told that he has to work for his bread by the sweat of his brow. Woman is told that she will have pain in childbearing. Then there is the greatest of all promises: The seed of the woman will destroy the Serpent, Satan.

By the Noahic covenant (Gen. 9:1–7) all people are told of God's promise that the world will never again be destroyed by flood. At its core is the sanctity of all human life: the symbolic prohibition against eating blood and the demand that murderers be put to death. That's about it! Those are all the covenants God has made with the world as such.

But with Israel, He has made several covenants: the Abrahamic covenant, the Mosaic covenant, the Davidic covenant, the new covenant. With the exception of the Mosaic Law, all of these are binding, unconditional, and eternal covenants. They are unilateral promises God has made to His people, Israel. No other nation can make that claim.

"and the giving of the law"

Where were our gentile ancestors and what were they doing when Israel was at the foot of Mount Sinai? When the ancient gentile nations were groping in blind idolatry, God gave to his covenant people a law, the Torah, the statutes, and the commandments that are perfect, that are righteous, holy, and good. They are the standard of all law that has ever been promulgated since then.

"and of the service of God"

The Lord chose one tribe out of Israel, Levi, and called them to be the priestly tribe. They would not own property within the land, but they would be the priests of the Lord and the Lord would be their inheritance forever. They would have the high calling of ministering through the sacrificial system, and intercessory prayer before the Lord on behalf of Israel. If any human being desired to worship God in the way God prescribed, he would have to do so through the Levitical priests. God chose one tribe out of all the nations and appointed them to be His priests. No other nation can make that claim.

"and the promises"

This is related to the covenants. God made promises to Israel: the restoration to the land, the national salvation of the people, and that God Himself would reign in person, on earth, from their capital city. Even in unbelief, religious Israeli Jews grasp for the land promises. In the modern state of Israel, it is interesting to note that the national anthem is called *"Hatkivah"* — the Hope. Hope in what? It must be the hope in the promises of God.

Query: Anyone have access to the words of the national anthem? It may not mean hope in the promises of God.

"whose are the fathers"

One thing that has kept the Jewish people going through centuries of persecution is a fiercely devoted identity in the patriarchs. It was with Abraham, Isaac, and Jacob that God communicated directly. With them He made binding, unconditional, and eternal covenants. These promises have not been transferred to any other national entity.

"and of whom . . . Christ came"

But the crowning glory of Israel, the capstone of Israel's past glory is the eighth prerogative: "And of whom as concerning the flesh, Christ came, who is over all, God blessed forever, Amen." When God became a man, when the Almighty took upon Himself human flesh, He didn't become an American, or an African, or a Russian, or an Englishman, or a Chinese. He took upon himself the seed of Abraham; He became a Jew: the Son of David, the Son of Abraham. No other nation can make that claim.

THE TRAGIC PRESENT STATE OF ISRAEL

The Jews' Need

The present state of Israel is revealed in Romans 10:1 where Paul writes, "Brethren, my heart's desire and prayer to God for Israel is, that they might be saved." Israel is lost. There are those who teach that Israel does not need its Christ. The Jews believe in God, they have the law, they have the synagogues. Paul does not take that position. He prays that Israel might be saved.

Israel needs the Messiah they missed. Practicing Jews do not lack faith, but they lack understanding of the object of that faith. "For I bear them record that they have a zeal of God, but not according to knowledge" (Rom. 10:2). Israel exists because Jews have had a zeal for God and their people throughout the four thousand years of its long history. The Jewish idea of a martyr is one whose dying words are the *Shema'*, "Hear O Israel, the Lord our God, the Lord is one" (Deut. 6:4), with *Torah* clutched to his chest. Jews would not bow down to idols, especially after the Babylonian captivity. Thousands were slaughtered for refusing to honor the Greek pantheon in the brutal hellenization campaign of the third century B.C.

One argument modern Jews give against believing in Christ is that it smacks of idolatry, the worship of a man. The abhorrence of idolatry is so strong that it even keeps them from their own Messiah. It has erected a wall against evangelism for Muslims as well. Muhammad learned his theology of radical monotheism from reading the Jewish Scriptures.

Their zeal for God is also a zeal for self-salvation, as Paul states: "For they being ignorant of God's righteousness and going about to establish their own righteousness, have not submitted themselves unto the righteousness of God" (Rom. 10:3). The Messiah is the one who gives the righteousness of God through submission to Christ, not to the law.[3]

Is God Through with Israel?

Paul asks rhetorically; "Hath God cast away His people?" (Rom. 11:1a). Many scholars over the centuries, answered that question, "Yes. God is through with Israel! Whatever covenants God had with Israel have been canceled and have been transferred to the church, the new Israel." Paul answers his own question, however, "God forbid" (11:1b). The words *mē genoito* express the strongest negative in the Greek language. John A. Witmer writes of this phrase:

> To that possibility Paul responded, Not at all (*mē genoito*, "Let it not be," a frequent exclamation by Paul; cf. vv. 6, 31; 6:1, 15; 7:7, 13; 11:1, 11). Though some Jews did not believe or were unfaithful (evidenced by their sinful conduct mentioned in 2:21–23, 25), God remains faithful to His Word (cf. Deut. 7:9; 1 Cor. 1:9; Heb. 10:23; 11:11; 1 Peter 4:19).[4]

How can anyone say that God is through with Israel when He appointed Paul, a Hebrew of the Hebrews, as one of the chief officers of the church (see Rom. 11:1c)? Paul, of course, could have added that all the apostles were Jews. So he concludes,

> *God hath not cast away His people which He foreknew. Wot ye not what the Scripture saith of Elias? how he maketh intercession to God against Israel, saying, Lord, they have killed Thy prophets, and digged down Thine altars; and I am left alone, and they seek my life. (Rom. 11:2–3)*

If anybody had a right to think that God was through with Israel, it was Elijah. Israel was in apostasy, caught up in Baal worship. Even after God had shown his power on Mount Carmel, showing the prophets of Baal to be false, Queen Jezebel issued a death warrant for Elijah. Elijah ran to the Sinai desert, crawled under a juniper tree and said, as it were, "Lord, I'm the only one left who is faithful to you" (1 Kings 19). The Lord appreciated Elijah's faithfulness but he told the prophet that his accounting was off by 6,999. The seven thousand God preserved were a faithful remnant within Israel.

Paul then draws the application that there remains a remnant "according to the election of grace" (Rom. 11:5). The remnant Jews are saved by grace, through faith into His church. Paul writes that the nation has not fallen so that no Jews will be saved. To the contrary, the fact that gentiles are coming to *their* God through *their* Messiah will draw some Jews to Christ by provoking them to jealousy (Rom. 11:11). There are many reasons why God has brought each gentile believer to himself, but Paul gives one reason—to be part of the salvation of Israel through their jealousy. Paul reminds his readers that he is speaking as the apostle to the gentiles, but also as a Hebrew Christian. Even his ministry among the gentiles has, as a prominent purpose, to provoke faith in his fellow Jews through jealousy (11:13–14). Paul sets the example for gentile and Hebrew Christians in this great effort.

THE ILLUSTRATION OF THE OLIVE TREE

The illustration of the cultivated olive tree (11:15–24) approaches Paul's point from another direction. The parts of the tree used in the example are the root, the attached natural branches, the broken-off natural branches, and the grafted-in wild branches. The root stock is what Paul describes in Ephesians 2:12 as the "commonwealth of Israel." The root is the Jewish spiritual identity in the fathers—Abraham, Isaac, and Jacob. The natural branches are the Jewish people, and the wild branches the gentile believers.

Some branches remained attached, the believing remnant, but others have been broken off for unbelief in Christ. So, "contrary to nature," the wild branches have been grafted in among the natural branches. Gentiles have been brought into the commonwealth, to become sharers in the benefits of the national covenants. Neither the church nor gentile believers *are* Israel, but they have come within the *sphere* of the commonwealth of Israel.

At the dawn of the twenty-first century, the fragmentation of world Judaism generally and the nation of Israel in particular shows the lost condition of the Jewish people. The hostility to gentile Christians who speak of their connection to the commonwealth—and especially to Jewish Christians regarded as traitors to their heritage, shows the provocation of jealousy still at work. Jews are, in fact, coming to Christ in record numbers, showing that God is not through with the Jewish nation. Matthew Henry emphasizes this when he states, "Throughout the argument based on the wild olive shoot Paul implies that the lopped off natural branch has not yet been cast on the rubbish heap. Israel has not been definitively rejected by God."[5]

THE MAGNIFICENT FUTURE OF ISRAEL

If God still has a future for His ancient covenant nation, what is the nature of this future of the chosen people?

A Sure Future

Paul continues, "For I would not, brethren, that ye should be ignorant of this mystery, lest ye should be wise in your own conceits (Rom. 11:25a). At this point Paul addresses the gentile Christians directly, telling them not to be ignorant of their relation to Judaism. Gentiles who are ignorant may become conceited. The truth is,

> *that blindness in part is happened to Israel, until the fulness of the Gentiles be come in. And so all Israel shall be saved: as it is written, There shall come out of Zion the Deliverer and shall turn away ungodliness from Jacob: for this is my covenant unto them when I shall take away their sins. (Romans 11:25b–27)*

The current situation of a partial spiritual blindness upon the people of Israel will not continue forever. Israel is blind in part; all of Israel is not blind, because the remnant is being saved in each generation. The nation is blind in part, but that situation will not go on forever. Henry asserts that Israel must be delivered to fulfill prophecy: "The final salvation of all Israel is God's own "mystery," but the certainty of it, and the terms on which it must take place, like those of all God's world, are disclosed in God's revelation of his righteousness in Jesus Christ" (11:28–32).[6]

There is the promise that when the gentile church is complete, then God's dealings with national Israel will resume. A Deliverer will come out of Zion. When the Messiah returns to Jerusalem He will remove ungodliness from Jacob. This is His promised covenant.

All Israel Will Be Saved

Obviously the statement of 11:26a, "And so all Israel shall be saved," does not mean that every Jew who ever lived will ultimately be saved. Israel always has been seen as the living cultural entity currently upon the earth. Jesus told the Jewish people of His generation, "If ye believe not that I am He, ye shall die in your sins" (John 8:24a). This prophecy has in view that generation living when Christ returns. Those who endure the horrors of the tribulation, what Jeremiah 30:7 describes as the "time of Jacob's trouble," will be the generation of "all Israel." The most horrible time for Israel's sad history is yet to come. But those who come through that will be broken and ready to acknowledge Jesus as their Messiah. The whole nation will receive Him: "They shall look upon Me whom they have pierced, and they shall mourn for Him. . . .

In that day there shall be a fountain opened to the house of David" (Zech. 12:10; 13:1). It will be a time of forgiveness and reconciliation, as Witmer explains: "Following this judgment God will then remove godlessness and sins from the nation as He establishes His New Covenant with regenerate Israel (cf. Jer. 31:33–34)."[7]

When Israel is again the head of the nations, there will be peace and righteousness on the earth and the knowledge of the Lord will cover the earth, as the waters cover the sea (Isa. 11:9; Hab. 2:14). The church will reign with Him, and the nations will walk in the blessings of the Lord. The Prince of Peace will reign and there will be peace, finally, upon the earth.

It is here, concerning the *future* of Israel, that there is the greatest difference of opinion about the chosen nation among Christian interpreters. I have described the premillennial interpretation. Amillennialists and postmillennialists understand the phrase "all Israel shall be saved" to mean that the church will be complete, or that there will be a large conversion of the Jewish people *within the church*. Matthew Henry proposes this view:

> We have here a prophecy of *the binding of Satan* for a certain term of time, in which he should have much less power and the church much more peace than before. The power of Satan was broken in part by the setting up of the gospel kingdom in the world; it was further reduced by the empire's becoming Christian; it was yet further broken by the downfall of the mystical Babylon; but still this serpent had many heads, and, when one is wounded, another has life remaining in it. Here we have a further limitation and diminution of his power.[8]

This view does not interpret Scripture as prophesying that Israel will have a distinct future apart from the church. Instead, Israel's widespread turning to Christ will come during the church's history. Henry indicates that this has not happened, but that Satan has been progressively bound in the first coming of Christ, the Christianization of the Roman Empire, and the Reformation.

However, the Scriptures present a considerably different picture. In accordance with normative dispensationalism, we believe the church age continues with its final stages ending in greatly increased apostasy, and concluding in the spectacular rapture of the church. The church will then be in heaven, and the world will go through the tribulation, which relates to Israel as the "time of Jacob's trouble."

At the end of the tribulation, Israel will turn to Christ. At that time Christ will establish His millennial kingdom on the earth, binding Satan in the Abyss. Israel will remain apart from the church, becoming, as God intended, the truly redeemed covenant nation of the Lord. There are many aspects of the prophesied future of Israel that show it will be distinct from the church.

Restoration to the Land

As noted above, the church is not tied to a land, but God gave to Israel a land grant of Canaan as an everlasting inheritance. Israel has never possessed the land to the extent promised. Its widest boundaries were during the reign of King Solomon. When Christ returns, the Jewish people will be restored to all of their ancient and future land. The vision in Ezekiel 37 describes this restoration as a process. The "whole house of Israel" is seen as bones that are coming out of the graveyards of the nations, putting on flesh, and becoming a live and vibrant host.

The Throne and Capital of the King

The Lord Jesus Christ is called the *Head* of the church, but never its *King*. When He returns to the earth, Jesus will sit upon the throne of His father David. He will rule as the King of Kings and the Lord of Lords. Jerusalem will be His capital, the city of the Great King. The twelve tribes of Israel will be ruled by the twelve apostles of the Lord, in their resurrection power. The church will participate in the millennial kingdom, co-reigning with Christ over Israel and the nations of the earth. Nevertheless, the church and Israel will be distinct entities.

The Temple

Christ will rebuild the temple in a manner that will surpass anything Solomon or Herod ever dreamed. This millennial temple is described in great detail in Ezekiel 40–48. Mount Moriah is elevated to a grand plateau, and the temple of the Lord will be resplendent. The Levitical priesthood and the animal sacrifices will be restored, and the Lord will be worshiped in the millennial temple. As Jesus has made the only all-sufficient sacrifice on behalf of the sins of the world, these sacrifices are apparently memorials, much as the Lord's Supper serves that purpose in the church age. Such a difference in worship is another indication that the future glory of Israel is not within the church.

The Feast of Tabernacles

The nations will demonstrate their subservience to the King of Kings by celebrating the ancient Feast of the Tabernacles every year throughout the Millennium. According to the prophet Zechariah, the nations will have to send delegations to Jerusalem each fall in order to give homage and thanksgiving to King Jesus.

EPILOGUE

The past, present, and future of Israel comprises one of the great themes of the Word of God. Another theme is the present and future of the church. These two peoples have been confused in the study of Scripture.

In light of the understanding that God has a glorious future for Israel, we need to dedicate ourselves to a renewed effort to evangelize the Jew. How much effort are we as the church putting out to evangelize the Jew? Are we showing compassion for the nation now that God has sovereignly reestablished them in their land? At the beginning of the twenty-first century these are good questions to answer in the light of Romans 9–11.

CHAPTER 11

The Person and Ministry of God the Father

Harold L. Willmington

Thomas A. Smail, vice principal of St. John's Theological College, Nottingham, England, wrote a penetrating book entitled *The Forgotten Father*. It is difficult to imagine a more appropriate title. How sad (indeed, tragic) to contemplate how few books are written on the Person and work of God the Father, while thousands are available on the second and third members of the Trinity.

Imagine yourself among a group of Christians who have been given a biblical test with but three essay questions:

1. Put down everything you know about the Person and work of Jesus Christ, the second person of the Trinity.

Probably most of the group could fill several pages of material about the Savior in a reasonable amount of time.

2. Put down everything you know about the Person and work of the Holy Spirit, the third person of the Trinity.

Now the pens do not move as rapidly or as confidently as before. There are long pauses between sentences. At the end of the given time period the average believer has probably written at least one-half page or more.

3. Put down everything you know about the Person and work of God the Father, first person in the Trinity.

How silent the room now becomes! One statement is written: "He is the Father of Jesus Christ."

It is my opinion that precious few in that group of Christians would be able to write even a half-dozen lines about the Father. This fact is incredible and absolutely inexcusable. The Father is mentioned 256 times in the New Testament alone. Jesus refers to the Father no fewer than seventeen times during the Sermon on the Mount alone (Matt. 5:16, 45, 48; 6:1, 4, 6 [twice], 8, 9, 14, 15, 18 [twice], 26, 32; 7:11, 21).

The Father is a primary focus of attention throughout the New Testament. References are found three times in Acts, forty-four in Paul's writings, two in Hebrews, three in James, four in the letters of Peter, sixteen in John's epistles, one in Jude, and five in the book of Revelation.

THE FATHER'S ROLE IN THE TRINITY

False Views

How can God be "one" and "three"? Scripture goes just so far in describing God; for the rest we simply must believe what is beyond our understanding. Over the centuries many have tried to helpfully go beyond what the Bible teaches. They want to explain God or they want to force God to fit their own theological preconceptions. Either way, these formulations are doomed to fail. For example, *tri-theism* and *monarchianism* are two errors that deal particularly with God as Father in relation to God as Son and God as Spirit. Such heresies are still around and are fatal to faith in the true God.

Tri-theism holds that the Trinity consists of three separate but cooperating gods. This grievous error reduces the Trinity to a crude kind of pagan pantheon. Jews and Muslims tend to believe that all Christians are tri-theists.

According to modalistic monarchianism or Sabellianism there is one, unitary God who reveals himself to us through three different modes, or roles. The classic modalistic illustration, occasionally used by Christians who should know better, is that at different times of the day a man may fill the roles of, and be recognized as, a husband, a father, and an employee. In one sense he is potentially all three at once, and in another those roles might be discussed as though filled by three people. But only one man is involved and he only works at one role at a time. The Father became the Son, but he was no longer the Father. The Son became the Holy Spirit, but he was no longer the Father or the Son.

This view, as in the case of tri-theism, has no scriptural foundation. To the contrary, it negates everything the Bible tells us about the Trinity.

True Views

Within the Trinity, the Father is incomprehensible to human beings. That doesn't mean, however, that we cannot know the Father personally. We also can make propositional truth statements about the Trinity, and the Father's place in it. Over the centuries theologians have studied Scripture carefully to arrive at helpful descriptions.

Within its larger, carefully defined chapter on God, the *Westminster Confession of Faith,* published in 1647, had this to say about the Trinity (2.3):

> In the unity of the Godhead there be three persons, of one substance, power, and eternity: God the Father, God the Son, and God the Holy Ghost. The Father is of none, neither begotten, nor proceeding, the Son is eternally begotten of the Father, the Holy Ghost eternally proceeding from the Father and the Son.

The *New Hampshire Baptist Confession* of 1833 made this concise statement:

> We believe that there is one, and only one, living and true God, an infinite, intelligent Spirit, whose name is JEHOVAH, the Maker and Supreme Ruler of heaven and earth; inexpressibly glorious in holiness, and worthy of all possible honor, confidence, and love; that in the unity of the Godhead there are three persons, the Father, the Son, and the Holy Spirit, equal in every divine perfection, and executing distinct and harmonious offices in the great work of redemption.

A propositional approach to confessing the Trinity has been taken by R. C. Sproul. Sproul makes the valid point that the doctrine of the Trinity is a fence around our intellect. It sets limits on human speculation about the nature of God. We can know that the Trinity affirms the "triunity" of God, and it is not a contradiction. God is one in essence and three in person.

Sproul notes that we need not understand what we have faith in because the Bible affirms it: first, God is one; second, the Father and Son and Holy Spirit are all three divine; third, we distinguish among the three by their work.[1]

Wayne Grudem observes the eternality of the relationships among the Father and the Son and the Spirit. The Son was the Son in relation to the Father before the Incarnation; in fact, before the world began. The Holy Spirit has proceeded from Father and Son through eternity. We know this because Scripture says so and because God does not change. If God exists now as Father, Son, and Holy Spirit, he always has existed as a Trinity.

Scripture has the most to say about the relationship between Father and Son for our salvation. John 3:16–17 shows the outworking of the relationship. The Son was "sent." He already was the Son, but when it was time he became human (Gal. 4:4).[2]

The Father's Role with the Son

Lewis Sperry Chafer summarizes the relationship between the Father and the Son in a comprehensive way:

> The relationship of the second person to the first person has from all eternity been that of a Son, and, like all else, related to the Godhead, is not only eternal but is unchangeable. He did not become a Son of the Father, as some say that He did, by His incarnation, or by His resurrection, nor is He a Son by mere title, nor is He temporarily assuming such a relationship that He may execute His part in the covenant of Redemption.
>
> He was the only begotten of the Father from all eternity, having no other relation to time and creation than that He is the Creator of them. It is evident that the Father and Son relationship sets forth only the features of emanation and manifestation and does not include the usual conception of derivation, inferiority, or distinction as to the time of beginning.
>
> It is probable that the terms Father and Son, as applied to the first and second persons in the Godhead, are somewhat anthropomorphic in character. That sublime and eternal relationship which existed between these two persons is best expressed to human understanding in the terms of Father and Son, but wholly without implication that the two Persons, on the divine side, are not equal in every particular.[3]

Father and Son in the Old Testament

The Old Testament focuses on the Father. These books give us our clearest picture of who he is. They have less to say about the Son and the Spirit, for the full work of the Trinity was hidden from the Old Testament saints in the mystery of the gospel, to be revealed in the Incarnation (Rom. 16:25; Eph. 1:9; 3:3–9; 6:19–20; Col. 1:26–2:3; 4:3–4).

But that is not to say that the Old Testament tells us nothing about this relationship. Jesus frequently used Old Testament references to it, especially two Psalms:

> *The kings of the earth set themselves, and the rulers take counsel together, against the Lord, and against his anointed, saying, "Let us break their bands asunder, and cast away their cords from us" . . . I will declare the decree: the Lord hath said unto me, "Thou art my Son; this day have I begotten thee." (Ps. 2:2–3, 7)[4]*

> *The Lord said unto my Lord, Sit thou at my right hand, until I make thine enemies thy footstool. (Ps. 10:1)*

Through the prophet Isaiah the "Son" speaks about the "Father" who sent him and the "Holy Spirit":

> *Come ye near unto me, hear ye this: I have not spoken in secret, from the beginning, from the time that it was, there am I, and now the Lord God, and his Spirit, hath sent me. (Isa. 48:16)*

And in Isaiah the Father and the Son and the Holy Spirit are seen at work in one text:

> *In all their affliction he was afflicted, and the angel of his presence saved them; in his love and in his pity he redeemed them; and he bare them, and carried them all the days of old. But they rebelled, and vexed his Holy Spirit, therefore he was turned to be their enemy. (Isa. 63:9–10)*

The Father in the Ministry of the Son

Even as a boy who had not yet begun His earthly ministry Jesus understood that he was sent by the Father. When his parents found him in the temple of Herod He chided them, "How is it that ye sought me? wist ye not that I must be about my Father's business?" (Luke 2:49). He concluded His earthly ministry on the Mount of Olives by stating, "And, behold, I send the promise of my Father upon you: but tarry ye in the city of Jerusalem, until ye be endued with power from on high" (Luke 24:49).

Jesus even began and concluded his agony on the cross by praying to the Father. He states, "Father, forgive them; for they know not what they do" (Luke 23:34a). And His final statement was, "Father, into thy hands I commend my spirit" (Luke 23:46a).

The Conversations in the Gospels

While Jesus was on earth the Father and Son spoke to one another on occasion in words audible to those around them.

> *Now when all the people were baptized, it came to pass, that Jesus also being baptized, and praying, the heaven was opened, and the Holy Ghost descended in a bodily shape like a dove upon him, and a voice came from heaven, which said, Thou art my beloved Son; in thee I am well pleased. (Luke 3:21–22)*

Here we are told that the Savior spoke to His Father who then answered from heaven.

At the end of Jesus' Triumphal Entry we hear,

Now is my soul troubled, and what shall I say? Father, save me from this
hour: but for this cause came I unto this hour. Father, glorify thy name.
Then came there a voice from heaven, saying, I have both glorified it,
and will glorify it again. (John 12:27–28)

Christ glorified and sought the presence of the Father in prayer continually. He prayed in connection with his ministry, such as before choosing the twelve (Luke 6:12), before going into Galilee (Mark 1:35; Luke 4:42), and after hearing the report of the seventy he had sent out (Matt. 11:25-27; Luke 10:21-22).

He prayed in connection with ministry to others, such as Mary and Martha (Luke 11:1), small children (Matt. 19:13-15; Mark 10:13-16; Luke 18:15-17), and the Greeks who came to him (John 12:20-28). He prayed for his disciples then and in the future (John 17:1-26). He prayed in connection with Peter's confession that he was the Christ (Luke 9:18).

He prayed in connection with miracles, such as healing a leper (Luke 5:16), feeding the multitude (Matt. 14:23; Mark 6:46; John 6:15), and raising Lazarus (John 11:41-42).

He prayed in the garden on the Mount of Olives before his arrest (Matt. 26:39, 42, 44; Mark 14:35-36, 39; Luke 22:41-42)

He prayed in the midst of his agonies on the cross (Matt. 27:46-47; Mark 15:34-35; Luke 23:34, 46)

In this unique triune relationship, the Father bestowed supreme honor upon His Son. After the Father sent the Son (John 3:16; 6:57; 8:16, 18; 12:49; Gal. 4:4; 1 John 4:14), He commanded the angels to worship His Son (Heb. 1:6; Luke 2:8-15). He himself bore witness to His Son (John 8:18) and glorified Him (John 12:27-28; 17:1, 5). The Father sealed His Son (John 6:27). He loved (John 10:17) and delighted in His Son (Isa. 42:1; Matt. 3:17; 17:5). He taught (John 8:28) and listened to His Son (John 11:41-42).

The Father anointed His Son (Luke 4:16-21). He offered up His Son (John 18:11; Rom. 8:32; 1 John 4:9-10). He raised His Son (Gal. 1:1; Eph. 1:20), exalted Him (Phil 2:9-11; Eph. 1:21), and made Him head of the church (Eph. 1:22) and Judge (John 3:35; 5:22, 27; Acts 17:31).

The Father and the Holy Spirit

That the Father and the Holy Spirit had an intimate relationship from the beginning is obvious from the second verse in the Bible where we read, "And the Spirit of God moved upon the face of the waters" (Gen. 1:2).

In His Upper-Room Discourse, Jesus asks the Father to send the Holy Spirit (John 14:16; 15:26). At Pentecost, the Father would send the Spirit in order that the Spirit would:

- make Christ real within them (John 15:26).
- seal them (2 Cor. 1:21-22; Eph. 1:13; 4:30).
- permanently indwell them (John 14:16).
- empower them (1 John 4:4).
- teach them (John 14:26).
- reassure them of their adoption by the Father (Rom. 8:15-16; Gal. 4:6).
- aid their prayer life and pray for them (Rom. 8:26-27).
- give them spiritual gifts (1 Cor. 12:4-11).
- usher them into the presence of the Father (Eph. 2:18).

THE FATHER IN CREATION AND REDEMPTION

Who created the universe? According to David, the Father created all things. "The heavens declare the glory of God, and the firmament sheweth his handiwork" (Ps. 19:1). However, John declares the Son did it. "All things were made by him; and without him was not any thing made that was made. In him was life; and the life was the light of men" (John 1:3-4). Finally, in other passages, the Holy Spirit is said to have performed the initial act of creation.

The answer to this seeming disagreement is that all three persons in the Trinity had a part. As long as the analogy is not carried too far, it is like an executive who determines to build a spacious home. He employs an architect to design the necessary plans. The architect secures a competent contractor to follow his blueprints. The executive would be the Father, the architect would be the Son, and the contractor would be the Holy Spirit in the sense shown in these texts:

> *Thou sendest forth thy spirit, they are created: and thou renewest the face of the earth. (Ps. 104:30)*

> *By his spirit he hath garnished the heavens; his hand hath formed the crooked serpent. (Job 26:13)*

> *The Spirit of God hath made me, and the breath of the Almighty hath given me life. (Job 33:4)*

In regards to creation, the Father, it would appear, has personally assumed responsibility in four areas: plant life (Ps. 104:14, 16; Matt. 6:28-30); animal life (Ps. 104:14, 16-18, 20-21, 27; Matt. 10:29); weather (Pss. 135:6-7; 147:8, 16-18; 148:8); and the seasons (Gen. 8:22; Acts 14:17)

The entire Trinity was involved in redemption. In particular, the Father is ultimately the source and reason for our salvation in Christ:

First, He foreknew and predestinated us.

Having predestinated us unto the adoption of children by Jesus Christ to himself, according to the good pleasure of his will, in whom also we have obtained an inheritance, being predestinated according to the purpose of him who worketh all things after the counsel of his own will. (Eph. 1:5, 11; cf. Rom. 8:29a; 11:2)

Second, He chose and elected us.

Who shall lay any thing to the charge of God's elect? It is God that justifieth. (Rom. 8:33)

According as he hath chosen us in him before the foundation of the world, that we should be holy and without blame before him in love (Eph. 1:4).

God hath from the beginning chosen you to salvation. (2 Thess. 2:13; see also Matt. 24:31; 1 Peter 1:2)

Third, He called and conformed us.

And we know that all things work together for good to them that love God, to them who are the called according to his purpose. . . . To be conformed to the image of his son. . . . Moreover whom he did predestinate, them he also called. (Rom. 8:28–30a)

Fourth, He justified and glorified us.

And whom he called, them he also justified, and whom he justified, them he also glorified" (Rom 8:30b).

Fifth, He sent his Son to us.

To wit, that God was in Christ, reconciling the world unto himself, not imputing their trespasses unto them; and hath committed unto us the word of reconciliation. (2 Cor. 5:19)

Thanks be unto God for his unspeakable gift. (2 Cor. 9:15)

Sixth, with the Son He gives peace.

Grace to you and peace from God our Father, and the Lord Jesus Christ. (Rom. 1:7b; cf., 1 Cor. 1:3; 2 Cor. 1:2)

Seventh, He is the source of all good gifts

Every good gift and every perfect gift is from above, and cometh down from the Father of lights, with whom is no variableness, neither shadow of turning. (James 1:17)

The Father and the Angels

The Father stands in special relationship to all his creation, from human beings and the created universe to the angels and their spiritual dwelling. This includes both the angels who stand before God in worship and those who have rebelled against his authority.

The unfallen angels are servants of the Father in four particular ways:

1. They worship and minister to Him (Dan. 7:9–10; Rev. 4:2–3, 10–11).
2. They worship the Son at his command (Heb. 1:6).
3. Their every action is obedient to Him (Ps. 68:17; Matt. 26:53).
4. They are commanded to be ministering servants to God's people (Heb. 1:14).

Satan was originally created as a powerful, brilliant and talented cherub angel called Lucifer (Isa. 14:12; Ezek. 28:12–14). But Lucifer rebelled; He was judged by the Lord and cast out of heaven's fellowship (Isa. 14:13–15).

After the Son came to earth, there were occasions when the Father protected Him from the wiles of Satan. Christ was also protected when Herod was seeking to kill Him. An angel of the Lord warned Joseph to flee to Egypt (Matt. 2:13).

Jesus was protected at the synagogue in Nazareth when the crowd realized He claimed to be the Messiah. They carried Him out of the city and wanted to throw Him over a cliff. "But passing through their midst, He went His way" (Luke 4:30). Throughout His life, Jesus was protected from death until the time had come when He was to die. Hebrews tells us "He offered up prayers and supplications . . . to the One able to save Him from death, and He was heard because of His piety" (5:7).

The time will come when the Father will imprison Satan for one thousand years (Rev. 20:1) and will crush his final rebellion after the Millennium and cast him into the lake of fire forever (vv. 7–10).

The Father and the Unbeliever

God is the creator, having fashioned humankind in His own image and likeness. There are some disagreements about what the image of God comprises, but there seem to be two elements—one that cannot be lost, and another that can be lost.

Scripture suggests that every human being bears God's image, whatever their relationship with him (for example, 1 Cor. 11:7; James 3:8–9). With Noah, God institutes capital punishment for the unwarranted taking of life of a human being. He justifies such a heavy penalty on the grounds that an image-bearer is holy before God. A murderer should die for taking the life of another creature because this act is a direct assault on the image of God (Gen. 9:6).

The Bible teaches that unsaved men and women still display traces of the original image of God's creation. It has been suggested that fallen man resembles a beautiful European cathedral after it had been gutted by a Nazi bomb.

Of course, Scripture speaks as well of the image that can be lost. Paul describes the "new man" as the image-bearer who has been created after God in righteousness and true holiness" (Eph. 4:24; cf. Col. 3:9–10).

His wrath is upon all unbelievers for their rebellion, which forfeits the divine image (John 3:36; Rom. 1:18; Eph. 5:6; Gal. 3:6). Yet at the same time His long-suffering mercy is extended to unbelievers, because he desires their repentance (Rom. 2:4; 1 Tim. 2:4; 2 Peter 3:9).

The Father and the Believer

> *And it came to pass, that, as he was praying in a certain place, when he ceased, one of his disciples said unto him, Lord, teach us to pray, as John also taught his disciples. And he said unto them, When ye pray, say, Our Father which art in heaven, Hallowed be thy name. Thy kingdom come. Thy will be done, as in heaven, so in earth. (Luke 11:1–2)*

In His Sermon on the Mount (see also Matt. 6:9–13) Jesus must have shocked His listeners by inviting each believer to personally pray to the Father. In the Old Testament the First Person in the Trinity is referred to as "Father" only fifteen times (Gen. 26:24; 28:13; 1 Sam. 7:14; 2 Chron. 17:13; 22:10; Pss. 68:5; 89:26; 103:13; Isa. 22:21; 63:16; 64:8; Jer. 3:19; 31:9; Mal. 1:6; 2:10). Israelites never thought of him as their personal father, though occasionally they looked to him as Father of the entire nation. What an amazing contrast to find scores of New Testament references to our personal relationship as Christians with the Father.

Paul carries this a step further, describing an incredible intimacy between each child of God and the Father (Rom. 8:15–16; Gal. 4:6). John summarized this wondrous truth:

> *Behold, what manner of love the Father hath bestowed upon us, that we should be called the sons of God, therefore the world knoweth us not, because it knew him not. (1 John 3:1)*

The following list overviews the ministries performed through the atonement of Christ by the Father in each son and daughter.

- He foreknew us (Rom. 8:28; 1 Peter 1:2).
- He chose us in Christ (Luke 18:7; Rom. 8:29, 33; Eph. 1:5, 11; 1 Thess. 1:4; Titus 1:1; 1 Peter 1:2).
- He gave us to Christ (John 6:37, 44; 10:29).
- He called us (Rom. 8:28, 30; 1 Cor. 1:9; 2 Thess. 2:14).
- He justified us in Christ (Rom. 8:33).
- He sealed us through the Spirit (Eph. 1:13; 4:30).
- He ordained our works for him (Eph. 2:10).
- He sends his spirit to be in our hearts (John 14:23).
- He reveals truth to us (Matt. 11:25; 16:17; Eph. 1:17).
- He supplies our needs (Matt. 6:32–33; Phil. 4:19).
- He blesses us with spiritual blessings (Eph. 1:3).
- He is glorified by our fruitfulness (John 15:8).
- He loves us (John 14:21, 23; 2 Thess. 2:16).
- He honors us (John 12:26).
- He comforts us (2 Cor. 1:3–7; 2 Thess. 2:16).
- He keeps us (John 10:29; 17:11).
- He chastens us (Heb. 12:5–11).
- He restores us (Luke 15:21–24).
- He gives victory from temptation (1 Cor. 10:13).
- He makes us holy (John 17:17; Jude 1).
- He seeks our worship (John 4:23).
- He will gather us in Christ (Eph. 1:10).
- He will reward us (Matt. 6:1; Heb. 11:6; 2 Tim. 4:8).
- He will bring us into his kingdom (Matt. 13:43; 25:34; 26:29; Luke 12:32).

THE APPEARANCES OF THE FATHER

The Scriptures declare that "No man has seen God at any time" (John 1:18), because He is a Spirit, but nevertheless He has made Himself manifest in visual fashion to His servants on special occasions. These appearances are called theophanies. In the Old Testament He appeared to Moses (Exod. 24:9–10), Isaiah (Isa. 6:1–2), Micaiah (1 Kings 22:19), Ezekiel (Ezek. 1:26–27), Daniel (Dan. 7:9–12), and Habakkuk (Hab. 3:4).

In his Revelation vision, John saw the Lord "sitting on the throne" in heaven (4:2). He saw the emerald-like glow surrounding the throne (v. 3) and the flashes of lightning, and he heard the clashes of thunder (v. 5).

In the Old Testament, the prophet Ezekiel saw the Lord as the wondrous Being in glory (1:27–28). Daniel visualized Him as the Ancient of Days (7:9a); Habakkuk witnessed rays of brilliant light flashing from the Lord's hands (3:4).

THE GOODNESS OF THE FATHER

Jesus' parable of the prodigal son illustrates the goodness of the Father as clearly as does any teaching in Scripture (Luke 15:11–32). The story shows the grace of God, not simply in providing salvation for lost sinners, but more, in His eagerness to restore the wayward son. The central individual in the account is not the prodigal or his selfish brother; it is the father of these two boys.

While the son is off rebelling against Him, the father is watching. While the son is still a long way off, his father sees him (v. 20a). He "felt compassion for him, and ran and embraced him, and kissed him" (v. 20b). He clothed him with the best robe (v. 22a) and placed his own ring on his finger (v. 22b). He immediately invites his friends to a feast of celebration (v. 23) because "this son of mine was dead, and has come to life again; he was lost, and has been found" (v. 24).

How better to show the compassion of the Father of glory for His own? One can immediately see the connection between the actions of this earthly father to those of the heavenly Father to claim his sons or daughters!

THE MISSING THEME IN MUSIC

We began by lamenting the absence of theological books that exalt the person and work of the Father, as contrasted to the abundance of volumes that speak of the Son and Holy Spirit. This dearth also applies to gospel songs and hymns written during the twentieth century. Note a few older gospel songs and hymns related to the Son: "Tell Me the Story of Jesus," "Fairest Lord Jesus," "The Name of Jesus," "May Jesus Christ Be Praised," and "Jesus Paid It All." Songs relating to the Spirit include "Come Holy Spirit, Heavenly Dove," "The Comforter Has Come," "Breathe on me, Breath of God," "Holy Ghost with Light Divine," and "Spirit of God, Descend Upon my Heart."

Such songs have an important place in the worship of God, but many hymnals print fewer hymns dedicated to the Father and very few that have been written during the twentieth century. In some church traditions they are few and far between.

It is interesting that one of the most popular songs dealing with God as "father" was written as poetry just after the turn of the last century in 1901 and scored in 1915 by Franklin Sheppard. The author of "This is My Father's World" was Maltbie Babcock. Babcock was an athletic baseball player and champion swimmer who entered the pastorate. He kept in shape by running in the early mornings from his home in Lockport, New York, to the brow of a hill two miles away that overlooked Lake Ontario. From there he would run to a deep ravine that was inhabited with about forty species of birds.

Is it any wonder that a hymn extolling God's hand in nature should come from such a man.[5] "This Is My Father's World" was the capstone for Babcock's ministry, written not long before his death. Though specifically dealing with the writer's feelings about nature, the words praise the hand of the Father behind the beauty:

> This is my Father's world,
> And to my listening ears
> All nature sings, and 'round me rings
> The music of the spheres.
>
> This is my Father's world:
> I rest me in the thought
> Of rocks and trees, of skies and seas—
> His hand the wonders wrought.
>
> This is my Father's world,
> The birds their carols raise,
> The morning light, the lily white,
> Declare their Maker's praise.
>
> This is my Father's world:
> He shines in all that's fair;
> In the rustling grass I hear Him pass,
> He speaks to me everywhere.
>
> This is my Father's world,
> O let me ne'er forget
> That though the wrong seems oft so strong,
> God is the Ruler yet.
>
> This is my Father's world:
> The battle is not done;
> Jesus who died shall be satisfied,
> And earth and heav'n be one.

Perhaps the twenty-first century will restore something that has been lost in our churches, so that God the Father will be lifted up even more than in the past. The Holy Spirit speaks not of Himself but He glorifies Christ (John 16:14). And from His death and resurrection, the Son glories the Father (17:1).

CHAPTER 12

The Deity, Attributes, and Eternality of God the Son

Paul P. Enns

The doctrine of the deity and eternality of Jesus Christ is a foundational, bedrock Christian doctrine. Any deviation from this historic doctrine represents a departure from historic Christianity. There can be no compromise on the absolute deity of God the Son. Without the doctrine of the deity and eternality of Christ, there is no Christianity.

THE THEOLOGICAL ENVIRONMENT

Among Liberals

The issue of Christ's deity and eternality remains at the forefront of theological discussion today as much as it has in centuries past because it impinges on other doctrines. In espousing religious pluralism, John Hick realized that the uniqueness of Jesus represented a theological roadblock. The resolution? Dethrone Christ from His historicity. To do so, of course, Hick must discredit the New Testament Scriptures, stating "We should not think of the four Gospels as if they were eyewitness accounts by reporters on the spot. They were written between forty and seventy years after Jesus' death by people who were not personally present at the events they describe."[1]

Hick further suggests that it was not unique to Jesus to be called a "son of God." He concludes that Jesus' statements expressing His exclusiveness "are not pronouncements of the historical Jesus. Rather, they are words put into his mouth sixty or seventy years later by a Christian writer expressing the theology that had developed in his part of the expanding church."[2]

This is also the method of John Dominic Crossan of DePaul University. Crossan rejects the historicity of the Gospels and attributes claims of Christ's deity to the influence of Greek-Roman mythology.[3] Likewise, John P. Meier, Roman Catholic priest and professor at Catholic University of America in Washington, D.C., suggests that Jesus was born in Nazareth and was possibly married.[4] Both Meier and Crossan refuse to acknowledge the central element of orthodox Christian faith: Jesus is God.

Bill Phipps, moderator of the United Church of Canada, the largest Protestant denomination in the country, commented in an interview, "I believe that Christ reveals to us as much of the nature of God as we can see in a human being. I don't believe Christ was God."[5] By his own admission, Phipps stands outside historic Christianity.

Of course, these men are in error. Even the liberal theologian John A. T. Robinson has recognized the integrity and early-date writing of the New Testament documents.[6]

Globalization, a dialog movement among different nations and religions, has on its agenda the destruction of the Christian understanding of the uniqueness of Jesus Christ. Not surprisingly, the Association of Theological Schools (ATS) in the United States and Canada has made globalization a high priority, including "dialogue with other religions."[7] Liberal theologians have moved to recognize other religions on a par with Christianity at the expense of the uniqueness of Christ. They particularly find offensive any claims to exclusivity based upon Christ's deity and eternality.

Among Evangelicals

Such talk is to be expected from the liberals, but one must wonder in such uncertain times where evangelicalism now stands as a movement. Because the majority of seminaries and the largest seminaries within the ATS identify themselves as evangelical, Willard Erickson believes there may come "a progressive movement back toward absolutizing the person of Jesus."[8] Such a movement will not be progress if it does not recognize as nonnegotiable Christ's eternality and deity.

Ironically, if theological schools may be showing some hopeful signs, the evangelical arts are more doubtful. Especially within evangelical music, there is a "detheologized Jesus"[9] that appears to reflect a change in thinking. A hint in this might be seen in the overwhelming preference in lyrics to use the name *Jesus*, rather than *Christ*, by an overwhelming margin. This became particularly noticeable in the last quarter of the century. In the popular 1983 *Maranatha! Music Praise Chorus Book* the name *Jesus* occurs 222 times but *Christ* appears only twenty-one times.[10] Erickson draws a conclusion:

> "Jesus" is usually understood as referring to the historical personage of Nazareth, while "Christ" is often understood to refer to his deity. The name *Jesus* frequently appears in songs that place a strong emphasis upon

his humanity. Jesus is beautiful, wonderful, great; he is the friend and helper who meets our needs. But the name *Jesus* rarely appears in contexts that refer to his divine origin and virgin birth. This being the case, we can expect that continued singing of the current songs will tend to underscore the reality of the historical Jesus and of his humanity at the expense of emphasis on his deity. The upshot is that in the years ahead we can expect to find evangelicalism encountering some difficulties with belief in the deity of Christ. It is my expectation that there will be, at least on the popular level, a movement toward belief in a Jesus who is human, and in some sense a very unusual human, but not fully divine.[11]

This is sobering analysis. To counter this dangerous pursuit, evangelicals must reaffirm their commitment to the integrity and inerrancy of Scripture and diligently pursue the serious study of Scripture as foundational to a belief system. Such a system must stress the verbal, plenary inspiration of the Word of God as an entirely trustworthy basis for developing the doctrine of the eternality and deity of Jesus Christ.

An attack on the deity of Jesus Christ is an attack on the bedrock of Christianity. At the heart of orthodox belief is the recognition that Christ died a substitutionary death to provide salvation for a lost humanity. Had Jesus been only a man, He could not have died to save the world. Because of His deity, His death had infinite value, whereby He could die for the entire world.

THE DEITY DEBATE

A History of Attacks on the Doctrine

The consensus of the early church was clear and firm: Jesus Christ is deity, the second person of the Trinity. He is, therefore, eternal.

Ignatius (d. c. 117) affirmed the deity of Christ, referring to Him as "Jesus Christ our God" (Ign. *Eph.* 1; Ign. *Rom.* 1). Ignatius taught that, through the indwelling Holy Spirit, "He Himself may be in us as our God" (Ign. *Eph.* 15; Ign. *Magn.* 12). He also referred to the Savior as being the "mind of the Father" (Ign. *Eph.* 3); and as the "knowledge of God" (Ign. *Eph.* 17). Ignatius proclaimed the eternality of Christ in stating He was "with the Father before the world" (Ign. *Magn.* 6).

Polycarp (c. 70–155/160), the disciple of the apostle John, proclaimed the deity of Christ by referring to Jesus as "our Lord and God Jesus Christ" (Pol. *Phil.* 12).

The epistle to *Diognetus* in the late second century is one of the early apologetic writings of the Church. One of the truths the author wanted Diognetus to understand was the eternality of Christ: "This Word, Who was from the beginning. . . . Who is eternal" (*Diogn.* 11).

Orthodox Christians rejected the heretical wing of the Ebionites, as well as Arians, because they denied the true deity of Christ.

False theologies during the early centuries of Christianity, the docetists and Apollinarians for example, denied that Jesus Christ was human at all. These religions were baptized forms of Gnostic platonic idealism.

Medieval theology acknowledged the deity and eternality of Christ. John of Damascus (c. 675-749) taught that,

> The Logos assumed human nature, and not *vice versa,* that is, the man Jesus did not assume the Logos. This means that the Logos is the formative and controlling agency, securing the unity of the two natures . . . there is a co-operation of the two natures, and that the one Person acts and wills in each nature. The will is regarded as belonging to the nature, but it is claimed that in Christ the human will has become the will of the incarnate God.[12]

Martin Luther (1483-1546), Ulrich Zwingli (1484-1531), John Calvin (1509-1564), and their colleagues among the Reformers all acknowledged the deity and eternality of Christ.

It was only with the Enlightenment and the rise of naturalistic deism, unitarianism, and liberal theologies, that there was significant departure from belief in the deity of Christ among people who seriously identified themselves as Christian. The antisupernatural conclusions of the Enlightenment heresies were not drawn from Scripture, but from experience and reason—the new sources of authority.

Such cults as the Jehovah's Witnesses also deny the historic, biblical doctrines concerning Christ in His deity and eternality. Jehovah's Witnesses teach that Christ was actually the angel Michael[13] who was a creation of God.[14]

Some modern practitioners of the "health and wealth" gospel have been good at hiding their deviation from biblical orthodoxy concerning the person and nature of Christ. Some of these popular preachers and teachers found within the prosperity movement seem to waffle, so as to be harder to pin down on teachings that take them beyond the pale of Christianity. However, the evidence is firm that at least some of these false teachers deny the uniqueness of Jesus as the God-man. They teach that Christians are also deity, having the same authority and power as Christ. Kenneth Copeland has written most clearly of this, saying,

> You need to realize that you are not a spiritual schizophrenic—half-God and half-Satan—you are all-God. . . . Jesus was in right-standing with the Father during His earthwalk and the results He obtained were outstanding. As a child of God and joint-heir with Jesus, you

should expect to receive the same results. . . . Because you are in
Jesus, God sees you the same way He sees Jesus. He wants to treat
you like He treats Jesus—so let Him! . . . *You* are to think the way
Jesus thought. He didn't think it robbery to be equal with God. . . .
Jesus is no longer *the only begotten* Son of God.[15]

Kenneth Hagin certainly has rejected the unique deity of Christ, teaching
that Jesus assumed Satan's nature in order to become sin:

Jesus is the first person ever to be born again. Why did His spirit need
to be born again? Because it was estranged from God. . . . Spiritual
death also means having Satan's nature. . . . Jesus tasted death—spiritual death—for every man. . . . He became what we were. . . . Jesus
became sin.[16]

These purveyors of false doctrine deny the uniqueness of Jesus Christ in
His undiminished deity and unblemished, sinless humanity.[17] These teachings
must be labeled apostate.

Liberal theology has so twisted the deity of Christ that people raised in the
church may confess "Christ is God" and mean He is "God-like." Christ is
absolutely equal with the Father in His Person and His work. Christ is undiminished deity. C. S. Lewis wisely remarked,

I am trying here to prevent anyone saying the really foolish thing that
people often say about Him: "I'm ready to accept Jesus as a great
moral teacher, but I don't accept His claim to be God." That is the
one thing we must not say. A man who was merely a man and said the
sort of things Jesus said would not be a great moral teacher. He
would either be a lunatic—on a level with the man who says he is a
poached egg—or else he would be the Devil of Hell. You must take
your choice. Either this man was, and is, the Son of God: or else a
madman or something worse.[18]

Biblical Evidence

A proper belief system concerning the person of Jesus Christ for the twenty-
first century can only be derived from the Scriptures. What do Scriptures
affirm concerning the person of Jesus Christ? Do they declare His deity, as
Christians have historically believed? The inductive study of Scripture is paramount to resolving these questions.

The Scriptures are replete with personal claims by Jesus Christ, as well as
the testimony of others concerning His deity. The gospel of John is particularly rich in its emphasis on Christ's deity.

His Names

God. Jesus is expressly called God in the Scriptures. In Hebrews 1:8ff. the writer states the superiority of Christ to angels and ascribes Psalm 45:6–7 to Christ:

> *Thy throne, O God, is forever and ever; A scepter of uprightness is the scepter of Thy kingdom. Thou hast loved righteousness, and hated wickedness; Therefore God, Thy God, has anointed Thee with the oil of joy above Thy fellows.*[19]

The writer of Hebrews frames the quotation from Psalm 45 with the words, "But of the Son He says . . ." Further, the Greek vocative *ho theos* in "Thy throne, O God is forever" addresses the messianic King as full deity.[20] The reflexive construction of Psalm 45:6–7, which is carried over into Hebrews 1:8–9, shows God to be the anointer and God also to be the one anointed.

Upon seeing the wounds of the resurrected Christ, Thomas confessed unequivocally, "My Lord and My God" (John 20:28). John records that Thomas said the words to Jesus. It is unmistakable that Thomas addressed Jesus with these unique words. The phrase appears similar to Psalm 35:23 in David's prayer to God. Jesus never rebuked Thomas for his words, thereby accepting the accolade of Thomas. Leon Morris writes,

> Here we must evidently give the term all that it will hold. "My God" is a quite new form of address. Nobody has previously addressed Jesus in this way. It marks a leap of faith. In the moment that he came to see that Jesus was indeed risen from the dead Thomas came to see something of what that implied. Mere men do not rise from the dead in this fashion. The One who was now so obviously alive, though He had died, could be addressed in the language of adoring worship.[21]

Jesus is clearly referred to as God in Titus 2:13 in the phrase, "our great God and Savior, Jesus Christ." The grammatical construction *tou megalou theou kai sōtēros hēmōn Iēsous Christou* reflects the Granville Sharpe Rule: When two nouns are joined by *kai* (and) and when the first noun has the definite article (*tou*) and the second does not, the two nouns refer to the same thing. Hence, "great God" and "Savior" both refer to Christ Jesus.[22]

John 1:18 presents an interesting reading. The text says, "No man has seen God at any time; the only begotten God, who is in the bosom of the Father, He has explained Him." The phrase under study is "the only begotten God." The third edition of the United Bible Societies' Greek text gives the phrase *monogenēs theos* a "B" rating. That means there is fairly strong evidence from study of the ancient manuscript families that this is the same form as the original. It suggests a degree of doubt.[23] The textual evidence suggests the correct reading of John 1:18 is "the only begotten God" rather than "the only begotten Son." That being the case, this is a strong statement concerning the deity of Jesus Christ.

Lord. In debating the Pharisees, Christ argued that Messiah is greater than simply a physical descendant of David. He reminded them that David himself called Messiah "my Lord" (Matt. 22:44). But what is the meaning of *Lord* (*kyrios*)? In religious usage, linguist Walter Bauer says, it is used "as a designation of God."[24] So strong is this connection that *Lord* is used in the LXX as a translation of the Hebrew *YHWH* or "Yahweh." The word *kyrios* is used to translate the name of the Lord 6,814 times in the Greek Old Testament. Any Greek-speaking reader at the time of the New Testament who had any knowledge of the LXX would immediately have recognized that, in appropriate contexts, *Lord* was the name of the Creator and Sustainer of heaven and earth.

Frequently the New Testament uses Lord in what can only connect Jesus to this strong Old Testament sense. "The Lord" is Yahweh or God Himself.[25] Significant in this regard is Romans 10:9, 13. In verse 13 Paul quotes Joel 2:32: "Whoever will call upon the name of the Lord (*kyriou*) will be saved." This clearly identifies *kyrios* as meaning deity. In the same context, in verse 9, Paul addresses Jesus as *kyrion*—clearly a reference to Christ's deity. The same term denominating God in verse 13 is used of Jesus in verse 9.

This returns us to Hebrews 1 and its series of statements after the superscription "But of the Son He says. . . ." Verse 10 applies Psalm 102:12, 25 to Christ as "Lord":

> But Thou, O LORD, dost abide forever;
> And Thy name to all generations. . . .
> Of old Thou didst found the earth;
> And the heavens are the work of Thy hands.

Leon Morris remarks that *kyrios* "could also be used with reverence and awe, as when applied to the Deity. After the resurrection it was used of Jesus habitually."[26]

As the risen, glorified Lord, Jesus Christ is the object of worship. Every being in heaven, on earth, and under the earth will acknowledge Him as Lord (Phil. 2:9–11). That is only possible if He is God. Only in recognition of God do people bow the knee and worship.

Several times John refers to Christ as "Lord of lords and King of kings" (Rev. 17:14; 19:16), a title that has its origin as an ascription of God the Father (Deut. 10:17). Within the context of Deuteronomy, the Israelites are warned "to fear the LORD your God, to walk in all His ways and love him, and to serve the LORD your God with all your heart and with all your soul" (Deut. 10:12). The Lord is unique—He alone is God; He alone is Lord. The culmination of this truth will become evident when the eternal Christ returns triumphantly to establish the millennial kingdom on earth. At that time all the nations will recognize that Jesus Christ is "King of Kings and Lord of Lords" and will bow in submission to Him (Rev. 19:16).

Son of God. Jesus claimed to be the Son of God on numerous occasions (for example John 5:17-47). The term *Son of God* is frequently misunderstood; some suggest sonship implies inferior status. The Jews, however, understood the claim that Christ was making. By saying He was the Son of God, they recognized that he was "making Himself equal with God" (John 5:18c).

Commenting on the phrase "[Christ] existed in the form of God" in Philippians 2:6, "Old Princeton" theologian B. B. Warfield (1851-1921) said, "He is declared, in the most express manner possible, to be all that God is, to possess the whole fullness of attributes which make God, God."[27]

In his New Testament linguistic guide, Fritz Rienecker defines *morphē* ("form) as "the outward display of the inner realities or substance. [In Phil. 2:6] it refers to the outward display of the divine substance, i.e., divinity of the preexistent Christ in the display of His glory as being in the image of the Father."[28] This glory is manifested in several attributes reserved only for God.

Eternal One. See the discussion on the preexistence and eternality of Christ.

Omniscient One. When the people at the Passover Feast in Jerusalem exhibited their superficial belief in Jesus, He did not entrust Himself to them because He knew their fickle hearts.[29] When Jesus knew the past of the Samaritan woman (John 4:18) she recognized His omniscience (v. 19). The apostles also recognized Jesus' omniscience (16:30). Jesus' omniscience is particularly evident in the detailed explanation He gave the apostles concerning His death. He knew He would die in Jerusalem (Matt. 16:21; 20:18; 26:2), that the Sanhedrin would cause Him suffering (16:21), condemn Him to death (20:18), that they would deliver Him into the hands of the Romans (17:22; 20:19), that He would be mocked and scourged (20:19), killed by crucifixion (20:19; 26:2), and rise from the dead on the third day (16:21; 17:22; 20:19).

Omnipotent One. The apostle John unfurls the omnipotence of Jesus in recording signs of Jesus' complete control over every sphere.[30] Jesus revealed His omnipotence in the realm of quality by changing water into wine (John 2:1-11), in the realm of space by healing the nobleman's son from a distance (John 4:46-54), in the realm of time by healing the man at the pool of Bethesda, who had been sick for thirty-eight years (5:1-18), in the realm of quantity by feeding the five thousand (6:1-14), in the realm of nature by walking on the water (6:16-21), in the realm of misfortune by healing the blind man (9:1–41), in the realm of death by raising Lazarus from the dead (11:1–44). These "signs are the logical expression of deity in action."[31]

The ultimate expression of Jesus' omnipotence is His power to forgive sins—a prerogative of God (cf. Mark 2:5, 7, 10; Isa. 43:25; 55:7). Jesus has all authority (*exousia*) of heaven and earth (Matt. 28:18), a clear reflection of His deity.

Omnipresent One. Jesus evidences His omnipresence in His final promise to the apostles: "I am with you always" (Matt. 28:20). The omnipresence of Jesus is a significant doctrine for New Testament believers. Though Christ will eternally be seen in His glorified body, His Spirit abides within the believer. It is this constant, abiding presence that provides hope and comfort; His omnipresence enables believers to live righteously (Rom. 8:10). Through His presence the believer is crucified with Christ to the old life and alive to the new life—Christ Himself through His omnipresence living through the believers (Gal. 2:20). Here also the Greek text is emphatic: "Living in me is Christ!"

Immutable One. Unchangeableness is an attribute of deity, taught in both the Old Testament (Mal. 3:6) and New Testament (James 1:17). As a human being, Christ took upon himself the mutability of growing mentally and physically. But his will and constancy of love are the same as before the world began. The writer of Hebrews encourages the suffering believers that because Christ is immutable (Heb. 13:8), He has never and will never desert them (Heb. 13:5).

Underived life. All life in our own experience is derived life—human beings, animals, plants, the world—every living thing derives its life from its parental source. But Jesus Christ is unique. He has life in Himself. His life is not derived (John 1:4; 14:6). The imperfect *hen* stresses that the eternal life was continually existing in Christ. This life is *eternal,* and it *exists* in Christ.[32] Life is an attribute of deity; God alone has life independent of any source. The life God possesses is not derived; it is native to His nature.

Head of God's People. The Atonement, Resurrection, and ascension to the right hand of the Father confirm the divine Christ as the source of everything the church needs. In Ephesians 4:8 Paul describes the distribution of spiritual gifts as a result of the ascension of Christ. Paul quotes Psalm 68:18 in teaching that Christ gave spiritual gifts to believers when he ascended; however, Psalm 68:18 is a majestic psalm, extolling the greatness of God. Plainly, Paul equates Christ with God in Ephesians 4:8.

Creator. In a grandiose statement, John declares, "All things came into being through Him; and apart from Him nothing came into being that has come into being" (John 1:3). "All things" stands in the emphatic position in the Greek text, stressing that there is nothing that exists that has not been created by Christ. In fact, the aorist *egeneto*, "came into being" [the second occurrence] emphasizes that creation was a singular event.[33] Since Genesis declares the fundamental truth that "God created the heavens and the earth" (Gen. 1:1), John reminds us that Christ is indeed deity.

Paul corroborates John's thesis. He delineates Christ's creation as involving "both in the heavens and on earth, visible and invisible, whether thrones or dominions or rulers or authority—all things have been created through Him and for Him" (Col. 1:16). Paul attributes creation of the heavens and earth, humans and angels, the visible and the invisible to Christ—He is the Creator of everything. As Creator, Christ is God.

Sustainer. Not only is Christ creator, He is also sustainer—a corollary truth. In Christ "all things hold together" (Col. 1:17). The verb *synestēken* is a compound word, combining "together" and "to stand," hence, "to stand together," or "continue, endure, exist, hold together."[34] Not only is Christ the Creator of the universe, but as God He sustains it, holding it together. He is the principle of cohesion in the universe. Through his unity and solidarity the cosmos does not become a chaos.[35] Hebrews 1:3b states that Christ "upholds all things by the word of His power."

Forgiver. Christ deliberately confronted His opponents, forcing them to consider who He is with the statement, "My son, your sins are forgiven" when He healed the paralytic (Mark 2:5). The scribes rightly recognized that only God can forgive sins—that is an attribute of deity (Mark 2:6). When the sinful woman wept at Jesus' feet, He told her, "Your sins have been forgiven" (Luke 7:48). In declaring He forgave people their sins, Christ was stating in the strongest language possible that He is God. Only God forgives sin.

Miracle Worker. The miracles of Christ are an attestation of His deity. In sending a response to John the Baptist when the forerunner was confused, Jesus reminded him, "the blind receive sight and the lame walk, the lepers are cleansed and the deaf hear, and the dead are raised up and the poor have the gospel preached to them" (Matt. 11:5). Jesus claimed His messiahship before John the Baptist by reminding John that He was performing messianic miracles. But who performs miracles? It is God who gives sight to the blind (Ps. 146:8), who stills the storm (Ps. 107:29–30), who raises the dead (Ps. 49:15), who feeds the multitudes (Joel 2:22–24). When He performed His miracles, Christ revealed His deity. He was doing the works of God.

Object of Worship. Fundamental to biblical teaching is the truth that God alone is to be worshiped (Deut. 6:13; 10:20; Matt. 4:10; Acts 10:25–26). The fact that Jesus accepts worship attests to His deity. Not only does Jesus readily receive the worship of men but He commands that He be worshiped. In the strongest possible language, Jesus Himself commanded, "that all will honor the Son even as they honor the Father. He who does not honor the Son does not honor the Father who sent Him" (John 5:23). The nature of the honor to be accorded Christ is established by the phrase "just as" (*kathos*). Christ is to be honored *equally* with God the Father.

Jesus' equality with the Father in receiving worship is also reflected in the healing of the blind man. When the healed man discovered who Jesus was, he worshiped Him (John 9:38). In the act of worship, the man bowed down (*proskynēsen*), which was, as Raymond Brown points out, the unvarying Old Testament reaction to a theophany. John uses *proskynēsan* in John 4:20–24 to describe the worship due to God (cf. John 12:20).[36]

THE ETERNALITY OF JESUS CHRIST

Eternality is only one attribute of the Father that is shared with the Son, but the eternality and deity of Jesus Christ are inseparable. Those who deny His eternality also deny His deity. One doctrine assumes the other. Therefore, this topic is a good case study for looking at the Bible's witness to the divinity of Christ. If the deity of Christ is established, there is no problem in accepting His eternality.

The word *preexistence* is also used to define Christ's eternality. However, preexistence and eternality are not precisely the same. According to Brown,

> Preexistence of Christ means that He existed before His birth. For some writers it means that He existed before Creation and before time. But strictly speaking, preexistence is not synonymous with eternality. Practically speaking, they stand for a similar concept, for a denial of preexistence almost always includes a denial of eternality and vice versa. . . . Eternality means not only that Christ existed before His birth or even before Creation but that He existed always, eternally. Usually eternality and preexistence stand or fall together, though Arius taught preexistence of the Son but not His eternality. He insisted that if Christ was the Only Begotten He must have had a beginning. Jehovah's Witnesses today have an Arian-like Christology which denies the eternality of the Logos.[37]

The importance of the eternality of Christ is self evident. For if Christ did not exist until the birth of Jesus, there is no eternal Trinity. Jesus cannot be God now if he is not eternal. And he is shown to be a liar, because he claimed eternality. Such claims by Christ Himself and the assertions of Scripture demand that we accept his eternality.

Direct Proof

New Testament

John 1:1–2. In John 1:1–2, the word *was* in the phrase "In the beginning *was* the Word" is the Greek *hen,* the imperfect tense of *eimi*, which stresses continual existence in past time. The phrase could thus be translated, "In the beginning the Word was continually existing." John's beginning probably goes back to the origin of the universe; John indicates that however far back one goes, the Word was continually existing. Morris sets it in plain terms: "There never was a time when the Word was not. There never was a thing which did not depend on Him for its very existence. The verb 'was' is most naturally understood of the eternal existence of the Word: 'the Word continually was.'"[38] John 1:2 emphasizes the same truth: "He was in the beginning with God." The verb *was* (*hen*) emphasizes "in the beginning" Christ was "continually existing with the Father."

John 8:58. In commenting on John 8:58, radical feminist Christian Lore Weber says the Incarnation was not restricted to Jesus alone. She suggests the incarnation is a continuing process, resulting "in what is earth-created matter becoming transformed into God. . . . What distinguishes Jesus from the rest of us is that he knew, was conscious of, who and what he was. He knew he was God's Word; that is not to say the rest of us are not."[39] Obviously these are heretical words, standing outside of biblical and historic orthodoxy. The biblical record judges such statements, affirming the absolute uniqueness of Jesus as the eternal Son of God.

Although Abraham lived two thousand years before Christ, Jesus could say, "before Abraham was born, I AM." The present tense *eimi* (I am) is significant. Before Abraham was born, Christ was continually existing. The statement *I am,* of course, is also a reference to His deity and a claim of equality with Yahweh. *I am* ultimately takes the reader back to Exodus 3:14. There God identifies Himself as "I AM WHO I AM." Jesus claims both eternality and deity.[40]

John 17:5. In eternity past Christ shared the glory of God with the Father (John 17:5). *I had* (*eichon*) is the imperfect tense, stressing continuous action in past time. Christ continually shared the glory of God in eternity past; there never was a time when Christ did not have the glory of God.

Philippians 2:6. Prior to the Incarnation, Christ "existed in the form of God" (Phil. 2:6). In affirming that Christ has the very "form of God," Paul is not referring to a physical shape. Form (*morphē*) refers to that which is intrinsic and essential; it applies to the attributes of the Godhead.[41] The present participle *existed* (*hyparchōn*) emphasizes the continual existence of Christ in eternity past. Paul provides a strong statement confirming Christ's eternal existence as the second Person of the Godhead.

Colossians 1:17. In stating "He is before all things" (Col. 1:17a) Paul once more stresses the eternality and pre-existence of Christ. The present tense *is* (*estin*) emphasizes His eternal existence and sustaining power. Since Christ exists before all things, and since He created all things (v. 16), Paul clearly infers that Christ Himself is uncreated and therefore eternal. Before anything came into being, "He is" (*autos estin*)—He is continually existing; there never was a time when Christ did not exist. The statement demands Christ's eternality. Colossians 1:17b builds on 17a. Since Christ is eternal, He holds all things together; if He was not eternal, He could not hold all things together through His sustaining power.

Hebrews 1:8. As noted above, in 1:8 the writer of Hebrews begins a series of Old Testament quotations, prefacing with the superscription "But of the Son He says. . . ." Hence, the statements of verses 8–13 refer to Christ. The first statement, "Thy throne, O God, is forever and ever," (v. 8a) refers to the eternality of the Son. This is a profound statement because it emphasizes not just eternality, but eternal sovereignty.[42] Not only is the Son eternal, but He is the sovereign God, ruling from eternity to eternity.

Revelation 22:13. It is noteworthy that God's declaration, "I am the Alpha and the Omega," is used by the Lord God Almighty in Revelation 1:8, and by the Son in Revelation 22:13. The triple statement, "I am the Alpha and the Omega, the first and the last, the beginning and the end," all refers to eternality. Therefore, it is the divine Son's self-attribution of Divine prerogatives.[43] A prerogative of Deity—eternality—is applied to Son.

Old Testament

Isaiah 9:6. Since the subject of Isaiah 9:6 is the child that will be born and the Son that will be given, the title *Eternal Father* must refer to the Son. That is not to suggest there is confusion within the Trinity. The members of the triune Godhead share some of the same titles as they share the same attributes. The Son is not the Father, but the Son has father-like qualities; hence, the Son is called the *Eternal Father.* One of those attributes is given in the qualifying term *eternal.* Since the phrase *eternal Father* refers to the Son, it is a clear statement of the eternality of Jesus Christ.

Micah 5:2. It is indisputable that the subject of Micah 5:2 is Jesus Christ. The verse predicts Messiah's birth will be in Bethlehem. Matthew quotes the verse in describing the fulfillment of this prophecy (Matt. 2:6). Significantly, Micah describes the coming Messiah as one whose "goings forth are from long ago, from the days of eternity." The peculiar phraseology in Micah 5:2 is so expressed because man is bound by time in thought, but this statement of Micah incorporates the concept of eternity.[44] The Messiah is eternal.

Indirect Proof

Other Scriptures infer the eternity of Christ. The following are examples:

In John 1:3, Christ's preincarnate work proves His eternal existence. John's emphasis here is the dependence of all things on Christ for their being. *All* stands in the emphatic position in the Greek text, emphasizing that Jesus Christ has created absolutely everything that has been created. The inference is evident. If Jesus Christ created everything that has been created, then of necessity, He is uncreated and therefore eternal. If He is not eternal but created all things, He would have had to create Himself. This is an impossibility.

Christ's heavenly origin proves His eternal existence. In John 3:13 Jesus announced that He had descended from heaven, implying He had an existence in heaven prior to coming to earth. This corresponds to His other statements, teaching His eternal existence with the Father (John 17:5).

Christ's titles prove His eternal existence. John 12:41 says that Isaiah "saw His glory, and he spoke of Him," referring to Isaiah 6:1–5. The antecedent of *His* and *Him* is Jesus Christ, the subject in the preceding verses. Hence, John says Isaiah saw *Yahweh*, the Lord, and John identifies *Yahweh* as Jesus Christ. The Lord of the Old Testament is the Lord of the New Testament. Since *Yahweh* is eternal, Jesus is eternal. Similarly, in Matthew 22:44 Jesus quotes Psalm 110:1, "The LORD said to My Lord," and applies it to Himself. The name "Lord" is *Adonai*, one of the Old Testament names of God. Since Jesus is designated *Adonai*, He is eternal, for Adonai is eternal. In calling Messiah *the Lord*, David recognized that the Messiah would be more than simply a physical descendant of David. He would be God and therefore eternal (Matt. 22:45).

CONCLUSION

What doctrinal stand will the twenty-first century believers take concerning Jesus of Nazareth? Will the new century bring continuing commitment to his deity and eternality? Or will the church continue to be led astray by those who prefer a human, sympathetic Jesus to a divine, sovereign Christ? Will Christians be led astray by the Christology of the cults or by the aberrations of charismatic theology or by liberal theologians of such groups as the Jesus Seminar? This study has focused on analyzing the *biblical texts* concerning Jesus Christ, for there can be no other source of knowledge. The basis for our Christology must be the Scriptures. Twenty-first century believers will hold a view of Christ that is just as strong as their commitment to the Scriptures as inerrant. The Scriptures are clear—Jesus Christ is God.

CHAPTER 13

The Virgin Birth

Edward E. Hindson

The doctrine of the virgin birth of Christ is foundational to the entire New Testament theology of the person of Jesus Christ. It has been accepted by Christian believers from the earliest times as a factual account of the incarnation of the divine Son of God in human flesh through the miraculous virginal conception of Mary, the mother of Jesus. He had no biological human father.

Matthew 1:18-25 and Luke 1:26-38 emphasize that the birth of Jesus resulted from a miraculous conception in which He was conceived in the womb of the Virgin Mary, without male seed, by the power of the Holy Spirit. John M. Frame points out,

> If one rejects the possibility of miracle in general . . . then one must reject the virgin birth as well. But such a generalized rejection of miracles is arbitrary . . . indefensible . . . and contrary to the most fundamental presuppositions of Christian thought. The virgin birth is no more miraculous than the atonement or the resurrection or the regeneration of sinners.[1]

THE BIBLICAL DATA

Biblical references to the Virgin Birth are found in Isaiah 7:14, Matthew 1:18-25, and Luke 1:26-38. Allusions to this idea may also be inferred from even the Old Testament reference to the coming divine Savior in Genesis 3:15; Isaiah 9:6; and Micah 5:2. It is clearly understood in John 1:13, implied in Galatians 4:4, and in the background of texts about Jesus' relationship to his family and others, such as Mark 6:3. Beyond this, the Bible has little else to say about the Virgin Birth. A. N. S. Lane observes,

223

The paucity of references in the New Testament is sometimes given as an argument against the historicity of the doctrine. But it should be noted that the virgin birth is almost the only point in common between the two narratives [the birth narratives of Matthew and Luke], a clear indication that it is based on an earlier common tradition.[2]

Actually, there are several points of agreement between the two birth narratives. F. F. Bruce points out the Gospels' agreement "that Christ was born in Bethlehem, the son of Mary, who was affianced to Joseph, a descendant of David; but more particularly that Mary conceived him by the Spirit of God while she was still a virgin."[3]

Both Matthew and Luke use the specific Greek term *parthenos* to designate Mary as a "virgin." Despite the tendency of a few modern versions to use the translation "young woman," this particular New Testament term always refers to a woman (or with masculine grammatical endings, a man) who has had no sexual intercourse.[4] Thus, the biblical data clearly supports the doctrine that the incarnation of Christ in human flesh was accomplished through the Virgin Birth.

"Confirming the antiquity of this tradition is the remarkably 'Hebraic' character of both birth accounts," Frame observes. "This fact renders very unlikely the hypothesis that the virgin birth is a *theologoumenon*—a story invented by the early church to buttress its Christological dogma."[5] Ironically, this hypothesis is the typical challenge to the biblical data, yet in Scripture there is no evidence anywhere that biblical writers ever felt the need to question or defend the doctrine of the virgin birth.

Because of the theology of the fall that is worked out throughout Scripture, the Virgin Birth is vital to the gospel. The very character of Christ's sinlessness demands a miraculous birth. James Orr wrote in the original *Fundamentals*,

What happened was a divine, creative miracle wrought in the production of this new humanity which secured, from its earliest beginning, freedom from the slightest taint of sin. . . . The birth of Jesus was not, as in ordinary births, the creation of a new personality. It was a divine Person—already existing—entering on this new mode of existence. Miracle alone could effect such a wonder.[6]

TESTIMONY OF THE EARLY CHURCH

That Matthew, a Jewish believer, and Luke, a gentile convert, both refer to the Virgin Birth emphasizes its wide acceptance throughout the early church. Aside from the unsubstantiated theories of a few modern scholars, there is no evidence that this doctrine ever was in question, except among heretical fringe elements (notably Ebionites and the docetic Gnostics) who denied the whole idea of the Incarnation. There was remarkably unanimous acceptance of the validity of the Virgin Birth. For example,

- In A.D. 110, Ignatius clearly accepted the Virgin Birth as a well-established fact.
- The *Apostles' Creed,* based on the old Roman baptismal confession (c. 117), preserves a very early affirmation of belief in the Virgin Birth.
- Clear references to a belief in the Virgin Birth may also be found in the writings of Aristides (A.D. 125), Justin Martyr (c. A.D. 150), Irenaeus (A.D. 170), Tatian (A.D. 170), Clement of Alexandria (A.D. 190), and Tertullian (A.D. 200).[7]

Catholic theologian, Raymond Brown, surveys the evidence of the early church fathers and concludes that "by the year A.D. 200 the virginal conception of Jesus was 'in possession' as a Christian doctrine."[8] Presbyterian scholar J. Gresham Machen notes, "At about A.D. 110 belief in the Virgin Birth was no new thing; it was not a thing that had to be established by argument, but had its roots deep in the life of the church."[9] Machen goes on to point out that Ignatius's testimony holds particular significance since he was the bishop of the church at Syrian Antioch—the mother church of gentile Christianity.

THE SIGNIFICANCE OF OLD TESTAMENT PROPHECY

As early as Genesis 3:15 we see a hint at the Virgin Birth in the *protoevangelium.* The reference to the "seed of the woman" seems to deliberately preclude the male counterpart. The obscurity of this prophecy does not eliminate its significance. The fact that it follows such a dramatic event as the Fall seems all the more reason to view it as pointing ahead to the coming Savior.[10]

Micah 5:2 has long been recognized for its prediction of the place of Christ's birth at Bethlehem (see Matt. 2:4–6). But we should also observe that Micah's prophecy also points to the One who is coming as the messianic ruler of Israel whose "going forth are from long ago, from the days of eternity." Charles Feinberg points out that the terminology of this passage emphasizes the pre-existence of the Messiah in the "strongest possible statement of infinite duration in the Hebrew language."[11]

Sign of Immanuel

The *Immanuel prophecy* (Isa. 7:1–12:6) is the foundational passage for the Old Testament doctrine of the Virgin Birth. In these chapters the prophet Isaiah introduces the sign of Immanuel, the virgin's son, as well as the coming child who will rule on David's throne. Children play a key role in the prophetic symbolism in these chapters, and each is mentioned as a "sign" from God.

Three basic positions have been taken historically by commentators in the interpretation of this passage: (1) Immanuel is the Messiah; (2) he is a person living in the prophet's own time; (3) he is somehow both. Roman Catholic and Protestant scholars held the first view exclusively prior to the eighteenth century. However, with the rise of a non-messianic view, some evangelicals, beginning with Albert Barnes (1840), began to suggest a dual fulfillment. This approach views the prophecy as both a reference to an immediate event in the prophet's own time and a distant reference to the coming Messiah.[12]

The prophetic portion of chapter 7 (vv. 10–16) begins by emphasizing that the "LORD spake again unto Ahaz" (v. 10) by the prophet Isaiah, who urged the Judean king to "ask thee a sign" (ʾōt) of God's miraculous intervention. Surprisingly, Ahaz refused to ask for God's help with the pious excuse that he would not "tempt the LORD" (v. 12).

In response to the king's refusal to ask for a sign from God, Isaiah announced that God would give the "house of David" (the royal Davidic line) a sign of His own. In view of the eventual conquest of Judah by the Babylonians, future generations of Jews would need the assurance that the Messianic line would survive. While the Davidic line will appear to be cut down, out of its roots will come the Branch, Immanuel, the Child Ruler who will fulfill all of these prophecies. Thus, the entire section (7:1–12:6) should be seen as a unit with one prominent person in view throughout.

Therefore (*lākēn*) is a connective word often used by the prophets to introduce a divine declaration. In this context it is a transitory word used to unify verse 14 with the preceding statements. *Behold* (*hinnēh*) is always used to arrest the attention. When used with a participle it is an interjection, introducing either present or future action. The term here calls attention to an important birth (see similar announcements in Gen. 16:11 and Judg. 13:5). Thus, one is to look with anticipation to the virgin and her son, who are announced as central figures of this prophecy.

Identity of the Virgin

The interpretive controversy in this passage hinges on the translation of the Hebrew word *ʿalmâ* and the time of action implied in her pregnancy. Since the nineteenth century, commentators have debated whether *ʿalmâ* should be translated "virgin" or "maiden." The underlying issue is whether the passage really predicts the Virgin Birth of Christ. The Hebrew text uses the definite article (*hā*) to indicate "the" virgin as a specific person, not a generalized idea. There can be little doubt that a definite woman is in view. Whoever she is, the prophet is clearly aware of her distinctiveness.

The argument in the interpretation of the passage has centered around the meaning of *ʿalmâ*. All agree that it denotes a young woman above the age of childhood who has matured sexually and is of age to marry. The word is unique and uncommon, appearing only nine times in the Old Testament. The more common Hebrew term for "virgin" is *bĕtûlâ*. But in spite of its frequent usage to denote a virgin, *bĕtûlâ* is used in at least two passages (Deut. 22:19 and Joel 1:8) to refer to a married woman or young widow.

The biblical usage of *ʿalmâ* consistently distinguishes it as a precise designation for unmarried girls. In the case of Rebekah (Gen. 24:43), she is called both an *ʿalmâ* and a *bĕtûlâ*, showing that both words could be used interchangeably to indicate an unmarried virgin. However, unlike *bĕtûlâ*, the term *ʿalmâ* is never used of a married woman. Therefore, Isaiah chose the more precise, though uncommon, term to identify clearly the nature and character of the "virgin." Linguistic scholar, Cyrus Gordon, writes,

> The commonly held view that "virgin" is Christian, whereas "young woman" is Jewish is not quite true. The fact is that the Septuagint, which is a Jewish translation made in pre-Christian Alexandria, takes *almah* to mean "virgin" (Greek, *parthenos*) here. Accordingly, the New Testament follows Jewish interpretation in Isaiah 7:14.[13]

While *ʿalmâ* may not be the common word for "virgin," there is little basis for denying that it means "one who is a virgin." At the same time, the common word for "virgin" (*bĕtûlâ*) lacks the precision of the more distinctive term *ʿalmâ*. If Isaiah intended to convey a prediction of the Virgin Birth he chose the right word with which to do it.

Another crucial issue in the interpretation of 7:14 is whether the verbal elements of the passage indicate present or future time. The standard translation has been "shall conceive and bear a son" (KJV). The Hebrew form *hārâ* is neither a verb nor a participle but a feminine adjective connected with an inactive participle ("bearing"). The verbal adjective describes the state of pregnancy, and the participle is used in Hebrew to denote the present tense.

Shall conceive should actually be translated "pregnant." Thus, the prophet points to a "pregnant virgin who is bearing a son." The scene, though future in its fulfillment, is present to the prophet's view. Edward Young discussed this point at length to show conclusively that the virgin is already pregnant and bearing a son.[14] The context makes it clear that the virgin is pregnant and is still a virgin.

One cannot escape the conclusion that this is a picture of the Virgin Birth of the Messiah.

Identity of Immanuel

Matthew forms a "bridge" to the Hebrew Scriptures from the life and ministry of Christ. More than any other gospel he quotes from the Old Testament and relates its theology, law, and prophecy to the events of Christ's life. So it is not surprising that in 1:23 Matthew quotes Isaiah 7:14. The Matthew text reads (NASB), "'Behold, the virgin shall be with child, and shall bear a son, and they shall call His name Immanuel;' which translated means, 'God with us.'"

There are three ways to look at Isaiah's conception of the Messiah in the light of Matthew's New Testament identification of Jesus as Immanuel:

1. Isaiah did mean to refer to Christ, and Matthew's interpretation is correct.
2. Isaiah did not refer to Christ, and Matthew is wrong.
3. Isaiah did not refer to Christ directly, but Matthew saw an application to apply to Him.

Immānû'ēl is the symbolic name of the child, meaning "God with us." He is undoubtedly the same one who is mentioned in connection with the land (Isa. 8:8) and the one who is the "Prince of" four titles (9:6–7). In regarding Jesus as Immanuel, Matthew quotes Isaiah 7:14 as being fulfilled in the Virgin Birth of Christ (Matt. 1:23).

Even if one attempts to argue that Matthew merely followed the LXX in using the Greek *parthenos* for *'almâ*, he followed the source that represented the oldest available interpretation of Isaiah 7:14.

Parthenos is also commonly used to translate *'almâ* in the Qumran (Dead Sea) Scrolls. G. A. F. Knight concluded that it is difficult to escape the fact that the oldest Jewish texts in Greek, the LXX and the Qumran scrolls, use *parthenos* to translate *'almâ*.[15] The significance of this observation is that *parthenos* is the most precise Greek word to indicate a "virgin."

The Coming Prince

Isaiah continues to look to the future coming of the Messiah as the solution to Judah's problems. His predictions of a coming child prince (9:6–7) and the branch of Jesse (11:1–5; 11:10–12:6) point to the Messiah.

The child who is to be born will be a light to the "nations" (*gôyim*, "gentiles") and will shine in Galilee (Isa. 9:1). Matthew (4:15–16) also takes this to be a Messianic prophecy fulfilled in Jesus' ministry in Galilee. The Gift-Child (9:6–7) is certainly the same person as Immanuel (7:14 and 8:8). Using the prophetic perfect, the prophet speaks of this child-ruler as though he were already born.

The fourfold title emphasizes the uniqueness of this Gift-Child. He is a "wonderful counselor" (*pele' yō'ēṣ*), the two words serving as an appositional genitive. He is "the mighty God" (*'ēl gibbôr*), clear reference to His deity and the explanation of how Immanuel could be "God with us" and miraculously born of a virgin. The Child is God Himself incarnate. He is also called "the everlasting Father" (*ʾăbîʿad*), literally the "father of eternity." Finally, He is designated as the "prince of peace" (*sar-shālōm*). Thus, His reign will be characterized by peace on earth because He is the embodiment of peace.

In the eleventh chapter, Isaiah sees him as the branch out of the rootstock of Jesse (David's father). He pictures the Davidic line as a tree that will be cut down, but out of its roots will spring up the "rod" and "branch" of future hope.

The prophet predicts that the Spirit of the Lord will "rest upon him" (11:2), and he will rule by the "rod [or scepter] of his mouth." Thus, he foresees the rule of the Messiah by the power of His Word and of the Spirit. Therefore, the Immanuel prophecy ends in a great crescendo of praise for His rule of peace on earth. "JEHOVAH is my strength" (12:2 KJV), and "the Holy One of Israel" is present with you (12:6).

NEW TESTAMENT FULFILLMENT

The context of Matthew 1:2–3 is the visit of the angel to Joseph to reassure him that Mary's condition of pregnancy is a conception "of the Holy Spirit," obviously implying that it is not the result of adultery.

The indication is also presented here that there is, therefore, no human father involved in this birth. Joseph is told that the child will be a boy and is to be named Jesus, "for it is He who will save His people from their sins." Next comes the quotation from Isaiah prefixed by the statement, "Now all this took place that what was spoken by the Lord through the prophet might be fulfilled" (v. 22). Awaking from his sleep, Joseph did as commanded and married Mary and "kept her a virgin until she gave birth to a son; and he called his name Jesus" (v. 25).

The purpose of biblical prophecy was to prepare for the coming of Christ so clearly that His coming would be recognized as a fulfillment of such prophecy when compared to it. Either this passage was clear to Matthew or else it was not. There have been those who think Matthew was not correct in what he was doing. Probably a more comfortable critical position is to attempt to retain Matthew's intent but reject his method.[16]

Pre-Christian Jewish interpretation of the Messiah in Isaiah 7:14 is supported in the Talmud. The Jewish writer J. Greenstone states that the Talmud reflects a concept of a divine Messiah with supernatural qualities and deeds. He sees the rabbinical interpretation of Isaiah 7:14 as a "development of the ideal of the Messiah child." He also finds reference to the birth of Messiah in the apocalyptic book of Zerubabel.[17]

Use of *Parthenos*

We have observed that the LXX, translated in the third century B.C., uses *parthenos* to translate the Hebrew *ʿalmâ*. This would indicate the interchangeable use of those terms in pre-Christian Judaism. Greek translations of Hebrew among the Dead Sea Scrolls show this to have been the case. The Qumran literature in Greek consistently uses *parthenos* to translate *ʿalmâ*.

Nearly all contemporary commentators maintain that Matthew's usage of *parthenos* in place of *ʿalmâ* in the quotation of Isaiah 7:14 reflects the LXX. However, the insinuation has frequently been made that the LXX translation (and therefore Matthew's use of it) is wrong. We have considered the argument over the Hebrew term *ʿalmâ*, which many feel should not be rendered "virgin." So they say Matthew should not have used the Greek term *parthenos*, which is always to be interpreted "virgin." The argument is not simply whether *parthenos* and *ʿalmâ* are interchangeable linguistically in ancient literature generally, but whether they are interchangeable specifically in Isaiah 7:14. Was the LXX wrong in using *parthenos*.

Its general use in literature is an important argument that *parthenos* was used properly in place of *ʿalmâ*. It certainly argues that Jews c. 200 B.C. believed that Isaiah was referring to a virgin. It is, then, unfair to conclude that Matthew is inaccurate in following this historic precedent. If *ʿalmâ* can possibly be translated "virgin," and if this was the interpretation of most ancient authorities, it would seem reasonable that the LXX and Matthew correctly use *parthenos*.

If the LXX, Qumran scrolls, and some early rabbinical commentators saw Isaiah 7:14 as a virgin-birth prediction, Matthew also had historical precedent for his interpretation of the passage. Frequently in the Gospels we encounter Jewish anticipation of the Messiah. Matthew's use of Isaiah 7:14 would probably have found ready acceptance by the general Jewish populace. The bulk of historical evidence supports an inter-testamental period view of Isaiah's prediction of a virgin-born Messiah. This evidence is the best early support of a messianic interpretation of Isaiah 7:14.

Usage of *Plērōthē*

Matthew's use of *plērōthē* (1:22) indicates that he definitely saw a predictive fulfillment of Isaiah's prophecy in Christ. This form, "to fulfill," is found frequently in the first gospel. Broadus states that the usual meaning implies real prediction.[18] Lenski adds, "The verb, *plērōthē* pictures the promise or prophecy as an empty vessel which is at last filled when the event occurs."[19] BAGD renders *plērōthē* in Matthew 1:22, "the fulfillment of divine prediction or promise."[20] Matthew stands in the way of anyone who wishes to deny early church acceptance of the predictive element of Isaiah. It cannot be done on a philological-grammatical basis, as has been attempted.

It is clear that Matthew regarded the prophecy's origin as being from God. He states that it was "spoken by the Lord through the prophet" (1:22). He, therefore, recognized that the sign given in Isaiah 7:14 was God's revelation, delivered to Ahaz through the prophet. When accompanied by a passive verb the preposition *hypo* ("by or by means of") introduces the direct agent of the action (in the genitive case). The second preposition, *dia*, shows the mediate agent for whatever action is being accomplished. Following this classic grammatical form, Matthew can only be saying that the actual speaker is *Yahweh* and the prophet is the one through whom He speaks. "God is the *cause efficiens* (*hypo*), God's agent the *causa instrumentalis* (*dia*)."[21]

Conservatives are criticized for accepting Matthew's statement at face value. Yet look at the evidence. If Matthew followed the LXX in using *parthenos*, he followed the oldest available interpretation (by translation) of Isaiah 7:14's ʿ*almâ*. His contextual usage of *plērōthē* is almost certainly indicative of his understanding the Isaiah passage to contain a predictive element. His recognition of the prophecy as coming from God shows that he believed his "interpretation" of it was also of God.

Within the Greek construction, it is even possible that verses 22–23 are not Matthew's narration at all, but are simply his recorded quotation of the angel's reassuring declaration to Joseph. Whether the angel or Matthew, we know that the apostles were taught the interpretation of messianic prophecy by the resurrected Jesus (Luke 24:27, 44–47). Therefore, to say that Matthew made a mistake is to say that either the angel also made a mistake or Jesus Christ made one and passed it on to Matthew.

THEOLOGICAL IMPLICATIONS

The doctrine of the Virgin Birth is inseparably related to the concept of the incarnation of Christ. The Incarnation at once affirms both the deity and humanity of Christ. F. F. Bruce states, "If there is, among the distinctive articles of the Christian faith, one which is basic to all the others, one is it this: that our Lord Jesus Christ, the eternal Son of God, became man for our salvation." Bruce goes on to explain that this means that "one Who had His being eternally within the unity of the Godhead became man at a point in time, without relinquishing His oneness with God."[22]

The Incarnation means that God became fully human without ceasing to be fully divine. The apostle John expresses this incarnation of the divine into the human when he writes, "And the Word became flesh, and dwelt among us, and we beheld His glory, glory as of the only begotten from the Father, full of grace and truth" (John 1:14 NASB). Jesus expressed it this way:" He who has seen me has seen the Father" (John 14:9b NASB).

The Virgin Birth is clearly taught in the New Testament as the means by which the Incarnation was accomplished. While some argue that the two are not necessarily mutually dependent, an Incarnation without the Virgin Birth is much more difficult to understand. The real issue is the sinlessness of Christ. Can a sinless God become truly human without Himself becoming sinful, since all human beings are sinful by nature. There would have to be an arbitrary declaration, but that would impugn the holiness and justice of God—the very reasons the Incarnation was necessary.

It is obvious that the New Testament writers and the early Christian believers accepted the Virgin Birth as the explanation of *how* the incarnation of the sinless Son of God was accomplished. So should we.

John Frame lists doctrines that are at stake in relation to the Virgin Birth:[23]

1. *Doctrine of Scripture.* If we cannot trust what the Bible teaches about the Virgin Birth, how can we trust what it says about the deity of Christ, His atonement for our sins, or His bodily resurrection?
2. *Deity of Christ.* Eliminating the Virgin Birth from the Incarnation leaves us at a loss to explain how the divine Son of God could enter the human race without the taint of sin and still be fully human and fully divine at the same time.
3. *Humanity of Christ.* Without a human birth, the true humanity of Christ would be in question. Early Christians emphasized that Jesus was really born and was really one of us, in contrast to the beliefs of the Gnostics. Even Ignatius of Antioch, a minister contemporary to the aged apostle John, went to great lengths in his epistles to stress that Christ was human as well as divine.
4. *Sinlessness of Christ.* If Jesus had been born of two human parents, how could he have been exempted from Adam's sin nature. How could he become a "second Adam," a new head for the human race. His sinlessness is possible by the sanctifying "parentage" of the Holy Spirit.
5. *Doctrine of Salvation.* There is no salvation as we know it without the Virgin Birth, the Incarnation, and the sinlessness of Christ. Only the virgin born, sinless Son of God can die for our sins. Otherwise He is, as some theologians suggest, a self-appointed, radical martyr—the victim of His own inadequacy.

TWENTIETH-CENTURY DEVELOPMENTS

Almost a century ago, the Scottish theologian and writer James Orr wrote on "The Virgin Birth of Christ" for the original volumes of *The Fundamentals*. In his article he emphasized that this doctrine "affects the whole supernatural estimate of Christ—His life, His claims, His sinlessness, His miracles, His resurrection from the dead."[24] In defending the importance of the doctrine, Orr observed, "Placed in its right setting among the other truths of the Christian religion, it . . . is felt to fit in with self-evidencing power . . . and to furnish the very explanation that is needed of Christ's holy and supernatural Person." Orr quoted A. B. Bruce, who had observed that "with the denial of the Virgin Birth is apt to go denial of the virgin life."[25]

This was perhaps the most insightful comment in his essay. The nineteenth century had known the skeptics "quest for the historical Jesus." Skeptics in the twentieth century imagined they had found him in their revisionistic theories of a fallibly human Jesus. It was the essence of what Bruce predicted. Both Karl Barth (1886–1968) and Rudolf Bultmann, (1884–1976), following J. G. Wilhelm Herrmann (1846–1922), abandoned hope of finding the "real" Jesus, and sought only an existential encounter with God.[26]

In most twentieth-century theologies, the real person of Jesus Christ is dethroned and replaced by an obscure and marginal reflection of changing societal values. John A. T. Robinson extended Bultmann's demythologizing of Christ to the Person of God Himself.[27] Others focused on the "self-understanding" of Jesus as the basis for the Christian proclamation.

In the second half of the twentieth century, Wolfhart Pannenberg, Jürgen Moltmann, Edward Schillebeeckx, and Hans Küng all proposed views of Christ that attempted to explain away the biblical explanation of his divine and human natures. In the 1980s the liberal "scholars" of the "Jesus Seminar" even made secular world news when they voted on which aspects of the biblical record they believed to be true, and which were fanciful and mythological additions by the early Church.

TWENTY-FIRST-CENTURY PROJECTIONS

We can suppose that radical reinterpretations of the person of Christ will continue. Tragically, however, in a society that is increasingly illiterate about the Bible, such interpretations are likely to be taken more seriously by the general public than ever before. The influence of the Jesus Seminar already shows that.

The liberal theological contingent now routinely dismisses or ignores the "myth" of the Virgin Birth. Catholic theologian Raymond Brown has pointed out that, in the past, the denial of virginal conception has often been accompanied by a denial that Jesus is the Son of God.[28]

The challenge to the doctrine of the Virgin Birth in the twenty-first century will be similar to the challenges facing all of Bible-centered Christology. T. W. Manson wrote,

> The supreme task of New Testament scholarship is to make Jesus Christ crucified a living reality in the . . . lives of men and women in these days, and to renew in them the awe, wonder, faith and courage He inspired in men and women who knew Him in the days of His flesh.[29]

Kenneth Kantzer observes, "The Jesus of history is the Jesus of the New Testament just as He is there portrayed—the virgin-born, miracle-working, vicariously dying and resurrected incarnation of God."[30] John R. W. Stott adds, "There is Jesus the Bultmannian myth and Jesus the revolutionary fire-brand, Jesus the failed superstar and Jesus the circus clown. It is over against these human reinterpretations that we need to recover and reinstate Jesus, the Jesus of history who is the Jesus of Scripture."[31]

Stott expresses it best when he says,

> The ultimate question is absolutely plain, even to the man on the street . . . it is this: Is Jesus to be worshipped or only admired? If he is God, then he is worthy of our worship, faith and obedience; if he is not God, then to give him such devotion is idolatry.[32]

In the generations to come, the temptation will be to qualify the doctrine of the Virgin Birth. With absolutism giving way to relativism, any waffling will be disastrous to the church of Christ on earth. Against forces who downplay Christ's unique birth there can be no compromise.

CHAPTER 14

The Nature and Purpose of the Suffering and Death of Christ

Russell L. Penney

The death of Jesus Christ, God and man, for the sins of lost human beings seems especially foolish to the unregenerate mind. Yet in his letter to the church in Corinth, the apostle Paul clarified the importance of Christ's death, burial, and resurrection. He wrote,

> Now I make known to you, brethren, the gospel which I preached to you . . . by which you are saved. . . . For I delivered to you as of first importance what I also received, that Christ died for our sins according to the Scriptures, and that He was buried, and that He was raised on the third day according to the Scriptures. . . . For if the dead are not raised, not even Christ has been raised; and if Christ has not been raised, your faith is worthless; you are still in your sins. . . . If we have hoped in Christ in this life only, we are of all men most to be pitied. (1 Cor. 15:1–4, 16–17, 19)[1]

Paul's point is that the content of *the gospel message* is the message of the death, burial, and resurrection of Jesus Christ, and it is the only message that brings salvation. It is a message about a death that brings life. But why is the death, burial and resurrection of Jesus Christ so vitally important in the salvation of a soul? This can only be understood if one is clear about what the Bible teaches about the nature of God, and the nature and purpose of the events of Christ's death, burial, and resurrection. The resurrection of Christ is dealt with in another chapter in this volume. This chapter deals specifically with the nature and purpose of the death and burial of Christ. Obviously, if this is part of the content of the gospel itself, holding to or denying an orthodox position in this area of doctrine will have a tremendous effect on evangelistic and missionary efforts in the twenty-first century. To deny what the Bible teaches in this area will destroy the faith, for this is the heart of the Christian faith.

THE NATURE AND PURPOSE OF THE DEATH OF CHRIST

Errant views throughout church history have failed either because they did not take into account all that the Scripture states about the death of Christ, or because they did not consider the scriptural evidence at all. A proper view of the nature and purpose of the death and burial of Christ must begin with a proper view of Scripture. The following evidence assumes that the reader holds to a strong view of inspiration and inerrancy (see ch. 4, "The Revelation, Inspiration, and Inerrancy of the Bible"). It follows an "authorial-intent" view of hermeneutics (see ch. 3, "The Importance of Hermeneutics"). Only an authoritative book can yield to us an accurate and authoritative message.

The Nature of God

God Is Holy

A proper view of the nature and purpose of the death of Christ must start with a proper view of the nature of God. It is the character of God that made the death of Christ necessary. The first attribute clearly attested to in Scripture that contributes to our understanding of the purpose for Christ's death is the holiness of God. Henry C. Thiessen said that the fact that God is holy "means that God is absolutely separate from and exalted above all His creatures, and He is equally separate from all moral evil and sin."[2] Much scriptural proof could be set forth to defend this doctrine but a few verses will verify our statement.

After God had done the mighty miracle of dividing the waters of the Red Sea allowing the children of Israel to escape and then had slammed the waters back down on the Egyptian army, Moses' song of response is recorded (Exod. 15:1–18). With the Lord's humiliation of the pagan gods of Egypt still fresh in their memories, "Moses and the sons of Israel" sang, "Who is like Thee among the gods, O Lord? Who is like Thee, majestic in *holiness*, Awesome in Praises, working wonders?" (v. 11).

Later, in giving the Levitical laws, in Leviticus 11:44–45, God emphasizes the reason for this all-encompassing ceremonial cleansing system when he states, "For I am the Lord your God. Consecrate yourselves therefore, and be holy; for I am holy. . . . For I the Lord brought you up from the land of Egypt, to be your God; thus you shall be holy for I am *holy*." The Leviticus text shows that God is holy and that those with whom God identifies Himself *must* be holy as well. The unholy cannot relate to him.

God Is Righteous

The Bible also tells us that God is righteous. Psalm 67:4 states, "Let the nations be glad and sing for joy; For Thou wilt judge the peoples with uprightness, And guide the nations on the earth. *Selah*." The psalmist writes in 145:7, 17, "They shall abundantly utter the memory of thy great goodness, and shall sing of thy righteousness. . . . The LORD is righteous in all his ways, and holy in all his works" (KJV; see also 2 Chron. 12:6; Dan. 9:14; 2 Tim. 4:8). Charles Ryrie writes,

> Though related to holiness, righteousness is nevertheless a distinct attribute of God. Holiness relates to God's separateness; righteousness, to His justice. Righteousness has to do with law, morality, and justice. In relation to Himself, God is righteous; i.e., there in no law, either within His own being or of His own making, which is violated by anything in His nature. In relation to His creatures He is also righteous; i.e., there is no action which He takes that violates any code of morality or justice.

Since righteousness is an essential part of God's character, He cannot dismiss sin without proper payment for that sin. Imagine a judge dismissing a murder case simply because the murderer said he was sorry, and showed deep remorse for his crime. Such a judge may be deemed compassionate toward the murderer (though certainly not toward the victim's family). He would certainly not be classified as righteous, since he did not carry out a sentence of justice. But God is righteous; He always deals with his creatures justly. As Thiessen writes, "The righteousness or justice of God is that aspect of God's holiness which is seen in his treatment of the creature."[3] Thus, since God is righteous it means that He demands punishment of sin.

The Nature of Man

The Fall

It is also impossible to understand the nature of Christ's death without understanding the nature of each human being. God's original creation of humanity was perfect (Gen. 1:31). Adam and Eve were made in the image of God (1:26–28). Although theologians disagree about all that this image comprises, at the very least it means that, of all God's creatures, only humankind shares with God the communicable attributes of spiritual life, personhood, and the ability to ethically comprehend truth, wisdom, love, holiness, and justice. Only people can reason logically, feel emotion, and relate spiritually to God. Adam and Eve had the added attribute of a favorable disposition toward God. They had direct fellowship with their Creator (1:28–30; 2:15–25; 3:8–9).

Adam and Eve in Eden received responsibilities and one prohibition. The responsibilities included being fruitful and multiplying, subduing the earth, and ruling over it (1:28). The prohibition was that they not eat of the tree of the knowledge of good and evil (2:17).

The fall into sin occurred when Satan, indwelling the serpent (cf. Rev. 12:9; 20:2), tempted Eve to disobey God's prohibition. Satan succeeded, through half-truth and seeds of doubt, in his aim of planting the fear that God is unjust. God diminishes in her mind as she half-heartedly defends him to the serpent (Gen. 3:1-3). Then Satan directly impugns God's character by calling him a liar: God's motive in the prohibition is that he doesn't want to share His own unique deity (Gen. 3:4-5). Satan had successfully created doubt in Eve's mind, and her response was to take her focus off God. She observed that the tree was good for food, it was attractive to the eyes, and that it could increase her wisdom. Once the woman ate of the fruit, she shared the fruit with the man and he, without any apparent deception, made a choice to eat. Thus did humanity fall into depravity (Gen. 3:14-19; Rom. 5:12).

Results of the Fall

Paul summarizes what happened in the Fall in his great theological treatise to the Roman believers. Paul describes a desperate spiritual state. He shows the need of the whole human race by condemning the gentile (1:18-32), the moralist (2:1-16), and even the Jew (2:17-3:8). Then comes his "grand finale" of condemnation on all humankind, which he accomplishes by stringing together a litany of Old Testament quotations:

> As it is written, "There is none righteous, not even one;
> There is none who understands,
> There is none who seeks for God;
> All have turned aside, together they have become useless;
> There is none who does good,
> There is not even one."
> "Their throat is an open grave,
> With their tongues they keep deceiving,"
> "The poison of asps is under their lips;"
> "Whose mouth is full of cursing and bitterness";
> "Their feet are swift to shed blood,
> Destruction and misery are in their paths,
> And the path of peace have they not known."
> "There is no fear of God before their eyes." (Rom. 3:10-18)

Romans 1:18-3:20 discloses the extent of human depravity as a result of the Fall. Corruption permeates human nature; there is no human action that could merit saving favor with God.[4] When Adam fell spiritually in the garden it plunged the entire human race into sin. Paul makes this clear in Romans 5:12 where he explains original sin and its results. He writes, "Therefore, just as through one man sin entered into the world, and death through sin, and so death spread to all men, because all sinned" (Rom. 5:12).

Paul's assessment is in line with the entirety of Holy Writ's description of unregenerate:

- They are apostates from the womb, and as soon as they are born they go astray (Ps. 58:3).
- The sin nature is part of the human composition, even in the womb (Ps. 51:5).
- The heart's intent is evil from childhood throughout life, even in those who outwardly live out a moral and even a self-sacrificial ethic (Gen. 8:21).
- Lifestyle and relationship and thought life are shaped by the evil heart (Prov. 4:23).
- Acts of sin freely flow as expressions of the natural heart, which is deceitful and "desperately sick" (Jer. 17:9).

Thus, not only do we commit sins; we are sinners by nature. *Sin (hamartia)* is defined as missing the mark: The term was used in athletic competition when a javelin missed the target. God has a target, a standard of morality, but none live up to it. God demands perfect righteousness in order for us to have a relationship with Him (Hab. 1:13). Martin Luther stated, "We are not sinners because we commit sins—now this one, now that one—but we commit these acts because we are sinners before we do so: that is, a bad tree and bad seed produce bad fruit, and from an evil root nothing but an evil tree can grow."[5]

THE ATONEMENT OF CHRIST

Our Sacrifice

After his condemnation of man in Romans 1:18–3:20, Paul returns to his central theme to more fully explain "the righteousness of God" (Rom. 1:16–17): "But now apart from the Law the righteousness of God has been manifested, being witnessed by the Law and the Prophets" (Rom. 3:21). Although God gave the Jews the Law, it was never meant to be a way of salvation (Rom. 3:20; Heb. 10:4), but the Mosaic law was given alongside the Abrahamic Covenant as a basis of fellowship with God for the Jews (Galatians 3). It spoke of the righteous demands of God. The sacrifices were a continual reminder of the penalty of sin. In fact, the sacrifices looked forward to the ultimate sacrifice by God's Son. In John 1:29 John the Baptist pointed out Jesus to two of his disciples and stated, "Behold, the lamb of God who takes away the sins of the world!" People have always been saved by God's grace through Christ's righteousness, as Paul shows in Romans 4.

Paul says the "righteousness of God" that has been manifested is "the righteousness of God through faith in Jesus Christ" (Rom. 3:22). Paul addressed the questions "How do we receive this righteousness?" and "To whom is this righteousness available?" Paul says that we receive this righteousness by faith and that it is available for all who believe. This righteousness is available because, as we have already seen, we are all in need, "For all have sinned and fall short of the glory of God" (Rom. 3:23). We all fall short of God's perfect standard of righteousness, and we have to meet that standard to stand before a Holy God. As we will see, this perfect standing of righteousness is provided by faith only on the basis of the shed blood of Jesus Christ (vv. 24–26). To solve our sin problem, Christ became the substitute for mankind.

Some modern scholars have asserted that the idea of the atonement is a pagan concept. B. B. Warfield, in his monumental work, *The Person and Work of Christ*, responds to those who attempt to argue that Christ's work on the cross was not a sacrifice for sin:

> Is there no sacrificial suggestion in such language as this: "Whom God set forth as a propitiation, through faith, in His blood"? [Rom. 3:25] Or in such language as this: "While we were yet sinners Christ died for us: Much more than having been now justified by His blood, we shall be saved by Him from the wrath"? [Rom. 5:8–9] Or as this: "And by Him to reconcile all things unto Him, having made peace through the blood of His cross"? [Col. 1:20]: Or as this: "In whom we have redemption through His blood, the forgiveness of sins"? [Eph. 1:7] Or as this: "But now in Christ Jesus you who once were far off have been made nigh in the blood of Christ"? [Eph. 2:13]. This is the very language of the altar: "propitiation," "reconciliation," "redemption," "forgiveness."[6]

In Warfield's day of a century ago, as today, liberal scholars attempted to explain away the substitutionary death of Christ by reinterpreting the emphasis the writers of Scripture place on the blood of Christ. Warfield reacts to such interpreters in bewilderment:

> It passes all comprehension how it could be suggested that the word "blood" could be employed in such connections [referring to the verses quoted above] "merely in allusion to Jesus' violent death." And that particularly when Jesus' death was not actually an especially bloody death.

". . . Why is precisely the "blood" of Jesus so often spoken of? Why is the redemption and the forgiveness of sins so often connected with the "blood" of Jesus? This is remarkable; for the death on the cross was not so very bloody that it should be precisely that blood of Jesus which so impressed the eye-witnesses and the first Christians. The Evangelists moreover (except John xix. 35 f.) say nothing about it. This special emphasis on the blood cannot be explained therefore from the kind of death Jesus died. If we really wish to know what the New Testament writers had in mind when they spoke of the blood of Jesus we have only to permit them to tell us themselves. They always adduce it in the sacrificial sense.[7]

Propitiation

If God is holy and just and man is sinful, the wrath of the judge against the lawbreaker is on all people. A. H. Strong writes that "though love makes the atonement, it is violated holiness that requires it; and in the eternal punishment of the wicked, the demand of holiness for self-vindication overbears the pleading of love for the sufferers."[8] The Bible uses at least twenty Hebrew terms to refer to God's wrath in the Old Testament. About 580 references have been counted (for example Job 21:20; Jer. 21:12; 23:25; Ezek. 24:13). Sin is the reason for God's wrath, especially the sin of idol worship (for example, Deut. 6:15; Josh. 23:16; 2 Kings 13:3; 23:25; Ezek. 8:18; 16:38).

Charles Ryrie, who made this study of the wrath of God, observes that in Romans 3:25 the Old Testament scholar Paul links propitiation of God's wrath with the death of Christ.[9] Paul states that Christ's death on the Cross was a *hilastērion* "propitiation." This interesting Greek word was used in the Greek Old Testament, the Septuagint (LXX), of the "mercy seat," over the Ark of the Covenant (Exod. 25:17–22, cf. Heb. 9:5). On the Day of Atonement each year the High Priest would enter the Holy of Holies and sprinkle blood on the "mercy seat" to cover the sins of the nation of Israel (Leviticus 16).

Leviticus 16:15–16a explains the reason for the Day of Atonement: "Then he [Aaron the High Priest] shall slaughter the goat of the sin offering which is for the people, and bring its blood inside the veil, . . . and sprinkle it on the mercy seat and in front of the mercy seat. And he shall make atonement for the holy place, because of the impurities of the sons of Israel, and because of their transgressions, in regard to all their sins."

This was to meet God's righteous demands to punish sin. This Old Testament "type" was ultimately fulfilled when Christ offered his blood on the cross to satisfy those same righteous demands to punish our sin. Christ became our "mercy seat."[10]

John and the writer of Hebrews also use derivatives of *hilastērion*. John writes, "Jesus Christ the righteousness . . . *is* the propitiation [*hilasmos*] for our sins; and not for ours only, but also for *those of* the whole world" (1 John 2:1b–2). The writer of Hebrews uses the verb form: "Therefore, He had to be made like His brethren in all things, that He might become a merciful and faithful high priest in things pertaining to God, to make propitiation (*hilaskesthai*) for the sins of the people" (Heb. 2:17). The word *propitiation* carries the meaning of "satisfaction." John communicates the truth that this propitiation was (*peri tōn hamartiōn ēmōn*) "for our sins." He means that the propitiation (satisfaction) of God's wrath is in relation to our sin. The writer of Hebrews confirms that the propitiation is directed toward God and His righteousness. It was a *substitutionary atonement* of the righteous demands of a holy God.

Although C. H. Dodd and other liberal scholars have argued against the idea that God requires satisfaction for His holy wrath, Leon Morris has shown conclusively that *hilasmos* carries the meaning of propitiation. Morris writes: "The uniform acceptation of the word in Classical Greek, when applied to the Deity, is the means of appeasing God, or averting His anger; and not a single instance to the contrary occurs in the whole Greek literature."[11]

The result of Christ's propitiatory work on the cross is that

1. God is justified in forgiving sins.
2. God is justified in bestowing righteousness. God imputes to us the righteousness of Christ by faith
3. God is2 justified in bestowing grace on sinners for whom the propitiation is applied.

The *first* reason for the death of Christ is clearly that the wrath of God should be satisfied through the blood of Christ. Paul Enns writes, "Propitiation is *Godward;* God is propitiated—His holiness is vindicated and satisfied by the death of Christ."[12]

One last note is that the resurrection of Christ verifies that the propitiatory work of Christ on Calvary was acceptable to appease God's holiness and justice and thus to avert His anger on those who appropriate redemption through faith.

Redemption

Such justification is a declaration of righteousness. Paul states that it is a gift "by His grace through the redemption [*apolytrōseōs*] which is in Christ Jesus" (Rom. 3:24). *Apolytrōseōs* is from *apolytrōsis*, a noun that means "release, pardon, dismissal, deliverance."[13] It is used nine other times in Scripture (Luke 21:28; Rom. 8:23; 1 Cor. 1:30; Eph. 1:7, 14; 4:30; Col. 1:14; Heb. 9:15; 11:35), but rarely outside the sacred text. Walvoord writes that of the ten occurrences of *apolytrōsis* in the New Testament, only Hebrews 11:35 does not refer to redemption in Christ. The nine occurrences that definitely relate to Christ's sacrifice "substantiate the idea of deliverance by payment of a price."[14] This is affirmed in Romans by Paul's point in 3:25 that God was propitiated ("satisfied") by the blood of Christ on our behalf. A payment was applied, so that freedom could be offered as a gift. This doctrine is affirmed in the other nine passages (cited above) where the term *apolytrōsis* is found.

The related verb form *lytroō*, meaning "to redeem or release by payment of a price," is used three times in the New Testament (Luke 24:21; Titus 2:14; 1 Peter 1:18-19).[15] The passage in Luke deals with Israel's national deliverance, but the references in Titus and Peter are most definite in meaning the individual release of believers by the payment of Christ's blood. Titus writes that the Christian looks for the appearing in glory of "our great God and Savior, Christ Jesus; who gave himself for us, that He might redeem *[lytrōsētai]* us from every lawless deed and purify for Himself a people for His own possession, zealous for good deeds." Peter uses a passive form of *lytroō* in discussing how his readers should conduct themselves, "knowing that you were not redeemed *[elytrōthēte]* with perishable things like silver or gold from your futile way of life inherited from your forefathers, but with precious blood, as of a lamb unblemished and spotless, the blood of Christ" (1 Peter 1:18-19).

The noun form, *lytron*, occurs two times in the New Testament, both clearly supporting the teaching that Christ's death was substitutionary and redemptive (Matt. 20:28; Mark 10:45). Christ Himself states that "the Son of Man did not come to be served, but to serve, and to give His life a ransom for many *[lytron anti pollōn*, lit. "a ransom instead of the many"]" (Matt. 20:28). In this verse and the nearly identical construction of Mark 10:45, there is a clear view that the death of Christ constituted the ransom by which the sinner is set free. The depraved man is a slave of Satan, this world, and bound in his nature, but at the point of faith he is set free, redeemed to serve God (Romans 6-8).

The New Testament uses two other Greek words to express and expand this idea. The first is *agorazō*, meaning to "buy at the market place" (1 Cor. 6:20, 7:23; 2 Peter 2:1). *Exagorazō* is a compound of *agorazō* and *ek* ("out of"), meaning that believers have been bought at the market place and released out of it (Gal. 3:13; 4:5). Paul writes, "Christ redeemed us from the curse of the Law, having become a curse for us—for it is written, 'Cursed is everyone who hangs on a tree'" (Gal. 3:13). The substitutionary and redemptive nature of Christ's death is clear.

The last word used in this regard is *peripoieō*. Luke writes, "Be on guard for yourselves and for all the flock, among which the Holy Spirit has made you overseers, to shepherd the church of God which He purchased *[periepoiēsato]* with His own blood (Acts 20:28). Walvoord writes,

> In contrast to the use of *agorazō* which would emphasize the idea of purchase, the verb used here has more the thought of the result of the

action, that the church has been "acquired." The idea is therefore one of possession rather than emphasis on the act of purchase. This is also true of 1 Timothy 3:13. [16]

The acquisition of the church was "with His own blood." This realization brings with it a great responsibility for those who oversee this body for the Savior. He died for it.

Ryrie succinctly summarizes the argument for our understanding of redemption: First, people are redeemed *from something* ("the marketplace of slavery to sin"). Second, they are redeemed *by something* (the blood of Christ). Third, they are redeemed *to something* (the freedom of slavery to the Lord). "Redemption is viewed *manward*," said Ryrie. "Mankind was in bondage to sin and in need of release from bondage and slavery to sin."[17]

This is a life transforming truth. We were released from an evil bondage to the privilege of enslaving ourselves to our Redeemer and a life of righteousness.

Reconciliation

Walvoord writes of the reconciliation aspect of the atonement:

> Few doctrines are more important in a total theology than the doctrine of reconciliation. Though based on comparatively few specific references, reconciliation has been hailed as a doctrine of "vital concern both for doctrinal clarity and pulpit vitality."[18]

In relation to this vital doctrine Paul writes, "We . . . exult in God through our Lord Jesus Christ, through whom we have now received the reconciliation" (Rom. 5:11). The term Paul uses is *katalassō*. It means "to exchange, to exchange enmity for friendship." Reconciliation means a change of relationship from hostility to harmony and peace.

Paul's emphasis in 5:6–11 is on the peace that God has accomplished between himself and the regenerate (5:1) through the death of His Son. He points out that in our unregenerate state we were "helpless" (v. 6), unrighteous (v. 7), sinful (v. 8), and enemies of God (v. 10). It is more than not being able to do anything to become reconciled to God; people in this state have no desire to be reconciled (cf. Rom. 3:10–18). With this context, it is clear that God had to initiate the reconciliation. God reconciled us ("through whom *we have now received* the reconciliation," v. 11) to Himself. The means of the reconciliation as being the death of Christ is stated over and over in the context (i.e., "Christ died for the ungodly," v. 6; "one will hardly die for a righteous man," v. 7; "Christ died for us," v. 8; "by His blood," v. 9; "through the death of His Son," v. 10). Since we were in a state of complete inability to reconcile ourselves to God, God reconciled us to Himself through the blood sacrifice of His Son on the cross.

Romans 5 is a central passage in the New Testament on reconciliation, but of equal theological weight is 2 Corinthians 5:17–21. Paul writes,

> *Therefore, if any man is in Christ, he is a new creature; the old things passed away; behold, new things have come, Now all these things are from God, who reconciled us to Himself through Christ, and gave us the ministry of reconciliation, namely, that God was in Christ reconciling the world to Himself, not counting their trespasses against them, and he has committed to us the word of reconciliation. Therefore, we are ambassadors for Christ, as though God were entreating through us; we beg you on behalf of Christ, be reconciled to God. He [God the father, v. 20] made Him [Christ, v. 20] who knew no sin to be sin [a sin offering] on our behalf, that we might become the righteousness of God in Him. (2 Cor. 5:17–21)*

Paul's statement in verse 17, "If any man is in Christ, he is a new creature," is built grammatically and theologically upon his point in verse 16. Paul writes in verse 16 that he now looks at each person he meets in relation to that person's standing in Christ. In Romans 5:6–11 the person without Christ was said to be helpless, unrighteousness, sinful, and in open enmity with God. In 2 Corinthians we see the positives to those negatives. If we are "in Christ" (v. 17) we are a "new creature," because the "old things [have] passed away." The old things are our helplessness, unrighteousness, sinfulness, and enmity with God. Since these things passed away, "new things have come." The new things are the direct opposite of the "old thing." We are empowered through the Spirit, we are righteous and holy in Christ before God, and we are at peace with God.

Our "new creature" status is in no way our own merit. It is "from God" (2 Cor. 5:18), "who reconciled [*katallaxantos*] us to Himself through Christ." God not only reconciled us to Himself, but He also "gave us the ministry of reconciliation." What a privilege this affords us to be used of God to take part in helping others partake of what we have received. Communicating the gospel to the ends of the earth is the mode through which God is reconciling the world unto Himself. In all our human frailty and inadequacy, God has given us the honor to have the ministry of reconciliation.

Paul goes on to clarify what it means that we have the ministry of reconciliation. In verse 19 he writes, "God was in Christ reconciling the world to Himself, not counting their trespasses against them, and he has committed to us the word of reconciliation." Of this, Richard Lenski comments,

> What does Paul say? That what God has finished from him and for his helpers (aorist *katallaxanto*) he is still busy with (durative present

participles) in regard to the world, namely that individuals in it; that in steadily working at this reconciling and not reckoning to men their transgressions God employed Paul and his helpers in the ministry which he gave them with the word of reconciliation that he deposited with them. This work began when Christ died, when "God was in Christ," when he wrought the objective reconciliation "through Christ" (v. 18). That objective reconciliation included the whole world. But it must be brought to the world, to be made a personal possession by Faith, a personal, individual reconciliation by means of the ministry of the reconciliation and the word of the reconciliation.[19]

God through Christ's death provided reconciliation for the world, but it is only effective individually after the one who needs reconciliation places personal faith in Christ. Paul tells the basis for reconciliation in 5:21: "He [God the father, v. 20] made Him [Christ, v. 20] who knew no sin to be sin on our behalf, that we might become the righteousness of God in Him." Here Paul points out the sinless nature of Christ (cf. Heb. 4:15). This sinless Savior took on himself the sin of the world (John 1:29; 1 Peter 2:24; 1 John 2:2).

Paul's literal statement in the Greek is that Christ was "made sin" (*hamartian epoiēsen*). This has been taken in different ways by expositors. Some believe that a good rendering here would be that Christ was "made a sin offering," in line with the sacrificial concept. But H. Vorländer and Colin Brown speak for the majority of conservative Bible scholars:

> It may be too specific to say that Paul is thinking here of Christ as a "sin offering." The normal LXX expression for "sin offering" is *peri hamartias* . . . "for a sin offering." The term *peri hamartias* is actually found at Rom. 8:3, but commentators generally prefer to take it in the wider sense of "for sin" rather than that narrower one of a particular OT type of sacrifice.[20]

Paul sets a parallel between Christ "becoming sin" and the believer "becoming righteousness." Just as the believer is reckoned as righteous (cf. Rom. 4:5), Christ was for a brief time in history reckoned as sin. Murray Harris adds, "Just as 'the righteousness of God' is extrinsic to us, so the sin with which Christ totally identified himself was extrinsic to Him."[21] Christ took our sin so that God's righteousness could be imputed (placed on our account); thus we could be reconciled to God. Walvoord summarizes,

> In its broadest sense, the work of reconciliation extends to the total work of God on the behalf of the believer, while redemption is active toward the payment of the price for sin, and propitiation is directed to

satisfaction of the righteousness of God. Reconciliation, then, deals with man's total need and total restoration.[22]

Above, Paul Enns observed that propitiation is "godward." The rest of his statement is that "reconciliation is *manward;* man was the one that had moved out of fellowship because of sin, and man needed to be reconciled to renew the fellowship."[23]

THE EXTENT OF THE ATONEMENT

Much debate has occurred over the extent of the Atonement. Even among these who hold to the radical depravity of humanity, there is disagreement. Some believe that Scripture teaches that the blood of Christ was shed only for the elect. Other's hold that Christ's blood was shed as a provision for the reconciliation, propitiation, and redemption of all—that it was without limit as to its provision for all. In this view, the whole human race was potentially reconciled to God.

Texts Indicating a Select Atonement

Both groups agree that some texts clearly mark out a group who are particularly atoned for, indicating that Christ died for that select group. For example, the following verses in context show an atonement for a specific group.

He was pierced through for our transgressions, He was crushed for our iniquities. (Isa. 53:5)

"And she will bear a Son: and you shall call His name Jesus, for it is He who will save His people from their sins." (Matt. 1:21)

"I am the good shepherd; the good shepherd lays down His life for the sheep." (John 10:11)

"I ask on their behalf; I do not ask on behalf of the world, but of those whom Thou hast given Me; for they are Thine." (John 17:9)

"Be on guard for yourselves and for all the flock, among whom the Holy Spirit has made you overseers, to shepherd the church of God which He purchased with His own blood." (Acts 20:28)

Husbands, love your wives, just as Christ also loved the church and gave Himself up for her. (Eph. 5:25)

In these passages it is clear that not all are included among those for which Christ died. If there were no other texts on the subject, it would be hard for those committed to an authoritative text to hold that Christ's atonement was unlimited. The problem one encounters is that other passages indicate that Christ did not die *exclusively* for an "elect."

Texts That Argue Against Exclusivity

John 3:16. Probably the most beloved and memorized verse of all the Bible is John 3:16: "For God so loved *the world*, that He gave His only begotten Son, that *whoever* believes in Him should not perish, but have eternal life." Many who hold to limited atonement teach that "the world" is here used in a restricted sense meaning "people from every tribe and nation—not only the Jews."[24] This seems to be an artificial restriction since in the same verse and the previous verse John uses the word "whoever" in reference to the potential believer who will receive eternal life. In addition, Enns points out, "The *world*, as John describes it, is God-hating, Christ-rejecting, and Satan-dominated. Yet that is the world for which Christ died" (cf. John 1:29; 3:16–17; 4:42; 1 John 4:14).[25]

Lewis Sperry Chafer notes that *whoever* occurs at least 110 times in the New Testament—always with an unrestricted sense (cf. John 3:16; Acts 2:21; 10:43; Rom. 10:13; Rev. 12:17.[26] Context does not support the conclusion of anyone who uses "whoever" in any limited atonement sense. Only if the verse is forced into a theological framework can one reach such a conclusion. Normal exegesis of the passage supports an unlimited atonement.

Those who hold to a limited atonement have more sticky textual problems with such passages as 2 Corinthians 5:14–15, 19; 1 Timothy 2:6; 1 Peter 2:1; and 1 John 2:2.

Second Corinthians 5:14–15, 19. We have discussed 2 Corinthians 5:14–15, 19 in considering reconciliation. It bears on our discussion here as well.

> *For the love of Christ controls us, having concluded this, that one died for all, therefore all died; and He died for all, that they who live should no longer live for themselves, but for Him who died and rose again on their behalf. . . . Namely, that God was in Christ reconciling the world to Himself, not counting their trespasses against them, and He has committed to us the word of reconciliation.*

Paul distinguishes between the *all* (occurring three times in vv. 14–15) for whom Christ died and "they who live." Jesus died for all (a universally sufficient provision) but it is efficiently applied only to the elect ("those who live"). Paul states on this basis, "Therefore, we are ambassadors for Christ." Using the conjunction *gar* ("therefore") in another equally valid sense, the phrase could be translated "for this cause" we are ambassadors for Christ.

The basis of our position as ambassadors is the fact the God has provisionally reconciled the world unto Himself.

First Timothy 2:6. In 1 Timothy 2:6, Paul writes to Timothy that Christ "gave Himself as a ransom for *all,* the testimony borne at the proper time" (1 Tim. 2:6). Paul had just stated in the context that "God our Savior . . . desires all men to be saved and to come to the knowledge of the truth" (2:4). The all in verse 6 would certainly be referring back to "all men" (v. 4) and "men [humankind]" (v. 5). It should be clear from this passage that Christ's ransom was for all people.

Second Peter 2:1. Another difficult passage for limited atonement advocates is 2 Peter 2:1. Peter writes, "But false prophets also arose among the people, just as there are also to be false teachers among you, who will secretly introduce destructive heresies, even denying the Master who *bought* ["redeemed," *agorasonta,* from *agorazō*] them, bringing swift destruction upon themselves." The immediate context is that false teachers are destined for eternal punishment. They are "bringing swift destruction upon themselves." God will "keep the unrighteous under punishment for the day of judgment" (v. 9). False teachers will be destroyed with all the other unreasoning animals (v. 12). They are "accursed children" (v. 14). Yet Peter states that the Master bought these very people. The word *agorazō* for "bought" is the same word that is normally translated redeemed. These false teachers then have been provisionally redeemed, but have not been effectively redeemed because they have not believed in the Master.

First John 2:2. First John 2:2 reads, "and He Himself [Jesus Christ the righteous, v. 1] is the propitiation for *our sins;* and not for ours only, but also *for those of the whole world.*" Here John is discussing the fact that as "little children" we have a provision for our sins through the propitiatory work of Christ. On that basis we can confess our sins to the Father through our Advocate, Christ Jesus. John states that "He Himself *is* the propitiation [satisfaction] for our sins." God's wrath was effectually diverted from us as "little children." But John goes beyond that when he states, "and not for ours only, but also *for those of the whole world.*" The word *world* is used in a similar way in 3:1 where John states, "For this reason, the world does not know us, because it did not know Him." Here John is clearly not referring to "classes of people" but to the unbelieving world as a whole.

In light of the above evidence, what can we say about the individual elements involved in the atonement of Christ previously discussed (i.e., propitiation, reconciliation, and redemption)? Each of these works of Christ were provisionally provided for the world but Scripture is also clear that they must be appropriated by faith by each individual before the benefits are applied. Regeneration and the impartation of faith to the believer must occur simultaneously for the benefits of Christ's work to be applied immediately to the believer.

RESULTS OF TRUST IN THE ATONEMENT

Forgiveness

Since Christ's death satisfied the righteous demands of God to punish sin, we can receive forgiveness through faith. Enns explains that "forgiveness is the legal act of God, whereby He removes the charges that were held against the sinner because proper satisfaction or atonement for those sins has been made."[27] In Ephesians 1:7 the apostle Paul states that in Christ "we have redemption through His blood, the forgiveness of our trespasses, according to the riches of His grace." The Greek word Paul uses here is *aphesis* which carries the idea of pardon or the canceling of an obligation or punishment or guilt.[28] Our sins are forgiven. As Paul puts it in Colossians, "He made you alive together with Him, having forgiven us *all* our trespasses" (Col. 2:13b).

Justification

In Romans 3:24 Paul states that justification is "a gift by His grace." The word *justify* (*dikaioō*) was a legal term in Paul's day as in ours. It meant "to be pronounced and treated as righteous." Even though we are not righteous *experientially* when we receive Christ as our Savior, we stand in the "position" of the righteous before the Father if we are in Christ. Enns gives this definition:

> To justify is to declare righteous the one who has faith in Jesus Christ. It is a forensic (legal) act of God whereby He declares the believing sinner righteous on the basis of the blood of Christ. The major emphasis of justification is positive and involves two main aspects. It involves the pardon and removal of all sins and the end of separation from God (Acts 13:39; Rom. 4:6-7; 5:9-11; 2 Cor. 5:19). It also involves the bestowal of righteousness upon the believing person and a title to all the blessings promised to the just.[29]

This forensic act does more than acquit us of sin. God places or imputes Christ's active righteousness into our spiritual account. "He [God the Father] made Him [God the Son] who knew no sin to be sin on our behalf, so that we might become the righteousness of God in Him" (1 Cor. 5:21). We are "adopted" as God's sons. Paul writes in his letter to the Galatians, "But when the fullness of time came, God sent forth His Son, born of a woman, born under the Law, in order that He might redeem those who were under the Law, that we might receive the *adoption as sons*" (Gal. 4:4–5). Lightner writes,

> In the New Testament the term adoption into the family of God means to be placed as an adult son in God's family with all the rights,

privileges, and responsibilities of sonship. The sinner who trusts the Savior has citizenship in heaven at once even though he is still on earth (Phil. 3:20; Eph. 2:19). Every child of God is, from the moment of faith on, a member with all the other saints in the household of God (Eph. 2:19; 3:15).[30]

Our faith in Christ's atoning work results in the Father justifying us. This involves the legal act of acquittal, as well as the imputing of Christ's righteousness to us and our adoption into the family of God.

SUMMARY

We are sinners by nature and in practice as a result of the Fall (Gen. 3:1–21; Rom. 5:12). We are utterly depraved (Rom. 3:10-18; 5:6-11; Eph. 2:1-3). Because of this we are separated from God, since God is holy and we are unrighteous sinners. God's wrath is upon us (John 3:36; Rom. 1:18, 24, 26, 28).

As a result of Christ's sacrifice, God's wrath against us is satisfied (Rom. 3:25; Heb. 9:5; 1 John 2:2; 4:10). Now through our faith (trust) in Christ's finished work on the cross and through God's grace toward us, we are saved. As a result, we are justified (declared righteous) before God (Rom. 3:24); are redeemed from our slavery to sin and Satan (1 Cor. 6:20; 7:23; 2 Peter 2:1; Rom. 6); are forgiven (Eph. 1:7; Col. 2:13); and are reconciled to God (Rom. 5:1; 2 Cor. 5:17-19; Eph. 4:24; 1 Peter 1:4).

THE TASK AT HAND

About a decade into the twentieth century, a group of godly men stood up in the face of liberalism and boldly proclaimed the authoritative truth of God's Word. The resulting outpouring of support struck a blow against liberalism in North America. These books gave hope that the spiritual heritage of our country might be saved. We who enter the twenty-first century are faced with a similar task. We must defend the authority of Scripture and its vital teachings against an onslaught of godless philosophies, despite spiritual apathy and scriptural ignorance in our churches.

If we lose the belief in the message of Christ's suffering and death, as well as His resurrection, we will have lost both the battle and the war. This message is the heart of the gospel. "Even though we, or an angel from heaven, should preach to you a gospel contrary to that which we have preached to you, let him be accursed" (Gal. 1:8). If our hope is built on anything less, we stand in a slippery bog that will only facilitate our way to eternal damnation.

CHAPTER 15

The Resurrection of Christ

Gary R. Habermas

Jesus Christ died by crucifixion, paying for human sin in the process. After-wards, He rose from the dead, appearing to His followers in His own, physi-cal body, although it was now immortal. This is the central, most fundamental doctrine of Christian theology, as well as the major fact in defense of its teachings. Further, the New Testament relates Jesus' resurrection to many areas of Christian theology and practice, too. In short, the resurrection of Jesus is the very center of Christianity. This was true in the New Testament, in the earliest church, and it should keep this chief position in the church today, especially as we look to the twenty-first century.

I will briefly survey this topic from several angles. We will look at the historicity of the Resurrection, and then the bodily nature of Jesus' appear-ances, followed by the centrality of this event both in the New Testament and in the earliest, post-apostolic church. Turning to the contemporary scene, we will also set forth several prospects for future study.

THE RESURRECTION AS HISTORY

Orthodox Christianity has insisted on the facticity of Jesus' resurrection. While this event is multifaceted in its application and meaning, very little remains if it did not literally occur in history, in the space-time world. Thus, believers should never tire of stating the historical case for the resurrection of Jesus.

Some will point out that the factual truth of the Resurrection and the con-centration on historical evidences for it are not exactly the same. Yet, especially for the centerpiece of Christianity, since its facticity is so crucial, it is also true that evidence always has a meaningful place. This was repeatedly recognized in the New Testament, so there is no need for us to be shy about it today.

Naturalistic Theories

Historical arguments for the resurrection have traditionally been based on two sorts of evidence. The first move is to deal with the non-miraculous alternative theories that have been offered as long as the Christian message has been proclaimed. Several of these are even reported in the Gospels. But these attempts have failed to explain away this event. In particular, each hypothesis has been disproved by the known historical facts.

Further, critical scholars have themselves attacked each of their own theories. For example, nineteenth-century liberal scholars who disbelieved the Resurrection still argued against the suppositions of their colleagues in detail, to such an extent that each approach was disproved, sometimes with a sneer. The non-miraculous alternatives were taken apart piece by piece.

In the twentieth century, the critical attitude has surprisingly changed even more radically against these critical attempts. Most thinkers, even across a variety of theological schools of thought, still reject these alternative hypotheses. In fact, this dismissal usually takes place in a wholesale manner, with the entire cartel of hypotheses being ruled out as unacceptable. What makes these rejections even more interesting is that these scholars do *not* accept the inspiration of Scripture, and yet they still believe that the known facts refute these objections.[1]

However, this naturalistic hypothesis has not been popular among critical scholars for over two hundred years. There are convincing reasons for this lack of interest:

1. If Jesus' disciples had stolen His dead body and then lied about the appearances, how do we explain their willingness to die for convictions that they *knew* were false? Are there any historical examples of a group in which each person was willing to die *for something they knew to be a lie*?
2. Would they have made this lie the very center of their faith, as critics admit the Resurrection was?
3. How do we explain their overall transformations? The disciples were paralyzed with fear and despair after Jesus was taken by the Romans and killed. It is difficult to understand how common fishermen and others recovered sufficiently to immediately challenge the authorities.
4. Are we to believe that none of them, as far as we know, ever recanted? In a world of Watergate and other scandals, this is difficult to conceive.
5. How are we to explain the convictions of James, the brother of Jesus and Saul of Tarsus, skeptics who were converted by what they believed were resurrection appearances of Jesus? How would the disciples explain their scheme in order to get these two skeptics on board? Paul had regarded persecution of these Christians to be his God-given min-

istry (1 Cor. 15:9; Phil. 1:4–6). It is no wonder that critics have never been impressed with the *plot theory* that the disciples stole the dead body of their Teacher.

In Luke 24:36–43, we are told that it occurred to the disciples, after they saw the risen Jesus, that He was some sort of disembodied spirit, or even an hallucination. Could they be sure that they were not seeing something that was not even there? *The hallucination hypothesis* was popular over one hundred years ago, but it is perhaps plagued by more problems than almost any other attempt to dismiss the resurrection appearances:

1. Since hallucinations are impressions in one's mind for which there are no corresponding realities (like dreams), they are private occurrences. Not even two people can share the same hallucinations. As a result, groups of people could not have had the same hallucinations of Jesus.
2. The fear, doubt, and despair that gripped these men after Jesus' death are the very opposite of the positive expressions of personal expectation and excitement that characterize experiences of religious fervor. The disciples did not believe either the women or each other when it was proclaimed that Jesus had appeared.
3. Hallucinations are rare, except in cases of extreme psychological or physical problems. Yet we are to believe that every person who saw Jesus was precisely in the proper state of mind.
4. Perhaps the most problematic issue is the variety of persons, times, and places of Jesus' appearances. Men and women, hard-headed Peter and soft-hearted John, singly and in groups, indoors and outdoors, walking and fishing—all reportedly saw Him. That all of these people would have been candidates for hallucination stretches the limits of credibility.
5. Hallucinations would not account for the incredible transformations of Jesus' followers—from despair to ultimate triumph.
6. Even if hallucinations occurred, the tomb should not be empty. So how will we explain the fact that Jesus' body was missing?[2]
7. Was James the skeptic a good candidate for these subjective experiences?
8. Are we to suppose that Paul the persecutor wanted to see the resurrected Jesus enough to imagine Him?

Other naturalistic hypotheses suffer similar fates; all are significantly flawed. The facts argue that each one is seriously mistaken. If this was not the case, why would critics who do not even accept the inspiration of Scripture still reject them?[3]

Historical Evidences

The second prong of an apologetic for Jesus' resurrection is the large number of historical evidences for this event. That the disciples thought they had seen Jesus after His death is the single most important fact in our entire discussion. Incredibly, the critical community widely admits it, too. Speaking about the Resurrection, Reginald Fuller boldly proclaims, "That within a few weeks after the crucifixion Jesus' disciples came to believe this is one of the indisputable facts of history."[4] James D. G. Dunn asserts that "[i]t is almost impossible to dispute" that the earliest disciples had experiences that they thought were appearances of the risen Jesus.[5]

What a report by the disciples! How can such records be explained?

First, if naturalistic theories cannot adequately account for them, then we are left with the appearances themselves as the best explanation, especially given all the evidence in their favor.[6] Jesus was seen alive after His horrible death by crucifixion. Is it any wonder that the lives of the disciples were forever transformed from that point onwards?

Second, this altered behavior requires an adequate explanation. Unlike other religious converts who believe that the message of their founder is true, the disciples proclaimed that Jesus' teachings were unique. More important to our discussion, they based their entire message on the fact that they had seen the risen Jesus (Rom. 1:3-4; Acts 17:30-31). Because they *saw someone*, they were willing to die to spread his teachings.

Third, the Resurrection was the central proclamation of the church from its beginning. Since this message was so crucial to them, we would think that they would repeatedly certify its truthfulness. This is exactly what we find them doing. For example, Paul said that he twice went to Jerusalem specifically for the purpose of speaking with the other apostles to ascertain the truth of the gospel message (Gal. 1:18-20; 2:1-10).

Fourth, the tomb in which Jesus' body had been placed was found empty. Early testimony confirms it (see below). Even the Jewish leaders admitted it, and historical facts are often established if one's opponents agree. Further, the earliest witnesses were said to be women. This made absolutely no sense since women were not even allowed to testify in a court of law. Why let the burden of this report fall on them. Jerusalem was the last place in which one would wish to proclaim such a resurrection unless it could be verified. Otherwise, an occupied tomb could easily be found to prove the truth. Another hypothesis is necessary to explain these facts.

With all of these fantastic claims floating around Jerusalem, one might think that the Jewish leaders would be able to disprove the disciples' message. After all, the Jews had both a motive and the power to do something about it. They were also in the physical location to carry out their desires—this all happened in their home town. The crucifixion of Jesus showed their ability to get the job done. Yet, according to Acts, they could not disprove the disciples' message (5:33-40), and even a number of Jewish priests rather mysteriously became believers (6:7). Could the report of Jesus' resurrection have contributed to this?

Fifth, we still need to explain the conversions and subsequent transformations of skeptics like James (the brother of Jesus) and Paul. But these events play havoc with the alternative theories. Sixth, we have to account for the birth of the church and why Sunday became the day of worship (Acts 20:7; 1 Cor. 16:1-2). This was all rather radical for law-abiding Jews who had been taught all of their lives that Saturday was the Sabbath (Exod. 20:8-11).

Seventh, another angle on the evidence comes from arbitrarily reducing the number of known facts that are admitted as historical by virtually all critical scholars. There are five such facts: (1) Jesus' physical death by crucifixion; (2) the resulting despair of the disciples; (3) their experiences with whom they believed was the risen Jesus; (4) their radical transformations; (5) and the conversion of Paul due to a similar experience. The disciples' experiences are crucial here. Historian Michael Grant agrees with Fuller and Dunn above. Historical investigation can prove that the earliest eyewitnesses were convinced that they had seen the risen Jesus.[7] Naturalistic theses do not adequately explain these experiences.

An Early Witness

However, contemporary studies have moved far beyond these issues to other arguments in favor of Jesus' resurrection. The center of recent attention has been 1 Corinthians 15:3-8, where Paul records material that he had "received" from others and "delivered" to his listeners (v. 3). Contemporary scholars are almost unanimous in holding that this data is from one or more ancient creed(s). The words are older than the book in which they are recorded. Evidence of an additional sort emerges here.

There are indications that Paul's material is exceptionally early.[8] Not only has Paul chosen rather technical terms that refer to receiving and passing on tradition, but the account also has a rather formal style, including Jewish parallelism. Additionally, it contains non-Pauline words and structure, the specific names of Peter and James, and possibly indications of an Aramaic origin. Most critical scholars who comment on the subject think that Paul received this creed within about five years after the Crucifixion.

These same scholars usually agree that Paul received this creedal material from the apostles Peter and James when he visited Jerusalem about five years after Jesus' death (Gal. 1:18-20). Additional corroboration comes from Paul's use of the term *historeō* (1:18). This term indicates that Paul conducted an investigative interview. The context of Paul's remembrance is 1:11 through chapter 2, in which the subject is the nature of the gospel message, including the resurrection of Jesus (1 Cor. 15:3-4).

As if one meeting with the Jerusalem apostles was not enough, Paul returned fourteen years later, also to discuss the nature of his gospel message. On this occasion, his theme was again confirmed by the church leaders (Gal. 2:1–10; cf. Acts 15).

Paul's report in 1 Corinthians 15 is important for other reasons. Here (15:8) and elsewhere (1 Cor. 9:1), Paul tells us that he saw the risen Jesus, too. Critical scholars, no matter how skeptical, rarely question Paul's own perception that he had an actual experience with the Christ.

Paul explains that both he and the other eyewitnesses agreed in their proclamation of the death and resurrection of Jesus (1 Cor. 15:11). So we have Paul's testimony that he and all the other apostles were teaching the same message. This is another piece of evidence that the report of eyewitness testimony is firmly anchored in early data, not in legendary reports that arose later.

THE BODILY NATURE OF JESUS' APPEARANCES

There is probably more scholarly agreement that something actually happened regarding Jesus and His disciples than there is concerning the form of His appearances. This is not only a dispute between the evangelical and higher critical groups of scholars. There also is a lack of agreement within these circles.

We have said that the pivotal fact, admitted as historical by virtually all scholars, is that the earliest disciples had real experiences of some sort. It is nearly always recognized that "something happened." As we have seen, the specific naturalistic theories are generally rejected on the basis of the evidence, even by contemporary intellectuals, so various opinions exist concerning the exact nature of these experiences.[9] Naturalistic critics, of course, continue to deny that any sort of miracle took place at all. Most say we just do not know what really happened.[10] Some scholars are willing to think that Jesus appeared in some unspecified non-bodily encounter, arguing that at the most Paul saw a light from heaven. Still others seem to think that Jesus revealed Himself as some sort of objective image in the minds of the early believers. These non-bodily views are probably the most popular opinions in recent decades, but they are rather ill-defined, often purposefully so.

Those who believe that Jesus appeared in an actual body often disagree concerning how physical that body was and whether it was the same body that was crucified. Discussions often concern the degree of change implied by Paul's statements and analogies in 1 Corinthians 15:35–51.[11]

The objective evidence points to the conclusion that Jesus was literally raised from the dead. Orthodox theology, with few exceptions, has supported the view that He was raised in His own body.[12] However, the body may have been changed, it was the physical body that had been crucified.[13] Nine lines of reasoning support this view.

First, although the New Testament speaks of the disagreement over the Resurrection within Judaism, most first-century A.D. Jews believed in it. It is in the context of this general understanding and acceptance that Jesus' teaching must be understood.

Second, the term *resurrection* (*anastasis*) usually refers to the physical body being raised. In Philippians 3:11, Paul specifically used another word, *exanastasis*, which literally can be translated "out-resurrection from among the dead." That Paul thought the body would be brought back to life confirms the earlier data on the dominant view of the times.

Third, Paul's word for Jesus' resurrection appearances to His followers is *horaō*, which is far more frequently used in the New Testament for bodily (rather than spiritual) sight. Both Luke (24:34) and John (20:20, 25) also use the term to report very physical resurrection appearances by Jesus.

Fourth, the majority of New Testament scholars who study this subject think that the disciples' experiences with the risen Jesus were *visual* for reasons mentioned above (see the statements by Fuller, Dunn, and Grant). While visual incidents do not require a resurrected body, hallucinations and related theses fail to account for the facts. This is also granted by most scholars. Viewed in conjunction with the earlier evidence for Jesus' resurrection, we are left with no better explanation than that the disciples *actually* saw Jesus. So the visual component of the appearances certainly argues against views that interpret these events as subjective experiences.

Fifth, Paul's early creed tells us that at least three *groups* of persons saw the risen Jesus (1 Cor. 15:4–6). This is further proof that certain persons really *saw* Jesus. This makes better sense than saying that Paul thought the five hundred individuals had arrived at a simultaneous, inner conviction that Jesus was raised from the dead. That He was standing in front of them is the most natural reading of the text concerning each of these three appearances.

Sixth, Pauline anthropology can only be understood if Paul believed in a physical resurrection. Paul taught that the entire person was raised from the dead, including the physical body. In an intricate and authoritative study on this subject, Robert Gundry deduces of Paul's concept of Jesus' resurrection body that "it is a physical body renovated by the Spirit of Christ and therefore suited to heavenly immortality."[14] Gundry concludes, "the raising of Jesus from the dead was a raising of his physical body."[15]

John A. T. Robinson reached a similar verdict after his own detailed study of Paul's anthropology. Like Gundry, he also addressed the specific nature of Jesus' resurrection body:

> All the appearances, in fact, depict the same phenomenon, of a body identical yet changed, transcending the limitations of the flesh yet capable of manifesting itself within the order of the flesh. We may

describe this as a "spiritual" (1 Cor. 15:44) or "glorified" (cf. 1 Cor. 15:43; Phil. 3:21) body . . . so long as we do not import into these phrases any opposition to the physical as such.[16]

We violate Paul's anthropology if we try to interpret his statements in 1 Corinthians 15:3ff. in terms of subjective experiences of the earliest Christians. Paul's view cannot have been anything but that Jesus was objectively and bodily raised.

Seventh, Paul's view of bodily resurrection is clarified by his identification with a theological position that strongly favored this stance. He repudiates the positions of theological rivals that did not hold this conviction. Paul explains that he had been a Pharisee, "a Hebrew of Hebrews," prior to his conversion to Christianity (Phil. 3:4–6). He was formerly committed to a specific theological agenda, which involved the teaching of the resurrection of the body. His writings show that Paul never changed his former position on the subject. He also confirmed it at a couple of crucial points.

Eighth, in spite of recent attempts to reject the testimony of the Gospels and Acts, there are excellent reasons to accept their historical facts in general and their testimony concerning the nature of Jesus' resurrection body in particular. Archaeological and linguistic analysis has shown that these volumes were written relatively soon after the events themselves and are the earliest and best texts on this subject. The passage of thirty-five to sixty-five years before all of these volumes were produced is a very brief time by ancient standards. Speaking about the Gospels and Acts, Roman historian A. N. Sherwin-White has noted that even two generations is too short of a time for myth to prevail over the historical core of oral tradition.[17]

C. H. Dodd is one critical scholar who has argued that several of the gospel accounts of Jesus' resurrection appearances are "concise" reports, indicating that they contain trustworthy material regarding Jesus' appearances to his disciples. He concentrates especially on Matthew 28:8–10, 16–20; John 20:19–21; and, to some extent, Luke 24:36–49.[18] Coming from more of an evangelical direction, biblical scholar Grant Osborne has shown that even contemporary critical techniques do not annul the data reported in the Gospels. In his extensive discussion, he relates that the gospel reports of Jesus' appearances provide trustworthy accounts of these crucial events.[19]

Ninth, the fact of the empty tomb points very strongly to the view that Jesus' body was raised. The most obvious intent of the gospel reports is to persuade that the body that had been crucified, had died, and was buried was the *same* one that had been raised and that appeared to the earliest believers. Particularly to Jewish ears, it would be even more difficult to teach an empty tomb followed by resurrection appearances without involving the physical body, since this was the dominant first-century Jewish view.

There is much attestation that the tomb was indeed empty. We will briefly mention a few proofs here, since this component of the early teaching has such a direct bearing on the fact that Jesus appeared in His own body. We have already seen how the Jewish authorities freely admitted the empty tomb (Matt. 28:11-15), but their explanation did not hold up. The gospel reports that women were the earliest witnesses to the empty tomb (Matt. 28:1-6; Mark 16:1-8; Luke 23:55-24:8; John 20:1-2). As noted above, women could not testify in a Jewish court, so they would not be anyone's first choice for witnesses.

Further, Paul's early report in 1 Corinthians 15:3-4 strongly implies an empty tomb, since he records the sequence from Jesus' death to burial to resurrection to appearances. It all happened to the body of the same person. Another early creedal passage explains that the tomb in which Jesus was buried was later empty. Jesus' body did not decay (Acts 13:29-30, 36-37). As noted, it would have been extremely difficult to proclaim Jesus' resurrection in the very same city where his body was entombed. A Jerusalem location for the early preaching ensures an empty tomb.[20]

In sum, we have several strong indications that, not only was Jesus raised from the dead, but He appeared to His followers in the same body in which He died and was buried. This is certainly not to say that every molecule was the same, for Paul's analogies (1 Cor. 15:35-51) indicate glorious changes from a perishable to an imperishable body. But to argue either that Jesus did not appear bodily at all, or that the body was not the same one that died by crucifixion, is opposed by a host of facts, as well as centuries of Christian historical theology.

THE CENTRALITY OF THE RESURRECTION

There is widespread agreement, even among the most skeptical theologians, that the resurrection of Jesus is the central claim of Christianity. In the New Testament, the Resurrection is the heart of Christian theology and apologetics.[21] Not as widely recognized is that more than three hundred verses relate this event to personal spiritual life and other areas of Christian belief.[22]

The New Testament

We have already see how Paul defines the nature of the earliest gospel message in 1 Corinthians 15:3-8. The Resurrection is an indispensable part of that message, along with Jesus' deity and atoning death. In 1 Corinthians 15, Paul goes on to explain the significance of the Resurrection. If Jesus was not raised from the dead, then Christianity is false (v. 14) and ineffective (v. 17). The apostles' preaching is valueless (v. 14), and their testimony is untrue (v. 15). No one's sins have been forgiven (v. 17), and believers have no hope in death (v. 18). Paul's pessimistic conclusion is that, without the

Resurrection, Christians are the most miserable of all persons (v. 19). Paul adds that, without the Resurrection, "Let us eat and drink, for tomorrow we die" (v. 32). This is perhaps the most dismal passage in all of Scripture.

Paul's point is that, if Jesus was not raised, believers may as well try hedonism or another outlook. The Resurrection makes Christianity a unique system, separating it from other beliefs. With it, we have everything that matters; without it, we have nothing.

The apostle Paul teaches the centrality of the Resurrection in other texts, too. In another early creed (Rom. 1:3-4) he gives Jesus three christological titles—Son of God, Christ (or Messiah), and Lord. Then he says that Jesus' resurrection showed that He was each of these (cf. Rom. 14:9). The Resurrection also provides salvation (Rom. 10:9-10) and is a model of the believers' resurrection (1 Cor. 15:20; 2 Cor. 4:14; Phil. 3:20-21; 1 Thess. 4:14).

For Paul, the Resurrection message was practical, too. He has already told of being energized by Jesus' appearance to him (1 Cor. 9:1). Now in chapter 15, which is sometimes called the "resurrection chapter," the apostle concludes with an exhortation: Because of the truth of the Resurrection, believers should stand firmly in faith, committing themselves to the work of the Lord (1 Cor. 15:58). The power of the Resurrection itself is available for believers, even as they go about doing ministry (Phil. 3:10-11).

Other New Testament authors expressed similar emphases. Jesus taught that His resurrection from the dead would be the chief sign of the truth of His teachings (Matt. 12:38-40; 16:1-4). He even used the hope of the Resurrection in speaking to Martha, Lazarus's grieving sister (John 11:21-26). Later, He comforted His grieving disciples with the same message (John 16:20-23). The risen Jesus directed the disciples to be witnesses to others (Matt. 28:19-20; Luke. 24:47-48; Acts 1:8). The Resurrection insures the believer's salvation and home in heaven, making it possible for us to rejoice during times of persecution (1 Peter 1:3). Because He was raised, Jesus can deliver us from the bondage of death's fear (Heb. 2:14-15). He now serves as the believer's high priest, making intercession for us (Heb. 7:23-25). And one day, we will have a new body like His (1 John 3:2).

These and other texts dramatically show the centrality of the Resurrection for the New Testament writers. Early believers such as Paul realized that this event provided the central claim of Christianity. It is related to our most treasured areas of theology and practice. With it, the Christian message of eternal life is secure, resting on the reality of Jesus' victory over death. Without it, the Christian message is reduced to human philosophy.

The Early Church

The earliest post-apostolic writings exhibit a very similar emphasis on the centrality of Jesus' resurrection. The writings of Clement of Rome in the late A.D. 90s is perhaps the closest to New Testament themes. He teaches that, by the will of God, Jesus delivered the gospel message to the disciples, who passed it on to the church. The importance of the Resurrection here is that it provides "full assurance," and thereby serves the role of confirming the truthfulness of the apostolic message. Clement clearly thinks that the Resurrection plays the key role in confirming the "glad tidings that the kingdom of God should come" (Clem. *Cor.* 42).[23]

In writing that is reminiscent of Paul's teaching in 1 Corinthians 15, Clement also reminds his readers that Jesus' resurrection is "the firstfruits" of the believer's resurrection. Using examples from night and day, planting seed, and the Phoenix (the bird in a Greek resurrection myth), Clement declares that God will raise believers in new bodies, which he refers to (citing Job) as "flesh" (Clem. *Cor.* 24–26). Therefore, we should be obedient, keeping God's commands, and trusting His promises (27).

Writing just a decade after Clement, Ignatius commands that believers "be fully persuaded" of the literal facts of "the birth and the passion and the resurrection, which took place in the time of the governorship of Pontius Pilate; for these things were truly and certainly done by Jesus Christ our hope" (Ign. *Magn.* 11; cf. Ign. *Phld.*, introduction).

Ignatius emphasizes that Jesus' flesh was raised. He appeared to Peter and the others, and told them to touch Him. Here Ignatius quotes from Luke 24:39, adding that those present did touch Him. Turning to a practical lesson, he explains that, as a result, the disciples "despised death, nay they were found superior to death" (Ign. *Smyrn.* 3).

Additionally, Ignatius taught that Jesus was not only raised from the dead, but God "in the like fashion will so raise us also who believe on Him—His Father, I say, will raise us" (Ign. *Tral.* 9). This is the believer's hope (Ign. *Tral.* Introduction)—the reason why Christians should despise death.

Writing about the same time, Polycarp reminds us several times that Jesus' resurrection is the basis of our faith (Pol. *Phil.* 1–2, 12). He also links the resurrection of Jesus to that of believers (2, 5). But those who pervert Jesus' teachings will not be raised (7). While being killed for his faith, we are told that Polycarp blessed God that he could be a martyr for his Lord, to whom he was looking for the "resurrection of eternal life" (*Mart. Pol.*, 14).

The issue of the nature of the body in which Jesus appeared was raised quite early. Clement, Ignatius, and later Tertullian thought it was Jesus' flesh that was raised.[24] The Alexandrine School and Origen, in particular, championed the position that Jesus' resurrected body only appeared to be physical. Rather, Jesus' body was of spiritual material.[25]

For many scholars today, the emphasis concerns Paul's concept of the "spiritual body." Biblically minded theologians wish to do justice to both the element of bodily continuity, and Paul's comments about the change. Thus, Jesus was raised in His own body, including certain new qualities.

FUTURE PROSPECTS

Several areas of study on the resurrection need more attention than evangelicals have given them. The effort is crucial to the twenty-first-century church if we are to defend and develop this doctrine that is so close to the center of Christianity. These suggestions concern both scholarly pursuits and practical application.

Areas for Research

Much work needs to be done to answer the ongoing challenges of various theses that question the truth of the resurrection of Jesus. Evangelicals have frequently not been watching these developments. They often fail to answer them when they are known.

One rather technical subject needing work is the philosophy of history. This territory covers ground that is absolutely crucial to the Christian message. We depend so much on historical underpinnings, yet we do relatively little to address the tough theoretical issues of fact and philosophy on which historical studies are founded.

We need to define history more carefully and look closely at historiography— how we actually *do* history. What checks and balances determine whether an event really occurred? What is the nature of human testimony? How should contrary experience be critiqued? What is the relation between events and their interpretation? To what extent can the past be known objectively?[26]

Such subjects may seem overly technical to the average Christian, but they have a direct bearing on how we establish the historical basis of our faith— especially when this basis is questioned.

We must carefully and strongly respond to the influences of epistemological syncretism and the intolerance in Western culture toward any questioning of a relative view of truth. The generations entering the twenty-first century tend to wonder whether anything is true. They question knowledge in general, and individual belief systems in particular. Favorite areas to question include any subject in which Christianity makes absolute claims or claims to uniqueness. The incarnation and deity of Christ, His exclusive salvation message, and His resurrection are of course front-line targets for criticism.

Since Jesus made claims to uniqueness, one cannot preach an inclusive acceptance of all or a gospel of universalism. Christian apologetics, with regard to Jesus, has a twofold emphasis: the uniqueness of His teachings and the historicity of His resurrection from the dead. The first is confirmed by the second.

Whatever is questioned by contemporary audiences needs to be addressed. We need to study and know these areas. Believers ought to educate themselves on the relevant issues and be prepared to provide a biblical defense (2 Cor. 10:5; Jude 3).[27]

Closely related to these trends is a new kind of gnosticism. There has been a concerted effort to set several Gnostic works on a par with Scripture. The effort tries to give them more credibility by setting their writing as much as a century before scholars have always dated it. Such writings as the *Gospel of Thomas* are frequently ranked with the four canonical Gospels as authoritative, or even given the edge in importance. The presumption is that Jesus' life and teachings were open to multiple interpretations, of which historical orthodoxy is one option. On the Resurrection, the tendency is to treat Jesus' appearances as manifestations of light instead of bodily appearances.

Evangelicals have produced relatively little in this area, ignoring the Gnostic texts as unimportant. Both the general thesis that the Gnostic volumes are reliable sources[28] and their alternative understanding of the resurrection appearances, need to be refuted.[29]

It will be increasingly important to defend the reliability of the Gospels, in particular. In recent critical thought, Paul is well accepted, but the Gospels are not. Evangelicals cannot allow any subtle excuse for disputing or neglecting these texts. We need more works that take on the critical questions, pointing out that higher critical procedures betray agnostic presuppositions.[30]

Next, we should mention the possibility that, from any of several angles, today's critic might question the historicity of the Resurrection. In recent years there has been a number of revivals of the naturalistic theories. Each one must be addressed, step by step. Another possible approach is that other religions might argue that their religious leaders were also resurrected. It is one thing to make charges, and quite another to provide historical demonstration for them.[31]

In spite of the many publications on the Resurrection, evangelical thought too frequently follows similar paths instead of launching out into current debates. Critics and believers ask questions that require viable answers.

Areas for Application

We also miss an important component of the resurrection of Jesus if we do not ask how we can build bridges between this event on one side and popular theology and Christian ethics and spirituality on the other. This is even more easily overlooked by evangelicals for whom this event sounds the charge in two main areas: apologetics or soteriology. There is much more to the Resurrection than these two areas alone, as indispensable as they are. We have argued above that the Resurrection applies to all the important areas of belief and growth, as well as to common Christian struggles?

If the Resurrection is the center of New Testament theology, it should serve as a guide for us. Regarding the bodily nature of Jesus' resurrection body, a doctrine about which there has been debate even in evangelical circles, the discussion must be held strictly accountable to Scripture.[32] We must not allow belief in this biblical distinctive to decline.

What about everyday life matters, particularly subjects that New Testament writers relate to the Resurrection? What is the connection between this event and transformed lives, as experienced by the apostles and early believers in Acts? How should it revolutionize believers today? What did Paul mean by his hope of exhibiting the power of Christ's resurrection (Phil. 3:10)? Can this power help believers to overcome sin (Rom. 8:5–11)? How about the roles of witness and teaching—commands of the risen Jesus (Matt. 28:19-20; Acts 1:8)?

Does the hope of the Resurrection lead believers to a deeper commitment and meaningful labor for the Lord (1 Cor. 15:58)? How can the truth of the Resurrection be used in counseling? What about dealing with the fear of death (Heb. 2:14-15) or with those suffering from grief, like Martha (John 11:20-27)? Are there other situations today (like persecution—1 Peter 1:3-9) where believers could grow by applying implications of the Resurrection? How does the Resurrection give us a taste of heaven (1 Cor. 15:50-57)?

Those who point out that the resurrection of Jesus extends beyond our apologetic efforts are certainly correct. It definitely has a wide application in the New Testament. These are only a few of the areas of practical theology in which the influence of this event needs to be implemented. We have lagged far behind the biblical emphasis by not noticing and applying this truth in everyday circumstances.

CONCLUSION

The Resurrection is a multifaceted diamond. Turn it one way to see strong historical evidences, even when using only a limited number of facts that are confirmed by the data and recognized even by critical scholars. Turn it another way and these facts disprove naturalistic alternative theories. Rotate it to concentrate on the bodily nature of Jesus' appearances. If we keep it revolving we can see how the resurrection focus of Christian theology makes it a point of integration in all of life. In the Resurrection we can catch a vision for the power that this event can make in our daily relationship with the Lord as we work through tough issues.

What more could a believer ask for? The resurrection of Jesus Christ is the capstone of the gospel and its guarantee for all who trust Him (1 Cor. 15:1-20). It is the center of Christian faith, theology, and practice (15:12-19), the key to the immortality of God's eternal kingdom for those who believe.

CHAPTER 16

Salvation by Faith Alone

George E. Meisinger

It is an ancient question, one that has ever burned through human minds in search of an answer: "How can I receive eternal life?" For those who have believed in a deity and a life after the grave, there have been three basic answers:

1. One can gain life after death through good works. If good works outweigh the bad, heaven is gained.
2. Some sort of faith is required, coupled with good works. One must both believe *and* do good deeds.
3. God saves by grace alone, through faith alone, in Christ alone.

THE FIRST-CENTURY BATTLE

Since the first century, a theological war has raged periodically between the second and third options. The antagonists were often fellow believers within the church and sometimes partisans of other groups identifying themselves with Christianity but theologically outside the pale of orthodox belief. Paul assaulted the issue frontally in the young church of Galatia. The Galatians, he warned, had turned away from the grace that belongs to each Christian in Christ (Gal. 1:6). In regard to the Gentile pastor Titus, Paul firmly resisted the ritual of circumcision.[1] Stressing circumcision even among the Gentile converts meant they would have to become Jews to be saved. This reliance on keeping the law confused the doctrine of salvation until grace was no longer grace (Gal. 2:3; cf. Rom. 11:6; 2 Peter 5:12).[2]

Paul was alarmed that someone had "bewitched" the Galatians into supposing that they must supply good works to accompany their faith (Gal. 3:1-6).

267

To the contrary, believing Christians are all children of God through faith alone (Gal. 3:26). The Galatians misunderstood the nature of grace and its relationship to obedience (Gal. 5:6–7). This was an important matter for three reasons:

1. Anyone who seeks justification by good works ("the law") must keep the whole law perfectly—an impossibility (Gal. 5:3).
2. The person who seeks justification by good works is alienated from Christ and all the benefits He died and rose again to provide (Gal. 5:4a).
3. The person who seeks to be just before God by good works has missed grace completely (Gal. 5:4b).

The unbeliever who declines grace cannot be declared righteous in Christ. There is neither eternal life nor justification on such a mistaken path. But even believers who have received grace and should understand it turn from the path and so miss out on the abundant life that grace affords.

Stand fast therefore in the liberty by which Christ has made us free, Paul concludes. Do not be entangled again with the restraint of bondage to law (Gal. 5:1).

THE GOSPEL ACCORDING TO THE CULTS

The siren's song of self-righteousness, and even self-salvation, by doing something has always been seductive to fallen humanity. Only biblical Christianity provides clear alternative to the keeping of a set of standards. Satan has set traps among the churches—false faiths that make claims about following Christ but in the end trade the Cross for self-salvation. There are many of these false Christian cults, but their anti-Christian messages can be discerned from the writings of adherents to two well-known cults—the Jehovah's Witnesses and the Latter-Day Saints or Mormons.

Jehovah's Witnesses

Jehovah's Witness doctrine is promulgated through publications of the Watchtower Society, whose pronouncements carry much the same authority that Christians ascribe to Scripture.

In the following quotation, notice that the writer says that baptism is no guarantee of salvation, but neither can faith stand alone. It must be accompanied by "godly sorrow over our past sins," abandonment of "any wrong course we followed," and endurance to the end.

> Compliance with God's laws, principles, and standards should move us to repent, expressing godly sorrow over our past sins. This leads to conversion, that is, to a turning around and abandoning any wrong course we followed when we did not have the knowledge of God.

(Acts 3:19) Naturally, if we are still secretly practicing some sin instead of doing what is righteous, we have not really turned around, nor have we fooled God.[3]

Although baptism is vitally important, it is not a guarantee of salvation. Jesus did not say: "Everyone baptized will be saved." Instead, he said: "He that has endured to the end is the one that will be saved" (Matt. 24:13).[4]

To JWs, "enduring" means following a prescribed lifestyle that is centered around acts benefiting "Jehovah God" and the kingdom hall. In this unitarian worldview, Christ is not fully God, so he could not die for the sins of all people. There is no foundation for grace.

The Mormons

Within the theology of the Church of Jesus Christ of Latter-Day Saints, God grants forgiveness, eternal life, and ultimately divinity through repentance. This break with sin is both emotional and physical. Salvation is accompanied by sorrow and regret for one's sin against God and other human beings. It is demonstrated in necessary obedience, submission, and resolute conformity to all of the laws of God. Contrary to Ephesians 2:8-9 salvation (and even godhood) is by grace through faith and works. Since Christ is no more or less a god than we can become, he is no basis for salvation.

> What is it, then, that the Lord asks of us to show our acceptance of his offer of salvation? [p. 39] . . . Repentance, means turning away from a sin and turning toward righteousness. Forsaking sin involves both an emotional and a physical break from transgression, giving rise to sorrow and regret. It also involves trying to repair the damage done by one's sins, as far as that is possible. Thus, in many instances, confession is necessary, as in going to a person one has wronged and confessing one's wrongdoing. The marvelous thing about repentance is forgiveness. Not only may we obtain forgiveness from others, but more important, God himself will forgive us.[5]
>
> All these glorious gifts, and many more that could be mentioned, come to us through his grace as free gifts and not of works, lest any man should boast. (See Eph. 2:8-9.) Nevertheless, to obtain these "graces," and the gift of eternal salvation, we must remember that this gift is only to "all them that obey him" (Heb. 5:9).[6]
>
> We are saved by grace through faith. We are also saved by grace through works, because we know that where there are no works, there is no faith. James's point in his discussion of faith and works is that they are inseparable. He said, "by works was faith made perfect" (James 2:22).[7]

In short, it is not a choice of either faith or works. The two are integral parts of a single whole, and, for reasons stated above, the writings of both Paul and James show this. Faith is the foundation on which we build, but it is not a foundation that springs into full-blown existence by pure chance.[8]

THE GOSPEL OF MODERN REFORMERS

One might expect to find such autosalvation in other religions and among the pseudo-Christian cults. Some questionable teachings, however, have also caused intense and sometimes rancorous debate within fundamentalist evangelicalism. This argument is called the "lordship salvation controversy." One of the leaders who take the lordship of Christ in an unbiblical direction in the estimation of this writer is the prominent pastor, author, and seminary president John F. MacArthur Jr.

According to MacArthur, one does not receive eternal life by the "easy believism" of faith without commitment to obedience. It is necessary to submit to Christ as Lord of life. True Christians, MacArthur teaches, seek to change their lives with all of their hearts. They surrender to the Lord's authority in a humble, emotionally broken, repentant faith. MacArthur's comments include the following statements:

> The message of Jesus cannot be made to accommodate any kind of cheap grace or easy-believism. The kingdom is not for people who want Jesus without any change in their lives. It is only for those who seek it with all their hearts.[9]
>
> [Jesus] is Lord, and those who refuse Him as Lord cannot use Him as Savior. Everyone who receives Him must surrender to His authority, for to say we receive Christ when in fact we reject His right to reign over us is utter absurdity. It is a futile attempt to hold onto sin with one hand and take Jesus with the other. What kind of salvation is it if we are left in bondage to sin?
>
> This then is the gospel we are to proclaim: That Jesus Christ, who is God incarnate, humbled Himself to die on our behalf. Thus He became the sinless sacrifice to pay the penalty of our guilt. He rose from the dead to declare with power that He is Lord over all, and He offers eternal life freely to sinners who will surrender to Him in humble, repentant faith. This gospel promises nothing to the haughty rebel, but for broken, penitent sinners, it graciously offers everything that pertains to life and godliness (2 Peter 1:3).[10]

Reformed theologian and ethicist John Gerstner and church historian Sam Logan are among those who have weighed in on the side of MacArthur.

According to Gerstner, "Good works may be said to be a condition for obtaining salvation in that they inevitably accompany genuine faith. . . . The question is not whether good works are necessary. As the inevitable outworking of saving faith, they are necessary for salvation."[11] Elsewhere Gerstner says that "Lordship teaching does not 'add works,' as if faith were not sufficient. The 'works' are part of the definition of faith."[12]

"Evangelical obedience is an absolute necessity, a 'condition' in man's justification," adds Logan.[13]

THE SEARCH FOR A BIBLICAL VIEW

In all the above quotations, we observe two things that seem to be held in common: (1) Good works are indispensably linked to faith; a faith without works is not a faith that saves eternally. (2) There is hostility toward those who claim that receiving eternal life and forgiveness is by faith alone, without consideration of works.

This is not to equate these theologies, for they represent two diametrically opposed movements. The cults are heretical and antibiblical, whatever their outward expressions of honor toward Scripture. The Christian theologians are thoroughly orthodox and biblically based. However, in one aspect of their soteriology they are disturbingly similar: Salvation is by faith plus works, regardless of how they with dexterity link works to faith. Some "front-load" the gospel by requiring works with faith from the beginning. Yet the others "backload" the gospel in requiring that works follow one's act of faith. Neither requirement is biblical.

Accordingly, the fundamental issue Paul confronted in the first century has swung full circle as we pass into the third millennium: Is a man saved by faith alone, or by a faith that produces good works? Some attempt to finesse the issue by claiming that works are not the basis of faith but are rather the necessary fruit. This is sophistry. Whether one integrates works at the beginning of the act of faith, or following after, God's grace is stripped of its glory: "If by grace, then it is no longer of works; otherwise grace is no longer grace. But if it is of works, it is no longer grace; otherwise work is no longer work (Rom. 11:6).[14]

Romans: Faith, Works, and Abraham

Two works of Scripture in particular—Romans and James—touch upon the question of faith and works and are crucial foundations for an understanding of the issue.

In Romans 4, Paul shows that, according to the Jewish Scriptures, even Abraham has no right to boast; we should conclude that no one has a right to vaunt himself before God.[15] The plan of God excludes all boasting before the Lord.

What then shall we say that Abraham our father has found according to the flesh? (4:1)

Paul's opening question is, "What shall we say about Abraham, who seems to have human grounds for boasting?" Of all the forefathers of Israel, here was the one God uniquely chose to originate the nation. Abraham must have been special in God's eyes; otherwise the Lord would not have selected him to be the father of the nation.

What was it that Abraham "has found," or obtained?[16] The answer of context is that Abraham obtained nothing by works. He did not find righteousness before God based on how much good he did, either before or after the point of regeneration. The next verse expands on this.

For if Abraham was justified by works, he has something of which to boast, but not before God. (4:2)

To be justified is to have God declare one to be innocent before heaven's tribunal, before the divine standards of right and wrong. Justification is defined by H. C. G. Moule as the "winning of a favorable verdict . . . the sentence of acquittal, or the sentence of vindicated right."[17] Justification is not an improvement of one's moral condition. Deuteronomy 25:1 takes the concept of justification into the courtroom, in which judges "justify the righteous and condemn the wicked." The decision of the judges does not alter the character or integrity of the accused. "The judges are not to make the righteous man better," Moule writes.[18] They are to vindicate his position as satisfactory to the law:

> In regard of "us men and our salvation" it stands related not so much, not so directly, to our need of spiritual revolution, amendment, purification, holiness, as to our need of getting, somehow—in spite of our guilt, our liability, our debt, our deserved condemnation—a sentence of acquittal, a sentence of acceptance, at the judgment seat of a holy God. . . . The direct concern of Justification is with man's need of a divine deliverance, not from the power of his sin, but from its guilt.[19]

Jews exalted Abraham and most would have answered Paul that Abraham's faith was grounds for boasting before God. If God justified Abraham by his merit, then he has a basis for pride, a sense of achievement. Yet the apostle quickly adds that this is not the case, certainly not before God. He uses the contrasting conjunction *but* to cut off any notion that there could be boasting before God.

For what does the Scripture say? Abraham believed God, and it was accounted to him for righteousness. (4:3)

To "believe" is to trust an object or a person, in this case God. Faith must always have an object. Moule strongly argues that faith is not the same as a practical confidence.

> To have faith in a commander does not mean merely to entertain a conviction, a belief, however positive, that he is skillful and competent. We may entertain such a belief about the commander of the enemy—with very unpleasant impressions on our minds in consequence. We may be confident that he is a great general in a sense the very opposite to personal confidence in him. No, to have faith in a commander implies a view of him, in which we either actually do, or are quite ready to, trust ourselves and our cause to his command. And just the same is true of faith in a divine Promise, faith in a divine Redeemer. . . . It means a putting of ourselves and our needs, in personal reliance, into His hands. [20]

Paul sharply contrasts *belief* in 4:3 with *works* in verse 2, with the point that faith and works are antithetical to one another. They are the sort of opposites, like water and oil, that do not mix. To do good works is one thing; to believe God is another. What did Abraham believe, according to Genesis 15? He put himself into God's hands, trusting the Lord who promised to be his shield (Gen. 15:1) and to give descendants who would become as innumerable as the stars (Gen. 15:3–5). The Lord responded to Abraham's act of trust by accounting it to him "*for* righteousness." The preposition *for* here expresses equivalence.[21]

Before he believed, Abraham was accounted by God to be an unrighteous man. However, with Abraham's first act of faith, God declared his faith as non-meritoriously and forever equivalent to righteousness; He accounted him a righteous man. This does not mean that Abraham no longer sinned. Yet in the heavenly bookkeeping system, God took Abraham's act of faith as preparing him to live forever in heaven. Abraham had no acceptable righteousness of his own to offer. All he had to offer was faith.

Romans 4:4–5 exhorts people not to mingle faith and works when seeking forgiveness and eternal life.

> *Now to him who works, the wages are not counted as grace but as debt. But to him who does not work but believes on Him who justifies the ungodly, his faith is accounted for righteousness. (Rom. 4:4–5)*

The negative side of the principle is that a person who works receives what is due, or owed. What is due is not given by grace. "To him who works" speaks of one who expends energy in order to produce. An employer rewards these efforts with payment for the work accomplished. The laborer deserves to be paid.

One who has earned a wage does not count it as grace. The pay did not come out of good will. Compensation is a matter of justice. However, if the boss goes beyond the contractual agreement for labor, and gives the employee a turkey for Thanksgiving, that turkey is an expression of grace. The employee did not earn or deserve the turkey; it was a token of the employer's grace attitude.

The positive side of the divine operating principle is that an ungodly person who does not work but still believes "is accounted for righteousness" in the accounting book. That is God's grace at work. God declares righteous, or innocent, each one "who believes on Him who justifies the ungodly."

The Lord does not justify "do-gooders," the decent religious types or those who turn over a new leaf. He justifies the ungodly who have no merit before God. Neither their thoughts nor their conduct measure up. Yet, regardless of their absence of personal righteousness, each believer discovers that faith is accounted for righteousness, which implies forgiveness.[22]

Just as David also describes the blessedness of the man to whom God imputes righteousness apart from works: Blessed are those whose lawless deeds are forgiven, and whose sins are covered; Blessed is the man to whom the Lord shall not impute sin. (Rom. 4:6–8)

David is an Old Testament illustration of the blessing of receiving righteousness freely. *Just as* introduces Old Testament evidence (Ps. 32:1–2) to show that God does not ground righteousness in works, but makes it a free gift of His grace.[23] Upon a person with such righteousness, God has conferred a great benefit, thus his *blessedness*. Imputed righteousness is *apart from* works, just as 3:21 said it was "apart from the law" and 3:28, "apart from the deeds of the law. Why does Paul keep repeating the concept that justification is *apart from* works? Perhaps it is because we are hopelessly lost if a right standing before God depends on works. No one can do enough to satisfy a holy God, including all the works following the new birth.

The next two verses (7–8) quote a parallel blessing from Psalm 32, elaborating on God's *bestowal* (what theologians call the "imputation") of righteousness apart from works. The bottom line is that when God imputes righteousness that is alien to the individual, it belongs to Christ alone. This bestowal of righteousness goes with forgiveness. Here is a strong platform for the assurance of one's eternal relationship with God. We could never have assurance of a righteous standing and forgiveness if our relationship to God required good works. Even if it were possible to satisfy God's need for righteousness, one would never know when enough had been done. Nevertheless, when we are persuaded that God imputes righteousness to believers, not to workers, genuine happiness is ours.

Luther says, "Blessed are they who by grace are freed from the burden of iniquity, namely, [liberated] of the actual sins which they have committed."[24] Accordingly, David illustrates the blessing of a man whose sin God does not impute (4:8). Bruce remarks that there was no question of David's sin, yet he received free pardon and is declared not guilty. "And if we examine the remainder of the psalm [51] to discover the ground on which he was acquitted, it appears that he simply acknowledged his guilt and cast himself in faith upon the mercy of God."[25]

Supposing that good works are necessary compels a candid person to high anxiety because deep inside he knows that he is not good enough. His thoughts are too often evil. His attempts to control his tongue are too often defeated. Moreover, keeping injurious emotions under control is like trying to press down a balloon: About the time he gets down part of it, another section pops up again. He may suppress anger, but covetousness pops up. In addition, these questions plague a sincere person: "How many good works are enough! When have I done enough? Do I have to do a thousand? Ten thousand? A million? Are the kind of works I do pleasing to God, or only to me and someone else? On the other hand, God forbid, have I committed one sin too many, so that God will not forgive me?"

Now Paul goes head-to-head with the self-righteous and religious people who claim that works are part of the package of eternal life. He does not say that those who are born-again should not do good works. He does not say that good works do not have a place in the Christian way of life. However, if any suppose that even one good work is necessary to receive God's justification, then that man terribly misunderstands Scripture. Such a person does not grasp the significance of Abraham's salvation. Thus in Romans 4, Paul illustrates by the life of Abraham that God justifies a man through faith alone and never by works.

> *Does this blessedness then come upon the circumcised only, or upon the uncircumcised also? For we say that faith was accounted to Abraham for righteousness. How then was it accounted? While he was circumcised, or uncircumcised? Not while circumcised, but while uncircumcised. (Rom. 4:9–10)*

Paul asks another rhetorical question, regarding blessedness: "Does this blessedness then come upon the circumcised only, or upon the uncircumcised also." He is linking back to 4:6–8 where the author featured blessedness apart from works. It is a magnificent blessing, an inner sense of joy and gratitude, knowing that God graciously forgives, without demand. It was the position of many rabbis that God blessed Israel alone.

> *And he received the sign of circumcision, a seal of the righteousness of the faith which he had while still uncircumcised, that he might be the father of all those who believe, though they are uncircumcised, that righteousness might be imputed to them also, and the father of circumcision to those who not only are of the circumcision, but who also walk in the steps of the faith which our father Abraham had while still uncircumcised. (Rom. 4:11–12)*

Despite justification being by grace through faith, the Jews were inclined to treat circumcision as a means to merit righteousness before God. The Lord never intended circumcision to serve such an end. Therefore, Paul explains that circumcision was to accomplish certain post-justification benefits.

The first purpose was to grant Abraham a *sign* and *seal*. The *sign,* according to Genesis 17:11, was a "sign of the covenant" with God by which the Lord promised to multiply Abraham's descendants, make him the father of many nations, add kings to his posterity, and grant him the land of Canaan. The affirming sign of this promise was *circumcision,* i.e., "the sign [that] consists in circumcision."[26] "Circumcision is an outward sign, a pointer to the reality of that which it signifies, namely (according to Gen. 17:11) the covenant made by God with Abraham and his seed."[27]

Circumcision was not only a sign, but also "a seal of the righteousness of the faith which he had while still uncircumcised." A "seal" is something that confirms what God did for Abraham.[28] The seal was the Lord's visible guarantee to Abraham of the righteousness he acquired by faith. God granted both the seal and imputed righteousness to Abraham while he was still uncircumcised, implying that circumcision did not confer a status of righteousness on him, but was valuable as an outward and visible attestation of the righteous standing he already possessed.

Hence, the *seal* was not the means of obtaining righteousness, but an accessory after the fact. Bruce sees Paul treating circumcision as "a subsequent and external seal of that righteous status which Abraham already possessed as God's gift; it neither created nor enhanced that righteous status."[29]

Abraham is the prototype of faith resulting in imputed righteousness for those who believe what Abraham believed. Remember that in John 8:39, the Jews said to Jesus "Abraham is our father." However, Jesus did not say, "Yes, that's right." Instead, He said, "You are of your father the devil "(8:44). Physical descent and circumcision do not assure entrance into heaven.

The faith that stands alone is *persuasion of the gospel's truthfulness and personal applicability.* This single-minded faith in Christ results in circumcision of the heart, which is what matters. Elsewhere Paul says, "We are of the circumcision, who worship God in the Spirit, rejoice in Christ Jesus, and have no confidence in the flesh" (Phil. 3:3).

Not only is Abraham the father of those who by one initial act of faith become the sons of God, but he is the father of a certain category of Christians, those who continue to believe the exceedingly great and precious promises. Paul calls him "the father of circumcision to those who not only are of the circumcision, but who also walk in the steps of the faith which our father Abraham had while still uncircumcised."

Those "who also walk in the steps of faith" are Abraham's natural descendants because walking *in the steps of the faith* is possible only for those who have been born-again, those the Holy Spirit enables. Hebrews 11 mentions three noteworthy acts of faith by Abraham: (1) He left Ur, not knowing where he was going (11:8). (2) He lived as an alien in Canaan. He was willing to give up security and status and depend on God's provision (11:9-10). (3) He offered up Isaac (11:17-18). Some walk in Abraham's steps of faith. The term *walk* is literally to march in line, or file, as soldiers on a drill field. It speaks of the decisions and steps one takes in life that flow from obedience to God's Word. If Abraham is our father or prototype *in practice*—in personal experience—we too will

- obey God's Word once we grasp its meaning, even if we have unanswered questions.
- believe God when He says that He will provide for all our needs in Christ Jesus, rejecting anxiety about the material things of life.
- move forward to do God's will, regardless of dangers, trials, and opposition.

And if by grace, then it is no longer of works; otherwise grace is no longer grace. But if it is of works, it is no longer grace; otherwise work is no longer work. (Rom. 11:16)

Paul stresses the point in Romans 11:6 that God's eternal election is by grace, God's favor to us, not works. "Otherwise grace is no longer grace." Election is favorable action to which God is not bound. God is bound only by the dictates of His own divine attributes, for example his faithfulness (immutability) to His promise (veracity) to save the one who believes. God graciously provides for eternal justification without cost through Christ's redemptive work (Rom. 3:24; Eph. 2:5, 8-9).

Since human nature is sinful and hostile (Rom. 3:23; 5:10), God's favor is a free gift toward those who have no legitimate reason to expect divine generosity. In Romans 3:24 we see the absolute freeness of God's provision of eternal life by the adverb *graciously* (δωρεάν), which denotes what is freely given, without cost, without paying.[30] The believer is "justified *freely* by His grace" (Rom. 3:24). In Revelation 22:17 the Lord invites everyone to "take the water of life *freely*" (Rev. 22:17).

If God's gift of eternal salvation is without cost, it is by necessity, unrelated to works. No human deed or accomplishment matters, before, during, or after the act of faith alone in Christ alone. Charles Hodge makes this clear:

> Grace and works are antithetical. "To him that worketh is the reward not reckoned of grace, but of debt." (Rom. iv. 4.) "If by grace, then is it no more of works: otherwise grace is no more grace." (Rom. xi. 6.) Grace of necessity excludes works of every kind, and more especially those of the highest kind, which might have some show of merit. But merit of any degree is of necessity excluded, if our salvation be by grace.[31]

The giving and receiving of eternal life must be this way, for if it were different, grace is no longer grace. If election to eternal life is by works, grace no longer has the nature of an unmerited free gift. It has become something other than grace, distorted beyond recognition.

James: Faith Applied

Because of centuries of misguided interpretation of James 2, some deploy this passage to support the notion that genuine faith *inevitably* produces good works. If good works are not present, they say, faith is dead. It is not a faith that saves.

James says nothing of the kind.

We should note, first, that James writes to Christians, not unbelievers. His purpose is not to show unbelievers how to be reconciled to God; he wants to show believers how to walk to please the Lord. We know that James is addressing Christians from his use of terms. Twelve times he calls them "beloved brethren," "my brethren," or "brethren." His basis for regarding them as brothers is that they "have been brought forth [born-again] by the Word of truth" (1:18). He assumes that God is their Father (3:9) and that the Spirit dwells in them (4:5; see Rom. 8:9–11; 1 Cor. 6:19–20). They look for the coming of the Lord (James 5:7).

Second, in 1:19 James gives a three-part outline for his Epistle. Christians are to be "swift to hear" (1:21–2:26), "slow to speak" (3:1–18), and "slow to become angry" (4:1–5:6). This outline tells us to understand chapter two in the light of the admonition "Be swift to hear." Chapter two explains what James means by hearing, teaching believers how to live now that they are God's people. This portion of Scripture says nothing about what it takes to receive eternal life.

Third, those born-again, whom he urges to walk in a worthy manner, must put aside sinful thinking and behavior and welcome the "implanted Word" (1:21a). The seed of the Word has the inherent power to take root in one's life, then bring about beneficial fruits. For example, James says the Word rooted within us "is able to save your souls" (1:21b), referring to his brethren in the Lord.[32] God has already saved his readers in the sense of granting forgiveness, new birth, and eternal life. Yet, they still need to be saved. From what do Christians need to be saved? James says that Christians need to be saved—delivered or rescued—repeatedly from *various trials* (1:2), lack of *wisdom* (1:5), and the death-dealing power of temptation and sin (1:14–15). If we are to be delivered daily from these problems, the Word must become implanted in our souls. We must be "swift to hear."

Being "swift to hear," or a "doer of the Word," means not becoming sidetracked with partiality, thereby neglecting the poor (2:1–13). In fact, if "my brethren" fail to minister to those with pressing needs, what, James asks, "does it profit" (2:14a)? If *a brother or sister* is destitute of life's necessities, and we do not minister to them, again, he asks, "what does it profit" (2:15–16)? His fellow believers who show partiality and lack compassion are not "swift to hear," not doers of the Word. There is no *profit*, no practical benefit, resulting from their faith.

In this light, James asks, "Can faith save him (1:14)?" Can faith, so entangled with partiality and disconnected from merciful works, deliver or rescue a believer from life's troubles and the death-dealing power of temptation and sin? The required answer is "No!" Instead, such a believer will experience overwhelming trials, along with temptation and sin that "bring forth death" (1:15; 5:19–20). He does not have eternal death in view, but rather temporal death-like experience (cf. Rom. 7:24; 8:6).

James concludes this subsection by saying, "Thus faith by itself, if it does not have works, is dead" (1:17). He does not say that an unbeliever does not have faith and needs the miracle from God of implanted faith. He does say that a believer who is indifferent to the pressing needs of fellow believers has a "faith by itself." This faith is lonesome; it has no works to keep it company. Moreover, when one's faith is not exercising itself though merciful deeds, it is dead in the sense that it is unproductive. A fruitless faith is like a barren fruit tree. It is without practical benefit to others. This point is reinforced in 2:20 where again James says "faith without works is dead." The best Greek manuscripts use a different term for "dead" here (ἀργό), than in verses 17 and 26 (νεκρό). The term in verse 20 does not mean "dead," but "idle or useless"—the Christian's faith without works is profitless.

This point is illustrated through the lives of Abraham and Rahab (2:21–25), both of whom were "justified by works." James has been challenging born-again believers and now underscores his challenge with positive examples of two Old Testament believers. When Abraham offered Isaac on the altar (2:21), he had been born-again for some forty years. God had imputed righteousness to Abraham for his faith years before and his eternal destiny was not in question. His "good work" regarding Isaac did not justify Abraham in God's eyes (vertical justification that is by faith alone), but in the eyes of other people (horizontal justification that is by faith plus works). Some writers throw in a cute expression here, saying that "faith alone saves, but the faith that saves is not alone." Their implication is that saving faith inevitably produces goods works, thus James says works justified Abraham. Moreover, they imply, if works are not there, then one has not received eternal life.[33]

However, chapter two addresses believers who are not swift to hear, that is, not doers of the Word. They are seriously compromising their testimony to the poor, not to mention in the eyes of the affluent unbeliever who benefited from their partiality. They are of no practical benefit to others, so that even the validity of their faith is in question. God alone knows that they have believed in Jesus as the Christ, the Son of God. None saw that transaction with God. If these believers are to recover their testimony before the poor and rich, they must do more than believe. Their idle, useless, dead, faith has to come alive in works. Then, as Abraham and Rahab, works will justify them in the eyes of the poor and rich. Only through faith plus works can they authenticate before the world their certain eternal relationship with God.

James wraps-up his challenge to believers who fall short of "swift to hear" with a subtle personal exhortation. "As the body without the spirit is dead, so faith without works is dead also" (2:26). James has urged believers to light a fire under their idle, useless faith in order to benefit others. He has told how an active faith vindicates one's faith (1:21), helps bring one's faith to maturity (1:22), and (c) makes one a *friend of God* (1:23).

In verse 26, an analogy gives us wonderful incentive for being *swift to hear*—a doer of the Word. As the human spirit is the body's animating source of physical life, so works animate faith. Good works not only profit fellow believers, they also profit the worker. They breathe life, vitality, and energy into our faith. Paul says in Romans 10:17 that faith comes by hearing. James adds that faith also comes alive by using. As we are swift to hear, we become doers of the Word, applying it in our lives.

THE NATURE OF FAITH

Ability to Believe

Ephesians 2:1 declares that unbelievers are "dead in trespasses and sins." Some infer that this means these dead cannot believe. Yet context does not say that. To be dead is to be alienated from God (in the sense of v. 12). God is the source of spiritual life. Accordingly, to be dead is to be cut off from eternal life. This says nothing about one's inability to believe. Though one might deduce that such a dead man cannot believe, we have the New Testament illustration of Lazarus responding to the voice of God (John 11). Since Lazarus in his grave responded to Jesus' voice, we may conclude that an unbeliever, who is spiritually dead, can respond to the illuminating voice of the Holy Spirit. The problem is not the unbeliever's inability to believe when the Spirit illumines; the problem is his inability to know and understand apart from the supernatural illumination of God the Holy Spirit.

Another illustration from life is Cornelius in Acts 10. This centurion is unregenerate, dead in sins. Yet he was not like a rock, unable to respond to God. To the contrary, Cornelius the non-Christian was "a devout man and one who feared God and he gave alms and prayed to God always" (10:2). He received revelation from God (10:3, 22) and the Lord recognized his prayers and alms (10:4, 31). When Peter preached the gospel to him, saying that "whoever believes in [Jesus of Nazareth] will receive remission of sins" (10:34–43), the Holy Spirit fell upon all who heard (10:44). Nothing suggests that Cornelius the non-Christian was spiritually insensitive. He was able to hear and believe the message.

Belief and Persuasion

One must either believe the gospel or reject it in disbelief. In Acts 28:24, Luke contrasts *persuaded* with *disbelieved,* showing that *persuaded* and *disbelieved* are opposite sides of a coin. Accordingly, not to believe *is* not to be persuaded. To believe *is* to be persuaded of the truth of the gospel, thus Luke expresses the concept of "believe," using its synonym.

What about the term *persuade* (πείθω)? The New Testament uses it both in active and passive senses. That is, Scripture speaks of trying to *persuade* someone that the gospel is true; this is the active use. Alternatively, the word is used of someone becoming convinced that something is true, the passive use.

Here are examples of someone taking initiative (active voice):

- Luke 11:22 speaks of armor in which a man trusted (lit. "had trusted," from πείθω), adding the nuance of *trust* (having been persuaded) to the notion of *persuade.*
- Acts 18:4 reveals that Paul persuaded, or convinced Jews and Gentiles.
- Acts 19:8 speaks of "reasoning and persuading" others of the things concerning the kingdom of God.
- Acts 28:24 shows the apostle trying to persuade, or convince the Jews of Rome.

Luke also uses the term in the passive sense of being persuaded, coming to depend on, trust, or rest confidence in something:

- Luke 16:31, the rich man was told that if his brothers would not believe Scripture, they would not be persuaded even by someone rising from the dead.
- Luke 20:6, the people are persuaded (sure, certain) that John was a prophet.
- Acts 17:3b–4, "this Jesus whom I preach to you is the Christ. And some of them were persuaded."
- Acts 28:24, be persuaded, be convinced, come to believe. Here "persuaded" opposes "disbelieved" (ἐπείθοντο . . . ἠπίστουν).

Did Paul persuade unbelievers by his ability to communicate? The Holy Spirit used his words—which were God's words—to persuade them. God is the One who says "Let there be light" (2 Cor. 4:6). Note how in John 3:36, being persuaded relates to eternal life: "He who believes in the Son has everlasting life; and *he who does not believe* [ἀπειθέω] the Son shall not see life, but the wrath of God abides on him."

To "not believe" (ἀπειθέω) is to refuse to believe the Christian message, even to refuse to be a believer, or to reject the Christian message (cp. Acts 14:2; Eph. 2:2).[34] Hodge defined faith, in keeping with the biblical emphasis on being persuaded, as "the reliance of the mind on anything as true and worthy of confidence." He elaborates that

> in the strict and special sense of the Word, as discriminated from knowledge or opinion, faith means the belief of things not seen, on the ground of testimony. . . . In the New Testament God is said to have borne witness to the truth of the Gospel by signs, and wonders, and divers miracles, and gifts of the Holy Ghost (Heb. ii. 4); and the Spirit of God is said to witness with our spirits that we are the children of God (Rom. viii. 16). The Word in these cases is marturevw, to testify. This is not a lax or improper use of the Word testimony; for an affirmation is testimony only because it pledges the authority of him who makes it to the truth. . . . When, therefore, it is said that faith is founded on testimony, it is meant that it is not founded on sense, reason, or feeling, but on the authority of him by whom it is authenticated.[35]

SALVATION AS A GIFT (EPH. 2:8–9)

By grace you have been saved through faith, and that not of yourselves; it is the gift of God, not of works, lest anyone should boast. (Eph. 2:8–9)

When Paul in Ephesians 2:8 uses the clause *that not of yourselves* we are naturally drawn to ask the question "What does *that* refer to?" According to Greek grammar, it cannot refer to the words *grace* or *faith* because the pronoun translated "that" has an ending in the neuter gender. Both *grace* and *faith* are in the feminine gender. Corresponding terms must agree in gender. Grammatically, *that* can only refer to the conceptual notion as a whole, God's provision of a salvation that is by grace through faith.[36] His salvation is of grace because He provides and initiates eternal life apart from all human effort; it is of faith because one must believe in the Lord Jesus Christ. Moreover, salvation is "not of ourselves" because the faith exercised has no virtue or merit in itself. Merit is drawn strictly from the object of faith, Jesus Christ.

Moule has a helpful illustration from his day and age:

> When lately the vast dam of the Nile was completed, with all its giant sluices, there needed but the touch of a finger on an electric button to swing majestically open the gates of the barrier and so to let through the Nile in all its mass and might. There was the simplest possible contact. But it was contact with forces and appliances adequate to control or liberate at pleasure the great river. So Faith, in reliance of the soul, the soul perhaps of the child, perhaps of the peasant, perhaps of the outcast, is only a reliant look, a reliant touch. But it sets up contact with Jesus Christ, in all His greatness, in His grace, merit, saving power, [and] eternal love.[37]

Paul prays for illumination (Eph. 1:17–18). As far as sequence goes, verse 18 indicates what happened when the Ephesians became believers: "The eyes of your understanding having been enlightened" (πεφωτισμένου τοῦ ὀφθαλμοῦ τῇ καρδία ὑμῶν). God enlightened them in the past, and enlightenment can continue to be their experience. Paul prays that God will give Christians an on-going spirit of wisdom and revelation in the knowledge of Him (2:17).

From the human side, remember that the ability to believe is not the problem. The problem is that the unbeliever does not know or understand the gospel, because Satan blinds him and seeks to pluck the seed of the gospel out of his heart.

To counter the blinding work of the devil, when one hears the gospel the Holy Spirit illumines the unbeliever's understanding. At the point of understanding—the moment of truth—three possibilities exist:

1. The person believes, resulting in the new birth and eternal life. If later he doubts, or even rejects, it has no effect on his status in God's family (2 Tim. 2:11–13).

2. The person doubts, thus is still not born-again, still in a searching mode.
3. The person rejects (disbelieves) and remains in danger of missing eternal life, yet so long as he lives the opportunity exists.

What is the result for those who believe? Universally, when one believes "that Jesus is the Christ, the Son of God" (John 20:31a), it results in belief and life in His name (v. 31b). One act of faith in Jesus Christ culminates in eternal life, imputed righteousness, and forgiveness. Moule notes that "faith is the way and means of our Justification. By Faith we are united to Christ. By that union we truly have a righteousness. And upon that righteousness the justice as well as mercy of God is engaged to justify and acquit us."[38]

Nowhere does John's Gospel add repentance. Nowhere does he include good works as an inevitable and necessary result of faith. Eternal life is a free gift by grace alone, through faith alone, in Christ alone; each person needs to establish this truth firmly in mind. Only then should the person attempt to advance in the Christian way of life and learn the importance of good works to meet pressing needs (Eph. 2:10; Titus 3:8, 14).

THE ROLE OF REPENTANCE

Most of the viewpoints sampled at the beginning of this chapter insist that, to be eternally saved, one must repent—turn physically and emotionally from sin. Usually they add a necessity for the emotional response of sorrow. The kingdom of God or eternal life, they allege, is not for people who want no change in their lives. Others see repentance, not as a change of lifestyle, but a change of mind, thus eliminating a logical tension between salvation by grace and salvation by works.

What, then, is the place of repentance in God's plan? John clearly states in the gospel that his purpose for writing is to show how one "may have life in [Christ's] name" (20:30-31). John was "moved by the Holy Spirit" to state his purpose, thus we must conclude that he accomplished his goal, recording everything one must do to have eternal life. To suppose otherwise assumes that John either misrepresented, or failed to achieve, his purpose. A proper view of inspiration does not permit such suppositions.

Nowhere does John mention or allude to repentance (μετανοέω; μετάνοια).[39] Since we must not suppose that John fails to teach us how to achieve eternal life, it is clear that God does not require repentance. This is not an argument *from* silence, but an argument *about* silence. John does not mention repentance precisely because it is not germane to his subject.[40] God does not require one to repent to receive eternal life; He requires faith alone in Christ alone, period.

What about the passages that mention repentance? It is obviously an important theme in the Bible. While we cannot here do a full exegesis of the biblical concept, we suggest two points for consideration. First, no New Testament text, not even Acts 11:18, directly links repentance and eternal life.[41] Second, many New Testament passages urge Christians to repent of sin that they might avoid divine discipline (see for example, the letters to the churches in Revelation 2–3). None of these occurrences makes repentance a prerequisite to receive eternal life.

If in order to be saved we must repent and believe, then believing is not the only condition of eternal life and *sola fide* is not true. Intellectual honesty would abandon the charade of justification by faith alone, if repentance is an independent condition. This is true whether we marry such repentance at the beginning of faith, or attempt to finesse it into the picture after the moment of faith as a so-called inevitable and necessary fruit of faith.

CONCLUSION

I have written to you briefly, exhorting and testifying that this is the true grace of God in which you stand. (1 Peter 5:12)

When he speaks of testifying to the "true grace of God," Paul implies that there is a false notion of the grace of God. Pseudo grace is grace that in any way seeks to wed works to faith alone in Christ alone for eternal life. Grace and works are antithetical ideas (Rom. 11:6). If someone teaches that we must have faith *plus anything* to be saved, that doctrine is not grace. Similarly, if anyone teaches that works are a necessary and inevitable result of faith, that is not grace. It is an erroneous notion of salvation by grace through faith. Neither Ephesians 2:8–9 nor James 2 teach such a doctrine.

The apostle says all that needs to be said for eternal life: "God loved the world in this manner that He gave His uniquely begotten Son, that every believer in Him should not perish but have eternal life" (John 3:16, author's translation). One needs no more than this simple yet profound message to pass from darkness and death to light and life. Accordingly, Jesus says, "Most assuredly, I say to you, he who believes in Me has everlasting life" (John 6:47).

CHAPTER 17

The Personality and Deity of God the Holy Spirit

Robert G. Gromacki

THE PERSONALITY OF THE HOLY SPIRIT

Who or what is the Holy Spirit? Some view Him as the personification of holy power in the same sense as they view Satan as the personification of evil power. In both cases, the Holy Spirit and Satan are not accepted as real, personal beings. Others see the Spirit as the *energy* of God, an impersonal influence that God uses to activate His will in the universe.

The erroneous doctrine of modalism teaches that God is one being, manifesting Himself in three modes: the Father, the Son, and the Holy Spirit. This position denies the eternal existence of three distinct centers of personhood within the one divine being. In stressing monotheism, modalism rejects trinitarianism. The Holy Spirit is merely a mode or manifestation of God. Advocates often use the illustration of water and its three manifestations as liquid, vapor, and ice. However, the water in question cannot be at the same time liquid, vapor, and ice. It can change from one form to the other. The Father does not change into the Son nor does the Son change into the Spirit.

In the unitarian monotheism espoused by liberal Christendom, there is a belief in one divine being and eternal person, God the Father. Jesus Christ is seen merely as a man with a strong God-consciousness. The Holy Spirit is a way of referring to God's activity in the world. Any unitarian approach denies the personality of the Holy Spirit.

Evangelicals believe in trinitarian monotheism. We believe in one God, eternally existing or subsisting in three Persons—God the Father, God the Son, and God the Holy Spirit. We believe in the intrapersonal oneness of the three Persons within the one divine Being. We also affirm that the Father is not the Son nor the Spirit, that the Son is not the Father nor the Spirit, and that the Spirit is not the Father nor the Son. We affirm eternal and distinct personhood of the Father, the Son, and the Holy Spirit.

What the Holy Spirit Is Not

The Holy Spirit Is Unlike the Spirit of Man

God formed the body of Adam from the dust of the earth, breathed into man the breath of life, and man became a living being (Gen. 2:7). Man, thus, is a physical-psychical being. Christ distinguished between the body and the soul of man (Matt. 10:28). Paul divided man into spirit, soul, and body (1 Thess. 5:23). In this life, the immaterial self is inseparably related to the material body. At death, the spirit-self separates from the lifeless body.

The Spirit of God, though, is not like the spirit of man. Paul made this distinction: "For what man knows the things of a man except the spirit of the man which is in him? Even so no one knows the things of God except the Spirit of God" (1 Cor. 2:11).[1] The spirit of man is *in man*. However, the same words, "which is in him," are not repeated for the Spirit of God, because the Holy Spirit is not *in God*.

The Spirit knows the things of God because He is God. The Father, the Son, and the Holy Spirit all know the things of God because they are all coequally God.

The Holy Spirit Is Not a Physical Being

Jesus Christ taught that God was spirit in essence (John 4:24). Likewise, Paul affirmed that God was both immortal and invisible (1 Tim. 1:17). The very name of the Holy Spirit refers to His immaterial nature. He is spirit, not corporeal. He has neither shape nor form.

The Holy Spirit is a pure spirit, a personal, eternal being. He is everywhere present in the totality of His divine essence. He has no physical properties.

The Holy Spirit Is Not a Thing

The designation of "the Holy Spirit" comes from the Greek *to hagion pneuma*. The term *pneuma*, usually translated "spirit" or "wind," is a noun that is grammatically neuter in gender.

Rules of Greek grammar classify nouns, pronouns, adjectives, and articles into masculine, feminine, or neuter gender. These three groupings have nothing to do with personality or sexuality. For example, the Greek word for "house" is *oikos*, which uses endings that are masculine in gender. All words modifying *oikos* likewise would have masculine endings. However, the house is a thing, thus an adjustment in translation is necessary to convey proper meaning in English. Literally, someone speaking Greek says "I see my house and am walking toward him." But that person means the same as an English speaker who says, "I see my house and am walking toward it."

Gender has caused problems for those who seek to work out a doctrine of the Trinity. Some deny the personality of the Holy Spirit, arguing that the *pneuma* is neuter; they conclude that the Spirit must be an "it"—an inanimate thing. The King James Version translators fell into this grammatical trap with the translation "The Spirit itself beareth witness with our spirit that we are the children of God" (Rom. 8:16; also see 8:26). The word for "itself" is the neuter pronoun *auto*, since to be grammatically correct it must agree in gender with *to pneuma* ("the Spirit"), a neuter noun. All modern versions have corrected this King James oversight to read: "the Spirit Himself" (e.g., NKJV, NIV, NASB).

Christ used both masculine and neuter pronouns to describe the Holy Spirit. On the night before His crucifixion, He said to His disciples, "When the Helper comes, whom I shall send to you from the Father, the Spirit of truth who proceeds from the Father, He will testify of me" (John 15:26). The title *Helper* or *Comforter*, is from the masculine noun *paraklētos*. The relative pronoun *whom* (*hon*) is also masculine, agreeing with *paraklētos*. The relative pronoun *who* (*ho*) is neuter, agreeing with *pneuma* ("Spirit"). The pronoun *He* is actually the demonstrative pronoun *ekeinos*, masculine gender agreeing with *paraklētos*.

Earlier Christ promised the disciples, "And I will pray the Father, and He will give you another Helper *[allon paraklēton]*, that He may abide with you forever" (John 14:16). The adjective *another* (*allon*) means "another of the same kind." Christ was a personal comforter and encourager to the twelve; thus the Holy Spirit would also be a personal helper. Christ contrasted Himself with another person, not with an impersonal thing.

Christ also said to the apostles, "These things I have spoken to you while being present with you. But the Helper *[paraklētos,* masculine], the Holy Spirit *[to pneuma to hagion,* neuter] whom *[ho,* neuter] the Father will send in My name, He *[ekeinos,* masculine] will teach you all things, and bring to your remembrance all things that I said to you" (John 14:25-26). The mix of masculine and neuter nouns and pronouns show that personality is definitely part of the nature of the Spirit. The teaching responsibilities of the Spirit also indicate that He is a person, just as Christ was a teaching person.

Christ later declared, "I tell you the truth. It is to your advantage that I go away; for if I do not go away, the Helper *[paraklētos,* masculine] will not come to you; but if I depart, I will send Him *[auton,* masculine] to you. And when He *[ekeinos,* masculine] has come, He will convict the world of sin, and of righteousness, and of judgment" (John 16:7-8). The usage of the masculine pronouns is based upon the gender agreement with *paraklētos*. The convicting ministry depicts the work of a real person.

Again, the Lord Jesus stated, "However, when He *[ekeinos,* masculine], the Spirit [*to pneuma*, neuter] of truth, has come, He will guide you into all truth; for He will not speak on His own authority, but whatever He hears He will speak; and He will tell you things to come. He [*ekeinos*, masculine] will glorify me, for He will take of what is Mine and declare it to you" (John 16:13–14). The use of *ekeinos* is significant because its nearest antecedent is *paraklēton* (16:7), whereas the neuter noun *pneuma* is found in the immediate context. Again, the easy exchange of masculine and neuter pronouns argue for the personality of the Holy Spirit. The activities of the Spirit mentioned in these verses also point to a person rather than to a thing.

What the Holy Spirit Is

The Qualities of a Person

The marks of personality include an awareness of self-existence, an awareness of self-consciousness and distinction from other persons and things, and a sense of moral "oughtness." The traits of personality also involve the capacities to think, to feel, and to choose. As humans, we are moral, mental, emotional, and volitional beings.

From our understanding of the personality of man and from an investigation of the Word of God, we can dogmatically declare that the Holy Spirit is a person.

He thinks. The Holy Spirit has intelligence. He is omniscient. He knows all things. Paul wrote, "Now He who searches the hearts [God the Father] knows what the mind of the Spirit is, because He [the Spirit] makes intercession for the saints according to the will of God" (Rom. 8:27). Thus, the Spirit has a mind, an infinite mind.

In his exposition of the indispensable ministry of the Holy Spirit in divine revelation, inspiration, and illumination, Paul declared: "But God has revealed them to us through His Spirit. For the Spirit searches all things, yes, the deep things of God. For what man knows the things of a man except the spirit of the man which is in him? Even so no one knows the things of God except the Spirit of God" (1 Cor. 2:10–11). The Holy Spirit knows. In order for Him to know the things of God completely, He must also be God. Only God can know God perfectly.

Obviously the Holy Spirit must have intelligence in order to teach (John 14:26), to testify (15:26), to convict (16:8), to guide (v. 13), to reveal (v. 13), and to glorify Christ (v. 14).

Isaiah identified the Holy Spirit as the one who would anoint, fill, and indwell the promised Messiah. He described Him thus: "The Spirit of the LORD shall rest upon Him, the Spirit of wisdom and understanding, the Spirit of counsel and might, the Spirit of knowledge and of the fear of the LORD" (Isa. 11:2). These features show that the Holy Spirit has a mind, an infinite capacity to think.

He feels. Paul cautioned believers, "And do not grieve the Holy Spirit of God, by whom you are sealed for the day of redemption" (Eph. 4:30). Deliberate sin by a Christian emotionally hurts the indwelling Spirit. The Greek word *lypeō* ("grieve") is the same word used for

- the sorrow of the apostles over the forthcoming crucifixion of Christ (Matt. 17:23).
- the sorrow of the rich young ruler after he left Christ in unbelief (Matt. 19:22).
- the sorrow of the disciples over the announcement that one of them would betray Christ (Matt. 26:22).
- the intense sorrow of Christ as He prayed in Gethsemane (Matt. 26:37).
- the sorrow of Peter over Christ's challenge of love and loyalty (John 21:17); the sorrow of the Corinthian church which led to repentance (2 Cor. 2:2, 4; 7:8-9, 11).
- the sorrow of believers over the deaths of loved ones (1 Thess. 4:13).
- the burden of heaviness produced by life's trials (1 Peter 1:6).

Parents have been grieved by the rebellion and disrespect of their children. Husbands and wives hurt each other by verbal assaults and deceitful or disloyal acts. Emotional hurt seems far more severe when the ones we love the most violate our relationship. So it is with the Holy Spirit. All sin grieves the Spirit, but those deliberate sins committed against Him by believers in whom He dwells hurt Him the most. Such grief shows the emotional aspect of His personality.

He decides. The Holy Spirit has a will; He can choose or decide. The Holy Spirit said to the prophets and teachers of the church at Antioch, "Now separate to me Barnabas and Saul for the work to which I have called them" (Acts 13:2). He chose two out of the five. His will was for Paul and Barnabas to be the first missionaries into the gentile world.

On his second missionary journey, Paul and his team were forbidden by the Holy Spirit to evangelize the Roman provinces of Asia and Bithynia (Acts 16:6-7). Again, the Spirit revealed His will as to the geographical focus of the preached word.

All believers have received spiritual gifts or abilities from the Holy Spirit. He also determines what gift will be imparted to each Christian. Paul wrote, "But one and the same Spirit works all these things, distributing to each one individually as He wills"(1 Cor. 12:11). It is as He wills, not as we will.

What we do says much about who we are. Animals do what they do because they are animals. Birds do what they do because they are birds. Humans do what they do because they are human. Likewise the Holy Spirit does what He does because He is a divine Person.

He guides. Christ promised His disciples, "However, when He, the Spirit of truth, has come, He will guide you into all truth" (John 16:13). The verb *hodēgeō* ("guide") occurs only five times in the Greek New Testament. Christ used it twice to depict the blind leading the blind (Matt. 15:14; Luke 6:39). It is used of Christ, the Lamb, who will lead the redeemed to "living fountains of waters" (Rev. 7:17). When Philip encountered the Ethiopian eunuch and asked the ruler whether he understood the text of Isaiah, the eunuch responded, "How can I unless someone guides me?" (Acts 8:31). The Holy Spirit can use yielded, knowledgeable believers to guide others into an understanding of the Word of God.

The verb is related to a common noun *hodos* (*road* or *way*). The concept of guidance involves destination, assistance, time, and determination to move forward in one's spiritual life.

He convicts. Jesus Christ, speaking about the Holy Spirit, said, "And when He has come, He will convict the world of sin, and of righteousness, and of judgment" (John 16:8). The verb *elenchō* ("convict") is a legal term. In a human courtroom, the prosecuting attorney must present evidence to the jury and the judge that the accused defendant is guilty beyond a reasonable doubt.

In the moral conviction of sin, righteousness, and judgment, the Holy Spirit does not attempt to convince a jury of the sinner's peers. Rather, He creates within the sinner an awareness of his own personal sin and guilt. He persuades the sinner to confess his guilty status before the Judge of the universe. Only then can the sinner receive the gracious gift of salvation through Jesus Christ. This process of moral and personal conviction can only be done by another moral person. It is life influencing life.

He works. After Philip baptized the converted Ethiopian eunuch, "the Spirit of the Lord caught Philip away, so that the eunuch saw him no more, and he went on his way rejoicing. But Philip was found at Azotus" (Acts 8:39–40a). Like a whirlwind, the Holy Spirit physically transported Philip from one geographic location to another. This unique miracle was the act of a divine Person.

He prays. Paul wrote, "Likewise the Spirit also helps in our weaknesses. For we do not know what we should pray for as we ought, but the Spirit Himself makes intercession for us with groanings which cannot be uttered. Now He who searches the hearts knows what the mind of the Spirit is, because He makes intercession for the saints according to the will of God" (Rom. 8:26–27). Such prayer is the effort of a person. True prayer goes from our hearts through the mind of the Spirit to the Father.

He searches. Paul wrote that "the Spirit searches all things, yes the deep things of God" (1 Cor. 2:10b). The verb *eraunaō* ("search") occurs six times. Christ challenged His critics to search the Scriptures concerning Him (John

5:39). The religious leaders criticized Nicodemus for partially defending the ministry of Christ and challenged him: "Search and look, for no prophet has arisen out of Galilee" (John 7:52). Both God the Father and God the Son search out the hearts of men (Rom. 8:27; Rev. 2:23). The prophet searched the Old Testament to understand the correlation of the sufferings and the glory of the promised Messiah (1 Peter 1:11). Searching involves mental analysis. Only persons can do it, so the Holy Spirit must be a person.

Luke recounted what happened to Paul and his team during the apostle's second missionary journey: "Now when they had gone through Phrygia and the region of Galatia, they were forbidden by the Holy Spirit to preach the word in Asia. After they had come to Mysia, they tried to go into Bithynia, but the Spirit did not permit them" (Acts 16:6-7). The actions of forbidding (*kōlyō*) and permitting (*eiasen*) are choices of persons.

He speaks. When God spoke, He could be understood by men and by angels (Heb. 1:1-2). Passages abound where the Father spoke and the Son spoke. There are also references to the speech of the Holy Spirit. We do not know whether the words of the Spirit were audible to all or just to the intended recipient. Luke wrote, "Then the Spirit said to Philip, Go near and overtake this chariot" (Acts 8:29). Philip understood, obeyed, and thus evangelized the Ethiopian eunuch.

God gave a vision to Peter in the city of Joppa. Luke then added, "While Peter thought about the vision, the Spirit said to him, Behold, three men are seeking you. Arise therefore, go down and go with them, doubting nothing, for I have sent them" (Acts 10:19-20). Peter obeyed the divine injunction.

The words of the Holy Spirit to the leadership of the church at Antioch produced the first missionary team. Luke recounted, "As they ministered to the Lord and fasted, the Holy Spirit said, 'Now separate to me Barnabas and Saul for the work to which I have called them'" (Acts 13:2). How did the Spirit say those words to a group? We do not know, but apparently the leaders discerned the will of God and commissioned the pair. The composition of Scripture is also related to the speech or word of the Holy Spirit.

Prior to the selection of Matthias to be the twelfth apostle, Peter announced, "Men and brethren, this Scripture had to be fulfilled, which the Holy Spirit spoke before by the mouth of David concerning Judas, who became a guide to those who arrested Jesus" (Acts 1:16). Paul used similar words: "The Holy Spirit spoke rightly through Isaiah the prophet to our fathers" (Acts 28:25). The text of Scripture thus is the voice of the Holy Spirit. His words have meaning and syntactical relationships. These are the properties of communication among persons.

The words of Jesus Christ are also equated with the words of the Holy Spirit. Christ addresses the seven churches of Asia (Revelation 2-3). Each letter concludes, "He who has an ear, let him hear what the Spirit says to the churches" (Rev. 2:7, 11, 17, 29; 3:6, 13, 22). These are shared words from two of the three Persons within the one divine Being.

He loves. We know that God the Father loves us (John 3:16) and that God the Son loves us (Eph. 5:25). God the Holy Spirit, being coequal with the Father and the Son, also loves us. Paul wrote, "Now I beg you, brethren, through the Lord Jesus Christ, and through the love of the Spirit, that you strive together with me in prayers to God for me" (Rom. 15:30). This love could be interpreted as either our love for the Spirit or His love for us. The latter seems probable. After all, His purpose in us is to produce spiritual fruit, namely love (Gal. 5:22–23). If He wants us to love others, then surely He must also love them and us.

The Holy Spirit Can Be Mistreated Like a Person

He can be blasphemed. Jesus Christ encountered a blind and mute man whose physical problems were caused by demonic possession (Matt. 12:22–23). Christ cast out the demon, and the man was then able to speak and to see. The multitude who witnessed the miracle questioned whether Christ could be the Son of David, the promised Messiah. The disturbed Pharisees rebutted, "This fellow does not cast out demons except by Beelzebub, the ruler of the demons" (Matt. 12:24). The Pharisees admitted the reality of the exorcism. The leaders affirmed that the man was indeed blind and mute, that he was indwelled by a demon, that demons did exist as supernatural evil beings, and that Satan or Beelzebub was the ruler of the demons. The Pharisees, however, sinned when they claimed that Jesus Christ performed the miracle by the evil spirit of Satan rather than by the Holy Spirit. Christ responded with this warning: "Every sin and blasphemy will be forgiven men, but the blasphemy against the Spirit will not be forgiven men" (Matt. 12:31). Only persons can be blasphemed, thus the Holy Spirit must be a person. Christ admitted that the Holy Spirit had energized Him: "But if I cast out demons by the Spirit of God, surely the kingdom of God has come upon you" (Matt. 12:28). The issue of that day was simple: Was Jesus Christ controlled by the Holy Spirit or by Satan?

Blasphemy against the Holy Spirit was the unpardonable sin of the Jewish leaders. Christ called them "a brood of vipers" (Matt. 12:34) and confirmed them in their position of condemnation. He warned, "Anyone who speaks a word against the Son of Man, it will be forgiven him; but whoever speaks against the Holy Spirit, it will not be forgiven him, either in this age or in the age to come" (Matt. 12:32). The phrase *this age* referred to the age when Christ was on earth, preaching, healing, and offering the messianic kingdom to Israel. The phrase *the age to come* referred to the church age, the age that would occur after Christ's death and resurrection. These same Jewish leaders, blinded by their spiritual hardness, repeatedly rejected the message of the apostles (Acts 4:1–21; 5:1–40).

He can be lied to. In the early history of the church at Jerusalem, Ananias and Sapphira sold some property, secretly kept some of the sale money, and gave the rest to the church (Acts 5:1–2). The couple deliberately gave the impression that they had given all of the sale money to the church. Luke then recorded this incident: "But Peter said, Ananias, why has Satan filled your heart to lie to the Holy Spirit and keep back part of the price of the land for yourself?" (v. 5:3). The couple through their planned deception sinned against the apostles and the church body, but ultimately they sinned against the Holy Spirit. The Spirit indwelled the believing couple, the apostles, and the Christians within the Jerusalem church. In that sense, they lied to the Holy Spirit.

He can be resisted. Stephen was one of the seven original deacons or servants who assisted the apostles in the church at Jerusalem. He was "full of the Holy Spirit and wisdom" (Acts 6:3). He also had an active outreach ministry. The Bible says, "And Stephen, full of faith and power, did great wonders and signs among the people" (v. 8). The religious leaders disputed with him, but "they were not able to resist the wisdom and the Spirit by which he spoke" (v. 10). In a public defense before his critics, Stephen reviewed the plan of God for Israel, her historical past, and her rejection of the prophetic messages.

He concluded, "You stiff-necked and uncircumcised in heart and ears! You always resist the Holy Spirit; as your fathers did, so do you" (Acts 7:51). The Jewish people resisted the Spirit in that they rejected the Spirit-filled prophets who proclaimed the Spirit-inspired word of God. The rejection of the personal prophets was really the rejection of the person of the Holy Spirit. Such resistance is deliberate, sinful, and culpable.

He can be grieved. Paul gave this prohibition: "And do not grieve the Holy Spirit of God, by whom you were sealed for the day of redemption" (Eph. 4:30). Only persons can be grieved, thus the Holy Spirit is a person. In this context, believers can grieve the Spirit by living as pagan gentiles (vv. 17–19), by yieldedness to the sinful disposition (vv. 22–24), by lying (v. 25), by anger (vv. 26–27), by stealing (v. 28), by using corrupt speech (v. 29), by bitterness (v. 31), by an unforgiving spirit (v. 32), and by sexual immorality (5:3–5).

He can be quenched. Paul gave this negative command: "Do not quench the Spirit" (1 Thess. 5:19). The verbal concept *sbennymi* is based upon the metaphor of fire. It is used eight times in the New Testament. In His tenderness, Christ would not quench any smoking flax, meaning that He would not stamp out the smallest amount of flickering faith and commitment (Matt. 12:20). The foolish virgins lamented that their lamps had gone out (25:8). Christ described Hell as a place where the fire would not be quenched (Mark 9:44, 46, 48). Believers can use the shield of faith "to quench all the fiery darts of the wicked one" (Eph. 6:17). Heroes of faith, like Shadrach, Meshech, and Abednego, were able to quench the violence of fire when they survived in the fiery furnace (Heb. 11:34; cf. Dan. 3:23–28).

He can be insulted. Persons can verbally reproach or insult other persons. The verb *hybrizō* (*insult*) stresses the shameful treatment of persons (Matt. 22:6; Luke 11:45; 18:32; Acts 14:5; 1 Thess. 2:2). Both Christ and Paul were thus treated (Luke 18:32; 1 Thess. 2:2). Unsaved persons are often violent, spiteful in their insults (Rom. 1:30). Paul confessed that he had been an insolent man, injuring others with his verbal insults, in his unsaved life (1 Tim. 1:13).

The book of Hebrews contains a dire warning: "Of how much worse punishment, do you suppose, will he be thought worthy who has trampled the Son of God underfoot, counted the blood of the covenant by which he was sanctified a common thing, and insulted the Spirit of grace?" (Heb. 10:29). The verb *enybrizō* is found only here in the New Testament. It is a compound verb, based upon the regular verb for insult, *hybrizō,* and the preposition prefix *en* (*in*). That preposition seems to indicate that the believer has insulted the Holy Spirit who dwells within him. That concept makes the sin more heinous than one committed by an unsaved person. Thus, the verbal insult against the gracious Holy Spirit shows that He is indeed a person, not an influence or thing.

The Holy Spirit Relates to the Father and to the Son

There are several passages where the Father, the Son, and the Holy Spirit are mentioned together. They are seen as three distinct persons, relating to each other in a divine work.

After His resurrection but prior to His ascension, Jesus Christ gave the great commission to the apostles: "All authority has been given to me in heaven and on earth. Go therefore and make disciples of all the nations, baptizing them in the name of the Father and of the Son and of the Holy Spirit, teaching them to observe all things that I have commanded you, and lo, I am with you always, even to the end of the age" (Matt. 28:18–20). The baptismal authorization is significant. The Father, the Son, and the Holy Spirit are joined together under a singular name (not *names*). Genuine believers should be baptized in the name of the triune God. God is one in being, thus He has one name. At the same time, there are three separate personal distinctions of persons within the one divine Being. If the Father and the Son are persons, then the Holy Spirit must also be a person.

Peter set forth the eternal redemption plan with these words: "Elect according to the foreknowledge of God the Father, in sanctification of the Spirit, for obedience and sprinkling of the blood of Jesus Christ" (1 Peter 1:2). The Father elected, the Spirit sanctified, and Christ redeemed us. Those are three blessed actions done by three blessed divine Persons. The Spirit must be seen as a person in the same sense that the Father and Jesus Christ are persons.

Jude identified the three divine Persons with this exhortation: "But you, beloved, building yourselves up on your most holy faith, praying in the Holy Spirit, keep yourselves in the love of God, looking for the mercy of our Lord Jesus Christ unto eternal life" (Jude 20-21). A cursory reading of these verses easily gives the proper interpretation of three separate persons.

The Holy Spirit Relates to Jesus in His Ministry

In the upper room discourse (John 13-17), Jesus Christ distinguished the Holy Spirit from Himself (John 14:16-17, 26; 15:26; 16:7-11, 13-15). Christ declared that the Holy Spirit would help believers, indwell them, teach them, assist them in their witness, and guide them. The Savior also pointed out that the Spirit would convict the world and that He would glorify Christ.

Christ regarded the Spirit as a person who could minister in the place of Christ, doing what Christ had previously done. The Lord Jesus did not give the impression that the Spirit was a mere divine influence or power, an impersonal entity.

The Holy Spirit Relates to the Church

At a council convened in Jerusalem, the apostles and the church elders in the presence of the congregation debated the relationship of physical circumcision to divine justification. They concluded that all, both Jews and gentiles were saved by grace alone through faith alone in Christ alone. They affirmed that the rite of circumcision was unnecessary and should not be imposed upon uncircumcised gentile believers.

The council then composed an authoritative letter to the gentile believers. "It seemed good to the Holy Spirit, and to us, to lay upon you no greater burden than these necessary things," their report read (Acts 15:28). They referred to themselves ("us") and to the Holy Spirit in a simple expression of personal equality. Of course, they knew that the Holy Spirit was divine and that they were human. Nevertheless, they agreed as beings who shared responsibility for the church.

THE DEITY OF THE HOLY SPIRIT

The Holy Spirit could be a person without being God. Angels and humans are personal beings without being divine. However, if the Holy Spirit is God, then He also must be a person, because God is a personal being. Deity implies the possession of personality.

Evangelicals relate the deity of the Holy Spirit to both the deity of God the Father and the deity of God the Son. As we argue for the oneness of the divine being (monotheism), we must also demonstrate the trinity of the

Godhead (trinitarianism). We maintain that the Father, the Son, and the Holy Spirit are three distinct, divine persons who have an intrapersonal unity within the one being of God.

Names of the Holy Spirit

Names Relating to the Trinity

The Holy Spirit is related to God the Father in these titles:

- "the Spirit of God" (Gen. 1:2; 1 Cor. 3:16) or "the Spirit of our God" (1 Cor. 6:11);
- "the Spirit of Yahweh" (Judg. 3:10) or "the Spirit of the Lord God" (Isa. 61:1; Luke 4:18);
- "the Spirit of the living God" (2 Cor. 3:3);
- "My Spirit" (Gen. 6:5), "His Spirit" (Num. 11:29), or "Your Spirit" (Ps. 139:7);
- "the Spirit of your Father" (Matt. 10:20);
- "the Spirit of Him who raised Jesus from the dead" (Rom. 8:11).

The Holy Spirit is related to God the Son through these titles:

- "the Spirit of Jesus" (Acts 16:7), "the Spirit of Jesus Christ" (Phil. 1:19), "the Spirit of Christ" (1 Peter 1:11);
- "the Spirit of His Son" (Gal. 4:6);
- "the Spirit of the Lord" (Acts 8:39).

These names definitely show a relationship between two distinct persons. They also imply the possession of equal deity in those special relationships.

Names and Divine Attributes

Holy. His most familiar name is the *Holy Spirit.* That title is indelibly inscribed within the formula of Christian baptism: "baptizing them in the name of the Father and of the Son and of the Holy Spirit" (Matt. 28:19b). God is holy (Lev. 11:44; 1 Peter 1:16). What He does manifests who and what He is. He is the eternal objective standard of personal holiness. This title for this divine person, *the Holy Spirit,* denotes His holy deity. He also is designated as "the Holy One" (1 John 2:20) and "the Spirit of holiness" (Rom. 1:4).

Eternal. God is eternal, neither beginning nor ending. The Holy Spirit is called *the eternal Spirit,* showing that divine attribute (Heb. 9:14).

Glory. The glory of God is the manifestation of all that He is. Only God has glory in that infinite sense. The Holy Spirit bears the name "the Spirit of glory" (1 Peter 4:14).

Life. God has self-sufficient life. He is not dependent upon anyone or anything outside of Himself for the creation or sustenance of His being. He immutably was, is, and always shall be. The Holy Spirit is called "the Spirit of life" (Rom. 8:2). Christ is life (John 14:6), as is the Spirit; both impart and sustain life in others without diminishing themselves.

Truth. God *is* truth, so he necessarily acts and speaks truthfully (John 17:17). There can be no duplicity in Him. Likewise, the Holy Spirit is named the Spirit of truth (John 14:17; 16:13). In the life of each child of God, the Holy Spirit teaches the truth revealed in the Scriptures—the word of truth—and guides the believer into all truth.

Grace. God is gracious in and of Himself. He bestows His grace upon undeserving sinners. The Lord Jesus Christ is full of grace (John 1:14), and so is the Holy Spirit. He is identified as the Spirit of grace (Heb. 10:29). He dispenses the grace of God as He works out the redemptive purpose of God in each converted sinner.

Wisdom. God alone is wise (1 Tim. 1:17). We can all exclaim with Paul, "Oh, the depth of the riches both of the wisdom and knowledge of God! How unsearchable are His judgments and His ways past finding out!" (Rom. 11:33). God knows everything actual and possible, and yet He has never learned. He is infinitely omniscient. With this understanding about the nature of God, Paul identified the Holy Spirit as the Spirit of wisdom and revelation (Eph. 1:17).

At the baptism of Jesus, God anointed His Son with the Holy Spirit. Christ then began His public ministry of preaching, teaching, and healing. Isaiah predicted this key messianic event: "The Spirit of the Lord shall rest upon Him, the Spirit of wisdom and understanding, the Spirit of counsel and might, the Spirit of knowledge and of the fear of the Lord" (Isa. 61:2). The role of the Holy Spirit in the life of Christ is inseparably linked to the concepts of wisdom and knowledge.

Other Names

On the day of His ascension, Christ equated the Holy Spirit with "the Promise of the Father" (Acts 1:4). The Savior had taught that the Father would send the Spirit once He had ascended into the presence of the Father (John 14:16-17, 26).

Christ also gave to the Holy Spirit the name *paraklētos* ("Comforter or Helper"; John 14:16, 26). Christ comforted, helped, and encouraged all of his disciples when He was on earth with them. The Holy Spirit would perform the same ministry within their lives after Jesus had ascended. In that sense, the Spirit would be *allos* ("another" of the same kind) comforter. To be another of the same kind, the Spirit would have to be as divine as Jesus Christ.

Each believer has received the Holy Spirit as a Spirit of adoption (Rom. 8:15). The indwelling presence of the Spirit, made possible through spiritual regeneration, enables each Christian to call God his Father.

His Attributes

The attributes of God are those qualities or characteristics that belong only to Him eternally and infinitely. They constitute who He is. God did not acquire them, nor can He lose them. He is immutable, therefore He can be nothing other than what He is.

God the Father, God the Son, and God the Holy Spirit coequally, eternally and infinitely possess the divine attributes. What is true of one divine Person is true for the other two. The Scriptures indicate that the Holy Spirit has those attributes that only the true God possesses.

He Knows All Things

No creature, by sense perception, logical reflection, or imagination, could ever know God's creative-redemptive plan. For us to know, God must reveal them. God has done exactly that through the ministry of the Holy Spirit. Paul explained, "But God has revealed them to us through His Spirit. For the Spirit searches all things, yes, the deep things of God. For what man knows the things of a man except the spirit of the man, which is in him? Even so no one knows the things of God except the Spirit of God" (1 Cor. 2:10–11). The Spirit knows exactly what God the Father knows. The Holy Spirit, therefore, must be God, because only God can know as God knows. There is no sense of learning within the eternal knowledge of the Spirit.

Jesus Christ declared, "However, when He, the Spirit of truth, has come, He will guide you into all truth; for He will not speak on His own authority, but whatever He hears, He will speak; and He will tell you things to come" (John 16:13). God is true, never false. The Spirit, whose essence is truth, speaks truth and guides into truth. There are no errors in His ministry due to misinformation or faulty reasoning.

Christ added, "He will glorify Me, for He will take of what is Mine and declare it to you. All things that the Father has are Mine. Therefore I said that He will take of Mine and declare it to you" (John 16:14–15). The Father, the Son, and the Spirit share this truth. What belongs to one belongs to the others. Any one of the divine persons can reveal the mind of God because each person knows the mind fully. The Father knows all things (Jer. 17:10), the Son knows all things (Rev. 2:23), and the Spirit knows all things (1 Cor. 2:11).

He Is Everywhere Present

All creatures can only be in one place at one time. They are localized, finite beings. God, however, can be everywhere present in the totality of His divine being. God can be present in heaven and on earth at the same time. He can be both here and there. He is omnipresent.

David wrote, "Where can I go from Your Spirit? Or where can I flee from Your presence? If I ascend into heaven, You are there. If I make my bed in hell, behold, You are there. If I take the wings of the morning, and dwell in the uttermost parts of the sea, even there Your hand shall lead me, and Your right hand shall hold me" (Ps. 139:7–10). No human, either before or after death, can escape the omnipresence of the Spirit. This truth is a blessing to the child of God. How wonderful to know that wherever we go, God is there, the God of all grace and comfort.

Another proof for the omnipresence of the Holy Spirit can be seen in His part in redemption. In order to enter the kingdom of God, a person must be born again of the Spirit of God (John 3:3–8). The Spirit bears believing sinners into the family of God. Unbound by time and space, He can do this in many different places at the same time, while simultaneously indwelling all believers (1 Cor. 6:19). Such individual ministries are possible because the Spirit can be everywhere present.

He Is All-Powerful

God inquired concerning Himself, "Is anything too hard for the Lord?" (Gen.18:14). When the angel Gabriel informed Mary of the forthcoming virgin conception and birth, he assured her, "For with God nothing will be impossible" (Luke 1:37). Only God is omnipotent. He can do anything consistent with His essence and will. The Bible affirms that the Holy Spirit has this divine attribute.

Elihu said to Job, "The Spirit of God has made me, and the breath of the Almighty gives me life" (Job 33:4). Elihu attributed his human existence to the procreative activity of the Spirit, plus His providential preservation of his life. All human life is derived from parents and eventually from Adam and Eve. God is the source of all life. The Spirit of God is involved in the giving of that life.

He Is Eternal

Only God is eternal. He has neither beginning nor ending. Angels and humans had a beginning in time, but they will continue to live forever in their creative existence.

The Holy Spirit is eternal as the Father and the Son are. The book of Hebrews stated, "How much more shall the blood of Christ, who through the eternal Spirit offered Himself without spot to God, cleanse your conscience from dead works to serve the living God?" (Heb. 9:14). Jesus Christ, full of the Holy Spirit offered Himself as the redemptive sacrifice for our sins through the ministry of the Spirit. The Spirit is here identified as the eternal Spirit.

He Is Called God

Acts 5

In discussing the personhood of the Holy Spirit, we have referred to Peter's testimony against Ananias and Sapphira in Acts 5 as showing that the Spirit is a person who can be lied to. But Peter says more as he sees the implications Ananias had not anticipated in his lie. A lie is a violation of truth. A lie is also a sin against the God of truth. The ninth commandment codified for Israel the divine prohibition of bearing false witness (Exod. 20:16). Paul instructed believers to tell the truth and not to lie (Eph. 4:25). In all ages, lying between persons is wrong because it ultimately is a sin against God.

In condemning Ananias and Sapphira, Peter said that they ultimately had not lied to the apostles and the church; they had lied to the Holy Spirit. "Why have you conceived this thing in your heart? You have not lied to men but to God" (Acts 5:4b).

1 Corinthians 6

In a personal sense, every believer is indwelled by the Holy Spirit. When believers come together as a local church, that corporate body also is indwelled by the Spirit.

Paul thus warned the Corinthian assembly, "Do you [plural] now know that you [plural] are the temple of God and that the Spirit of God dwells in you [plural]? If anyone [singular] defiles the temple of God, God will destroy him. For the temple of God is holy, which temple you [plural] are" (1 Cor. 3:16–17). Believers, individually and corporately, constitute the temple of God. God dwells in them individually and as a corporate assembly because the Spirit of God is in them. Paul thus equates God with the Holy Spirit.

His Work

God manifests who He is by what He does. His works are divine because He is divine. His works are supernatural and unmatched. The Holy Spirit thus discloses His deity.

In Creation

"In the beginning God created the heavens and the earth. The earth was without form, and void; and darkness was on the face of the deep. And the Spirit of God was hovering over the face of the waters" (Gen. 1:1–2). Other translations give the sense that the Spirit was brooding or moving over the waters. To be sure, the Holy Spirit was present and actively involved in the creation event and process.

Later, God decreed, "Let Us make man in Our image, according to Our likeness, let them have dominion over the fish of the sea, over the birds of the air, and over the cattle, over all the earth and over every creeping thing that creeps on the earth. So God created man in His own image; in the image of God He created him; male and female He created them" (Gen. 1:26–27). The two phrases, "in Our image" and "in His own image," refer to the triunity of God. God is one being, thus the creation of man is in His (singular) image. God exists in three Persons, thus the creation of man is in Our (plural) image.

His sustaining ministry in creation was affirmed by the psalmist: "You send forth Your Spirit, they are created; and You renew the face of the earth" (Ps. 104:30). The Spirit is both life-giving and life-sustaining.

In the Incarnation

Paul identified the manifestation of God in the flesh as the first part of "the mystery of godliness" (1 Tim. 3:16; cf. John 1:14). The Incarnation was achieved by the conception and birth of Jesus Christ through a virgin (Isa. 7:14). *Parthenogenēsis* (fr. Gk. *parthenos*, "virgin," and *genetē*, "birth") is a biological impossibility. Yet in the creative-redemptive purpose of God, this divine work in Mary was accomplished through the ministry of the Holy Spirit (Luke 1:30–33).

Only through this ministry could the Messiah, Jesus Christ, be both divine and human. God the Son, a divine person with a divine nature, obtained a human nature through Mary. Theologians call this a *hypostatic union*, two natures united within the single person of Christ. This impossibility was made possible through the Holy Spirit (Matt. 1:19–20; Luke 1:34–35). The Holy Spirit superintended the act of conception as God the Son entered the womb of Mary as a miraculously fertilized ovum. The miracle of the Incarnation occurred at the conception. Mary underwent a normal pregnancy climaxed by a normal birth. We can assume that the Holy Spirit continued to minister to her, protecting her from miscarriage, birth defects, or other complications.

Although the Holy Spirit was sovereign in the act of conception, Christ is never called "the son of the Holy Spirit." God the Father was the eternal Father of God the Son. Because the Spirit represented the Father in the conception, Mary could pass her human nature to Jesus Christ without contaminating the fetus with depravity. Thus the divine human Son of God could be a second Adam, holy in all aspects of personhood.

In Inspiration

God is true, thus He speaks truth (John 17:17; Rom. 3:4). His words are infallible and inerrant. The Bible equates the oral word of God with the written word of God. Paul asserted, "All Scripture is given by inspiration of God, and is profitable for doctrine, for reproof, for correction, for instruction in righteousness" (2 Tim. 3:16). Inspiration technically refers to what is written, not to the human authors who wrote.

The Holy Spirit superintended the production of the Scriptures. Peter wrote, "Knowing this first, that no prophecy of Scripture is of any private interpretation, for prophecy never came by the will of man, but holy men of God spoke as they were moved by the Holy Spirit" (2 Peter 1:20–21). No person, unaided by God, can determine the divinely intended meaning of the Scriptures. No writer of a biblical book determined by his own initiative and intelligence to write.

Therefore, the biblical canon of the sixty-six books did not originate within the human impulse or imagination. God providentially set the writers apart for their task and prepared them through genetic inheritance, family background, educational opportunities, and life experiences. This divine action, executed by the Holy Spirit, changed these men into "holy men of God." The Holy Spirit then guided them in what they spoke and wrote. The Spirit burdened their hearts and minds. The divinely prepared and enabled men then wrote exactly what God wanted them to write, adding nothing and leaving out nothing.

The result is that the Bible is a divine-human book, the revealed truth of God written in human vocabulary and grammar, apart from error in the original documents. The Bible is without error in all matters, from theology to history, geography, and science.

In Redemption

The Holy Spirit's active role in redemption also reveals deity. The works of the Father and of the Son would be incomplete without the work of the Holy Spirit. Redemption is the work of the triune God.

All believers are born of God into His family (John 1:13). That act of spiritual regeneration is directly attributed to the Holy Spirit. Jesus said to Nicodemus, "Most assuredly, I say to you, unless one is born of water and the Spirit, he cannot enter the kingdom of God" (John 3:5; cf. 3:6–8). To be born of God is to be born of the Spirit; thus the Holy Spirit must be God.

Paul described the essence of salvation:

> *But when the kindness and the love of God our Savior toward man appeared, not by works of righteousness which we have done, but according to His mercy He saved us, through the washing of regeneration and renewing of the Holy Spirit, whom He poured out on us abundantly through Jesus Christ our Savior, that having been justified by His grace we should become heirs according to the hope of eternal life." (Titus 3:4–7)*

All three divine Persons are inseparably involved in our salvation. The Father, the Son, and the Holy Spirit each has a distinctive role in the execution of the plan of redemption, but it is the work of the one God to whom we give glory and worship.

His Association Within the Trinity

In the divine program of progressive revelation, the Old Testament stresses the monotheistic nature of God, whereas the New Testament emphasizes God's Trinitarian nature. The concept is not unknown in the Old Testament, however.[2]

Indications of Plurality

First, the Hebrew name that is often used for *Yahweh* in the Old Testament, *Elohim,* has a plural ending (*im*) added to the singular noun that generically refers to "a god," *el.* Plural pronouns also were ascribed to God at very key points in Scripture. God said, "Let us make man in our image" (Gen. 1:26). The plural cannot refer to both God and a non-divine being. It can only refer to multiple persons within the oneness of God.

Singular and plural pronouns are used in the same grammatical contexts to describe the one action of the one God. At the creation of man, God said, "Let us make man in Our image, according to Our likeness. . . . So God created man in his own image; in the image of God He created him; male and female He created them" (Gen. 1:26, 28).

God commissioned the prophet Isaiah with the question, "Whom shall I send, and who will go for Us?" (Isa. 6:8). Since God is one, He can say "I." Because of the plurality of the Persons, He can also say "Us."

Even in the *Shema* (*šĕmaᶜ*) of Israel, the very foundational confession of *Yahweh* as "one," the use of the adjective *one* (*eḥād*) in Deuteronomy 6:4 is significant.[3] The adjective can refer to a single person—or to a single people. The corporate usage (one people) implies that there is more than one person within the singular group. This usage was common in the Old Testament (Gen. 2:24; Exod. 24:3; 26:11; Judg. 6:16; Ezek. 37:19). These occurrences reveal a plurality in unity, not a single undiversified sameness.

Indications of Three Persons

The first suggestion of three persons is seen in the priestly blessing which God directed Aaron to pronounce upon Israel: "The LORD bless you and keep you; The LORD make His face shine upon you, and be gracious to you; The LORD lift up His countenance upon you, and give you peace" (Num. 6:24–26). Here is a triple blessing with a triple mention of God's name. It was not given once, twice, or four times; rather, it was stated three times.

The second suggestion is found in the worship and praise of the angelic seraphim: "Holy, holy, holy is the LORD of hosts, the whole earth is full of His glory" (Isa. 6:3). This triple invocation coupled with the later plural pronoun usage argue for three Persons (Isa. 6:8).

Mention of Three Names

Isaiah revealed a distinction of three persons. God said through the prophet, "Come near to Me, hear this: I have not spoken in secret from the beginning; from the time that it was, I was there. And now the Lord God, and His Spirit have sent me" (Isa. 48:16). Here is the mention of one person, the speaker (I, me), a second person (Lord God), and a third person (His Spirit).

In a prediction, Isaiah recorded the words of the promised messiah:

> The Spirit of the Lord God is upon Me, because the Lord has anointed Me to preach good tidings to the poor; He has sent Me to heal the brokenhearted, to proclaim liberty to the captives, and the opening of the prison to those who are bound; to proclaim the acceptable year of the Lord, and the day of vengeance of our God; to comfort all who mourn. (Isa. 61:1-2)

Jesus Christ applied this prophecy to Himself when He taught in the synagogue at Nazareth (Luke 4:16-21). This significant passage mentions one person, the speaker (Me), a second person (the Spirit), and a third person (Lord God, Lord, our God).

The New Testament clarified the Old Testament allusions to the plurality of divine persons. At the baptism of Jesus by John the Baptist in the Jordan River, all three Persons were active and identified. Matthew wrote that "the heavens were opened to Him, and He saw the Spirit of God descending like a dove and alighting upon Him. And suddenly a voice came from heaven, saying. 'This is my beloved Son, in whom I am well pleased'" (Matt. 3:16-17). There is the mention of one person, Jesus (He, Son), a second person (the Spirit), and a third person (God the Father through the heavenly voice). This event does not demonstrate that all three persons are coequally divine, but it does show three separate persons at the same event.

At His temptation by Satan, Jesus was led by the Holy Spirit into the wilderness (Matt. 4:1). As the divine-human Son of God, He knew that it was wrong to tempt the Lord God by presumptuous acts (Matt. 4:7). He also recognized that true worship must always be directed toward the Lord God (Matt. 4:10). All three Persons of the Trinity figure into this narrative, although this Scripture does not attribute deity to all.

On the night before His crucifixion, Jesus Christ made a distinction among the three Persons: "And I will pray the Father, and He will give you another Helper, that He may abide with you forever—even the Spirit of truth" (John 14:16-17a). He repeated the distinction twice in John 14:26 and 15:26. He placed the Father, the Holy Spirit, and Himself together as separate Persons in heaven.

Paul ended an epistle with this glorious benediction: "The grace of the

Lord Jesus Christ, and the love of God, and the communion of the Holy Spirit be with you all. Amen" (2 Cor. 13:14). The names of these three distinct Persons are presented in this sequence: Lord Jesus Christ, God the Father, and the Holy Spirit.

Peter explained the activity of the three Persons in the program of redemption: "Elect according to the foreknowledge of God the Father, in sanctification of the Spirit, for obedience and sprinkling of the blood of Jesus Christ" (1 Peter 1:2).

In an exhortation to believers to safeguard their spiritual experience, Jude appealed; "But you, beloved, building yourselves up on your most holy faith, praying in the Holy Spirit, keep yourselves in the love of God, looking for the mercy of our Lord Jesus Christ unto eternal life" (Jude 20-21). The order of name presentation here is Holy Spirit, God the Father, and Lord Jesus Christ.

Interpersonal Equality

Among the New Testament references there is not a set order for the names of the three Persons. This hints at their equality within the divine oneness. In normal evangelical expression, we identify the Trinity as the Father, the Son, and the Holy Spirit. We use that order because of the familiar baptismal formula (Matt 28:19) and because of the logical progression of roles in redemption. The Father sent the Son, and Father and Son sent the Holy Spirit. Quite often we speak of the first Person (the Father), the second Person (the Son), and the third Person (the Holy Spirit). The danger with these non-biblical designations is that they may convey the impression that the Father is superior to both the Son and the Spirit and that the Son is superior to the Spirit. That perception is false. There is an ontological equality of the three Persons within the oneness of the being of God. They are coequal, eternal, infinite, omnipotent, omniscient, omnipresent divine Persons.

All three are named as God. In greeting the readers of his epistles, Paul usually extended a blessing of grace and peace from the Father and the Son (Rom. 1:7; 1 Cor. 1:3; 2 Cor. 1:2; Gal. 1:3; Eph. 1:2; Phil 1:2; Col. 1:2; 1 Thess. 1:1; 2 Thess. 1:2; 1 Tim. 1:2; 2 Tim. 1:2; Titus 1:4; Philem. 3).

Applying Psalm 8 to Jesus, the writer of Hebrews shows the Father saying, "But to the Son He says: Your throne, O God, is forever and ever; a scepter of righteousness is the scepter of Your kingdom" (Heb. 1:8). God the Father calls the Son "God." Paul speaks of the Jewish nation in Romans 9:5: "Of whom, . . . according to the flesh, Christ came who is over all, the eternally blessed God."

Peter identified the Holy Spirit as God when he confronted Ananias: "Why has Satan filled your heart to lie to the Holy Spirit. . . . You have not lied to men but to God" (Acts 5:3-4). Ananias and Sapphira conspired to test the Spirit of the Lord (Acts 5:9). According to Christ, such testing is a sin against the Lord God (Matt. 4:7).

The Bible repudiates polytheism, including the existence of three separate gods. The above passages, therefore, must teach a trinity in unity, a plurality of three Persons within the divine oneness. Only then could the one divine Being be called God and simultaneously three separate Persons be called God. The early church had to face the problem of how to state its Trinitarian belief.

The Nicene Creed (325) stated, "We believe in one God—and in one Lord Jesus Christ, the Son of God, begotten of the Father, light of light, very God of very God, begotten, not made, being of one substance with the Father—and in the Holy Ghost." The Nicene-Constantinople Creed, formed A.D. 381, reaffirmed this position. These creeds stood for centuries as the standard of doctrinal orthodoxy.

The Athanasian Creed, formulated in the fourth or fifth century, is one of the strongest Trinitarian confessions.[4] It states in part, "We worship one God in Trinity, and Trinity in Unity, neither confounding the Persons, nor dividing the Substance." Earlier the church fathers had used such words as *one, unity,* and *substance* to stress their monotheism and such terms as *trinity* and *persons* to confess their Trinitarian faith. They were careful to point out that God could not be divided into three parts ("dividing the substance"). They also declared their belief in three Persons who had an intrapersonal oneness within the one divine Being. They did not want to confuse or confound the Persons. The Father is neither the Son nor the Holy Spirit, the Son is neither the Father nor the Spirit, and the Holy Spirit is neither the Father nor the Son.

As the sixteenth-century Protestant Reformation progressed, various church groups set forth their own doctrinal confessions. The *Augsburg Confession* (1530) reflected the belief system of Philip Melanchthon, an associate of Martin Luther. The Augsburg Confession set the direction theologically for the Lutheran Church. It states, "There is one Divine essence which is called God and is God, eternal, without body, indivisible, of infinite power, wisdom, goodness, the Creator and Preserver of all things, visible and invisible, and yet there are three Persons of the same essence and power, who also are coeternal, the Father, the Son, and the Holy Ghost."

The Reformed churches, sometimes called Calvinist, look to several confessions. Two of the most extensive and influential are the *Canons of the Synod of Dort* (1619) in the Netherlands and the *Westminster Confession of Faith* (completed in 1647), which are followed by British and especially Scottish Calvinists. Both of these documents contain strong Trinitarian definitions. For example, the *Westminster Confession of Faith* begins its confession of the person of God: "There is but one only, living and true God" (2.1). This chapter ends with a definition of the Trinity: "In the unity of the Godhead there be three Persons, of one substance, power, and eternity—God the Father, God the Son, and God the Holy Ghost: The Father is of none, neither begotten, nor proceeding; the Son is eternally begotten of the Father; the Holy Ghost eternally proceeding from the Father and the Son" (2.3).

Procession

The *Westminster Confession* uses the term *procession*, which is one way church councils and theologians have tried to verbalize how the Holy Spirit relates in role and function within the Trinity. They affirmed the eternal generation of the Son by the Father (Ps. 2:7; Acts 13:33) while denying that Christ was made or created. They also affirmed the eternal procession of the Holy Spirit from the Father and the Son. They used the terms *generation* and *procession* to designate the functional differences. The Constantinopolitan Creed, 381, stated that the Holy Spirit proceeded from the Father. At the Synod of Toledo in 589, the Latin word *filioque* (and Son) was added by the Western Church to show that the procession of the Spirit came from both the Father and the Son. The eastern half, which looked to the bishop of Constantinople rather than Rome and grew into the Greek Orthodox Church, claimed that the procession was only from the Father.

The term *procession* comes from a promise made by Christ in John 15:26: "But when the Helper comes, whom I shall send to you from the Father, the Spirit of truth who proceeds from the Father, He will testify of Me." The verb *ekporeuetai* (proceeds) literally means "to go out of." Christ taught that the Father would give the Spirit in answer to the Savior's prayer (14:16–17). He said that the Father would send the Spirit in the name of Christ (v. 26), that He would send the Spirit from the presence of the Father (15:26), and that He would send the Spirit once He had departed from earth (16:7).

Part of the difficulty in understanding this relationship is that we must distinguish between an ontological Trinity and an economic Trinity. The ontological Trinity deals with God as He is. The Father, the Son, and the Holy Spirit are ontologically equal in person, sharing the same divine essence. Jesus Christ could thus affirm, "I and my Father are one" (John 10:30).

The economic Trinity refers to God as He acts. Christ set forth this principle of function: "Most assuredly, I say to you, a servant is not greater than his master; nor is he who is sent greater than he who sent him" (John 13:16). With that principle declared, Christ later said, "My Father is greater than I" (14:28).

Thus, the procession or sending of the Holy Spirit by the Father and the Son in principle is similar to the sending of the Son by the Father. The Spirit has come to do the will of the Father and the Son. The only "subordination" of the Holy Spirit refers to His role within the economy of the Trinity, the way God acts. Ontologically the Holy Spirit is "very God of very God,"[5] equal to the Father and the Son in eternal attributes and essence.

CONCLUSION

A Christian must affirm belief in Trinitarian monotheism along with other foundational doctrines in order to be known as orthodox, evangelical, or fundamentalist. A person who denies the Trinity, the deity of Jesus Christ, or the deity of the Holy Spirit will be classified as liberal or apostate. Fringe cults, such as the Jehovah's Witnesses or the Mormons, deny the deity of the Holy Spirit. Belief in the personality and deity of the Holy Spirit has historically been a test of orthodoxy in the Christian faith.

With the rise of mysticism and the departure from serious study of Scripture and theology in churches, the twenty-first century may see a diminishing emphasis on the Trinity. To diminish these vital doctrines will be to diminish the greatness of God Himself and tragically lead to a denial of the triunity of God. There must be a renewed emphasis on all the cardinal doctrines of the faith, including the doctrine of the Holy Spirit.

CHAPTER 18

The Work of the Holy Spirit Today

Paul N. Benware

Since the human being feels as well as thinks, the saving response to Christ is both emotional and intellectual. Mind and heart are in balance in a vibrant, healthy faith. However, there is no aspect of Christian life in which one is more likely to depart from a healthy balance and swing to an extreme than in relating to the Holy Spirit. On one hand, the believer can become unduly intellectual, analyzing and trying to structure the Holy Spirit and His work. This often leads to a cold deadness that is unattractive, unsatisfying, and so unlike Jesus Christ.

PROBLEMS CONCERNING THE HOLY SPIRIT

Every area of Christian doctrine has been affected by error during the history of the church. Satan is committed to damaging and confusing the church with doctrinal errors (see 1 Tim. 4:1). The doctrine of the Holy Spirit has not escaped this attack. From the second century, a variety of errors have been introduced into the life of the church. These have distorted teaching and encouraged destructive, sinful practice. In relation to the Holy Spirit, four basic errors have periodically beset the church.

First, the Holy Spirit has wrongly been presented as simply a force from God or a created being. He has been seen as simply a mode, or expression of God, but not as a person of the Godhead. Both His deity and personality have been denied by a number of groups during church history. But the Scriptures reveal that the Holy Spirit is both a person and deity. See chapter 17 of this volume for Robert Gromacki's discussion of the deity and personhood of the Holy Spirit.

Second, teachings and practices in the church sometimes have overemphasized the Holy Spirit. This is a wrong focus, for the Spirit's ministry in this church age is to glorify Jesus Christ, the head of the church. Jesus declared that the Spirit would bear witness to and glorify Him as Christ (John 15:26; 16:12-14). Whenever the emphasis of a theology is on the Spirit and alleged manifestations of the Spirit, there inevitably is a diminished emphasis on Jesus Christ. This is contrary to Scripture.

If we are told that the Holy Spirit will not speak of himself but of Jesus, we may conclude that any emphasis upon the person and work of the Spirit that detracts from the person and work of Jesus Christ is not the Spirit's doing. In fact, it is the work of the spirit of Antichrist, whose endeavors are to minimize Christ's person (1 John 4:2-3). Important as the Holy Spirit is, he is never to preempt the place of Christ in our thinking.[1]

The apostles did not stutter when they declared that the Word of God is the final authority in all areas pertaining to life and godliness (2 Peter 1:2-4; see also 2 Tim. 3:15-17). The Word brings a believer to maturity and evaluates all experience.

In the realm of spiritual mysticism, some have left the authority of the Word of God and established the authority of experience. The authority is claimed because the experience is attributed to God the Holy Spirit. Herein lies great danger. Dr. Joseph Chambers, a pastor in one of the denominations in which this sometimes has been a problem, wisely observes that "we do have experiences in the subjective realm, but never do they take precedence over truth as established in the Bible. Living in the world of the subjective experience, or great emotional feelings is the most dangerous area of the believer's life."[2]

It is so dangerous because the Spirit is asked to do something that Scripture never promises He will do, offer an authority for the believers practice that is independent of Scripture.

THE MINISTRY OF THE HOLY SPIRIT PRIOR TO PENTECOST

The church age began with the outpouring of God's Spirit at Pentecost (Acts 2:1-4) and it will continue until the Rapture (1 Thess. 4:13-17). This is the period discussed in this study, rather than the Holy Spirit's ministries in this world since the Creation. However, in order to understand today's ministry, it is helpful to contrast it with the Spirit's work in the days prior to His coming at the Feast of Pentecost.

There are about one hundred references to the "spirit of God" in the Old Testament. It is difficult to be confident of an exact number, for some of these are unclear as to meaning. The Hebrew word translated "spirit" is the same word that can be translated "breath" or "wind." It is, therefore, somewhat tenuous to establish clear doctrinal positions on these verses. While people in the Old Testament era could not understand the person and the work of the Holy Spirit as we do, that does not mean that the Spirit was not present and at work (cf. Acts 7:51; 2 Peter 1:21). But the emphasis in the Old Testament was on the role of God the Father, rather than on the Son Jesus Christ or the Holy Spirit.

The Old Testament writers did not directly reveal the doctrine of the Trinity but allowed for it and prepared for it when they used the plural for *God* (*Elohim*). The Holy Spirit who presided over the development of revelation apparently had the plural used with a view to the future unfolding of the doctrine of the triune God.

The Holy Spirit came in sovereign power upon selected Old Testament saints from time to time as they were called to perform specific tasks. Not all believers knew such an indwelling. This special filling, when it did occur, tended to be temporary. The Spirit's ministries were limited in extent.[3] Not only did a minority of God's people enjoy the Spirit's filling, but the working of the Spirit was generally focused on tasks pertaining to the nation of Israel. And, as noted, there was a limit to the duration of the Spirit's indwelling. Finally, the ministries were limited in number. Some ministries found in the church age are never mentioned as having occurred in the Old Testament period.

At the Jewish Feast of Tabernacles, six months before the crucifixion, the Lord Jesus spoke of a coming time when the Spirit would be "given" to His followers (John 7:37-39). Since the Spirit was in fact present and active in their lives, this "giving" of the Spirit is not a reference to an initial coming. The Holy Spirit, being fully God, is omnipresent and therefore never could be absent from the earth. Rather, Jesus statement was looking at the full, unique ministries of the Spirit that would begin at Pentecost. Jesus declared that in a new way believers would be the Holy Spirit's channel of blessing to others. The apostle John links this "giving" of the Holy Spirit with the glorification of Christ—His resurrection and ascension back to the Father. While John 7:37-39 is not a full and complete discussion of the Spirit's ministries in the church age, it does make it clear that there would be some obvious differences between the old and new dispensations.

The night before the Crucifixion, Jesus spoke in greater detail about the Spirit's coming and ministries (John 14-16). When Jesus returned to the Father, the Spirit would be sent to be the "helper" of the believer. Jesus reminded the disciples that the Spirit had been "with" them. But soon the Spirit would be "in" them (John 14:16-17). This statement made it clear that a significant change in the Spirit's role was about to take place. This significant change took place, as promised by Christ, on the day of Pentecost (cf. Acts 1:5-8; 2:1-4). The permanent indwelling of the Holy Spirit in every believer, along with other new manifestations of His active participation, would be unique to this present age.

THE HOLY SPIRIT AND THE UNBELIEVER

It should not be assumed that the Holy Spirit only labors on behalf of the believer and that He is uninvolved in the experience of the unbeliever. All unsaved people benefit from the gracious activities of the Spirit, even if they are not aware of His working. The Spirit deals in the realm of common grace—God's unmerited favor toward all, as displayed in His general care for them. For example, the restraint of sin and the sending of rain and fruitful seasons are great blessings to the unsaved, whether the individual ever acknowledges them (Gen. 6:3; Psalm 19; Matt. 5:45; Acts 14:17).

The Spirit reveals the gospel (John 16:8–11). He presents evidence that condemns the world of their unbelief regarding Jesus Christ. And He convicts the unsaved of the reality of righteousness, the righteousness God requires, and the righteousness He provides through the resurrected Christ.

THE HOLY SPIRIT AND THE BELIEVER

The emphasis in the New Testament, of course, is on the Holy Spirit's workings in and through the believer who has placed his trust in Jesus Christ alone. On the day of Pentecost (Acts 2) the church began. Until the Holy Spirit came that day with new and expanded ministries, no one (including the apostles) was in the church. The church did not exist until the head of the body, Jesus Christ, had risen from the dead, ascended back into heaven, and sent the Holy Spirit (Eph. 1:22–23). A believer enters this body of Christ, through baptism (cf. 1 Cor. 12:12–13). That particular ministry of the Spirit did not and could not exist until Pentecost. On that day, the Holy Spirit came with His new ministries and expanded ministries as they now related to that new entity called the church.

To some degree, the grace of God is experienced by all people. But since this common grace does not bring salvation, another aspect of grace is needed. Efficacious grace (also called particular grace or effective grace) is the work of the Spirit of God, which brings about salvation. This grace operates at the moment of salvation. It is an act of the Holy Spirit's work on the will of a person to desire to receive Christ as savior.

The work of efficacious grace is a catalyst, as in a chemical reaction. Two substances combined in a test tube might not react until another element (a catalyst) is introduced. Then reaction occurs. An unsaved individual has a will (the ability to choose) and hears the gospel message (the capacity to understand). But nothing happens until the Holy Spirit enters the process. The Spirit enables the person to choose to trust Jesus Christ. Without the Spirit's work of grace the individual would not and could not make that decision. This ministry of the Spirit is clearly connected to the doctrine of the radical depravity of man. Every unsaved person is spiritually dead—unable to choose holiness and salvation.

This ministry of the Spirit is based on *grace* and *call*. *Grace*, of course, is God's unmerited favor, extended to His creatures. Ephesians 2:8 relates that "by grace you have been saved." We neither deserve nor work for God's salvation; it can only be a gift to us (cf. Rom. 3:24). If one could contribute in any way to his salvation, then salvation is no longer a matter of grace. The word *call* is also important. Occasionally the word *call* is used of the general invitation to receive Christ, but usually it has a more restricted use. Charles Ryrie comments,

> The vast majority of occurrences [of the term *call*] concern the effective call that leads to salvation. From such verses as Romans 1:1; 8:28; 1 Timothy 6:12; and 2 Peter 1:3, 10 it is clear that the calling is not merely a general invitation but is that mysterious yet effective work of God through the Holy Spirit which brings man to saving faith in Jesus Christ. To those who are not called in this effectual sense, the gospel remains foolishness (1 Corinthians 1:21–25).[4]

In regeneration the Holy Spirit imparts eternal life to a person who trusts in Christ (Titus 3:5). It is an instantaneous change from spiritual death to spiritual life that is miraculously and powerfully brought about by the Spirit, the agent of regeneration.

In Titus 3:5 the word *regeneration* is used in teaching that this rebirth is the direct ministry of the Holy Spirit. Scripture also speaks of the "new birth" (John 3:3), of "being born" (John 1:13), of being made a "new creation" (2 Cor. 5:17), and being "made alive" (Eph. 2:5). The nineteenth-century Princeton theologian Charles Hodge observed that in regeneration there is

> a new life communicated to the soul; the man is the subject of a new birth; he receives a new nature or new heart, and becomes a new creature. As the change is neither in the substance nor in the mere exercises of the soul, it is in those immanent dispositions, principles, tastes or habits which underlie all conscious exercises, and determine the character of the man and of all his acts.[5]

The permanent, universal indwelling of believers, a chief mark of the Spirit's ministry, is the basis for many other ministries. All who have come to faith in Christ have the indwelling of the Spirit. Those who do not have the experience are not believers (John 14:16–17; Rom. 8:9, 11; 1 Cor. 3:16; 6:19; Jude 19). The New Testament never warns that the Spirit's presence can be lost because of sin. Sin will negatively influence the power for living and the believer's fellowship with the Lord, but it will not expel the Spirit.

The teaching of the New Testament is that in this age the Holy Spirit lives permanently in each believer. Important implications accompany this truth. Ryrie notes that "whether or not we feel it, God the Holy Spirit lives within our beings constantly. This ought to give us (a) a sense of security in our relationship with God, (b) a motivation to practice that presence of God, and (c) a sensitivity to sins against God."[6]

Also, the indwelling presence of the Spirit is God's "pledge" that He will complete the work of salvation in our lives (Eph. 1:14). This "down payment" of the Spirit's presence in the believer's life is the guarantee of future blessing. Further, the indwelling of the Spirit makes the believer's body a temple for the Spirit (1 Cor. 6:12–20). This changes the way in which believers are to view and treat their bodies. This truth should have a profound affect on Christian living.

The Holy Spirit places the believer into the universal church, the "body of Christ" by a spiritual baptism. By this means all true Christians are brought into organic union with Christ; a union that is essential for holy living. This ministry of the Holy Spirit automatically takes place at regeneration.

A variety of teachings have muddied this truth for many believers. Some have not differentiated between baptism by the Spirit and filling by the Spirit. Others have confused the baptizing work of the Spirit with regeneration, indwelling, or anointing. Some Christians seek a different baptism of the Spirit subsequent to salvation.

Another reason there has been a lack of clarity is that some do not maintain the distinction between Israel and the church, teaching instead that the church is the elect of all ages. If the church began at some point in the Old Testament, Holy Spirit baptism has no relation to the New Testament church since Spirit baptism did not begin until Pentecost.

Only a careful analysis of the Scriptures can bring about a clear understanding on this work of the Spirit. Ryrie writes that a proper understanding of this ministry of the Spirit does make a difference:

> Confusion results in misunderstanding and divisions among Christians. Additionally, a lack of understanding of this doctrine obscures the important and wonderful truth of our union with Christ and consequently wrecks the foundation of Christian living. If one does not understand the baptizing work of the Spirit, then he cannot understand the only sure basis for holy living. The baptism joins us to Christ, and this is the basis for a holy walk with the Lord.[7]

All four Gospels quote the words of John the Baptist regarding the baptism of the Spirit (Matt. 3:11; Mark 1:8; Luke 3:16; John 1:33). John the Baptist foretold that the Christ would baptize believers in the Spirit. His question in Luke 7:18–20, as to whether Jesus was the Messiah, indicates that John poorly understood this baptism. He knew nothing of the concept of the church as the "body of Christ" (1 Cor. 12:13). He did see Christ as the agent who would baptize men in the Holy Spirit at some future time.

It may be that John was simply declaring that when Messiah came He would immerse believers into the many and varied ministries of the Spirit prophesied in Joel 2:28–32 and by the Lord Himself in John 7:37–39 and 14:16–17. When he speaks of Jesus baptizing with the Holy Spirit and fire, he seems to be making the same point that Jesus made in John 5 when He said that all men would face Him either as the giver of life (baptism) or as the judge (fire). John's statement is general, probably not as significant to the discussion as one might initially think.

The most important scripture in the discussion of the baptizing work of the Holy Spirit is 1 Corinthians 12:13. This verse is a didactic (teaching) passage and not one that simply describes an event. This is an important distinction, as shown by such theologians as John R. W. Stott:

> We should look for the revelation of the purpose of God in Scripture in the teachings of Jesus, and in the sermons and writings of the apostles, and not in the purely narrative portions of the Acts. What is described in Scripture as having happened to others is not necessarily intended for us, whereas what is promised to us we are to appropriate, and what is commanded to us we are to obey.[8]

Since it is the only text that specifically instructs us on the matter of Spirit baptism, we must listen carefully to the apostle in 1 Corinthians 12. First, Paul teaches that all believers have been baptized by the Spirit. It is a universal experience. No unbaptized believer exists. Second, the use of the aorist tense suggests that it is an unrepeated experience. Nowhere is any believer rebaptized. That would necessitate being removed from the body of Christ and then returned into the body. Third, it is a ministry that automatically occurs at regeneration. There is no evidence anywhere that believers existed who were not Spirit baptized. And it should be noted that nowhere in the Scriptures is a person commanded to be baptized by the Spirit or to seek Spirit baptism. This is to be expected since the believer is never told to seek an experience that has already occurred.

There is a teaching that tries to avoid the thrust of 1 Corinthians 12:13. This view attempts to distinguish between being baptized "by" the Spirit and being baptized "in" or "with" the Spirit. It is said that all believers are baptized "by" the Spirit into the body of Christ but that is not enough. Believers subsequent to their conversion need to be baptized "in" or "with" the Spirit if they would know the power of God. In such a post-conversion experience Christ would be the agent who baptizes believers into the sphere of the Holy

Spirit. In the initial, universal baptism at conversion the Holy Spirit is the agent and Christ is the sphere into which believers are placed.

In answering this teaching it must be noted that the same Greek preposition (*en*) is found in each passage that touches upon this question. It is highly questionable that two radically different kinds of Spirit baptism would be taught by the identical phrase.[9] The legitimacy of this interpretation must be called into question. The truth observed by Stott above must also be remembered. The more important evidence used in interpretation must come from the didactic passage and not the narrative portions. The differences between the agents and spheres found in 1 Corinthians and the Gospels and Acts can be understood without stretching the phrase "in the Spirit."

The sealing ministry of the Spirit is referred to three times in the New Testament, revealing a significant work of the Spirit on behalf of the Christian (2 Cor. 1:22; Eph. 1:13; 4:30). The Holy Spirit is shown to be both the seal and the One who seals. Also, all believers are sealed by the Spirit at regeneration. There are no exhortations that the believer should be sealed. It is particularly noteworthy that Paul allows for no "unsealed believers" among the Corinthian Christians, who were not noted for their godliness. The exhortation not to grieve the Spirit in Ephesians 4:30 assumes that all believers are sealed.

The King James Version of Ephesians 1:13 states "after that ye believed, ye were sealed." This text is a problem for any who teach that the Holy Spirit ever seals someone to God's promises subsequent to conversion. Paul sees believing and sealing as coordinate actions: "having also believed you were sealed" (NASB).

Security is perhaps the most significant truth communicated by the sealing of the Spirit. God committed himself to keeping believers safe until their final salvation on "the day of redemption." Something that is sealed is made secure, and only the one with authority can break a seal. This means that only God could break the seal and cause the loss of salvation, and this He will not do since He intends to bring His children to glory.

The image of the seal also underscores the reality that no human or angel or demon can bring about the loss of a believer's salvation, since they do not have the authority to do so. Nor can the individual break the seal of the Spirit of God. The believer, purchased and owned by God, is guaranteed safe keeping by the Spirit until final redemption is secure. There are no losses along the way.

In anointing, oil was poured on persons or things to set them apart for God's service. Kings and priests were anointed with oil as they began their life of service (e.g., Exod. 30:22–33; 40:13–15; 1 Sam. 16:1–13). Oil was important in the lives of God's people Israel, and it referred to the ministry of the Holy Spirit. The anointing oil poured on a person's head is a picture of the Spirit flowing over that person to set them apart to serve God effectively.

Today, all believers are permanently anointed (2 Cor. 1:21b; 1 John 2:20, 27). Never are believers told to seek or pray for an anointing. This anointing is as permanent as the anointing of an ancient king or priest. Believers are anointed to be priests, representing the Lord in this world (1 Peter 2:9). Following the pattern found in Scripture, it is not surprising that we believer-priests have been anointed for sacred service. The New Testament writers never explained this anointing; they assumed that we would understand the meaning from the Old Testament.

The word *anoint* is sometimes used in a different manner to speak of praying that the Lord will "anoint someone" for a particular ministry. We actually are praying that the person would be empowered by the Lord for the work. We probably are not denying that this person has been anointed as a believer priest, according to 2 Corinthians 1:21, but we sometimes think of these as similar operations of the Spirit. Anointing is not the same as being empowered for ministry, nor is the concept ever used that way in the New Testament.

Anointing has to do with our ability to serve the Lord. Anointing gives the believer two capacities that are needed for effective service. First, the capacity to understand the truth is essential, and anointing concerns an enabling to understand truth (1 John 2:20, 27).[10] Prior to conversion a person's mind is darkened; God's truth cannot be understood (cf. 1 Cor. 2:14; Eph. 4:18). At conversion the capacity to understand is given. Having the capacity to understand does not negate the need for growth in knowledge. It prepares our minds so that the Spirit can illumine with the knowledge that we need to serve.

The Ministry of Filling

At conversion the Holy Spirit regenerates, baptizes, indwells, seals, and anoints each Christian. Believers are never commanded to pray or seek these ministries. The believer is commanded to be *filled with the Spirit*. Not all believers experience this ministry, but the filling of the Holy Spirit directly affects the fruit of the Spirit and set-apart living.

Clearly this filling is not about obtaining more of the Holy Spirit, since He fully indwells the believer. When the apostle Paul commands believers to "be filled with the Spirit" (Eph. 5:18) he uses the comparison and contrast of a person being intoxicated with wine. As long as we do not take this illustration beyond Paul's intent, it is helpful. A person filled with wine will behave in a manner that is different than when he is sober. His thinking, words, and actions will be noticeably changed. Being filled with the Spirit means the believer is controlled and will behave in a different manner. A believer controlled by the Holy Spirit acts and thinks differently. Being filled with the Spirit means being controlled by the Spirit and not somehow "getting more" of the Holy Spirit.

The New Testament reveals two aspects of this filling, controlling ministry. First, there is a filling for special situations. The book of Acts relates dramatic times in which believers are instantaneously controlled by the Spirit (Acts 2:4; 4:8, 31; 7:55-56; 13:9). These particular instances are related to serving Christ in an unusual situation in which the Spirit's control was particularly needed. These fillings were not the result of prayer. No one asked to be filled with the Spirit, but that is what took place. Being filled with the Spirit was not an end in itself nor was it a permanent thing. The same individual could be filled again.

The second aspect of filling is a progressive spiritual growth. When a believer is progressively being controlled by the Holy Spirit the fruit of the Spirit becomes more evident (cf. Gal. 5:22-23).

This aspect of the filling of the Spirit must be tied to the Word of God. The Holy Spirit is the "Spirit of truth," and it is the Word that He uses to gain control in the believer's life. The believer must study to understand Scripture. The Word reveals sin to confess and areas of life that need to be brought into conformity with God's wisdom. With understanding comes the choice of whether to submit or rebel. When the mind submits to the Word, the Spirit gains control in that area.

Other Ministries

Other ministries of the Holy Spirit are important to all believers. As the Spirit exalts Christ, He does not always fit neat categories. He will never operate outside the parameters of the Scriptures and never call attention to Himself.

Teaching

Without the aid of the Spirit believers would not come to understand the truth of God found in Scripture (1 Cor. 2:10-13). The indwelling Spirit who has anointed the believer gives the capacity to understand truth and continues to illumine that truth. As a believer meditates on the Word of God, the "Spirit of Truth" opens and transforms the mind. The Holy Spirit does not originate the message but leads believers to truth (John 16:12-15). Since the Spirit has distributed the spiritual gift of teaching to believers within the church, it is reasonable to expect that the Spirit would also teach through fellow believers in the church.

Guiding

The will of God for the believer is always found within the parameters of the Word of God. But specifics regarding a particular life application are not found in Scripture. That is not to say that these life decisions make no difference to the Lord. A benefit of the Spirit's presence is that He guides us into the will of God. God's will is good and perfect. The Spirit leads us to what is best for us and what brings the greatest glory to the Father.

Praying

Prayer sometimes seems paradoxical. The youngest child can approach God with the simplest prayer, and the most mature can be baffled by prayer's complexity. Prayer is commanded and important, but there is much about it that is not understood. The Holy Spirit helps us in our praying "for we do not know how to pray as we should" (Rom. 8:26). Often the believer approaches his heavenly Father with uncertainty. It is encouraging to know that the indwelling Holy Spirit knows what we do not know and can communicate what we are unable to communicate. The Spirit helps us enter into the will of the Father in all areas of life.

Helping

The night before the Crucifixion, the Lord Jesus told His men that the coming Spirit would be to them "another Helper" (John 14:16). While we have mentioned some of the Spirit's work, we simply cannot "neatly package" it. As the Holy Spirit ministers to and through other believers, some things defy categorization; they are works of "the Helper." The Greek word *paraklētos* was used by the Lord when speaking of the Spirit. Vine's dictionary of New Testament words gives a simple explanation of a term that literally means "called to one's side." It

> suggests the capability or adaptability for giving aid. It was used in a court of justice to denote a legal assistant, counsel for the defense, an advocate; then, generally, one who pleads another's cause, as intercessor, advocate . . . In the widest sense, it signifies a "succorer, comforter." Christ was this to His disciples, by the implication of His word "another" (*allos,* "another of the same sort," not *heteros,* "different") Comforter," when speaking of the Holy Spirit, John 14:16.[11]

Alleged Supernatural Works of the Spirit

There were many supernatural works and manifestations of the Holy Spirit in the New Testament church, and much controversy about the continuation of such workings. As the church began, the apostles were the primary individuals commissioned to carry on the work of Christ in the power of the Holy Spirit. The word *apostle* means that they were ones sent out with Christ's authority. They indeed were given authority by the risen, ascended Christ to proclaim the gospel and to work miracles.

Apart from the Twelve, the Holy Spirit also performed many supernatural acts in and through a number of men and even through angels. Acts records many of these workings.[12] The question faced today has to do with the continuation of those kinds of workings. Are we to expect the Spirit to do the same miraculous works today as He did in the church of the first century?

Although it is not possible to answer this question in a detailed way, certain points ought to be kept in mind:

1. A miracle is a suspension of natural law by supernatural intervention. God can work miracles if He so chooses. The issue is never "*Can* God do it?" but rather what He has said about the meaning and purposes of miracles.
2. The Bible reveals only a few times when God employed miracles. Miracles would certainly lose their impact and significance if they occurred daily, as some believe they do. The scriptural record shows that God rarely suspends natural law.
3. The criteria for evaluating the truthfulness of an alleged supernatural event must be the Word of God. Satan will always attempt to masquerade as the Holy Spirit, and we can be sure that the Spirit will never do anything apart from the Scriptures. The Word of God must define experience—not the other way around.
4. The primary purpose of miracles has been to authenticate the message and the messenger. Many have claimed to be sent with a message from God. Miracles showed that the messianic claims of Jesus and the ministries of the Apostles were different from those of false prophets (John 5:36; Rom. 15:18-19; 2 Cor. 12:12; Heb. 2:3b-4). Once a message has been authenticated (as the entire Bible has been), continued authentication is not needed.

CONCLUSION

Believers have the Word of God in its fullness and the gift of the Holy Spirit. When we consider the presence of the Holy Spirit in our individual lives and the fact that He continually helps us and points us to Christ, we can understand why Jesus said to the disciples (John 16:7), "It is better for you that I go away." We really have no excuse for succumbing to the world, the flesh, and the Devil. With the aid of the Spirit we can increasingly become more like Christ and effectively minister for Christ. May we live by means of the Spirit until we see the Lord Jesus.

CHAPTER 19

The Nature and Purpose of the Church

Robert P. Lightner

THE CHURCH AND THE CHURCHES

The church that is Christ's body did not exist until the Day of Pentecost. It follows that there were no local churches until that time. The New Testament clearly distinguishes between the universal church, which is Christ's body, from the local church. The natures of the two differ, as do their reasons for existing. To be sure, there are similarities and things true of both, but one is distinguished from the other by their differences. Here are some reasons for seeing that these two exist as different entities.[1]

Christ told Peter that He would build His church, and the gates of Hades would not overpower it (Matt. 16:18). Here, *church* is singular. Surely our Lord was not saying He would build a local church. Further, He guaranteed success of the church He would build. To which local church would this apply?

Christ is said to have given Himself for the church (Eph. 5:25). If there is no universal church, for which local church did He die?

Christ, we are told, is head over the church, which is His body (Eph. 1:22; 3:10, 21; Col. 1:18). The statement is that He *is* Head, not that He wants to be head. Over what local church is he head?

Along with others, the church of the firstborn is said to occupy the heavenly Jerusalem in the future (Heb. 12:22–23). Which local church will have that honor?

According to Scripture, all who are in the body of Christ are children of God (Romans 6; 1 Corinthians 12). Are all in every local church regenerate?

THE UNIVERSAL CHURCH

Two Programs of God

Israel and the church universal are contrasted in Scripture. These are not just two distinct people-groups sharing in the same soteriological program of God. Rather, God has a distinct and unique plan and program for the church and one for Israel that includes more than salvation, although there are similarities, and the two relate to one another.

Amillennialists, postmillennialists, and progressive/modified dispensationalists do not accept the view that God's program for the church is different from His program with Israel. That the church's program is distinct from Israel's is basic and essential to premillennial pretribulation dispensationalism.

There are several reasons for belief in the two-program view and not the one-program view of amillennialism, postmillennialism, and progressive dispensationalism. These reasons follow and highlight the nature and the purpose of the church that is Christ's body.

Beginning on the Day of Pentecost

Several steps lead to this conclusion. First, Jesus said the church was future from the time He spoke to Peter when He said, "I will build my church" (Matt. 16:18). If words mean anything, this means the church that Christ would build was not then in existence but would be in the future. Second, the promise of the baptism of the Holy Spirit originally given by John the Baptist (Matt. 3:11) was reaffirmed by Luke in Acts 1:5 in conjunction with the ascension of Christ: "For John baptized with water, but you will be baptized with the Holy Spirit not many days from now."[2] This promise relates directly to the question of when the church began, as we shall see.

Third, the Acts 1:5 promise of the baptizing work of the Holy Spirit was quoted by Peter as he vindicated his ministry to the gentiles (Acts 11:15–17). Peter recalled for his Jewish critics how God led him in that ministry to the house of Cornelius: "And as I began to speak, the Holy Spirit fell upon them, just as He did upon us at the beginning. And I remembered the word of the Lord, how He used to say, 'John baptized with water, but you will be baptized with the Holy Spirit'" (Acts 11:15).

The promise of Spirit baptism given in Acts 1:5 was first fulfilled sometime between when it was given and Peter's visit to the house of Cornelius, where it was realized again. This is what Peter meant by the Holy Spirit falling upon the gentiles "as He did on us at the beginning" (11:15). The meaning of "at the beginning" is a reference to the Day of Pentecost described in chapter 2.

By itself, this, of course, does not prove that the church began on the Day of Pentecost. What it does mean, however, is that the promise of the baptizing work of the Spirit was fulfilled at that time.

Fourth, we learn from Paul's instruction to the Corinthians that the Holy Spirit's baptizing work formed the body of Christ: "For by one Spirit we were all baptized into one body, whether Jews or Greeks, whether slaves or free, and we were all made to drink of one Spirit" (1 Cor. 12:13).

There is no parallel to Spirit baptism anywhere in the Old Testament. Spirit baptism is the unique work of the Spirit of God, by which He identifies or unites each believer with Christ the head of the body, the church (Rom. 6:1-10), and at the same time identifies or unites believing sinners with each other in that body (1 Cor. 12:12-13). Jews and gentiles are on equal footing in the body of Christ. Of the two, God has made one new man. This was a mystery, which means it was completely unrevealed, not just unrecognized in the Old Testament (Eph. 3:1-5).

Fifth, this body of Christ formed by the baptizing work of the Spirit is the church. Paul described it as such on at least two occasions: "And He put all things in subjection under His feet, and gave Him as head over all things to the church, which is His body" (Eph. 1:22-23a). And again, "He is also head of the body, the church" (Col. 1:18a).

Christ promised He would build the church. There was promise of the baptism of the Spirit at the time of the ascension. Peter affirmed that in the house of Cornelius the Spirit came upon them as the Spirit had earlier and he quoted the promise in Acts 1:5, which was then realized. The baptism of the Spirit formed the body of Christ. The body of Christ is the church.

New Testament Contrasts

Lewis Sperry Chafer lists twenty-four contrasts between the church and Israel.[3] Of those, seven are particularly significant in that they highlight the contrast between the nation and the church: (1) Headship—Abraham is designated the head of the Jewish race and Christ the head of the church. (2) Covenants—Four unconditional covenants were made with Israel. None of these was made with the church, though she does share some of the blessings related to some of those covenants. (3) The Holy Spirit—The Spirit came upon Israelites, and believers of the church age are indwelled by Him permanently. (4) A governing principle—The Law of Moses governed Jewish life for fifteen hundred years. The church is not under the Law of Moses as a rule of life. (5) Farewell addresses—Christ speaks of the nation before His departure from the earth (Matt. 23:37-25:46). In the discourse He relates Israel's future to His return. On the eve of His death Christ gave the Upper Room Discourse, which concerns the church and individual's relationship to Him. (6) The promise of Christ's return—Christ will return as Israel's King and for the church as the Bridegroom for His bride. (7) Priesthood—Israel as a nation *had* a human priesthood. Not every Israelite was a priest. The church on the other hand *is* a priesthood by our relation to Christ, the great High Priest.

Contrasts between Israel and the church such as those listed above point clearly to a separate divine program for each.

Critics of Chafer and those who hold the two-program view often ignore the similarities Chafer saw between Israel and the church:

> There are similarities between these two groups of elect people. Each in turn has its own peculiar relation to God, to righteousness, to sin, to redemption, to salvation, to human responsibility, and to destiny. They are each witnesses to the Word of God; each may claim the same Shepherd; they have doctrines in common; the death of Christ avails in its own way for each; they are alike loved with an everlasting love; and each as determined by God will be glorified.[4]

New Testament Designations

Israel is still addressed as a nation after the church began. Shortly after Pentecost, Peter and John were used to heal a man who had never walked. Peter responded to the people who were in amazement at what they heard and saw and addressed them as "men of Israel" (Acts 3:12). Soon after this, Peter and John were jailed overnight. The next day the authorities asked them how they had been able to perform such a miracle. Again, Peter responded to those officials as "rulers and elders of the people" (4:8).

The apostle Paul informed the Roman Christians that the church did not rob Israel of her promised blessings (Rom. 9:4-5). Though set aside for a time, "God has not cast away His people" (11:1). There is a future for Israel. The church has not replaced Israel. The church is never identified with spiritual Israel.[5] Gentile Christians are never included in the term *Israel* in Scripture.

THE MYSTERY NATURE OF THE CHURCH

The Greek *mystērion* (mystery) occurs twenty-seven times in the New Testament and twenty of these instances are by the apostle Paul. Clearly then, *mystery* is a New Testament concept related to the church. Paul defines the word in his benedictory praise in Romans: "Now to Him who is able to establish you according to my gospel and the preaching Jesus Christ, according to the revelation of the mystery which has been kept secret for long ages past" (16:25). A mystery, therefore, in biblical usage is not "mysterious," but rather something unknown until revealed.

Based on occurrences of *mystery* in the New Testament, J. B. Lightfoot defined it as "a truth which was once hidden but now is revealed, a truth which without special revelation would have been unknown."[6] It is a secret imparted only to the initiated.

The Church as Mystery

The most extensive passage from the apostle Paul in which the church is described as a mystery is Ephesians 3:1–10. Paul says that God made known to him and the other apostles and prophets of the church, the mystery of Christ, which was not known before, "that the Gentiles are fellow heirs and fellow members of the body, and fellow partakers of the promise in Christ Jesus through the gospel." This mystery was being made known through the church even "in the heavenly places."

Covenant theologians, whether amillennialist or postmillennialist, have always held "that the church existed in the old dispensation as well as in the new, and was *essentially* the same in both."[7] Such a concept is contrary to the clear statements of Paul to the Ephesians.

Just what is the "mystery" of which Paul wrote? Is it that gentiles would be blessed along with Jews? Is it that gentiles would be recipients of God's great salvation? Neither of these answers can be correct, because gentile blessing and salvation were predicted and experienced in the Old Testament (i.e., Gen. 12:3; Isa. 42:6–7). This would therefore not be a mystery, a new truth hidden in God but now made known.

Key Terms

Paul relied on three terms to explain the mystery, each appearing in Ephesians 3:6: *sygklēronoma*, "fellow heirs"; *syssōma*, "fellow members of the body"; and *symmetocha*, "fellow partakers." These descriptive nouns each begin *syn-*, which means "together." Of *sygklēronoma*, John Eadie explained,

> Their heirship was based on the same charter and referred to the same inheritance. Nor . . . were they only residuary legatees bound to be content with any contingent remainder that satiated Israel might happen to leave. No; they inherited equally with the earlier sons. Theirs was neither an uncertain nor a minor portion.[8]

Equally forceful is Eadie's comment on *syssōma*:

> The Gentiles were of the same body—not attached like an excrescence, not incorporated like a foreign substance, but concorporated so that the additional were not to be distinguished from the original members in such a perfect amalgamation. The body is the one church under the one Head, and believing Jew and Gentile form that one body, without schism or the detection of national variety or of previous condition.[9]

The third term, *symmetocha,* also stresses the equality of the two groups which form the one body. Both partake of the Savior. The word means "a joint partaker."[10]

The body formed by the joining together of these two groups did not exist prior to the union. It was not an already-existing entity to which a new group was added. Our Lord made "the two into one new man" (Eph. 2:15).

Those who do not believe the church is completely unrevealed in the Old Testament—amillennialists and postmillennialists—find reason for their view in the phrase, "As it has now been revealed to His holy apostles and prophets in the Spirit" (Eph. 3:5). Progressive dispensationalists hold a very similar view but do not appeal to this phrase to defend it.

Is the church partially revealed in the Old Testament? Is the church simply unrealized in the Old Testament, as progressive dispensationalists say? Robert Saucy, a popular voice for the movement, answers: "A mystery may be hidden in the sense that its truth has not yet been realized."[11] Such a statement from one who claims to be a premillennial dispensationalist sounds confusingly similar to the explanation of Princeton Seminary founder Oswald T. Allis (1880-1973), a staunch defender of covenant theology: "It [the church] was a mystery in the sense that, like other teachings which are spoken of as such, it was not fully revealed in the Old Testament and was completely hidden from the carnal minded."

The truth is, Paul said the mystery of which he wrote—that said Jews and gentiles were equal members in the same body—was "hidden in God" (Eph. 3:9). He did not say it was simply hidden from the carnal or that people had not realized the truth. He did not even say the mystery was hidden in the Old Testament Scriptures. The reason it was not revealed in the Old Testament is because it was hidden in God; He kept it secret until the divinely appointed time.

Just what did Paul mean by the "as" clause in Ephesians 3:5? Could the *hōs,* the "as," possibly mean there is in the Old Testament a partial revelation of the church? Is the issue one of degrees of revelation—less in the Old, more in the New?

Those who understand the "as it has now been revealed" (Eph. 3:5) in a *restrictive* sense are within grammatical bounds to do so. However, that is only one of its uses. But that is by no means the only legitimate way to understand it. A. T. Robertson lists its various uses, one of which is the *descriptive* sense.[12] When understood as descriptive, there is no comparison of the degrees of revelation. Rather, the descriptive use of the *hōs* clause means there was no revelation at all in an earlier time, which harmonizes well with the contrasts Paul sets forth in the context. He does not make a contrast between degrees of revelation but between that which was not revealed at all and that which is now revealed.

The "as" does not give a comparison between degrees of revelation in the former time and "now." It denies that there was any revelation at all of the mystery in that former time; just as if one should tell a man born blind that the sun does not shine in the night as it does in the daytime. It does not shine at all by night.[13]

Paul told the Colossian Christians the same thing about the church being a mystery (Col. 1:25-26). There is one striking difference, however, from what he told the Ephesians—there is no "as" clause in the message to the Colossians. It is simply "the mystery which has been hidden from the past ages and generations, but has now been manifested to His saints" (Col. 1:26). The omission of the "as" clause in Colossians further supports its *descriptive* use in Ephesians 3. Added to this is the fact that major elements of the church that is Christ's body are called mysteries also. These further support the argument that the church did not exist in the Old Testament. Beyond that, they argue for a unique, separate, and distinct program of God in the church.

Parallel Mysteries

In the mystery of one body, the Jews and gentiles have absolute equality (Eph. 3:1-12). In addition, the indwelling of Christ in each believer is also called a "mystery." Such indwelling is foreign to the Old Testament. There, only Christ's external manifestation was spoken of. The living organism resulting from Christ's indwelling is a complete mystery and absent from the Old Testament (cf. Col. 1:24-27; 2:10-19; 3:4-11).

There is the mystery of the bride of Christ (Eph. 5:22-32; Rev. 19:7-9). Paul exhorted the Ephesian Christians that the unity and love that ideally characterizes the human family is based upon the relationship between Christ and His church. The church is now the bride and will become the wife. The *bride*, the *wife*, the *body*, and the *church* are synonymous terms in Ephesians 5. The mystery is the union of Christ with saved Jews and gentiles in the body. There is no hint of such in the Old Testament.

Finally, there is the mystery of the translation of living saints at the rapture (1 Cor. 15:51-52). Resurrection was not unknown in the Old Testament (cf. Isa. 26:16-19; Dan. 12:1-2). However, the idea that the living would be caught up with the resurrected dead to meet the Lord in the air is not found in the Old Testament.

Is the church completely unrevealed in the Old Testament or just not revealed there fully and therefore unrecognized, as amillennialists, postmillennialists, and premillennial progressive dispensationalists insist? The case has been set forth that there is no revelation of the church in the Old Testament. This we base upon the Ephesians 3:1-12 and Colossians 1:24-27 passages and the mysteries of the body, the organism formed by Christ's indwelling, the bride, and the translation at the Rapture.

FIGURES USED OF CHRIST AND HIS CHURCH

Of the many metaphors used to describe the relationship between Christ and the church, seven figures particularly describe the unique relationship between Christ and members of His body.

Shepherd and Sheep (John 10:1–16)

It is important to observe the difference between the "fold" (Gk. *aulēn*) and the "flock" (*poimēn*) in John 10. It seems clear that the fold represents Judaism.[14] It was out of the nation that Jesus called His sheep by name and led them out (v. 5). Shepherds did this because several shepherds would have their sheep in the "fold" for the night. Each shepherd's sheep knew the voice of their shepherd and responded to him when he called them in the morning.[15]

Not all the sheep in the "fold" responded to a particular shepherd's call. Not all the Jews responded to Jesus' call as the chief Shepherd either. In addition to the Jews who responded to His call Jesus said He had "other sheep which are not of this fold" (John 10:16). These "sheep" referred to gentiles who would hear His voice and whom Jesus would also bring so that they and believing Jews would "become one flock with one shepherd" (v. 16).

Here again, we see from this figure that the nation did not become the church; neither was the nation dissolved when the church was formed. Our Lord brought into existence a totally new entity called His flock from believing members of Israel and the gentile nations.

Vine and Branches (John 15:1–7)

Clearly Christ describes Himself here as the Vine and His apostles with Him the branches.[16] The major point of the figure that Christ used here is to teach His own of the union that exists between Himself and His people. Along with that is the responsibility of service to be rendered by the branches. Christ sets forth Himself and believer here as one. Indeed, the vine and the branches in a vineyard are difficult to distinguish. It is hard to tell where the one ends and the other begins. Nevertheless, Christ is illustrating here that He as the true Vine and believers as the branches form one organic whole.

Two major themes are stressed in this figure. One is expressed in the words, "in me," and the other in the words of exhortation, "abide in me." To be in Christ speaks of our relationship with Him. To abide in Him describes the fellowship we are encouraged to have with Him. It is impossible to abide in Him without being in Him. It is, however, altogether possible to be in Him and not abide in Him. Unless we abide in Him, we cannot bear fruit anymore than a branch can bear fruit without being united to the vine from which it receives its nourishment.

Cornerstone and Stones (Eph. 2:19–22)

Our Lord Jesus Christ is referred to as a stone several times in Scripture. To the gentiles He is seen as the smiting stone that struck the image in Nebuchadnezzar's dream (Dan. 2:34). Peter presents Christ as a "stone of stumbling" (1 Peter 2:8) for the Jews. For the church Christ is seen as the foundation stone (1 Cor. 3:11) and the "cornerstone" (Eph. 2:20).

It is this last one of the above metaphors with which we are concerned here. Believers are seen as a building in contrast to a body. This great structure is built upon Christ. Believers are said to be "living stones" (1 Peter 2:5) in the building.

The universal church "building," Paul said, was "built upon the apostles and prophets" (Eph. 2:20). Is this statement not in conflict with Paul's affirmation to the Corinthians: "No man can lay a foundation other than the one which is laid, which is Jesus Christ" (1 Cor. 3:11)? No, the two statements are not in conflict because Paul uses the building metaphor in two different ways. In the Corinthian passage Paul is referring to the local church and the doctrine of Christ on which it was built. In the Ephesians passage he is talking about the universal church. His emphasis there is on the people who make up the universal church.[17]

The context of Ephesians 2:19–22 seems to support the fact that through Christ the building or the church is united in and by Christ. Each stone or believer in the church is dependent on Christ for strength and stability. He has brought unity, oneness, to the body. It is our job as living stones to reflect that unity.

High Priest and Kingdom of Priests (Heb. 5:5–10; 1 Peter 2:5, 9)

This metaphor more than any of the others highlights some similarities between Israel and the church. These are seen in Peter's description of the church as "a chosen race, a royal priesthood, a holy nation, a people for God's own possession" (1 Peter 2:9). Does this mean the church and Israel are not distinct? Does it mean that God does not have a separate program for each? The answer to both of these questions is no.

Indeed there are similarities between the church and Israel as indicated earlier. These have always been recognized by dispensationalists. Similarities between the two does not mean the two are equated or do not have separate divine purposes. An automobile and a farm wagon have similarities. For example, both are means of transportation. Both have four wheels. These and other similarities do not make the two the same, however. It is the distinctions and differences that set the one apart from the other one. It is the same with the church and Israel.

The nation Israel had a priesthood and the entire nation was to function as God's kingdom of priests before the other nations around them. The nation and the priests within that nation were God's mediators on earth to advance His cause. Both the nation and the priesthood within that nation failed miserably to fulfill their responsibility.

Old Testament priests in the nation of Israel were to give of themselves and their talents to the service of Jehovah God. There was the service of sacrifice, the service of worship, and the service of intercession.

> The contribution which is made to the doctrine of the Church by the figure of the high priest and the kingdom of priests is that, in this life, the believer is not only closely associated with Christ positionally, being in Him, but is closely associated in those activities which He is undertaking on the plane of infinity and which may be extended, by His grace, into the finite sphere. As has been seen, these activities are: service, sacrifice, and intercession. Again, it is made clear that it is given to the members of His Body to share in the great achievement of the outcalling and perfecting of the Church of Christ. The Savior has a glory which accrues to Him because of His great accomplishment, but His own who are in the world are His instruments who will share with Him in His merited glory. Theirs is not merely a glory which is a benefaction, but is one which is due to a partnership fruition.[18]

Head and *the* Body (1 Cor. 12:12–27; Eph. 1–5)

Paul calls the church not *a* body, but *the* body of Christ. The Holy Spirit of God led him to do this. The metaphor of the head and the body serves again to distinguish the church from Israel and to set forth the nature and purpose of the church.

Just as man's physical head and the rest of his body are distinguished, so Christ as the head of the church is kept distinct from His body in this metaphor. Unity and union, yes; but identity of the one with the other, no. Christ as head over the church places Him in a definite position of preeminence. Each of the members in the body of Christ, just as in the physical body, is needed. That is true even though the members often hold diverse theological views. They must all, of course, agree on the essentials of the faith in order to be members of the body. Each member is related to every other member of the body.

Life, nourishment, and growth result from being united with Christ. The body of Christ in Scripture is not the local church. There have always been and continue to be local assemblies where Christ is not the head. He is to be made the head of each local church. But no such responsibility is given to us with regard to the universal church. He is the head of the body.

What then is our responsibility stemming from the metaphor? How can we apply this truth to our everyday walk with God? As the Head, our Lord provides direction, guidance, and control to the members. Our responsibility as members of His body is to follow His direction, guidance, and control. How do we do that? There is only one way—live according to Scripture.

Last Adam and New Creation (1 Cor. 15:35–50)

This figure stands in some contrast to the previous one. Chafer put it this way:

> In the New Creation reality, Christ is seen to be the all-important part of it, whereas, in the figure of the Body, that entity is viewed as a thing to be completed in itself and separate from, and yet to be joined to, the Head. The Body is an entire unit in itself, which is vitally related to Christ. Over against this, the New Creation is a unit which incorporates the resurrected Christ and could not be what it is apart from that major contribution—the Source of all the verity which enters into it.[19]

The first Adam is the head of the old creation. God endowed Adam and Eve with the powers of procreation and told them, "Be fruitful and multiply, and fill the earth" (Gen. 1:28). Their disobedience of God in eating the forbidden fruit resulted in their own separation from God and a curse upon all of creation. The moment they ate they died spiritually; they began to die physically and became subjects of eternal death apart from God's gracious provision for them. All of mankind since then suffers from the same three forms of death.

God through His Son has provided a way of salvation. Christ, the eternal Son of God, is set forth by Paul as the "last Adam" (1 Cor. 15:45). Christ is the Head of a "new creation" (Gal. 6:15) and each one in Him is "a new creature" (2 Cor. 5:17). In the first Adam all died. All in the Last Adam will be made alive (1 Cor. 15:22).

The reality of this figure rests solidly on the resurrection of Christ. If He did not come forth from the dead, the believer's "faith also is vain" (1 Cor. 15:14). "If we have hoped in Christ in this life only, we are of all men most to be pitied" (v. 19).[20]

No Old Testament saint was ever said to be "in Christ." The phrase is a Pauline term used only of post-Pentecost saints. The phrase with its equivalents is used 132 times in the New Testament. "To be in Christ is to be in the sphere of His own infinite Person, power, and glory. He surrounds, He protects, He separates from all else, and He indwells the one in Him."[21]

How is this stupendous truth to be fleshed out by the believer? Each is to live in the power of the resurrected Christ (cf. Eph. 4:21–24; Col. 3:9–10).

The believer must exercise his/her will and "put on the Lord Jesus Christ, and make no provision for the flesh in regard to its lusts" (Rom. 13:14). Positionally, Christ is put on by faith at the time of salvation. However, Paul's exhortation here is to put Him on experientially.

Bridegroom and Bride (Eph. 5:23–32; Rev. 21:9)

The "bride of Christ" does not refer to the future triumphant church.[22] Nor does it refer to the past Jewish church.[23] Rather, the "bride of Christ" is the church that was not revealed in the Old Testament. It was a mystery that Jew and gentile would be equal, joint partners, in the church. This church is composed of all who have trusted Christ alone as their Savior between the Day of Pentecost and the Rapture. This church is also called the bride of Christ and the body of Christ. The "body" and the "bride" are indistinguishable in Ephesians 5. This figure, perhaps as no other, speaks of the union that exists between Christ and His people.

The meaning and significance of the metaphor of the bride and bridegroom can best be seen by observing the culture surrounding the oriental marriage. First, there was the legal contract into which the pair entered. This was described as the betrothal. This involved the parents of the couple and the arrangement was sealed by the giving of money or at least a letter to indicate that the woman was espoused to be married. The respected Bible scholar Alfred Edersheim explained it this way: "From the moment of her betrothal a woman was treated as if she were actually married. The union could not be dissolved, except by regular divorce; breach of faithfulness was regarded as adultery."[24]

The presentation of the bride to the bridegroom was the second stage of the oriental marriage. Usually this was done at night. Paul's word to the Thessalonian Christians describes how Christ will come for His bride, the church. "For the Lord Himself will descend from heaven with a shout, with the voice of the Archangel and with the trumpet of God, and the dead in Christ will rise first. Then we who are alive and remain will be caught up together with them in the clouds to meet the Lord in the air, and so we shall always be with the Lord" (1 Thess. 4:16–17).

The third stage of the oriental marriage was the marriage feast. The bride would accompany the bridegroom on this occasion. The apostle John describes this as it relates to the church: "Let us rejoice and be glad and give the glory to Him, for the marriage of the Lamb has come and His bride has made herself ready. It was given to her to clothe herself in fine linen, bright and clean; for the fine linen is the righteous acts of the saints. Then he said to me, write, Blessed are those who are invited to the marriage supper of the Lamb" (Rev. 19:7-9).

The two programs of God—the mystery nature of the church and the figures used of Christ and the church—all highlight the church's unique nature and purpose.

We now turn briefly to the biblical doctrine of the local church to examine its nature and purpose.

THE LOCAL CHURCH

Our goal here is not to present a full-orbed doctrine of the local church but simply to set forth its nature and purpose as given in the New Testament.

All that we have discovered of the nature and purpose of the universal church applies directly to the local church. This is true because the local, at least in the New Testament, is made up of members of the universal. Therefore all the admonitions springing from being a member of Christ's body find their implementation in the local assembly.

The local churches are the visible manifestations of the universal church, the body of Christ. They are the functional units by which God now carries out His will in the world. Only these churches, as the working agencies of the body of Christ, have the assuring promise of God that the "gates of hades" will not prevail against them. Every believer, then, should be part of, and serve through, a local church. Such labors have God's first blessing and will accomplish lasting results.

The definition that follows is broad and is not intended to reflect any particular denomination. It could easily be made to describe a particular church by specifying, for example, the kind of New Testament offices and the names of the ordinances.

A local church is a group of professed believers in the Lord Jesus Christ as Savior, organized with New Testament offices of elder and deacon, observing New Testament ordinances, united in covenant to engage in the public worship of God, educate and edify the members with the Word of God, and evangelize the lost.

Practices and Precepts

One's doctrine of the local church, to be true to the Scriptures, must be built upon the practices and precepts given in the New Testament. Most of what we see there is recorded practices of the early church. There are some precepts or exhortations that are binding across cultures and times but a lot fewer than we may think. For example, no specific form of church government is commanded. Neither are we told how often to observe the Lord's Table, or what prerequisites beyond salvation to require for membership or even to have a formal membership. In view of these realities it seems best to view the recorded practices as precepts except those that can be demonstrated to be culturally peculiar.

The Nature of the Local Church

There is in the New Testament no hierarchy with authority over the local church. Each of the churches referred to were completely independent, self-sustaining, and self-perpetuating. Each local church chose its own leadership. Each one conducted its own affairs and made its own decisions. Each one also, of course, was to allow Christ to be the head and the Holy Spirit the teacher. Voluntary fellowship between churches and joint efforts to promote the work of the Lord was encouraged in the New Testament.

In the services of the churches much emphasis was placed upon the careful reading of God's Word. Christ and the Scriptures were central. The leadership in the churches was encouraged to both exhort and rebuke in accordance with the needs. Prayer was also a vital part of the church service. There is no evidence of entertainment in the New Testament assemblies. No effort was made to make people feel comfortable in their sin. There was no effort to build large and complex church organizations. Discipline was also commanded and exercised in New Testament churches. There was an obvious effort to strive for purity both of doctrine and of life in the local churches.

New Testament Purposes

Why does the local church exist in the world today? What was its purpose in New Testament times? Both classic writers and contemporary ones differ on what the local church is here to do? How can it be and do what the Spirit of God intends for it in the modern world? Our basis for the answer to such questions must be found in the New Testament. Our God-given purposes do not arise from a particular culture. Cultures should guide us in how we can implement the assignments God has given us to do. These are cross-cultural and are not for us to decide or to alter.

Here is a sampling of purposes as seen by writers of yesterday and today:

Augustus Hopkins Strong (1836–1921) wrote: "The sole object of the local church is the glory of God, in the complete establishment of his kingdom, both in the hearts of believers and in the world."[25]

The definition worked out by John Calvin (1509–1564) shows its purpose from his perspective. He says the church

> is the multitude of men diffused through the world, who profess to worship one God in Christ; and are initiated into this faith by baptism; testify their unity in doctrine and charity by participating in the Supper; have consent in the Word of God, and for the preaching of that Word maintain the ministry ordained by Christ.[26]

In the Protestant Reformation, a set of three "marks" of the local church was used to distinguish true from false bodies: "The true preaching of the

Word," "The right administration of the sacraments," "The faithful exercise of discipline."[27]

> In examining the New Testament, four Greek words stand out in connection with the nature of the mission of the church: *martyria*, or witness; *diakonia*, or service; *koinonia*, or fellowship; and *leitourgia*, or worship.[28]

John Patten, who teaches on the doctrine of the church at Faith Baptist College, Ankeny, Iowa, gives a helpful list, with some explanation regarding the missions of the local church:

1. To worship God (John 4:23-24 with Phil. 3:3; Heb. 10:25).
   The assembling together of believers has as its primary purpose the paying homage to God. It expresses the heart attitude of the believer toward the living God.—*P. B. Fitzwater*
2. To be a constant witness to Christ's saving grace and to the truth (Acts 1:8; 8:1-4; 2 Cor. 5:20; 1 Tim. 3:15).
3. To perfect the saints unto the work of ministering (Eph. 4:11-16 ASV; 1 Thess. 5:11).
   a. That there should be unity of faith and knowledge of the Son of God.
   b. That there should be developed the full-grown man attaining to the measure of the stature of Christ.
   c. That there should be strengthening of believers against man's craftiness.
   d. Failure to attend and function in the church leads to certain apostasy.
4. To evangelize the world with the gospel (Matt. 28:19-20; Acts 1:8; 5:42; Eph. 3:8).

Paul understood clearly that his mission was to preach the gospel to the heathen. The purpose for which the church exists is missions. If you take the missionary idea out of the church, you have a life without an objective, a barren tree that cumbers the ground. Limit the gospel in its scope for power and you have cut out its heart. Everyone who accepts the invitation "come" must immediately hear the imperative command "go." The supreme business of the church is to make Christ known to all.

I believe the four purposes expressed above can be reduced to three without omitting anything. I not only believe strongly in this three-fold mission and purpose of the local church, but I also believe they should be stressed in the order given.

1. *The Exaltation of God.* This is what worship is (John 4:23-24; Phil. 3:3).

2. *The education, edification, and equipping of the saints in and through the Word of God* (Eph. 4:11-16; 1 Thess. 5:11). Both the written Word of God and living Son of God need to be central in every facet of the local church's ministry. To be Bible centered and Christ centered is to be true to the Scriptures. The local church ought to be the place where God's people can be built up in the most holy faith. Here they also ought to be encouraged to be involved in personal Bible study and a consistent walk with God. The local church is not a religious social club. It is not where we go to impress people or to discharge our religious duties. Rather, it is where we are instructed in God's Word, edified or built up in the most holy faith and equipped to go out into the world as salt and light.

3. *The evangelization of the lost* (Matt. 28:19-20; Acts 1:8; 2 Cor. 5:20; 1 Tim. 3:15). This should be done both in the church and outside it. Members of the church need to be instructed and encouraged on how to share the good news of salvation with the lost. They need to know God expects them to do this with their lives and their lips. The one teaching or preaching the Word of God should be sensitive to the Holy Spirit's ministry and open to His prompting to invite people to accept the Lord Jesus Christ as personal Savior. Opportunity to do this ought to be made available either through a public invitation, an invitation to remain after the service for counsel or meet with church personnel in a designated place for counseling, or even by receiving Christ as Savior where they are in the pew.

An old Anglican benediction summarizes well the nature and purpose of the local church.

> Now go into the world in peace;
> Have courage;
> Hold on to what is good;
> Honor all men;
> Strengthen the faint-hearted;
> Support the weak;
> Help the suffering and
> Share the Gospel.
> Love and serve the Lord
> In the power of the Holy Spirit,
> And may the grace of our Lord Jesus Christ
> Be with you all.
> Amen.

CHAPTER 20

In a Pagan World: The Mandate for Evangelism and Missions

Albert T. Platt

It used to be that when asked their favorite verse, most Christians would reply John 3:16. Now it seems that the verse is Matthew 7:1, "Judge not that ye be not judged." Tolerance takes away the foundation of conviction and is not a biblical concept. If the Lord Jesus Christ were to preach His message today, people would not wait the thirty-three years to crucify Him; it would happen in a matter of thirty-three days! We are not now living in a post-Judeo-Christian era but rather in an anti-Judeo-Christian era.

—Josh McDowell[1]

The "post" phenomenon is not just a fad. We have truly entered into an epoch fundamentally at variance with anything we have experienced to date. Likewise, there can be no doubt that the new situation is confronting the Christian church with unprecedented challenges.

—David J. Bosch[2]

A recent Gallop Poll determined that more Americans believe in hell today than did in the generally more wholesome and pious 1950s. Yet with the increasing belief of those not committed to biblical Christianity, there is a corresponding unbelief (or uncertainty) of those who profess to be committed Christians. . . . Several surveys reflect a "softening of doctrinal certainties" among undergraduate and seminary students who describe themselves as fundamentalist Christians. There is especially, "a measurable degree of uneasiness within this generation of Evangelicals with the notion of an eternal damnation"

—Larry Dixon[3]

If the early twenty-first century continues the past century's trends of uncertainty and the anti-Christian bias described above, Christians face great challenges in evangelism. We will, in fact, have difficulty just maintaining the status quo of acceptance for God's message. What will happen if future seminarians have the same lack of confidence as those surveyed? What foundational authority will be reflected in the message evangelicals disseminate? What will be taught and believed in the churches they plant, if they plant churches?

At the beginning of the new century the consensus is that things will get worse, rather than better. Things will be worse in the world (which is, after all, what God's Word has predicted). Certainly things will be worse in the West, for without divine intervention, that snowball is becoming an avalanche.

THE EVANGELISM/MISSIONS *SINE QUA NON*

For the true believer, the "fundamentals of the faith" are fixed. They do not result from hypothetical projection but from careful reflection upon an authoritative source.

The themes of evangelism and missions are integral to that part of systematic theology termed *ecclesiology*. No school of thought, religious entity, denomination, or mission board can stake a creative or proprietary claim to the evangelistic commission. They can only obey it. Neither can any culture or generation escape the responsibilities imposed in Scripture. Certainly people have always looked for loopholes to avoid obedience to the revealed will of God. Since the temptation of Adam, Satan has demeaned the requirements of God's words. So it is not surprising that the Bible's soteriological message and the church's responsibility for its dissemination should be among his targets. The closer the church gets to the Rapture and the world to the Tribulation, the greater will be the satanic pressure to dilute Scripture or trade it for a delusion.

It is not difficult to see the damage this attack already has inflicted on the evangelistic mandate. When he commented on "the crucial problem of authority in the contemporary situation," D. Martyn Lloyd-Jones specifically stressed the implications of lost biblical authority on evangelism. "We are concerned about the matter because it involves the whole question of evangelism," he observed. [4]

Without authoritative statements—propositional, revealed objective truths—there is no need for evangelism. The church has nothing to say about humanity's disease or the cure. There can be neither mandate nor mission.[5] The primacy of the Bible as authoritative communication from God is the *sine qua non* for a true theology and a valid anthropology—not to mention the indispensable platform from which to disseminate that communication.

Who is this God who has spoken and what has he said? The Bible makes it clear that its message is from and about a personal, provident God, the Creator and Sustainer of the universe. It is His auto-revelation, something mankind could not possibly have known without His intervention. What is written is not authoritative because the men who wrote it down were wise or noble, or because they insightfully analyzed the sad state of affairs in the world. Scripture is authoritative only because God is its ultimate author.[6]

THE GOD/MAN/WORLDVIEW CRISIS

We can define *evangelism* as the effective presentation of God's good news, the unique plan of salvation by grace through faith made possible because of the substitutionary death of Christ. We can define the *mandate* to evangelize as the command to take that good news to all people. Such definitions, of course, are intimately based in the New Testament. In this chapter we view evangelism and its mandate as elements of *ecclesiology*—the biblical teaching of the church as the body and bride of Christ. Ecclesiology connects the evangelism mandate to theology proper, our thoughts about the person of the triune God.[7]

THE DIVINE PERSPECTIVE: GOD ON GOD

The *issues* with which evangelism and mandate must wrestle today and tomorrow require a clear understanding of theology. The situation demands a solid, biblically derived authority. All that the Scriptures teach about God must be salient. The missions enterprise rests on the divine revelation of what is true about God. All of what God does reflects what He is. It would be impossible for Him to act in any way contrary to the absolutes of His character.

God's *holiness* is the resplendent theme of Scripture (Lev. 11:44; Ps. 99:3; 1 Peter 1:15). This characteristic is more than just the absence of evil, or possession of the highest morality. He *is* the absolute norm. This sets Him apart from anyone or anything humankind could know. The very definition of sin is any lack of conformity to that absolute. God's holiness is the rule and norm against which all humankind from Adam on is measured (Rom. 3:23). This fact aptly describes God's *righteousness* or *justice*. Do not expect the God of Scriptures to act in any other way than on the basis of His absolute holiness properly applied. One will need to keep this in the forefront as one considers the eternal destiny of anyone, whatever the time, culture, or place.

"[The] God is *love*" (1 John 4:8b). In the original Greek, the word *love*, being anarthrous (lacking an article), speaks of a quality. The article before *God* stresses his being. John heads off the human tendency to somehow substitute the quality for the Person. As Charles Ryrie observes, "Love in God is seeking the highest good and glory of His perfections."[8] He *is* love and He loves. He has loved the world and the sinful people in it enough to send His Son to die while we were yet sinners (John 3:16; Rom. 5:8). Yet people debase such love to the level of a human emotion. Since God is love, love is God. This leaves a sinful-man-friendly Creator who winks at evil. Here is false hope to a lost world.

God is *immutable* (Mal. 3:6; James 1:17). He is consistently, invariably, irrevocably, unchangeably, absolutely, and eternally as the Bible describes Him. His perfections preclude improvement. God cannot become holier than He now is nor better than his goodness (Ps. 100:5). Nor can he become less holy or less good. His love is not fickle. Believers can be assured that God feels now toward them as He did in eternity past, as He did when He sent His Son to die for them. His love will not lessen in intensity over time and eternity. "God never changes moods or cools off in His affections or loses His enthusiasm," notes Ryrie. [9]

God is *infinite* (1 Kings 8:27; Acts 17:24–28; Rom. 11:33). He is limitlessly all that the Scriptures say He is. Obviously this places full comprehension of God beyond the capabilities of even the most brilliant and best educated finite human mind. His ways *are* past finding out (Rom. 11:33). Infinitude is easily predicated for holiness, righteousness, and love. However, the term also concerns God's omnipotence, omniscience, and omnipresence.

God has the power to do anything and everything (*omnipotence*) that is in accordance with the attributes of His nature. Scripturally, the concept is derived from the fifty-seven occurrences in Scripture of *almighty* (Heb. *shaddai*; Gk. *pantokratōr*). The essence of this attribute means that he has the power and is self-sufficient to accomplish all his will. He has demonstrated this as seen throughout the biblical record. [10]

The second big "O" is *omniscience.* God knows everything; He is eternal, and therefore has known everything always and never had to learn about anything. Indeed, Tozer reminds us that God cannot learn. "Could God at any time or in any manner receive into His mind knowledge that He did not possess and had not possessed from eternity, He would be imperfect and less than Himself."[11]

We need not inform God of our situation in world evangelism. He knows all about the "10/40 window," whether Eastern Europe will ultimately open or close itself off from Christ, and the situation in China before, during and since Chairman Mao. He knows each missionary who is murdered and each who is taken hostage by a rebel army. He knows the confusion caused by false Christian sects and the ebb and flow of Christian concern for a lost world. Isaiah informs us, "Who hath directed the Spirit of the LORD, or being his counselor, hath taught him? With whom took he counsel, and who instructed him, and taught him in the path of judgement, and taught him knowledge, and shewed to him the way of understanding?" (40:13–14).

Omnipresence. God, being infinite, has no limits. All that is true about God is always, everywhere, and completely present. No geography is too remote or inimical, no culture is too idolatrous or indifferent, and no people are too erudite or ignorant that he is not at work among them. He is not "there" as in pantheism, nor "there" approving of sin committed before his eyes, but he is there. Neither is omnipresence a matter of "feeling" or "experiencing," although there are times of intimate fellowship with Him. It is a matter of *knowing reality* (Psalm 139:7–12; cf. Matt. 28:20).

The sovereignty of God answers the question, "Who is in control?" It is the court of last appeal for those who live under the cloud of "I don't understand!" The God who possesses all the characteristics the Scriptures ascribe to Him in absolute perfection is the one whose plan is in action and who will see to it that it moves to full completion without a misstep. All of this is a strong reminder that the themes under consideration here, evangelism and mandate, are His work. There are others. The Exodus 17 account of the battle with the Amalekites shows victory dependent on a most significant element. Moses was to be on the top of the mountain overlooking the battle, not merely imploring God for victory, but holding up the rod of God over the battlefield (Exod. 17:9–11). That rod was the symbol of His authority. Though Joshua and the men of Israel were in the field, the battle was the Lord's. As His authority was lifted up, there was victory.

So, is one's knowledge of the true God really all that important? Any conception of God that does not conform to the theology of Scripture is an idol. Tozer said of the idolatry in his day,

> Left to ourselves we tend immediately to reduce God to manageable terms. We want to get Him where we can use Him, or at least know where He is when we need Him. We want a God we can in some measure control. We need the feeling of security that comes from knowing what God is like, and what He is like is of course a composite of all the religious pictures we have seen, all the best people we have known or heard about and all the sublime ideas we have entertained.
>
> The God of contemporary Christianity is only slightly superior to the gods of Greece and Rome, if indeed He is not actually inferior to them in that He is weak and helpless while they at least had power.[12]

Such a god could not energize evangelism; He would not even have evangelism on his agenda.

THE DIVINE PERSPECTIVE: GOD ON MAN

Anthropology as "Man on Man"

The social sciences most simply define anthropology as "the study of man in time and space." This definition describes that discipline's deficiency: Man on man suffers from severe limitations since man is a finite creature. There is no possible way even the most intelligent could go beyond being finite man. Pursue and analyze as they may, mankind has yet to master the complexities of man's study of man from the material at hand, and there is still more material to collect. And for all the study and new insights, no one has improved the race.

The Bible on Man

The beginning found man created (a significant departure from the thesis of secular anthropology) in the image and likeness of God. He was placed in a perfect environment, ideal for the development of a God-honoring lifestyle. Sin inflicted upon Adam physical and spiritual death and infected the rest of the race with the same nature and punishment. "For all have sinned and come short of the glory of God" (Rom. 3:23). The Bible gives all the details, though the social sciences do not take them into account. Apart from God, each human being stands dead in sins (Eph. 2:1) and is dying in every other respect (John 3:16; 2 Cor. 4:3). They are slaves to darkness, in the grasp of Satan (Col. 1:13; 1 John 5:19). They commit deeds against God and hate the light (John 3:17–20, cf. Rom. 3:10–18). Therefore, God's wrath is on them (John 3:36). They are all that Romans 1:29–31 declares them to be:

> *Being filled with all unrighteousness, fornication, wickedness, covetousness, maliciousness, full of envy, murder, debate, deceit, malignity; whisperers, backbiters, haters of God, despiteful, proud, boasters, inventors of evil things, disobedient to parents, without understanding, covenant-breakers, without natural affection, implacable, unmerciful.* [13]

This is God's anthropology. *Lost* aptly describes people who are without Christ, no matter what their religion, station in life, cultural heritage, education, or geographical location. For most of the unsaved and many within the religious community, even believers, such words as *lost, the wrath of God, dead in sin,* and *perishing* cannot really mean what they seem to; such words could never reflect a God who is love.

> There is disagreement on the state of the unevangelized even among those who appear vitally interested in missions. At one of the Urbana conferences, out of 5000 replies to over 8000 questionnaires distributed, only 37 percent believed that a "person who doesn't hear the gospel is eternally lost." Only 42 percent believed that "unbelievers will be punished in a literal hell of fire," and 25 percent believed that "man will be saved or lost on the basis of how well he followed what he *did* know.[14]

The Bible on Human Destiny

If the Bible is clear about the condition of lost human beings, we should heed its words about their destiny. There will be a judgment (Heb. 9:27). This judgment will be according to an absolute, determined from all eternity by a sovereign God. "Therefore the ungodly shall not stand in the judgment, nor sinners in the congregation of the righteous. For the Lord knoweth the way of the righteous; but the way of the ungodly shall perish" (Ps. 1:5-6). The righteous need not fear this judgment; those without God will perish. Unbelievers live under a terrible sentence of God's righteous anger (John 3:36).

The Lord on Human Destiny

Jesus taught that hell is a place (Matt. 24:51; Luke 16:28; cf. Acts 1:25; Rev. 21:8) that should be avoided at all cost (Matt. 5:22, 29, 30). Hell is utterly separated from God's presence (Matt. 7:23; cf. 2 Thess. 1:8, 9). It is a place of darkness and sorrow for all (Matt. 8:12), though its punishments will vary in severity (Matt. 11:22-24). Spiritual death in hell is a fate far worse than physical death (Matt. 10:28).

When considering the vivid imagery employed by the Lord Jesus Christ in depicting the character of a destiny without God, it needs to be remembered that the literal historico-grammatical interpretation of Scripture understands completely the use of figures in the science and art of communication. They are not the license for the receptor to use his imagination but convey in the idiom of the day a picture of some aspect of the truth. Figurative language, if it has any meaning at all, intends something literal. So when our Lord speaks about fire in the future of the unrepentant ungodly, and indeed of unquenchable fire (Matt. 3:11-12), he refers to unending conscious misery. He refers to the ungodly as weeds that will be thrown "into the fiery furnace, where there will be weeping and gnashing of teeth" (Matt. 13:42). They are like bad fish to be thrown away (13:47-50).[15]

Christ also presents a vivid picture in the parable of the rich man and Lazarus (Luke 16:19-31). His parable assumes a conscious existence after death (thus refuting annihilationism), in which believers are alive and fully conscious and in which the unbeliever's state is an unalterable condition of agonizing suffering.[16]

The biblical doctrine of a literal hell remains a potent stimulus for world evangelism, despite what missiologist David Hesselgrave calls the "'kinder gentler' evangelicalism [that] seems to question such a motivation for salvation."[17] The bad news accompanying the good news is carefully spelled out in Scripture. Christians are not free to add to it or subtract from it in their worldview.

THE DIVINE PERSPECTIVE: GOD ON WORLDVIEW

Worldview—how a person sees and responds to all that is around him—is the composite of a myriad of subtle elements that more often than not are unconsciously assembled. Many elements of worldview will be the individual's mindset or philosophy of life that are already in place early in childhood. They are refined and supplemented during later childhood and adolescence. By adulthood a worldview can be challenged and adjusted only with difficulty.

The worldview thus constructed makes bigots and bullies, philosophers and philanthropists, do-gooders and do-nothingers, atheists and devout religionists. The modern Western worldview almost inevitably totes the baggage of materialism, self-realization, and a love for innovation and distrust of the old. The *new* that is desired never goes so far as new life in Christ. In addition, each generation is shaped by social structure and current events. In the late twentieth century West, for example, there were worldview nuances among "Baby-boomers," "Busters," and "Gen-Xers" and most recently "Gen-Yers."

Seeing Through God's Eyes

Only Christians with a thorough knowledge and understanding of what the Scriptures teach, who are totally committed to those truths, can possess a truly in-touch-with-truth worldview. Such knowledge and understanding provides foundational base and focus, a real perspective of how God sees the world. Plus, under the guidance of the Holy Spirit, the Christian mind filters out unwanted, unnecessary, even harmful elements. The Word teaches what believers are (John 17:3; 1 Thess. 1:9–10), how they behave (Gal. 5:22–26; Eph. 4:1–3; Phil. 2:3–5), and what has no part in their lives (Romans 6; 12:2; Gal. 5:16–21). The Bible is even clear as to how this transformation comes (2 Cor. 5:17).

A Root Deficiency

A faulty worldview, then, can be attributed to a deficient understanding of, and yieldedness to, biblical authority. Anyone who elects to view the world first (or exclusively) through the lens of culture (personal, another's, or some nebulous hybrid one-world type) will have that world grossly out of focus.

The only lens that puts everything into correct perspective is that of God's auto-revelation. "The fear of the Lord is the beginning of wisdom and the knowledge of the Holy One is understanding [discernment]" (Prov. 9:10 NASB). Biblical absolutism can accept a culture only up to that point where those absolutes begin to be compromised. Eating with chop sticks, forks, or fingers offers no biblical compromise. Idolatry, lying, murder, adultery, and blasphemy do.

Limits to the "Soft Sciences"

When it comes to world evangelization, observations from a variety of disciplines, especially the social sciences, aid in communicating the gospel message so that it can be better understood. These sciences must not be permitted to vitiate, abrogate, impede, substitute for, or ameliorate the Scriptures. Evangelical missiologists also agree that we must not allow "the science of missions" to undercut the real mission. Our work is first and foremost to communicate God's self-revelation with a view to seeing the lost come to a saving knowledge of Jesus Christ.

The problem comes with a tendency to assume that the social sciences and anthropology are "foundational to the discipline of missiology."[18] I take issue with such a sentiment. Too often the "discipline" becomes caught up in the "foundation." Enamored with their own analyses, missiologists are far too given to rumination. This lack of discipline shows itself when techniques are tried without first being submitted to Scripture, and results are judged to be successful or a failure on subjective grounds that follow trendy "new parameters." In general, we are too ready to produce yet another book.[19]

It is totally unfair to apply such complaints to all those who formally study missions. Nevertheless an unhealthy, even "unholy," trend is at work.

When "Culture" Controls

Another danger area involves the politically correct tolerance and pluralism that are now so passionately promulgated. Revivals of universalism and annihilationism also fly in the face of God's Word. These concepts represent a finite and fallen perspective, based on gross ignorance or denial of what Scripture teaches. Obviously these errors have had a definitive role in shaping the deficient worldview of many, nonbelievers and believers alike.[20]

So do other trends in the West. One mission's magazine made the thesis that "today's young people could become the best missionaries ever." But the magazine went on to ask what might keep the new generation from its task.[21] A survey identified major barriers:

First, parents resist interest in long-term missions by their children. There is nothing really new there. Second, Christian colleges and even seminaries have slimmed down Bible and theology offerings in favor of marketable-skills courses. This too has been going on for generations in colleges that no longer accept the authority of Scripture. It is shocking when it occurs in colleges that claim to have strong statements of faith.

Third, some aspects of the church growth movement, especially in "megachurch" circles, consider cross-cultural evangelism to be "traditional," and therefore old-fashioned. Related to that is the general "doctrine divides and love unites" error. This encourages a philosophy of ministry that is programmed to meet every conceivable felt need of a culture dedicated to self, but it is not exactly conducive to reaching out to a lost world. The same emphasis on self and its gratification brings with it a low level of perseverance and peripatetic church attendance.

Worldview and the Family

It is hard to imagine a positive institution beset by more problems than the late-twentieth-century family. In the West, misunderstanding about God's view of the family looms everywhere. Ominous shadows seem larger still on the future horizon. Thus, this will be the rare voice that cautions Christians not to become so centered in family relationships that the call to serve God is avoided or postponed to some later "empty-nest" time. Evangelical families so react to the cultural disintegration of parent-child relationships that in some circles service to God is not appropriate if it takes children beyond easy visiting distance.

Of course family is important to God, and the Bible has much to say on marriage and child-parent relationships. It is hard to escape "Honor thy father and thy mother" (Exod. 20:12a) or its New Testament expression, "Children, obey your parents in the Lord: for this is right. Honor thy father and mother; which is the first commandment with promise" (Eph. 6:1–2). The synopsis in Colossians 3:18–21 is succinct, and of course the Ephesians 5 passage focuses on the relationship of husband and wife. However, the relatively recent and noble emphasis on the family has mushroomed to over-emphasis as the West generally has begun reaping the harvest of generations of narcissistic, self-indulgent parenting and open marriage.

Usually this reactionary pendulum swing is set off by well-meaning and sometimes godly writers, teachers, and preachers. It sounds biblical, though much of the teaching does not consider all of Scripture. An out-of-focus out-of-balance analysis misses the real issues. One is reminded of Luke 14:20 and 26: "And another said, I have married a wife, and therefore I cannot come. . . . If any man come to me, and hate not his father, and mother, and wife, and children, and brethren, and sisters, yea, and his own life also, he cannot be my disciple." Jesus speaks here of priorities. "Love-hate" metaphors in Scripture often deal with the will. We are said to "love" what we have surrendered ourselves to; we "hate" what we attempt to gain mastery over or are willing to repudiate. Obviously God expects family to figure in worldview but not to control it.

MANDATE

The New Testament Orders

Finally, worldview, mind-set, or philosophy of life will certainly be shaped by the way each of us understands the Christian "mandate."

We should first mention problems in the ways in which we approach Scripture in discerning. The mandate for believers is so explicitly set forth in the New Testament that one wonders why missiology seems preoccupied with justifying world evangelization from the Old Testament. It is easy to confuse mandates and commands that appear throughout Scripture. The Old Testament contains a multitude of commandments or mandates, general and specific. Genesis begins with a divine requirement on the race (1:28; cf. 2:15).

George Peters points out, though, that these general mandates from God should not to be confused with the responsibility God has laid upon the church:

> I do not find anywhere in the Bible that the first mandate comes under the biblical category of missions. It is man's assignment as man and is to be fulfilled on the human level. It is not implied in the Great Commission of our Lord to his disciples nor do any of the spiritual gifts (*charismata*) as presented in Scriptures relate to it. It is therefore unscriptural to confuse the two mandates and speak of them on equal terms as missions and church ministries . . . It should not be downgraded as unworthy or secular service, though it is not missionary service in a technical sense.[22]

Further, it is said that we should interpret the Bible with a "missionary" hermeneutic, even suggesting that one needs to understand Scripture in the light of world missions. To approach the Word of God with any preconceived idea is eisegesis, not exegesis, and infers an inaccurate view of the principles of hermeneutics. There is no more need for a "missionary" hermeneutic than for an "ecclesiological" hermeneutic or a "feminist" hermeneutic or perhaps a "geriatric" one. For world missions none is needed. A proper "biblical" hermeneutic leads inexorably to the New Testament missions mandate.

Centripetal/Centrifugal

The nature of testimony for Israel in the Old Testament was *centripetal*. The nation was to be holy, to draw the nations to God by demonstrating radical holiness. Those who make "bless the nations" of the Abrahamic Covenant (Gen. 12:2; 22:18) into a missionary commission miss the point. Abraham is promised that he will bless the nations through his progeny, the Savior. Israel did fail to do what God required of them, but their requirement was not to go out in a *centrifugal* outreach to the nations. Therefore, God's requirements upon them should not be construed as mission in the New Testament sense.

The Son: The Father Sent Him! He Came! Why?

The question arises as to the *overriding purpose* of the Father's sending of the Son, a most significant factor since a comparison is made involving the mandate to the disciples. Many references are made to the soteriological purpose of Christ's coming (for example, Matt. 1:21; Luke 19:10; John 1:29).

Jesus also came for other reasons. Among them, he was to fulfill the Davidic covenant (Luke 1:32–33), to reveal God to people (John 1:18), to be a qualified judge (John 5:22–27), to become a sympathetic high priest (Heb. 4:14–16), and to destroy the works of the Devil (1 John 3:8). These reasons are associated with the soteriological purpose.

There is, however, one reason for His coming that encompasses all of the others: "I have glorified thee on the earth; I have finished the work which thou gavest me to do" (John 17:4). The overriding purpose was to glorify God the Father. The Westminster Catechism captures this by beginning its Shorter Catechism with the question, "What is the chief end of man?" The answer is, "The chief end of man is to glorify God and to enjoy Him forever."

It is typical of our ego to assume that our salvation should have been uppermost in God's plan. Surely the chief end of God is to save us. It is only a short journey from that self-centered idea to a belief that God will save everyone in the end. Noble and appealing as it might sound, universal salvation impinges upon God's absolute character and the plan His absolute wisdom put into action. If human salvation were the chief end of God, then He has known something less than complete success, for some are already in torment (Luke 16:19–31), and according to the Scriptures others *will* join them (Rev. 19:20).

The overriding purpose for the Son's being sent from heaven by the Father was to glorify God, to be in agreement with Him, and to follow through on that agreement. That meant the ignominy of the cross. On the very night of His betrayal, Christ stated that He had fulfilled the purpose of His coming (John 17:4) and charged His followers with the same kind of commission (v. 18). They also were to be in agreement with the display of His attributes and to demonstrate that agreement. There was to be identification with the crucified One, without another substitutionary death. The plan for the followers was different. They had been chosen out the world system and no longer belonged to that world system. Nonetheless, they were sent back into it.[23]

John 17:18 says nothing of geography. *Kosmos* (world) in the Greek text refers to the world system. That element is established in Acts 1:8, a statement that should end for all time the arguments of those who would downplay the imperative force of Matthew 28:19. One cannot get to "Samaria," let alone "the uttermost parts of the earth," without definitive movement, and the Lord's followers are expected to go.[24]

The Assignment Is Clear

While many dissect, discuss, and differ on the Matthew 28 assignment, the Acts reference, though general, is clear. There is to be a witness with regard to Jesus Christ. This witness must agree with the revealed will of God in the

Bible and then demonstrate that agreement. The mission mandate is "to the praise of his glory" (Eph. 1:12). Scripture tells us that we praise the glory of God by accepting and complying with the task of world witness (Matt. 28:16–20; Mark 16:15; Luke 24:44–48; John 17:18; and Acts 1:8).

Motivating Factor?

What then should be the motivating factor or factors in evangelism and missions? Obviously the believer's reason for being, to glorify God, is a prime factor, as is obedience to his Word. To glorify and obey accompany being "bought with a price" (1 Cor. 6:20). That which is bought becomes the property of the buyer, to be used as it suits his purpose. The revealed will of the owner, God, tells the believer how to serve.

One could say then that obedience should be the greatest motivator to become involved in evangelism and missions. Instead, in a shameful copying of the world, the modern missions enterprise often feeds on marketing, blatant pragmatism, and human invention. Hesselgrave makes a good point that what lends meaning and urgency to missionary appeals is the "perception, purpose and plan of Almighty God."[25] In the final analysis compliance or obedience to that plan is required, and the appeal to do so should frequently be framed in those terms. Neither "compliance nor obedience is popular with fallen human beings," as Woodrow Kroll writes in *The Vanishing Ministry.*

> Who is in charge? The honest answer to that question could spell an immediate turnaround for the vanishing ministry. Ownership is a concept with which we have become quite familiar. We own cars—"It's my car!" We own clothes—"How do you like her sweater?" We own houses—"It's the bank's and mine!" We own businesses—"He's in business for himself." In fact, we have little or no aversion to the concept of ownership, as long as it doesn't apply to us.—"You don't own me!" But that's the point! The Bible says it does apply to us. Until we grasp what that means and internalize it into our thinking about lifetime service, the vanishing ministry will continue.[26]

Send Money, Not Missionaries!

There is a particular and growing element in the world church that would prefer for the ministry of missions to vanish. Especially in third world and impoverished countries, voices call the Western church to send their money, for the missionaries are neither needed nor desired. This not new, and sometimes it grows out of indigenized evangelical churches that are becoming theologically self-sufficient. But that is often not the motivation.

Even among believers in some receiving countries, extremist political influences have tended to energize the statement, "Keep your missionaries, but send your money!" Some modern agencies, professing great interest in getting "more bang for the mission buck" irresponsibly suggest that we uncritically listen to these social justice movements. The human need is undeniable. The cause is noble. We are told, "There is a new paradigm." However, the problem stems from not submitting the plan to Scripture.

The commission is for *people* to go, not just money. Yes, it does *cost* great amounts of money to send someone from the West, but it *pays* in God's economy, simply because it is obedient. As good stewards of what God has entrusted to us, and following biblical priorities, we also can share responsibly with national ministries. But we must follow priorities established in Scripture.

Western Christians must also keep in mind that believers in third-world countries have the same privilege and responsibility to send and support. That should not be denied to them by keeping them dependent on foreign sources. Those who espouse the "send-money-only" position, not submitting it to the Word while still urging missions, keep national churches in dependency.

Spiritual Mapping

A final warning needs to be sounded about the late-twentieth-century concept of "spiritual mapping," which has become alarmingly popular in designing the methods to fulfill the mandate.

> A majority of missions-focused seminarians in America now take courses in which such new understandings are being taught as the basis for the cutting-edge, essential strategy for effective evangelism. The number of new books and articles by missiologists about spirits and spiritual warfare is voluminous. These understandings are being institutionalized in various ways. The Prayer Track of the A.D. 2000 Movement, for example, is being organized directly upon the assumptions of these new understandings of spirit realities—in this case assumption of territorial spirits and the need for spiritual mapping.[27]

Sincere and concerned, but mislead and deceived, believers suggest and actively pursue a strategy of spiritual warfare that is not in accord with the Scripture. Ephesians 6:12 tells us that there is indeed warfare and that the nature of it is spiritual. However, the sources of information that the proponents of this aberration cite are *extra-biblical*—observations in the field and even demonic interviews. Demons themselves are consulted with the naive notion that they can be forced to tell the truth. The oxymoronic demon/truth combination certainly is not in accord with Scripture (cf. John 8:44). Neither is the pursuit of information from demons (Isa. 8:19; 1 Tim. 4:1).

The net result of the strategic warfare program is "spiritual and territorial mapping." These demonic spirits of an identifiable nature and specific area can then be prayed over, restrained, overcome, or eliminated, thus freeing the area for the penetration of the gospel. This evangelical animism is based on experience and does violence to Scripture.

Though purporting to enhance the cause of evangelism and missions, in reality the spiritual warfare movement's current practices debilitate the mission by placing emphasis and resources on a scripturally unsupported method. It is aggressive, and one could hardly oppose the concept of prayer support for the preaching of the gospel, but this is an errant way to go about it.

CONCLUSION

The Old Testament "preacher" was correct; "there is no new thing under the sun" (Eccl. 1:9). The twenty-first century will see no new kind of sin or opposition to the gospel. There will be no new deterrent to missions nor a new potion to be released that will overcome all obstacles. Sociology and religion may elect to describe the world as "post-" everything. But needs and questions around the world are the same, and the answers are found in God's Word.

CHAPTER 21

The Uniqueness of Christianity over Other Religions

Erwin W. Lutzer

"Unite or Perish!"

That message seemed to dominate every session of the 1993 Parliament of the World's Religions in Chicago. Clearly the group most often targeted for criticism—the folks who could not be expected to buy into this united agenda— were those who belonged to the historic Christian faith. I'm convinced that a religious tidal wave is sweeping America. The message I heard at the Parliament was that we had better get on board or be left to swim (or drown) on our own.

The gods are "on a roll," and woe to those who stand in the way of their agenda. With lofty ideals and utopian plans to unify religions for the common good, this Parliament met to break down barriers in the path of an accelerated march toward unity. Six thousand delegates came to learn from one another, explore areas of agreement, and grasp a better understanding of one another's religious heritage. They promoted a global ethic designed to alleviate the suffering and end wars. Their time, they say, has come.

What place did Jesus of Nazareth have among the more than seven hundred workshops at the eight-day conference? He was admired, quoted, and favorably compared to other religious teachers, ancient and modern. He was touted as one stage in the evolutionary development of religion, indeed a very important stage. He was one of the enlightened. He has since been overshadowed by others, but He should be admired as the *special* man for His times.

With only a few exceptions, speakers expressed reverence for the contributions of Jesus to the history of religion. He was even described by some as a revealer of God, a man who had achieved the highest degree of enlightenment. Others allowed that He was the master of masters, the one who shows us the way, the one who is to be loved and followed. He was respected; He was not worshiped.

Instead, the delegates were often encouraged to shout "I AM!" as an affirmation of their own godhood. People who still believed in prayer were told that they should pray to their "god of choice." A religious edifice was being constructed that was flexible enough to house all the world's faiths under one spiritual roof. We were told that religious unity would end war, feed the hungry, and save the environment.

One woman claimed healing through mystical meditation; another said her New Age beliefs had saved her marriage. One man said that only when he delved into Hinduism did he "find the other half" of his soul. *Fulfillment, peace,* and *energy* were the words of power. There were plenty of testimonials to say, "It works!"

If so, what should we do with our doctrinal beliefs, those stubborn convictions that are roadblocks to unity? In one session of the Parliament one leader said, "Hold on to your chairs tightly, as if you might go through the ceiling if you were to let go. Now think of one of your most cherished beliefs—now let go of both your chair and your cherished belief! Nothing happened, right? Now you've got the feel of it!" Then we were told that we could have our beliefs back, thank you very much. We just had to get used to "letting go!"

In Chicago I saw a microcosm of schools, businesses, and communities. The people who live next door and your associates at work most likely believe that it doesn't matter what god you pray to, because every deity is ultimately the same, only shrouded in a different name. According to the 1993–1994 Barna research report, nearly two out of three adults contend that the choice of one religious faith over another is irrelevant because all religions teach the same basic lessons about life

HOW DIFFERENT IS CHRIST?

Now if Christ is indeed only one among many, if He is but one of the gods, it is time for all the religions to unite. Let all religious leaders stand on equal ground and pool their insights to fight our battles with a unified army. Enough of division! Enough of fruitless arguments! Enough of bigotry! Does Christ belong on the same shelf with Buddha, Krishna, Bahaullah, and Zoroaster? Such leaders have taught lofty ethics. If we simply say Christ stands taller than the rest, on a higher shelf so to speak, have we given Him His due?

When Gustav Doré (1832–1883) completed a painting of Christ a passerby paused to admire his work and remarked, "You must love Him to paint Him so well!" The artist replied, "Yes, I do love Him, but if I loved Him more, I'd paint Him better!" Those who consider Christ against the backdrop of the world's religions should come to love Him more and paint Him better.

IN DEFENSE OF THE UNIQUE CHRIST

The Bible draws a definitive line through the peoples of the world. Christ and His followers are on one side of that line, and all other religious and philosophical choices and adherents are on the other. The Bible gives reasons why Christ cannot be placed in the same cupboard, let alone on the same shelf, as Buddha, Krishna, or Zoroaster. Leaders of the other religions can only bow in worship.

A Sinless Savior

The Bible begins presenting its case with us. It teaches, and experience confirms, that we are sinners, separated from God. Our own efforts at self-transformation can improve our lifestyle or even our attitudes, but fundamentally we are left unchanged. Our greatest need is to be forgiven, reconciled to God, and in short, rescued from the tyranny and consequences of our sin. We need a Savior. Other religions have prophets, teachers, or gurus who tell us how we can better ourselves, be our own savior. In effect they tell us we are drowning, but they can only make our descent to the bottom of the ocean more comfortable. They might even give swimming lessons. But only a qualified Savior can reach out to snatch us from the power of the undertow.

The purpose of Christ's coming was stated before His birth when the angel said to Joseph, "And [Mary] will bear a Son; and you shall call His name Jesus, for it is He who will save His people from their sins" (Matt. 1:21).[1] Years later Jesus stated his own job description: "For the Son of Man has come to seek and to save that which was lost" (Luke 19:10).

Of course there have always been those who wanted to strip Christ of his qualifications. In the twentieth century, liberal scholars and media gurus insisted that Christ was Himself drowning, just as we are. When Martin Scorsese directed the film, "The Last Temptation of Christ," he said, "I tried to create a Jesus, who in a sense, is just like any other guy on the street." His Christ was not a prophet, much less a Savior. His "Christ" was not even worthy of respect as a guy on the street. Those searching for a Savior do not want to have to trust someone who is in the same predicament as they.

Understandably, none of the religious leaders I spoke with at the Parliament of Religions claimed to have a Savior. Their prophets, they said, showed the way; they made no pretense of personally forgiving sins. They could not transform a human being.

Jesus challenged anyone to find imperfection in his life and to believe the truth he proclaimed if there was none (John 8:46). He pointed out hypocrisy in the lives of His critics, but none of them could charge him. Even Judas, who knew Jesus on a daily basis, said, "I have sinned by betraying innocent blood" (Matt. 27:4a). Pilate confessed, "I find no guilt in this man" (Luke 23:4). Peter knew Jesus intimately for three years, yet he quoted the prophet

Isaiah in describing his master. Jesus had "committed no sin, nor was any deceit found in His mouth" (1 Peter 2:22). Paul said that God the Father "made Him who knew no sin to be sin on our behalf, that we might become the righteousness of God in Him" (2 Cor. 5:21). Jesus was either sinless or the great deceiver.

Luke records, "And Mary said to the angel 'How can this be, since I am a virgin?' And the angel answered and said to her, 'The Holy Spirit will come upon you, and the power of the Most High will overshadow you; and for that reason the holy offspring shall be called the Son of God'" (1:34–35). The unborn child was already holy. "His Holiness," the Dalai Lama does not live up to his name and he knows it. One woman who shook hands with him at the Parliament ran back to touch us to "share his energy." I said, trying to smile but still hoping she would get the point, "Why are you doing this? Do you realize that he is a sinner like the rest of us, and if he doesn't have a sinless Savior he's in big trouble?" The Dalai Lama said in an interview, "I'm not the best Dalai Lama there ever was, but I'm not the worst either!"[2] How should we interpret this candid remark? According to his own reincarnation theology he should be the *only* Dalai Lama who ever was. Best or worst, he himself knew that he was not "His Holiness."

Scan the religious horizons; read about the great religious teachers, what they taught, and what they had to say about themselves. Most called themselves "prophet," but look for a qualified sinless savior, and none are even competing against Christ for the title. If another claimed sinlessness, we could check out his credentials, but none even claim it. And Christ has satisfied the requirements.

> *For it was fitting that we should have such a high priest, holy, innocent, undefiled, separated from sinners and exalted above the heavens; who does not need daily, like those high priests, to offer up sacrifices, first for His own sins, and then for the sins of the people, because this he did once for all when He offered up Himself. (Heb. 7:26–27)*

Only a perfect Savior is able to save forever those who draw near to God through Him, since He always lives to make intercession for them (7:25). Not only can Christ save great sinners, but He saves us completely and eternally. And who benefits from His salvation? Given what we know about Him, it makes sense that he is the only way to the Father.

Christ According to Christ

At a Bible study I met a Jewish woman, Adriane Millman, who told how desperately she had prayed every day to find how to have a personal relationship with God. The very thought that Jesus might indeed be the Son of God, the Messiah, frightened her. "O God," she often prayed, "please be anyone but Jesus!"

"Truly, truly, I say to you, if anyone keeps My word he shall never see death" (John 8:51). His listeners could not believe what they heard. A man who was perhaps thirty years old promised that those who believed in Him would have eternal life. These seemed the words of a lunatic:

> Now we know that you have a demon. Abraham died, and the prophets also; and You say, "If anyone keeps My word, he shall never taste of death." Surely you are not greater than our father Abraham, who died? The prophets died too; whom do You make Yourself out to be? (8:52–53)

Christ replied that His critics really did not know God as they claimed. If they did, they would know who was speaking to them, for "before Abraham was born, I AM" (v. 58).

The Jews knew that Christ claimed to be God. His words could be interpreted in no other way. He had identified Himself with the "I AM," Yahweh, who appeared to Moses in the burning bush (Exod. 3:14). If He wasn't God this was the highest blasphemy. Jesus also said, "Not even the Father judges anyone, but He has given all judgment to the Son, in order that all may honor the Son, even as they honor the Father. He who does not honor the Son does not honor the Father who sent Him" (John 5:22–23).

A Hindu might accept Christ as an incarnation of whatever gods there be, but as Gandhi put it, "He cannot be given a solitary or supreme throne." It is precisely such solitary preeminence that Christ claims: if there is but one God and Christ is the second Person of what we call the trinity, there cannot be other thrones that He must share.

Affirm the deity of Christ who is the incarnation of the One true God and Christ stands alone without a single rival on the horizon; deny it and Christ is reduced to a false prophet who was deluded about His own person and mission. If He was not the one personal God manifest in the flesh, He falsely claimed to do what only God can do; He was a deceitful man who promised more than He could deliver.

The Divinity Chasm

The deity of Christ gouges a clean and unbridgeable chasm between Christianity and other religious options. Other religions cannot logically make the claim that they frequently do make: Christ is one of a long line of prophets. Islam, for example, professes great respect for Christ. Indeed, Muslims affirm Christ as one of the great prophets who preceded the greatest prophet, Muhammad. They admire Christ, but they do not worship Him.

The Qur'an denounces the Christian teaching of the deity of Christ as the greatest of tribulations. The Qur'an is quite right in teaching that the divinity of Christ sharply divides Christianity from Islam, as from all other religions. If it is false, it is a curse; if it is true, it is the best news—perhaps the only really good news—available on planet earth.

Christianity, then, cannot be combined with Islam; only Christianity affirms the Trinity, and therefore only in Christianity can God become man. No wonder Christ taught that He alone was qualified to be our Sin-bearer. He affirmed that the eternal destiny of men and women depended on their relationship to Him.

Christ taught that there were two paths, an attractive broad way that led to destruction and the narrow way that often was overlooked. "Enter by the narrow gate; for the gate is wide, and the way is broad that leads to destruction, and many are those who enter by it. For the gate is small, and the way is narrow that leads to life, and few are those who find it" (Matt. 7:13-14). The broad way of autosalvation is deceptive because many so-called enlightened religious leaders have labeled it "the way to life." Christ confronted us with two paths, two gates, and two separate destinations.

Persian mystic Bahaullah (1817-1892), founder of the Bahai faith, claimed that his vision of the nature of man and society superseded the teachings of Christ. Could it be that his revelation from God had supplanted Christ's? Did he have more direct or more up-to-date contact with the Almighty?

The problem is that Christ and Bahaullah teach mutually exclusive doctrines, so both could not speak for the same changeless God. Bahaullah believed in the fundamental goodness of the human soul. None who believe in God's unity, he taught, should discriminate among all the truth claims of those God has used as channels of light. Christ said, "Truly, truly, I say to you, he who does not enter by the door into the fold of the sheep, but climbs up some other way, he is a thief and a robber. . . . All who came before Me are thieves and robbers; but the sheep did not hear them" (John 10:1, 8). Whole chapters in the New Testament are devoted to the identification of false teachers, who are to be rejected. Indeed, doctrinal discrimination is given as a mark of spiritual maturity.

This is just one central difference between Christ and Bahaullah. Logically, both Bahaullah and Christ may be wrong, but both cannot be right. So-called later revelations cannot be another step in God's progressive revelation. They must originate from an entirely different source. The choice is between Christ and a prophet who is walking on a different road.

The New Testament predicts that, for a brief time, a unified world religion will be attempted. Through this religion, Antichrist will be worshiped for bringing economic stability and peace. There will be signs and wonders, and a giddy optimism about humankind's transformation. But Christ will return as judge, and those who have rejected Him will suffer.

A Step Beyond

At the end of the twentieth century, people speak of moving beyond Christianity to something better. New Age disciples say that Christianity is like a boat that is necessary to take one across the river, but once you disembark you are free to transcend it and enter into a whole new existence. From the baby steps of Christianity we must move on to something more mystical, satisfying, or complete.

One must always be cautious when considering steps beyond the barriers. To move beyond love is to lust; to move beyond rationality takes one into irrationality or even insanity. Beyond wholesome curative medicines are substances that harm instead of heal. The Bible teaches that to move beyond Christianity is to enter a shadow world of error and gross deception. One never can get beyond Christ without falling into a deep pit.

Strictly speaking, it is not possible to move beyond Christianity without abandoning it. Those who surrender the uniqueness of Christ surrender the religion entirely. We cannot remove the foundation and profess that the building is still intact.

An Extraordinary Death

The death of Christ and its meaning also sets apart Christianity from other options. All other religions believe that some form of human effort is involved in the salvation process, however *salvation* may be defined. Regardless of what they believe about the *Religious Ultimate*, other religions teach that we have to save ourselves or at least help the god or gods do it.

Christianity sets aside all hope of human merit and any deeds that make us feel better about ourselves as a basis for reconciliation with God. From God's viewpoint, we are not filled with latent good but rather with evil. Our hearts, Christ taught, are deceitful and our moral blemishes can neither be covered nor changed by us or through religious rituals. We have nothing in common with the holiness of God. Augustine (354–430) said, "He who understands the holiness of God despairs of trying to appease Him." The moral gap between us and God is infinite.

We have used the metaphor of a drowning swimmer. Actually now it must be abandoned, for the Bible teaches that sinners are not drowning but are rather dead in sins. We don't need a rope; we need someone to scoop us out of the water and give us life. Other religions speaks of trying to be better. Christianity speaks of Christ making dead people alive.

It is not that we contribute little to our own salvation, but that we can contribute nothing. If God did not save, we would never be saved; if He did not reconcile us to Himself, we would never be reconciled.

Paul wrote that God set forth Christ publicly "as a propitiation in His blood through faith. This was to demonstrate His righteousness, because in the forbearance of God He passed over the sins previously committed; for the demonstration, I say, of His righteousness, at the present time that He might be just and the justifier of one who has faith in Jesus" (Rom. 3:25-26). God remained just and became the justifier of those who believe.

God's holiness could neither be tainted nor compromised to achieve His desired result. He couldn't lower His standards because of love; He couldn't choose to be reconciled to those who were still unrighteous. Nor could He pretend that sin does not exist. Who could satisfy His justice? Only God Himself could meet His own requirements.

God the Father demands perfection that we do not have, but God the Son came to die on the cross to provide such perfect righteousness. He lived a life of perfect obedience, gave a perfect sacrifice, which the Father accepted on our behalf. No human works are involved, no human merit can be added to the completeness of Christ's work.

A Complete Work of Connection

The God of Christianity, is different from the gods of other religions in his connection to Christ. Allah, the tribal God of Muhammad, is not a trinity and therefore could never be incarnated. Since there are many gods in eastern religions, they cannot claim exclusivity, nor can any one of them promise their adherents the gift of forgiveness and personal reconciliation with the Religious Ultimate. No other religion lays claim to a Creator God who becomes a man to redeem humanity.

In fact, Buddhism could survive without Buddha. When Buddha was asked how he would like to be remembered, he answered that his followers should not trouble themselves with that, since only his teaching really mattered. The teachings of Hinduism survive far removed from those who originated the teachings. Islam could survive if the revelations had come through some other prophet. But Christianity could not survive without Christ as the second person of the Trinity coming to earth and dying on the cross and rising from death. His mission was redemption and that was not accomplished by His teaching but by His death. To empty the Cross of its meaning is to strip it of its power.

"For by grace you have been saved through faith; and that not of yourselves, it is a gift of God; not as a result of works, that no one should boast" (Eph. 2:8-9). God requires faith because He appreciates being believed. Faith is not itself a meritorious act; the merit is in the One to whom it is directed. It is gift given to those to whom God would show His mercy. Faith does not set out to earn God's favor but depends solely on the undeserved favor of God. He does all the giving, we do all the receiving. Our contribution is to admit our sins and our helplessness. God's contribution is to give us Christ's righteousness and make us members of God's family forever.

The uniqueness of this grace extends to its permanence. Once the gift is received it can never be lost through rebellion. When God bridges that infinite chasm and makes a fallen member of the human race his child, the process cannot be undone.

Too much is at stake for God to lose a child that belongs to Him. Just as I do not disown my children when they are disobedient, so God is committed to us for now and eternity. We are sealed with the Holy Spirit until the day of redemption (Eph. 4:30). This gift, once given, is ours forever.

Assurance of Reconciliation

Is it possible for a person to be confident of acquittal before God, so that a blessed eternity is assured? Non-Christian religions and even some false teachings among Christian sects that make works a part of salvation insist that full assurance is impossible. The reason is obvious: As long as human merit contributes to the salvation process, not one of us can know that we have done enough to earn our way.

New Testament Christianity asserts that we can have personal assurance because all of our requirements are met by Christ, who has impeccable credentials. If we believe that Christ did all that will ever be necessary for us to stand in Christ's presence, we will have the assurance that we belong to God. For this to happen we will have the settled conviction that our debt has been paid, and that we have been reconciled to God.

Now we can better understand why Christianity stands apart from all other theories of salvation. The strength of the gospel is in it's purity; whenever we add, we subtract; whenever we combine, we dilute.

The Personal Evidence

Atheist Antony Flew uses a parable to illustrate what he thinks is the lack of evidence for the existence of God.

Once upon a time two explorers came upon a clearing in the jungle in which there were both flowers and weeds. One explorer says, "Some gardener must tend this plot." The other disagrees, insisting that there is no gardener. So they pitch their tents and set a watch. No gardener is ever seen.

But the believer insists that there is an invisible gardener. So they set up a barbed wire fence, electrify it and patrol it with bloodhounds, reasoning that even an invisible man could be smelled though he could not be seen. But the fence is never tripped and the bloodhounds never cry out. No matter how long the explorers keep their vigil, no gardener is ever detected.

Yet the believer is unconvinced. He insists, "But there is a gardener, an invisible, intangible, elusive gardener; a gardener insensible to electric shocks, who has no scent and makes no sound, a gardener who comes secretly to look after the garden which he loves."

But the skeptic despairs, "Just how does what you call an invisible, intangible, eternally elusive gardener differ from an imaginary gardener, or even from no gardener at all?"[3]

Flew makes two points. First, there is no evidence that an invisible, intangible, elusive God who tends the world exists. He has never been detected with scientific equipment. This world, like an unkempt garden, has both weeds and flowers; both evil and good. There is, says Flew, no reason to believe that someone tends the plot.

Second, Flew says believers are unwilling to allow any evidence to count against their faith. They refuse to stipulate the conditions under which they would surrender their belief. Flew asks us, "What would have to happen before you were to disbelieve in the existence and love of God?" If nothing will count against your faith, it proves you have given it a privileged position immune from proof or disproof. Such a belief, he says, which is compatible with anything and everything, is meaningless.

Every religion has the responsibility to respond to Flew's challenge. We have every right to ask a Buddhist, Hindu, or Muslim, What would have to happen before you would give up your belief? What evidence would you accept that would count decisively against your creed? If we give our religious convictions a privileged position that is closed to rational investigation we relegate our beliefs to private opinions and personal preferences. Unless we can point to evidence outside of ourselves, evidence accessible to everyone, we have no reason to say that our beliefs are true for us and for others.

You'd think that Paul was responding directly to Flew when he wrote,

For I delivered to you as of first importance what I also received, that Christ died for our sins according to the Scriptures, and that He was buried, and that He was raised on the third day according to the Scriptures, and that He appeared to Cephas, then to the twelve. After that He appeared to more than five hundred brethren at one time, most of whom remain until now, but some have fallen asleep; then He appeared to James, then to all the apostles; and last of all as it were to one untimely born, He appeared to me also. . . . But if there is no resurrection of the dead, not even Christ has been raised; and if Christ has not been raised, then our preaching is vain, your faith also is vain. . . . and if Christ has not been raised, your faith is worthless; you are still in your sins. (1 Cor. 15:3–8, 13–14, 17)

Paul is strident in his argument: A man who claimed to be God was put to death and was raised to prove that His claims were valid. And if it be proven that Christ is still dead, if the grave still contains His body, we will stop preaching and humbly admit we have been misled. Our faith is not compatible with anything and everything, but is based on reliable historical events.

Why is the physical resurrection of Christ so important to our faith? First, it fulfills His prediction that this is the final sign He would give to the world (Matt. 12:40; 16:21). Reason requires that if Christ is God, He could not stay in the tomb indefinitely. Second, this is proof of our own final resurrection. Strictly speaking, Christ is the only person in history who was resurrected. Lazarus was simply resuscitated; he had to die again. Christ was resurrected with a new, indestructible body, a prototype of the body we shall receive.

Christianity does not teach reincarnation but resurrection (1 Cor. 15). This respect for the human body contradicts the Gnostic claim that matter is evil. And it contradicts the Eastern claim that we lose individuality in a cycle of rebirths. Our disintegrated bodies will be reconstituted so that we will have an eternal body. Our soul (the mind with its memories and affections) will be rejoined to the body so that we shall be whole people, personally in fellowship with other people and God forever. Eternity is neither vague nor shadowy, but individual, conscious, and eternal. Despite receiving new indestructible bodies and a new nature, we will be the people we are now for all of eternity.

The skeptic David Hume (1711-1776) thought that his essay on miracles would disprove the resurrection. He argued that we have uniform experience against miracles and there can be no exceptions to this rule! But his basic premise assumes the conclusion. How can he know that we have "uniform experience" against miracles? Obviously if a resurrection has occurred, we do not have "uniform experience" against such a miracle. Our responsibility is not to pontificate about what can or cannot happen in the world, but to simply look at the evidence to see what has happened. No philosophical argument keeps Christ in the tomb.

Karl Marx (1818-1883) took the stone of economics and rolled it in front of the tomb, hoping to keep Christ out of sight. He was reared in the Rhineland of Germany and baptized a Lutheran. But with his friend Friedrich Engels (1820-1895) he wrote *The Communist Manifesto* and *Das Kapital.* He said that religion was the opiate of the people, and that within time these myths would be exterminated.

But he didn't do very well in keeping Christ in the tomb. Today, countries that officially adopted Marxism are turning to Christianity with growing faith in a resurrected Savior. How could Christ be kept out of economics and politics when His shoulders will eventually bear the governments of the world?

"For unto us a child is born, unto us a son is given: and the government will be upon His shoulder" (Isa. 9:6a).

Sigmund Freud (1856-1939) rolled the stone of psychotherapy in front of the tomb. He claimed that our idea of God was a figment of our imagination, an idea we grasp to give us hope. Driven by aggression, sex drives, and a strong desire for a father image, we create God. He believed that psychoanalysis would be the answer to the distressed human spirit.

Today, psychiatry is itself on the couch; the entire discipline is in a disarray of conflicting theories about what works. Freud didn't understand that Christ is the master psychoanalyst, who is aware of the minute details of personality and has the power to restore the mind to God.

Voltaire (1694-1778) rolled the stone of culture in front of Christ's tomb. He had good reason to be critical of the church of his day; but he rejected Christ with the unspiritual churches. Within one hundred years, he wrote, the Bible would be a forgotten book, yet the house in which he lived became headquarters for the Geneva Bible Society.

Charles Darwin (1809-1882) rolled the stone of science in front of Christ's tomb. Though he himself professed belief in some form of god, he thought evolution could explain the origin of life. The next generation of scientists made God the unnecessary hypothesis. Yet today evidence is accumulating that the complexity of life cannot be explained by blind chance. Paul Leman, editor of the French Encyclopedia, said candidly, "Evolution is a fairy tale for adults." The reasonable scientific explanation for what is continues to be, "For by Him all things were created, both in the heavens and on earth, visible and invisible, whether thrones or dominions or rulers or authorities—all things have been created by Him and for Him" (Col. 1:16).

DOUBT AND REASON

The disciple Thomas reminds us that Christ accommodates skeptics whose hearts are open to embrace the truth. Doubt is not unbelief. Unbelief is usually rebellion against evidence. Doubt is stumbling over an insufficient understanding.

Iron! Wood! Blood! As far as Thomas was concerned it was all over; he had witnessed a tragic end to a beautiful life.

Was he justified in his doubt? There were good reasons to believe in the resurrection of Christ even without seeing the Lord. First, Christ had predicted that He would die and be raised. He had explained this in detail to His disciples (Matt. 16:21). Second, the miracles should have given Thomas confidence that the grand miracle of the Resurrection was both possible and necessary. Third, he should have believed because of the credibility of the witnesses. The disciples all shouted, "We have seen the Lord!" This was a lawyer's dream—ten testimonies in perfect agreement. But Thomas seems to have been the pessimist. The prediction of Christ and the word of his friends did not meet the needs of his hopeless heart. He needed personal encounter.

Thomas is not the kind of disciple who was so gripped with what higher critics call "messianic fever" that he was looking for reasons to make Christ into God. He was a hard-headed fisherman who wanted the evidence "beyond reasonable doubt."

Christ let Thomas brood for eight days before accommodating Thomas's stipulations (John 20:25–28). Why did Thomas believe when confronted by the face, the body, and the scars? He did want to believe. He didn't say, "I dare you to convince me!" He set what he thought were reasonable stipulations. When they were met he went beyond mere agreement to worship. He confessed whole-heartedly, "My Lord and My God!" (John 20:28).

In presenting and judging the evidence for Christ's resurrection, modern doubters must set reasonable stipulations. We are not in the realm of simple mathematical formulae. Mathematics simply joins abstract numerical concepts logically ($2 + 2 = 4$). Natural sciences do the same with concrete physical properties. The evidence for the Resurrection is *forensic*, rooted in the same proper historical investigation as any past event. Such evidence is sufficient for the honest doubter, but not enough for the dishonest one.

CONCLUSION

Christian faith is unique because it alone is centered in Christ, and Christ alone is God. Christ's truth claims can be held confidently and they are open to investigation. Religious truth is robbed of its power when given a privileged position that is immune from rational evidence.

There are good reasons to believe the truth claims of Christianity. There are the best reasons for giving our hearts to the Christ who is so proven. The alternative is to flounder in life, and to have no hope in death. "He who believes in the Son has eternal life; but he who does not obey the Son shall not see life, but the wrath of God abides on him" (John 3:36).

———————————

This chapter is adapted by permission of copyright holder from Erwin W. Lutzer, *Christ Among Other Gods* (Chicago: Moody, 1994).

CHAPTER 22

Unmasking the Many Faces of Pluralism

Gary P. Stewart

Pluralism—to most theologically conservative and evangelical Christian leaders it is a threat to biblical integrity; to theological liberals and some evangelicals it is a concept promising hope and unity in a world that needs peace. To one side, it means compromise; to the other, cooperation. To one, it is an excruciating push away from theological exclusivity to compatibility; to another, it is an encouraging push away from totalitarian authoritarianism to tolerance. To one it is corruption, to the other, compassion. To some these lines are clearly drawn in the sand, to others any lines at all appear extreme.

One thing is clear: Pluralism will be the defining issue in much of the Christian world, and especially in North America, for the coming decades.[1]

As the world becomes a smaller place due to advanced transportation and communication technology, national boundaries conjoin and cultures collide. The vast mountain ranges and the great oceans that historically have separated people no longer are barriers to connection or conflict. Peace conferences can be conducted through teleconferencing, and war can be waged "over the horizon." Economic, political, sociological, and religious differences among cultures are better understood. Humanity has become one huge "Tower of Babel." Many believe we could somehow unite the whole.

The concept responsible for this drive for unity is *pluralism*. We live among a plurality of views and lifestyles that both intrigues and threatens us. We are intrigued by the dress, song, architecture, and history of others. We are threatened by ideologies that these societies bring with them. *Pluralism* describes a situation of disunity, according to E. D. Cook, in which a world is marked by a variety of diverse views and outlooks. "Different moral, religious and political philosophies and ways of life compete with each other. This creates a smorgasbord effect, where those in the society [world] find it hard to decide between the competing views."[2]

Pluralism also is evidence of disunity because it is the natural product of a world that seeks God and truth through human reason. Ecumenism as a form of pluralism is evidence of an unacceptable attempt at unity. It is unacceptable because it blurs the essential distinctives that must be understood if we are to achieve unity. On the other hand, biblical Christianity is an acceptable evidence of unity, because it is the divinely ordained channel through which peace ultimately will come to the world.

This view is itself unacceptable to a great many within Christendom, for it seems exclusivist and thoroughly authoritarian. It is incompatible with a liberal view of theology. My primary objective here is to encourage evangelicals to resist the temptation to forego biblical distinctives for the sake of unity. Such unity, in my opinion, is at most a peripheral attempt at a temporal earthly peace.

TERMINOLOGY

"Buzz words" have become the handles by which we grasp the meaning and purpose of pluralism. This discussion will not look at all the terms that accompany the concept of pluralism. It is intended to describe the major ideas that shape the controversy. One immediately notices in defining terms that *pluralism* is a more narrow and technical concept than its contemporary use would indicate. It is more helpful as it is used correctly. The same can be said for the entire topic, which has been expanded upon so frequently that we cannot truly understand it without greater clarity. [3]

Pluralism

What most writers have generally referred to as *pluralism* is understood here as encompassing tolerance, diversity, and religious and political ecumenism. We will use the term *pluralism* in its more limited, proper sense as describing a given society or global perspective that recognizes the reality of differing races, languages, values, religions, and ideologies. *Pluralism* refers to what is, not what should be. It does not imply how people should relate to one another or whether any religion or cultural ethic is superior to another. Pluralism understands that there are many different animals in the zoo who live in many different cages.

Pluralism is a fact of life since the Tower of Babel. What is different about our modern world is that the cultural differences encounter each other much more frequently. In ancient history, cultures remained more or less isolated, until war brought subjugated peoples and their cultures into the societal mix. Pluralism was always present, but tolerance of differences and concern for national autonomy was never regarded as a redeeming human quality.

Today access to differing cultures and their views has become a way of life, particularly in the industrialized East and West. War and subjugation still mix cultures, along with the immigration social upheavals cause. Especially in Canada, the U.S., and the European Community countries, relaxed immigration has poured together peoples of various ethnic backgrounds, nationalities, and religious persuasions. *Descriptive pluralism*, or *empirical pluralism* as D. A. Carson refers to it, describes the communal presence of peoples from differing cultures and perspectives.[4]

What happens when pluralism has no national boundary, as in the melting pot societies, when people are not only personally aware but are personally experiencing this world situation? The paradox of pluralism is that the greater the national or global pluralism, the greater the potential for partisanship. And the greater the partisan division, the more pressure to seek a unanimity that will erode the uniqueness of all the cultures that have come together.

How can a pluralistic society achieve unity? Can people come together while holding their own uniqueness? This is the primary struggle that pluralism brings to modern politicians and theologians alike.

Multiculturalism

One of the world's most pluralistic nations achieved an amazing degree of unity for about 180 years by building upon a unified ethical/worldview religious foundation. With relatively few exceptions, the U.S. Constitution was interpreted fairly consistently from a Christian moral perspective. There certainly were intercultural struggles, but to the extent that the Christianity-based legal system was respected, the resulting social structure tolerated considerable diversity.

All of that fell apart with the rise of postmodernism and its theory that all truth is relative. If one truth is no more valid than another, the strength of a national Constitution is left to the worldview discretion of individual judges, legislators, and attorneys. The courts became obligated to address the opinions of all interest groups who claim to be objects of negative discrimination, and there are no clear boundaries to objectively determine what negative discrimination is.

So words relating to justice have been traded for a new language with the terms *accommodation, sensitivity, inclusion, cooperation,* and *harmony*. These virtuous sounding concepts have become the sole end for social justice, and they are to be reached without any consideration of moral values or consensus regarding standards of conduct. Even virtues common to most religions are ignored in the name of sensitivity. This is the picture of society dominated by *multiculturalism*, a skewed, totally secular understanding of the world. Multiculturalism is no ultimate answer, though as a concept, it does possess a commendable respect for all of humanity. Without any possible moral underpinning, it becomes divisive and perpetuates disorder.

Multiculturalism is no longer simply an attempt to conjoin various cultures within a society. It is becoming a worldview in its own right, a secular worldview free of referent to God or absolutes. It is becoming another culture within the culture, a worldview among conflicting worldviews. It attempts to join peoples for the sake of politics and commerce, rather than for reasons of truth and justice. Where there is no absolute truth, people have nothing left to them but a smorgasbord of ideas that are equally valid. For a secular mind-set, this removes the shackles of morality, but ultimately ends in social chaos. Gene Edward Veith Jr. comments,

> Eager to accommodate all oppressed minorities, many college campuses today segment them all the more. After all the hard fought battles to integrate higher education, today we see a re-segregation of the university. Racial minorities often have separate dormitories, separate dining areas, separate student unions, separate yearbooks, and separate graduation ceremonies. Affirmative action programs base admissions and scholarships on race, unfairly stigmatizing qualified minority students by implying that they could not succeed on their merits alone. Though all this multiculturalism aims at promoting tolerance, more racial tension and animosity exists on campuses today than ever.[5]

Multiculturalism's relativistic roots have focused so much on accommodating and tolerating distinctives that it has overlooked similarities. The result is a society full of distinctly independent cultural groups each demanding the right to live according to their own dictates.

Along these lines, it is interesting to note Samuel P. Huntington's prognosis. Basically people tend to identify themselves "in terms of ancestry, religion, language, history, values, customs, and institutions. They identify with cultural groups: tribes ethnic groups, religious communities, nations, and, at the broadest level, civilizations."[6]

Huntington's model identifies eight distinctive civilizations: Islamic, Sinic (centered on the "core state" of China), Western (with the United States as its core), Orthodox (with Russia at its core), Japanese, Hindu, Latin American, and somewhat tentatively, African. Of these eight, the latter two count for little in geopolitics, and the greatest clashes and struggles are foreseen between Islam, the West, and China. The conflicts between these cultures will arise in part, due to "Western arrogance, Islamic intolerance, and Sinic assertiveness."[7] Some distinctives are dangerous to national or international peace. The attitudes and policies of some culture groups (civilizations) are not only incompatible with pluralism, but also intolerant of pluralism. A multiculturalism that genuinely seeks uniformity amidst a plurality must never lose sight of humanity's more sinister side. One particular religiously based culture group that is a threat to other groups is Islam.

Where Islam becomes dominant, it negates pluralism, i.e., the presence of cultural differences, by applying Shari'a (Islamic Law) to the non-Muslim population. Nina Shea reports just a few Islamic atrocities of the 1990s:

> The militant Islamic government's tactics in its religious war in the southern part of the country [Sudan] have resulted in the deaths of about 1.5 million people and the displacement of more than three million. Sudanese agents have burned and looted villages, enslaved women and children, forcibly converted non-Muslim boys before using them as shock troops in battle, relocated entire villages into concentration camps called "peace villages," and withheld international food aid to non-Muslim communities until they convert.[8]

Multiculturalism cannot work where people ascribe to doctrines that demean and subjugate those of the human family who hold "heretical" positions. "Since the early part of this century the number of Christians in Iraq has decreased from 35 to 5 percent of the population; in Iran, from 15 to 2 percent; in Syria, from 40 to 10 percent; and in Turkey, from 32 percent to 0.2 percent." Christians in America have good reason to be concerned with the eradication of its perspective from the public square. Shea argues that Christians are the most persecuted religious group on earth.[9]

As a secular system, multiculturalism does not offer much hope for Christians in America. The reality of Islamic persecution in Sudan is grim evidence of the ideological threat to the West. Huntington writes, "The underlying problem for the West is not Islamic fundamentalism. It is Islam, a different civilization whose people are convinced of the superiority of their culture and are obsessed with the inferiority of their power."[10]

Tolerance

When one hears the word *tolerance*, mental and emotional reactions immediately begin to surface. What is actually meant by the word is left to each individual's philosophical perspective on life and truth. Those from a more traditional background tend to view tolerance as a virtue that undermines and diminishes their orthodox belief in the transcendent, while those who espouse progressivism view tolerance as an opportunity to pursue a personal and autonomous agenda without interference. To the traditionalist, tolerance is seen as a threat to morality and objective truth; to the progressivist, it is a key that unlocks the shackles of moral restraint and intellectual narrowness.

People have forgotten that genuine tolerance is dependent on a predefined standard. Tolerance is extended to people who, because of personal or cultural ignorance, are yet unaware of all that a preexisting standard requires of them. For this reason, emotional and intellectual growth is expected within a broad, but limited, time frame, at the end of which tolerance is gradually replaced by some form of discipline, ranging in severity according to the extent of the discrepancy.

To ignore or not expect personal growth and to remain silent about a behavior that is detrimental to the welfare of a given community confuses tolerance with timidity. Society must have a moral standard around which tolerance operates, truth is honored, and justice prevails. The Christian tolerance of those who live outside of the evangelical faith tradition is appropriate and understandable.

Though we do not accept much of their behavior and often must make our sentiments known, we understand the theological blindness (2 Cor. 4:1-7) from which their worldview originates. Therefore, we treat them compassionately, and mercifully leave their ultimate fate in the hands of God. This is genuine tolerance. However, when tolerance is not framed within accepted moral standards, such concepts as grace, mercy, unconditional love, and forgiveness become confused and lose their meaning. Don Eberly notes,

> To love unconditionally and forgive is not to be confused with tolerance, a term that can imply moral neutrality and consent. The spirit of forgiveness accepts others while rejecting their conduct or convictions. Few terms are more loaded with self-deception and distortion than the contemporary concept of tolerance. The growing calls for Americans to be more tolerant have not produced citizens who act with genuine benevolence toward one another.[11]

This was clearly demonstrated in the mid-1990s by the political and moral upheavals that resulted from U.S. President Bill Clinton's covered-up and then admitted sexual indiscretions. Requests to forgive the moral impropriety or to show mercy because of his human weakness were not appeals for genuine tolerance. Rather, there was a mandate for establishing personal and private behavior as off limits to public and judicial scrutiny.

In the name of tolerance, America is eliminating standards for morality to achieve sexual and economic gratification. True tolerance may delay justice as an expression of mercy in hopes of producing genuine repentance or change in behavior, but it never permits an injustice or rolls over to allow an adjustment in a transcendent standard.

With the world getting smaller, there is a need for peoples to be tolerant of one another, but we must be aware that tolerance is not an isolated phenomenon. James Hunter notes that "it coincides with the slow but steady expansion of political and ideological tolerance (such as tolerance of communists and atheists), racial tolerance (of blacks and Hispanics), and sexual tolerance (of homosexuals and those cohabiting outside of marriage)."[12]

We live in a country that is proposing "indiscriminate inclusion" apart from a moral foundation. Everything is accepted, so nothing can be identified as "right." And so, S. D. Gaede observes,

> we deny the need for such a foundation of rightness and hope against hope that we can build a decent society undergirded by relativism. For that reason we promote multiculturalism—not as an effort to establish justice based on some moral vision, but simply to achieve indiscriminate inclusion. But what we end up with instead is not tolerance, nor inclusion, and certainly not justice. What we get is Robespierre: people with power deciding what is best for all and executing their will accordingly.[13]

In a world of unfettered tolerance, someone will grasp ultimate power and press their own will. If that someone has a philosophy that is anti-Christian, tolerance will be selective. Believers must be people of conviction who take responsibility for what they know, and share it with the world rather than look at their knowledge as an achievement that deserves respect.

We forget the power inherent in the gospel and its ability to thwart the powers of evil. Gaede warns us to be inclusive of people, but not of beliefs. We should listen to all people, without agreeing with all. We should embrace the speaker but not the spoken lie.[14] Gaede explains,

> The modern world does not know how to deal with the issue of differences. It doesn't have the categories to do so. And so it vacillates between a blind affirmation of differences and an equally blind affirmation of similarities, looking to politics of inclusion or exclusion to save us. But they will not save us. Only Jesus saves. And it is only as we take our cue from him, and build our policies on the truth that he has given us, that we will be able to serve a very needy world.[15]

Hunter accurately describes a valid multicultural playing field in his suggestion that a "principled tolerance" is what life in North America is all about. "But this is only possible if all contenders, however much they disagree with each other on principle, do not kill each other over these differences, do not desecrate what the other holds sublime, and do not eschew principled discourse with the other."[16]

Autonomy

The desire to be autonomous human beings is as old as the fall of Adam and Eve. Since that time, humanity has sought tenaciously to create its own sovereignty, whether on the level of nations or as individuals. The issue is anthropological; what is to be done with the self and how much control over the self can, or should, one have? Does the term *autonomy* provide the answer, or is it confusing, deceptive, and misleading? The philosophical debate over autonomy throughout the twentieth century led to the atrocity of the holocaust and legalization in the United States of abortion in 1973 and physician-assisted suicide in Oregon in November of 1997.

Scholars are not blind to obvious shortcomings with the idea that society will survive if everyone behaves as autonomous entities. James F. Childress and John C. Fletcher, while believing that biomedical ethics must provide a central place for the principle of respect for self-determination, know that the demands of autonomy are often unclear. The motivations for personal actions and values can be difficult to decipher, and there are multiple sources for moral guidance. [17]

The respect for personal autonomy is individual and context driven. Scholars maintain that the autonomous human being is self-determining but limited by other people's autonomy and perhaps other moral constraints.[18] The word is too directive or determinative to satisfy the moral care of the individual and the moral responsibility that individual has toward others. Thomas Murray correctly reminds us of the paternalistic treatment patients received from health care professionals and of the importance to protest:

> Autonomy was a powerful and handy concept with which to do that. Because it touched such deep currents in American character and culture, autonomy cast a dazzling glow that many hoped would be able to illuminate all the dark corners of our shared moral life. Some still retain that faith; others, such as myself, believe that autonomy remains a vital moral bulwark against oppression, but that it is not an all-encompassing guide to living good lives or building good communities.[19]

Murray well identifies the disrespectful abuses of the individual by medicine; he has a point that autonomy is not a "guide to living good lives." Yet his argument from the perspective of self-rule or autonomy is misleading and ill-advised. The term has taken on so much meaning that it is not helpful in balancing the issue of paternalism.

Relativism is a logical extension of autonomy. Relativism claims that there is no truth or that truth is personally or culturally determined. To rule oneself (autonomy) demands that one decides truth for oneself (relativism), which eventually leads to self-divination or self-destruction. Studies of the late twentieth century showed that relativism, and therefore personal autonomy, is prevalent in the West.

North America provides a good example. In one U.S. study, only 13 percent of the respondents expressed belief in all ten commandments. Forty percent were willing to believe in the force of five of the ten. As recently as the 1950s, institutions commanded respect. By the end of the century there was little respect for law. People were a law unto themselves, the authority over church and God and government, laws, and police. Ninety-three percent of respondents to one survey declared that they alone determined what was moral for them. Almost as many (84 percent) did not feel constrained to obey the established rules of whatever religion they identified as their own.[20]

Respect for fellow human beings has nothing to do with autonomy; it has to do with the value of each individual as the image-bearer of God. The sacrifice of choosing "never to pay back evil for evil," but to "respect what is right in the sight of all men," and "so far as it depends on you" to "be at peace with all men," (Rom. 12:17–18 NASB) ultimately brings peace and freedom. Without God's instruction, we will not gain mutual respect.

Religious Pluralism

Religious pluralism is a confusing term. It appears simply to refer to a multiplicity of differing religions; however, it is much more. From its most prominent proponent, we are able to understand that ultimately it is a multireligious approach to universal salvation. John Hick contends that all theology is a human creation that does not accurately reflect the heart and will of the "Ultimate Reality." Each religion represents a human attempt to describe the Ultimate Reality, and therefore each is of equal value.

> God is known in the synagogues as Adonai, the Lord God of Abraham, Isaac, and Jacob; in the mosques as Allah rahmin rahim, God beneficent and merciful; in the Sikh gurudwaras as God, who is Father, Lover, Master, and the Great Giver, referred to as war guru; and in the Hindu temples as Vishnu, Krishna (an incarnation of Vishnu), Rama, Shiva, and many other gods and goddesses, all of whom, however, are seen as manifestations of the ultimate reality of Brahman; and in the Christian churches as the triune God, Father, Son, and Holy Spirit. And yet all these communities agree that there can ultimately be only one God![21]

Having dismissed the value of Christian Scriptures, Hick is free to create any theology of his pleasing to satisfy his personal understanding of God. In fact, no Scripture from any faith can convince Hick of a theological position since all are of human origination. It is the position of the religious pluralist that sincerity of faith is the grounds for acceptance by the "Real." Hick compares the morality of non-Christians with Christians and concludes that there is no visible difference between the two. Non-Christian religions experience the same "fruits of the Spirit" that Christians do. Their desire to seek out God has produced a morality that is evidence of their salvation.

If Christians can accept the fact that God has never accurately revealed himself in any particular way or to any particular people, then any means of acquiring salvation, including Hick's, is open for consideration. If personal experience, observation, and a "cosmic optimism" are all that is required to create a view of salvation, and if salvation is ultimately universal as Hick states, then the "Real" is the most brutal of gods to delay ending the senseless human tragedy of history.[22] To love a god of my own creation, whether I am a Christian or Buddhist, is to commit to a contrived figment of human imagination. I might as well create a religion that satisfies more of my human desires and requires fewer risks, and then be sure to follow it with sincerity. As long as my morals are consistent with the moral systems of others who are trying to know the Real, I'll be fine; from a universalist perspective, all will work out anyway.

Religious pluralism is a postmodern *universalism* that promotes relativism and diversity without unity. Like most postmodern philosophies, universalism accepts contradiction as normative, so it is intellectually deceitful and irresponsible.[23] A "radical hermeneutic" has been employed to dismiss objective truth in order to set the worlds of politics and religion upon equal footing. To avoid the superiority of any one group, the salvific plan of God in Christ is reduced to a socially constructed sincerity.[24] One wonders if a universalist considers universalism superior to other religions or whether members of other religions are willing to submit to the superiority of Western universalism.[25]

Inclusivism and Exclusivism

Neither universalism nor any other inclusivist faith is compatible with Christian teaching. The Old and New Testaments simply will not tolerate the idea that Christ exists in all religions in some anonymous way. Carl F. H. Henry echoes this sentiment:

> The notion that God's historical covenants embrace all world religions as a part of the church that finds fulfillment in Christ, and that Christ is present in nonbiblical religious history from the beginning, is alien to biblical teaching and arbitrarily correlates religion in general with redemptive religion. The New Testament does indeed represent the whole cosmos and all history as finding its final reconciliation in Christ. But from this emphasis we cannot logically infer that nonbiblical religious writings point to Christ in some hidden way. While God's saving design in the Bible has certain universal implications, it does

not welcome the world's works-religions as prefatory to the propitiatory work of the Redeemer.[26]

Exclusivists do maintain a limited view of salvation, holding that salvation is found only in Christ and that knowledge of him is essential to avoid damnation. Carson comments of Christian faith,

> Normally it is also held that salvation cannot be attained through the structure or claims of other religions. It does not hold that every other religion is wrong in every respect. Nor does it claim that all who claim to be Christians are saved, or right in every respect. It does insist that where other religions are contradicted by the gracious self-disclosure of Christ, they must necessarily be wrong.[27]

Exclusivists seek to stay true to the intent of Scripture. They do not try to reinterpret or dismiss the text through deconstructionism.[28] The apostle Paul reminds us that "there is none righteous, no, not one; there is none who understands; there is none who seek after God" (Rom. 3:10 NKJV).

The suggestion that people in all cultures and countries are genuinely seeking after the one true God, or that they are able to find him in any religion, is not simply inconsistent with the biblical record. The belief that morality is synonymous with righteousness is inconsistent with human experience. My life before Christ was as moral as that of any Christian, Muslim, Buddhist, or Hindu I have ever known, but my righteousness was my own and not Christ's. I believed in God, but did not know that I needed the righteousness of Christ until I heard the gospel message. The Lord had to draw me to a place where I could hear and respond to the gospel and receive the righteousness of Christ.

Now I strive to live a moral life to honor him for what he has done for me, not from fear of parental discipline and disappointment or because of a personal preference. Morality, styles of worship, religious spirituality, and commitment to one's beliefs occur in people's lives for many reasons, both good and bad. To suggest that they are evidences of salvation in those who have not heard or who practice a non-Christian faith gives salvific quality to these traits that is not supported biblically. If human righteousness was an evidence of salvation, why would Christ have condemned outwardly righteous Pharisees with such contempt (Matt. 23:13–36)? The Scriptures are clear: Christ and his righteousness are imputed solely to each individual who trusts in him for salvation (Luke 24:47; John 1:12; 3:16–18; 14:6; 17:20; Acts 4:12; 26:15–18; Rom. 5:1; 6:23; 10:1–15; 2 Cor. 5:18–21; Eph. 1:7; 2:8–9; Phil. 2:5–11; Col. 1:9–14; 1 Tim. 2:4–5; Heb. 1:2–4; 1 Peter 1:17–21).

It grieves me to think of the suffering that awaits those who reject or do not hear the Good News (see Luke 16:19–26). Among them are friends and members of my own family. I wish I could believe in their annihilation or conditional immortality or that God would save them in spite of themselves. But the Scriptures do not allow such a position. So I pray, trusting in the goodness and wisdom of God who knows the hearts of all men and women and whose discernment far outweighs my own. Who am I to question what He has set in place? I am the messenger, not the message or its drafter.

CONCLUSION

Throughout history, pluralism has been necessary to bring about peace between differing religions and philosophies. However, the way in which our postmodern world chooses to define and use the concept of pluralism will create many challenges for those who continue declaring that there is absolute truth and that humanity is responsible to live according to it.

The next century is our moment in history. God has commissioned us, who are his imagebearers, to represent him honestly and compassionately. We are not called to victory but to faithfulness. Our guide is an inerrant and holy Bible, our strength is in the Holy Spirit, and our hope lies beyond these corruptible bodies in the redemptive work of a unique Savior.

CHAPTER 23

The Worldviews of Destruction in the Twentieth Century

David A. Noebel

*Beware lest any man [educator, politician, musician, news reporter]
take you captive through vain and deceitful philosophy [naturalism,
materialism, existentialism, hedonism, pragmatism], after the tradition of men [Marx, Darwin, Nietzsche, Wellhausen, Freud, Dewey,
Foucault], after the rudiments of the world [socialism, natural evolution, higher criticism, humanism, moral relativism, deconstructionism,
collectivism], and not after Christ. (Col. 2:8)*

The twentieth century provided a laboratory for the praxis of Paul's warning
to the Colossians. Those sectors of civilization that had traditionally been
open to Christ had replaced their historic faith with any of a number of
philosophies. Ideas have consequences, and the twentieth century reaped devastating fruit of these utopian schemes.

Over one hundred years ago (1890–1891), James Orr presented the Kerr
lectures in Edinburgh, Scotland. *The Christian View of God and the World*
argued forcefully for the proposition that biblical Christianity is a worldview
(Ger. *Weltanschauung*). By this term he meant that Christianity is more than
a two-hour emotional experience on Sunday morning. Rather Christianity is
a twenty-four-hour-a-day relationship with God through Jesus Christ.

At approximately the same time Orr presented his work, three men and
one woman were about to emerge on the world's stage. By the time they
finished speaking, writing, and living out their worldviews, millions of human
beings lost their lives. Millions more will perish in the twenty-first century
because of ideas contained within these worldviews.

The twentieth century was incredible for its advances in inventions, medical science, transportation, communications, expansion of the Christian gospel, higher living standards, and freedom from tyranny. But there was incredible devolution in political oppression, poverty, drug use, pornography, homosexuality, venereal diseases including AIDS, illegitimate births, and abortions. It was a century of lawlessness and immorality, an era of mass murder unequaled in previous human history. In fact, more human beings died because of lawlessness and injustice during those one hundred years than in all previous centuries combined. The twentieth century was the century of slaughter.

Up to the time he wrote the words, the first eighty-eight years of the century, historian R. J. Rummel related that

> almost 170 million men, women and children have been shot, beaten, tortured, knifed, burned, starved, frozen, crushed or worked to death; buried alive, drowned, hung, bombed, or killed in any other of the myriad ways governments have inflicted death on unarmed, helpless citizens and foreigners. The dead could conceivably be nearly 360 million people. It is as though our species has been devastated by a modern Black Plague. And indeed it has, but a plague of Power, not germs.[1]

Rummel estimated that the abuse of power had killed at least 203 million people.[2] This does not include the final twelve years of the century. Nor does it take into account the slaughter brought about by abortion—a foundation stone of the secular humanist worldview. Most of these millions died at the ideological hands of the three men and one woman whose worldviews inflicted the world.

The three men are Josef Stalin (b. 1879), Benito Mussolini (b. 1883), and Adolph Hitler (b. 1889). The woman was Margaret Sanger (b. 1879).

Mussolini and Hitler held fascist/national socialist worldviews. Stalin was a Marxist/Leninist. Margaret Sanger was a secular humanist.

The dead were sacrificed on altars with a variety of labels, all born of one of those three worldviews. Ideas exploded from the fevered brows of the intelligentsia, taking such forms as atheism, naturalism, dialectical materialism, ethical relativism, class morality, social Darwinism, euthanasia, eugenics, collectivism, statism, "new man" ideologies, new social/world orders, national and international socialism, positive law, and sociological jurisprudence.

At the beginning of century twenty-one, we must admit a dark secret: The ideas responsible for a century of terror are still taught in Western public institutions of lower and higher education. Ironically, the worldview frequently proscribed is biblical Christianity, the one that is not responsible for the slaughter. All other worldviews have their voices and defenders in academia.

David Horowitz reminisces in his autobiography, "The situation in the universities was appalling. The Marxists and socialists who had been refuted by historical events were now the tenured establishment of the academic world. Marxism had produced the bloodiest and most oppressive regimes in human history—but after the fall, as one wit commented, more Marxists could be found on the faculties of American colleges than in the entire former Communist bloc. The American Historical Association was run by Marxists, as was the professional literature association."[3]

Horowitz was speaking particularly of one nation, the United States, in which one worldview still monopolizes public education; however, other nations face a similar educational disaster. It is perhaps more noticeable in the U.S. because the architects of the national educational system were American humanists Sanger and John Dewey (1859-1952). Secular humanism thus became the celebrated worldview of professors and teachers and professional organizations. Secular humanist values predominate in the power centers of society.[4]

The result of this power base in education, entertainment, the courts, and government was that various humanistic worldviews campaigned vigorously and systematically to eradicate the biblical worldview from the public square.[5] If this continues one can expect the same results during the twenty-first century—death and destruction.

NAZISM

This trend has been international. For example, Protestant pastors across Bavaria delivered an official blessing of Nazism on Easter Sunday, April 16, 1933. Churchmen passed the collection plate in honor of Hitler's birthday, flew the Reich flag on state holidays and marched in national parades with swastikas stitched to their vestments. This national church movement ignored the fact that the national socialist worldview was pagan, occult, anti-Jewish, and anti-Christian. They were uncritical of the government's socialist, collectivist, or evolutionist principles.[6]

In fairness to these pastors it should be noted that in 1918 the Marxist Kurt Eisner staged a coup in Munich and held the city for over three months. The Nazi party played on fears of Marxism, insisting that Christianity and Nazism fight the Red terror together.[7] What the pastors did not realize was that Hitler's militant socialism and Marxist socialism were blood brothers— one national, one international. Nazis were quick to adopt methods imported from the USSR: the one-party system; the position assigned to the secret police, concentration camps; policies of administrative execution or imprisonment of all opponents; extermination of families of suspects; and propaganda methods. Notes Ludwig von Mises, there were no more docile disciples of Stalin, V. I. Lenin (1870-1924), and Leon Trotsky (1879-1940) than the Nazis.[8]

Anyone reading Hitler's *Mein Kampf* (My Struggle) can see how completely he was controlled by Darwinian views of human development. These framed his racial and militaristic policies. Hitler thought he could help nature a little with the evolutionary struggle for existence.[9]

It is no secret that these concepts of Darwinism still dominate natural science education throughout the world.[10] In most countries no competition from creation-based science is tolerated. In the U.S., for example, Christians continually challenge this monopoly in the courts, usually without much success. The teaching of creationism, since it assumes some sort of creating deity, was ruled to be an unconstitutional mixing of church and state. The writer of that decision, Justice William Brennan, was a vocal secular humanist.

A number of scholars have noted the strong connection between naturalistic evolutionary theory and Nazi objectives. In one of the foremost studies of Hitler, Werner Maser found that Darwin was the general source for Hitler's biology, worship, philosophy of the use of force. It informed his rejection of moral causality in history.[11]

Darwin wasn't Hitler's only god, however. Socialism was as much a part of the national socialist worldview as was evolution. Socialism is consistent with collectivism or statism. It requires a dictator to abolish or control private property and to nationalize the means of production.[12] Friedrich A. Hayek's *The Road to Serfdom* observes the mental collectivizing of students in Nazi Germany. Hayek writes that, "Many a university professor during the 1930s has seen English and American students return from the continent uncertain whether they were Communists or Nazis and certain only that they hated Western liberal (in the traditional sense) civilization."[13]

Youth flocked to the Nazi and Communist causes, and some observed the incredible "susceptibility of university-trained people in Germany to totalitarian appeals."[14] Twenty-five percent of the SS had Ph.Ds. Germany's intellectual community prepared the German people and especially the German youth for the acceptance of some form of militant socialism. Hans Kohn writes in *The Mind of Germany* that "within little more than a decade German intellectuals succeeded in leading German people into the Abyss."[15] Kohn says it was primarily the philosophy of Martin Heidegger, the political theory of Carl Schmitt, and the theology of Karl Barth that convinced German intellectuals that Germany's future was not with the West.

Barth, of course, later joined forces with the anti-Nazi movement and was a signer of the Barmen Declaration. But as John Robbins notes, while Barth's theological views changed over the decades, his political and economic views did not. Barth admitted that he chose theology to find a better basis for social activism. "Socialism," claimed Barth, "is a very important and necessary application of the gospel."[16] Barth commented,

> If you understand the connection between the person of Jesus and your socialist convictions, and if you now want to arrange your life so that it corresponds to this connection, then that does not at all mean you have to "believe" or accept this, that, or the other thing. What Jesus has to bring us are not ideas, but a way of life. One can have Christian ideas about God and the world and about human redemption, and still with all that be a complete heathen. And as an atheist, a materialist, and a Darwinist, one can be a genuine follower and disciple of Jesus. Jesus is not the Christian worldview and the Christian worldview is not Jesus.[17]

Unfortunately for Barth and his defenders he supported Marxism and even Stalin. He was the ultimate anti-anti-Communist.[18]

So it was not just Marx, Heidegger, Johann Fichte (1762–1814), Ferdinand Lassalle (1825–1864), and Friedrich Nietzsche (1844–1900) who prepared Germany for Hitler and Nazism. Barth, Rudolf Bultmann (1884–1976), Friedrich Delitzsch (1813–1890), Emanuel Hirsch (1888–1972), Gerhard Kittel (1888–1948), and Paul Tillich (1886–1965) all played a role in turning the German people from Christ and biblical Christianity to Darwinism, national socialism, and sometimes Marxist socialism.[19]

Germany's higher critical scholars taught that the resurrection of Jesus Christ was only a spiritual vision, and that the resurrection accounts in the Gospels were later additions. Hirsch thought the idea of a physical resurrection distorted Christianity by focusing attention on the hereafter instead of the present. He stressed the importance of community in the Christian life.[20] Tillich, a member of the Marxist Frankfurt School, was never friendly to biblical Christianity and Bultmann is known for his advocacy of "demythologizing" the New Testament.[21]

How much have we learned from this portion of history? Not much according to historian Franklin Littell:

> The lessons to be learned from the Church Struggle and the Holocaust have hardly penetrated our Protestant seminaries, our liberal Protestant press, our church literature, the thinking and writing of even our ablest older theologians . . . American Liberal Protestantism is sick, and the theological form of its sickness can be summarized by saying that it stands solidly on ground but lately vacated by the German Christians . . . who collaborated with Nazism.[22]

Significantly, the nineteenth and twentieth century "quests for the historical Jesus," which began as German theological liberalism, were replayed in the 1980s and 1990s in the so-called "Jesus Seminar," primarily a U.S. movement.

David Frederick Strauss, whose *Life of Jesus* (1835) influenced Marx and the first "quest" movement, was extensively quoted by Jesus Seminar scholars.[23]

FASCISM

A worldview quite similar to Nazism, fascism was a pagan religion with worship of the state on its list of major ingredients.

Fascism, says Stanley G. Payne,

> was above all a product of the new culture and intense international Social Darwinism of the early twentieth century, normally (though not in every instance) wedded to war and fundamental international changes. Its pagan warrior mentality sometimes conflicted with the norms and processes of modernization, but fascist states eagerly incorporated major functions of rationalization and modern development.[24]

Evolution was as important to Mussolini as it was to Hitler. A. E. Wilder-Smith states that both "Hitler and Mussolini glorified struggle and war on the basis that the fittest would survive and the race would be thus cleansed."[25] Both sought to assist nature in its inevitable progress. Evolutionary doctrine gave Mussolini the excuse to enslave whole peoples, or wipe them out as less highly evolved than his own people. The concept of evolution, says Wilder-Smith, justifies tyranny.[26]

George Bernard Shaw, a founder of the socialist British Fabian Society, characterized the Jews as "the real enemy, the invader from the East, the Druze, the ruffian, the oriental parasite, in a word the Jew." Henri Bernstein, the French Jewish writer, sarcastically referred to Shaw as "dear socialist, multimillionaire and anti-Semite." Shaw's advice to the Nazis on the Jewish question was "Force the Jews to wed Aryans." Thus, he claimed, would the Jewish question be solved.[27]

Shaw's fascistic bent was coupled to an intense sympathy for Communism. All totalitarianism fit his plans for a rigid collectivism. Therefore, he could announce to the world, "We, as socialists, have nothing to do with liberty. Our message, like Mussolini's, is one of discipline, of service, of ruthless refusal to acknowledge any natural right of competence."[28]

It is grossly unjust that social and theological conservatives are often labeled fascist. None of the individuals or movements we have looked at could be regarded as conservative in any meaningful sense.[29] *Conservative* implies limited government. Fascism, Nazism and Communism were brutal socialist dictatorships. Mussolini's father was a socialist revolutionary, and Mussolini was an orthodox Marxist before he became a fascist.[30] In fact, says von Mises,

"Nobody could surpass Mussolini in Marxian zeal. He was the intransigent champion of the pure creed, the unyielding defender of the rights of the exploited proletarians, the eloquent prophet of the socialist bliss to come."[31]

Says Vetterli and Fort,

> Fascists theory thus exemplified much of the philosophy of Nietzsche. To Nietzsche, the will to power, the desire to dominate gave meaning to life. Truth is relative. It is freed from moral connotations. Truth is whatever aids the will to power. . . . This superman would be beyond the pale of moral restraint. He would himself create the standard of value. The cult of power was to replace traditional religion and moral values. There is no doubt that Benito Mussolini (as Hitler after him) believed himself to be the personification of Nietzsche's superman.[32]

The will to power, moral relativism, relative truth, and the replacement of traditional religion and moral values, are all fundamental planks of postmodernism, the latest rage of intellectuals at the end of the twentieth century.[33]

MARXISM/LENINISM

The third destructive worldview of the twentieth century, Marxism/Leninism, is a well-developed application of materialistic atheism and social evolutionary principles. It is the socialist worldview. Marxism/Leninism has been the greatest killing machine in recorded history. And history has recorded some unbelievable mass killings.[34]

While Hitler has the distinction of eliminating 21 million human beings, V. I. Lenin, Josef Stalin, Mao tse-Tung, and other Communist dictators have eliminated more than 86 million.[35] The suffering and stark terror behind this statistic is impossible to comprehend. Robert Conquest's *Harvest of Sorrows* describes Stalin's slaughter in the Ukraine. "Evolution," said Stalin, "prepares for revolution and creates the ground for it; revolution consummates the process of evolution and facilitates its further activity."[36] In effect, Stalin determined that the human race would be advanced if the Ukrainians did not survive. But before Stalin could move into the high stakes of death and destruction he needed Marx and Lenin.

In *The Communist Manifesto* (1848), Karl Marx called for elimination of the bourgeoisie (property owners). Said Marx, they must "be swept out of the way, and made impossible."[37] Later in the document he wrote, "the Communists everywhere support every revolutionary movement against the existing social and political order of things. . . . They [communists] openly declare that their ends can be attained only by the forcible overthrow of all existing social conditions."[38]

Lenin took one step further and set up the state apparatus to eliminate the bourgeoisie. While Lenin was responsible directly for much killing, it was Stalin and Mao who took Marx's teaching and Lenin's state apparatus to their ultimate extent.

Marx's atheism, dialectical materialism, naturalistic evolution, and socialism are the heart of the Communist worldview. These ideas brought the slaughter of the twentieth century. Marxist ideas are still very much alive in the twenty-first century. Postmodernists, for example, propagate atheism, materialism, evolution, socialism, and even a collectivism. These views have immediate access to the West's public education institutions. The message of theist and creationism is usually excluded from the educational marketplaces.

The philosophy that empowers Marxism/Leninism/Stalinism is dialectical materialism. The heart of the philosophy states that (1) matter is reality, and (2) matter behaves dialectically.[39] Dialectical materialism attempts to explain all of reality down to the subatomic level. Dialectical processes govern the organic world (including life and even mind or consciousness) and social life (including economics and politics). All of nature reflects, illuminates, and illustrates Communist dialectical philosophy, and the system is built wholly upon atheistic and evolutionary understandings.

The psychology of Marxism centers in materialistic behaviorism. Humankind is looked upon as a conditioned, evolving animal, or as Lenin says, "Matter is primary nature. Sensation, thought, consciousness, are the highest products of matter organized in a certain way. This is the doctrine of materialism, in general, and Marx and Engels, in particular."[40]

Marxist sociology demands the abolishing of all social structures that reflect a theistic worldview. As Marx says in *The Communist Manifesto,* "The Communists disdain to conceal their views and aims. They openly declare that their ends can be attained only by the forcible overthrow of all existing social conditions."[41] The three social institutions to be overthrown are the family, the church and the state. Marx and Engels called for "an openly legalized community of women," in *The Communist Manifesto.*[42]

Marxist/Leninist/Stalinist law is applied evolutionary law. There are no legal absolutes because law evolves alongside mankind. There is no eternal lawgiver, so there are no eternal legal principles. Just laws are those that advance evolutionary, socialist history; all others are unjust. "Law, morality, religion, are to [the proletariat] so many bourgeois prejudices, behind which lurk in ambush just as many bourgeois interests," Marx wrote.[43]

The Marxist/Leninist/Stalinist interpretation of history consists of one major mover and a few minor players. The dialectical nature of matter rules history. All reality is the outworking of this concept. Dialectical matter is eternal, so only dialectical matter determines history. Communists do believe in nudging the dialectical processes of history toward their own ends.[44]

SECULAR HUMANISM

Secular humanism also is a worldview. John Dewey said in *A Common Faith*, "Here are all the elements for a religious faith that shall not be confined to sect, class, or race. Such a faith has always been implicitly the common faith of mankind. It remains to make it explicit and militant."[45] Margaret Sanger represents an aspect of secular humanist that ultimately could kill more human beings than Nazism, fascism, and Communism combined. Sanger founded and provided the philosophical basis for Planned Parenthood, an organization that has promoted the abortions of millions of unborn human beings.

Secular humanists became intimately involved with the proabortion movement in accordance with their desire to further the sexual revolution. Sanger is one of the foremost figures of the humanist power struggle. Other names in that leadership include Mary Calderone and Faye Wattleton. Those three and many others have been heavily involved in promoting the revolution aimed at breaking down the family and establishing a free-love ethic in its place. Of Sanger's importance, Elasah Drogin wrote, "If it is possible for one person to change the very foundations of civilization from a moral one to an immoral one, then Margaret Sanger should rightfully be known as the founder of modern culture because today's culture is characterized precisely by the values she and her admirers taught."[46]

H. G. Wells agreed, "Margaret Sanger made currents and circumstances. When the history of our civilization is written, it will be a biological history and Margaret Sanger will be its heroine."[47] As part of the Wantley Circle, a free-love association, Wells was not only an admirer of Sanger, but her sexual partner, as was Harold Child and Hugh de Selincourt.[48]

A goal of Planned Parenthood was candidly to help "young people obtain sex satisfaction before marriage. By sanctioning sex before marriage, we will prevent fear and guilt."[49] The Planned Parenthood publication *You've Changed the Combination* states, "There are only two kinds of sex: sex with victims and sex without. Sex with victims is always wrong. Sex without is always right."[50]

When Wattleton accepted the Humanist of the Year award, she paid the ultimate tribute to Sanger: "To a great extent Sanger epitomizes the Secular Humanist worldview. Nothing in her teaching or lifestyle falls outside of Humanism in theory or practice. All are proud of her and her accomplishments."

Sanger founded the publication *The Woman Rebel*, whose slogan was "No Gods! No Masters!" In the first edition she denounced marriage as "a degenerate institution" and sexual modesty as "obscene prudery."[51] Sanger read the seven volumes of Havelock Ellis's *Studies in the Psychology of Sex* and told her husband that she wanted liberation from the bonds of marriage. She ultimately deserted him to practice free love in Greenwich Village.

Sanger shows a close connection between secular humanism and the Nazi worldview because of her belief in eugenics as a tool to achieve racial purity. In

1933, *Planned Parenthood Review* published the article "Eugenic Sterilization: An Urgent Need" by Ernst Rudin, director of the Nazi Society for Racial Hygiene. Later in 1933 it published an article by Leon Whitney defending the Third Reich's racial program.[52]

Sanger's eugenic solution was to limit the number of children born to members of the lower class. In her ideal, parents would apply for licenses to have babies, and the poor would be sterilized, forcibly if necessary. This included limiting births among races deemed inferior. The more successful human types would inaugurate a new world order without the crime and poverty caused by genetically inferior people. The difference between Sanger and Hitler was that she found peaceful methods of racial purification.

While we are using Margaret Sanger as the representative of secular humanism, every student of this worldview knows that Dewey is the most famous voice. In the United States his influence cannot be overstated, because Dewey's thought has dominated educational philosophy, especially since the 1930s. At the end of the century, owing largely to Dewey, secular humanism is the only worldview allowed in the public schools. Humanist Charles Francis Potter writes in *Humanism: A New Religion*,

> Education is the most powerful ally of Humanism, and every American public school is a school of Humanism. What can the theistic Sunday Schools, meeting for an hour once a week, and teaching only a fraction of the children, do to stem the tide of a five-day program of humanistic teaching.[53]

In nation's influenced by Dewey, students are immersed in the doctrines and dogmas of secular humanism from kindergarten through graduate school. The U.S. Supreme Court inconsistently has promoted this worldview monopoly, despite designated secular humanism as a religion in 1961.[54]

Dewey was a leader in the North American counterpart to the British Fabian Society, the League for Industrial Democracy. Dewey epitomizes Secular Humanism since he was an atheist in theology, a naturalist in philosophy, an ethical relativist in morals, an evolutionist in biology, and a socialist in economics. Humanists have been clear about the implications of various areas of their worldview. A collection of their statements includes

- *In theology atheists*: "Humanism cannot in any fair sense of the word apply to one who still believes in God as the source and creator of the universe."[55]
- In *philosophy naturalists*: "[Naturalistic humanism] is the Humanism that I have supported through the written and spoken word for some forty years."[56]

- *In ethics relativists*: "No inherent moral or ethical laws exist, nor are there absolute guiding principles for human society. The universe cares nothing for us and we have no ultimate meaning in life."[57]
- *In origins and science Darwinian*: "Evolution is a fact amply demonstrated by the fossil record and by contemporary molecular biology. Natural selection is a successful theory devised to explain the fact of evolution."[58]
- *In psychology proponents of self-actualization*: "For myself, though I am very well aware of the incredible amount of destructive, cruel, malevolent behavior in today's world–from the threats of war to the senseless violence in the streets–I do not find that this evil is inherent in human nature."[59]
- *In sociology radical social evolutionists*: "Marriage, for most people, has outlived its usefulness and is doing more harm than good."[60]
- *In civil rights positivists*: "No matter how misperceived as natural they may be, rights . . . are the works of human artifice."[61]
- *In politics globalists*: "It is essential for UNESCO to adopt an evolutionary approach. . . . The general philosophy of UNESCO should, it seems, be a scientific world humanism, global in extent and evolutionary in background. . . . Thus the struggle for existence that underlies naturals selection is increasingly replaced by conscious selection, a struggle between ideas and values in consciousness."[62]
- *In economics socialists*: "A socialized and cooperative economic order must be established to the end that the equitable distribution of the means of life be possible."[63]
- *In historiography materialists*: "The laws of biology are the fundamental lessons of history."[64] "War is one of the constants of history and is the ultimate form of natural selection in the human species."[65]

CONCLUSION

Every believer, says Erwin W. Lutzer in *Hitler's Cross*, must be able to give a rationale for defending the supremacy of Christ over alternatives.[66] This is in keeping with 1 Peter 3:15: "But sanctify Christ as Lord in your hearts, always being ready to make a defense to everyone who asks you to give an account for the hope that is in you, with gentleness and reverence." The alternative to humanistic worldviews is Christ. Lutzer writes,

> We do not know where all this [efforts to cleanse the public square of biblical Christianity] will end. What we do know is that we have the high honor of representing Christ in the midst of this ideological mega-shift. Our challenge is to rise to this hour of incredible challenge and opportunity.[67]

Lutzer agrees with Dietrich Bonhoeffer's sentiments:

> We Lutherans have gathered like eagles around the carcass of cheap
> grace, and there we have drunk the poison which has killed the life of
> following Christ. . . . In such a Church the world finds a cheap cov-
> ering for its sins; no contrition is required, still less any real desire to
> be delivered from sin. . . . Cheap grace means the justification of sin
> without the justification of the sinner; . . . it is grace without dis-
> cipleship, grace without the cross, grace without Jesus Christ, living
> and incarnate.[68]

Cheap grace demands the soft life. Living for Christ twenty-four-hours-a-
day is hard. It demands discipline, sacrifice, purity, prayer, witness, study,
standing alone, confrontation (Acts 17:16f.). But the very "being" of life
involves theology, philosophy, and ethics. It demands that we follow Christ in
these areas. This is exactly what the Bible teaches.

For example, in theology, Christ is "the fulness of the Godhead" (Col.
2:9); in philosophy, Christ is the "logos" of God (John 1:1–3); in ethics,
Christ is "the true light" (John 1:9); in biology, Christ is "the life" (John 1:4;
11:25); in psychology, Christ is "the Savior" of the soul (Luke 1:46–47); in
sociology, Christ is "the son" (Luke 1:30–31); in law, Christ is "lawgiver"
(Gen. 49:10); in politics, Christ is "King of kings and Lord of lords" (Rev.
19:16); in economics, Christ is "owner" of all things (Ps. 50:10–12); and in
history, Christ is the "Alpha and Omega" (Rev. 1:8). No area is secular; all are
sacred because Jesus Christ is involved in them all. Since Christ is the foun-
tainhead of all wisdom and knowledge (Col. 2:2–3) all areas are open for
living and study.[69]

If the twenty-first century is not to be a slaughter similar to the twentieth
century, Christians need to listen carefully to Lutzer, who has learned some
valuable lessons from the surrender of the Christian church under Hitler. It is
time, says Lutzer, that Christians take the lead in art, education, politics, and
law. He could have added theology, philosophy, ethics, the natural and social
sciences, and history. "Let's not make the mistake of the German church,"
says Lutzer,

> and isolate the spiritual sphere from the political, social, and cultural
> world. Bonhoeffer was critical of the church when its only interest
> was self-preservation. We should be characterized by giving, not with-
> holding. Since we share this planet with all of humanity, we must
> reestablish leadership in all of those areas where Christians often led
> the way.[70]

The Spiritual War for the Soul of the West

Tim LaHaye

Anyone familiar with Bible prophecy knows that moral degeneracy is one sign of the "last days" or "the end of the age" (Matt. 24:1–5), that brief period just prior to the return of Christ. The apostle Paul called the times "perilous" (2 Tim. 3:1). He goes on (3:2–5) to list eighteen tragic characteristics that make the period perilous. Notice how many of those characteristics seem descriptive of our own day. Men will be

1. lovers of themselves
2. lovers of money
3. boasters
4. proud
5. blasphemers
6. disobedient to parents
7. unthankful
8. unholy
9. unloving
10. unforgiving
11. slanderous
12. without self-control
13. brutal
14. despisers of good
15. traitors
16. headstrong
17. haughty
18. lovers of pleasure rather than lovers of God

Like the society Paul described, Western culture has turned morality on its head. [1] For example, law and social pressure now accept or even honor those who practice a perverted homosexual lifestyle. The media and liberal elite who control communication condemn those who disapprove of that immoral and dangerous sexual lifestyle.

The apostle Peter made a similar prophecy that in the last days people will walk after their own lusts, and be "scoffers." "Knowing this first: that scoffers will come in the last days, walking according to their own lusts" (2 Peter 3:3). [2] These people will be blind to the obvious warnings of their Creator God, but in their rebellion will choose a lifestyle that satisfies their own lusts rather than obey His commands.

CULTURAL CONDITIONS WILL GET WORSE

This is before the Holy Spirit is taken out of the world in the church at the Rapture. "For the mystery of lawlessness is already at work; only He who now restrains will do so until He is taken out of the way" (2 Thess. 2:7). Today the single morally restraining influence in Western civilization is the Holy Spirit in the church. That is why the world so hates the church; the church calls culture back to a respect for biblical morality as a basis for conduct, through law, virtue, and absolute truth.

AMERICA THE GOOD

My own nation is the ultimate example of how far culture can fall. The U.S. was founded on strongly theistic and even biblical principles. As a result the country has enjoyed more freedom for more people for a longer period of time than has any other nation in history. From the period of earliest settlement, almost four centuries ago, American citizens have done what no other major body politic on earth has done for so long—elect our own city, state, and national rulers. In those early settlements the people, Christian or not, had been profoundly influenced by the Protestant Reformation concept of the priesthood of believers. They read their own Bible translations and other publications made possible by the printing press.

The result was what it always is when people read or hear the Word of the Lord. Northern Europe experienced a spiritual revival that invaded their culture. It produced the highest standards of civic morality in those countries where the people were most exposed to the Bible.

What had not changed was that the people were subject to the "divine right of kings," dictators who usurped government control. Government was used by ruthless individuals to dominate the citizenry while the elite ruling class lived in luxury. So, in 1620, the first wave of religious volunteers left tyranny to come to what Abraham Lincoln described in his Gettysburg Address as the conception in liberty of a new nation. The government was normally committed to enabling all its citizens to pursue rights that would be inscribed into the national Declaration of Independence as "life, liberty and the pursuit of happiness." From the earliest Puritan "Pilgrims," immigrants arrived with the Bible in one hand and a musket in the other. They were determined to provide a better nation for their children than the one they had left. They founded government on the principle of human equality through creation. They recognized God-established moral values around which their society should function.

Despite revisionist historical arguments to the contrary, the evidence is irrefutable that America enjoyed the strongest biblical roots of any country ever founded. These roots shaped laws and policies through about the first 250 years of American history. The U.S. Constitution was so well-framed that several countries have copied it whole or in part for their own governments. The constitution alone did not produce unprecedented blessing, however. God worked through churches, Christian-directed education, and faith centered families. It would be difficult to exaggerate the influence of the Bible and the church on the writing of the amazing document we call the Constitution of the United States. An amoral or biblically illiterate people could never have produced it.

American historians often forget that during the first one hundred years of colonial history, starting with the founding of Harvard College by Rev. John Harvard in 1636, one hundred twenty-eight colleges or Bible schools were founded. A religious group, a church, or a body that stood for the propagation of the gospel and the teaching of biblical principles founded each school. Harvard, Princeton, and Yale, all established as Christian schools, served as the leading source of teachers for the first two hundred or more years. Its graduates fanned out and became the nations' schoolteachers, imparting not only the three "R's," but also morality, character, and biblical literacy.

George Washington, president of the Constitutional Convention (1787), knew the importance of the Christian religion. He observed in his Farewell Address that national morality cannot prevail apart from religious principle:

> And let us with caution indulge the supposition that morality can be maintained without religion. Whatever may be conceded to the influence of refined education on minds, . . . reason and experience forbid us to expect that national morality can prevail in exclusion of religious principle.[3]

John Jay, the first chief justice of the U.S. Supreme Court, spoke of the indispensability of the Christian religion to the nation when he said, "Providence has given to our people the choice of their rulers, and it is the duty, as well as the privilege and interest, of a Christian nation to select and prefer Christians for their rulers."[4]

French official Alexis de Tocqueville visited America to study the nation's prisons in 1831. As he toured the country, he became so impressed with the culture and society that he published a two-volume description that is widely quoted today for its observations about the American spirit. Regarding the religious life of the nation he wrote,

> On my arrival in the United States the religious aspect of the country was the first thing that struck my attention; and the longer I stayed there, the more I perceived the great political consequences resulting from this new state of religion and the spirit of freedom marching in opposite directions. But in America I found they were intimately united and that they reigned in common over the same country. . . .
>
> The sects that exist in the United States are innumerable. . . . Moreover, all the sects of the United States are comprised within the great unity of Christianity, and Christian morality is everywhere the same. . . .
>
> In the United States the sovereign authority is religious, and consequently hypocrisy must be common: but there is no country in the world where the Christian religion retains a greater influence over the souls of men than in American; and there can be no greater proof of its utility and of its conformity to human nature than that its influence is powerfully felt over the most enlightened and free nation of the earth. . . .
>
> In the United States the influence of religion is not confined to the manners, but it extends to the intelligence of the people. Among the Anglo-Americans some profess the doctrines of Christianity from a sincere belief in them, and others do the same because they fear to be suspected of unbelief. Christianity, therefore, reigns without obstacle, by universal consent; the consequence is, as I have before observed that every principle of the moral world is fixed and determinate, although the political world is abandoned to the debates and the experiments of men. Thus the human mind is never left to wander over a boundless field.[5]

A WAR FOR A CULTURAL SOUL

The freedom and prosperity of the United States was under attack from the time of its national beginnings. I have documented that attack in several of my books, including *The Battle for the Mind*, and *A Nation Without A Conscience*.[6] As America grew in influence in the 1800s, the nation was a primary source of missionaries to the uttermost parts of the earth. At one time, it is estimated, eighty-five percent of the evangelistic work in foreign countries was done by Christians from the United States.

The Climax of the Cultural War

The war for the soul of our culture is the ageless war between God and Satan. The human suffering has been incalculable. In the area of military conflict alone, about fifteen thousand wars have killed or maimed uncounted millions of people.

That the war for control of our world is heating up is shown by the fact that the twentieth century, supposedly the very climax of civilization, was also history's most violent. More have died from wars during the twentieth century than in all the combined wars in the history of the world before 1900. Zbigniew Brzezinski, national security adviser to U.S. president Jimmy Carter (and first executive director of the Trilateral Commission) estimates that 180 million people were killed at the hands of governments during the twentieth century. So much for the progress of humankind under the leadership of the secular elite; current world conditions lead Christians and many secularists to realize that some kind of supernatural intervention must occur or humanity will cease to exist.[7]

To really understand the cultural war in which we are engaged, we must go back to the beginning.

The Tales of Two Cities

I would like to write a book by the title "The Tales of Two Cities" and show the past, present, and future of the two most influential cities of all time. Those cities have served as the working capitals for God and Satan. The entire world is under the influence of one or the other.[8]

Jerusalem is the city of God, where He revealed Himself to Abraham, Melchizedek, kings, prophets, and other holy men. Through the city of God He provided His people with a holy book. This book contains instruction on how people should live, conduct their families, run their countries, and enjoy freedom and the blessing of a moral culture.

Satan chose *Babylon* to launch his ancient diabolical attack on mankind. There he spread his lies about God, creation, sin, salvation, moral values, culture, and eternity. His objective was to draw worship and service that was due to God alone. That is why he produced polytheistic idolatrous religions and modern humanistic idolatry based on the theory of evolution. Satan hopes to satisfy the yearning for God in the heart of every person. Satan operated from the strategy that a God that can be seen is more appealing than one who must be worshiped by faith "in spirit and in truth."

This original Nimrodism or Babylonian mysticism happened before God began to reveal Himself by special revelation. In the midst of that idolatry God raised up Abraham and through him the nation of Israel. This nation would be the torchbearers of His truth to the world. It was at Jerusalem and through Israel that He revealed His plan to send His only begotten Son into the world to be the divine sacrifice for mankind's fall and subsequent sin. It was a magnificent plan, but the people disowned it in the days of the judges and the kingdom. During the rule of David and part of Solomon's reign it seemed that the plan might be coming into operation. Then Solomon was drawn into idol worship and the nation returned to pagan religions. Babylon supplanted true worship, and the culture became evil. God sent judgment on His chosen people, allowing Jerusalem to be taken captive into Babylon.

Return from Babylon

After their Babylonian exile, Israel was so occupied with repairing the damage to their country that their more fervent worship did not extend to being torchbearers to the pagan nations as God had planned. While that seventy-year bondage in Babylon cured Israel of the penchant for idolatry, it did not take away their rebellious self-will. During the period between the testaments, when there were no writing prophets and few spiritual leaders, Satan filled that vacuum with the polytheistic religions in Eastern culture and Hellenistic philosophy of humanism in Western culture.

The Period of Jesus

Jesus Christ came into a world filled with heathen paganism and a Greek humanism that masqueraded as philosophy but was actually a godless religion. Greek humanism has always been the best human attempt to be independent of God. But history shows that where humanism and idolatry prevail, personal freedom is lost, family values and morality are despised, womanhood is degenerated, and true worship is forbidden or ridiculed.

In this pagan world Jesus Christ, God's own Son, came to die for the sins of mankind. His sinless, miraculous, and sacrificial life was climaxed by the miracle of his bodily resurrection. Jesus made this unique impact on the world in only three years.[9] His most world-altering act after His resurrection was His establishment of His church. When there were just twelve disciples and a few other followers He predicted that, "the gates of Hell will not prevail against her" (Matt. 16:18). Within three hundred years that little body of believers had spread over the known world.

Those Christians of the first three centuries were driven by the conviction they received from the apostles and the Holy Spirit that their Lord could return at any time. That apostolic challenge continues to drive the true Church toward Scripture and an expectation that Christ could come at any time. The early church was so filled with this expectation that they filled the whole world with their message, leading millions to faith in Christ.

Conversion of Constantine

When Constantine, the Roman emperor (c. 280–337), professed faith in Christ in 312 and signed the Edict of Milan in 313, Christianity became recognized as the state religion of Rome. Historians get so caught up in wondering whether the conversion of Constantine was genuine that they lose sight of the incredible achievement that culminated in the Edict of Toleration (311) and the Edict of Milan. During three hundred years of persecution, Jesus had made the churches in truth "lampstands" of the world (Revelation 1-3). He was walking, through His spirit, among the lampstands.

Allegorizing the Bible

Due to an allegorizing hermeneutic for interpreting Scripture, theologians influenced by the school of interpretation of Alexandria, Egypt, including Augustine (354-430), opened the church to pagan practices that eventually subverted the church of Rome. Eventually it became more Babylonian than Jerusalem. In addition, Augustine brought enough residual Greek philosophy into the church that it became vulnerable to Greek humanism. Over the many centuries since, this philosophical bent became the secular humanism that is the official religion of the West today. Thomas Aquinas (c. 1225-1274), a theologian and philosopher, followed a long line of advocates of Augustine's teaching. Aquinas did more to revive interest in the thought of Aristotle than he did the use of Scripture. While he personally held the Scriptures on a high plane of inspiration, he elevated the philosophy and writings of Aristotle to the same level, considering true learning to be a balance of human wisdom and Scripture.

Only a short time after Thomas's death, Rome's theologians elevated him to sainthood and Aristotle and Greek philosophy above scripture. The scholasticism that developed ultimately resulted in a tradition that was part Greek philosophy, part Babylonian paganism, and part Scripture. Today the official teaching of the Church of Rome is based on "fifteen hundred years of tradition and scripture." The decline in accepting the early church doctrine of *sola scriptura* (Scripture alone) invited skepticism and secularism into the church and institutions of learning.

The Dark Ages

The Dark Ages, from around 400 to 1500, were spiritually dark, and the people lived in ignorance and poverty because the Bible was kept from them. The official policy of the Roman Church was that Bibles should be kept in monasteries or in seminaries. Only priests and scholars could "interpret" Scripture properly. Schools for the common people were rare or non-existent, and it has been suggested that during much of that time only one European out of twenty thousand could read. Except for very rare Greek manuscripts, the Bible was available in Latin, which was only known by scholars. It is plain to see that the Bible had little or no influence on Western culture for much of those eleven hundred years.

The Bible and the Reformation

Through these centuries valiant saints within and without the Roman Church fought bravely to release the Word of God from its ecclesiastical prison. John Wycliffe, "the morning star of the Reformation" (1329-1384), oversaw translation of an English Bible. Bohemian Jan Hus (1374-1415) and Englishman William Tyndale (1494-1536) were only two of hundreds who died to preach or translate Scripture for the lay Christian. In so doing they changed the face of Europe, North America, and eventually through world missions, the rest of the world. The Bible continues to transform people of all nationalities and walks of life. No other book comes close to influencing people as has this international best-seller. The only time the Bible does not influence people or culture is when it is kept closed or under glass in museums so that it cannot be read and studied regularly by the people.

Martin Luther (1483-1546) is best known for the Ninety-five Theses he nailed on the door of the University of Wittenberg parish church in 1517, which sparked the Sixteenth-Century Reformation. He should also be recognized for his pioneering work in education, so that common people might be able to read the German Bible he translated. He realized that to give the next generation a Bible-centered life and faith, there must be a literate people. Trained preacher-teachers spread education even as they spread the Reformation. The influence of his schools on the future generations of Germany was incredible. John Calvin (1509-1564) opened Geneva Academy to train both Bible preachers and educators, who were especially successful in Britain and Scotland. They started church related schools to teach the Bible and Christian doctrine to the next generation of children. A literate clergy led the new Protestant churches.

The Bible changed the world more quickly because of the printing press. The first book printed with movable type was the Latin Bible in 1456. With the Reformation, Bible translations, tracts, and religious books were suddenly available everywhere, leading European culture and civilization.

But Satan was not asleep during this period. In addition to the violent opposition faced by the early Protestants, a generation of skeptical philosophers arose in the Enlightenment. Philosophical humanism had been developing since before Aquinas in the earliest universities. French skepticism and German rationalism was an outgrowth of this training in religious educational institutions. Many philosophers rejected Christ because they were offended by the decadent conditions in the church. René Descartes (1596-1650), Françoise Voltaire (1694-1778), Jean-Jacques Rousseau (1712-1778), G. W. F. Hegel (1770-1831), and others influenced the skeptical direction of the Enlightenment which prepared the way for the French revolution. Socialistic philosophy swept like wildfire through the academic institutions, the arts, governments, and the new mass-market publications.

CULTURAL DECLINE

Many times over human history Satan has seemed to be poised for a final strike. At each attack a greater power has intervened. The interventions have included the ark and world deluge, the judges of Israel, or the return of the children of Israel to their homeland. God shows himself to be in control at those moments when things most seem out of control. We could see such an intervention in the twenty-first century. It could be the rapture of the Church followed by the seven-year tribulation and culminating in the final victory of Christ. These events will precede the thousand years of peace that prophets and apostles predicted. God will have to intervene soon to keep Satan from utterly taking over the world's governments and cultures.

Of one thing I am certain, Western culture cannot sustain another fifty years of decline like the last half of the twentieth century. I have been in the ministry for fifty years. At the end of the century I see examples of moral decay that would have been unimaginable fifty years ago. No place is safe from violence. Women once could walk on any street of Britain, Canada, or the U.S. after dark. The word *damn* caused community outrage if it was considered for radio and movie scripts. At the end of the century even the situations depicted had become unprintable. No consumers of Western culture can be unaware of what happens on the evening news and in primetime television. Through internet access and world media satellites, the worst of Western culture is spreading its influence through the world.

Someone has said, only partly in jest, that medieval people showed how inhumane they were by putting mentally handicapped people on stage to laugh at. In the late twentieth-century morally handicapped people are in the places of influence in the media, the government, and education. They are destroying our culture.

IS THERE HOPE FOR AMERICA?

Unfortunately, the spiritual climate of most of the world at the dawn of the twenty-first century can best be described as dead. But I believe that the Lord is still working his plan to use Christians even in the West to win many to Christ before He comes. Let me share four reasons for such hope.

1. Our God Is Merciful

Even the rebellious prophet Jonah knew God was merciful, for he said, "I knew that you are a gracious and compassionate God, slow to anger and abounding in love, a God who relents from sending calamity" (Jonah 4:2 NIV). If God had dealt with this country on the basis of what we deserve, we would have ceased to be a nation long ago.

If God would save Ninevah because of one hundred twenty thousand innocents who didn't know "their left hand from their right," why would he not also save the U.S., where there are 47 million children, many of whom do not know right from wrong. They have been brainwashed by secularists who teach that there are no moral absolutes.

I believe that our merciful God will yet spare the West because of who and what He is.

2. God Remembers the Abrahamic Covenant

Many believe that God will save the West, especially the U.S., because of his promise to Abraham. God performed a biological miracle on the bodies of Abraham and Sarah, and created the Hebrew nation. A part of God's promise was to "make you a great nation; I will bless you and make your name great; and you shall be a blessing. I will bless those who bless you, and I will curse him who curses you; and in you all the families of the earth shall be blessed" (Gen. 12:2–3; cf. Gen. 27:29; Num. 24:9).

One of the most worthwhile accomplishments of the United States has been a consistent regard for the plight of the Jewish nation. No nation has a better record of treating individual Jews with respect and of befriending Israel as a nation. America has committed many sins against the Jews, for which we may well deserve judgment, but as a nation we have been a consistent friend.

For example, in 1948 President Harry Truman helped persuade the United Nations to recognize the nation of Israel. By the end of the century the U.S. had contributed over $50 billion of aid to that government. Without U.S. support and protection, the nation of Israel probably would not have been able to exist. If we have any reason to expect God to bring a revival to America, it is that we have blessed Israel.

3. God Has Shown a Strong Hand of Providence

We again single out the United States as key to a Western revival, because God has placed a strong hand upon America from the nation's beginning. As the framers of the U.S. Constitution believed, the country has been a miracle nation. Without "the strong hand of Providence," as Washington called it, we would never have survived. Even the Pilgrims, the earliest European settlers, claimed that they would not have survived the first long, cold winter without divine intervention.

During the American Revolution, God supernaturally arranged a fog through which Washington led seven thousand troops and eighteen hundred wounded soldiers to safety during a British siege. Had the force been captured, any chance of a Colonial army victory would effectively have been destroyed. Our fledgling country's victory against England was a miracle, as was the second victory in the War of 1812. God had a plan in founding this nation, and a great part of His plan, no doubt, involved using the United States as a beacon and bearer of the gospel around the world (Acts 1:8).

4. There Still Are Many Christians

Speaking with Abraham (Genesis 18), God agreed to spare Sodom and Gomorrah if he could find within the city ten righteous souls. Ten could not be found. In some Northern European countries Christians probably feel that lonely. There still are millions of Christians in the U.K., however, a higher percentage in Canada, and between sixty million and seventy million U. S. residents claim to have been "born again." Those millions may be preserving the Western nations, and especially North America, from God's destruction.

The judging hand of God has never fallen on any people with so high a percentage of Christians. That does not mean that the U.S. and Canada will not be disciplined. Nations, as individuals, can rarely be trusted with great blessing, and all the Western countries, especially North America, have been greatly blessed. Such a "good life" is not conducive to faith in God. Old Testament Israel had that problem and went through the cycles of blessing and punishment (most notably in the time of the judges). They strayed from God and his moral values, and God sent a nation to humble them and bring them back to him. Time after time God heard their cry and sent them a deliverer.

Personally, I believe the future of the nations with a Christian heritage is in the hands of their pastors. If enough of them take seriously their Christian citizenship responsibilities, to the extent many of them now take their evangelistic responsibilities, we could return to some degree of moral sanity. The Church needs to evangelize, pray, and vote if we are to reverse Satan's fifty-year demolition of our culture. Only the church can save its culture, with God's help. It is up to pastors to lead their congregations to pray, evangelize, and vote as if the future depended upon their actions, for it does.

We owe our God and our children no less.

CHAPTER 25

Technology and Theology: Reality and Hope for the Third Millennium

Timothy J. Demy

As we enter a new century and also a new millennium, it is appropriate that Christians reevaluate and reaffirm their commitment to the Bible; the fundamental doctrines of orthodox Christianity; and the application of those beliefs in a personal, local, and global context. The Christian view of, and response to, technology is only one of the many areas of life that we must examine if we are going to be effective in our Christian witness in the future. D. A. Lyon observes, "The debate over technology will continue to be central to political life in the twenty-first century. Christian contributions to this debate become increasingly important in contexts where secularization has eroded and excluded the sense that there are any real norms to guide technological development."[1]

Though at first glance technology and theology might appear to be mutually exclusive, a very strong connection has been present throughout history. Christian thinkers, at least since the time of Augustine, addressed issues of science and technology, recognizing the importance of understanding the physical world. The argument that Christianity was inherently antiscientific and thwarted the pursuit of science and technology is one that arose in the eighteenth and nineteenth centuries and is inaccurate.[2] For example, in the twelfth century, a treatise entitled *The Various Arts* by a monk, writing under the pseudonym Theophilus, became a standard reference for craftsmen. Thus, the technology employed in building the cathedrals of Europe was also understood to have theological underpinnings.[3] Later, such men as Isaac Newton and Jonathan Edwards would also integrate science, theology, and technology. Christian history is filled with examples of an acceptance of technology and attempts to understand it within a biblical perspective.

With the turning of a page of the calendar, the dawn of a new era of human history begins. The question that remains to be answered in A.D. 2000 and beyond is whether the Christian witness in the future will shine forth, permeating culture, or be eclipsed by the gathering clouds of neopaganism. In a post-Christian culture in the West and a non-Christian culture in the East, the challenge to the Christian testimony is formidable. Perhaps we are not so unlike the Israelites in the wilderness to whom God said, "I have set before you life and death, the blessing and the curse. So choose life in order that you may live, . . . by loving the LORD your God, by obeying His voice, and by holding fast to Him" (Deut. 30:19b–20a). The decisions we make now will affect not only ourselves but also our posterity.

TECHNOLOGY'S CHALLENGE

The greatest technological challenge of the twenty-first century and the third millennium as we await the return of Jesus Christ will not have been the resolution and aftermath of the computer Y2K problem or "millennium bug" (though it is an excellent illustration of the dependency of much of society on technology). Rather, the challenge will be the extent to which technological processes and objects will be molded to God's normative will rather than to pride and selfishness.[4] Will technology and technological activity be pursued within a biblical or secular framework? The extensive presence of technology in Western society is a reality that must be considered within the framework of the Christian worldview. Technology directly or indirectly affects every area of our lives. Whether we consider this good or bad, it is a fact.[5]

One area of concern that Christians should address is the hope that individuals and society as a whole place in technology. For some, technology (with science) has become a false god of hope, the vaunted path toward human perfection. For much of the secularized West, there has been, and continues to be, a pursuit of human perfection and salvation that is technologically based rather than theologically based. Jeremy Rifkin writes of the contemporary ideological quest for a techno-paradise: "In the modern age, the idea of a future technological utopia has served as the guiding vision of industrial society. For more than a century utopian dreamers and men and women of science and letters have looked to a future world where machines would replace human labor, creating a near-workerless society of abundance and leisure."[6]

Rifkin further argues that in the last one hundred years technology has become the "new secular god."[7] How are we, then, to view technology? What are the promises and perils of the future of technology when viewed from a biblical perspective? Is technology a tool, a toy, or a tyrant? The answers we give to these questions can have significant effects on our personal, spiritual, vocational, or professional and social lives.

Numerous helpful volumes have been written on the history of technology, on the phenomenon of technology as a system, and on its nature as a social and political phenomenon, especially with regard to ideas of progress. There have been, however, far fewer investigations of technology from a theological perspective. The majority of the theological writings have not come from the pens of evangelicals; conservative theological critiques have been rare.[8] Yet, within a biblical perspective, technology falls under the responsibilities of the divine mandate to care for and open up the possibilities of the creation. This is because science and technology arises out of an understanding of and inter-action with creation. Commonly referred to as the "cultural mandate," we read in Genesis 1:26–28,

> *Then God said, "Let Us make man in Our image, according to Our likeness; and let them rule over the fish of the sea and over the birds of the sky and over the cattle and over all the earth, and over every creeping thing that creeps on the earth." And God created man in His own image, in the image of God He created him; male and female He created them. And God blessed them; and God said to them, "Be fruitful and multiply, and fill the earth, and subdue it; and rule over the fish of the sea and over the birds of the sky, and over every living thing that moves on the earth."*

With regard to technology and the cultural mandate, Stephen Monsma notes,

> Few systematic reflections on modern technology have been initiated by Christian theologians. Indeed, Christians have often not seriously concerned themselves with either the negative or the positive conse-quences of modern scientific-technological development. They have viewed technology either as something that is naturally good or as a development that is neutral in relation to the Christian faith. The point is that even Christians—who in theory accept the cultural man-date as a duty to be carried out in subjection to God's normative will—have in practice often emphasized the theme of progress and cultural development for its own sake, without reference to the divine constraints within which proper and responsible cultural development is sought.

These tendencies—all too often present within Christendom—have been strengthened and reinforced by a secularization movement that has its roots in the Renaissance, the Enlightenment, and modern philosophy. They have come to play a powerful role in modern society in the past two centuries.[9]

The neglect of Christians in addressing technology from a theological perspective has resulted in domination by secularism's view of technology. This view is accepted uncritically by users and developers of technology. As evangelicals view technology and its effects on culture and society, we are left with the dilemma voiced by Carl F. H. Henry more than a quarter of a century ago:

> We live in the twilight of a great civilization, amid the deepening decline of modern culture. Those strange beast-empires of the books of Daniel and Revelation seem already to be stalking and sprawling over the surface of the earth. Only the success of modern science hides us from the dread terminal illness of our increasingly technological civilization. . . . The barbarians are coming; the Lord Jesus Christ is coming. *Christians are here now; do they know whether they are coming or going?*[10]

What is our response to this question, and in what areas of technology should Christians exert major efforts? The barbarians may indeed be coming, but they are also coming in full technological force (literally as well as figuratively).[11] Before we can answer these questions, we should briefly view the different perspectives regarding technology.

THE GOOD, THE BAD, THE UGLY

Though we think of technology as machines or computers, it also refers to systems and processes. The word *technology* is derived from the Greek roots *techno* (art, skill, or craft) and *logos* (word, study). When we think of technology today, we think not only of tools but also of crafts or techniques for doing something. Thus, technology may be defined as "the application of organized knowledge to practical tasks by ordered systems of people and machines."[12]

Within the history and philosophy of technology there have been three major views—*technology as liberator, technology as threat,* and *technology as instrument of power.* Three comments from representatives of these views illustrate the positions respectively:

> Technology, the source of the problem, will once again prove to contain within itself the germs of a solution compatible with the betterment of man's lot and dignity.[13]

> Our enslavement to the machine has never been more complete.[14]

> What we call Man's power over Nature turns out to be a power exercised by some men over other men with Nature as its instrument.[15]

Most Christian thinkers have supported the second and third perspectives—technology as a threat or as an instrument of power. Though aspects of the technology-as-threat perspective are appealing, the third viewpoint is accepted in this essay.

Technology as Liberator

The arguments of those who see technology as a liberator are fourfold:

1. Technology provides higher living standards and quality of life.
2. Technology provides opportunity for choice.
3. Technology provides more leisure.
4. Technology provides improved communication.[16]

Critics of the view reply that these four benefits come at a great cost to individuals and society. This cost entails

- environmental liabilities and human risks;
- alienation from nature and the created order;
- concentration of economic and political power in the hands of the few rather than the many;
- large-scale technologies that are capital intensive and vulnerable to error, accident, or sabotage;
- creation of a society with a very high dependence on experts;
- a linear view of the science-technology-society relationship in which technology is normally understood to have a one-way impact on society.[17]

While aspects of the technology-as-liberator view are attractive at first sight, as a philosophical framework for understanding technology this view is inadequate and underestimates the broken nature of humanity due to sin. Technological optimism does not match well with theological reality.

Technology as Threat

At the opposite end of the spectrum are those who view technology essentially as a threat. Adherents of this view are such notable and diverse religious representatives as Jacques Ellul, Paul Tillich, Martin Buber, and the Amish. Technological pessimists, who see technology primarily as a threat to contemporary society and individuals, suggest five major human costs of technology:

1. Technology creates uniformity in a society at the expense of individuality.
2. Technology creates narrow criteria for efficiency, minimizing meaningful work roles.
3. Technology promotes impersonality and manipulates people.

4. Technology creates its own social momentum that tends to make technology itself uncontrollable.
5. Technology contributes to the impoverishment of human relationships, the loss of community, and alienation in the workplace.[18]

Three replies have been offered against the technological pessimists:

1. The great variations among technologies defy generalized condemnation.
2. A negative view of technology neglects possible avenues for the redirection of technology.
3. Technology, if properly used, can serve human values.[19]

Aspects of this view also have merit. However, as an overall philosophy of technology, it does not adequately address all of the concerns and issues.

Technology as Instrument of Power

The third view of technology, technology as an instrument of power, "holds that technology is neither inherently good nor inherently evil but is an ambiguous instrument of power whose consequences depend on its social context."[20] This is not to say that technology is neutral even though it often appears to be so. Because there is a historical context for its development and ethical decisions were made regarding it, technology is not neutral. Ian Barbour illustrates this:

> A knife can be used for surgery or for murder. An isotope separator can enrich uranium for peaceful nuclear reactors or for aggression with nuclear weapons. But historical analysis suggests that most technologies are already molded by particular interests and institutional goals. Technologies are social constructions, and they are seldom neutral because particular purposes are already built into their design. Alternative purposes would lead to alternative designs. Yet most designs still allow some choice as to how they are deployed.[21]

Because technology is not developed in a social and ethical vacuum, nor used in one, it is not neutral for either the creator or the consumer. Ethical decisions are always included in the development of new technologies, either directly or indirectly. Research and development of one technology means that those same resources will not be used for other areas. Choices always entail consequences. Proponents of this third view include Barbour, Monsma, Egbert Schuurman, Roger Shinn, C. S. Lewis, and H. Richard Niebuhr. Barbour writes of the relationship of this position to Christianity:

This third position seems to me more consistent with the biblical outlook than either of the alternatives. Preoccupation with technology does become a form of idolatry, a denial of the sovereignty of God, and a threat to distinctively human existence. But technology directed to genuine human needs is a legitimate expression of human kind's creative capacities and an essential contribution to its welfare.[22]

Technology influences human life but is also a part of the social and cultural system. It is therefore an instrument of power that serves the purposes of those who control it and use it—either for good or for evil.

Among the most significant areas of life affected by technology are food, health, work, and personal fulfillment. In each of these areas there is potential for great good and great abuse. Each of these also relates significantly to the broader issues of justice, freedom, rights, and democracy.[23] Technology is therefore inextricably linked to the realm of economics and politics as well as theology. Without a biblical perspective, confusion, chaos, and manipulation will soon prevail in any of these areas.

A BIBLICAL PERSPECTIVE

Within a Christian worldview, our perspective of technology must be seen in the context of the cultural mandate. David Gill notes that "any theological critique of technology must return to the biblical sources. There we find that technology is an expression of divinely created human creativity and imagination, of doing and making good and helpful life-enhancing things."[24] As a means of assisting in human endeavors, technology, if used within its purposes and limits, is good. As an example of this, we find in Deuteronomy 22:8 the requirement to incorporate safety features in building design. As a means of fulfilling the cultural mandate, technology is a good thing but, like everything else, it is also affected by the intrusion of sin into the world. The potential for the misdirection of technology is always present. As a result of the Fall, some technology came to be used for destructive purposes, especially in warfare, and there arose also a dependence upon technology. Lyon writes,

Not only are tools used destructively as weapons, but an element of transferred trust is also present, later to be denounced by prophetic woes on those who *rely on* their chariots and spears (Isa. 31:1–3). The story of the tower of Babel (Gen. 11:1–9) represents a particularly low point in technological history, where the whole project is both breathtaking in conception and idolatrous in intention.[25]

Just as technology was affected by the Fall, so also will it be affected by the final redemption of creation in the millennial kingdom (Rom. 8:22). It is at this time that the effects of the Fall will be reversed. Technology that has been used for destructive purposes will be transformed for socially constructive uses. It will be at this time that "they will hammer their swords into plowshares and their spears into pruning hooks; nation will not lift up sword against nation, and never again will they train for war" (Mic. 4:3). As an instrument of power, technology can be used for good or evil by fallen humanity. "The biblical viewpoint, significantly, stresses the salience of all three features—creation, broken covenant and redemption—in interpreting technological activity."[26]

A biblical perspective of technology is far different from a secular perspective in which there is a drive for human autonomy and mastery of the environment apart from God and the will of God. This latter perspective might best be called *technicism*, not technology. Such a view "reduces all things to the technological; it sees technology as the solution to all human problems and needs. Technology is a savior, the means to make progress and gain mastery over modern, secularized cultural desires."[27] Similarly, Lyon defines *technicism* as "the belief in human autonomy and power, manifest in technological development."[28] Within technicism, there is an assumption of human sovereignty and human progress. In technicism, technology becomes its own reason for existing. In essence, technicism says that if something can be done, it should be done. No questions should be asked, and it is understood that "You can't stop progress!" Technicism believes that the fate of men and women rests in their own hands and that progress is not only possible but also inevitable in every area of existence. With the assistance of technology, a techno-paradise, if not perfection is just over the horizon.[29] Such a perspective is antithetical to a biblical perspective, yet it is the prevailing philosophy of technology in the world. Technicism becomes a theological problem that is manifested in the economic, political, and social realms of daily life in the industrialized world. Monsma writes,

> Because society as a whole has adopted the faith of technicism, government is unable to play an effective role in justly directing technological structures. The heart of the problem turns out to be religious. The command to love God above all and one's neighbor as oneself needs to be followed. Not that technology and its fruits are always evil. In fact, they are often good. What is needed is a means to properly evaluate and judge technologies, and that comes from following biblically based normative principles. Such principles need to replace technicism as humankind's guiding principles.[30]

A biblical perspective of technology is soundly at odds with our contemporary culture and is unlikely to ever become the prevailing perspective. Yet we still have the obligation to practice and preach the principles of such a view. To the extent that we are competent and have the opportunity to influence our society, we must do so. Monsma is correct when he states,

> The cadence of our culture is set by the beat of the technological drum. In and of itself, this basic fact should be cause for neither great rejoicing nor great alarm. The crucial question is, if this is so, who or what is determining the beat? . . . In modern society this beat is largely determined by a drive for power, for human mastery apart from the will of God. Humankind has revolted against its Maker, has declared its independence from him and his will, and all too often drives ruthlessly for a salvation of material prosperity brought about by technological prowess.[31]

As we look toward a biblical perspective of technology, there are two extremes we must avoid. The first is trying to deduce a complete system of social knowledge and societal structure from Christian principles—the facts are too diverse, society too complex, and the human mind too limited. This does not mean however, that there are no Christian principles of social action and social order. A second extreme is complete withdrawal from society and culture and a view that all perspectives and judgments are personal, subjective, and private.[32]

Characteristics of Technology

What are the characteristics and principles that we might look for in a biblically based view of technological activity? There are three characteristics of Christian normative principles for technological activities that should be considered as a foundation.[33] First, an adequate Christian normative character must be broad in its scope. Since everything in a theistic universe is value-laden, there is no neutrality and there are many points of contact between technology and other aspects of life. "Indeed, opposing the idea that technology is neutral implies that technology neither begins nor proceeds in a value-free manner, nor are its effects on society neutral."[34] Because it affects so many areas of life, we cannot look at technology in isolation. Technological activity must be firmly rooted in the love of God and others (Matt. 22:37–39). The overarching principle or umbrella for technological activity is love: love of God above all and love of one's neighbor as oneself.

Second, Christian normative characteristics for technological activities must differentiate between God and humans and between humans and other aspects of creation. There is diversity within the creation, and Christian normative principles for technology must recognize this and make necessary distinctions within creation.[35] The principle of love that is to be expressed is done so in varying ways within the spheres of human existence. For example, love of neighbor is different from love of family. Because there are so many facets to our lives and because technology affects all of these facets, we must make distinctions regarding the created diversity of human existence. Third, and finally, having recognized diversity within creation, Christian normative principles for technology must "integrate the diversity found in society so that there is no conflict among its facets."[36] Each of the three characteristics for doing technology, however, comes under the umbrella or mandate of love.

Because technological activity is a form of cultural activity, it is a way of partially fulfilling the cultural mandate and reflecting the commandment of love. Our pursuit of technology is, first, a form of service to God, then care and concern for other human beings, and finally, care and cultivation of the natural creation. "We are called to do technology in such a way that the creativity and joy for which God created men and women can exist in abundance, the riches of the physical world can be uncovered and utilized, and the plant and animal worlds can be perceived and used for what they are and for what God intends them to be."[37] A biblically based perspective such as this means that in technological activity, humans are to show respect for the various entities of creation and use them according to divine intent. Thus, appropriate use or development of a resource or technological process will require evaluation and discernment that extends beyond economic feasibility or profitability. Additionally, technological activity from a biblical perspective means that such activity reflects a love of God and neighbor by expanding rather than limiting opportunities for human freedom and action. Technology should assist others as well as us to fulfill responsibilities before God.[38]

Principles for Technology

What are the principles that should guide us in technological activity? As we attempt to construct a biblical philosophy of technology that incorporates love, recognition of created diversity, and integration of diversity, there are several principles that should guide technological endeavors. All of the principles found on this list are present in varying degrees in the writings of religious and secular philosophies of technology. A distinctively biblical perspective includes some, excludes others, and values each differently. These principles are developed at length by Monsma et al., in *Responsible Technology: A Christian Perspective*. While other principles might be added and some combined, a biblical perspective should include, in some manner, seven principles:

1. *Cultural appropriateness:* Technologies that erode or destroy cultural activities reflecting biblical values should not be used. This means that there must be careful thought and discussion in public and private forums before pursing the research and development of technology.

2. *Communication and openness of information:* The development and use of technology involves language and numbers. Therefore, if it is going to be developed and used responsibly, there must be accurate information about it.

3. *Stewardship:* Technological development and use of human and natural resources must be done from an attitude of respect rather than from reckless exploitation. Stewardship recognizes that there is more at stake than economics.

4. *Delightful harmony:* Technological development and activity should relate to humans and the rest of creation in manners that aesthetically satisfy and functionally promote right relationships.

5. *Justice:* All activity pertaining to technology must give people and creation that which is rightfully due them, including proper respect.

6. *Caring:* In conjunction with stewardship and justice, there must be the moral aspect of care regarding the use and results of technology. Technology should serve and safeguard that which is entrusted to us.

7. *Trust:* The product or activity must be dependable and safe enough that it earns trust. Also, there must be trust or faith in God so that technology and activity does not become an altar at which to worship human autonomy.[39]

Each of these principles must be pursued simultaneously, and each is an aspect of the single norm of love. We are not at liberty to choose which principles we will apply and which we will ignore. Though the "final product" of their application will vary, depending upon circumstances, they must all be applied in every circumstance.

Application of the principles presents an enormous challenge, but it is necessary if we are to uphold a Christian worldview. A biblical perspective of technology does not say that technology is good or bad. Rather, it argues that technology is an instrument of power that sometimes brings good and sometimes brings evil. A biblical perspective strives to replace the perspective of technicism and to articulate normative principles for judging technological activities and endeavors.

Because technology affects so many areas of human existence, it necessarily touches on many areas of theology. Theology and technology intersect at many points. Biblical perspectives regarding humanity intersect with contemporary bioethics and biotechnology, environmental concerns, and issues of energy and agriculture. The doctrine of sin intersects with issues of technology and privacy, technology and economics, technology and justice, technology and government, and technology and warfare. The doctrine of soteriology and evangelism intersects with communications and transportation. The doctrines of the church and spiritual life touch on the broad realm of cultural engagement, worship, idolatry, and values. Doctrines of the person and work of Christ affect how we view technology and the redemption of creation. The doctrine of eschatology relates to technological concerns of power, progress, and peace. The doctrine of creation is important to technology and humanity and to technology and the environment.

Directly or indirectly, technology and theology correspond at every turn. Yet there are also vast differences, primarily between technicism and a biblical perspective. In technicism, we find both worship and abuse of technology. Technicism, in effect, places the future in the human hand, rather than God's hand. It holds that failure to resolve global dilemmas are failures of the human intellect rather than of the human heart.

"Technicism is the attempt to locate technical solutions to nontechnical problems," observes Robert Wauzzinski, who stresses that such tragedies as the radioactivity released at Chernobyl or the loss of life in the Challenger explosion can be avoided only when *humility* reduces the scope of technology. They are not stopped by *adding* new systems. Because optimists find their remedies for all of life's problems in technology, they saturate culture with technical objects.[40] Technicism produces an uncritical and undiscerning optimism for both the short-term and the long-term future of humanity. Such optimism is at odds with the biblical perspective. The arrogance of science and technology has rendered God and theology irrelevant for many in contemporary society. Though not all who work in these fields share this perspective, it is the prevailing viewpoint.[41] Christian cultural critic Craig M. Gay writes of the secular perspective:

> From a scientific and theological point of view, God's existence is largely irrelevant. He has been left to inhabit only that space defined by our ever-diminishing scientific ignorance, and so has become the doubtful "god-of-the-gaps." And what little need we may still have for this god-of-the-gaps should, at some point in our technological future, diminish practically to the vanishing point.[42]

Science and technology have influenced the spiritual life as well as the material life:

> Science and technology have substantially reinforced the *plausibility* of practical atheism in modern society and culture. They have made it easier for us to go about our daily business and even to live our entire lives without giving God much thought. . . . This is largely because science and technology define the world in such a way as to render God *practically* irrelevant. Science and technology also encourage us to become so preoccupied with our own knowing and making that

we tend to forget that we are ourselves creatures within a larger Creation.[43]

Though the prevailing winds of society and culture are blowing away from God and theology, there remains, as always, individual responsibility and accountability before God.

Technology and science will certainly enhance life for much of the world's population in the future. Christians must not turn their backs on these endeavors. Rather, we must support responsible technology based on a Christian worldview and biblical principles. Technology can be a great asset in the proclamation of the redeeming work of Christ. Technology inevitably changes lives and lifestyles, but it does not change the gospel of Jesus Christ, doctrines of orthodoxy, or other Christian commitments.

Areas of Concern

In the future, several areas of technological endeavor will have enormous effects within industrialized societies: (1) biotechnology and bioethics; (2) communications and computers; (3) wealth, energy, and environmental concerns; and (4) warfare. Concerns related to the biomolecular revolution and the computer revolution will be briefly noted to illustrate the concerns found in many areas of inquiry.

BIOTECHNOLOGY AND BIOETHICS

Science and technology have brought enormous medical advances and benefits to humanity. The ability to diagnose, prevent, and treat many medical conditions has enriched and saved millions of lives. There have been great leaps in medical care, due in part to technology. No reasonable individual would suggest abandoning such progress. Yet advances in medicine and technology do raise new ethical issues that need to be continually refined and answered.

Many issues previously were not major concerns, for example end-of-life decisions, fetal-tissue research, genetic engineering, genetic testing, gene therapy, biopatents, cloning, and reproductive technology. In each of these areas, there are many ethical decisions. These can be complex problems without simple solutions—ethically or medically. But decisions must be made, with or without Christian responses. It is critical that Christians understand the issues and influence the decision-making process at every level.[44]

New abilities create new questions. Questions of "Can we?" must always be followed by "Should we?" Mathematician and minister John Polkinghorne, a member of the Human Genetics Advisory Commission in the United Kingdom, in an extended but insightful passage, writes,

Not everything that can be done should be done. The technological imperative, encouraging the continuing pioneering of new techniques, must be tempered by the moral imperative, requiring that such techniques should be achieved by ethically acceptable means and employed for ethically acceptable ends. The search for wise decisions must involve the relevant scientific experts (for only they have the access to the knowledge on which the assessments of possibility and consequences can be based), but it cannot be delegated to them alone (for they possess no necessarily unique insight beyond the topic of their professional expertise). There must be other parties in the debate, which centers on the nature of the respect and restraint due to human life and to human moral dignity. Here theology, with its insight that the good and perfect will of God the Creator is the true origin of all value, has an important contribution to make. Theology will not seek to stifle advances that could benefit humankind in acceptable ways, but it will insist that the means by which these desirable ends are achieved must themselves be of ethical integrity.[45]

With regard to the debates over genetic engineering and human cloning, it is essential that Christians be informed and responsible, rather than ignorant and reactionary. Theologian R. Albert Mohler Jr. correctly observes, "Christians should engage in this debate on biblical terms and contend for the sanctity of all created life as well as for the distinction between the creature and the Creator. All technologies, including modern genetics, must be evaluated in terms of the biblical revelation and the totality of the Christian worldview."[46] Christians cannot afford to ignore the social debates and concerns of the age. Our hope is indeed, in the person, work, and return of Jesus Christ. However, we have responsibilities in the present world, regardless of the transitory nature of our presence.

While we await the realization of the kingdom of God, there is another world coming upon us in which we may bear witness of the gospel of Jesus Christ. It is not a world that is ushered in by God; it is by humans. It is not in the distant future; it is tomorrow. Mohler warns that,

the troubling tangle of ethical issues involved in genetic technologies represents an urgent challenge to the Christian church as the people of truth. The new technologies cannot be naively dismissed or blissfully embraced. This generation of Christians must regain the disciplines of moral discernment and cultural engagement. The Brave New World is upon us.[47]

It is indeed a new world, and Christians cannot afford to ignore the signs of the times. There is too much at stake.

Over a half century ago, in the aftermath of World War II and the war crimes tribunal at Nuremberg, Dr. Leo Alexander, a psychiatrist who worked with the Office of the Chief of Counsel for War Crimes at Nuremberg, published a landmark paper entitled "Medical Science under Dictatorship."[48] In this paper, he reviewed the medical practices and propaganda employed by the Nazis as they suspended ethical principles and pursued aberrant procedures and gruesome techniques under the guise of medical science. What concerned him was the relative ease with which such research and practices were initiated. What is so troubling to many observers today is that procedures and perspectives that fifty years ago brought judgment as war crimes are today widely accepted. They are both legal and topics of general discussion.

COMMUNICATIONS AND COMPUTERS

The computer revolution of the last two decades has radically changed the world and the way many of its inhabitants live. Rifkin observes, "Throughout the world there is a sense of momentous change taking place—change so vast in scale that we are barely able to fathom its ultimate impact. Life as we know it is being altered in fundamental ways."[49] The amount of information and kinds of information we can communicate globally is phenomenal. Computers have touched every area of life. We now have a truly global economy, and global concerns rapidly become personal concerns. Staggering amounts of information are available to anyone with a phone line and a personal computer.

But information is also power. For all the good things that we receive because of computers, there should also be concerns of privacy and power. The ability that we now have to gather vast amounts of information leads to the question of what information should become public and what should remain private. How much should other people, institutions, or governments be allowed to know about your life? What are the boundaries, and who will establish them?

The amount of information that someone has about you is a factor in determining how much influence or control there will be over you. Privacy is the door through which power must pass in order to gain access to information about us. Once that door is opened, we become vulnerable to manipulation and control.[50] A decade ago, Alvin Toffler wrote that the control of knowledge "is the crux of tomorrow's worldwide struggle for power in every human institution."[51] Nothing in the realm of communications and computers has negated his prediction.

We must remember that not all problems have technological answers. Nor do all people benefit from current technology. We must never confuse the technology of the industrialized countries with the living standards of the emerging countries. More than half the world's population still lives more than a two-day walk from a telephone. Over 65 percent of the world's households do not have telephones.[52] Medical resources and capacities at the Mayo Clinic in Minnesota are vastly different from those of a missionary clinic in Mogadishu, Somalia. In the former, medical breakthroughs are anticipated and experienced routinely; in the latter, the allocation of scarce resources means that patients will die for lack of medication that we can buy over the counter at the local pharmacy.

TECHNOLOGY AND PROPHECY

For Christians who firmly believe the Bible and its prophetic teachings, there are often questions raised about technology and the horrors that may be perpetrated with it. Certainly there is cause for concern about the potential uses of some technologies. However, one thing we must not do is rush to condemn all technological advances and practices because of our views of the future. It is wrong to think that because something may or will be used for evil in the future, we should therefore avoid it or resolutely reject it in the present. It is much more important that we identify, understand, and nurture the attributes of Christian maturity than it is that we attempt to identify the mark of the Beast (Rev. 13:11–18). What is written on the heart is more important than what will be written on the head. Ultimately, people will lead to Armageddon, not armor. Our interpretation of the events of Revelation must not dissuade us from responsibly pursuing or using technology.[53]

An understanding of the Bible and its worldview does not forbid the use of technology. But we must be aware of technology's potential. The technology that we use today is always subject to be used for evil tomorrow: that which is intended for good is always in danger of being abused and corrupted by the heart. The problem of evil is not an issue of technology but of theology.

BETWEEN EDEN AND BABEL

We have often heard the expression "between a rock and a hard place" used to express the dilemmas that we sometimes face because of the circumstances in which we find ourselves. Though we might use such an expression to describe the technological quandaries of the present age, there is more accurate imagery from the pages of Scripture.

Two images stand out in relation to Christian ethics and technological power—Eden and Babel.[54] In Eden there was dominion over the garden and the responsibility to maintain it (Gen. 1:26; 2:15). There were also limits to that dominion (Job 39–41; Amos 5:8). There was a responsibility to maintain the creation, and there were boundaries to human control. In Babel we find the second image (Genesis 11). In this image, we see ambition, arrogance, the quest for power, and the desire to be like God. In this instance, technological endeavor and pride resulted in chaos with enduring effects. Though we cannot replicate the grandeur of the garden, we can easily succumb to the boastful building of Babel.

In Genesis 12, the chapter following the account of the tower at Babel, we find other construction projects. After the calling of Abraham, two altars were constructed to commemorate the blessing received from God (Gen. 12:7-8). At Babel, technology was used to serve human desires and plans. In Eden, at Shechem, and between Bethel and Ai, technology was used to serve God. We have the same option in our day; we can either serve God or self. David Gill writes of this contrast:

> As Christians we know we cannot go back to Eden. We must go forward either to Babylon, where Babel's project is fulfilled, or to the New Jerusalem, where Abraham's project is fulfilled. The afterlife is depicted in the form of a city, not a new garden, into which the nations bring their glory. We must pray and work that something of our own generation's technology might be worthy of a place in that city of God.[55]

The choices we make in life carry vast consequences, and we must make them carefully and prayerfully.

Technology is carrying us to new frontiers in many areas of life. We therefore need to continually critique our culture and our society from a biblical perspective. Not all that is labeled "progress" is morally and ethically acceptable. Christians categorically reject some technologies because they violate biblical principles. Individual Christians can decide not to use others because to do so would violate conscience, even though it is in an area of Christian liberty. We must know what we believe, why we believe it, and attempt to understand the ramifications of those beliefs.

PROPHETIC LIVING TODAY

As one watches the news, reads the papers, and considers one's own life, one frequently can wonder whether the world is experiencing the dawn of a new and glorious age or the eve of destruction. The Bible has the answer and will serve as our guide if we permit it to do so. It will also serve as our critic in all of life's endeavors—technological or otherwise. Carl Henry writes, "The Bible is still the most incisive critic of our age. It confronts our broken love of God, our dull sense of justice, our shameful moral nakedness, our waning sense of ethical duty, our badly numbed consciences, our clutching anxieties, the ghastly horrors and brutal violence of this era."[56] We must strive daily to understand the foundation of our beliefs and our actions.

Public and private actions and personal values have consequences. There is truly "a world of difference" between a Christian and a non-Christian worldview. The purpose and role of technology is part of that worldview. We must ask not only what new technologies will be but also how they will be used. Carl Mitchum, who has written extensively on philosophy and technology, notes,

> We do not live in order to make and use technologies; we make and use technologies in order to live—that is, to live one way rather than another. Given our medical, industrial, and computer technologies, we can seek to assess their benefits and risks and to submit them to the principles of justice, or leave them in the hands of amoral market forces. . . . No matter how we decide to treat the environment, no matter what we decide to do with our computers, it will have an ethical, not just a technical, impact on our lives.[57]

Though most of us will not create technology, we all will consume technology. Responsibility is therefore not an option; it is incumbent upon us as human beings. Writing to all citizens of democratic societies, Barbour states, "In sum, citizen participation in a technological society is a difficult but not impossible task. Even a relatively small number of informed and active citizens can contribute to greater public awareness and can enhance the accountability of legislators and officials. Public debate may delay decisions, but it is the lifeblood of democracy."[58]

What is true for all citizens, in this instance, is even more a mandate for Christians, who should have a national, global, and heavenly perspective.

If we are going to speak the truth to a technological age, we must be prepared to warn against the idolatry of technicism, remind our materialistic and technological culture that Jesus Christ offers liberation from the status quo, and stand willing to condemn the excesses and evils that technology may produce.[59] Writing of the Christian responsibility to confront secular society in one realm of technological activity, Monsma observed that "Christians will not always agree on which public policies best sort out the permissible from the impermissible. But the uncertainties of gray issues do not preclude a condemnation of those immoral genetic experiments that wantonly disregard the sacredness of personhood."[60]

This is true in other areas of technology as well. To the extent that we have the ability and opportunity, we should set forth technological advances that we believe should be developed. Gay reminds us, "We do not need to renounce human creativity, therefore; nor do we need to completely forgo technological making; rather, we need only insist that this creative activity be informed by the love of Christ, by the love of neighbor, and by the love of the

world for the sake of both."[61] We must also be careful to avoid idle speculation over far-fetched ideas. However, if we apply principles rather than looking at projections that may or may not come to pass, we will be on much
firmer ground and retain the credibility of the biblical worldview.

The hope of the future rests firmly in the person and work of Jesus Christ
and in His return. The present and future ramifications of technology are
extremely important for us to understand. However, the greater challenge is
that of the reality of a present Christless society. Though the ethical concerns
of technology's influence on our culture are significant, their importance
fades in the light of the urgency of the gospel of Jesus Christ.

IT'S TIME TO PRAY AND ACT

The mechanical clock had its origin in the Benedictine monasteries of the
late Middle Ages. Daniel Boorstin finds that both interesting and significant:
"The first steps toward the mechanical measurement of time, the beginnings
of the modern clock in Europe, came not from farmers or shepherds, nor
from merchants or craftsmen, but from religious persons anxious to perform
promptly and regularly their duties to God. Monks needed to know the times
for their appointed prayers."[62] Because they prayed at intervals during the
night as well as the day, monks needed to have an instrument that could be
heard in the darkness as well as in the light. Thus, the first mechanical clocks
were designed not to *show* the time but to *sound* it.

Though it was originally designed to assist the monks in regulating their
prayer lives, the clock was soon used by those outside the monastery walls for
their own purposes. Originally designed to call men and women to prayer in
adoration of God, it soon called men and women to work in adoration of
wealth. The original desire for the technology that led to the mechanical
clock was not wrong, nor was the design or the initial usage. There was even
benefit and positive application by the larger society as the technology spread.
What was faulty were those human hearts that used it solely for the glory of
gold.

Therein is the challenge for us today as we seek to wisely use technology
and develop the resources that God has entrusted to us. As we do so, may we
continually remember that our ultimate hope is not in this life but in the one
to come. "For we know that if the earthly tent which is our house is torn
down, we have a building from God, a house not made with hands, eternal in
the heavens" (2 Cor. 5:1).

CHAPTER 26

The Spread of Mysticism and Biblical Spirituality

Thomas D. Ice

Sometime during the 1980s Western culture shifted from "What do you think about . . . ?" to "How do you feel about . . . ?" Since then the evangelical church has been drifting with the secular tide. This transformation of the culture is usually described as the shift from modernism to postmodernism. The postmodern mentality directs forces that make a huge impact upon evangelicalism, especially in Christian living and spirituality. Even among some circles of evangelicals, spirituality has gone from a focus upon character development to a metaphysical mysticism.

THE AIR WE BREATH

First John 4:15 commands believers not to love *the world* nor *the things in the world*. John's warning against the world has in view the non-Christian mentality that dominates humanity. The things in the world include everything from the physical universe to what human craft has made.

In the New Testament, the word *world*, from which we derive our English words *worldly* and *worldliness* (lit. "world-likeness, or resembling the world) translates the Greek noun *kosmos*, from which we get our English word *cosmetics*. It was used to signify the orderly arrangement of individual parts into an integrated whole, as of the orderly arrangement of soldiers in battle formation.

Greek thought linked the concepts of beauty and order. So *kosmos* often expresses the idea of a beautiful arrangement or an adornment or decoration. The Holy Spirit chose an apt term, for Satan loves to decorate his ideas with the most beautiful, external attire. We should understand *world*, *worldly*, and *worldliness* to refer to the external arrangement of nonbiblical thinking. Worldliness connects with the organized and superficially attractive system of ideas, concepts, attitudes, and methods Satan uses to compete with God's view of life. Satan sits at the head of this system of thinking. Whenever we think like the world we are thinking as Satan wants us to. Lewis Sperry Chafer writes,

> The *cosmos* is a vast order or system that Satan has promoted, which conforms to his ideals, aims, and methods. It is civilization now functioning apart from God—a civilization in which none of its promoters really expect God to share, who assign to God no consideration in respect to their projects. This system embraces its godless governments, conflicts, armaments, jealousies, its education, culture, religions of morality, and pride. It is that sphere in which man lives. It is what he sees, what he employs. To the uncounted multitude it is all they ever know so long as they live on this earth. It is properly styled *the satanic system,* which phrase is in many instances a justified interpretation of the so-meaningful word, *cosmos.* It is literally a *cosmos diabolicus.*[1]

Worldliness is often presented as beautiful, desirable, or enlightening. As Eve thought after agreeing with Satan's temptation, "it was a delight to the eyes, and . . . desirable to make one wise" (Gen. 3:6). Eve was ready, willing, and able to sin when she starting looking at things from Satan's point of view rather than God's. Worldliness is Satan's window dressing. It presents evil in a way that seems good, right, and proper.

FROM RATIONALISM TO MYSTICISM

The Lord told Israel, "You shall not add to the word which I am commanding you, nor take away from it, that you may keep the commandments of the LORD your God which I command you"(Deut. 4:2).[2] This passage lays out three possible responses to God's Word: (1) adding to it, (2) taking away from it, or (3) obeying it. This passage makes it clear that God's Word is to be obeyed.

The logical outgrowth of modernism's rationalism is the current postmodern mysticism, which desires to add human wisdom to God's Word. Those who practice this theology insist that there new revelations now supplement God's Word. The progression of attack on God's Word throughout history has been (1) rationalism exalts human reason above revelation, (2) skepticism questions everything, (3) mysticism substitutes almost anything for belief. In the late twentieth century, even evangelicals had drifted toward this most serious of violations of Scripture.

Biblical Christianity looks neither to rationalism or mysticism as its basis for authority. It begins with revelation—God's Word—as a basis for truth.

God's Word is above human thought or feeling. "Since He [God] could swear by no one greater, He swore by Himself" (Heb. 6:13). God's revealed Word is the Bible. Psalm 36:9 says, "For with Thee is the foundation of life; in Thy light we see light." Psalm 119:130 declares, "The unfolding of Thy words gives light; it gives understanding to the simple." The Bible tells us that we come to know truth by God's gracious revelation of Himself. We can either respond to His Word by submitting in dependence upon it and thinking God's own thoughts, or by rebelling against His light and thinking our own thoughts.

There may be two ways to *search* for truth, but there is only one way to *find* truth, for "Thy word is truth" (John 17:17b). To look for truth in any other place is to guarantee that it will not be found. Christ spoke of the two ways to search for truth: "Everyone who comes to Me and hears My words, and acts upon them. . . . is like a man building a house, who dug deep and laid a foundation upon the rock" (Luke 6:47–48a).

The believer who is truly grounded upon God's Word will not be wiped out by the flood of life's problems. Those who do not have confidence that God's Word is the rock will fail, along with those who have not built upon that bedrock; "and the torrent burst against it and immediately it collapsed, and the ruin of that house was great" (6:49b).

FROM RATIONALISM TO HUMAN REASONING

The starting point and continuing authority for the believer is the written revelation from God. The God who knows everything provides a solid framework for developing confident perspective on life. The understanding of truth starts with dependence upon God and his truthfulness.

This approach to life and faith was challenged early in the history of the church through rationalism and mysticism. Marcion (d c. 154) was likely the first rationalist within the church. He set human reason above revelation, applying what amounted to a higher critical approach to the New Testament canon. In the end he threw out all New Testament Scripture that disagreed with his theology. At about the time Marcion died, the opposite heresy was being preached in Asia Minor through Montanus. It reached Rome in about 170 and by 200 had followers even among the church fathers. This ascetic Christianity stressed Platonic rejection of the physical and stress on miraculous gifts of the Spirit, including new direct revelation from God. The Montanists added to Scripture.

In the twentieth century, particularly after the two World Wars, both North American and European Christians across the theological spectrum disavowed the rationalism of pre-World War I classic liberalism. They replaced it with the more mystical teachings of neoorthodoxy. Among more conservative Christians, the Pentecostal/charismatic movement that began in 1907 continued to grow in influence. The cumulative result was a decline, sometimes almost to the point of death, of Bible-centered theology as the defining aspect of evangelicalism and fundamentalism.

Evangelicalism and fundamentalism were expressions of biblical Christianity that arose to counter liberalism. They were built primarily around theology— what one believes. Now *what* one believes is usually relegated to the back seat by the focus upon *how* something is done.

David Wells has provided a sober warning in *No Place For Truth: Or What-ever Happened to Evangelical Theology?* that the loss of authority leaves evangelicals where liberals once were—absorbed into the conventions of the world. Instead of "cognitive dissidents" in the culture, evangelicals are becoming partners with it:

> This transition has entailed banishing theology from its place in the center of evangelical life and relegating it to the periphery. Behind this banishment is a greatly diminished sense of truth. Where truth is central in the religious disposition, theology is always close at hand. . . . They are in fact, now beginning to retread the path that the Protestant Liberals once trod, and they are doing so, oddly enough, at the very time when many of the descendants of the Liberals have abandoned this path because of its spiritual bankruptcy.[3]

If evangelicals are turning away from theology and God's Word, toward what are they moving? Wells tells us that "many in the Church have now turned in upon themselves and substituted for the knowledge of God a search for the knowledge of self."[4] "Psychologized preaching" shifted the central focus of faith from God to the self. This naturally eroded conviction; a pragmatic people, unable any longer to think incisively about culture, instead reveled in the nonrational.[5]

Increasingly in evangelical circles, churches are drifting from the sufficiency of Scripture as they equip believers for works of ministry. The pattern is often the same: The Bible does not speak specifically enough in a particular area, so one must dip into the secular pool of wisdom. Areas in which this trend appeared included

1. *Personal living.* Sanctification was replaced by psychology and psychotherapy in an effort to understand the individual rather than God.
2. *Giving.* Fund raising programs became part of marketing strategy.
3. *Evangelism.* Personal witness was replaced by felt-need marketing.
4. *Christian outreach.* Sociology-based church growth sought to understand neighborhood demographics rather than God's view of society.
5. *Missions.* Anthropology became as important in some programs as was theology.

6. *Pastoral theology*. A redefining of pastoral professionalism turned church leaders toward a preoccupation with leadership and management skills.
7. *Theological education*. For working pastors "how to" training seminars, worked on all the pragmatic matters that had not been covered in seminary.

The leaven of existential idealism and pragmatism permeated late twentieth century church life, often erecting a barrier to sound biblical theology and godliness in much the same way liberal rationalism placed barriers in the church of a century ago. During the 1980s and into the 1990s, there appeared to be fewer areas in which evangelicals proclaimed authoritative Bible teaching. Instead, outside consultants provided "invaluable information" to be synthesized into a balanced blend of high octane "truth." Evangelical professionalism was often justified by the often heard slogan that "All Truth is God's Truth," while leaders seemed to be finding less of God's truth in the Bible.

Our evangelical heritage is supposed to follow the Reformation principle of *sola scriptura* (Scripture alone). This precept led Protestants to oppose ecclesiastical authority, the natural theology of Romanism, and the authority of human reason. Later biblical Christians used Scripture to oppose the experiential skepticism of liberalism. Evangelicals leave a place for reason and experience, but it is supposed to be subordinate to Scripture. Paul told the wayward Corinthians that he was teaching them "not to exceed what is written" (1 Cor. 4:6). So often evangelicals seem to become caught up in an "experimentalism," as if God has not given us a clear theological framework from which to interpret life.

SELF-FULFILLING PROPHECY

What Wells has observed within American evangelicalism is an ongoing fulfillment of 2 Timothy 3:1–5:

> *But realize this, that in the last days difficult times will come. For men will be lovers of self, lovers of money, boastful, arrogant, revilers, disobedient to parents, ungrateful, unholy, unloving, irreconcilable, malicious gossips, without self-control, brutal, haters of good, treacherous, reckless, conceited, lovers of pleasure rather than lovers of God; holding to a form of godliness, although they have denied its power; and avoid such men as these.*

Paul's thesis is that the difficult times will be the result as men love themselves (v. 2), rather than God (v. 4). The seventeen characteristics listed in verses 2–4 illustrate what lovers of self are like. Paul adds in verse 5 the further reason why many within the church will adopt a narcissistic emphasis upon self-love, self-worth, and self-esteem by "holding to a form of godliness, although they have denied its power." In chapters 1 and 2, Paul has been relating the power of God to the gospel. Thus, this self-virtue will not be based upon the gospel; it will be religious, but not biblical.

Reconstructionist theologian R. J. Rushdoony has predicted where an emphasis upon self leads:

> Perhaps the clearest area of success in the modern pulpit is in the preaching of psychology. Indeed, it can be said that psychology has in the main replaced theology and the social gospel in most pulpits. Today man is more interested in himself than in God or society.
>
> Psychology was once a branch of theology, as was anthropology. With the rise of humanism, psychology began to develop new orientations. In the 19th century, with Wilhelm Wundt, who was the son of a Lutheran pastor, psychology became the science of experience. Evangelical pietism and scientific experimentalism came together to exalt experience as the new area of reality and truth.
>
> The exaltation of experience meant that *life* now meant experience; in its truest, fullest sense, the meaning of life was sought in experience, not in God's enscriptured word. Experience became the new means of revelation.
>
> To cultivate experience means to cultivate also sensitivity to experience.[6]

Just such a narcissistic selfism provides the momentum for a mystical approach to Christianity and the Christian life. At the turn of the twentieth century the church was battling rationalism and its implications. At the turn of the twenty-first century the greater threat is from mysticism. Too many within the church either don't understand its danger, or they do not think that it will have such a negative impact upon the life of the church.

In his provocative book, *Christianity and Anti-Christianity in Their Final Conflict*, Samuel J. Andrews predicted that the final apostasy at the end of the church age will not be some form of rationalism. Instead he believed the disaster would come from mysticism. This would be a "pantheistic revolution" (as opposed to the previous "atheistic revolution"), and it would arise from several trends:

- New institutions would be established upon new (unbiblical) principles.
- Through these institutions pantheistic principles would take on a revolutionary power.
- The influence of this pantheism would grow with a stress on democra-

tization, establishing a more absolute equality among people and even between people and God.

- This equality would give the religious tone to life and affect human relationships.
- Although based on a universalism that believes one Infinite Spirit resides in all human beings, the result would be a self-exalting individualism. Legal restraints would be thrown off, since ultimately the divinity that is within the individual rules and guides. The self-sufficient individual will feel no thanks to another, nor reverence. He will owe nothing to God.[7]

Andrews provides insight into the type of mysticism that infects the church. An emphasis upon self leads to the journey within. That journey leads to the fulfillment of Scripture's prophetic overview of the church age.

MYSTICISM AND SPIRITUAL WARFARE

In a Christian television broadcasting studio, I watched the taping of an interview with a "Christian psychologist" who was sharing experiences from his practice to show how the spiritual blends with the psychological. He was attempting to anecdotally support his new therapeutic techniques.

The doctor told a story of a Christian woman whom he diagnosed as demon possessed. As he rebuked the evil within her, he said, she had lapsed into a trance in which she went into the contractions of labor as though she was about to give birth. He described the whole delivery performance: heavy breathing, cries of pain, and finally the pushing. The psychologist was her coach through the whole event, which was acted out in his counseling office. This episode resulted in the expelling of five demons through the woman's reliving the act of giving birth.

Such disturbing stories are becoming common within church traditions that have been part of the Evangelical Christian community. Such episodes are said to be "spiritual warfare" encounters. Christians are said to be casting off the blinders of Western rationalism, which for too long has held the Church captive. They are awakening to an enlightened view of the spiritual realm. Almost every aspect of the Christian life is being taught as an aspect of spiritual warfare because the worldview interprets life from a mystical framework instead of from biblical categories.

Arthur L. Johnson's description of mysticism is helpful in describing the dynamics at work in some areas of evangelical spirituality:

When either the psychological attitude alone, or the more complete philosophical grasp, is translated into theological terms, the resulting view leads the person to equate his inner impressions or subjective states with the voice of God. Such a person, if he is a Christian, tends to believe that the activity of the Holy Spirit within us is expressed primarily through emotional or other noncognitive aspects of our being. Having and "obeying" such experiences is what "being spiritual" is all about.[8]

MYSTICISM AND SPIRITUALITY

Ethical spirituality teaches that our relationship with God is mediated indirectly and develops in a way analogous to physical growth. Christian growth begins with a direct, metaphysical act of God through the new birth. However, as in a newborn, all of the necessary capacity has been imparted, and the baby grows in that capacity through eating (learning the Word) and exercise (obedience). This results in spiritual fruits of the Spirit. Progress in the spiritual life focuses upon ethical progress outside of the believer as he measures spirituality in terms of character development.

I believe that every instance of teaching and illustration about spirituality in the New Testament supports the ethical or growth approach to sanctification. Yet many evangelicals have taught a blend of both views. Perhaps this explains why the last few decades have seen a steady stream of evangelicals who have moved toward charismatic spirituality. A metaphysical interpretation sometimes is used for Ephesians 5:18, but proper exegesis of the passage supports an ethical spirituality. At issue is the meaning of the Greek phrase πληρόω ἐν πνεύματι (*plēroō en pneumati*), usually translated "be filled with the Spirit," found in Ephesians 5:18. We must first examine the term "filled."

The term for filling is used six times in the New Testament outside of Ephesians 5:18 in the following passages:

1. Luke 4:1, of Jesus
2. Acts 6:3, of Seven men
3. Acts 6:5, of Stephen
4. Acts 7:55, of Stephen
5. Acts 11:24, of Barnabas
6. Acts 13:52, of the disciples (verb)

In each occurrence except Acts 13:52 the word appears in the Greek as an adjective and emphasizes the abiding condition or state of fullness achieved. Luke does not present this phrase as a spiritual method or as any kind of special endowment of the Spirit to do a specific task. The phrase describes someone who is already Spirit-motivated. One does not *become full* in order to achieve a great measure of spiritual motivation; one *is full* when already spiritually motivated. This is much the same in the case of a man who is exceedingly wise; we describe the greatness of his wisdom by saying "He is full of wisdom." He does not *become full* in order to be wise; he already *is full*.[9]

Notice how these six uses of *filled* in Luke stress abiding result; they do not support the notion of a mystical infusion kind of filling:

1. Luke 4:1: "Jesus, full of the Holy Spirit, returned from the Jordan."
2. Acts 6:3: "But select from among you, brethren, seven men of good reputation, full of the Spirit and of wisdom."
3. Acts 6:5: "They chose Stephen, a man full of faith and of the Holy Spirit."
4. Acts 7:55: "But being full of the Holy Spirit, he [Stephen] gazed intently into heaven."
5. Acts 11:24: "for he [Barnabas] was a good man, and full of the Holy Spirit and of faith."
6. Acts 13:52: The disciples "were continually filled with joy and with the Holy Spirit"

We see from the New Testament occurrences that someone full of the Spirit has consistently exhibited a high degree of control by the Holy Spirit. This state did not come instantaneously, but rather through a process of spiritual maturity. No conditions are explicitly set down. The steps of spiritual maturity would be the means of achieving "fullness." The fullness is not a means for accomplishing an end, but is an end in itself. After a study of the New Testament work of the Spirit, Timothy Crater said that "one does not become full in order to live the victorious life, but one becomes so submitted to and influenced by the Holy Spirit that the extent of the Spirit's influence over his life may be described by saying 'is full of the Holy Spirit.'"[10]

As long as someone manifests the Spirit's control, he would be characterized as "full of the Spirit." A young or immature believer may exhibit the Spirit's influence, but not to the extent that would be called "full." The fullness of the Spirit appears to be the normative truth that could *potentially* be true of every follower of Christ.

Luke strongly supports an ethical dimension of the filling of the Holy Spirit by his use of double objects (e.g. "full of the Spirit and of wisdom" (Luke 4:1), "full of the Spirit and of wisdom" (Acts 6:3), "full of faith and of the Holy Spirit" (Acts 6:5), "full of the Holy Spirit and of faith" (Acts 11:24), "filled with joy and with the Holy Spirit" (Acts 13:52). Clearly, one does not obtain wisdom, faith and joy through a mystical connection. Wisdom, faith, and joy are character qualities, so the term linked to them also must be used in that way.

The only other time the phrase is used in the Greek New Testament is by Paul in Ephesians 5:18. However, the phrase ἐν πνεύματι (*en pneumati*) (by the

Spirit) is found also in Ephesians 2:22; 3:5; and 6:18. These all refer to the Holy Spirit as a personal agent. Some hold that *spirit* in Ephesians 5:18 refers to the human spirit. While this is a grammatical possibility, it is not the proper rendering according to the context. It does refer to the Holy Spirit, because Paul only uses this phrase in reference to the Holy Spirit. The phrase *en heni pneumati* ("in one spirit") is found in Ephesians 2:18. There are no New Testament references to the filling of the human spirit.

Ephesians 5:18 refers to an ethical filling of the Spirit because the description that follows this command (5:19–21) describes abiding characteristics of a person that are developed over time. These character qualities correspond with Luke's use.

In Greek grammar, endings dictate how a noun is used. The *nominative* is the "naming case" and is the form the subject of a sentence would take. The *genitive* is the "case of description and separation." It is usually translated with the prepositions *of* or *from*. The *dative* denotes interest, location, or means and is translated with the prepositions *to, in,* and *by*. The *accusative* designates or limits the context to the person/thing addressed. Words with these endings are shown to be the object in the sentence.

With some Greek verbs, including πληρόω (*pleroō*, "to fill") there are very specific endings that distinguish what is being filled, by whom, and how. The case endings of the nouns accompanying *pleroō* enable more precise communication than in English. So when *pleroō* is used with various cases (1) the *genitive* denotes the material that fills, in the texts we are discussing meaning the content of the Holy Spirit, (2) the *dative* refers to the agent or instrument that effects the filling, (3) the *accusative* refers to the thing filled.

With these rules I conclude that most English translations incorrectly render the phrase in Ephesians 5:18 as "be filled *with* the Spirit." This would make the English reader think that the genitive case in the Greek is behind this English translation. However, the Greek uses the dative case. It would be more proper to translate it "be filled *by* the Spirit," the dative denoting the agent of the filling, not the content of the filling. Likewise, Ephesians 2:22 should be translated "You are built together for an habitation of God *by* the Spirit." The Holy Spirit is the One who fills, not what the person is filled with.

I believe the text assumes that the real presence of the Holy Spirit is mystically imparted in the believer's life at spiritual birth. Paul's exhortation to the Ephesians is not that they receive more mystical filling, but that they allow the Spirit more control. A stronger relationship will produce the effects set forth in the Epistle. The Spirit is involved in the same way that human life animates our physical bodies. It is the means by which we do all kinds of things. The fact that we are animated by means of the Holy Spirit, as opposed to the flesh, should produce visible behavior that indicates that we are alive spiritually—the fruit of the Spirit or Christlike character.

Paul presents filling as a process that progresses toward a goal; it is not complete (cf. Luke 2:40; John 16:24). The filling of the Holy Spirit does not mean total control by the Spirit. This would necessitate sinless perfection, since the believer would not be able to resist the sovereign work of God. Neither does the filling of the Holy Spirit denote "Spirit possession" as some suggest. If God the Holy Spirit completely controlled the person's life, it would be impossible for that one to sin, because God cannot even be tempted to sin (James 1:13). Thus, the filling of the Spirit is not total control, but rather a progressive and dominant control by the Spirit through the yielding of one's volition to the will of God. The person so yielded is described in the New Testament as being full of the Spirit. The goal is the Spirit's control of the Christian. This rules out a *state of being filled*, coupled with being "in" or "out" of fellowship.

Further, the filling of the Holy Spirit emphasizes the effects of the Spirit in one's life (metonymy of cause for effect). Our focus should be on whether we are "speaking truth each one with his neighbor" (Eph. 4:25); "being kind to one another, tender hearted, forgiving each other" (4:32); "trying to learn what is pleasing to the Lord" (5:10), "making the most of [our] time" (5:16); "Speaking to one another in psalms and hymns and spiritual songs" (5:19–20); "being subject to one another" (5:21); and more, of which Ephesians 5:18 is just part.

The illustration of becoming drunk indicates a progressive process. Each drink brings one closer to drunkenness. Earlier in the history of the English language, when a man was described as being drunk he might be described as "full of wine or strong drink." Likewise, the Spirit gains such control of our lives that others notice that we are "full of the Spirit."

The verb *plēroō* (to fill) has certain implications:

1. It is plural in number: "Be all of you filled by the Spirit." This is not a privilege reserved for a few; it is potentially available to all believers.
2. It is in the present tense: "All of you be continually filled by the Spirit." The present tense in Greek describes continuing action. Again this fits well with our understanding that this filling is an abiding characteristic of a person's life.
3. It is a command: This is not an option. Paul commands us to be spiritually mature, which is the same as saying, "be filled by the Spirit."[11]

To be filled with the Spirit means to be a mature "Christ-like Christian" who exhibits the fruit of the Spirit. It means to be occupied with Christ, not with oneself or one's experience with the Spirit.

CONCLUSION

The New Testament teaches that, during the seven-year Tribulation, there will be false signs, wonders, and miracles (Matt. 24:4–5, 11; Rev. 13:11–15). At the same time, 2 Thessalonians 2:7 says that "the mystery of lawlessness is already at work" in preparation for the working of the Antichrist "whose coming is in accord with the activity of Satan, with all power and signs and false wonders" (2 Thess. 2:9).

Thus, it is clear that Satan is working to prepare the world for his program of false mysticism during the Tribulation. Such knowledge should lead believers to be careful spiritually so that they follow as closely as possible the biblical teaching of spirituality. Not to do so could mean that even believers are involved in facilitating the false mysticism of Satan that seems to be spreading like wildfire throughout the church. The apostle John recognized a similar danger when he ended his Epistle with the final warning, "Little children, guard yourselves from idols" (1 John 5:21).

CHAPTER 27

The Christian Family in the Twenty-First Century

Beverly LaHaye

Nations most often fall from within, and this fall is usually due to a decline in the moral and spiritual values in the family. As families go, so goes a nation. This has been the main premise of thinkers from British historian J. D. Unwin to Russian sociologist Pitirim Sorokin who have studied civilizations that have collapsed.[1]

J. Kerby Anderson's point from history has obvious and frightening implications for anyone living in Western culture today. True morals and ethics find their source in Scripture. God's design for the family can be found only in that same inerrant source. The strength of the family is in direct proportion to how it lines up with this divine design.

THE FAMILY IN THE NEW CENTURY

Carl Wilson, in his book *Our Dance Has Turned to Death,* chronicles the pattern of decline in the ancient Greek states and the Roman Empire. Observe the parallels to modern Europe and North America.

1. *Loss of male spiritual leadership in the home; humanistic worldview.* Men ceased to lead their families in worship. Spiritual and moral development became secondary. Their view of God became naturalistic, mathematical, and mechanical.
2. *Materialism without any leadership; humanism (selfism).* Men neglected their families to pursue wealth, power, and cultural concerns.
3. *Male sexual immorality and perversion.* Men thus preoccupied with business or war either neglected their wives sexually or became involved with other women or homosexual liaisons. There was a double standard of morality.

4. *Feminism and female immorality; loss of role identity.* Traditional roles of homemaker and mother lost status. Neglected and devalued, women revolted to gain access to material wealth and freedom for sex outside marriage. The emphasis of sexual relationships changed from conceiving children to sex for pleasure. Marriage laws were changed to make divorce easy.

5. *Angry, neglected children; defiance of authority.* As husbands and wives competed for money, leadership status, and the affection of their children, marriage relationships had a low success rate, and children became angry and frustrated. Homosexuality became more common, replacing family relationships.

6. *Family unit breakdown, followed closely by the larger society.* Children were unwanted, aborted, abandoned, molested, and undisciplined. There was social pressure not to have children. The breakdown of the home produced social anarchy within the community.

7. *Self-esteem movement; anarchy.* Selfish individualism grew, fragmenting society into group loyalties. The internal conflicts among groups weakened the nation. The lower birthrate produced an older population less able and willing to defend itself. The nation was more vulnerable to its enemies.

8. *Fragmentation; dictatorship.* Unbelief became complete, parental authority low, and ethical principles nonexistent. Economy and government fragmentation left society ready to receive a dictator or ready to fall to invaders.[2]

Who Defines the Family?

Satan knows that if he can destroy God's design for the family, he can destroy the society and neutralize the Church. This is clear from the fact that his first attack on mankind was against God's design in relationships. With this in mind, it is imperative that Christians understand the God-given design for the family as well as our roles in the biblical family. If our society is to survive into and through the twenty-first century, we must return to the divine design.

Equality of the Sexes at Creation

One way modern European and North American society has tried to destroy the biblical family is to diminish the distinctive sexual identity roles built into the family in God's original design. Thus, we must be aware of God's teaching so our thinking does not become conformed to the culture's design. The only way to understand God's design for biblical manhood and womanhood and their place as family is to look at key sections of Genesis 1–3. It is here that God defines manhood and womanhood. This is our foundation for evaluating and resisting conformity to the predominantly godless cultural understanding with which we are constantly bombarded. A study of this account shows that God intended distinct gender roles that complement one another in the family unit.

The feminist movement in Western culture and it's influence in government, education, and media has resulted in an obsessive cultural call for "equality of the sexes." The exact meaning of this term varies. Most of those influenced by feminist propaganda would say that this goes beyond equal work for equal pay to the opening of any and every occupational position. Women are encouraged to seek positions outside traditional lines in order to further this agenda.

The Bible has much to say about equality issues. We should begin by defining the terms *male-female equality* and *male-headship* that will be used in our discussion. Raymond C. Ortlund Jr. defines biblical male-female equality by saying, "Man and woman are equal in the sense that they bear God's image equally."[3] Of male-headship he says, "In the partnership of two spiritually equal human beings, man and woman, the man bears the primary responsibility to lead the partnership in a God-glorifying direction."[4] Ortlund also gives us a helpful distinction between *male-headship* and *male-domination*. He writes, "The model of headship is our Lord, the Head of the church, who gave Himself for us. The antithesis to male headship is male domination. By male domination I mean the assertion of the man's will over the woman's will, heedless of her spiritual equality, her rights, and her value."[5]

The Genesis Mandate

Now that we have defined some terms, let us look at what God's Word says about male-female equality and male-headship. Genesis 1:26–28, the record of God's creation of mankind, indicates several important things about people in general, and about the equality of men and women in particular.

First, we should note that the man and the woman were made in *the image of God*. At least one implication of this image is that, of all God's creatures, only human beings share God's communicable attributes: life, personality, truth, wisdom, love, holiness, and justice. Thus, only mankind can logically reason, feel emotion, and have a spiritual relationship with God. Genesis 1 particularly notes that mankind was created with dual sexuality. We exist as male and female, two distinct sexes. God had stated, "let *them* rule," involving both in the ruling process. In verse 28 Moses records mankind's responsibilities:

1. They are equal image-bearers of God.
2. They are equally called to be fruitful and multiply; to fill the earth and subdue it.
3. They are equally called on to rule over creation.

Did God Specify Male Headship?

In Genesis 1–3 we see full equality as far as bearing the image of God is concerned and carrying out the command to rule over the rest of God's creation by being fruitful and increasing the population of the world with godly progeny.

Now, the question is this, "In the context of this passage that clearly teaches the spiritual equality of the sexes, is there any hint of male-headship?" Ortlund writes that in the context of what Moses is about to say in Genesis 2, "God's naming of the race 'man' whispers male headship." This is not explicit, but it does suggest a logic for the language construction by which God refers to humans from the start. The generic term is *man*.

> God did *not* name the human race "woman." If "woman" had been the more appropriate and illuminating designation, no doubt God would have used it. He does not even devise a neutral term like "persons." He called us "man," which anticipates the male headship brought out clearly in chapter two, just as "male and female" in verse 27 foreshadows marriage in chapter two. Male headship may be personally repugnant to feminists, but it does have the virtue of explaining the sacred text.[6]

Genesis 2:18–25 establishes clearly what has been hinted at. As Genesis 1:26–28 stresses that male and female bear the image of God equally, Genesis 2 assumes equality and goes on to a clear difference in *functionality*. God makes man the head and woman the helper. Now we return to Ortlund's definition of male headship: "In the partnership of two spiritually equal human beings, man and woman, the man bears the primary responsibility to lead the partnership in a God-glorifying direction." God's call is to leadership within partnership. The man is called to lead with counsel and help from the woman. The partnership is not intended to serve God, not the sinful urges of either partner.[7]

Genesis 2:18–25 amplifies the creation set forth in Genesis 1:26–28. God has created the male (Gen. 2:7) and placed him in the garden (Gen. 2:15) to cultivate and keep it. In addition to the requirements to cultivate and keep, a prohibition has been given not to eat from the tree of the knowledge of good and evil (Gen. 2:17). Adam existed in a garden of paradise, but God quickly points out his one problem: "it is not good for the man to be alone."

God first asked Adam to name each kind of animal. This process of naming encouraged Adam to reflect on the particular natures of each sort of creature. From this exercise he learned that nothing among them shared his nature. Now that Adam realized that he was alone, God stated His promise of Genesis 2:18: "I will make a helper suitable for him." The Hebrew ʿēzer, translated "helper," means, "a helper, help, support."[8] This woman would be "suitable for him" in the sense that only she, of all the creatures, shared Adam's nature.

Verse 22 tells us what happens next: "So the LORD God fashioned into a woman the rib which He had taken from the man, and brought her to the man." [9] The first recorded words of mankind follow (v. 23): "This is now bone of my bones, and flesh of my flesh; she shall be called Woman [Heb. *Ishshāh*], because she was taken out of Man [Heb. *Ish*]." What a beautiful expression of love to the first man was the creation of the woman. Adam must have carefully observed the woman, just as he had all the other creatures that God had created. He must have marveled at her beauty and been overwhelmed when he realized that this new creature was his equal. This creature truly met his need for companionship. This new creature could meet his inner longing.

Moses goes on to explain that this is why man and woman have paired off and created families. Moses writes, "*For this cause* a man shall leave his father and mother, and shall cleave to his wife; and they shall become one flesh" (2:24). For what cause? For the cause that woman was taken out of man. The institution of marriage is not a result of tradition; it is God's sovereign design. Within the attraction between a man and a woman is the reuniting of what was originally one flesh is God's natural design. They were naked and not ashamed within the perfection of the original creation (v. 25) because they perfectly complemented each other.

What are the implications of these texts, especially of the phrase "a helper suitable for him" (Gen. 2:18, 20)? That the woman alone was suitable for the man shows equality. She was the only creature that shared his nature. Only she could provide companionship on an equal level. At the same time she is called his "helper." Returning once more to Ortlund's helpful discussion, the point is made that the language of Genesis 2 strongly speaks of gender roles that are distinct and nonreversible.

To summarize the principles of Genesis, (1) man and woman are equal image-bearers of God, (2) with the functional difference of male headship. (3) They are equal in nature, but different in functionality. (4) This is God's blessing, for it designs roles that blend and coexist in complete unity, the perfect complementary relationship. This is the basis for Ortlund's observation that man and woman are to love each other as equals, but they are not to love each other in the same way. "The man is to love his wife by accepting the primary responsibility for making their partnership a platform displaying God's glory, and the woman is to love her husband by supporting him in the godly undertaking."[10]

THE FALLEN DESIGN

If God's design for the family was so perfect, what happened to alter that perfect complementary relationship? Why is there such turmoil in the family today? The answer, of course, takes us to Genesis 3 and the tragic result of sin and the Fall on family relationships.

The Curse on Woman

The first judgment of the man and woman after they had rebelled against God was directed at the woman. She will have increased pain in childbirth. Apparently God's original design of procreation included some mild pain in the birthing process. But now God states, "I will greatly multiply your pain in childbirth, In pain you shall bring forth children" (Gen. 3:16a).

Second, the woman will have a strong desire for her husband. The meaning of the phrase, "your desire shall be for your husband" (Gen. 3:16b), is debated. The Hebrew word translated "desire" has two other occurrences in the Old Testament. One is Genesis 4:7, where sin's "desire" is for Cain. The other is Song of Solomon 7:10 where the husband's sexual desire is for his beloved wife. Genesis 3:16 seems to carry a similar sense. H. C. Leupold writes,

> The second part of the penalty is: "Unto thy husband thou shalt be attracted." *Teshûqah* might be rendered "desire" or even better "yearning." This yearning is morbid. It is not merely sexual yearning. It includes the attraction that woman experiences for man which she cannot root from her nature. Independent feminists may seek to banish it, but it persists in cropping out. . . . It is a just penalty. She who sought to strive apart from man and to act independently of him in the temptation finds a continual attraction for him to be her unavoidable lot.[11]

So, the woman has a deep yearning or craving that, although it includes the sexual aspect, is not restricted to merely sexual desire. It is a deep yearning to meet her needs through a relationship with the man.

Third, the man will in turn "rule over" his wife. The Hebrew word translated "rule" here carries the meaning of "to have dominion, to reign, rule."[12] In the pre-fall condition there was a beautiful complementary relationship, with full spiritual equality and comfortable male headship as the two worked together to fulfill God's design. But, because the woman usurped the headship role in taking the forbidden fruit, she will have to deal with the tendency of the male to dominate her. The woman's sinful reaction to sinful male domination is to rebel, resulting in feminist movements through history.

The Curse on Man

God then metes out punishment for the man. His punishment perfectly fits his sin. First, because he submitted to his wife (Gen. 3:17), whom he should have been lovingly leading, he will now have to deal with the insubordination of the soil. No longer will tillage be easy. Now it will involve "misery." Only through toil could enough food be produced to sustain him. It will be more grievous (Heb. ʿiṣṣābôn, "misery, toil, or sorrow") because the ground will be cursed, producing "thorns and thistles." The imperfect man will now live in an imperfect world, not knowing the blessing of the perfect creation. Leupold makes the point that God gives the curse on the plants of the field as an example of the curse on all creation, not just vegetation (Rom. 8:18-25).[13] Second, through the man, all the human race would be infected by sin (Rom. 5:12).

The Curse on Family

The fall of the man and woman in the garden had tragic implications on the family. Instead of the harmony of two spiritually equal individual's carrying out their sex roles in a complementary nature, a sinful man and an equally sinful woman attempt to live together while being driven apart by their selfish natures. Instead of working together, either partner is naturally disposed to put self first.

The exciting news is that God has provided a solution for those who are His children. As R. Kent Hughes writes, "Marriage ideally produces two people who are as much the same person as two people can be! Christians in marriage have the *same* Lord, the *same* family, the *same* children, the *same* future, and the *same* ultimate destiny–an astounding unity."[14]

MAN, HUSBAND, AND FATHER

The Character of a Christian Man

The specific biblical roles and responsibilities of the man in the family, the society, and in the church grow from character. Certain traits characterize the Spirit-filled Christian man who is walking in obedience to Jesus Christ. Paul twice lists qualifications for the elders of the church (1 Tim. 3:1-7; Titus 1:5-9). Several of these qualifications deal specifically with leadership, but others deal with character qualities that any man who is striving to make Christ the Lord of his life should possess. They form a check list for what God desires of us as men of God.

Paul states that a man should be "above reproach" (1 Tim. 3:7; Titus 1:7). The Greek word means "not able to be taken hold of." The man has a good reputation and deserves it. The other character qualifications listed simply amplify this qualification. The ideal in Christian character is to be above reproach.[15]

What puts a man above reproach? Paul says,

- A man who is married should be the husband of one wife (1 Tim. 3:2; Titus 1:6).

- He must know how to manage his own household (1 Tim. 3:4–5; Titus 1:6–7).
- He must be temperate (also Titus 1:8).
- He must be prudent and sensible (1 Tim. 3:2; Titus 1:8).
- He must be respectable (1 Tim. 3:2).
- He must be hospitable (1 Tim. 3:2; Titus 1:8).
- He must not be addicted to wine (1 Tim. 3:3; Titus 1:7).
- He must not be quick tempered or pugnacious (1 Tim. 3:3; Titus 1:7).
- He must be gentle, and uncontentious (1 Tim. 3:3; Titus 1:8).
- He must not be motivated by the love of money (1 Tim. 3:3; Titus 1:7).
- He must not be conceited or self-willed (1 Tim. 3:6; Titus 1:7).
- He must love what is good (Titus 1:8).
- He must be just (Titus 1:8).
- He must be devout (1 Tim. 3:9; Titus 1:8).

The Christian Man as Husband

An exciting part of life for a Christian is to partake of God's solution for our fallen state. This solution helps the husband and wife overcome the sinful effects of the Fall and live out the pre-Fall design for marriage. The apostle Paul deals with the key to a successful marriage in Ephesians 5:15–21. The Christian can walk, "not as unwise men, but as wise" as he lives in this sinful world (v. 15). Being controlled by the Spirit is the key to a wise life that expresses itself in God-honoring speech (v. 19a), internal joy (v. 19b), a grateful heart to God the Father (v. 20), and mutual submission among believers (v. 21).[16] Only when each partner is submitted to the control of the Spirit of God and is subject to His will (v. 17) can there be a return to the pre-Fall harmony and the carrying out of complementary sex roles according to God's original design.

Leaving and Cleaving

The first step for the Spirit-filled man to have a successful marriage is given in Genesis 2:24, which states, "For this cause a man shall *leave* his father and mother, and shall *cleave* to his wife; and they shall become *one flesh*" (cf. Eph. 5:31). When this leaving and cleaving does not occur, it spells disaster for the marriage. By leaving father and mother, the man and woman show that their conjugal union is a spiritual communion of heart as well as of body.[17] Leupold writes, "'Becoming one flesh' involves the complete identification of one personality with the other in a community of interests and pursuits, a union consummated in intercourse."[18]

Loving as Christ Loved

Paul, in his discussion of the role of the man in marriage (Eph. 5), again states the divine design that we saw in Genesis 1–3: Wives are to be subject to their husbands (v. 22), and husbands are to bear the responsibility of headship in the marriage (v. 23). Remember our definition of *headship*: "In the partnership of two spiritually equal human beings, man and woman, the man bears the primary responsibility to lead the partnership in a God-glorifying direction."[19] Paul summarizes the role of the husband in one simple phrase: "Husbands, love your wives." John MacArthur writes,

> The word Paul uses here for "love" is *agapaō,* the strongest, most intimate, most far-reaching, and most qualitative term for love. Yes, there is to be authority in a marriage. Yes, there is one who is the head and one who follows. But verse 25 does not say, "Husbands, rule your wives," or "Husbands, subject your wives," or "Husbands command your wives." No! Paul says, "Husbands love your wives."[20]

The way that the husband is to love his wife is the same way Christ loved the Church (v. 25), by giving Himself for her. The love of a husband for his wife is to be a self-sacrificial love. This command alone should make Christian divorce almost non-existent. MacArthur gives three practical and scriptural ways from 1 Peter 3:7 to express that love:

1. *Consideration.* MacArthur comments that to love one's wife demands sensitivity, understanding, and consideration. "Women often complain about their husbands, 'He never understands how I feel.' Lack of consideration often builds a wall in a marriage. Peter tells us to tear it down. He says, in essence, 'Be sensitive, be understanding, feel what she feels.'"
2. *Chivalry.* "Men need to remember that physically they are stronger than women. Do you practice courtesy and thoughtfulness, such as opening the car door for your wife? Or are you fifteen feet out the driveway while she still has one foot hanging out the door? Remember, your wife is the weaker vessel."
3. *Communion.* Peter reminds each husband to honor his wife as a "fellow-heir of the grace of life." MacArthur says, "This phrase 'the grace of life' means marriage is like the hot fudge on a hot fudge sundae. Marriage is the topping, the best part of life. And since you've inherited marriage, fulfill it together, will you? Commune together, talk together, share together. . . . 'so that your prayers may not be hindered.' A wrong marriage relation closes the windows of heaven."[21]

A Love That Sanctifies

Paul continues with his description of Christ's love for the church, the parallel for a husband's love for his wife. Christ's desire is to sanctify the church, "that He might present to Himself the church in all her glory, having no spot or wrinkle or any such thing; but that she should be holy and blameless" (Eph. 5:27). True love always seeks to purify. As a husband follows Christ's example, his life and leadership should always seek to sanctify and purify. He should do nothing that would lead her into sin. Writes MacArthur, "If a man really loves his wife he seeks that which keeps her feet clean from the dust of the world, doing everything in his power to maintain her holiness, her virtue, and her purity."[22]

R. Kent Hughes gives challenging questions for self-examination in his comments on this passage: "Is my wife more like Christ because she is married to me? Or is she like Christ in spite of me? Has she shrunk from His likeness because of me? Do I sanctify her or hold her back? Is she a better woman because of me? Is she a better friend? A better mother?"[23]

Love That Nourishes and Cherishes

Paul continues, "So, husbands ought also to love their own wives as their own bodies. He who loves his wife loves himself; for no one ever hated his own flesh, but nourishes and cherishes it, just as Christ also does the Church, because we are members of His body" (Eph. 5:28–30). We naturally do all we can to care and make provision for our needs. This is not stimulated by emotion but by an inner drive. This is Paul's point. A husband loves his wife as his own body since they have become one body (v. 31). The Hebrew word translated "cleave" in Genesis 2:24 literally means "to glue something together." As men we are to provide for, protect, and preserve our wives and families. The buck stops with the husband.

The Greek word translated "nourishes" here is used to refer to the nurture and raising of children. The word translated "cherish" means "to warm with body heat." These are responsibilities of the husband. The husband should provide for the material needs of the family—food, clothing, and physical shelter, as well as an emotionally safe and warm environment. MacArthur writes,

> Remember Genesis 3? The woman was cursed in childbearing and submission, activities involving the home. The man was cursed in having to work hard to provide for his family. From the very beginning it was assumed the woman would be at home with the children, meeting the needs there, and the man would be giving warmth and security to her. This is God's design—the husband provides security for his wife as Christ provides for His church.[24]

Decision-Making and Headship

This brings us to the question of responsibilities and processes for decision-making. A delicate balance must be maintained among the husband's leadership function, husband-wife equality as fellow image-bearers of God, and a husband's honoring of his wife as "a fellow-heir of the grace of life" (1 Peter 3:7). The husband must respect his wife's views, opinions, feelings, and contributions about the issue at hand, and he must do so in a way that takes into account both his and her strengths and weaknesses (1 Peter 3:8). On the other hand, he must not give over leadership, as did Adam, or God's rebuke will apply (Gen. 3:17).

Knight recognizes the difficulties inherent in this balancing act:

> In a world of sin in which both husband and wife are beset by the limitations sin brings to our understanding and to the evaluative and decision-making process, there will be times when a consensus may not be reached. In this situation, it is the husband's responsibility to exercise his leadership role and make the decision. The wife needs to submit to that decision (unless the decision is clearly and intrinsically evil).[25]

The Man as Father

In Deuteronomy 6, after Moses' recap of the ten commandments, verses 4–9 instructs us to pass on our godly heritage to successive generations:

> *Hear, O Israel! The Lord is our God, the Lord is one! And you shall love the Lord your God with all your heart and with all your soul and with all your might. And these words, which I am commanding you today, shall be on your heart; and you shall teach them diligently to your sons and shall talk of them when you sit in your house and when you walk by the way and when you lie down and when you rise up. And you shall bind them as a sign on your hand and they shall be as frontals on your forehead. And you shall write them on the doorposts of your house and on your gates.*

God has made it clear through the psalmist that children are His gift to us. The psalmist writes of the privilege and blessing it is to raise children:

> *Behold, children are a gift of the Lord;*
> *The fruit of the womb is a reward.*
> *Like arrows in the hand of a warrior,*
> *So are the children of one's youth.*
> *How blessed is the man whose quiver is full of them;*
> *They shall not be ashamed,*
> *When they speak with their enemies in the gate.*
> *(Psalm 127:3–5)*

In Ephesians 6:4, Paul summarizes God's plan for parenting: "And, fathers, do not provoke your children to anger; but bring them up in the discipline and instruction of the Lord." The instruction is addressed to fathers. This should be no surprise since we have seen that male headship is clearly taught from the beginning of creation. At the same time, the term *pateres* indicates that this is the responsibility of both parents. It is used that way in Hebrews 11:23.

Do Not Embitter

Paul begins with a negative command: "Do not provoke your children to anger." Here the Greek compound translated "provoke" (*parorgizō*) means, "to anger, or to bring one along to a deep-seated anger." MacArthur suggests nine ways in which parents embitter children:

1. *Overprotection.* Smothering; never trusting; always questioning their truthfulness. Never allowing them to develop independence.
2. *Favoritism.* Negatively comparing a child to a sibling or someone outside the family.
3. *Demands for achievement.* Pressuring a child to excel in school, sports, or other activities.
4. *Discouragement.* Withholding approval; only telling the child what he or she is doing wrong.
5. *Failure to sacrifice.* Making a child feel like an intrusion in your life.
6. *Failure to allow childishness.* Putting a child down for doing anything that is not mature and intellectual; condemning them for being children.
7. *Neglect.* Being too busy or not being available to share their lives.
8. *Withdrawing love.* Withholding or threatening to withhold love as punishment.
9. *Cruel words and punishment.* "You can destroy the heart of a child by your verbal barrage."[26]

Discipline and Instruction in Godliness

Paul's positive command for parents in Ephesians 6 is to "bring them up in the discipline and instruction of the Lord." The word translated "discipline" is the Greek *paideia*, a term generically referring to the upbringing and training of a child. God's example in Hebrews 12:5–11 is a good one to follow since He is the perfect Father. It reveals that God so loves us that He is committed to training us through godly counsel as well as administering chastisement when we stray from that freeing counsel. That chastisement should be part of the overall training process is made clear from several texts, among them Deuteronomy 21:18 and Proverbs 13:24; 19:18; and 23:13. At the same time, our motivation must be love as seen in our Heavenly Father's dealings (Heb. 12:6). The word translated "instruction" is the Greek *nouthesia*, which is almost synonymous with "discipline," but seems to stress the verbal side of the disciplinary process. "It refers to the training by word—by the word of encouragement, when this is sufficient, but also that of remonstrance, of reproof, of blame, where these may be required."[27]

THE WOMAN AS WIFE AND MOTHER

The Character of the Christian Woman

As in our discussion of the role of the man as husband and father, it is important to see what the Bible says about character traits specifically belonging to the Christian woman. Our discussion begins in 1 Timothy 3:9-10. In the church at Ephesus some women came to public worship dressed extravagantly and adorned with costly jewelry. Not only was their manner of dress distracting, but it betrayed their attitudes of worship. Their motivation was either a prideful display of wealth, or sexual enticement. Paul says that the proper apparel for a Christian woman is a godliness that shows through her everyday life in care and concern for her family and others (cf., Prov. 31:10-31; Eph. 5:22-23; Col. 3:18; 1 Tim. 2:9-10; 5:4, 10, 16; Titus 2:4-5).

Apparently churches of northern Asia Minor were experiencing the same problem as the church in Ephesus. In 1 Peter 3:3-4, Peter's admonition would suggest that some women were more concerned with what was external. Peter tells them to concern themselves with adornment of the "hidden person of the heart." This adornment should be "a gentle and quiet spirit." Such a spirit is imperishable and precious to God. The Greek word translated "gentle" (*praus*) "refers to the humble and gentle attitude which expresses itself in patient submissiveness."[28] A. T. Robertson points out, "[Christ] calls himself "meek [*praus*] and lowly" (Matt. 11:29) and Moses is also called meek. It is the gentleness of strength, not mere effeminacy."[29] R. C. H. Lenski writes,

> "Meek and quiet" go together, the doubling intensifies the virtue. This meekness is always quiet; loudness, intemperate, irate speech and action are foreign to it. A steady, balanced strength keeps it on an even keel. Such a Christian wife is a treasure for any husband. When a heathen husband sees that by conversion his wife is changed from vanity, love display, and other feminine vices to the true beauty of a new spirit, he must surely be drawn to a religion that is able to produce such wonders of grace. . . . God regards such virtue and conduct as *poluteles*, as valuable indeed. In order to produce this inner, spiritual excellence and beauty in every wife and woman He sends us His Word and Spirit.[30]

Solomon describes a godly woman in Proverbs, when he writes:

An excellent wife, who can find?
For her worth is far above jewels.
The heart of her husband trusts in her,
And he will have no lack of gain. . . .
Her children rise up and bless her;
Her husband also, and he praises her, saying:
"Many daughters have done nobly,
But you excel them all."
Charm is deceitful and beauty is vain,
But a woman who fears the Lord, she shall be praised.
Give her the product of her hands,
And let her works praise her in the gates.
(Prov. 31:10–11, 28–31)

The Woman in the Family

The God-given role of the woman in marriage has been much maligned in secular society. The lies of the satanically controlled culture have been voiced so often and so loudly, that they have influenced even the Christian community. We have seen that in God's creation design the man and woman are (1) equal image-bearers of God, (2) both called to be fruitful and to multiply, filling the earth and subduing it, and (3) both called to rule over the rest of God's creation.

God's particular design for the woman was that she be a suitable helper for the man (Gen. 2:18, 20). She was not to be the "head" but the "helper." Thus, when the man allowed the woman to usurp his headship in the garden, part of the curse that came upon her involved the biological aspect for which God created her (an increase in the pain associated with childbirth, 3:16).

The Woman as Wife

We have dealt with the role of the husband and father from Ephesians 5. We return to that passage's two instructions for the wife. Ephesians 5:22–23, 33 calls upon the wife to be subject to her husband. Here the verb "to be subject" is implied from its use in verse 21, but the meaning is confirmed by the explicit parallel passages (1 Cor. 11:3; 14:34; Col. 3:18; Titus 2:5; 1 Peter 3:1), as well as from the creation order and design (Gen. 1:26–28; Genesis 2–3). The form of the verb here, as well as in parallel passages, indicates that the wife is under the husband's headship. Fritz Rienecker defines the word as, "to line one's self up under, [or] to submit. . . . [The word was] used in a military sense of soldiers submitting to their superior or slaves submitting to their masters. The word has primarily the idea of giving up one's own right or will, i.e., 'to subordinate one's self.'"[31]

Ephesians 5:24 states that the wives are to submit to the husband "in everything." Like every passage in the Bible, this one needs to be interpreted in light of overall teaching of Scripture. If a husband tells his wife to do something that violates God's Word, then the principle that Peter stated in Acts 5:29 applies: "We must obey God rather than man." In Ephesians 5:33, Paul writes, "And let the wife respect her husband." The word translated "respect" means "to reverence," "to show respect." This does not imply that the wife should be afraid of the husband. This "fear" [KJV] or "respect" refers to a reverence for her husband's God-ordained leadership role. Mary Kassian writes,

> Respecting one's husband is similar in meaning to fearing him. To show respect for one's husband is to honor and esteem him, to show consideration or regard for him. Again, this is a response to the position God has placed him in. Respect is due, even though husbands may not *always* deserve it. The Christian wife gives respect out of obedience to God.
>
> Failure to fear and respect one's husband undermines his ability and/or desire to lead. A woman fails here when she belittles her husband's ideas, nags him, mocks him, reminds him of his inadequacies and past failures, or criticizes him. A wife who sarcastically tears down her husband in front of others (even in fun), and who constantly resents her husband and draws attention to his faults, does not know how to obey this Biblical directive. An attitude of fear and respect leads to words and practical actions of courtesy and thoughtfulness. A woman who fears and respects her husband will always treat him as someone special. [32]

The Woman as Mother

Regarding public worship in 1 Timothy 2–3, Paul prohibits women from teaching or exercising authority over men during corporate worship (2:11–12). Paul gives two reasons for this prohibition. First, in 1 Corinthians 14:34–35, Paul applies the creation order. "It was Adam that was first created, and then Eve" (1 Tim. 2:13). Second, a literal rendering of 1 Timothy 2:14 is, "And Adam was not deceived ('misled'), but the woman after being completely deceived, has come to be in transgression." Therefore, Paul reasons, a woman should not teach and exercise authority in the local church. Although many commentators avert making a judgment on Paul's thinking regarding this second reason, the only conclusion that can be drawn is that the woman, because of the way she was created for her role, is more easily deceived.

Paul then mentions the positive role that the woman holds in the Christian community. He states, "Saved, however, she shall be through childrearing, if they continue in faith and love and sanctity together with self-restraint." This is a difficult verse, but taking into account the immediate context of presenting woman in the negative light of her being "completely deceived," Paul is now pointing out the positive aspect of her staying within her God-given role, that of child-rearing and nurturing. Lenski writes,

> "Childbearing" includes the rearing of the children, which means Christian rearing to every Christian woman. Paul has in mind what we read in his other letters: the Christian family and home, the mother surrounded by her children, happy in these outlets for her love and affection, in this enrichment for herself and for them, Eph. 6:1, etc.; Col. 3:20. "By way of childbearing" speaks of the highest ideal of Christian (and even secular) womanhood. Nothing shall erase or even dim that for us. Yet the subject is "the woman," which includes also women of all ages, also girls who die before maturity, and women who my never marry, and those who are married but remain childless. God's providence in individual lives in no way destroys his creative purposes.[33]

A good paraphrase might be, "But women's role in society is preserved through the bearing and rearing of children, if they continue in faith and love and sanctity with self restraint." Paul's point is that the godly woman, instead of usurping the authority of the man, should be exercising her God-given role.

This role is affirmed elsewhere. One such passage is Titus 2:4–5, which describes this nurturing role: "that they may encourage the young women to love their husbands, to love their children, to be sensible, pure, workers at home, kind, being subject to their own husbands, that the word of God may not be dishonored." Here older women are assigned to teach and encourage the younger women. Part of this instruction is to be "workers at home." This Greek noun literally means "working at home or domestic [work]" and the verb form means "to fulfill one's household duties."[34] Again the emphasis is that the woman's primary responsibilities lie within the home. She is to love her husband and children and to carry out these responsibilities at home. The phrase "be workers at home" should not only emphasize that she is to be at home, but also that she is to *work* at home. She is not to fill her hours with TV, neglecting the care and instruction of her children. Additional passages, such as 1 Timothy 5:10, 14 and Proverbs 31 give added support to the scriptural teaching that the primary responsibility of managing the home is assigned to the woman.

THE ROLE OF THE CHILD

What does the Bible have to say about the spiritual standing of a child at birth? This is an important question considering that secular psychologists tell us that the child is born with a "clean slate." Environment will primarily determine whether he grows up as a productive member of society or as a criminal. If a child is born a "clean slate" the reasoning might be true, but if the assumption is faulty in understanding a child's nature, then the entire child-rearing construct collapses. Since our world is so saturated with antibiblical thinking, with even Christians "buying into" such philosophy, it is important to see what the Bible says about the nature of a child.

Paul strings together sever Old Testament quotations to tell the Roman believers that there is no empty slate; every single human being is depraved:

> *There is none righteous, not even one; there is none who understands, there is none who seeks for God; all have turned aside, together they have become useless; there is none who does good, there is not even one. . . . Their throat is an open grave, with their tongues they keep deceiving. . . . The poison of asps is under their lips. . . . Whose mouth is full of cursing and bitterness; . . . their feet are swift to shed blood, destruction and misery are in their paths, and the path of peace have they not known. . . . There is no fear of God before their eyes. (Rom. 3:10–18)*

Obviously children are born with a natural bent or propensity to sin. They do not have to be taught to disobey their parents or to selfishly cling to toys. They do this naturally. They will only learn to obey and share if taught. As God is involved in the process of disciplining and instructing us, parents are called on to discipline and instruct their children, so that they will learn to control their natural sinful tendencies (Heb. 12:1–13; Eph. 6:4).

Commands Directly to Children

Obey Your Parents

In Ephesians 5:19–6:4 we must turn our attention to the three verses in chapter 6 we have not yet examined: "Children, obey your parents in the Lord, for this is right. Honor your father and mother [which is the first commandment with a promise], that it may be well with you, and that you may live long on the earth" (Eph. 6:1–3).

In our passage, the term used for child (*tekna*) is a broad term used to refer to any offspring. In addition, the Greek word translated "obey" *(hypakouō)* means "to follow, or be subject to." The term is a compound noun from *hypō,* "under," and *akouō,* "to hear." The child is to get under the parents' authority by listening and heeding their instructions. The parent-child relationship is, in a sense, the foundational interpersonal relationship for a healthy society. If a child has been trained to revere and respect parents, that child will have little problem respecting the authority of teachers, police, government leaders, and others. On the spiritual level, that child will grow up with a reverence and respect for God and His Word.

How serious is God's command? Listen to the punishment God required for those who made a decision to not heed this command.

> *And he who strikes his father or his mother shall surely be put to death. . . . And he who curses his father or his mother shall surely be put to death. (Exod. 21:15, 17)*

> *If there is anyone who curses his father or his mother, he shall surely be put to death; he has cursed his father or his mother, his bloodguiltiness is upon him. (Levit. 20:9; cf. Prov. 20:20)*

> *If any man has a stubborn and rebellious son who will not obey his father or his mother, and when they chastise him, he will not even listen to them, then his father and mother shall seize him, and bring him out to the elders of his city at the gateway of his home town. And they shall say to the elders of his city, "This son of ours is stubborn and rebellious, he will not obey us, he is a glutton and a drunkard." Then all the men of his city shall stone him to death; so you shall remove the evil from your midst, and all Israel shall hear of it and fear. (Deut. 21:18–21)*

> *"Cursed is he who dishonors his father or mother." And all the people shall say, "Amen." (Deut. 27:16)*

This command regarding the execution of a rebellious child may sound extreme, but it demonstrates God's warning that a child who grows up in rebellion to parents is a rebel to society. Although these punishments were part of the Law of Moses and are not in force today, the principle remains. The child who does not learn obedience to, and respect for, the authority of his parents will become an adult with a rebellious nature. A child born in sin must be trained to obey. Several texts in Proverbs summarize parental responsibility and the natural results of proper training and discipline:

> *He who spares his rod hates his son, but he who loves him disciplines him diligently. (13:24)*

> *Discipline your son while there is hope, and do not desire his death. (19:18)*

Do not hold back discipline from the child, although you beat him with the rod, he will not die. (23:13)

Correct your son, and he will give you comfort; he will also delight your soul. (29:17)

As we have seen, children come into the world with a sin nature and a natural bent toward evil. They are totally self-centered individuals. No child grows up to be obedient if left alone. Obedience must be taught. But how long are children under the authority of the parents? MacArthur writes,

> So God's basic design is for children to be obedient to their parents. If your children are still living at home, whether they are in elementary, junior high, high school, or college, they are still under responsibility to obey you. And it is your responsibility as parents to teach your children to be obedient. Why? . . . Children do not normally come into the world ready to obey. They arrive fully bent toward disobedience! You don't have to describe disobedience to them. Children are disobedient because they inherited a sin nature like yours. The only way they will learn obedience is to be taught it.[35]

Honoring Father and Mother

The second command given in Paul's instruction to the child is a quote from the fifth commandment given to the children of Israel (Exod. 20:12). MacArthur comments,

> Notice that this is the only statement in the Ten Commandments relative to how the family is to function. Why? Because given the first four [commands] it is sufficient in addition to produce right relationships in the home and in society. This is the key to everything, since a person who grows up with a pattern of obedience and discipline, and a sense of reverence, awe, and respect for his parents will be a person who can make any human relationship work on any other level. And his life will flourish.[36]

The Greek word translated "honor" is *tima* from the verb *timaō*. The previous command, to obey, dealt with what a child's *response* should be toward his parents; this command deals with the child's *attitude* toward the parents. This Greek word has two shades of meaning. The word primarily means "to count as valuable, honor, or revere," but it can also have the sense of money or payment (cf. 1 Tim. 5:17). Jesus indicates that honoring one's parents carries with it a financial commitment to care for them also. MacArthur writes,

So the Old Testament law of honoring one's parents meant that so long as a person lived he was to respect and support his parents. Let's face it, during the first half of our lives our parents give everything they have to supply their children's needs. The other side of the coin is that when they are no longer able to meet their own needs, it becomes their children's responsibility to take care of them. Do you see the overlapping of generations. The cycle never ends. It is God's way of producing families that stick together and pass along the inheritance of an unselfish love.[37]

The responsibility of an adult child to financially care for his parents is also brought out strongly in Paul's discussion of the care for widows in his first letter to Timothy (5:4). Paul has strong words for the child that does not provide for his parents: "If anyone does not provide for his own, and especially for those of his household, he has denied the faith, and is worse than an unbeliever" (1 Tim. 6:8).

The Promise of Blessing

Paul reminds us in Ephesians 6:2–3 that there is a specific blessing promised to those who honor their father and mother. What does this mean to the child that honors his father and mother? MacArthur writes that obedient, honoring children "will have a full and rich life here on earth, and live with God in His Kingdom and for eternity in the new heavens and the new earth. In every possible way that promise will be fulfilled!"[38]

The bottom line is that those children who honor their parents throughout their lives, even by caring for their parents in their old age, will be honored by God in the quality and longevity of their own lives.

CONCLUSION

What is the outlook of the family in the twenty-first century? The answer to this question will depend heavily on how much society chooses to return the biblical pattern given above for the family. At this point, what will occur is anyone's guess. Joyce Brothers, in some 1980s predictions for 1990s America, noted that "Holding down a job, raising a family, and being Betty Crocker and Playmate of the Month isn't all it's cracked up to be." She predicted that there would be more emphasis on romance, courtship, and marriage. Women would demand that their husbands support the family, and they would return to traditional wife and mother roles. Brothers called this the "She Generation."[39]

Although by all appearance, Dr. Brothers's prophecy was not fulfilled on a grand scale, there does seem to have been some shift of the working woman back to the home, and a recommitment to the "traditional" family, at least in that arena.

But these trends are really superficial. Unless there is a return to a theistic worldview, the future for the family will be bleak (see Dave Noebel's chapter in this volume, "The Worldviews of Destruction in the Twentieth Century"). Secular humanism, based on Darwinian evolution is the dominate national worldview, and as a result, there is no impetus to return to the pattern set forth in—according to the thinking of a majority at least—a book of myths.

CHAPTER 28

The Nightmare of Abortion

Renald E. Showers

Abortion is one of the most controversial issues to confront the world during the last quarter of the twentieth century. The very mention of the word generates strong emotions. The issue has polarized parts of European and all of North American society into vocal opposing camps. Pro-life people claim that abortion destroys a complete human life and therefore is morally wrong. Pro-abortionists assert that abortion simply destroys impersonal tissue and therefore is not morally wrong. Other people take an agnostic approach by declaring that they do not know which view is correct.

The conflicting assertions of the pro-life people and pro-abortionists indicate that the key to the abortion issue is the point at which the human fetus is a complete human being (that is, at what point it is a person possessing a human soul).

Medical science has shed considerable light on this crucial question through its significant research concerning the development of the human fetus. However, in addition to this medical information man should give attention to divine revelation. God created man and the Scriptures teach that conception ultimately is controlled by God and is a gift of God (Gen. 16:2; 29:31; 30:22–23; Ruth 4:13). In addition, Psalm 139:13–16 praises God for superintending development of the human fetus within the womb. God is the ultimate authority about when the fetus is a complete human being who possesses a soul.

God has given divine revelation concerning this matter in the Scriptures. Two factors in the Bible bear significantly upon the issue of when the fetus is a complete human being. The first is the fact that man is created in the image of God. The second is the origin of the human soul.

IN THE IMAGE OF GOD

The Scriptures state six times that man was created in the image or likeness of God (Gen. 1:26, 27; 5:1; 9:6; 1 Cor. 11:7; James 3:9). The fact that four of these six statements are in the first book of the Bible emphasizes this truth from the very beginning. Human creation in the image of God has considerable significance.

Creation in the image of God does not mean that we are physically like God. Jesus declared that God is a Spirit (John 4:24) and that a spirit does not have flesh and bones (Luke 24:39). Thus, it is not the nature of deity to have a physical body. Since God has no physical body, the image of God cannot refer to the physical aspect of being.

The fact that man is made in the image of God means that each person is created to be a personal and moral being. The divine Trinity of Father, Son, and Holy Spirit possesses intellect, emotions, and will. In addition they possess a perfect sense of morality. When God created man, He created an intellectual, emotional, and free moral being. A sense of right and wrong makes us responsible for our conduct (Rom. 2:14–16; 13:1–7). It is in the personal and moral sense that man bears a resemblance to God.

God's creation of humanity in His image is significant for several reasons. First, it places us at the highest form of God's earthly creation. The fact that man is created in the image of God, but animals and plants are not, places human beings in a different category from either animals or plants. Human life is distinct from any other earthly life-forms. Man is a personal moral being; animals and plants are not.

As a personal moral being, man is superior to all other forms of life in God's earthly creation. In the personal realm for example, human intellect is able to communicate ideas by arranging words in logical thought. In the moral realm God has revealed moral standards to humans alone. Only people can use mathematics, compose music, paint pictures, or design and build airplanes and computers. Only human beings understand what it means to lie, steal, or abuse sexuality.

Second, man's creation in the image of God provides the basis for dominion over the earth. Genesis 1:26–27 shows that God gave to human beings the cultural mandate in the context of being His image bearer. Ruling authority was given over all other living things and over the earth itself. God intended Adam to be His representative, administering His rule on His behalf over the earthly province of His universal kingdom. To know how to administer that rule, it was necessary that humans be personal beings with whom God could communicate. To administer that rule in an ethical manner, the representatives had to be morally responsible. The fact that God gave dominion over all other living things on the basis of his image indicates again that God regarded these beings as distinct from, and superior to, all other earthly forms of life.

Third, creation in the image of God is the basis for capital punishment of murderers. God ordained capital punishment for murderers of human life: "And surely your blood of your lives will I require; at the hand of every beast will I require it, and at the hand of man; at the hand of every man's brother will I require the life of man. Whoso sheddeth man's blood, by man shall his blood be shed; for in the image of God made he man" (Gen. 9:5-6).[1]

The reason God instituted capital punishment of murderers of human life was that "in the image of God made he man." The person who murders another person is thereby striking the image of God in that other person. He is putting to death a personal moral being. God regards this as a very serious offense. Although God ruled that in some instances an animal should be destroyed for killing a human being, at no point did he ordain capital punishment for killing an animal. God regards man as different from and superior to all other earthly life forms

Fourth, creation in the image of God is significant because it provides the basis for human government as a tool for exercising dominion over the earth. Scripture teaches that when government uses the sword to exercise capital punishment, it is functioning as the minister of God (Rom. 13:4). It can therefore be concluded that human government is also based on the image of God. Government has the God-given task of protecting the lives and property of image bearers from harm (Rom. 13:1-7). Executive, legislative, and judicial governmental structures, political elections of officials, and decisions about use of the earth's resources are all governmental functions unique to the human realm on earth. Human government is far from perfect in its existing form, but its function in contrast to what exists in the animal realm indicates superiority.

Fifth, the image of God provides the basis for social conduct. James 3:9 relates that we should be careful in our conduct regarding other human beings, since they are made in the similitude or image of God. By contrast, nowhere do the Scriptures declare that a person should be careful about what he says concerning animals or plants.

All of these five points are true because of a person's unique image bearing relationship to God. Also, the image of God does not refer to physical aspects of being, but rather to personal and moral aspects. Since the personal and moral aspects of being relate to the realm of the soul, we can conclude that the image of God relates to the soul. God's statement in Genesis 9:5-6 that it is wrong to murder a human being because God made man in His image affirms that it is wrong to murder a human being because of the presence of the soul in that person.

In light of that fact, the *real* issue related to abortion is the point at which the human fetus has a soul.

THE ORIGIN OF THE HUMAN SOUL

Two facts bear upon the issue of when the fetus possesses a human soul. The first fact is that man is created in the image of God. The second is the origin of the human soul.

In light of the fact that it is wrong to murder a human being because of the presence of the human soul, if the soul is present from the moment of conception, then the fetus is always a complete human, and abortion at any time is murder. By contrast, if the soul is not present until some time after conception, then the fetus is not a complete being until that point, and abortion before that point does not involve the taking of a complete life.

At what point does the fetus possess a human soul? The answer to this question is dependent upon the answer to another question: What is the origin of each soul? Historically there have been at least three major views concerning the origin of individual souls.

The Preexistence Theory

The *preexistence theory* asserts that a community of bodiless souls exists somewhere. Some proponents of this theory believe that these bodiless souls have existed eternally. Other advocates claim that these souls were all created at one time. Still others propose that originally souls are not distinct from each other, but are all part of one universal world soul.

Proponents of the preexistence theory claim that a soul leaves the community of bodiless souls and enters a body, either at the time of conception or at birth. The preexistence concept is a pagan theory. It is advocated by Hinduism and other Eastern mystical philosophies and religions, by proponents of reincarnation, and by some secular philosophers and psychologists.

The preexistence theory must be rejected by those who hold to the authority of God's biblical revelation. It has no biblical support; in fact it is contrary to the Bible's anthropology, which states that all human beings sinned in Adam. According to Romans 5:12-19, sin entered the world through the first man's sin; physical death came to all as a result of that original sin. All people are condemned to die, not because of individual acts of sin they commit after birth, but because all people were represented by the first man in his rebellion. In Romans 5:12, the active voice of the verb *sinned* in the expression "for all have sinned" teaches that all of Adam's descendants participated in his original sin. First Corinthians 15:21-22 declares that death came by man, so that all human beings die "in Adam."

Although sin brings death upon the body, it is related primarily to the soul. It was in the realm of his soul, where his mind and will resided and functioned, that Adam decided to sin against God. All decisions to sin are made in the realm of the soul, because decisions are functions of the mind and will and the mind and will are aspects of the soul.

Since sin is related primarily to the soul, the only way that all people could have sinned in Adam is if their souls are related to or derived from Adam. If, as the preexistence theory asserts, individual souls exist before conception, then they are not related to Adam.

The Creation Theory

Proponents of the *creation theory* believe that each body is procreated by parents, but each soul is created directly and individually by God and embodied into the fetus at some point between conception and birth. The creation and embodiment of each soul would take place at the same time. Each body is derived ultimately from Adam through parents, but the same is not true of the soul. The creation theory of the soul is considerably better than the preexistence theory. It has been proposed by several secular philosophers and advocated by many Christians.

The creation theory has several problems, however. First, it does not explain the biblical teaching that all people sinned in Adam. Since sin is related primarily to the realm of the soul, how could all people have participated in Adam's original sin if each of their souls was created directly and individually by God sometime after that original sin?

Second, the creation theory does not explain the sinful nature of all people from the time of conception on. The Scriptures teach that all are sinful by nature and that all have sinned against the holy God (Rom. 3:9–19, 23; 5:19; Eph. 2:1–3). Each person is in this state of sin from conception (Ps. 51:5). Since sin is related primarily to the realm of the soul, the fact that all people are soul by nature from the time of conception indicates that each soul is in a state of sin from the time of its being. How can the creation theory explain the fact that each soul is in a state of sin from the time of its beginning if, as that theory asserts, God creates each soul individually and directly? Does the holy God create sinful souls? No, the source of human sinfulness is man, not God.

Third, the creation theory finds it difficult to explain the fact that children inherit qualities of intellect and character from parents. If God creates each soul directly and individually, why do children often resemble their parents in qualities that belong to the realm of the soul, not to the realm of the body?

The Traducian Theory

The *traducian theory* is that each soul is procreated by parents. The individual soul is brought into existence at the time of conception through the union of the male sperm with the female egg. Thus, entire persons, not just bodies, are propagated by parents. This theory has also been advocated by many Christians.

Certain Scripture passages strongly imply this theory. Genesis 46:26 states,

"All the souls that came with Jacob into Egypt, which came out of his loins, . . . were threescore and six." The Hebrew word translated "souls" in this passage is the same word used in Genesis 35:18 and 1 Kings 17:21–22 for the immaterial aspect of a human being that depart from the physical body at death. Thus, the statement in Genesis 46:26 that sixty-six souls came out of Jacob's loins indicates that it was more than physical bodies that came out of Jacob's loins. The implication is that Jacob played a significant role in procreating total people—souls and bodies. Therefore, souls are procreated by parents.

Hebrews 7 says that in some sense Levi, the great-grandson of Abraham, paid tithes to Melchizedek "in Abraham" when Abraham paid those tithes to Melchizedek, even though Abraham paid the tithes years before Levi was conceived. How could Levi have participated in this action of his ancestor before he was conceived? Hebrews 7:9–10 provides the answer: "For he was yet in the loins of his father, when Melchizedek met him." Like many other languages, ancient Hebrew used the term *father* to apply to any male ancestor. This implies that Levi was present in seminal form in Abraham's loins, and, therefore, there was a seminal participation by Levi in Abraham's act of paying the tithes.

Two things imply that more than an impersonal body was present in seminal form in Abraham's loins. First, how could an impersonal body perform the act of paying tithes? Second, the passage indicates that it was Levi, a person, not just Levi's body, who was present in seminal form in his ancestor's loins. The implication of Hebrews 7:10 is that souls as well as bodies are passed on in seminal form from generation to generation through ancestral lines until procreated by parents at the moment of conception.

A second line of evidence for the traducian theory is that it comfortably fits the biblical teaching that all people sinned in Adam (Rom. 5:12–19; 1 Cor. 15:21–22). Since sin is related primarily to the realm of the soul, all people could have sinned in Adam if their souls are related to or derived from him. According to the traducian theory, each soul is related to Adam in the same way that Levi's soul was related to Abraham. Just as Levi's soul was present in seminal form in Abraham's loins when Abraham paid tithes, so every soul procreated was present in seminal form in Adam's loins when he sinned his original sin. Thus, just as there was a seminal participation by Levi in Abraham's act of paying tithes, so there was a seminal participation by all people procreated in Adam's original sin. In this way, all souls are related to or derived from Adam.

The third line of evidence for the traducian theory is that it comfortably fits the biblical teaching that all people have a sin nature from the moment of conception. In Psalm 51:5 David declared, "Behold, I was shaped in iniquity, and in sin did my mother conceive me." Two significant things should be noted about David's statement. According to Franz Delitzsch, an Old Testament scholar, the meaning of David's statement is that "his parents were sinful human beings, and that this sinful state (*habitus*) has operated upon his birth and even his conception, and from this point has passed over to him."[2] Each person inherits a sinful state with a sin nature from parents through procreation at the moment of conception. If sin is related primarily to the realm of the soul, and each person inherits his sinful state from his parents through procreation at the moment of conception, then each person derives his soul from parents through procreation at the moment of conception. This conclusion agrees with the traducian theory.

Also, in Psalm 51:5 David used the personal pronoun me when referring to his conception within his mother. He thereby indicated that his mother conceived a total person, including a soul. This indication of the procreation of the soul by parents substantiates the traducian theory.

IMPLICATIONS FOR ABORTION

God created man in the beginning, and He, therefore, is the ultimate authority and source of knowledge concerning when the fetus is a complete being possessing a soul; He has revealed in the Scriptures that each soul is procreated by parents at the moment of conception. It can be concluded, therefore, that the fetus is a complete person with a soul from the moment of conception. The fetus does not become a complete person at some time after conception. Thus, divine revelation does answer the *real* issue related to abortion.

Since the fetus is a complete person possessing a soul from conception, abortion at any point involves the destruction of a complete life. From God's perspective, the deliberate killing of a complete life after conception is the same as a deliberate killing after birth; it is the same act of murder. It strikes at the image of God, and is a very serious offense (Gen. 9:5–6).

Christians must understand that God has authoritatively revealed his opposition to abortion, so they have no option but to oppose abortion. Society has given itself over to abortion rights for two reasons. First, there has been a persistent erosion of biblical authority. Abortion is a tragic consequence of that rejection. In Romans 1:18–32 God reveals that when the ungodly willfully reject divine revelation, abuse of human life, including murder, results. The second, ultimate reason society has legalized abortion is an inherent spirit of rebellion against God and His rule. In Romans 8:7 God revealed that unsaved man has a self-centered mind-set that makes him hostile toward God. Rebels refuse to submit, thinking that life exists for their own benefit, happiness, convenience, and pleasure. Outside Christ, each person wants to reject God's moral absolutes, ways, and authority. Abortion is a symptom of this sinful disease of rebellion.

At the very least, since God is opposed to abortion, Christians should not practice, condone, or encourage it. Instead, they should communicate their opposition through whatever legitimate, peaceful means are available. This opposition ranges from speaking out on governing laws and policies to supporting qualified alternative agencies that meet the needs of those who feel pressure to have an abortion.

Violence or threats are not legitimate. Jesus never advocated or condoned the use of violence or threats by His followers to do His work. And from a practical standpoint, the only effective way to eliminate a symptom is to cure the disease causing that symptom. Abortion is a symptom of the disease of rebellion against God and His authority. The only effective way to stop abortion is to cure its ultimate cause. The only cure for the disease that causes abortion is the spiritual salvation through faith in Jesus Christ of those who practice and favor abortion. The most effective way to combat abortion is to invest time, resources, and energies in reaching the unsaved with the gospel of Jesus Christ.

Whatever a sinner's past participation in abortion, salvation is readily available. Jesus Christ died for all the sins of all people (for example, 1 Cor. 15:1–4; Gal. 1:4; 1 Peter 2:24; 3:18; 1 John 2:2; 3:5; 4:10), so people can be delivered from their guilt by trusting Him to save them (John 3:16; Acts 16:30–31; Eph. 2:8–9).

If the Lord tarries, the prayer of believers should be that abortion should end. If it does not, the numbers of aborted children in the next generation will be astronomical, ripening the world for terrifying judgment.

This chapter adapted from a two-part article, Renald E. Showers, "Abortion" *Friends of Israel Magazine*, June–July 1990 and August–September 1990. Used by permission.

CHAPTER 29

Church and State in America: What Does the Future Hold?

H. Wayne House

The community of faith and the institution of government have shared an uneven relationship over the last two thousand years. This is particularly true among Christians and governments in the West. Before the rise of the Christian church, the state and religion were wed—in Rome this went so far as emperor worship. But after Christianity became a major influence, this association of religion and state became complicated. The Roman Church remained ever ready to wield both spiritual and secular swords. The Reformers unveiled new ideas of political theology. They tended to see church and state operating in divergent spheres, each with their own God-given mandate.

The two-kingdoms doctrine of the Reformation introduced new ground rules for the institution of the church and the institution of the state. As this political theology found fertile soil in the Unites States in the eighteenth century, a working agreement was forged between church and state that seemed to be the fulfillment of Christ's teaching on separate jurisdictions of God and Caesar.

THE EXAMPLE OF THE UNITED STATES

In early America it seemed that the various religious communities had discovered the promised land. Many of these groups had left religious persecution in Europe for the new Israel. Now the Christian immigrants, predominantly Puritans, considered themselves to be establishing a "City on a hill."

At the time there was little ethnic or religious diversity. Such is no longer the case. With vast diversity has come confusion regarding the nature of Christianity and the civil government. In the words of Justice Joseph Story,

Probably, at the time of the adoption of the Constitution, and of the amendment to it, now under consideration, the general, if not the universal, sentiment in America was, that Christianity ought to receive encouragement from the State, so far as such encouragement was not incompatible with the private rights of conscience, and the freedom of religious worship. An attempt to level all religions, and to make it a matter of state policy to hold all in utter indifference, would have created universal disapprobation, if not universal indignation.[1]

In a predominantly Christian populace the concern was that government act evenhandedly toward the various denominations. According to Justice Story,

The real object of the First Amendment was not to countenance, much less to advance, Mahometanism, or Judaism, or infidelity, by prostrating Christianity; but to exclude all rivalry among Christian sects, and to prevent any national ecclesiastical establishment which should give to a hierarchy the exclusive patronage of the national government. It thus cuts off the menace of religious persecution (the vice and pest of former ages), and of the subversion of the rights of conscience in matters of religion which had been trampled upon almost from the days of the Apostles to the present age.[2]

At the Constitutional Convention in 1787 there was no question about which worldview guided culture and the law. In the late twentieth century the issue involves vastly different worldviews. To what extent can they be accommodated, while retaining some shared heritage with the forefathers' perspective on law and freedom? The problem became obvious after a series of Supreme Court decisions in the second half of the twentieth century disestablished the Christian religion from any influence in the public sphere.

Even after judicial efforts to sanitize the public sphere of religious influence, the U.S. churches retained considerable presence. Even in public life there remained a civil religion. Religion had so pervaded American life and the public square, that the best efforts could not stamp it out. Many terms and practices reflect the Christian heritage. This ranged from sayings ("Thank God its Friday!") to such holidays as Christmas, Easter, and even Halloween (All Saints' Eve). St. Paul and Corpus Christi retained their ecclesiastical names. Religious themes still dominated music and visual arts.

So pervasive was religion on so many facets of private and public life, that one would think church and state could find some common ground. Instead they engaged in a shooting war, with secularists fighting to raise higher Thomas Jefferson's "wall of separation." Even jurists, who should have known better, proclaimed the impractical dogma that law can and must operate in a religionless vacuum. Their task was to create a safe zone, so that all checked at the door their personal worldviews and value systems when dealing with the law. Few over the first two centuries of the republic would have shared this perspective. Even those inimical to faith knew that government does not exist apart from worldview. Perfect valuelessness was certainly not the reality encountered in the academy, the courts, or the marketplace.

Assault on Christian Values

Any attempts of religious citizens, particularly Christians, to be heard in the political and legal processes were perceived as an attack on the "establishment clause" of the First Amendment to the Constitution. The argument that Christians also had rights of expression in the free exercise of religion carried little weight. In the jurisprudence of the postmodern courts, the establishment clause is absolute. It always trumps the free exercise clause, which is more narrow as to conduct, though not belief.[3]

The judicial rebuff of efforts to have one's deepest convictions heard in the culture or marketplace of ideas would have been unheard of in former days. The court has come to believe that religious views, apart from clearly stated secular purposes, necessarily violate the establishment clause. And federal courts have come to believe that they have the responsibility to keep religion from every corner of public life. Once federal government was far more limited in jurisdiction. The states, before the incorporation doctrine, had the freedom to make decisions relating to religious liberties at the behest of their citizenry. States provided a more open forum for political debate and were more truly pluralistic in fairly treating all religions within their borders.[4]

With incorporation this is no longer the case, and uniformity rather than diversity is enforced on all.[5] With the ever enlarging growth of government at all levels, the area of the public has increased so that religious expression finds fewer and fewer places in which persons can express their views without inviting charges of violation of "separation of church and state."[6]

Marginalized in the Public Square

Christianity has come on hard times in America, in contrast to its pervasive influence on law and culture for most of the country's first two centuries. Judge Robert Bork says that there is even a fear of Christian morality in the public square:

It thus appears, at least for society as a whole, that the major and perhaps only alternative to "intellectual and moral relativism and/or nihilism" is religious faith. That conclusion will make many Americans nervous or hostile. While most people claim to be religious, most are also not comfortable with those whose faith is strong enough to affect their public behavior.[7]

But if religious meaning is divorced from the public arena, this does not mean that the square will be empty. Rather, other ideologies will vie for prominence, ideologies that may escape scrutiny by judges who are looking for "holy books" instead of worldviews in defining religion.

Though separatists in the media or the courts desire to limit the influence of religion, particularly in public schools, they are not so fastidious about other ideologies. So hostile has this debate grown that the free exercise clause has been turned on its head. The concern is "freedom from religion" rather than "freedom of religion." It is significant that some of the most influential twentieth century jurists have candidly stated their opposition to religious influence. Felix Frankfurter described religious freedom as "freedom from conformity to religious dogma." Justice Harry Blackmun describes the establishment clause as protecting secular (not religious) liberty. We have come far from the view of those founders who understood religious freedom as willing obedience to the sovereignty of God.[8]

Why should Christian values have more moral authority than any other system? The obvious answer is that American law, society, and culture are built upon a Christian base, and it has served the country well. To change the moral foundation of the nation may undermine the liberty that such a foundation provided. Some have argued that the intention of the framers was to create a "godless constitution" to minimize the influence of Christianity in the formation of the new government.[9] Most evidence is to the contrary, as Presser explains:

> Indeed, the commonplace view until very recently that the United States was a "Christian Nation" was repeatedly acknowledged by the United States Supreme Court and on countless public occasions by spokesmen for a myriad of political views. For most of our history, then, most of our leaders appeared not to have believed in a Godless constitution at all.[10]

One can support a broad understanding of religious freedom in today's pluralistic society, yet still see that it is flawed thinking that the Constitution does not have a particular religious worldview. The framers inherited perspectives from both the Enlightenment, especially the thinking of John Locke, and the Bible and Western Christianity. The Constitution looks to the Declaration of Independence and to a broad, non-sectarian view of the nature of God and reality.

Pre-*Everson* America

Some would deny any reliance of U.S. law and government on Christian principles, but this position is hard to sustain. It is not the intent of this chapter to catalog the data regarding the Christian influences on Western law, but a few examples will illustrate how this influence played out in Europe, England, and all of North America.

Jean-Jacques Rousseau was surely correct to write that "no state was ever founded without having religion as its basis."[11] For example, Greek religion was connected to the religious preferences of the city-state—as Socrates fatally discovered.[12] In Rome religion was identified with the state, especially the state cult. The state religion, with occasional tributes to the gods of Greece and Rome, was primarily dedicated to the genius of the emperor who embodied the divine Rome.[13]

The connection of religion with the state is also true with the Roman world of the fourth century on. With the triumph of Christianity in the Roman empire the tie of this new faith to Roman law seemed natural. Christianity already had a natural affinity to law in view of the Old Testament so that, as Walter Ullmann has said regarding Roman law, "the law, could, as indeed it did, effortless penetrate into the very matrix of the rapidly growing Christian doctrinal body."[14]

The union of Roman law with Christianity began after the time of Constantine, and in approximately 534 the Emperor Justinian had the Roman laws compiled, edited, and wedded to Christianity. After the fall of the West to the barbarian hordes was complete, Roman law and Christian theology were adopted by the barbarians, though not systematized. In about 1100 the first modern law school was founded in Bologna in northern Italy. Thousands of students from all over Europe came to this school to study law as a "distinct and coherent body of knowledge," and the Justinian Code and Christianized Roman laws, were the basis for instruction. Western Europe's civil code looked mostly to these beginnings.

At least four major influences directly shaped American law. A fifth, European legal history, also brought an organizational structure to the development. These four are (1) the conservative enlightenment as manifested in John Locke, (2) the common law of England, (3) the influence of the Bible, and (4) Protestant Reformation views of law and government.[15]

Christianity was embedded in the common law,[16] provided the philosophy behind criminal law and punishment,[17] and was at the root of tort law.[18]

The Influence of John Locke

John Locke is generally considered to be a major influence on the leaders of the American Revolution. Regarding law and government, Locke believed that the "law of nature" had its source and authority in the Creator:

Thus the Law of Nature stands as an Eternal Rule to all Men, Legislators as well as others. The Rules that they make for other Men's Actions, be conformable to the Law of Nature, i.e., to the Will of God, of which that is a Declaration, and the fundamental Law of Nature being preservation of Mankind, no Human Sanction can be good, or valid against it.[19]

The Common-Law Tradition

When William of Normandy conquered England in 1066 he found a nation already rich in culture, including a basic legal system, far in advance of Normandy's. Common law emerged in the twelfth century from institutions that had been in place prior to 1066. The laws of the English, combined with Norman administration ability, eventually developed into the court systems that dispensed judge-made law, called common law.[20]

"While the Roman law was a deathbed convert to Christianity, the common law was a cradle Christian,"[21] wrote John C. H. Wu. Wu, an international statesman, jurist, and law professor, traced English common law from Henry de Bracton (d 1268) to William Blackstone (1723–1780). As indebted as the common law is to men such as the systematizer Bracton and the jurist Edward Coke (1552–1634), no person had as much influence on the framers of the American Declaration of Independence and the U.S. Constitution than did Blackstone.

Blackstone, Professor of Common Law, and Christian

Probably no person, other than Montesquieu, had as much influence on the framers of the U.S. Constitution than did Blackstone. Locke was the man read and discussed during the period leading up to the Declaration, but Blackstone is quoted more than two and one-half times as often as Locke in the period surrounding the drafting of the Constitution. This is probably because of his masterful discussions of governmental process, operation, and interaction among institutions.[22]

Often it is thought that the radical Enlightenment philosophers, such as Voltaire, Diderot, and Helvetius, wielded the most influence on those who worked on the document. In fact the American Revolution was a conservative insurrection, which owed more to Locke for the formation of the new government and such men as Montesquieu and Blackstone for its structure.[23]

Key statements of the Declaration of Independence reflect Blackstonian thought. The phrase "laws of nature and of nature's God" in the opening paragraph particularly reminds one of Blackstone's emphasis on this two-fold view of law. Blackstone believed nature is governed by God-established laws that reflect his will and are superior to any contrary human law.[24]

Many American students returning from England brought Blackstone with them. So popular did he become that one thousand copies of *Commentaries* were sold at ten pounds a set before the first American edition was printed. Prepublication sales for the first American edition were 1500. Blackstone's *Commentaries* became the chief (or only) law book, in law offices throughout New England. Daniel Webster read Blackstone before beginning the study of law in 1804. Law professor James Kent, wanted to become a lawyer after reading Blackstone at age sixteen. In 1835 Abraham Lincoln came into possession of the *Commentaries* and read them intently.[25]

Christianity and the Documents

Scholars have long recognized the influence of the Bible and the Christian religion on the development of Western law, but many have rejected any claims to their direct influence on the American Declaration of Independence and the Constitution of the United States. It is thought that the Declaration was written from purely an Enlightenment perspective, relying on natural law, and that the Constitution is intentionally secular, to avoid the religious divisions that had occurred in other lands.[26]

The Declaration of Independence is unarguably theistic, whatever its connections to Christian thought. This alone lays a theistic base for the Constitution, since historians argue cogently that the Declaration may be understood as the preamble to the Constitution. Donald Lutz summarizes this view:

> After approving the Declaration, the Continental Congress turned to writing a national constitution. The Articles of Confederation that resulted proved defective in important respects. As a result, the new Constitution of 1787 replaced the Articles. The Declaration, however, continued to stand as the preface to the American national compact. The Constitution begins, 'We the people of the United States, in order to create a more perfect union . . . .' The people already exist, and exist in a political union. This can be only if there is a first part to a compact of which the Constitution is the second part. There is no document that can be pointed to as fulfilling such a role other than the Declaration of Independence. To say that we live under a national compact of which the Declaration is the first part may sound a bit strange at first, but it would be stranger still to have begun our national bicentennial in 1976 if the Declaration of Independence was not part of our national founding.[27]

The Constitution also reflects a Christian worldview. The Constitution is, first of all, a document intended to give structure to the government begun by the Declaration. The primary force of that structure was to set limits on the power of national government in deference to state governments.

It is not a theological document, nor is it an anti-Christian document. One would be surprised to find in the Constitution the terminology found in the Declaration.[28]

However, there are internal signs of the influence of Christian ideas and practices. These include prohibiting at the national level the practice of religious tests, so as not to intrude upon such tests within state laws.[29] Also, oaths in the eighteenth century were regarded as solemn statements before the Supreme Being. Michael McConnell observes that these two elements— no religious tests and the affirmation exception to the taking of oaths— "reflect a spirit and purpose similar to that of the (First Amendment's) free exercise clause."[30] Another minor implicit indication of the framers concession of Christianity is provision for a Sunday exception in the signing of legislation.[31]

The Two Kingdoms

The doctrine of the two kingdoms is first seen in the history of the kingdom of Israel. Although Old Testament Israel is commonly thought of as having been a theocracy, in practice it was more like a constitutional monarchy than a people under the direct rule of God. The king himself was subservient to Yahweh and to the covenant Yahweh made with Israel (Exodus 19). The king was strictly a secular governor, who entered into the cultus functions of worship on the same basis as every subject. This differs from the normal practice of the ancient world, in which church and state were indistinguishable. Rulers had special prerogatives and responsibilities in leading worship. Israel's first king, Saul, ran afoul of this difference when he usurped the role of Samuel, the prophet-priest of Yahweh, to offer sacrifices at Gilgal before going into battle. Knowing the practices within "king cults" of other nations, Saul saw no problem with his action, yet it was one of the sins for which Yahweh cut off Saul and his line from the kingship (1 Sam. 13).

When King Uzziah attempted to burn incense at the altar of God, Yahweh inflicted him with leprosy which remained with him the rest of his life (2 Chron. 26:16–21). One might say that Yahweh erected a wall of separation between the religious cultus of Israel and the state, though it was never intended to separate Yahweh from the state.

Jesus assumed the doctrine of separate kingdoms when he was approached by certain Jewish leaders regarding whether one should pay taxes to Caesar (Luke 20:22). He said, "Render to Caesar the things that are Caesar's and to God the things that are God's" (Luke 20:25). Jesus thereby acknowledged that the state had legitimacy and jurisdiction, though all things belong to God.

The other major New Testament presentation of the two kingdoms is found in Romans 13:1-4, though the emphasis there is on "the kingdom of the left," to use Luther's designation. The power of the state is by divine design. Christians were to obey the civil ruler, at Paul's time the emperor Nero, though this obedience was not absolute. This separation of kingdoms was in Peter's view when he recognized the Christian's duty to government and God, with the latter taking preeminence (Acts 4:19).[32]

Such texts set forth the view that the state has God-ordained legitimacy, but that authority is limited in scope to those areas instituted by God and separate from the duties imposed by God on the religious community and the religious individual.

Though Christians have generally held to a two-kingdom doctrine, there has been disagreement as to how this doctrine should be understood, and the respective jurisdictions of church and state.

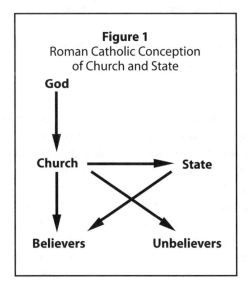

Figure 1
Roman Catholic Conception of Church and State

The Roman Catholic View

Roman Catholic theologians have generally differentiated between what Luther called the "two kingdoms," but they have been quick to qualify that by making the church's role preeminent, with the state subject to it. One framer of the Catholic understanding, Augustine, argued for the superiority of the church since it is eternal and the state temporal, and because the church must answer to God for the conduct of the state. The two kingdoms, or two swords, perspective was given by Pope Boniface VII in his papal bull, *Unam Sanctum,* in 1302.[33]

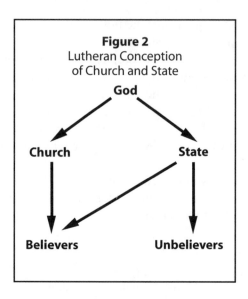

Figure 2
Lutheran Conception
of Church and State

The Lutheran View

In contrast to the Roman Catholic view, Luther believed neither church nor state to be superior. Both are established by God, but for different purposes. The state restrains evil. Believers belong to both church and the state, and have responsibilities to each. Believers relate to the first kingdom, the church, by faith, and to the second kingdom, the state, by reason.[34]

Unlike Calvin, Luther did not believe that Christians had the right to use the state to promote Christianity. Christians in government should use Christian principles inasmuch as the principles could also be justified by reason. A prudent though evil ruler is to be preferred to an imprudent virtuous ruler, since the latter may bring ruin while the former may at least resist evil.

The Calvinist View

Both Luther and Calvin believed that the state's authority came from God directly, and so it was not mediated by the church. Calvin accepted the legitimate separations of these spheres:

> For the Church has no power of the sword to punish or coerce, no authority to compel, no prisons, fines, or other punishments like those inflicted by civil magistrates. Besides, the object of this power is not that he who has transgressed may be punished against his will, *but that he may profess his repentance by a voluntary submission to chastisement.*[35]

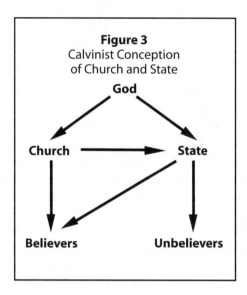

Figure 3
Calvinist Conception
of Church and State

Though Calvin had no difficulty with the government maintaining the official public church, he believed in limiting government's activity in reference to religion. This differentiation of separate jurisdictions for the church and the state is strikingly similar to the philosophy found in the First Amendment establishment clause. Calvin said,

> Nor let anyone think it strange that I now refer to human polity the change of the due maintenance of religion which I may appear to have placed beyond the jurisdiction of men. *For I do not allow men to make laws respecting religion and the worship of God* now, any more than I did before: though I approve of civil government which provides that the true religion which is contained in the law of God be not violated, and polluted by public blasphemies with impunity.[36]

It may very well be that Calvin's words "laws respecting religion" were picked up by the framers, since his writings were ever present among the predominantly Calvinist colonists. These colonists also sought to extend "freedom of conscience," believing that every person should worship God "according to his own conscience."

This view of Calvin had already found a firm footing in England. King James II saw a need for toleration of religious sects, as shown in his letter to Thomas Dongan in 1682, in which he used the phrase, "free exercise" of religion:[37]

> You shall permit all persons of what religion soever quietly to inhabit within your government without giving them any disturbance or disquiet

whatsoever for or by reasons of their differing opinions in matters of Religion, provided they give no disturbance to ye public peace, nor do molest or disquiet others in ye *free Exercise* of their Religion.

Though the doctrine of two kingdoms was held differently by various Christian traditions, the impact of the two kingdoms was ideally suited to the federal form of government inaugurated in the U.S. The founders desired a state limited in power that could not meddle in the institutional church. They did not want a "Church of New England." Unfortunately, the relationship between church and state, and between religious values and beliefs and the state became more complicated during the twentieth century.

ESTABLISHMENT CLAUSE CONFUSION

There is unprecedented confusion in the U.S. courts today regarding the interpretation and application of the religion clauses of the First Amendment to the Constitution. The First Amendment seems straightforward but has engendered considerable debate. The amendment reads simply, "Congress shall make no law respecting an establishment of religion, or prohibiting the free exercise thereof."

Until the *Everson* decision of 1947, the courts gave little consideration to the establishment prong and instead dealt with certain free exercise claims of minority religious groups that had arisen on American soil. The general view of the courts was that the first part of the amendment forbid Congress, the only law-making body of the federal government, from establishing a national religion or preferring one religious group or religious tenets over other groups or doctrines. This seems to have been the understanding of those who actually wrote and adopted this amendment based on the debates and revisions that occurred in the summer and early fall of 1787.

The Establishment Clause in the Courts

How then did the U.S. courts get to the current constitutional malaise observable at the end of the twentieth century? In 1947, the United States Supreme Court embarked on a course that would prove both controversial and, at times, paradoxical when it decided the seminal *Everson v. Board of Education.*[38] The majority decision purported to be consistent with the framer's understanding of the establishment clause. The Supreme Court, for the first time in its history, found the establishment clause to be applicable to state actions through the Fourteenth Amendment. The Fourteenth Amendment was ratified at the end of the American Civil War and was intended primarily to guarantee the rights of former slaves and to guarantee that insurrection would never again be tolerated at the state level. Section 1 of this amendment reads,

All persons born or naturalized in the United States and subject to the jurisdiction thereof, are citizens of the United States and of the State wherein they reside. No State shall make or enforce any law which shall abridge the privileges or immunities of citizens United States; nor shall any State deprive any person of life, liberty, or property, without due process of law; nor deny to any person within its jurisdiction the equal protection of the laws.

Since this case, many have criticized, and others praised, the Court's application of the establishment clause to state actions.

Whether initially legitimate, the reading of the First Amendment via the Fourteenth is now a permanent fixture of Constitutional law. Now the question becomes one of its meaning and significance to claims brought under the clause, specifically, the proper model or test that ought to be used in establishment clause adjudication.

As quoted above, the operative words in the establishment clause are *respecting*, *establishment*, and *religion*. *Respecting* identifies the object, about which Congress cannot make laws: "an establishment of religion." This would imply both proscriptive and prescriptive legislation. One author has suggested that, regarding establishment of a religion "there was to be a total lack of legislative power insofar as Congress was concerned." The term *respecting* is synonymous with "concerning, and regarding." The implication is that the First Amendment did not prohibit an establishment of religion *per se*. It merely prohibited Congress from usurping state authority by making any law "concerning or regarding an establishment of religion."[39]

The word *establishment* is synonymous with "institution, organization, business, company, or enterprise." Thus, an establishment of religion would involve a religious organization or institution. As shown below, this definition is substantiated by the records covering the proposed versions of the establishment clause.

This concept of "establishment" is linked inseparably to the term *religion* in the establishment clause. Yet the shifting meaning of the term *religion* in the First Amendment has made it difficult for the Court to determine exactly what is not to be established by the Congress. This failure to adequately define religion makes one wonder whether we are at the conundrum of Justice Potter Stewart when he said that he could not define *obscenity*, but he knew it when he saw it.

The Court seems to jostle from definitions for *religion* that have traditional theistic elements to views that seem to be little different from the basic beliefs that anyone and everyone in society might hold. With so little precision, the Court has effectively robbed religion of any protection from the state.

John Eidsmoe has compiled a series of quotations from decisions that show the stark changes in the definition of *religion* by the U.S. Supreme Court:

Holy Trinity (1899): "This is a Christian nation."

Zorach (1951): "We are a religious people whose institutions presuppose a Supreme Being."

Torcaso (1961): "neither can aid those religions based on a belief in the existence of God as against those religions founded on different beliefs."

Seeger (1965): "whether a given belief that is sincere and meaningful occupies a place in the life of its possessor parallel to that filled by the orthodox belief in God."[40]

The Court has thus moved from Christian, to religions presupposing a Supreme Being, to any belief at all that seems meaningful to the individual. Those who drafted the original document would shake their heads in disbelief.

Everson v. Board of Education

The line of demarcation for church-state law was established in *Everson v. Board of Education of Ewing Township* (1947). This decision limited the states' ability to define church-state relations. A "wall of separation" was placed between the two previously friendly spheres of American life.

Ewing Township Board of Education, pursuant to authority granted by New Jersey statute, authorized reimbursement to parents of money spent for public bus transportation of their children to and from school. Part of this money went to parents of parochial school students. A taxpayer in the school district brought the suit, claiming a violation of provisions in the state and federal constitutions because the action of the school board violated the due process clause of the Fourteenth Amendment and the establishment clause of the First Amendment as made applicable to the states by the due process clause of the Fourteenth Amendment.

The first contention was readily dismissed by the Court on the grounds that the "fact that a state law, passed to satisfy a public need, coincides with the personal desires of the individuals most directly affected is certainly an inadequate reason for us to say that a law has erroneously appraised the public need." This is the same reasoning found in the *Cochran* (Louisiana "Textbook") case that held a tax may be constitutionally valid even if the people against whom it is levied are not directly benefited by the money collected.

The second contention was the establishment clause issue. After a brief analysis of the various persecutions of sects that had allegedly flowed from government favored churches, the Court looked at the history of establishment of church states and state-churches in the colonies with particular emphasis on Virginia. Justice Hugo Black saw in Virginia the paradigm for proper analysis, concluding his historical analysis with this often quoted passage:

> The "establishment of religion" clause of the First Amendment means at least this: Neither a state nor the Federal Government can set up a church. Neither can pass laws which aid one religion, aid all religions, or prefer one religion over another. . . . No tax in any amount, large or small, can be levied to support any religious activities or institutions, whatever they may be called, or whatever form they may adopt to teach or practice religion. Neither a state nor the Federal Government can, openly or secretly, participate in the affairs of any religious organizations or groups and *vice versa*. In the words of Jefferson, the clause against the establishment of religion by law was intended to erect "a wall of separation between church and State."[41]

Black also used Jefferson's now famous "wall of separation" metaphor from a letter to the Danbury, Connecticut Baptists. The letter, which Jefferson wrote in anger, is oddly unreflective of the treaty Jefferson signed the next year with the Kaskaskia Indians. In that treaty Jefferson pledged federal money to build a Roman Catholic parish church for the Indians and to support its priest.

In addition to the selective use of the historical record to produce a strict separationist perspective, a further question is raised by the last lines of the majority opinion. Justice Black writes, "The First Amendment has erected a wall between church and state. That wall must be kept high and impregnable. We could not approve the slightest breach. New Jersey has not breached it here."[42] If Justice Black's earlier statement was applicable to the existing facts, how could he conclude that this wall was not breached? In fact the dissenting justices, led by Wiley Rutledge, criticized the majority's opinion for not following the logical conclusion of its analysis. However, the analysis given by the majority, and the principle that aid given to all citizens may only coincide with the desires of some of them, is similar to the argument in the *Cochran* case. In *Cochran*, the Court upheld a Louisiana statute that gave secular textbooks to all children in the state. The textbooks happened to benefit those children going to the parochial schools.

It should be noted that the dissenters in *Everson* accepted the selective use of historical arguments to conclude that the establishment clause requires strict separation of church and state.[43]

McCollum v. Board of Education

Although the majority upheld as constitutional the program of the school district in *Everson,* it was only a matter of time before the strict separationist dicta of *Everson* was used to defeat state action under the establishment clause. In fact the very next year, 1948, the Court in *McCollum v. Board of Education* ruled that a release time program for religious instruction violated the establishment clause.[44] The Court relied on the conclusion reached in *Everson* that the "wall of separation" between church and state "must be kept high and impregnable."[45] The justices rejected the state's argument that the First Amendment had been intended to forbid "only government preference of one religion over another."[46]

In subsequent cases, the Court gradually developed some tests for the application of the establishment clause to suspect state action. In *Engel v. Vitale,* the Court held that a nondenominational prayer, drafted by a state agency to be recited at the beginning of each school day, violated the establishment clause.[47] The Court used the same historical analysis as *Everson* and concluded that strict separation of church and state must be sustained.[48] Justice William O. Douglas, in a concurring opinion, stated that "the great condition of religious liberty is that it be maintained free from sustenance as also from other interferences, by the state."[49] He found support in Rutledge's dissent in *Everson.* Douglas's statement moved toward the test he would demand in the *Lemon* case.

One year later, *School District of Abington Township v. Schempp,* the Court ruled that a statute requiring the reading of ten verses from the Bible without comment at the beginning of each school day in public school classrooms violates the establishment clause, even if individual students may be excused.[50] The Court again squarely rejected the state's contention that the First Amendment forbids only national government preference of one religion over another. Further, the Court expanded on the *neither aiding nor inhibiting of religion* test set forth by Justice Douglas in *Engel.* The Court found,

> The test may be stated as follows: what are the purpose and the primary effect of the enactment? If either is the advancement or inhibition of religion then the enactment exceeds the scope of legislative power as circumscribed by the Constitution. That is to say that *to withstand the strictures of the Establishment Clause there must be a secular legislative purpose and a primary effect that neither advances nor inhibits religion.*[51]

The Court felt that this test was consistent with the interpretation of the establishment clause that they adopted in the ruling and, for that matter, the reasoning in *Everson, McCollum,* and *Engel.*

Lemon v. Kurtzman

Prior to its decision in *Lemon v. Kurtzman* (1971), the Court applied a rough test of several factors including purpose and effect, but not entanglement.[52] In *Lemon*, the Court held that a proper establishment clause analysis of any state or federal action should include a three part test:

> First, the statute must have a secular legislative purpose; second, its principal or primary effect must be one that neither advances nor inhibits religion, *Board of Education v. Allen, 392 U.S. 236, 243 (1968);* finally, the statute must not foster "an excessive government entanglement with religion."[53]

Under the tripart test, the establishment clause allegedly takes a "neutral" stand towards religion, promoting government activity in extending general benefits to nonreligious and religious interests alike.[54]

In most of the decisions that soon followed *Lemon*, the Court upheld the application of the tripart test in an establishment clause analysis. In *Committee for Public Education and Religious Liberty v. Nyquist*, the Court analyzed a New York statute which permitted financial aid to non-public elementary and secondary schools.[55] The Court reaffirmed the analysis of *Everson*, and it adopted the test as expounded in *Lemon*. The Court determined that the New York statute, "as written," violated the second prong of the *Lemon* test by having a "primary effect that advances religion."[56] In *Wallace v. Jaffree*, the Court characterized the establishment clause as requiring "complete neutrality towards religion," citing the strict separation decisions.[57] The Court found that the Alabama statute, which allowed for a voluntary moment of silence, not to exceed one minute, at the beginning of each school day violated the first prong of the *Lemon* test by having *"no* secular purpose."[58]

Finally the fourth prong suggested in *Lemon*—the "political divisiveness" test that William J. Brennan and Thurgood Marshall sought—entails difficulty in that it takes the providence of political interaction within a democratic society away from the people and legislatures and places it with the life tenured Court. I find it hard to believe that Brennan, Marshall, and Warren Burger are attempting to save us from a political controversy they feel we just don't have time to consider. Chief Justice Burger announced that it "goes against our entire history and tradition to permit questions of the Religion Clauses to assume such importance in our legislatures and in our elections that they could divert attention from [other issues]."

Deviations from Lemon

Not all the Court's decisions have so willingly followed the *Everson* line. Some have significantly deviated from the strict separationist approach. *Zorach v. Clauson*, for example, though relatively similar in issue addressed to the *Everson* decision, departed from the strict separation approach. In *Zorach*, the Court examined a release-time program that enabled public school students to receive religious instruction off school grounds during the school day for an hour each week. The Court ruled that this release-time program did not violate the establishment clause, because it merely accommodated religious belief and acknowledged the nation's religious heritage:

> The First Amendment, however, does not say that in every and all respects there shall be a separation of Church and State. Rather, it studiously defines the manner, the specific ways, in which there shall be no concert or union or dependency one on the other. That is the *common sense* matter. Otherwise the state and religion would be aliens to each other—hostile, suspicious, and even unfriendly. . . . The government must be neutral when it comes to competition between sects.[59]

In *Aguilar v. Felton,* the United States Supreme Court held that a New York City program to use public school teachers for remedial instruction in parochial schools was an excessive entanglement of church and state.[60] In a companion case, *School District of Grand Rapids v. Ball,* the Supreme Court held that a "shared time" program was analogous to New York City's Title I program and, therefore, was invalid.[61]

First, the Court found in both cases that providing government funding for religious organizations violated the third prong of *Lemon.* Since parochial schools were deemed to have an atmosphere dedicated to the advancement of religious belief, any instruction in that atmosphere was perceived to create the potential for impermissible fostering of religion.[62]

According to *Ball,* the presence of public teachers on parochial school grounds had a second impermissible effect: It created a "graphic symbol of the 'concert or union or dependency' of church and state,"[63] especially when perceived by "children in their formative years."[64] The Court feared that this perception of a symbolic union between church and state would indicate endorsement of religion and violate a "core purpose" of the establishment clause.[65]

Third, the Court found that the shared time program impermissibly financed religious indoctrination by subsidizing "the primary religious mission of the institutions affected."[66] The Court separated its prior decisions evaluating programs that aided the secular activities of religious institutions into two categories: those in which it concluded that the aid resulted in an effect that was permissible because it was "indirect, remote, or incidental," and those in which the aid was not permissible because it resulted in "a direct and substantial advancement of the sectarian enterprise."[67]

The New York City Title I program challenged in *Aguilar* closely resembled the shared time program struck down in *Ball,* but the Court found fault with an aspect of the Title I program not present in *Ball:* The Board had "adopted a system for monitoring the religious content of publicly funded Title I classes in the religious schools."[68] Even though this monitoring system might prevent the Title I program from being used to inculcate religion, the Court concluded, as it had in *Lemon* and *Meek,* that the level of monitoring necessary to be certain that the program had an exclusively secular effect would in itself entangle church and state.

In *Agostini,* the Court also acknowledged that it had departed from the idea found in *Ball* that all governmental aid that directly assists the educational function of religious schools is invalid. Thus, *Agostini* acknowledges that it is no longer, as a matter of law, presumed that governmental aid results in a "symbolic union" of church and state.

The Court also looked at whether such aid would result in excessive entanglement. The Court found that not all entanglements have the effect of advancing or inhibiting religion. The Court states, "Interaction between church and state is inevitable, see *id.,* at 614, . . . and we have always tolerated some level of involvement between the two. Entanglement must be 'excessive' before it runs afoul of the Establishment Clause."[69]

The Court concluded by holding, first, "that a federally funded program providing supplemental, remedial instruction to disadvantaged children on a neutral basis is not invalid under the Establishment Clause when such instruction is given on the premises of sectarian schools by government employees pursuant to a program containing safeguards such as those present here." Second, "a carefully constrained program also cannot reasonably be viewed as an endorsement of religion."[70]

CONCLUSION

The U.S. Supreme Court has taken two distinct directions in establishment clause analysis. The first, represented by the strict separationist sentiments of *Everson,* tends to use the tripartite test as an instrument to root out any vestige of church-state partnership. The second, represented by *Zorach,* and cases following it, especially *Agostini,* presents an accommodation view of history that allows nonpreferential aid to religions.

The sitting Court at the beginning of the twenty-first century appeared to be willing to define the role of church and state in America as one of cooperation rather than hostility. Just how long this will last largely depends on the future make-up of the Court. If Justices are approved for the Court who will be more sensitive to the historical heritage of America and to the importance of religion in defining the national morality and law, then the relationship of church and state will fulfill more nearly what the framers intended.

If, on the other hand, the Court seeks to act as though the public law is somehow neutral, void of religious guidance, then a religion of secularism, often very hostile to individual rights, will direct the country.

This chapter includes excerpts from H. Wayne House, "A Tale of Two Kingdoms: Can There Be Peaceful Existence of Religion with the Secular State," *Brigham Young University Journal of Public Law* 203 (1999): 13; and H. Wayne House, *Christian Ministries and the Law: What Church and Para-Church Leaders Should Know* (Grand Rapids: Baker, 1992). Used by permission.

CHAPTER 30

The Relationship of the Church to the State

Paul R. Fink

In the new millennium, how will government relate to religious and church autonomy? The last decade of the twentieth century saw some of the most blatant persecution against true believers since the Reformation. Thousands of Christians died for their faith. China intensified persecution of house-church Christians, confining many to prison. And though the Communist empire of the USSR collapsed, state-supported Orthodox churches in the newly independent countries successfully urged governments to tightly restrict evangelical assemblies.

In the U.S. there was good news and bad news. The California Supreme Court refused to hear an appeal by a homosexual who was forced out as a leader of the Boy Scouts of America. Gay rights groups in other states continued to sue the Scouts over alleged discrimination against homosexuals. How some state courts would react was anyone's guess.

QUESTIONS TO CONSIDER

For this discussion the concept of the church and state will be defined as the relationship of the believer to the state. Answers to three questions help us understand Christian responsibility to the state:

1. What does the Old Testament teach regarding the state's authority?
2. What does the New Testament teach?
3. In which realms does the believer have responsibility?

STATE AUTHORITY IN THE OLD TESTAMENT

The seed of human government begins wherever authority is vested. This vesting of authority can be seen first in the Edenic, Adamic, and Noahic covenants.

The Edenic Covenant (Gen. 1:28–2:17)

In the Edenic covenant Adam is charged to (1) populate and (2) subdue the earth and (3) exercise dominion over the animal creation (1:28). He was to (4) care for the garden and enjoy its fruit (1:29; 2:15), and he was to (5) refrain from eating the fruit of the tree of the knowledge of good and evil (2:16–17).

While the focus of the Edenic covenant is not human government as we usually think of it, the following relevant factors can be observed:

The Origin of Human Government

As the first human beings, Adam and Eve arrived on the scene by direct divine creation. However, God charged them with the responsibility to "be fruitful, and multiply, and *fill* [Heb., *mālē*, which means "to fill," not to replenish or refill as in KJV] the earth" (1:28a).[1] Implicit within this command is Adam's headship as the responsible agent for the society that will develop.

The Scope of Human Government

In the Edenic covenant, Adam is charged to subdue the earth and "have dominion over the fish of the sea, and over the fowl of the air, and over every living thing that moveth upon the earth" (1:28b). Had the Fall never taken place, Adam would still have had a responsibility to discharge before God. As the head of God's creation he was to cultivate the earth and maintain his dominion over God's creatures. Unfallen, Adam could have maintained this role forever. However, with the entrance of sin and death, Adam's dominion was carried on by successors and ultimately formalized in the institution of human government. Government is responsible for the care of God's earth and creatures.

The Responsibility to Human Government

God puts some definite restrictions upon the man to whom He has given responsibility over His creation:

> And the LORD God took the man, and put him into the garden of Eden to dress it and to keep it. And the LORD God commanded the man, saying, Of every tree of the garden thou mayest freely eat: But of the tree of the knowledge of good and evil, thou shalt not eat of it: for in the day that thou eatest thereof thou shalt surely die. (Gen. 2:15–17)

Adam was given responsibility to dress and keep the garden and he was given restrictions as to what he could and could not eat. Had sin not entered the world, these responsibilities and restrictions would have continued forever. With the entry of sin and death the Edenic obligations were terminated because no human remained in the garden. This responsibility to God for the care of creation did not end, however, and ultimately was given to the institution of human government.

The Noahic Covenant (Gen. 9:1–17)

The Noahic covenant includes God's blessing upon Noah and his family (9:1a), God's general revelation of His covenant (9:1b–7), and God's specific revelation of His covenant with Noah (9:8–17). While the Noahic covenant is concerned with much more than governmental authority, some principles for human authority are set out.

The Authority to Govern

God's general revelation of His covenant to Noah and his family concerns his progeny (9:1b), his dominion over creation (9:2), food (9:3-4), capital punishment of beast and man (9:5-6), and an additional word concerning Noah's descendants (9:7). The revelation concerning capital punishment provides the clue to the origin of human government and its responsibility. God states in verses 5 and 6,

> *And surely your blood of your lives will I require; at the hand of every beast will I require it, and at the hand of man; at the hand of every man's brother will I require the life of man. Whoso sheddeth man's blood, by man shall his blood be shed: for in the image of God made he man.*

Three times in this text God says, "I will require it" (Heb., *dārash*, "require, or, demand an accounting"). Thus it is God who demands an accounting of human government for its protection of life.

The Recipients of Governmental Authority

The text indicates that every beast and man that sheds human blood will be held accountable. The requirement of life for life is to be extracted of either people or animals. There are to be no more Cains (cf. Gen. 4:8-15). The shedding of an animal's blood (9:4) is not to cause an indifference to blood-shed. Whenever someone dies by man or by beast, God demands an accounting. The accountable agency is human government.

The Executor of Governing Authority

Genesis 9:6 explains 9:5 and shows how God demands that the accounting be done. This is human government as the basic institution for the welfare of the individual image bearers of God. This approach to government argues from the greater to the lesser. Government was instituted with power over the highest good—human life; therefore government has a claim to power for the good of humans over the lesser things, such as property and service.

The Necessity of Governmental Authority

The giving of capital punishment revolves around the phrase "by man shall his blood be shed." This construction is in the *niphal* imperfect tense, which is best understood to have imperative force: "By man his blood *must* be shed." Capital punishment by human government is not a matter of choice or preference, but a divine command. To fail to exercise it, whether on an individual or a national scale, is to reject the authority of God. Those who would tamper with this law are trying to be wiser than the Lawgiver and to overthrow the pillar of safety He erected for human welfare.

The Vindication for Governmental Authority

Governmental authority is an absolute necessity in protecting life "for in the image of God made he man." This shows the value of each person in God's sight. God does not require an accounting for the shedding of an animal's blood; He does require an accounting for wrongful death.

QUESTIONS CONCERNING AUTHORITY

From the exegetical considerations of this passage, four logical questions arise:

First, doesn't this command conflict with "Thou shalt not kill" in the Mosaic Law (Exod. 20:13)?

Government is here given limited power over human life in an official capacity. The Ten Commandments deal with personal morality. Here it is official conduct. The only time one has the right to take a life is when properly authorized to do so as an agent of human government.

Second, is capital punishment cruel and inhumane punishment?

To remove a cancer from the body of a patient, a physician dons surgical garments, takes surgical instruments in hand and cuts into the patient's body. The cutting injures the patient, but the physician is not charged to be cruel. By injuring his patient's body he has cut the growth that would otherwise destroy the whole body. So it is with capital punishment: If the "cancer" is not destroyed and cut out, it will destroy the rest of the body.

Third, what if the human government is corrupt?

God does not hold the individual responsible as an individual for the corruption of human government. He does hold the individual responsible for obeying Him. A believer called to serve on a jury has the Holy Spirit within to guide in reaching a verdict. Under such direction, the believing juror who considers a defendant to be guilty of murder must vote for capital punishment, even if this stand "hangs the jury." On the other hand, if the believer considers that the charge remains unproven, regard for the defendant's life as God's image bearer demands that the juror vote to acquit, even if all others vote to convict.

Fourth, what about wars?

Wars are an extension of this command. In war, one human government executes capital punishment upon another nation who has offended. A soldier who kills in the line of duty is acting as God's agent. He is not guilty of murder because he is acting in an official capacity.

Summary

From Genesis 9:1–17 it can be seen that human government originated with God's command to Noah following the universal flood. At that time God specifically gave corporate human government the responsibility for avenging wrongful death, either by another human being or by a beast. This represents the epitome of the authority of human government and also speaks for governing authority in the lesser realms that help protect human welfare.

STATE AUTHORITY IN THE NEW TESTAMENT

There are three central New Testament examples of the recognition of governmental authority, one each from Jesus, Paul, and Peter.

Jesus (Matt. 22:21)

If anyone could claim immunity from the authority of human government, it would be Jesus. In response to the Herodians' question as to whether it was lawful to give tribute to Caesar, Jesus replied, "Render therefore unto Caesar the things which are Caesar's; and unto God the things that are God's." (Matt. 22:21). Jesus delineates the two realms in which each person has obligations: (1) under government and (2) under God. There is a difference between the Herodians' question and Jesus' answer. They asked whether it was lawful to give (*dounai*, "to give as a gift") tribute to Caesar. Jesus' response is that one should render (*apodote*, "to give as an obligation") to Caesar the things that are his. Giving to Caesar is not voluntary. Eternal obligation to God does not discharge one from temporal obligations to the government.

Paul (Rom. 13:1–7)

Paul amplifies on Jesus' words in Romans 13, Scripture's most definitive word about the believer's relationship to government. Verses 1–7 teach,

Let every soul be subject unto the higher powers. For there is no power but of God: the powers that be are ordained of God. Whosoever therefore

resisteth the power, resisteth the ordinance of God: and they that resist shall receive to themselves damnation. For rulers are not a terror to good works, but to the evil. Wilt thou then not be afraid of the power? Do that which is good, and thou shalt have praise of the same: For he is the minister of God to thee for good. But if thou do that which is evil, be afraid; for he beareth not the sword in vain: for he is the minister of God, a revenger to execute wrath upon him that doeth evil. Wherefore ye must needs be subject, not only for wrath, but also for conscience sake. For this cause pay ye tribute also: for they are God's ministers, attending continually upon this very thing. Render therefore to all their dues: tribute to whom tribute is due; custom to whom custom; fear to whom fear; honour to whom honour.

From this passage several facts are evident:

First, subjection to government—whether local, county, state, or federal—is an absolute necessity for Christians and non-Christians alike. Christians should be the government's best citizens. Note that Paul wrote these words as a citizen under the Emperor Nero who would, in about a decade, order his execution.

The origin of governmental authority is God. The authorities that exist have been established by God (lit., "have been, are, and will be put into place by God"). Whatever the manner of his assuming power, no ruler governs by personal power and initiative. God establishes individuals in places of leadership as He pleases, in keeping with His plan.

The purpose of governmental authority is to preserve moral order. The state is to judge the wrong and approve the right. If it does not, it is disobedient. Ideally, the state should get its values for judging right and wrong from God, but often it does not. This is why it is important for Christians to be involved in their governmental processes. A governmental leader is God's servant (lit., "deacon, servant, minister").

Christians should obey and support government financially. The Christian's subjection is to be motivated not only by threat of punishment, but also because of a desire to honor God and present a consistent testimony. Taxes are paid to support the governmental authorities because they are God's servants and give their full time to governing. That is how they serve God.[2] Christians should support governmental officials appropriately. Taxes are paid to support the governmental official's salary. Revenue (*to telos*) refers to tolls paid for use of government facilities such as roads and bridges. Respect (*phobon*, "fear") is reverential awe paid to one who has power entrusted into his hands. Honor is the reverence and respect due to one who holds office.

Peter (1 Peter 2:13–17)

Peter's teaching concerning the Christian's responsibility to the state supplements Paul's:

> *Submit yourselves to every ordinance of man for the Lord's sake: whether it be to the king, as supreme; or unto governors, as unto them that are sent by him for the punishment of evildoers, and for the praise of them that do well. For so is the will of God, that with well-doing ye may put to silence the ignorance of foolish men: as free, and not using your liberty for a cloak of maliciousness, but as the servants of God. Honour all men. Love the brotherhood. Fear God. Honour the king.* (1 Peter 2:13–17)

Peter makes two assertions concerning the Christian responsibility to the state:

The first is 1 Peter 2:13–14: Subjection to the state is commanded by God. In principle this applies "to every ordinance of man."[3] This it to be done for the Lord's sake.[4] Jesus' life was one of obedience. He showed respect to Pilate and commanded His people to obey those in authority over them. He submitted to Caiaphas and Herod. Pacifists have damaged the Lord's cause by failing to recognize the difference between the spiritual (religious) and the state (governmental).

As long as the state legislates within its God-ordained realm, the believer is to be subject to it and obey its laws. However, if the state tries to legislate in the realm of the spiritual, the believer is to obey God rather than man (cf. Acts 5:29, 40–42). He is still not to resist with force but rather is to take the punishment that might be given out by the state that would result from his obedience to God as the higher authority. Though both ideas (subjection because of [1] the Lord's example or [2] for the Christian cause) might be included in Peter's thought, the context favors the former, for this is the very line of reasoning that Peter follows in 2:21–24.

The second is 1 Peter 2:15–17: Subjection to the state is the will of God. This is specifically proclaimed in 2:15a: "For so is the will [lit. "something specifically willed"] of God." What God specifically wills is subjection to the state, so "that with well-doing ye may put to silence [lit. "muzzle"] the ignorance of foolish men" (2:15b–16). It is better to prevent evil-speakers from speaking than to silence them after they have spoken.

The believer, then, is to conduct himself or herself in such a way that unbelievers will have no opportunity to speak against the body. The "ignorance" (*agnōsian*) of the foolish stems from the fact that they have not accurately observed the believers, nor do they share the believers' new birth experiences. They are totally ignorant of what is transpiring in life. The foolish are in want of mental sanity and have an inconsiderate habit of mind. They never stop to think that they might be making an inaccurate assessment.

Instead, they conclude that they are right, and anyone who does not conform to their ideas is insane. Such are muzzled (1) by well doing, (2) by contact with true freedom, and (3) by seeing freedom used properly (2:15–16). Well doing in this context is to subject oneself to the God-ordained authority of the state. It isn't resistance (whether passive or active) that will silence the foolish, but rather subjection—a concept quite foreign to the human mind.

"As free" sets forth the believer's relationship to the state. Within this freedom, however, the believer is God's slave. Ownership by God is to govern the relationship to the state. God's slave will be subject to the state because this is the will of God and the example of Christ. The believer who is not subject to the state is not subject to God. This is true even if he lives in a totalitarian state. This subjection on the part of the believer is designed to put to silence the ignorance of foolish men.

The believer is not to use his freedom in Christ "for a cloak of maliciousness" against the state. This might include resistance movements that depart from subjection to God-ordained authority. The believer's freedom from the state, rather, is to be used as befits a servant of God. Since God is Master and the state is God's creation for the orderly discharge of human affairs, the believer is to be subject to the realm of jurisdiction God has given to the state. Writes Edward Selwyn in his commentary on this text, "Christian freedom rests not on escape from service, but on a change of master."[5]

In this subjection, the Christian never forgets the motivation is not the innate goodness of the state but simple obedience to God. The idea that men are free and servants of God has always been an offense in the eyes of totalitarian political philosophy, even when Christian citizens practice subjection. This accounts for so many attempts, both ancient and modern, to suppress Christianity. The Christian citizen's act of submission to civil power is the act of a free man, for which he has good reasons in his knowledge of the true character of the state, and is further conditioned by the fact that he knows that he is the slave of God.

What governments find distasteful is that the believer's continuous attitude in service and subjection is not ideological, but rather reverence toward God. This reverence tempers patriotism and becomes the motive for doing certain things and abstaining from doing certain things. In the older English conception this was called "fear" of the Lord, but it is not a cringing fear that wonders what God might do at any given moment. It is a fear that holds God in highest awe and reverence.

In the political sphere the believer is to direct honor to the rulers, rather than the reverence due only to God. Honor is the believer's continuous attitude toward one who has human authority. Honor, of course, is the practical outworking of the submission enjoined in 2:13. The believer who is subject to the supreme authority will give appropriate honor.

THE REALMS OF A CHRISTIAN'S RESPONSIBILITY

First Peter 2:13–3:12 sets forth three spheres of responsibility in the life of a believer:

1. The state, or public affairs (2:13–17)
2. The household, or professional affairs (2:18–25)
3. The home, or private affairs (3:1–7).

In each of these spheres the believer is to be in subjection for the Lord's sake (cf. 2:13). The believer is to recognize that over all of these realms is the spiritual, his own personal responsibility to God. God has a specific will concerning the believer's conduct in each of these realms. It is the believer's responsibility to be in subjection to the proper authority in each of these realms. In the realm of the state, subjection is to God-ordained rulers (vv. 13–16). In the world of work it is subjection to the God-ordained master (v. 18). In the home subjection goes to the God-ordained head, the husband and father. The husband/father is likewise in subjection to Christ for his God-ordained responsibility of headship. For example, he is to accept his wife in every aspect of his life and render to her due honor as God-given wife and fellow heir of salvation (3:7).

As long as the God-ordained authority is operating according to God-ordained responsibility in public affairs, work, and home, all is well. The believer only has one responsibility-subjection. Confusion comes when one realm seeks to operate in the domain of another. This might happen, for example, in a country where the state forbids the worship of God in the household. God has commanded the worship, and the believer is obligated to obey.

The state, however, may say that in its value system the worship of God is evil, and those who worship Him are criminals deserving of punishment. The believer is faced with the quandary as to how to obey the authority structure as God has commanded. The believer may understand that God is the higher authority, but even though he does "good" so far as God is concerned, he becomes an evil-doer so far as the state is concerned. In such an instance the believer is not to resist or to overthrow the state or to thwart its effort at punishment. Rather the believer accepts without complaint whatever punishment the state metes out. The state is operating within its God-given authority (cf. Rom. 13:3–4).

This principle in action is seen in the lives of the Old Testament heroes Hananiah, Mishael, and Azariah, who refused to worship Nebuchadnezzar's image (cf. Daniel 3), and Daniel when he refused to give up praying to Jehovah (cf. Daniel 6). In modern days when governments have forbidden such activities as distributing Bibles, those who would smuggle Bibles must be willing to accept the potential outcome of their actions. Any time a believer determines to undertake an action out of obedience to God that is against the law the consequences should be embraced without complaint.

CONCLUSION

The proper biblical relationship between the state and believers (the church individually as well as corporately) may be summarized in six principles:

1. The church is not to dominate the state.
2. The state is not to dominate the church.
3. The church is to be independent of the state.
4. The state is to be independent of the church.
5. The church is to give the state its value system.
6. The state is to protect the church so that it can worship God freely.

Only the Lord Himself knows what the next one hundred years will bring in relation to these principles. So many Christians have never experienced freedom from government interference. Some argue that persecution only fans the flames of evangelism and causes the church to grow stronger. But whatever the level of freedom or persecution in our national context, we have the mandate to pray for those in authority that we may live peacefully with all, in order that the gospel may be heard.

CHAPTER 31

The Church, Government, and Civil Disobedience

Kerby Anderson

Should Christians be involved in politics? What should be the Christian's relationship to government? Should Christians ever disobey government? If so, under what circumstances? Such questions have swirled around the Christian community for decades. Individual Christians and the church as a whole question their responsibility toward government and the political process.

While there is room for intramural debates about strategy and tactics, fundamental principles in Scripture do help us develop a Christian view of government and political action. As developed at length in chapter 30, government is not an invention of man, but a divinely ordained institution, established by God to bring order and justice to a fallen world.

A CHRISTIAN VIEW OF GOVERNMENT

Government affects our lives daily. Laws passed within the governing processes tell us how fast to drive and regulate commerce. The defense function is meant to protect us from foreign and domestic strife. Yet we rarely take time to consider government's basic function. What is a biblical view of government? Why do we have government? What kind of government does the Bible allow?

Precise details of a biblical view of government are never exhaustively discussed in the Bible. This is itself instructive, showing that God allows for latitude as leaders establish institutions around the needs and demands of a situation. Because the Bible does not speak directly to every area of public policy, Christians often hold differing views on particular issues. However, Christians are not free to believe whatever they want, and they should not abandon the Bible when they begin to think through matters touching on politics and government. There is a great deal of biblical material to apply.

The Old Testament teaches that God established government after the flood (Genesis 9). The Old Testament provides clear guidelines for a theocracy. These guidelines, however, covered God's direction in particular circumstances involving a unique covenant people. Modern governments are not recipients of the promises God made to the nation of Israel. Apart from that unique situation, the Bible does not propose, nor does it endorse, a specific political system.

God does provide a basis for evaluating political philosophies to the extent that it clearly delineates a view of human nature. Every political theory rests on some view of human nature. The Bible describes two elements of human nature. Because humans are created in the image of God (Gen. 1:26–27), they are able to exercise judgment and rationality. However, humans are also fallen creatures (Genesis 3). Civil government has become necessary to restrain this human sinfulness (Rom. 3:23).

Many theologians have suggested that the only reason we have government today is to control sinful behavior because of the Fall. But there is every indication that government would have existed in a sinless world. There was structural authority in the Garden (Genesis 1–2). We notice indications in the Bible that even the angelic host is organized into levels of authority and purpose. In the creation God ordained government as the means by which human beings and angelic hosts are ruled. The rest of the created order is governed by instinct (Prov. 30:24–28) and God's providence. Insect colonies, for example, may show a level of order, but this is due merely to genetically controlled instinct.

Human beings, on the other hand, are created in the image of God and are responsible for obeying the commands of God. We are created by a God of order (1 Cor. 14:33); therefore we seek order through government structures.

A Christian view of government differs significantly from other political theories, because only the Bible roots civil government in our created nature. We are rational and volitional beings. We are not determined by fate, as the Greeks would have said, nor are we determined by environment as modern behaviorists say. We have the power of choice. We can exercise delegated power over the created order. A biblical view of human nature requires a governmental system that acknowledges human responsibility.

While the source of civil government is rooted in human responsibility, the need for government derives from the necessity of controlling sinfulness. God ordained civil government to restrain evil (as noted, for example, in Genesis 9). Anarchy is not a viable option because all have sinned (Rom. 3:23) and are in need of external control.

Christians must reject political philosophies that ignore human sinfulness. Many utopian theories are based upon this flawed assumption. Plato proposed in *The Republic* an ideal government in which enlightened philosopher-kings would lead. The Bible, however, teaches that all are sinful (Rom. 3:23). Plato's proposed leaders would not always have the benevolent and enlightened disposition necessary to lead the republic because they are fallen.

Christians should also reject a Marxian socialist view of government. Karl Marx believed that human nature was conditioned by society—in particular by the economic realities under which the society functions. His solution to social problems was to change human nature by changing the economy. We have greed, he taught, because capitalism conditions people to be greedy. Under socialism and ultimately its communist millennial kingdom, greed would cease. This utopian vision is based upon an inaccurate view of human nature. The Bible does teach that believers can become new creatures through spiritual conversion (2 Cor. 5:17), but that does not mean the effects of sin vanish, even among Christians. We will continue to live in a world tainted by sin. The Marxian new man in a new society, self perfected, simply will not work.

Since civil government is necessary and divinely ordained (Rom. 13:1-7), it is ultimately under God's control. He has given three political responsibilities: the sword of justice to punish criminals, the sword of order to thwart rebellion, and the sword of war to defend the state. Christians share in these responsibilities. They are called to render service and obedience (Matt. 22:21). Because it is a God-ordained institution, they are to submit to civil authority (1 Peter 2:13-17) as they submit to other institutions of God. Christians are not to give total and final allegiance to the secular state. Other God-ordained institutions exist in society alongside the state. The Christian's final allegiance is to God. Christians are to obey civil authorities (Rom. 13:5) in order to avoid chaos, but sometimes they are forced to disobey (Acts 5:29).

Because government is a divinely ordained institution, Christians have a responsibility to work for change within government structures. Government is part of the creation order and a minister of God (Rom. 13:4). Christians are to obey government authorities (Rom. 13:1-7, 1 Peter 2:13). Christians are also to be the salt of the earth and the light of the world (Matt. 5:13-16) in the midst of the political context.

Although rulers may be guilty of injustice, Christians should not stop working for justice or cease to be concerned about human rights. We do not give up on marriage as an institution simply because there are so many divorces, nor do we give up on the church because of its internal problems. Each God-ordained institution manifests human sinfulness and disobedience. Our responsibility as Christians is to call political leaders back to this God-ordained task. Government is a legitimate sphere of Christian service, and so we should not look to government only when our rights are being abused. We are to be concerned with social justice and should see governmental action as a legitimate instrument to achieve just ends.

Human rights in a Christian system are based on a biblical view of human dignity. In the U.S., John Locke and the Declaration of Independence did not grant rights to individuals. The dominant reasoning was that these rights already existed and simply needed acknowledgment. Government was, in fact, based on inalienable individual rights. Government based on humanism sees no rights as inalienable; therefore the state defines and redefines what rights its citizens may enjoy. The Bill of Rights adopted at the beginning of the U.S. government was concerned not with giving rights but with articulating what rights were inalienable and not to be restricted by government. This is far different from totalitarian systems in which citizens have only such rights as they are given, and power ultimately resides in the government.

A Christian view of government also recognizes the need to limit the influence of sin in society. Controls on government authority protect citizens from the abuse or misuse of power. The greatest threat to inalienable rights is the corrupting force of power on fallen humans. In the Old Testament theocracy there was less danger of abuse because the head of state was God. The Bible amply documents the dangers that ensued when power was transferred to a single king. Even David, a man after God's own heart (1 Sam. 13:14; Acts 13:22), abused his power and Israel experienced great calamity (2 Sam. 11–21).

LIMITATIONS TO SOVEREIGNTY

A key question in political theory is how to determine the limits of governmental authority. With the remarkable growth in the complexity, size, and scope of governments throughout the world during the twentieth century, it is necessary to define clearly the lines of governmental authority. The Bible provides some guidelines. However, it is often difficult to see these proper limits. Although human nature is the same, drawing biblical principles from an agrarian, monolithic culture and applying them to the technological, pluralistic cultures in which we live requires discernment.

This difficulty can be eased by identifying two issues: First, should government legislate morality? Second, what are the limits of governmental sovereignty? Taking the second question first, one can find a few general principles.

As Christians, we recognize that God has ordained other institutions in addition to government. Each is given authority by which to function in its particular sphere. This is in contrast to other political systems, in which the state has sovereignty in all spheres of life and over every other human institution.

The Church

The first institution is the church (see, for example, Heb. 12:18-24; 1 Peter 2:9-10). In Matthew 22:21 Jesus clearly set a line of demarcation between Caesar and God. Throughout Acts and the Epistles the apostles demonstrate, from the Christian side at least, a desire for government and church to work in harmony. Government has divinely-ordained civil authority, and the church exercises sovereignty in spiritual matters (e.g. 1 Peter 3:8–17).

The Family

While governing authority can be seen in the cultural mandate (Gen. 1:26–27), the first institution we see functioning in Scripture is the family (Eph. 5:22–32; 1 Peter 3:1–7). The family is an institution under God, and it has its particular sphere of sovereignty in marriage and parental relationships under His authority (Gen. 2:20–25). When the family breaks down, the government often has to step in to protect the rights of the husband or wife (in cases of spousal abuse) or children (in cases of child abuse or parent incapacity). The biblical emphasis, however, is not so much on rights as on responsibilities and mutual submission (Eph. 5:21).

A function of the institution of family is education. Children are not wards of the state, even in the matter of being educated. They belong to God and are given to parents as a gift (Ps. 127:3–5). Parents are to teach their children or see to their education (e.g., Deut. 4:9).

In a humanistic system of government, the institutions of church and family are usually subordinated to the state. In an atheistic system, ultimately the state becomes a substitute god and is given additional power to adjudicate disputes and bring order. Since institutions exist by permission of the state, there is always the possibility that a new social contract will allow government to intervene in the areas of church and family.

A Christian view of government recognizes the sovereignty of these spheres. Governmental intervention is sometimes necessary, where there is threat to life, liberty, or property. Otherwise civil government should respect the sovereignty of other God-ordained institutions.

THE MORAL BASIS OF LAW

Law should be the foundation on which government stands. Whether law is based upon moral absolutes, consensus, or totalitarian whim is a crucial matter. Western culture had an edge in legal theory in this, for the societies have generally held to the concept of a common law, founded upon moral absolutes. In a Christian view of government, those absolutes are God's revealed commandments. Law is not based upon human opinion or sociological convention. Law is rooted in God's unchangeable character and derived from biblical morality.

In secular humanistic theories of law, humanity is the source of law. Law is merely the expression of human will or consensus. Since ethics and morality are not transcendent, neither is law. Rooted in human opinion, humanist law is relative and arbitrary.

Two figures in the history of law are Samuel Rutherford (1600–1661) and William Blackstone (1723–1780). Rutherford's *Lex Rex* (1644) profoundly shaped British and American law. This treatise challenged the foundations of seventeenth-century politics by proclaiming that law must be based upon the Bible, rather than upon the word of any man. This was still the period of absolute monarchs, and Rutherford stirred great controversy by attacking the ancient theory of the "divine right of kings." The divine right doctrine held that the king-state ruled as God's appointed regent; thus, the king's word had the force of law. Rutherford argued from such passages as Romans 13 that the king, just as anyone else, was under God's law and not above it. Law was the true king.

An English jurist, Blackstone is famous for this *Commentaries on the Law of England* (1765), which became the definitive treatise on common law for England, Scotland, Ireland, Wales, Australia, New Zealand, Canada, and the U.S. According to Blackstone, the two foundations for law are nature and revelation through the Scriptures. Blackstone taught that God was the source of all laws. It is interesting that even the humanist Rousseau noted in his *Social Contract* that one needs someone outside the world system to provide a moral basis for law. He said, "It would take gods to give men laws."

Unfortunately, in the twentieth century each of the above countries drifted from the importance of "natural law" and based the modern legal structure on relativism and utilitarianism. Relativism provides no secure basis for moral judgments. There are no firm moral absolutes upon which to build a secure legal foundation. Utilitarianism looks merely at consequences, ignoring moral principles.

This legal foundation has been further eroded by the relatively recent phenomenon of *sociological law*. In this view, law should be based upon relative sociological standards. No discipline is more helpless without a moral foundation than law. Just as contractors and builders need the architect's blueprint in order to build, so legislators need theologians and moral philosophers. The problem is that most lawyers today are extensively trained in technique, but ill prepared in moral and legal philosophy.

The institutions of legal justice in the West still look back to a biblical understanding of human nature and responsibility. We hold criminals accountable for their crimes, rather than excusing their behavior as part of environmental conditioning. We also acknowledge differences between willful, premeditated acts (such as murder) and so-called crimes of passion (i.e., manslaughter) or accidents. A problem in society is that we do not operate from assumptions of human choice. The influence of the behaviorist, the evolutionist, and the sociobiologist are profound. The evolution-assuming sociobiologist finds most human behavior to be genetically determined. The behaviorist, taking evolutionary assumptions in a different direction, says that human behavior is environmentally determined. Neither posits free choice. Personal responsibility, then, has been diminished in the criminal justice system by secular perspectives.

Not by accident have we seen a dramatic change in our view of criminal justice. The emphasis has moved from a view of punishment and restitution to one of rehabilitation. If our actions are governed by something external, we cannot justly punish criminals, since they cannot help themselves. We must "rehabilitate" them. But such a view of human actions diminishes human dignity. A person who cannot choose is merely a victim of circumstance and must become a ward of the state.

As Christians, we must take the criminal act seriously and punish human choices. While we recognize the value of repentance and change (especially through Christ), we also recognize the need for punishment. The Old Testament punishment/restitution model makes more sense in light of the biblical view of human nature. Yet the legal system is so enamored with no-fault divorce, no-fault insurance, and excusable offenses that the notion of human responsibility is lost.

CIVIL DISOBEDIENCE

What should Christians do when government exceeds its authority? Do Christians have a right—even the responsibility—to disobey? Those who would quickly dismiss this question as irrelevant should realize the implications of civil disobedience on Christian discipleship and obedience to God's law. If there is never a circumstance under which a Christian would disobey the state, then ultimately the state has become god. Civil disobedience must be permitted; the question is to what circumstances force Christians across the line.

The best articulation of biblical principles is in Rutherford's *Lex Rex*. Arguing that God's law, not kings, had the ultimate authority, Rutherford wrote that when kings or legislative bodies disobey the law, then they are to be disobeyed. According to Rutherford the civil magistrate is a "fiduciary figure" who holds his authority in trust for the people. If that trust is violated, the people have a political basis for resistance. Not surprisingly, *Lex Rex* was banned in England and Scotland as treasonous and inflammatory.

The Bible provides prominent examples of civil disobedience. When Pharaoh commanded the Hebrew midwives to kill all male Hebrew babies, they lied to Pharaoh and did not carry out his command (Exodus 1-2).

The book of Daniel has a number of instructive examples. When three young Jews refused to bow down to Nebuchadnezzar's golden image, they were cast into a fiery furnace (Daniel 3). The commissioners and satraps persuaded King Darius to make a decree that no one could petition any god or man for thirty days. Daniel nevertheless continued to pray to God three times a day and was cast into the lions' den (Daniel 6).

The most dramatic example of civil disobedience in the New Testament is recorded in Acts 4–5. When Peter and John were commanded not to preach the gospel, their response was, "We must obey God rather than men" (Acts 5:29).

Biblical examples each include at least two common elements: *First, a direct, specific conflict arose between God's law and human law.* Pharaoh commanded the Hebrew midwives to kill male Hebrew babies. Nebuchadnezzar commanded his subjects to bow before the golden image. King Darius ruled that no one could pray. And in the New Testament the high priest and the Sanhedrin forbade the apostles to proclaim the gospel.

Second, in choosing to obey God's higher law, believers paid the consequence for disobedience. Although several of them escaped consequences through supernatural intervention, this liberation was not promised. Many others have paid for their disobedience with their lives.

Some critics argue that civil disobedience is prohibited by the clear admonition in Romans 13:1, "Let every person be in subjection to the governing authorities. For there is no authority except from God, and those which exist are established by God." Yet even this text provides the hint of an argument for disobedience when government exceeds its authority.

The following verses speak of the government's role and function. The ruler is to be a "servant of God," and government should reward good and punish evil. Government that fails to do so is outside of God's mandated authority and function. Government is not autonomous; it has delegated authority to restrain evil and punish wrongdoers. When it does violate God's delegated role and refuses to reward good and punish evil, it has no proper authority.

The apostle Paul called for believers to "be subject" to government, but he did not instruct them to "obey" every command of government. When government commands an unjust or unbiblical injunction, Christians have a higher authority. One can be subject to the authority of the state but still refuse to "obey" a specific law.

CIVIL DISOBEDIENCE: A PRO-LIFE EXAMPLE

Although civil disobedience has been debated in various arenas, the primary discussion of its use among Christians of the late twentieth century has been in the abortion debate. Millions of unborn babies are killed every year and political means to redress this evil have been stymied in the nations allowing abortions. Pro-life Christians, therefore, have debated whether civil disobedience is an appropriate action.

Proponents argue that we cannot wait for long political processes when infants are perishing daily now. Therefore, we should "rescue those being led away to death" (Prov. 24:11). Christians must follow the dictates of James

4:17: "Therefore, to one who knows the right thing to do, and does not do it, to him it is sin."

The activities done under pro-life civil disobedience have depended upon the philosophy of individual pro-life groups and leaders. Peaceful action has included picketing abortion clinics or doctors' homes and providing sidewalk counseling to women visiting the clinics. Some call for physical intervention by blockading clinics. Some call for stronger uses of force. Critics of the use of civil disobedience usually draw the line at trespassing and physical intervention (e.g., blockading clinics). Four criticisms usually surface in their critique of the use of civil disobedience to protest abortion:

First, the law being broken has nothing to do with abortion. Picketers are not arrested because they are protesting abortions, but because they are infringing on rights that are honored in society, for example, access to property. If protesters blocked the entrance to their church, wouldn't these Christians use the same ordinance to have the protesters arrested?

Second, Roe v. Wade *neither requires nor prohibits abortions but makes them permissible within certain restrictions.* Women who choose to have an abortion are free moral agents responsible before God for their actions, including the killing of their unborn children. The Christian's role is to use moral arguments to save the life of the unborn child. Using physical intervention is not an option.

Third, Christians are not permitted to disobey a just law in order to minimize the effects of unjust laws. When there is a clear contradiction between God and Caesar, Christians must obey God. In other cases, Christians should render obedience to civil authority. If they do not, then a state of anarchy would develop. Each person would do whatever seemed right and disobey whatever laws seemed wrong or inconvenient.

Christians must resist the tendency to rebel at the first provocation, especially in light of the scriptural admonitions to obey those in authority. This is especially true in light of our sin nature (Rom. 3:23). All of us have some rebellion in us. A good self check is to ask whether breaking a civil law is required. If not, we should give obedience the benefit of the doubt (Rom. 7:14).

Fourth, Christians should not use physical force. Proponents of using force believe that physical force is ethically correct to intervene in a life-or-death situation where innocent life is in danger. Likewise, force can be used to restrain evil. What are the limits to the use of physical force? If blocking clinics is justified, what about burning them down or blowing them up? Once any form of physical force is justified, how do we define the limits of its use?

Another question is this: If physical force can be justified in fighting abortion, what about using physical force in restraining idolatry or adultery? Should Christians block the entrances to New Age bookstores or pornography shops?

Some critics concerned that the use of physical force fear it would lead to unintended consequences, to justify all sorts of violent actions by Christians. Christians are not to fight with "the weapons of the world" (2 Cor. 10:4), but instead are to fight social evil with moral persuasion.

PRINCIPLES FOR CIVIL DISOBEDIENCE

Five principles should guide an individual's decisions about civil disobedience. *First, the law or injunction being resisted should clearly be unjust and unbiblical.* Christians are not allowed to resist laws merely because they disagree with them. Given our sin nature and our natural tendency toward anarchy, it seems appropriate for Christians to make a strong case for civil disobedience before they act. The burden of proof should be on the person advocating civil disobedience. In a sense, we should be talked into disobedience. If the case is not compelling for civil disobedience, then obedience is required by default.

Second, all lawful means of redress should be exhausted. One of the criteria for a just war is that the recourse to war must be the last resort. Civil disobedience should follow the same rigorous criterion. When all recourse to civil obedience has been exhausted, then and only then can discussion of revolution begin. Even then minimum resistance should be used if it can achieve a just result. If peaceful means can be used, force should be avoided. The only exception may be when the injustice is so grave and immediate that time for lengthy appeals is impossible. This exception is the appeal of many who propose the use of force to "rescue" unborn lives.

Third, Christians must be willing to accept the penalty for breaking the law. The biblical models, without exception, show those who stand for God submitting to the authority of the government they were disobeying. Such an attitude distinguishes civil disobedience from anarchy. By accepting punishment, believers often provide a powerful testimony to nonbelievers and awaken concern.

Fourth, civil disobedience should be carried out in love and with humility. Disobeying government should not be done with an angry or rebellious spirit. Bringing about social change requires love, patience, and humility, not anger and arrogance.

A fifth (somewhat controversial) principle is that civil disobedience should be considered only when there is some possibility for success. This has been seen since Augustine as an ethical criterion for waging a just war. In the case of civil disobedience success may not be the ultimate criterion, but it should be a concern if true social change is to take place. An individual certainly is free to disobey a law for personal reasons, but any attempt to change a law or social situation should enlist the aid and support of others. Also Christians should prayerfully evaluate whether the social disruption and potential promotion of lawlessness that may ensue is worth the positive result desired. Christians usually will be more effective by working within the social and political arenas to affect true social change.

BIBLICAL PRINCIPLES FOR SOCIAL ACTION

How then should Christians be involved in the social and political arena? They should be distinctively Christian in their approach, and they should learn from the mistakes of others so that they might be effective without falling into compromise or sin.

First, Christians must remember their dual citizenship. On the one hand, their citizenship is in heaven and not on earth (Phil. 3:17-21). Christians must remind themselves that God is sovereign over human affairs, even when circumstances look dark and discouraging. On the other hand the Bible also teaches that Christians are citizens on this earth (Matt. 22:15-22). They are to obey government (Rom. 13:1-7) and work within the social and political circumstances to affect change. Christians are to pray for those in authority (1 Tim. 2:1-4) and to obey those in authority.

Jesus compared the kingdom of heaven to leaven hidden in three pecks of meal (Matt. 13:33). The meal represents the world and the leaven represents the Christian presence in it. We are to exercise influence within the mass of society, seeking to bring about change that way. Though the Christian presence may seem as insignificant as leaven in meal, nevertheless we are to bring about the same profound change.

Second, Christians must remember that God is sovereign. As the Sovereign over the nations, He bestows power on whom He wishes (Dan. 4:17) and He can turn the heart of a king wherever He wishes (Prov. 21:1). Christians are often guilty of believing that they alone can make a difference in the political process. Christian leaders claim that the future of the country depends on the election of a particular candidate, the passage of a particular bill, or the confirmation of a particular Supreme Court justice. While it is important to be involved in public affairs, God is ultimately in control.

Third, Christians must use their specific gifts within the social and political arenas. Christians have different gifts and ministries (1 Cor. 12:4-6). Some may be called to a higher level of political participation than others (e.g., a candidate for school board or for Congress). All have a responsibility to be involved in society, but some are called to a higher level of social service, such as a social work professional or the crisis pregnancy center staff member. Christians must recognize the diversity of gifts and encourage fellow believers to use their gifts for the greatest impact.

Fourth, Christians should channel social and political activity through the church. Christians need to be accountable to each other, especially as they seek to make an impact on society. Wise leadership can prevent zealous evangelical Christians from repeating mistakes made in previous decades by other Christians.

The local church should also provide a context for compassionate social service. In the New Testament, the local church became a training ground for social action (Acts 2:45; 4:34). Meeting the needs of the poor, the infirm, the elderly, and widows is a responsibility. Ministries to these groups can provide a foundation and a catalyst for further outreach and ministry to the community.

Christians are to be the salt of the earth and the light of the world (Matt. 5:13–16). In our needy society, we have abundant opportunities to preach the gospel of Jesus Christ and meet significant social needs. By combining these two areas of preaching and ministry, Christians can make a strategic difference in society.

CHAPTER 32

The Coming Apostasy of the Church

Mal Couch

Despite the best intentions and desires of those who trust Jesus as Savior, there will come, on some day, a great departure from truth. This apostasy will leave Christianity with little substance. The church as a set of organized bodies will exist only as a shell, without spiritual power and meaning. The New Testament speaks often of this coming day. In 2 Thessalonians 2:3 it is called the *apostasia*, translated "the apostasy" (NASB) or "the falling away" (KJV). Similar language is used in 1 Timothy 4:1. The idea given in such texts is that there will be a departure from the faith.

The language used by the apostle Paul suggests that the great departure will become fully ripe probably sometime just before the rapture of the church (2 Thess. 2:2, 7–9; 2 Tim. 3:1). Paul also wrote that a form of this apostasy in some ways was already evident in his generation. Though this would climax in the last days, there would always be "departures" throughout the ages of the church (2 Thess. 2:7).

Paul's words introduce several questions: Has there been ongoing apostasy for the last two thousand years of church history? Does it come upon various generations of Christians in different ways? Is there apostasy in Christendom today? How might it be different in the twenty-first century? Could the next one hundred years be the countdown to the ultimate apostasy and its accompanying blessed hope for the rapture of the church? At some point in the next one hundred years, could the prophesied seven-year tribulation fall upon the world?

APOSTASY DEFINED

In its theological meaning with reference to the church, *apostasia* is used only in 2 Thessalonians 2:3. Here Paul writes, "Let no one in any way deceive you, for [the day of the Lord] will not come unless the apostasy comes first." Earlier in the New Testament, *apostasia* is used in a charge against Paul by the Jewish believers in Jerusalem. They accused him of "teaching all the Jews who are among the gentiles, to 'forsake' (*apostasia*) [the law of] Moses" (Acts 21:21a). We get an additional sense of the word from a related term, *apostasion*, which deals with the end of a marriage and is translated three times in the Gospels as "divorcement" (Matt. 5:31; 19:7; Mark 10:4).

In *A Greek-English Lexicon of the New Testament (BAGD)*, Walter Bauer defines *apostasia* as "rebellion, [or] abandonment."[1] The *Greek English Lexicon* of Liddell and Scott carries such meaning as "to depart, to stand aloof, to detach, to forsake."[2]

Etymologically, the word is a compound of the Greek preposition *apo* (away from) and the noun *stasis* (stand). Its literal meaning is "to leave or depart from."[3]

Usage

In 2 Thessalonians 2:1–12, Paul describes the work of Satan and the Antichrist at the mid-point of the seven-year tribulation. "In accord with the activity of Satan, with all power and signs and false wonders" (v. 9), the "man of lawlessness" will reveal his true colors and take "his seat in the temple of God, displaying himself as being God" (vv. 3b–4).

But the apostle Paul warns the believers in Thessalonica not to be disturbed because the Day of the Lord, the tribulation, has not come yet (v. 2). Before that day, the "departure" (*apostasia*) must take place first (v. 3a). Paul tells the Thessalonian church that they may see an "apostasy" long before the Antichrist makes his move in the tribulation. A blindness will overtake the professing church, but that same blindness to spiritual matters and what is true has already darkened the moral and biblical senses of those who have rejected Christ.

The apostle has already addressed in detail the issue of the Rapture before the great period of wrath (1 Thess. 5:1–11; cf., 2 Thess. 1:6–10). Here he does not mention that the believers themselves will not see the Antichrist.

On the doctrine of apostasy, Charles C. Ryrie writes, it is "a departure from truth previously accepted, involving the breaking of a professed relationship with God. Apostasy always involves willful leaving of previously known truth and embracing error."[4]

In the final hours of the dispensation of the Church, there will be those who have "confessed" biblical truth and who have "professed" a relationship with God. But they will simply be acting out, living a lie, walking as religious charlatans. Apostasy will be intense in the final days before the rapture of the church.

Illustrations of Apostasy

The apostles John, Peter, and Paul all speak of apostasy in their own day and another apostasy coming, in later times and in "the last days."[5] Ryrie describes these facts well:

> Beyond any question, apostasy is both present and future in the church. It was present when Paul wrote to Timothy, and Paul looked forward to a future great apostasy distinctive enough to be of the present-future antichrist. There were antichrists present in the church in John's day, and still he looked forward to the coming great Antichrist (1 John 2:18). Apostasy is something that plagues the church in every generation, though at the end of the church age the great apostasy will come on the scene before the Day of the Lord. [6]

In 1 Timothy 4:1–3, Paul writes that the Spirit explicitly speaks of a later falling away from faith. The words "falling away" come from the Greek verb *aphistemi* and can be translated, "they shall dismiss themselves" from the faith. By the expression "the faith," I believe the apostle is saying they will remove themselves from the faith profession. These people are not believers in Christ. He continues that they will be "paying attention to deceitful spirits and doctrines of demons." Their consciences will be seared as with a branding iron (vv. 1b–2).

In this passage Paul writes of a "later times" but he also seems to write that some of these things were happening at that time to the church. He urges those who "believe and know the truth" (v. 3), and who are good servants of Christ Jesus, that they be "constantly nourished on the words of faith and [on] sound doctrine which you have been following" (v. 6).

In 2 Timothy 3:1–9, Paul speaks of "the last days" in which difficult times will come (v. 1). He writes of men being lovers of self and money. He calls the people of that future day revilers, boastful, arrogant, disobedient to parents, ungrateful, unholy, "lovers of pleasure rather than lovers of God" (vv. 2–4). They are "holding to a form of godliness, although they have denied its power" (v. 5).

To Timothy, Paul speaks of a "last days" apostasy but also describes a present spiritual falling away during the period of his own ministry:

> *For the time will come when they will not endure sound doctrine; but wanting to have their ears tickled, they will accumulate for themselves teachers in accordance to their own desires; and will turn away their ears from the truth and will turn aside to myths. (2 Tim. 4:3–4)*

In 2 Peter 2:1–3, the apostle Peter describes false teachers who "secretly introduce destructive heresies, even denying the Master who bought them, bringing swift destruction upon themselves." He speaks of their sensuality, how they maligned the truth and exploit with false words (vv. 2–3). He continues this warning through verse 22 and writes,

> *Know this first of all, that in the last days mockers will come with their mocking, following after their own lusts, and saying, "Where is the promise of His coming? For all continues just as it was from the beginning of creation." (2 Peter 3:3)*

Peter reminds his readers that the day of judgment and destruction of the ungodly, who have attempted through the ages to mislead the saints, is certain (3:7–10).

John the apostle witnessed other apostasies coming against the churches. He writes about Gnosticism, the new cult that believed in secret knowledge and held that Jesus surely did not have a human-like body because flesh is sinful. John speaks out and warns the churches to test the spirits (1 John 4:1). He reminds believers that only those who confess that Christ came in the flesh can be from God (vv. 2–3a).

The spirit of antichrist is coming, John adds, and in fact, "now it is already in the world" (v. 3b). His summary warning is "whoever denies the Son does not have the Father; the one who confesses the Son has the Father also" (2:23).

In the Revelation, John writes of apostasy that even then was choking the life from the churches. He speaks of the Nicolaitans (Rev. 2:15), and the cult-like immorality of a "Jezebel" who was sapping the spiritual strength of churches such as Thyatira (2:20–23). Yet through such apostasy God was preserving the truth and working out His eternal purposes. The true church would survive, though it nearly drown in a sea of false teaching.

THROUGH THE AGES

Though not continual at any one place or always on an empire-wide scale, the Church suffered persecution almost continually from the 60s until the emperor Constantine issued the Edict of Milan in January 313. The Edict of Milan decreed that "the Christians among the rest, have the liberty to observe the religion of his choice, and his peculiar mode of worship."

One would imagine that in a new climate of safety Christendom would flourish in spiritual purity. It did not. In this reborn atmosphere of tolerance, apostate cults almost rooted out orthodoxy. New errors sprang up like weeds. Space allows us to mention but a few.

The Ebionites brought many back under the law of Moses. They rejected Paul, viewed Christ as a mere man, and in the New Testament accepted only a mutilated version of Matthew. The Gnostic-like cult of Cerinthus made a distinction between the earthly Jesus and the heavenly Christ. His views spread throughout Asia Minor.

Many fell victim to the Pseudo-Clementine Homilies. These taught that God dwelt on high in bodily form. His spiritual image was seen in man here below. The writings also speak of the feminine side of God.

Also serious competitors to the truth were the Gnostic systems of Basilides, of Valentinus, and of Marcion. Manichaeans syncretized a Zoroastrian version of Christianity. Monarchians solved the problem of the Trinity by teaching that God became Father and then Son and then Holy Spirit, but never more than one at a time. Many such doctrines rose up, planted spiritual confusion, and then vanished. Variations on the theme of apostasy seem endless.

This ledger of events seems bleak, but it must be remembered that the true church marched on through each new storm of error. Some always refused to believe the lie. The Holy Spirit gave them grace and stability to withstand the onslaught of doctrinal confusion.

A greater apostasy eventually would overtake the young church. Many centuries later it is called Roman Catholicism. Small steps of confusion led to giant steps of departure. A system began to develop around the bishopric of Rome that would become cast in unmovable iron. A system of bishops under the Roman bishop assumed organizational control of the people of God, and slowly their hierarchy was seduced toward unbiblical notions of faith and tradition. This hierarchical organization continued to focus on Rome, with the Roman bishop called the "father," or *pope.*

Doctrinal deviation grew: baptismal regeneration; Mary given worshipful adoration as the mother of God and a mediatrix for salvation alongside Christ; the mystical sacrifice of Christ in the Mass; purgatory; sainthood; prayers for the dead; dispensation of grace through the church; stigmata, apparitions, and infallibility of the pope. All this grew over long centuries. Infallibility did not become dogma until the middle of the twentieth century. But it all was built upon a foundation of works-righteousness salvation.

By the time Martin Luther first offered to debate his Ninety-five Theses in 1517, Roman Catholicism had become an institution of evil. No wonder Reformers frequently wrote of the pope as Antichrist, for the system enforced in the Roman Church was the epitome of departure from truth.

Many courageous men and women understood from Scripture that the Catholic Church was apostate and even pagan in its doctrines. They stood up against the system and a great many paid for their stand with their lives.

Though Catholicism remained almost intact, with a few minor reforms along the way, the light of the Reformation blazed brightly for a few centuries. At the end of the twentieth century that torch of truth is nearly extinguished. With the ecumenical rapprochement of Vatican II, Catholicism put on a new face. She is beckoning her wayward Protestant sheep to come home. Many are falling victim to her seduction.

THE APOSTASY OF HUMANISM

While Catholicism reached its pinnacle during the Middle Ages, a new apostasy emerged from ancient Greek culture to do immeasurable damage on Europe and North America. In the 1400s, Europe rediscovered itself in the Renaissance movement called humanism. Humanist artists put the human person at the center of life and art. They produced glorious sculptures, paintings, and buildings. Florence, Italy, was the center of this humanist, creative activity.

For centuries the favorite subjects of the master artists were superficially religious, but most had an underlying message of glorified personhood. They sought the perfect and the ideal within humanity and human surroundings. This philosophy was a neo-Platonism (or new Platonism) because it adapted the constructs of Plato to the Renaissance spirit. Neo-Platonism taught that the soul could ascend toward union with God through the contemplation of beauty. This mystical, naturalistic spirituality could be seen everywhere in Renaissance Europe.

Some thinkers resisted the trends, yet in the end most hammered out their own version of humanism. Fifteenth century cardinal Nicholas of Cusa (1401–1464) stressed the limits of human beings in trying to come to knowledge of God. Nicholas was a mathematician, and he believed we discover God through intuition, insights, and reason.

Writing on the dignity of human beings, John Pico della Mirandola (1463–1494) said people can be reborn to a higher life and become more like God Himself. To the human being it is granted "to have whatever it chooses, to be whatever it wills."[7]

Technology and industry combined with humanism in the eighteenth and nineteenth centuries to give rise to theological liberalism. If humankind could overcome poverty and disease by creativity, there was no need for God. At first, the Scriptures were attacked, then doctrinal Christianity. It was argued that the genius of humanity rendered obsolete the Bible, traditional morality, and God. Long before the turn of the twentieth century, such thinking had gained a serious hearing in traditionally Bible-centered circles.

THE "NEW" HUMANISM

At the beginning of 1900 in Europe, the Reformation of Calvin and Luther was but a shadow of its former self. A very traditional Catholicism held sway, especially in southern countries along and near the Mediterranean Sea. Protestantism had become basically political, for its most visible expressions were cold, lifeless state churches.

Classical liberalism dominated biblical studies in Europe's colleges and divinity schools, many of which were also state controlled. Humanism, skepticism, and doubt had polluted the spiritual climate of such institutions. The Bible was torn apart by intellectual criticism. Human had replaced divine reasoning.

Before 1800, liberalism and humanism were creeping their way across the ocean to America; by 1900 German philosophy and theology was one of the greatest imports of North America. The first to succumb were the universities of the East Coast. Harvard was leaving its faith foundation by the time of the first Great Awakening in the 1730s. By degree, the denominations slipped from their biblical roots and began to elevate the abilities of man. The liberals would argue that the wonders of the Industrial Revolution gave good reason to be optimistic in the hand of human enterprise.

By the early twentieth century, Unitarians, liberals, and conservative Christians all realized that Christianity was permanently changing. "Modernism is the result of a religious revolution," liberals wrote. "The present revolt [is] against doctrinal theology," professor Edward Ames of the University of Chicago noted.[8]

Others asked the religious to believe in themselves, "in the dignity of men, in the greatness of the human soul."

Some argued that we must ascribe divinity to people, because human nature was one with God's. People only needed to awaken to that supposed fact. To many, such thoughts were not shocking, because they had no authority base to evaluate these beliefs and find them damning and ridiculous. The authority of Scripture had been undercut by the overzealous application of naturalistic evolution and other parts of "objective" science. We were drifting from the idea that the Bible has any special significance or authority.[9]

Earlier, the British evangelist and preacher, Charles Haddon Spurgeon, saw the direction in which things were going: "If we have in the Word of God no infallible standard of truth, we are at sea without a compass, and no danger from rough weather without can be equal to this loss within."[10]

In 1915, Bible scholar J. Gresham Machen (1881–1937) saw the outcome of the victory of liberalism for his generation and for the future. He wrote, "Let us not deceive ourselves, . . . the Bible is at the foundation of the church. Undermine that foundation, and the church will fall."[11]

The modern trend, Arthur Pink wrote in the 1920s, was deification of the creature rather than the glorification of God. Rationalism had permeated Christendom. Darwinian evolution was influencing both the culture and the church. Pink also noted the fatal effects of unscriptural teaching in churches. The craving of his day was for something light and spicy from the pulpit. There was little demand upon the hearts and mental powers of believers.

Pink was right. Apostasy was changing how Western Christians thought.

So weak was the spiritual climate that the study of the deeper things of God was about over in church settings. False teachers with their injurious beliefs would follow shortly behind.[12] By mid-century, most traditionally biblical Protestant denominations had capitulated to some form of existentialistic modernism. Apostasy had reached the institutional structure of Protestantism as it had of the Roman Church.

THE FINAL APOSTASY?

Behaviorism, pantheism, naturalism, and related forces have ripped at the very foundation of biblical Christianity. The last fifty years of the twentieth century have been traumatic for Christians. Could this be a step toward *the* apostasy, that final great period of deception before the rapture of the church? There are forces now in place signaling that this is a possibility.

If so, we are certainly not at the beginning. The first steps were planted in another time. Look, for example, at the implications of only one influence from secularism that has infected churches: behaviorism, and its mechanistic understandings that have influenced much of psychology. Such men as Sigmund Freud and B. F. Skinner applied naturalistic forces to the study of human thought and action. The result was a mechanistic cause-response set of behavioral theories. Human volition, and then responsibility, are denied.

Behaviorism is part of a complex of psychological theories that denies the existence of a human soul as defined in Scripture. In the twentieth century behaviorism has been most profoundly influenced by the philosophy of pragmatism expounded by the social reconstructionist John Dewey (1859–1952). Humankind is seen as simply an evolving creature that is not essentially different from any other animal. With this and similar nonbiblical ideas in its background, secular psychology sets out to destroy the innate human understanding of immortality. John Horsch made the descriptive comment that "God is bowed out of existence."[13]

By the 1980s, even evangelical seminaries had begun to wed themselves to the godless theories of secular psychology under the guise of "integration," which integrated secular theories with biblical passages and principles.

Many evangelical seminaries that were at one time considered to be doctrinally solid now offer masters and doctoral counseling degrees that are based largely on these secular theories. As a result, some counseling centers, even in churches, are extremely humanistic and eclectic in practice. The average Christian seeking help feels safe in the cocoon of "Christian professionalism" and will accept as biblical the rhetoric of self-esteem, self-actualization, and self-love.

Ultimately, humanistic psychological theory appeals to the secular mentality. It gets rid of God. It makes human beings less morally responsible. Consequences are minimized. And there is no higher authority to answer to than self.

As the twentieth century began, these theories already would be packaged differently by a variety of theorists, from Sigmund Freud to Carl Jung, Alfred Adler, Karen Horney, and Erik Erikson. But the name that stands out in America as this century comes to a close is Carl Rogers.

Born in Oak Park, Illinois (1902), Rogers had leanings toward spiritual things. But at the age of twenty his Christian beliefs seem to have been shattered. From that point, he writes, he realized that Jesus was just another man and not divine. He gave up plans to be a missionary and in 1931 received his Ph.D. as a psychologist. He pioneered in understandings and therapies designed to bring one to "self actualization." "Experience is, for me, the highest authority. . . . Neither the Bible nor the prophets—neither Freud nor research—neither the revelations of God nor man—can take precedence over my own experience."[14]

Rogers added that humans should be able to trust their feelings over their senses or intellect. The only reality one can possibly know, he concluded, is one's experience at the moment. An experience cannot be thought of as "sinful" or ethically wrong, for such negative self-analysis clashes with one's full awareness. Our self-worth should be considered greater than the cultural mores or attitudes. Therefore, what is right for me is right.

Secular universities now brainwash their students in Rogerian philosophy and psychology. In popular form, even the world calls the society of the mid-1970s through the 1980s the "Me Generation." Does this not remind us of Paul's words of men being lovers of self, arrogant, ungrateful, unloving, without self-control, conceited, "lovers of pleasure rather than lovers of God" (2 Tim. 3:1–4).

Such a philosophy is a secular apostasy that has the seductive power to pull all the churches to its grasp and set up the kind of last-days "difficult times" described by Paul to Timothy.

1990'S SPIRITUAL REVIVAL?

In the mid-1990s, a CBS television series called *Touched by an Angel* achieved high ratings in its Sunday-night time-slot. Millions watched very human angels help humans out of precarious situations. These angels only rarely referred to God, and when they did it was to an accepting grandfather who lived to serve, never the God of Scripture. Rabbi Mark Bleiweiss caught the stupidity and self-indulgence of the concept and its attendant view of people, God, and reality. In his brilliant satire, "Slugged by an Angel," he describes these angels as "mainly of the savior variety, rescuing their charges from hijackings and hurricanes as well as from the perils of long lines and varicose veins.[15] They're God's little seraphs for the self-indulgent."[16]

Bleiweiss continues by noting that one CBS television executive justified this sorry pot of cold gruel by arguing that there is a growing trend in spirituality and even a mainstream "religious revival of the '90s." Apparently with such teachers as Rogers on his mind, Bleiweiss concludes,

> Modern angels, far from reuniting us with our Maker, sugar-coat the profound religious alienation in the world today. Angels of prime time iconography are little more than fairy godmothers with an affirmation action attitude. . . . No doubt many folks are bothered by the consuming emptiness of their lives, but not enough to do much about it. . . . [Angels] are the antithesis of the modern media heroes who make us feel so good about ourselves that serious spiritual reckoning seems somehow beneath us. God is eternity's "Good Guy." [17]

As the twenty-first century begins, the New Age movement is wrapping itself around the self with all kinds of techniques for finding one's way to an Eastern/Native American concept of godhood. New Age philosophy does not promote sacrifice of self but the fulfillment of self. The altered state of consciousness, through meditation, can put one into harmony with oneself and the universe (not the God of Scripture). Transcendental meditation is more fashionable than ever. The Unification Church promises thousands a spiritual redemption for humankind that even Jesus was not able to provide or complete in His work of redemption.

Pampering the self, the New Age movement promises a new world through psychics, astrologers, goddess worship, holistic health, and ecology. "Be happy and fulfilled" is the goal of whatever technique used for actualization.

Marianne Williamson's *A Course in Miracles* has sold 1 million copies since 1976. The book boasts "No religion has a monopoly on the greatest story ever told," and, "truth is in all religions." Williamson writes that our ultimate reality is at the core of who we are. Shades of Carl Rogers.

The lie continues to explode as millions are sucked into the vortex of a false religion of selfism. They are taught that Christ is but a common thread of divine love that is in every human mind. Within our minds, there is no place where God stops and we begin. Love is but an energy, an infinite continuum.

STEPS TOWARD THE RAPTURE?

The rapture of the Church is not simply a doctrine of easy escapism for believers in Christ. The church—those who belong to Christ and are part of his spiritual body—are removed from this earth just before the wrath of God is poured out upon rebellious and self-driven humanity.

The wrath will fall upon last-day mockers who follow after their own lusts and deny the promise of the return of Christ (2 Peter 3:3–4).

Though some disagree, it seems clear that the Bible teaches the pretribulational rapture of the Church. That is, all believers who are alive when it takes place will be lifted up from the earth. The dead in Christ will be raised first (1 Thess. 4:16). "Then we who are alive and remain shall be caught up together with them in the clouds to meet the Lord in the air, and thus we shall always be with the Lord" (4:17). Paul speaks of the Day of the Lord as the wrath (5:9; cf. Rom. 2:5) and clearly promises that, for all believers alive at that time, "God has not destined us for wrath, but for obtaining salvation through our Lord Jesus Christ" (1 Thess. 5:9). The wrath is the seven-year period of tribulation so vividly described in the book of Revelation. From the beginning, those events that are up front in the tribulation are collectively called "the wrath." This wrath originates from God who sits on His throne and from the Savior, Christ the Lamb! (Rev. 6:16-17).

With great zeal and anticipation, the apostle Paul describes the rapture of the church:

> *Behold, I tell you a mystery; we shall not all sleep, but we shall be all changed, in a moment, in the twinkling of an eye, at the last trumpet; for the trumpet will sound, and the dead will be raised imperishable, and we shall be changed. For this perishable must put on the imperishable, and the mortal must put on immortality. (1 Cor. 15:51-53)*

PROMISED WRATH

How terrible it will be for family members, friends, and neighbors who miss the rapture of the Church. How awful to contemplate that some we know would be left behind if the event were to occur now. They must then enter a world-wide tribulation, experiencing the wrath of God. The only way to escape this danger is by accepting Jesus Christ as personal Savior from sin, and as Lord.

We return to the question, "What will bring on the rapture of the Church, and then, the wrath?" The answer seems to be found in what is already beginning to happen in human hearts. They will increasingly turn to self-love and humanism to an extent greater than in any other generation.

Paul writes of stubborn and unrepentant hearts "storing up wrath for yourself in the day of wrath" (Rom. 2:5). He speaks of selfish ambition and tribulation and distress "for every soul of man who does evil" (vv. 8-9). And finally he writes, because of all kinds of sins, "passion, evil desire, and greed, . . . the wrath of God will come" (Col. 3:5-6).

WHAT SHOULD WE DO?

Since we could rapidly move into these events of the consummation of history, how should believers live? Part of that answer can be found in Paul's words to the persecuted church at Thessalonica. The apostle wrote how the Christians in that city "turned to God from idols to serve a living and true God, and to wait for His Son from heaven" (1 Thess. 1:9–10). They were discovered to be active and as well, looking upward for the return of Jesus. They were both serving and waiting. Ed Hindson offers this message for Christians of the next century:

> Since we can never be sure when God's purposes for His church will be finalized, we must remain obedient to our Lord's commands regarding His church. This was made clear to the disciples at the time of Christ's ascension to heaven. They had asked if He was going to restore the kingdom to Israel at that time, and Jesus told them, "It is not for you to know the times or dates the Father has set by His own authority" (Acts 1:7). Two facts are clear in this statement: (1) the date has been set; (2) we aren't supposed to know it because we have a responsibility to fulfill in the meantime.[18]

Though he would probably not believe all of our scenario about the return of the Lord, Scottish pastor Samuel Rutherford (1600–1661) held a great living hope of seeing the Lord bring all things to a blessed conclusion. In 1648, he wrote to a dying friend, George Gillespie, a superb poem, which in part reads

> The night, you say, is dark and long,
> The city out of sight;
> Yet lift your eyes: look to the east
> Where shadows take their flight.
> And though the goal seem wreathed in mists
> Still cleave to Christ your Guide
> Whose hidden love reserves for you
> Those comforts now denied.
>
> But one fight more—one fight of faith—
> The bravest and the last;
> One act of firm believing then
> The conflict shall be past.
> On Christ's strong righteousness rely
> Nor gaze on all your sin;
> Grace signs each debt as fully paid,
> Declares the guilty clean.
>
> To Him commit your deathless soul,
> Your weakness to His strength,
> Until your faltering steps shall gain
> Immanuel's land at length.[19]

CHAPTER 33

The Blessed Hope of the Church: The Rapture and the *Bēma* Judgment

Mal Couch

As we enter a new millennium, many believers in Christ sense that the next one hundred years could certainly herald the coming of Christ. All Christians have a longing for His appearance. From the human standpoint, one wonders how the ecological destruction of the earth can go on for another one hundred years. Other difficult problems plague the world, such as overpopulation, the development of therapy-resistant DNA strands in microbiology that could bring horrendous epidemics of disease. This is not to mention the ongoing work of evil that could bring wars of unimaginable scope. Someone has well noted that Scripture offers signs to look for regarding the second coming of Christ but no signs for the rapture of the church. This event can happen at any hour.

Among the body of Christ there are divergent views as to how He will come, or even if there will be a rapture. The majority of the church thinks He will simply come suddenly, end human sorrow, establish a court of judgment, purge the world, and inaugurate eternity.

Yet with the Reformation, Protestant Bible scholars who had greater access to Scripture in the original languages and in translation, began seeing issues related to the Rapture. Joseph Mede (1586-1638), considered the father of English premillennialism, saw a separation between the Rapture and the second coming of the Christ. Others who saw similar threads in the Bible included Thomas Collier, John Gill (1697-1771), Peter Jurieu (1637-1713), and Increase Mather (1639-1723).

With renewed interest in prophecy at the beginning of the nineteenth century, Bible scholars began to look intently at 1 Thessalonians 4:13-18. They noted how the apostle Paul speaks of a resurrection of those who had died in

Christ and then writes about those alive being "caught up." Students of prophecy realized that the body of Christ was to go up and meet the Lord in the air. This was distinctly different than saying that Christ would come to earth to reign or judge.

By the end of the nineteenth century, many scholars were paying more attention to principles of sound biblical interpretation. They began to see a pattern of how God worked differently in various ages of history. With this came a definite prophetic outline concerning the events of the last days. It became very clear that Christ's coming to "rapture" away the church saints was an entirely different event than was His coming to judge sinners and to rule and reign for a thousand years.

One scholar who led the way was John Nelson Darby (1800–1882). Born in London of wealthy Irish parents, his early studies were at Trinity College, where he was graduated in 1819 as a classical gold medallist. During a period of spiritual struggle, he gave up a career in law to enter the priesthood in the Church of England. Dissatisfied with the church-state relationship, he became a missionary and pastor among the Plymouth Brethren, a group that had split off from the dissenting churches in 1831.

Because of the plight of persecuted Jews, Darby and others began to understand more clearly God's plan for restoring Israel to the holy land. Seeing the beginnings of Zionism in their day, they could understand better the Old Testament prophecies that spoke of the literal coming of the Messiah to reign on the throne of David. Other prophetic patterns fell into place, including the idea that the Rapture would take place before the period known as the tribulation. Floyd Elmore summarizes Darby's teaching:

> The Rapture occurs before the final time of trial to come upon the earth. The church must already be with Christ in heaven to be able to appear with Him at His glorious return. . . . The first resurrection of the just coincides with the Rapture. Thus all those who have died in faith from both the Old Testament and New Testament eras will be raptured with the living church saints. Although all who have a resurrection body will be related in some way to the New Jerusalem, Darby called only the church the bride so as to give it the chief position among those glorified.
>
> After the Rapture, several things transpire in heaven. First, Satan is cast out of heaven to the earth. Then the saints will experience the judgment seat of Christ in preparation for the marriage of the Lamb.[1]

Many Bible teachers could see that the rapture of the church and the second coming of Christ would be literal comings that could not be spiritualized away. The doctrines of the pretribulational Rapture and the premillennial return of Christ to reign began to sweep across the larger conservative Christian world. The 1909 *Scofield Reference Bible* systematized these teachings as study Bible commentary that was written for the church at large. Many thousands learned about the prophetic message of Scripture in the *Scofield* notes.

THE BLESSED HOPE

Scholars have counted as many as fifteen clear and indisputable Scripture passages referring to the rapture of the church. In addition to 1 Thessalonians 4, one of the clear rapture passages is Titus 2:11-15. Paul writes of godly living and "looking for the blessed hope and the appearing of the glory of the great God and Savior, Christ Jesus" (v. 13). The context gives both rapture teaching and important references to the deity of Christ. In 3:4 Paul speaks of the "kindness of God our Savior." In 3:6 he speaks of "Jesus Christ our Savior." In 2:13 the Savior is both God and Christ Jesus. Paul says we ought to be looking for Christ who is God to appear. This means coming down to earth.

"The glory" in Titus 2:13 is a descriptive genitive, translated as an adjective, thus, "the glorious appearance." The Greek connects "the blessed hope and glorious appearing" under one article, suggesting that the reference is to one event viewed from two aspects. The reference to the Lord should read, "the great God even Savior, Christ Jesus."[2]

Paul makes it perfectly clear that the Rapture removes the church, the spiritual body of Christ from the earth just prior to the tribulation, a terrible seven-year period of wrath. In 1 Thessalonians 1:9-10 the apostle writes of the Thessalonians as serving and waiting for God's Son from heaven, "that is, Jesus who delivers us from the wrath to come." The wrath (*orgēs*) is equal to the tribulation period. The *from* (*ek*) is strong in Greek and could read "away from" or "out of."

Paul repeats this when he says, "For God has not destined us for wrath, but for obtaining salvation through our Lord Jesus Christ" (5:9). This wrath is "the day of the Lord" (v. 2) that will come on "them," the world. "But you, brethren, are not in darkness, that the day should overtake you like a thief" (v. 4).

What Defines a Rapture Passage?

Ten important key elements are identified as indicators for rapture verses. Though these elements are certainly not in every rapture context and passage, they show up often enough to become common markers.[3]

1. The Body of Christ

The rapture is for those "in Christ" and takes place at the end of the dispensation of the church. The Rapture closes the church age. Thus, the believers in Christ are taken home before the tribulation begins. This is termed the *pretribulation rapture doctrine.* Paul writes of "those who are Christ's at His coming" (1 Cor. 15:23b) and of those who will obtain salvation "through" our Lord Jesus Christ (1 Thess. 5:9).

2. Hope and Comfort

Rapture texts describe the great blessing of Christ's return for His own, the church, to take them to heaven. This is hope and comfort, a different scenario than that of the Lord returning to judge and rule as Messiah. When James writes "be patient" (James 5:7) the Greek is best translated "be eagerly expecting." The same is true in 1 Thessalonians 1:10. As well, Paul tells the Thessalonian church that "they need to be comforting each other right now and until the Lord comes. This is an exercise in faith in order to recognize the certainty of ultimate triumph."

3. The Change of the Body

The apostle writes to the Corinthians, "We shall not all sleep [physically die], but we shall all be changed. . . . The dead will be raised imperishable, and we shall be changed" (1 Cor. 15:51b, 52b; see vv. 51–53). To Philippi he writes of Christ, "who will transform the body of our humble state into conformity with the body of His glory" (Phil. 3:21). He will do this by His divine power, authority, and ability, because all things are subject to Him. This must be good news to those who suffer physically. "To transform" can literally mean to change the schematics, "turn about" the present body into something new.

4. A Going Home to Heaven

Jesus is emphatic about this in that very first rapture passage (John 14:2–3). The Greek could read "I will be coming again . . . where I am, I and you [together]." Because of context, it may also read as a future tense, "I will be coming again." This happening is stated as so absolute that in thought it may be contemplated as already coming to pass. When Paul writes of "our gathering together to Him," he refers to our going home to heaven (2 Thess. 2:1). Many speak of this passage as the "mustering of the saints to heaven!" In Greek the phrase "to Him" can be translated "up to Him."

5. Taken Directly to the Lord Jesus

This idea in these verses is similar to the idea of going up to heaven, but it emphasizes and punctuates the fact that the saints are brought into His very presence. When Paul writes that Jesus will deliver us from the wrath to come (1 Thess. 1:10), the word deliver (*ruomai*) conveys the idea of being rescued, dragged or drawn away from danger. It can even be translated "to draw to one's self." Paul and John add, "We eagerly wait for a Savior, Christ Jesus" (Titus 2:13). Stay with Him, "so that when He appears, we may have confidence and not shrink away from Him [from His face] in shame at His coming" (1 John 2:28). "We shall see Him just as He is" (3:2).

6. Taken Directly Before the Father

Jesus said "In My Father's house are many dwelling places; . . . I go to prepare a place for you" (John 14:2). This house could not dwell in an earthly kingdom. Jesus is about to go to His death, and thence to His Father's house. He will come for His own and take them back to heaven. Though the Father and the Son are separate persons in the Godhead, they share the same essence and attributes. We are thus raptured by God the Son and taken to the very presence of God the Father. As we have previously noted, in the same epistle Paul writes, "God [is] our Savior" (Titus 3:4) and "Christ [is] our Savior" (v. 6). As noted above, Titus 2:13 states this profoundly in speaking of the glory of our great God and Savior, Jesus Christ.

7. Those in Christ Are to Live Differently

In six distinct passages, godly living is tied to the rapture hope. Some claim that those who teach the doctrine of the rapture simply look for an escape. But the apostles James and Paul both make it an incentive for living because He could appear to take us to Himself at any moment. But the evidence is overwhelming that this expectation should stimulate Christian maturity and properly balanced anticipation. For example, James tells the believers to stop complaining against each other because they may soon be judged. "The Judge is standing right at the door" (James 5:9). Paul urges those in Christ "to keep the commandment without stain or reproach until the appearing [*epiphaneias*] of our Lord Jesus Christ" (1 Tim. 6:14). The truth of God's grace and its accompanying salvation through the rapture should cause us to look for the blessed hope (Titus 2:12–13). It should help us to deny ungodliness and worldly desires.

8. The Imminence or Immediacy of the Rapture

The early church looked for Christ's soon return. In the passages, the use of the pronouns *we, you,* and *us* are proof that the Rapture could have happened to Paul's generation. But how do we explain that it did not come to them? As with some engagements, a wedding date may not have been set, yet the bride and groom long for and anticipate their coming union. The disciples had this longing but were given no hint as to the time of the Rapture. Since it did not come upon them, we do not question their hope nor the Lord's revelation about the doctrine itself. It simply means that it is yet to come. John Walvoord writes,

The hope of the return of Christ to take the saints to heaven is presented in John 14 as an imminent hope. There is no teaching of any intervening event. The prospect of being taken to heaven at the coming of Christ is not qualified by description of any signs or prerequisite events. Here, as in other passages dealing with the coming of Christ for the church, the hope is presented as an imminent event.[4]

9. The Rapture as Parousia

Some critics confine their arguments against the Rapture by referring to the Greek word *parousia*. This word is translated as "the coming" as in "the coming of the Lord." Parousia can be translated "the event," the "appearance," or "the visit." It is, in fact, used of both the rapture coming and the second coming of Christ to reign. But one of the most important factors in interpretation is "context." *How* a word is used is more important than its original root meaning—though its etymology is significant. The contexts for the rapture verses are clear; it is hard to mistake what they are saying. From the Greek text, James 5:7–9 and 1 Thessalonians 3:13 can be read,

> *Be waiting steadfastly then, until the time of the visitation arrives. Be waiting steadfastly . . . because the visitation of the Lord has progressively been drawing near. [author's translation]*

> *That [He may] firm up the hearts of you faultless, . . . in the [very] presence of the God and Father of us with the arrival of our Lord Jesus. [author's translation]*

10. The Resurrection and the Rapture

Various resurrections are described in the Word of God. But concerning the church age, and those described as being "in Christ," the Lord is called the first fruits after His resurrection from the dead (1 Cor. 15:20). This agricultural term pictures a spring harvest in Palestine in which Christ is the first "of the crop" to come forth from the grave. If we die "in Christ" before the Rapture, we will rise from the dead, just as He did.

Paul spells this out in 1 Thessalonians 4. Those who have fallen asleep in Jesus will go before or ahead of those who are still alive when He descends from heaven. A shout will come from the archangel of heaven, a trumpet will sound, "and the dead in Christ shall rise first" (v. 16). Those still alive when this happens will be caught up, raptured to join the resurrected with the Lord in the clouds (v. 17). Obviously there is a miraculous change, a transformation of the dust that is in the ground. The spirit and soul are joined to this new body. The body of those of us still alive will also be transformed, with the result that "we shall always [from then on] be with the Lord" (v. 17b). Paul is adamant about the resurrection of the church saints. He reminds us not to grieve about those who have died in Christ (v. 13). He adds that it is the unbelievers who have no hope of life after death. The blessed truth of the Resurrection makes Christianity different. Milligan points out,

> No mention has been made of the reason of Gentile hopelessness, but it is clearly traceable to ignorance of the revelation of the one God, . . . and accordingly the Apostles proceed to lay down the real ground of Christian hope. That ground is the death and resurrection of the historic Jesus.[5]

Other Rapture Views

Four other views have limited acceptability. These come and go in influence. Their common weakness is that they place believers to some degree in the seven-year tribulation. Here is a brief survey of these teachings:

The Partial Rapture Theory

The partial or "sanctification" rapture has been advocated by pretribulationists who believe Christians must be morally prepared to go to heaven. They argue that, with the many exhortations to be faithful and live Spirit-filled lives, the translation to heaven is a reward. Christians are taken to heaven during the tribulation as they become spiritually mature. Some are raptured early, and others must wait until they become worthy.

Besides the issue as to whether the church will face the wrath of God, this Protestant purgatory view rejects the imputed righteousness of Christ. Believers do not earn perfection or righteousness. We get to heaven on the basis of Christ's declared righteousness, not our own. In living out the Christian experience, every believer walks imperfectly. But God is finished with all of our sins through Christ's imputed righteousness. They were all purged and paid for at the cross of Christ.

The Postribulation Rapture Theory

The postribulation rapture view believes that the church remains on earth during the entire seven-year tribulation. But as Christ descends to begin His kingdom reign, the church meets Him in the air and immediately returns back down with Him. This position conflicts with Christ's words in John 14:3 where He states that He will receive the church from the earth and take it to His Father's house in heaven. It also violates the promise that the church will not experience the wrath of God in the tribulation (see almost any of the central tribulation texts).

The Midtribulation Rapture Theory

The midtribulation rapture view is that the church stays on earth through the first three and one-half years of the seven-year period of wrath. Jesus then comes and raptures the church halfway through the seven years. Again, the biblical promise that the church will not go through the wrath is ignored.

The Pre-Wrath Rapture Theory

This pre-wrath view is similar to the midtribulation rapture teaching. The pre-wrath position says the church remains on earth until sometime between the middle and end of the seventieth week of Daniel. Thus, Christ will not come and rapture the church from the earth until perhaps three-fourths of the way through the seven-year period.[6] This view has inherited the same weaknesses as the other teachings. Basic passages are ignored or twisted in order to have the church go through at least a part of the seven-year wrath of God. Though this view is one of the most recent attempts to leave the church on earth during the tribulation, it has already been weighed and found wanting when all passages are given equal weight.

Answering the Views

The pretribulational rapture theory is the only one that seems consistent with all teachings in Scripture on the subject. Very strong evidence, as already shown, makes it clear that the church is taken away before any part of the Tribulation begins. Though even some premillennialists may disagree, it seems Paul makes the Day of the Lord (1 Thess. 5:2) equal to the wrath of God (v. 9).

Paul notes that *the world* ("they") will say "peace and safety" but the destruction (the Day of the Lord) still comes on *them* suddenly like birth pangs, "*and they shall not escape*" (v. 3). He goes on to say that this day will not overtake like a thief, the believers in Christ. We do not belong to darkness but are the sons of light (vv. 4–5). Because of this, we are not destined to wrath (v. 9); we are instead to obtain salvation from the wrath that is on its way (1:10).

In 2 Thessalonians 2 Paul comforts the church at Thessalonica that they are not in the Day of the Lord, as they think. In this chapter he teaches that the Day of the Lord has not come (v. 2), but before it arrives, the apostasy of the church must first take place (v. 3) and the Antichrist, the lawless one, must then come "who opposes and exalts himself above every so-called god or object or worship, so that he takes his seat in the temple of God, displaying himself as being God" (v. 4).

As already pointed out, the final and most convincing argument is found in Revelation 6:16–17. The apostle John writes of the wrath of God and of Christ Jesus, the Lamb. The context clearly suggests that the six seal judgments are all together taken as the wrath. With the tribulation wrath just beginning in this chapter, and with the previous promises that the church will not face this terrible wrath judgment, the pretribulational rapture seems to be the only biblical option that makes sense.

The rapture of the church is not simply an escape. It should be the blessed hope for all who trust Christ as Savior.

THE *BĒMA* SEAT JUDGMENT

Immediately following the rapture of those who are in Christ Jesus, the gathering of these true believers will stand in heaven before what is described in Romans 14:10 and 2 Corinthians 5:10 as the "judgment seat of Christ." Revelation 19:8 pictures Christ's bride, the church, as already having received their rewards when He returns to earth at His second coming. Therefore, many argue that this event will be subsequent to the Rapture but before that second coming.

The Greek word *bēma,* used to describe this rewarding event, portrays a seat or raised platform where a judge or governor of the Roman world sits to adjudicate a case (Matt. 27:19; John 19:13; Acts 18:12). This word was also used to describe such a platform on which the referee sat during the Isthmian sporting events at Corinth. Before this platform the rewards were passed out to the winners of the various athletic events. Without question the apostle Paul knew of such scenes and had this in mind when he used the phrase, "judgment seat of Christ." Putting all this together with the context and the historical background, the term *bēma* clearly implies this time and place for rewarding believers for their service to the Lord. First Corinthians 3:10–4:5 also supports this doctrine.

It is the believer in the Lord who has built upon the foundation of his Savior Jesus Christ, who will participate and be so honored at this judgment for rewards. No unsaved or even Old Testament saint will be so blessed.

The Bēma and Eternal Destiny

This is a judgment for rewards, not for salvation. Our eternity has already been settled once we accept Jesus as personal Savior. The believer in the Lord is legally acquitted or justified by faith. The apostle writes, "There is therefore now no condemnation for those who are in Christ Jesus" (Rom. 8:1). The context of Paul's words has to do with the forgiveness of *all* of the sins of a Christian, based on Jesus' work at the Cross.

All of the sins of the child of God are forgiven in terms of his "eternal position" in Christ. Yet the believer's works will stand scrutiny by the Lord who will judge His own children and then distribute rewards for service rendered during life. Douglas Moo relates,

Condemnation has been removed from the believer, and no more will condemnation of any kind threaten him or her (cf. 8:34). How can this happen for those "in Christ"? Because those in Christ experience the benefits of Christ's death "for us": "He was for us in the place of condemnation; we are in Him where all condemnation has spent its force" (cf. 2 Cor. 5:21).[7]

Do All Believers Stand Before the Bēma?

Paul writes "For we must all appear before the judgment seat of Christ, that each one may be recompensed for his deeds in the body, according to what he has done, whether good or bad" (2 Cor. 5:10). This *bēma* judgment cannot be confused with the "great white throne" judgment of Revelation 20:11–15. This judgment is of all unbelievers. Since Christ's blood has not covered their sins, they must answer for "all" their works.

The scene is a sobering one. The sea, death, and Hades give up all the lost for this final tribunal of their souls. There is no appeal. All who stand in the presence of the Lord at this judgment are cast into the lake of fire (v. 14), which is the conclusive spiritual "second death." What a horrible pronouncement: "If anyone's name was not found written in the book of life, he was thrown into the lake of fire" (v. 15).

Is the Bēma Immediately After the Rapture?

The apostle Paul desires that the saints in Christ not prejudge each other. He writes "Do not go on passing judgment before the time, but wait until the Lord comes" (1 Cor. 4:5). James likewise urges believers to "not complain against each other" because "behold, the Judge [Christ] is standing right at the door" (James 5:9).

Both passages appear to speak of the imminence of the Rapture for those to whom the apostles are writing. In other words, Christ's coming to rapture His own should be expected. And with this return, the church saints would suddenly face Him at the *bēma*.

Is the Bēma for Service to Christ?

At this judgment "each one may be recompensed for his deeds in the body, according to what he has done . . ." (2 Cor. 5:10). The Greek word for "recompense" (*komizō*) has the idea of receiving a "pay, wage." It is in the middle voice and would better read "he should receive to himself a wage." Some have translated this as "receive as his due." Each saint in the Lord will stand alone and be accountable to the Master. These works are judged as to whether they are "good or useless" (*phaulos*, 2 Cor. 5:10).

In 2 Corinthians 4:1–5, Paul seems to be drawing a picture of a servant or steward who must give account. He portrays an overseer, commonly a slave, who is charged with taking care of the household. He is responsible, not to others, but to the Lord, whose high trust demands a strict accounting. With perfect fairness, "each man's praise will come to him from God" (v. 5).

Will Actual Awards Be Given?

Paul pictures the Christian life as the struggle of an athlete who must discipline himself, in order not to receive a perishable wreath, "but . . . an imperishable" (1 Cor. 9:25). He goes on and speaks of "that day" when the Lord will appear at the Rapture (2 Tim. 4:8) and give to him a *crown of righteousness* presented by the "righteous Judge" who will reward with the crown reserved for his service to Christ.

Finally, James speaks of the crown given for how one lived the Christian life, in self-glory or humility, being double-minded or without reproach (James 1:5–10). The apostle continues to write about endurance that produces maturity, "lacking in nothing" (v. 4). He concludes his exhortation by writing "Blessed is a man who preserves under trial; for once he has been approved, he will receive *the crown of life,* which the Lord has promised to those who love Him" (v. 12).

CONCLUSION

Why is the Rapture and the doctrine of rewards so important to the Christian generations growing up in the century 2000? These truths of Scripture constrain the believer in Christ to live the Christian life. It is so easy to be caught up in what the world has to offer. Many of those who trusted Him as Savior in the final decades of the 1900s became caught up in the "Me Generation." Materialism and cultural conformity profoundly affected the church. If we are near the end, these temptations will only intensify. Apostasy and confusion will grow and doctrinal departure will only further weaken the church morally and spiritually.

But thank God some will understand what is happening around them. They can comprehend the nature of the growing spiritual darkness. They will not be passive, but will be standing firm, serving and waiting for the Lord from heaven. And though persecution may intensify during this next century, and the witness of the Christian may be taunted, there are rewards for those who persevere.

The hope of coming generations, if the Rapture does not take place soon, is not with human progress—particularly in the fields of science. The next generations must be reminded of the words of Isaiah and Paul when they wrote, "Stop regarding man, whose breath of life is in his nostrils; for why should he be esteemed?" (Isa. 2:22), for after all, they "set their minds on earthly things" (Phil. 3:19b).

Paul continues with his great reminder: "For our citizenship is in heaven, from which also we eagerly wait for a Savior, the Lord Jesus Christ" (v. 20). On these words of Paul, *Ellicott's Commentary* on Philippians well states that with the lost,

> "Their mind is on earth; our country is in heaven," and to it our affections cling, even during our earthly pilgrimage. . . . As all the citizens of Philippi, the Roman colony, were citizens of the far distant imperial city, so the Philippian Christians even now were citizens of the better country in heaven.[8]

CHAPTER 34

The Coming Millennial Reign of Christ

John F. Walvoord

Will the third millennium see a return of the Lord Jesus Christ to establish His thousand-year reign? We could be close to the time when Christ will rule the nations with rod of iron from His throne in Jerusalem. Some of the things Scripture says will occur in the seven-year tribulation period are for the first time possible today.

For the first time in history we can see how a one-world government and a one-world religion could function through an intricate web of communication and information access. The technology for interactive world commerce not only exists but is rapidly growing in use. A world banking system exists by which a few leaders could extend or withhold credit to world governments. Immense commercial and trade monopolies in which individual government policies are irrelevant have only recently been possible.

THE MILLENNIUM

Defining the Term

The word *millennium* means "one thousand years." While the word itself never occurs in the Bible, the span of time is mentioned six times in Revelation 20. Both orthodox Jews and Christians identify this period with Old Testament promises of a coming kingdom of righteousness and peace. In this earthly kingdom, the Jews will be leaders and all the nations will have great blessing spiritually and economically. A study of the Millennium involves an understanding of much prophetic Scripture.

One's view on the Millennium rests heavily on how one interprets Scripture. The premillennial view is derived from taking the Scriptures at face value and applying a natural, normal hermeneutic. This "literal interpretation" is the view presented in this volume.

Students of the early church agree that premillennialism (or chiliasm) was the view held by many church fathers. It is the oldest of the various millennial views. Chiliasm is from the Greek word for one thousand, *chilias*. It is a teaching that Christ will reign on earth for one thousand years following His second advent. *Premillennialism* derives its meaning from the belief that Christ will return before the beginning of this millennium. Both terms refer to the same doctrine.[1]

An Important Doctrine

The question has been raised whether the discussion of the millennial doctrine is in itself important and worthy of the consideration of the scholarly world. There remains today a tendency to dismiss the whole subject as belonging to another age and as being foreign to intellectual studies of our day. On the other hand, the continued production of books on the subject points to a growing realization that the issue is still regarded by many as important.

There is a growing realization that premillennialism is more than a dispute about Revelation 20. For the first time it seems to be commonly recognized that premillennial theology is a system of theology, not an alternate view of eschatology that is unrelated to theology as a whole.

Premillennialism not only takes the Bible as authoritative in opposition to liberalism, but believes that an ordinary believer can understand the main import of Scriptures, including the prophetic Word. Premillenarians are sometimes charges with "bibliolatry" or worship of the Bible. Thus, it is inevitable that defense of premillennialism becomes a defense of the sole authority of the Bible in speaking of future events and programs of God.

The Premillennial Hermeneutic

The premillennial system of interpretation of Scripture interprets prophecy in the same way as other Scripture. It denies the Augustinian separation of the literature of prophecy into a genre requiring different principles of interpretation. Though recognizing that some Scriptures contain figures of speech that are not intended for literal interpretation, premillennial interpretation finds no need for spiritualizing prophecy any more than any other portion of Scripture. This literal interpretation leads the premillenarian to affirm a future millennial reign of Christ.

The doctrine of a future millennium on earth affects interpretation of the Abrahamic covenant, with its promise that racial Israel will inherit the land promised to Abraham. It is by careful distinction of the promises made to Abraham, the promises made to Abraham's physical seed, and the promises made to Abraham's spiritual seed as contained in both the Old and New Testaments, that a full premillennial explanation is given of the Abrahamic covenant.

Even more specific in its relation to premillennialism is God's covenant with David in which David is promised that his descendants will rule over the house of Israel forever. This covenant is reiterated in the Old Testament and is specifically repeated to Mary in connection with the birth of Christ. If interpreted as a literal earthly kingdom, the covenant leads inevitably to the doctrine of a future reign of Christ on earth to fulfill these promises.

Premillennialism is also related to literal fulfillment of the covenant revealed in Jeremiah and Ezekiel. This covenant pictures a period when God would replace the Mosaic covenant with a new covenant that He would write upon the hearts of the people. It would be fulfilled when Israel would no longer need to teach the truth of Jehovah to every neighbor, for "they shall all know me, from the least of them unto the greatest of them, saith Jehovah" (Jer. 31:34).[2] The promises to Abraham, the promises to David, the promises to Israel of future possession of the land, and the promises to Jeremiah that Israel would continue as long as the sun and moon endure (Jer. 31:35–36) combine to provide a grand prelude to the millennial reign of Christ.

To the Old Testament picture the New Testament adds its revelation of future things. Of prime importance to the premillennial interpretation of Scripture is the distinction provided in the New Testament between God's purpose for the church and His purpose for the nation of Israel. Descendants of Jacob in this age who come to Christ join gentiles in forming the body of Christ, the church. The Bible makes clear, however, that Israel will have an expanded role in the future reign of Christ. At that time Israel will be His people and God will be their God. The New Testament makes plain, according to the premillennial interpretation, that God's present purpose is not to fulfill the kingdom prophecies of the Old Testament. Those prophecies will be fulfilled during the era in which Satan is bound and all the nations will come to worship at the feet of the King of Kings.

EVENTS BEFORE CHRIST'S REIGN

At least two significant events will precede Christ's glorious reign on earth. The first deals primarily with God's program for the Church and the other deals primarily with His program for the nation Israel.

The first of these events is the *rapture* of the church. This event will take place before the entire seven-year period of Daniel's seventieth week and can be expected at any moment of any day. This emphasizes the imminence of the Lord's return. At this event, as described by Paul in his first letter to the Thessalonians, the "Lord Himself will descend from heaven with a shout and with the voice of the archangel, and with the trumpet of God; and the dead in Christ will rise first" (1 Thess. 4:16). The "dead in Christ" refers to all Christians who have died before the moment when he returns for His Church (1 Cor. 12:12–13). Their spirits, which are with the Lord (Phil. 3:23; 2 Cor.

5:8), will return with Christ and they will be united with their resurrected and glorified bodies (1 Cor. 15:51-53). Believers alive at the time of this event will be "caught up" at the same time and glorified as well (vv. 51-53). This will be followed by the "judgment seat of Christ," which will be an evaluation of the believers for rewards (1 Cor. 3:11-15; 2 Cor. 5:10). See chapter 33 of this volume for a detailed discussion of these events.

The second major event that will precede Christ's second coming and His millennial reign is the *Tribulation*. This term refers to the seven-year period before the Jewish nation recognizes their Messiah and Christ's millennial reign will be established. According to Daniel's prophecy (9:24-27), the last seven years will begin with a covenant between the Antichrist and the people of Israel. This will evidently be a covenant of protection and of religious liberty, under which Israel is free to reestablish the sacrificial system.

In the middle of the seven years, the covenant will be broken and sacrifices will cease. This may be done in connection with an effort to deify the world ruler, outlawing worship of God by Jews and Christians. Thus begins a period of trial such as was never before experienced by those who would worship the true God.

BEGINNING CHRIST'S REIGN

The Second Coming

The most important step toward the Millennium will be the personal return of Jesus Christ to the earth. The preceding Tribulation will be a dramatic preparation for the coming by the Lord, accompanied by the saints and angels. Though the Second Coming may not be as important to the total program of God as the first coming, it will be without precedent in showing God's glory and power.

Several Old Testament Scriptures deal with Christ's return to establish his reign on earth (Deut. 30:3; Psalms 2; 24; 72; 96; 110; Isa. 9:6-7; 11-12; 63:1-6; Dan. 2:44; 7:13-14; Zech. 2:10-11; 14:3-11). One out of every twenty-five verses in the New Testament refers either to the rapture of the church or to Christ's coming to reign over the world. Many of these passages clearly present a premillennial coming at the close of the Tribulation, with judgment and the righteous reign of the King. Scripture suggests that

1. Christ's return to reign will follow the Tribulation (Matt. 24:21-29; Mark 13:24-26; Luke 21:25-27; Revelation 19).
2. Christ himself will return in body (Zech. 14:4; Acts 1:11).
3. Christ's return will be visible (Matt. 24:27-30; Acts 1:11; Rev. 1:7; 19:11-12).

4. Christ will return to a place (Pss. 14:7; 20:2; 53:6; 110:2; 128:5; 134:3; 135:21; Isa. 2:3; Joel 3:16; Amos 1:2; Zech. 14:1–4; Rom. 11:26; Rev. 19:11–21).
5. Christ will be accompanied by angels and saints (Matt. 25:31; 1 Thess. 3:13; Rev. 19:11–21).
6. Christ will return to judge (Matt. 19:28; 24:29–25:46; Luke 17:29–30; 2 Thess. 1:7–9; 2:8; Jude 15; Rev. 2:27; 19:11–21).
7. Christ will deliver the elect (Zech. 14:1–4; Matt. 24:22; Rom. 11:26–27).
8. Christ will bring spiritual revival to Israel (Jer. 31:31–34; Rom. 11:26–27).
9. Christ will reestablish the Davidic kingdom (Ezek. 37:26; Amos 9:11–12; Luke 1:31–33).

Resurrection and Judgments

It should be clear from Scripture that the Second Coming will be one of the most important events of all time. That Christ will sit in judgment gives the event tremendous significance (see chapter 35 of this volume for an extended discussion of this subject). At Christ's return, several groups will be judged:

1. those who undergo the Tribulation (Rev. 20:4–6)
2. Old Testament saints (Dan. 12:2)
3. living gentiles (Ps. 2; Joel 3:1–2; Zeph. 3:8; Zech. 14:1–19; Matt. 25:31–46)
4. the Jews (Ezek. 20:33–38)
5. Satan (who will have a final judgment later, Rev. 20:1–2, 10)

As a result of the judgments, those who survive the Tribulation, both Jew and gentile, will enter the millennial reign in their physical bodies. The Old Testament saints will inherit the promised kingdom in their resurrected bodies. The tribulation saints and church saints (whose judgment took place in heaven while the tribulation raged on earth) will inhabit the millennium in resurrected bodies.

CHRIST'S GOVERNMENT

The millennial kingdom is a rule of God on earth, as distinguished from his reign from heaven through history and his rule in eternity future. Psalm 2:8 records the invitation of the Father to His blessed Son: "Ask of me, and I will give thee the nations for thine inheritance, and the uttermost parts of the earth for thy possession."

Isaiah 11 paints the graphic picture of the reign of Christ, a scene that cannot be confused with the present age, the intermediate state, or the eternal state. The righteous government of Christ is depicted in Isaiah 11:4:

"But with righteousness shall he judge the poor, and reprove with equity for the meek of the earth: and he shall smite the earth with the rod of his mouth, and with the breath of his lips shall he slay the wicked." The description that follows describes such animals as wolves, lambs, leopards, kids, calves, and young lions. All of these are creatures of earth, not heaven. They are pictured in a time of tranquillity, such as only can apply to the millennial earth.

The sweeping statement of Isaiah 11:9 confirms this judgment: "They shall not hurt nor destroy in all my holy mountain: for the earth shall be full of the knowledge of the LORD as the waters cover the sea." Various countries of earth are mentioned as having some part in the dealings of God, showing that the earth is in view, not heaven (see also Isa. 42:4; Jer. 23:3–6; Dan. 2:35–45; and Zech. 14:1–9).

The Supreme King

In Psalm 2:6, in spite of the opposition of the kings of the earth, God declares His purpose: "Yet I have set my king upon my holy hill of Zion." This purpose will be fulfilled in the millennial kingdom in the reign of Jesus Christ as the Son of David. As Lewis Sperry Chafer has succinctly stated,

> Every Old Testament prophecy on the kingdom anticipates His kingly office: (a) Christ will yet sit on the throne as David's heir (2 Sam. 7:16; Ps. 89:20–37; Isa. 11:1–16; Jer. 33:19–21). (b) He came as a King (Luke 1:32–33). (c) He was rejected as a King (Mark 15:12–13; Luke 19:14; cf. Gen. 37:8; Exod. 2:14). (d) He died as a King (Matt. 27:37). (e) When He comes again, it is as a King (Rev. 19:16; cf. Luke 1:32–33).[3]

The fact that Christ will reign over the earth is of course imbedded in practically every prophecy concerning the millennial kingdom. The absolute character of His reign is indicated in Isaiah 11:3–5. This central prophecy is confirmed by the angel to Mary in announcing the coming birth of Christ in these words: "He shall be great, and shall be called the Son of the Highest: and the Lord God shall give unto him the throne of his father David: and he shall reign over the house of Jacob for ever; and of his kingdom there shall be no end" (Luke 1:32–33). It should be clear from the details surrounding these predictions that these prophecies are not being fulfilled now, nor are they a description of the sovereignty of God in the heavenly sphere. Many Scriptures substantiate the reign of Christ as King in the Millennium, among them Isaiah 2:1–4; 9:6–7; 11:1–10; 16:5; 24:23; 32:2; 40:1–11; 42:3–4; 52:7–15; 55:4; Daniel 2:44; 7:27; Micah 4:1–8; 5:2–5; Zechariah 9:9; 14:16–17.

The Millennial Government

From a governmental standpoint, the reign of Christ in the Millennium will have three characteristics. First, it will be a rule over the entire earth. It was God's intent from the beginning of the creation that the earth should be ruled over by man. Adam forfeited his right to rule, so God's purpose is fulfilled in Jesus Christ. In Psalm 2:6-9 God declares His purpose to set His king in Zion who will have as His possession "the uttermost parts of the earth."

The "stone" in Daniel 2:35 anticipates the universal rule of Christ. Daniel 7:14 is explicit: "And there was given him dominion, and glory, and a kingdom, that all peoples, nations, and languages, should serve him: his dominion is an everlasting dominion, which shall not pass away, and his kingdom that which shall not be destroyed." This idea is repeated in Daniel 7:27 and becomes a frequent theme of prophecy (for example, Ps. 72:8; Micah 4:1-2; Zech. 9:10). The title of Christ given in Revelation 19:16, "King of Kings and Lord of Lords," makes it plain that He is supreme ruler over the earth.

The second characteristic of the millennial rule of Christ is that His government will be absolute in authority and power. This is demonstrated in His destruction of all who oppose Him (cf. Ps. 2:9; Isa. 11:4). Such an absolute rule, of course, is in keeping with the person and majesty of the King in whom is all the power and sovereignty of God.

The third important aspect of the government of Christ in the Millennium will be that of righteousness and justice. Millennial passages emphasize this feature of the Millennium. Isaiah 11:3-5 assures the poor and the meek that their cause will be dealt with righteously in that day. The wicked are warned to serve the Lord lest they feel His wrath (Ps. 2:10-12).

The subjects of the millennial rule of Christ at the beginning of the Millennium will consist in those who survive the searching judgments of both Israel and gentiles as the Millennial reign of Christ begins. It may be gathered that all the wicked will be put to death, and only saints who have lived through the preceding time of trouble will be eligible for entrance into the Millennial kingdom. This is demonstrated in the judgment of the gentiles in Matthew 25:31-46, where only the righteous are permitted to enter the Millennium. According to Ezekiel 20:33-38, God will also deal with Israel and purge out all rebels, that is, unbelievers, permitting only the saints among Israel to enter the millennial kingdom.

Israel in Christ's Government

In the church age, Jews and gentiles are on an equal plane of privilege, but Israel clearly will have prominence in the Millennium. Though many passages speak of gentile blessing as well, Christ will reign as the Son of David, and Israel as a nation will be exalted.

Passages of the Old Testament that have been studied previously anticipating a future day of glory for Israel find their fulfillment in the millennial reign of Christ. The regathering of Israel, a prominent theme of most of the prophets, has its purpose realized in the reestablishment of Israel in their ancient land. Israel as a nation is delivered from her persecutors in the time of tribulation and brought into the place of blessing and restoration.

J. Dwight Pentecost gives an excellent summary of the important place of Israel in the Millennium in the following statement:

> Israel will become the subject of the King's reign (Isa. 9:6-7; 33:17, 22; 44:6; Jer. 23:5; Mic. 2:13; 4:7; Dan. 4:3; 7:14, 22, 27). In order to be subjects, Israel, first, will have been converted and restored to the land, . . . Second, Israel will be reunited as a nation (Jer. 3:18; 33:14; Ezek. 20:40; 37:15-22; 39:25; Hos. 1:11). Third, the nation will again be related to Jehovah by marriage (Isa. 54:1-17; 62:2-5; Hos. 2:14-23). Fourth, she will be exalted above the Gentiles (Isa. 14:1-2; 49:22-23; 60:14-17; 61:6-7). Fifth, Israel will be made righteous (Isa. 1:25; 2:4; 44:22-24; 45:17-25; 48:17; 55:7; 57:18-19; 63:16; Jer. 31:11; 33:8; 50:20, 34; Ezek. 36:25-26; Hos. 14:4; Joel 3:21; Mic. 7:18-19; Zech. 13:9; Mal. 3:2-3). Sixth, the nation will become God's witnesses during the millennium (Isa. 44:8, 21; 61:6; 66:21; Jer. 16:19-21; Mic. 5:7; Zeph. 3:20; Zech. 4:1-7; 4:11-14; 8:23). Seventh, Israel will be beautified to bring glory to Jehovah (Isa. 62:3; Jer. 32:41; Hos. 14:5-6; Zeph. 3:16-17; Zech. 9:16-17).[4]

Spiritual Life in the Millennium

Of central importance in the spiritual life of the millennial kingdom is that Christ will be present and visible. This was the burden of Old Testament prophecy according to Peter. The prophets "prophesied of the grace that should come unto you: searching what time or what manner of time the Spirit of Christ which was in them did signify, when it testified beforehand the sufferings of Christ, and the glory that should follow" (1 Peter 1:10b-11).

The glories that were predicted to follow are not only that glory that is Christ's in heaven but that which is manifested to the earth at His second advent. It is stated also in Matthew: "Then shall all the tribes of the earth mourn, and they shall see the Son of man coming on the clouds of heaven with power and great glory" (Matt. 24:30b).

Imbedded in countless prophecies of the Millennium are predictions of the glory of the millennial earth. Isaiah writes, "Every valley shall be exalted, and every mountain and hill shall be made low: and the crooked shall be made straight, and the rough places plain: and the glory of the LORD shall be revealed, and all flesh shall see it together: for the mouth of the LORD hath spoken it" (Isa. 40:4-5).

It was a prayer of Solomon relative to the future kingdom: "And blessed be his glorious name for ever: and let the whole earth be filled with his glory" (Ps. 72:19). How the glory of the God of Israel will be shown in Christ has been summarized by H. C. Woodring.[5] The glory of the humanity of Christ is shown in His dominion (Heb. 2:8-9), government (Pss. 2:8-9; 72:19; Isa. 9:6-7; 11:4), and inheritance of the promised land (Gen. 15:7; 17:8; Dan. 8:9; 11:16, 41). He is the glorious Prophet and Lawgiver (Deut. 18:18-19; Isa. 2:2-4; 33:21-22; 42:4; Acts 3:22). His reign will fulfill the Davidic covenant (2 Sam. 7:12-16; Isa. 9:6-7; Matt. 25:31; Luke 1:31-33). Glory will adhere to his kingdom (Ps. 72; Isa. 9:7; 11:10; Jer. 23:6).

Because Christ the Ruler is in the world, the Millennium is characterized as a time immersed in the truth of God. Isaiah writes, "The earth shall be full of the knowledge of the LORD as the waters cover the sea" (Isa. 11:9). Jeremiah writes of the new covenant,

> *I will put my law in their inward parts, and write it in their hearts; and will be their God, and they shall be my people. And they shall teach no more every man his neighbor, and every man his brother, saying, Know the LORD: for they shall all know me, from the least of them unto the greatest of them, the LORD: for I will forgive their iniquity, and I will remember their sin no more. (Jer. 31:33b-34)*

We cannot now say that all know God, but it will be true in the Millennium.

Righteousness is another feature of the millennial earth. Psalm 72:7a predicts that "in his days shall the righteous flourish" (cf. Isa. 11:3-5). Coupled with righteousness is universal peace: "And he shall judge among the nations, and shall rebuke many people: and they shall beat their swords into plowshares, and their spears into pruning-hooks; nation shall not lift up sword against nation, neither shall they learn war any more" (Isa. 2:4). The desire for peace among nations will be a reality in the Millennium.

Joy will characterize the millennial earth. Isaiah predicts, "Therefore with joy shall ye draw water out of the wells of salvation. And in that day shall ye say, Praise the LORD, call upon his name, declare his doings among the people, make mention that his name is exalted" (Isa. 12:3-4). Isaiah declares God's purpose: "To appoint unto them that mourn in Zion, to give unto them beauty for ashes, the oil of joy for mourning, the garment of praise for the spirit of heaviness." Shortly thereafter, he adds, "For your shame ye shall have double; and for confusion they shall rejoice in their portion: therefore in their land they shall possess the double; everlasting joy shall be unto them" (Isa. 61:3, 7).

THE MILLENNIAL TEMPLE

A major section of Ezekiel (40:1-46:24) describes a temple in detail as well as the ritual and priesthood connected with it. This temple pertains to the future millennial period, inasmuch as no fulfillment of this passage has ever taken place in history. If a literal interpretation of prophecy be followed, it would be most reasonable to assume that a future temple will be built in the millennium as the center of worship. Such premillenarians as Merrill F. Unger, Arno C. Gaebelein, and James M. Gray have argued that a temple will be built in fulfillment of Ezekiel's prophecy.[6] Some have been troubled by the dimensions of Ezekiel's temple. Though it is true that the dimensions would not fit the historical temple site, a changed topography of Palestine would permit rearrangement of the amount of space assigned to the temple. Other views do not provide an explanation for the dimensions either, except to deny that they are meant to be taken literally.

The real problem in connection with a literal future temple is not the question of whether such a temple could be built, but the implication that temple ritual and sacrifices would be restored. This introduces problems.[7] Allusions are made to these sacrifices in the details of the construction of the temple (Ezek. 40:39-42) with further details on the sacrifices themselves (Ezek. 43:18-46:24). Isaiah 56:7 implies that the institution of a sacrificial system includes observance of the Sabbath (Isa. 66:20-23). Jeremiah 33:18 refers to the same thing (see also Zech. 14:16-21). The details such as are offered for these sacrifices make it clear that it is a system distinct from the Mosaic, but it involves animal sacrifices and other forms of worship similar to those provided under the Mosaic law.

Those who consider the millennial sacrifices as a ritual that will be literally observed in the Millennium invest the sacrifices with the central meaning of a memorial that looks back to the one offering of Christ. The millennial sacrifices are no more expiatory than were the Mosaic sacrifices that preceded the Cross. If it has been fitting for the church to have a memorial of the death of Christ in the Lord's Supper, it would be suitable to have a memorial of a different character in the Millennium in keeping with the Jewish characteristics of the period.

A. C. Gaebelein writes in support of this view:

But what is the meaning and the purpose of these animal sacrifices? The answer is quite simple. While the sacrifices Israel brought once had a prospective meaning, the sacrifices brought in the millennial temple have a retrospective meaning. When during this age God's people worship in the appointed way at His table, with the bread and wine as the memorial of His love, it is a retrospect. We look back to the Cross. We show forth His death. It is "till He comes." Then this memorial feast ends forever. Never again will the Lord's Supper be kept after the Saints of God have left the earth to be with the Lord in glory. The resumed sacrifices will be the memorial of the Cross and the whole wonderful story of the redemption for Israel and the nations of the earth, during the kingdom reign of Christ. And what a memorial it will be! What a meaning these sacrifices will have! They will bring to a living remembrance everything these sacrifices will have! They will bring to a living remembrance everything of the past. The retrospect will produce the greatest scene of worship, of praise and adoration this earth has even seen. All the Cross meant and the Cross has accomplished will be recalled and a mighty "Hallelujah Chorus" will fill the earth and the heavens. The sacrifices will constantly remind the peoples of the earth of Him who died for Israel, who paid the redemption price for all creation and whose glory now covers the earth as the waters cover the deep.[8]

If a literal view of the temple and the sacrifices be allowed, it provides a more intimate view of worship in the Millennium than might otherwise be afforded. Though the system as revealed is different from the Mosaic in many particulars, it obviously has at its center the redemptive and sacrificial system.

Spiritual life in the Millennium will be characterized by holiness and righteousness, joy and peace, the fullness of the Spirit, and the worship of the glorious Christ. The fact that Satan will be bound and demons will be inactive will provide a world scene in which spiritual life can abound. Far from denying the spiritual character of the Millennium, premillennialism affirms its high standard of spiritual life, which in many respects is far above that of any previous dispensation.

SOCIAL, ECONOMIC, AND PHYSICAL LIFE

The reign of Christ on earth during the Millennium, featuring as it does His righteous and universal government over all nations and characterized by spiritual blessing, obviously will affect all phases of life on the earth. Though the principal effects of the reign of Christ will be manifested in righteous government and in the spiritual realm, the rule of Christ will have extensive impact on the economic and social aspects of life on the earth.

Universal Justice and Peace

The fact that wars will cease during the Millennium will have a beneficial effect upon both the social and economic life of the world. Instead of large expenditures for armaments, attention can be directed to improving the world. Even under current world conditions, a relief from taxation due to military expenditure would have a great effect upon the economy. This, coupled with an absolute justice that assures government protection for all and a greatly reduced incidence of crime, will establish a social and economic order far different from anything the world has experienced. Such prophetic Scriptures as Psalm 72 and Isaiah 11 testify to these unusual millennial conditions.

An Outpouring of Salvation

Due to the unusual conditions in the world, in which all will know the great truths concerning Christ and redemption (Isa. 11:9), we assume that most of the earth's population will be saved. The testimony of Scripture is that at the beginning of the Millennium all unsaved people are put to death. In the parable of the wheat and the tares (Matt. 13:24-30, 36-43) and in the parable of the good and bad fish (Matt. 13:47-50) it seems clear that only the righteous survive. This is confirmed by the judgment of Matthew 25:31-46. What is here pictured for the gentile nations seems also true for the judgment of Israel, in which all rebels or unbelievers are purged (Ezek. 20:33-39). The enemies of Christ are eliminated (cf. Rev. 19:11-21).

The Curse on the Earth Lifted

The curse, which descended upon the physical world because of Adam's sin, apparently is lifted during the Millennium. According to Isaiah 35:1-2,

> *The wilderness and the solitary place shall be glad; and the desert shall be glad for them; and the desert shall rejoice, and blossom as the rose. It shall blossom abundantly, and rejoice even with joy and singing: the glory of Lebanon shall be given unto it, the excellency of Carmel and Sharon, they shall see the glory of the LORD, and the excellency of our God.*

The rest of the thirty-fifth chapter of Isaiah continues in the same theme. Abundant rainfall characterizes the period (Isa. 30:23; 35:7) and abundance of food and cattle are pictured (Isa. 30:23-24). The curse on the earth is only partly lifted. People will die until the new heaven and the new earth (Rev. 22:3). Palestine will once again be a garden. The world in general will be delivered from the unproductiveness that characterized most of the globe in prior dispensations.

General Prosperity

Widespread peace and justice, spiritual blessing, and abundance of food will result in a general era of prosperity, such as the world has never known (Jer. 31:12; Ezek. 34:25-27; Joel 2:21-27; Amos 9:13-14). The factors that produce poverty, distress, and unequal distribution of goods will be nonexistent. Everyone will receive just compensation for labor (Isa. 65:21-25; Jer.

31:5). Thus the curse that creation has endured since Adam's sin (Gen. 3:17-19) will be in part suspended, as even animal creation will be changed (Isa. 11:6-9; 65:25).

Health and Healing

One prediction regarding the coming of the Messiah was that healing from sickness would characterize His reign. Though Christ healed many, the prophecies of healing seem to point to the millennial situation. Thus Isaiah writes, "And the inhabitant shall not say, I am sick: the people that dwell therein shall be forgiven their iniquity" (Isa. 33:24). Blindness and deafness will be healed (29:18), and healing will be experienced in a similar way by others (35:5-6).

The brokenhearted will be comforted and joy will replace mourning (61:1-3). Longevity apparently will characterize the human race for Isaiah compares the death of a person one hundred years old with the death of a child (65:20).

A TIME OF CHANGE

The Mount of Olives

As noted, Palestine will experience topographical changes in connection with the establishment of the millennial reign of Christ. While some of these changes may be due to the lifting of the curse upon the earth, the alterations seem to be more extensive than can be explained simply by this.

In connection with the return of Christ, Zechariah 14 pictures a battle for possession of Jerusalem, which at first will appear to be a victory for the gentiles. Then Christ will return:

> *Then shall the LORD go forth, and fight against those nations, as when he fought in the day of battle. And his feet shall stand in that day upon the mount of Olives, which is before Jerusalem on the east; and the mount of Olives shall cleave in the midst thereof toward the east and toward the west, and there shall be a very great valley; and half of the mountain shall remove toward the north, and half of it toward the south. (Zech. 14:3-4)*

In view of the fact that the Mount of Olives nowhere in Scripture is given a spiritual interpretation, it seems clear that this refers to the physical Mount of Olives east of Jerusalem. When Christ returns, there will be, where the Mount of Olives now stands, a great valley extending toward the east, for the Mount of Olives will have split in two.

Other phenomenal things will occur at the same time. A long day is described when "at evening time there shall be light" (Zech. 14:7). Subsequent description pictures the "living waters" that "shall go out from Jerusalem; half of them toward the eastern sea, and half of them toward the western sea: in summer and in winter shall it be" (v. 8). It should be clear from this description that the character of the land to the east of Jerusalem shall be much different, and that the changes mentioned will be a preparation for other features of the millennial kingdom. Ezekiel adds more details concerning the river, with special attention to the eastward flow of the river into the Dead Sea (cf. Ezek. 47:1-12). The source of the river also will be a miracle, and it will bring fruitfulness to the land (cf. vv. 7-12). The river will bring healing to the Dead Sea. Trees and vegetation will grow on its banks, and fish will thrive in its waters.

Though other scholars have tended to give this a figurative meaning, the details are such that a literal meaning makes sense in the millennial context. James M. Gray writes, "The whole thing is literal in fact, and yet supernatural in origin."[9]

The City of Jerusalem

More important than the changes concerning the Mount of Olives are those involving the entire land of Palestine. According to Zechariah 14:10, "All the land shall be turned as a plain from Geba to Rimmon south of Jerusalem: and it shall be lifted up, and inhabited in her place, from Benjamin's gate unto the place of the first gate, unto the corner gate, and from the tower of Hananel unto the king's winepresses." The effect of all the changes will be to elevate Jerusalem above the surrounding territory and to change the topography of Palestine to suit millennial conditions. This will accommodate the temple of Ezekiel, which would not fit the current topography.

Palestine Generally

The topographical changes seem to be a preparation for the new division of the enlarged land of Palestine, embracing all the area promised to Abraham (Gen. 15:18-21). Palestine will be divided into three parts. The northern part will be divided into areas for Dan, Asher, Naphtali, Manasseh, Ephraim, Reuben, and Judah (cf. Ezek. 48:1-7). The southern portion will be devoted to the tribes of Benjamin, Simeon, Issachar, Zebulun, and Gad (vv. 23-27). In between the northern and southern parts of the land is placed the "holy oblation" of Ezekiel 48:8-20, set apart as holy to the Lord. This portion is described as a square, twenty-five thousand reeds on each side. Two-fifths of the area will be for the Levites (45:5; 48:13-14), another two fifths will be for the temple and priests (45:4; 48:10-12), and the remaining one fifth for the city (45:6; 48:15-19).

THE HEAVENLY JERUSALEM

The Eternal Home of the Saints

Much of the confusion regarding the Millennium and the eternal state stem from a failure to distinguish between promises to the last generation of saints who are on the earth at the time of the Second Advent and promises given to all the resurrected or translated saints. The prophecies of the Old Testament give adequate basis for the doctrine that Israel has an earthly hope. The prophets in Israel's darkest hours painted the most glowing picture of the coming earthly kingdom in which Israel would participate as a favored nation and possess the land under the reign of the Son of David.

The promises clearly refer to those who were not resurrected and are directed to the nation of Israel as it is to be constituted at the time of the Second Advent, that is, the Israelites who survive the Tribulation. They and their seed will inherit the land and fulfill the hundreds of prophecies that have to do with Israel's hope in the Millennial kingdom. These promises are delineated in the Abrahamic, Davidic, Palestinian, and new covenants.

The Old Testament, however, also records promises to the saints as individuals. They are promised resurrection (Job 19:25–27; Isa. 26:19–20; Dan. 12:2–3). They are promised such rewards as characterize God's dealings with the saints in eternity (Dan. 12:3; Mal. 3:16–17). A few promises specifically relate to the new heaven and the new earth and help us know something of the eternal state that will follow the Millennium (Isa. 65:17–18; 66:22). From these passages it is evident that the millennial reign of Christ on earth is not the ultimate hope of the resurrected saints, but rather of the saints who enter the Millennium in their natural bodies and who are fitted for the earthly scene.

This conclusion seems to be confirmed by the New Testament revelation concerning the heavenly city. In stating the faith of Abraham in Hebrews 11 it is stated, "For he looked for the city which hath foundations, whose builder and maker is God" (Heb. 11:10). It is further stated of Abraham and his Old Testament descendants that they did not receive the promises while on earth. In fact they were seeking, not earthly benefits, but a heavenly city:

> These all died in faith, not having received the promises, but having seen them afar off, and were persuaded of them and embraced them, and confessed that they were strangers and pilgrims on the earth. For they that say such things declare plainly that they seek a country. And truly, if they had been mindful of that country from whence they came out, they might have had opportunity to have returned. But now they desire a better country, that is, an heavenly: wherefore God is not ashamed to be called their God; for he hath prepared for them a city. (Hebrews 11:13–16)

Interpretations of Revelation 21:9–22:5

The heavenly city of Jerusalem is described in detail in Revelation 21:1–22:5. Most conservative expositors agree that Revelation 21:1–8 refers to the eternal state, the new heaven and new earth, and the new Jerusalem as it will exist in eternity. Difference of opinion, however, has arisen regarding the express application of Revelation 21:9–22:5. Three principal interpretations have been advanced. First, some believe that this portion of Scripture is a retrospect, like certain other portions of the book of Revelation, and is in fact a description of the millennial scene in figurative language.[10] In support of this position it is noted in Revelation 21:24 that nations and kings of the earth are mentioned that some think would be incongruous with the eternal state. Further, in Revelation 22:2 reference is made to the leaves of the tree of life which are for the healing of the nations, and from this it is inferred that the reference is to the millennial scene because no healing will be necessary in the eternal state.

A second view is advanced that Revelation 21:9 and following describes the eternal state introduced in the first eight verses of the chapter.[11] Inasmuch as there is in the context a new heaven and a new earth to which the holy city is coming down, it would imply that the description of the city is contemporary with the eternal state. According to this view, the city is proceeding from heaven to the earth as seen in Revelation 21:10 and is established with its foundations on the new earth. It is evident from any careful study of the millennial scene that the heavenly Jerusalem does not correspond to the earthly Jerusalem of the Millennium.

A third view, however, is sometimes offered that mediates between the first two. This view contemplates the heavenly Jerusalem as in existence during the millennium over the earth as the habitation of the resurrected saints, and is in contrast to the city of Jerusalem located on earth. The heavenly Jerusalem apparently is withdrawn at the destruction of the present earth and heaven. Then, as pictured in Revelation 21:2, it returns to the new heaven and new earth. This interpretation regards Revelation 21:9–22:5 as the heavenly city in the eternal state, though recognizing its existence in the Millennium. This seems to solve most of the exegetical problems and some objections to the premillennial interpretation of Scripture as a whole.

Resurrected Saints and Millennial Earth

Though the major difficulty of the relationship of resurrected saints to those who are still in their natural bodies in the Millennium is explained by the residence of the resurrected saints in the heavenly Jerusalem, Scripture hints of some relation of resurrected saints to millennial citizens.

For one thing, Christ promised His followers that they would participate with Him in judging Israel in His kingdom.

Christ declared, "Verily I say unto you, that ye who have followed me, in the regeneration when the Son of man shall sit on the throne of his glory, ye also shall sit upon twelve thrones, judging the twelve tribes of Israel" (Matt. 19:28). A larger promise is given by reminder to the Corinthians when Paul wrote them: "Know ye not that the saints shall judge the world? and if the world is judged by you, are ye unworthy to judge the smallest matters?" (1 Cor. 6:2).

The objection frequently raised that any mingling of resurrected with nonresurrected beings is impossible must be denied. Christ in His resurrection body mingled freely with His disciples. Though there evidently was some change in their relationship, he could talk with them, eat with them, and have physical contact with them.

Further, even now there is a ministry of angels to human beings, though angels are of an entirely different order of beings. Though the free mingling of resurrected and nonresurrected beings is contrary to our experience, there is no reason they should not be associated in the millennial earth.

Undoubtedly the millennial kingdom will differ from any previous dispensation. Certainly it will have unique features. It will be climactic, a divine preparation for the eternal state. Such a kingdom will be the answer to the world's longing for peace, righteousness, and equity.

THE CLOSE OF THE MILLENNIUM

Satan will be bound during the Millennium. According to Revelation 20:7–9, he then will be loosed, permitted once again to deceive.[12] Those who are deceived evidently will have been born in the millennial kingdom among those who entered the millennium in their natural bodies. Some of the children born no doubt will merely profess to follow Christ under the compulsion of His absolute reign.

With the renewed activity of Satan, these will rebel. According to Revelation 20:8, they will gather themselves to battle against the Lord and surround earthly Jerusalem. Satan will "deceive the nations which are in the four corners of the earth, Gog and Magog." This should not be confused with a similar reference in Ezekiel 38:2 to *Gog* and *Magog* fighting a battle that probably will precede the Millennium. The similarity of terms is best explained by defining *Gog* as the prince and *Magog* as the people of the prince, or the land over which he rules. So interpreted, the passage states that Satan will deceive the nations in all parts of the earth, both rulers and people. Apparently the defection against Christ will extend even to some involved in the political government of the world at the close of the Millennium.

The White Throne

In Revelation 20:11–15 one of the saddest passages of Scripture is found. Subsequent to the Millennium a great white throne is established. Both earth and the starry heavens flee from it in the destruction of the earth and heavens. Before this throne are assembled the dead, small and great. It is implied that this is a judgment of the wicked dead who have not previously been raised from the grave. They are judged according to their works as written in "the books," the divine record of human activity.

The dead are brought back to this judgment, their bodies being delivered from the grave, whether in the sea or on the land. Their souls are brought up from hades for summary judgment: Those whose names are not recorded as belonging to God are cast into the lake of fire (Rev. 20:15). This is defined as "the second death" (v. 14). Just as physical death is separation of the immaterial part of man from his physical body, so the second death is eternal separation of the wicked from God.

There has been some debate as to the exact character of the "book of life" referred to in 20:15, but whatever it is, the book of life records the names of those who are God's. Though the wicked will be judged according to their works as to degree of punishment, the fact that their names are not in the book of life is the ground for final judgment (see chapter 35 in this volume).

New Heaven and New Earth

According to Revelation 21:10, following the judgment of the great white throne, a new heaven and a new earth is apparently created to replace the current earth and heaven. Very little description is given. Isaiah 65:17 states that when the new heavens and the new earth are created, the former will no longer be remembered. The new heavens and the new earth differ greatly from the old. For one thing, there will be no sea (Rev. 21:1).

The glory of the Lord will illumine the new creation, so that there will be no night. It is a scene of release from earth's sorrows. God "shall wipe away all tears. There shall be no more death, neither sorrow, nor crying, neither shall there be any more pain: for the former things are passed away" (Rev. 21:4).

An astounding feature is the dimension of the city: fifteen hundred miles square and fifteen hundred miles high. Such a dimension is quite foreign, even in a world of urban high-rise construction. This impressive and spacious city will be the seat of God's eternal government and dwelling place for the saints. Expositors differ as to whether the city is a cube or a pyramid, though the latter seems more likely. If a pyramid, it is possible that the throne of God will be at the top and the river of life will wend its way down the various levels of the city. For further discussion, see chapter 36 in this volume.

CHRIST'S REIGN AND A NEW MILLENNIUM

There are several reasons why we should understand this doctrine as we enter the twenty-first century. That this period covers such an extensive amount of Scripture should make us want to know it well. If sheer amount of Scripture shows emphasis, and I believe it does, then God believes that the thousand-year reign of His Son is important.

Also, our understanding of the rapture of the church should compel us to live holy lives, and so should an understanding of the Lord's millennial reign. Our Lord is the sovereign of the universe and will someday rule in righteousness. What a privilege we have to serve Him.

Finally, we should be motivated by the fact that during his reign we will be given the honor to rule with Him. Revelation 20:6 states, "Blessed and holy is he that hath part in the first resurrection: on such the second death hath no power, but they shall be priests of God and of Christ and shall reign with Him a thousand years" (see also 2 Tim. 2:12; Rev. 5:10).

What a humbling privilege. "Even so, come, Lord Jesus" (Rev. 22:20b).

This chapter is adapted by permission of copyright holder from John F. Walvoord, *The Millennial Kingdom* (Grand Rapids: Zondervan, 1992).

CHAPTER 35

The Biblical Doctrine of the Judgments

Paul N. Benware

Death and God's judgment are two topics that people avoid. Apparently it is hoped that somehow these two issues will not have to be faced if they are ignored. Both, however, are universal realities. Those who do not wish to consider them would be wise to do so. This is, perhaps, why King Solomon suggested that it is better to go to a funeral than to a party (Eccl. 7:2-6). Parties promote a false, superficial view of life. Funerals bring us face to face with ultimate reality. The Bible succinctly declares that "it is appointed for men to die once and after this comes judgment" (Heb. 9:27).[1]

Since Scripture does give clear, declarative statements, the wise person will study them to understand and be forewarned. Coming judgment may be an avoided doctrine—even by theologians and pastors—but Jesus spoke often on the subject, warning of what lies ahead.

THE NECESSITY OF JUDGMENT

Because God Is Creator

All human beings are accountable to the One who created them, since their very existence depends on God. It is both logical and Scriptural that what they have done with the gift of existence should be evaluated by the One who made them. Paul argued that, because God made the world and everything in it, He will judge the world (Acts 17:24, 31). The apostle John, in the book of Revelation, declares that since God is the Creator, He has the right to do what He chooses with His creation. That includes judging men, angels, and the material universe itself (e.g., Rev. 4:11; 10:6; 14:7).

Because of God's Character

The most significant attribute of God related to the issue of judgment is His holiness. Holiness means that God is free from moral evil. He is absolute moral perfection. The righteous law imposed on the creature is that which comes from the nature of the holy God. Perfect righteousness is the moral requirement. Rational creatures must be like Him in moral character, or else God must enforce his law against them for violating his moral absolutes. Since He is infinitely pure, He is, in His very nature, opposed to all sin and must deal with sin. God's justice and righteousness bind Him to punish the sinner. According to A. H. Strong, "Justice and righteousness are simply holiness exercised toward creatures. The same holiness which exists in God in eternity past manifests itself as justice and righteousness, so soon as intelligent creatures come into being."[2]

The wrath of God is essential to his holiness. It means he cares about justice. But God's wrath must not be thought of in terms of outbursts of human anger. The wrath of God is not like any emotion that humans experience, observed James Boice:

> It is, rather, that necessary and proper stance of the holy God to all that opposes him. It means that he takes the matter of being God seriously, so seriously that he will not allow any thing or personality to aspire to his place . . . When men and women refuse to take the place that God has given to them, they will be judged also.[3]

"There is in God no selfish anger," adds Strong. "The penalties he inflicts upon transgression are not vindictive but vindicative. They express the revulsion of God's nature from moral evil, the judicial indignation of purity against impurity, the self-assertion of infinite holiness against its antagonist and would-be destroyer."[4]

So, because the creatures have violated the righteous laws of the holy God, He must judge them. Not to judge would violate His own nature. A nonjudgmental God would not be God. Some have objected that God's attribute of love prohibits God from judging especially judgments that are eternal in duration. But it must be remembered that God's love already has provided full redemption for sin in the Cross. If many refuse to respond to God's love in Christ to deal with their sin, they will face God's justice. As Strong said, "though love makes the atonement, it is violated holiness that requires it; and in the eternal punishment of the wicked, the demand of holiness for self-vindication overbears the pleading of love for the sufferers."[5] God's love has indeed been shown in an extraordinary way, as God himself took the punishment for the violation of his righteous law. But those who refuse to respond to the work of Christ on the cross, must face the holiness and justice of God without Him.

Because of Discrepancies in Life

A great ethical problem faced by the Bible's human writers was the injustice and unrighteousness around them. The apparent triumph of evil troubled God's people. In light of this, it is important that all of creation clearly understands that what God has said is true. Violators of His righteous laws must face consequences.

Notwithstanding the prosperity of the wicked and the afflictions of the righteous, the conviction is everywhere expressed that God is just. Somehow and somewhere He will show that He is righteous and holy.[6]

THE JUDGE OF FUTURE JUDGMENTS

The Judge of the coming judgments is the Lord Jesus Christ. According to John 5:21–27, all judgment has been given to the Son of God and all those who do not come to Him as the giver of life will face Him as Judge. Louis Berkhof wrote,

> Naturally, the final judgment . . . is a work of the triune God, but Scripture ascribes it particularly to Christ. Christ in His mediatorial capacity will be the future Judge. . . . Such passages as Matt. 28:18; John 5:27; Phil. 2:9, 10, make it abundantly evident that the honor of judging the living and the dead was conferred upon Christ as Mediator in reward for His atoning work and as part of His exaltation.[7]

Jesus Himself declared that His judgments would be just and be in harmony with the will of the Father (John 5:30). He would judge righteously and fairly and with complete knowledge. It is said of Jesus that His eyes are like a flame of fire. He sees all and knows all (Rev. 1:14; 2:18). It is essential that the judge at these future judgments knows everything, that He will not overlook facts and that He cannot be fooled or misled.

Evidently both holy angels and redeemed people will assist in these judgments (cf. Matt. 24:31; 25:31; 1 Cor. 6:2-3; Rev. 20:4). Their role is unclear, but it appears that they will actively participate in the times of judgment.

QUESTIONS ABOUT FUTURE JUDGMENTS

Do These Judgments Determine Anyone's Final Destiny?

The judgments do not determine the final destiny of individuals. That is determined during their lives. Those who have become children of God through faith are forever saved and those who died in their sins are forever lost. Their eternal fate is not decided at these future judgments. Rather, the judgments will display before all of creation the glory of God, magnifying His holiness, righteousness, goodness, and mercy. The judgments are also important to determine varying rewards and punishment.

How Many Judgments Will There Be?

No millennial view is without some difficulties in answering this question. The premillennial view best handles the combined theological, exegetical, and hermeneutical considerations. The premillennial position sees several times in the future for God's judgments and not simply one general judgment. It will be seen that a number of judgments take place, involving different people.

The Rapture Judgment of Believers

Immediately following the rapture of the church, all of the church age saints will stand before their Lord (Rom. 14:10; 1 Cor. 3:11–4:5). It will not include unbelievers or Old Testament saints. This is a time of recognition, when the Lord Jesus evaluates the works of His people.

The issue is not individual salvation, but works. Deeds that are good and acceptable will receive reward. If works are considered worthless there will be a loss of reward, though not the loss of salvation. The consequences of rewards may carry on through the Messiah's thousand-year kingdom and into the eternal state. Loss probably will have an impact on life, responsibility, and privilege. The Lord will reward on the basis of standards He has set forth in Scriptures. He will test the faithfulness of believers' use of his gifts to them, as well as their motivation for serving.

For some believers this will be a time of unparalleled joy, while for others it will be a time of deep regret. For more on this judgment, see chapter 33 in this volume.

TRIBULATION JUDGMENT

Soon after the removal of the church at the Rapture, the world will experience seven years of judgment. This period is called the Tribulation, the Day of the Lord, the wrath of God, the seventieth week of Daniel, or the time of Jacob's trouble. This period will be unprecedented in ferocity and cannot be compared to any other time of earth's history. Jesus said that if God had not limited it to seven years, no one on the planet would survive (Matt. 24:22). While the salvation of Israel and others is the first great purpose of this time, punishment is the second purpose. The wicked who have refused God's message of grace and arrogantly refused to live in obedience to the Creator will be punished.

God will pour out three series of judgments, killing most of those on earth (Revelation 6–16). These are referred to as judgments of the "seals," "trumpets," and "bowls." They will increase progressively in intensity and frequency. These judgments will be so clearly divine that all will have to acknowledge that God is God, even though many refuse to repent (Rev. 16:9–11, 21).

SECOND-COMING JUDGMENTS

When the tribulation period is over, the second coming of the Lord Jesus Christ will establish His messianic kingdom on earth. At this time three judgments will take place: judgment of the gentile nations; judgment of Israel; and judgment of Old Testament and tribulation believers.

The Gentile Nations

Time

Daniel 12:11–12 suggests that there will be a period of seventy-five days between the Second Coming and the actual start of the millennial kingdom. During this interval the judgment of the nations as well as the judgments of Israel and Old Testament saints apparently take place. Joel 3:1–3 and Matthew 25:31–46 also speak of this judgment at the Second Coming.

Joel connects the judgment of gentile nations with the "Day of the Lord," saying that this judgment will take place when Judah and Jerusalem have their "fortunes restored." As a result of the judgment, some will get to participate in the millennial kingdom, while others will be excluded.

Place

This judgment will take place on the earth, where Christ has come to set up His throne (Matt. 24:27–31; 25:31–32). Joel specifically places the judgment in the "Valley of Jehoshaphat" (Joel 3:2, 12). Some identify this with the Kidron Valley next to Jerusalem; others believe it will occur at the place where God brought delivered King Jehoshaphat from his enemies (2 Chron. 20:14–30). The exact geographic location is difficult to determine because this name has not been attached to a specific place. Likely the name, which means "Jehovah judges," is intended to be symbolic. It will be in Israel, where the recently returned Lord Jesus will gather the nations to judge them. The site may come into existence in connection with topographical changes that will take place at the Second Coming (Zech. 14:4). It likely will be near Jerusalem.[8]

Participants

Both of the primary Scripture references to this judgment state that the "nations" are gathered before the Lord. The word translated "nations" can also mean "gentiles." It is used mainly as a category for those who do not belong to the nation of Israel, so it is called the judgment of gentiles.

Only those who are living when Christ returns at His second coming will be judged. Those brought before the Lord are gathered from the various parts of the earth from which Israel has been regathered (Joel 3:2). These gentiles will be judged for what they have done immediately before Christ's return (cf. Joel 3:2–3; Matt. 25:35–40).

Most will perish during the terrible days of the Tribulation (Revelation 6, 8, 9, 16). More will die as God's wrath is poured out in the three series of judgments and the campaign of Armageddon. Others will perish because of the activities of Satan and the Antichrist. Most gentiles alive at the beginning of the seven years will die before it is over. But when Jesus Christ returns millions still will live. These will stand before Him.

The Basis of Judgment

The situation of those terrible days of the Tribulation is important in understanding this judgment. During the last half of that period an active, satanically energized anti-Semitism will spread across the earth (Rev. 12:13–16). The Antichrist will attempt to thwart the plan and purposes of God by annihilating the covenant people. John Walvoord says,

> Under the widespread anti-semitism that will prevail in the Great Tribulation, anyone who befriends a Jew in trouble will be distinguished as a person who has trust in the Bible and trust in Jesus Christ. Accordingly, while their works do not save them, their works are the basis of distinguishing them from the unsaved.[9]

According to Walvoord, the spiritual lives of individual gentiles will be revealed by how they treat Israel during the Tribulation. Jews forced to flee death and destruction will have no means of caring for themselves. Righteous gentiles, at great risk to themselves, will provide food and shelter and show other acts of kindness.

Jesus refers to these gentiles as righteous (Matt. 25:37). The good deeds done to Jesus validate that designation of "righteous." However, it is apparent that these righteous gentiles (the sheep) are somewhat confused because they know that they did not do any good deeds to Jesus personally. But the Lord instructs them that when they did these good, selfless acts to "these brothers of mine" they were also doing them to Jesus Himself (Matt. 25:40).

It must be noted that the "brothers" of Jesus is not a reference to humanity in general, but rather to the Jews who believe and are subject to satanically inspired persecution. Jesus usually had in mind spiritual relatives when he spoke of connections to him in the Gospels. He referred to His followers that way in His earthly ministry (Matt. 12:46–50). These righteous gentiles will be welcomed into the millennial kingdom by the King. They are saved by grace, but they demonstrate their righteousness in heroic care for Jesus' "brothers" (the saved Jews) during great persecution.

Purposes for Judgment

All of the times of judgment vindicate God's character. Scripture records that all will bow the knee and submit to the Creator (John 5:22–23; Phil.

2:9–11). When the judgments are completed, no creature will challenge or speak against the character or the deeds of the one and only God.

It is also important that God will always do what He says He will do. The judgment of the gentiles, based upon how they treat Israel, brings to remembrance the promise to Abraham in Genesis 12:3. In that initial giving of the Abrahamic covenant, God has said that He would bless those who bless Abraham's descendants but would curse those who curse his descendants. This has held true through history. The judgment of the gentiles is as clear an application of this word as one can find.

This judgment also determines who from the period of the Tribulation will be welcomed into the kingdom of Jesus the Messiah. The righteous gentiles will be received with joy. But the wording of the text also suggests that there is more here than the righteous merely entering the kingdom. The phrase "inheriting the kingdom" (Matt. 25:34) may include the giving of rewards to faithful gentiles.[10] It is argued that "inheriting the kingdom" in the Scriptures is always conditioned upon some good works done by the individual. And since one's salvation is never conditioned upon good works, it must be that the phrase is focusing on rewards. "Entering the kingdom" itself refers to justification by faith (cf. John 3:5) and is unrelated to works.

The unrighteous reveal their rejection of the gospel message by refusing aid and comfort to Jesus' "brethren." These gentiles were not passive in their dealings with the people of Israel (Joel 3:2–3). They brought great distress and suffering to the Jews as they drove them out of their land, divided up the land, and enslaved the people. These unrighteous committed the crime of taking the Lord's portion for themselves. They will have to bow the knee to the One they have treated with contempt.

The Nation of Israel

If there is a judgment on the gentiles, a similar judgment for Israel might be anticipated. In their unique covenant relationship with the Lord, the Jews would have greater accountability to Him. So a distinct judgment of Israel is revealed in Ezekiel 20:33–38, Matthew 25:1–13, and other passages. There are similarities between this judgment on Israel and that on the gentiles.

Time

In His Olivet Discourse, Jesus gave a chronology: (1) the Tribulation; (2) gathering; (3) beginning of millennial reign. The angels will gather "His elect" from all parts of the earth (Matt. 24:31). The parables that follow this statement of the gathering of the elect focus on the need to be ready and alert for the return of the Lord. They teach that it is critical that one be ready for the Lord's return because it will determine one's future relationship with King Jesus in His kingdom.

Place

Since this judgment follows the return of Christ to the earth, the judgment must take place on the earth (Matt. 24:27–31; Zech. 14:4). The prophet Ezekiel states that when God's people are regathered, God will bring them into the wilderness to judge them (Ezek. 20:35–36). Ezekiel saw these future dealings of God with Israel in light of His past dealings with them in the days of Moses. The parallel in the judgments, as given by Ezekiel, suggests that this judgment will take place geographically on the earth and outside the borders of the Promised Land as given in the covenants. The Old Testament emphasizes the land as the inheritance of the righteous. It is, therefore, not surprising to learn that the unrighteous will not be allowed to enter.

Participants

The judgment involves those Israelites who are alive on the earth at the end of the Tribulation period. Those who are to be judged will have been brought back from the gentile nations. "And I shall bring you out from the peoples and gather you from the lands where you are scattered, with a mighty hand and with an outstretched arm and with wrath poured out" (Ezek. 20:34). "And I will bring them out from the peoples and gather them from the countries and bring them to their own land." (34:13a). Living Israelites will be judged by the Lord, face to face (20:35–37; 34:16–22).

Basis of Judgment

The purpose of the seven years of tribulation is to bring the nation of Israel into the covenant of salvation (Jer. 31:31–34). Through the preaching of the gospel of the kingdom (Matt. 24:14) with the accompanying miracles and displays of power, God will redeem many Israelites. In Romans 11:26 the apostle Paul declares that "all Israel will be saved." This does not mean every individual Israelite, but rather Israel as a whole.[11] Millions from Israel will turn in faith to Jesus the Messiah, which, according to Jesus, is the prerequisite for His return to the earth (Matt. 23:39). It is possible, however, that of all those who are regathered by the Lord for this judgment, two thirds are unbelievers (cf. Zech. 13:8). Charles Ryrie explains:

> When the Lord returns they will be gathered and judged, the rebels (possibly two thirds, Zech. 13:8) to be excluded from the kingdom, and those who turn in faith when they see Him to enter the kingdom (Ezek. 20:33–44). Those believing survivors constitute the "all" of all Israel that will be saved at the Second Coming (Rom. 11:26).[12]

Jews who are identified as standing with Jesus will face intense, universal persecution by the forces of Satan (Matt. 24:9; Rev. 12:13–17). Many believing Israelites will die. However, others will flee the land of Israel and find safety among the gentiles (Rev. 12:16; Matt. 25:34-40). It will mostly be these who remain alive to participate in the judgment of living Israelites. Many unsaved Jews who have thrown in with the Antichrist also will be alive.

Those who enter the millennial kingdom will be redeemed while the unredeemed will be excluded. In the parable of the "ten virgins" the five wise virgins are those who have oil, which is commonly interpreted to be a reference to the Holy Spirit (Matt. 25:4-9). These with the Spirit are allowed into the wedding feast while the others are shut out and not allowed in.

Purpose of Judgment

This judgment of living Israelites will determine who will enter the millennial kingdom. While nationally Israel is in covenant relationship with God, only those who are saved will enter into the full blessings of the Abrahamic covenant, and more particularly the new covenant (Ezek. 20:37). Righteous Israelites will be joyful participants in the long awaited kingdom of the Messiah, experiencing the blessings of the kingdom spoken about in the prophets. These Israelites will be important participants in the kingdom. They will not yet receive resurrection bodies. They will enter the kingdom in their earthly bodies and be parents of the first millennial Jewish babies.[13]

Old Testament and Tribulation Saints

All righteous people will be raised prior to the millennial kingdom in order to participate in the reign of Christ (e.g., Matt. 8:11; 16:27; Luke 14:14; Rev. 20:4-6). Two other groups of righteous people must be raised at the Second Coming. These two groups are the believers from the Old Testament and those believers who died during the Tribulation.

Believers from Old Testament times probably await the Second Coming to be raised and rewarded. Some have suggested that these saints are raised at the same time as church age saints, coming to resurrection life at the rapture event before the Tribulation begins. But the resurrection that takes place at the time of the rapture involves those who are "in Christ," which is to be understood as a designation only for those who have been baptized into the church, the body of Christ. The righteous of the Old Testament do not have that position.

Also, it does seem that since the Church is viewed in the Scriptures as a "mystery" (Eph. 3:1-6), God concludes His dealings with the church before He returns to fulfill His covenant commitments to the nation of Israel. Furthermore, Daniel 12:2-3 and Isaiah 26:19 place Israel's resurrection at the end of times (cf. Dan. 12:1). In the immediate context, Daniel is speaking of events that take place during and after the Tribulation ("time of distress"), and therefore, the raising and rewarding of the righteous in Israel takes place at that time.

The Bible is clear that many believers will perish during the Tribulation but that these will be raised when Christ returns. Revelation 20:4 says that those who had stood for Christ, resisted the Antichrist, and subsequently were beheaded "lived and reigned with Christ a thousand years." This scripture follows the pattern of other scriptures that link Christ's second coming with resurrection and judgment (cf. Dan. 12:2; Luke 14:14; Matt. 16:27; 19:28-29).

AFTER THE MILLENNIAL KINGDOM

When the thousand-year Messianic kingdom is over, three more judgments will take place. These are necessary to prepare for the eternal phase of the kingdom of God that will follow the millennial kingdom of Christ.

Satan and the Fallen Angels

Reason

Satan and his angelic followers will be judged for their sin and rebellion (cf. 2 Peter 2:4; Jude 6-7; Rev. 20:10). Satan rebelled against God and was joined by many angels in this rebellion (cf. Isa. 14:12-17; Ezek. 28:12-19). These evil beings have resisted the purposes of God and fought against Him and His people. For this willful, active wickedness they will be judged.

Time

Satan and his fallen followers have had other judgments pronounced upon them. Some of these demons are now confined with no access to heaven or earth. For previous sins committed some are temporarily confined while others are in a confinement that is permanent (cf. Luke 8:31; 2 Peter 2:4; Jude 6; Rev. 9:1-11). When Jesus Christ died and rose again the final fate of Satan was sealed (cf. Luke 10:18; Col. 2:13-15).

When the Tribulation is half over, another aspect of Satan's judgment will take place. Satan and his followers will be forcibly removed from heaven by the holy angels (Rev. 12:7-9). When Jesus Christ returns, yet another phase of judgment takes place. Satan is cast into the abyss for a thousand years.

After the millennial kingdom is over, Satan will be released. He instigates a rebellion against the reigning Messiah, gathering a multitude of unbelievers (Rev. 20:7-9). This last futile rebellion against the Messiah is God's final object lesson, showing that the heart of man is incurably evil and rebellious. Satan will be defeated and thrown into the lake of fire (Rev. 20:10).

The text is clear that there will be no escape and no end to this judgment. Satan will be "tormented day and night forever and ever." Also, the demons will face the Judge at this time. Jude 6 states that the fallen angelic followers of Satan will be judged in "the great day." This refers to the coming "Day of the Lord," which terminates all the judgments of the creation. The apostle

Peter declares that the angels that sinned await a coming judgment (2 Peter 2:4). It is necessary for Christ to judge all sin of all creatures in preparation for the perfect eternal kingdom of God.

Participants

In this judgment believers will assist the Lord (1 Cor. 6:3). In some way this will be a vindication for the trouble and pain brought to believers during their lives by these evil beings.

The judgment will include Satan and all of those angels who chose to rebel with him. Confined angels will be released to face their Creator and Judge (2 Peter 2:4; Jude 6; Rev. 20:10).

Results of Judgment

This judgment concludes God's dealings with the rebellious angelic beings. All will be consigned to the lake of fire, the "second death." This is the place of eternal, conscious torment (Rev. 19:20; 20:10, 14–15).

The Old Heavens and Earth

The entire universe has been contaminated by sin and needs purification and restoration (Rom. 8:20–21; Col. 1:20; Heb. 9:23). Because of the remaining elements of the curse on creation and because of the presence of sin in the universe, such a judgment is needed. This second judgment to take place after the millennial reign will be the destruction by fire of the old heavens and the old earth (2 Peter 3:10; cf. Matt. 24:35; Rev. 20:11).

Robert Thomas calls the picture in Revelation 20:11 "a sudden and violent termination of the physical universe" as it disappears from before the presence of the omnipresent God.[14] In Revelation 21:1 the old order is said to have "passed away," pointing to a complete disappearance of the old. "The unavailability of any 'place' (*topos*) for the earth and the heaven following their departure indicates that theirs is a flight from the present existence," writes Thomas.[15] The Lord will create a new heaven and earth in preparation for the eternal state.

The Unsaved

Time

In the chronology of the book of Revelation, the judgment of those who have not been redeemed takes place after the millennial reign and the short-lived rebellion of Satan (Rev. 20:1–9). Sometimes this is called the Great White Throne Judgment. It occurs after the judgment on the old heavens and earth, since the apostle John has said that these have "fled away" (Rev. 20:11). It takes place prior to creation of the new heavens and new earth (Rev. 21:1).

John has this final judgment in mind in Revelation 20:5 when he says that the unbelieving dead will come to life only after the thousand years are completed. So this judgment will be after the millennial phase of the final kingdom of God and prior to the eternal phase.

Place

The location of this judgment is uncertain, since the earth and the heavens have just been destroyed. Somewhere in limitless space this throne of judgment will exist and men will stand before the Judge there.

Participants

Those appearing before the throne are declared to be "the dead" (Rev. 20:12). They are clearly resurrected since they have come out of the sea, death, and *Hades* (v. 13). After Satan's unsuccessful rebellion at the end of the Millennium, there will be no living unsaved dead since all the rebels were destroyed by the heavenly fire (v. 9). All of the righteous dead have been raised. The only ones left unresurrected are the unsaved dead. By implication the resurrection of the unsaved is the second resurrection (Dan. 12:2; John 5:29; Rev. 20:5). That these will experience the second death automatically excludes the righteous (cf. Rev. 20:5-6).

Apparently the only unsaved who will not appear here at the Great White Throne are the Antichrist and the False Prophet, who have already been judged and dispatched to the lake of fire (Rev. 19:19-21).

Basis of Judgment

This judgment has often been viewed as determining who goes to heaven and who ends up in hell. As noted, however, the eternal destiny of each man and woman is based on one's acceptance or rejection of God's gift of salvation in Christ. Justification is always by faith alone in Christ alone.

> This judgment, contrary to popular misconception, is not to determine whether those who stand before this judgment bar are saved or not. All those that are to be saved have been saved and have entered into their eternal state. . . . As in the judgment of the Gentiles the works demonstrated faith or lack of faith, so here the works demonstrate the absence of life. That there will be degrees of punishment meted out to these unsaved is suggested from other Scripture (Luke 12:47-48). But the sentence of the second death will be passed on all.[16]

This Great White Throne Judgment, therefore, is for unbelievers. There will not be a separation of believers from unbelievers.

Results of Judgment

The result of this judgment is the final and forever separation of the unbeliever from God. Everyone who appears before the Judge at this judgment will be cast into the lake of fire, the "second death" (Rev. 20:6, 14). Scripture teaches that the duration of the punishment is eternal (e.g., Matt. 18:8; 25:41, 46; 2 Thess. 1:9; Rev. 14:11). In Matthew 25:46 Jesus declared that the wicked "will go away into eternal punishment, but the righteous into eternal life." He used the same word (*aiōnios*) of the eternal destiny of both the righteous and the wicked. Since the same word cannot mean entirely different things in one context, Jesus must be declaring that the existences of the righteous and the wicked are both forever.

The Lord Jesus also spoke of "everlasting fire" and "everlasting punishment" as He warned people of coming punishment, using the term *Gehenna* (e.g., Matt. 18:8; 25:41; Mark 9:43). *Gehenna* was the name given to the valley south of Jerusalem, commonly called the Valley of Hinnom. It has commonly been identified with the fiery judgment of apocalyptic literature, because human sacrifices were made there in the days of Ahaz and Manasseh (2 Kings 16:3; 21:6; 2 Chron. 28:3; 33:6). Jeremiah 7:32 and 19:6 declares that coming judgments will take place there. A distinction should be noted between *Gehenna* and *Hades* (hell). Hades receives the ungodly temporarily between death and resurrection, while Gehenna is eternal—the place of final disposition.[17]

Before the unsaved are sent to the lake of fire, they are judged at the Great White Throne on the basis of the "book of life" and books that record their deeds (Rev. 20:12–15). The books make it clear that this is no arbitrary judgment, since all the evidence is there. The Book of Life will give testimony in that the names of these individuals are not written in it. They do not possess God's eternal life and therefore may not spend eternity with the One who is Life. The statement that "every one of them" will be judged emphasizes their individual responsibility (20:13). Not a single human being will avoid facing the Creator.

CONCLUSION

With the Great White Throne Judgment comes the end of God's judgments. All people have now been resurrected and judged. With creation of the new heavens and earth, God will begin the eternal kingdom that seems to restore His original plan and desire for fellowship with His creatures in Paradise.

As we enter this new millennium, the specter of coming judgment is a sobering thought. God does require that we live according to His righteous laws. When we violate those laws we face His just punishment. The evidence against us will be clear and overwhelming. This judge cannot be mistaken, misled, or bribed. Our wrongdoing will be judged to the full extent of His righteousness. What happens in that future day is determined by what happens today, a thought we should keep continually in mind.

CHAPTER 36

Eternity: The New Heavens and the New Earth

Henry Holloman

Both the Old and New Testaments point forward to new heavens and a new earth where God will dwell eternally with His people (Isa. 65:17; 66:22; 2 Peter 3:13). John the apostle envisioned this eternal state when He wrote:

> *I saw a new heaven and a new earth; for the first heaven and the first earth passed away, and there is no longer any sea. And I saw the holy city, New Jerusalem, coming down out of heaven from God, made ready as a bride adorned for her husband. And I heard a voice from the throne, saying, "Behold, the tabernacle of God is among men, and He shall dwell among them, and they shall be His people, and God Himself shall be among them." (Rev. 21:1–3)[1]*

The reality of this eternal state is based on the eternity of God who is faithful and able to fulfill His promises (Num. 23:19; Rom. 4:20–21; 2 Cor. 1:20).

The eternal God revealed His solution to the problem of human mortality "by the appearing of our Savior Christ Jesus, who abolished death and brought life and immortality to light through the gospel" (2 Tim. 1:10). God gives eternal spiritual life to all believers in Christ (John 3:16; 5:21, 24; Rom. 6:23). And when Christ returns, believers will receive immortal bodies so that they can live forever with God in His eternal kingdom (1 Cor. 15:50–53; Phil. 3:20–21).

ETERNITY AND TIME

Erich Sauer studied the philosophical relationship between eternity and time and came to the following conclusion:

Eternity is not the negation of time but, on the contrary, the substantial form of time; the sequence of one thing after another remains in force in eternity also. It is only the limitations of time which are absent, its restricting narrowness, its unreliable changeableness, its vanishing evanescence. . . . Time-less eternity is therefore God's alone, the time-full He has granted to His creatures.[2]

Eternity is more than quantitatively different from time; it is *qualitatively* different because it is another dimension of reality. God dwells in eternity (Isa. 57:15), so He transcends the temporal order of the universe. This distinguishes the true God from pantheism, which identifies God wholly with the universe. Pantheism is a powerful force at the beginning of the twenty-first century, particularly through Eastern and New Age thought.[3]

The infinite God alone possesses and experiences timeless eternity, for He is "the High and Lofty One Who inhabits eternity, whose name is Holy" (Isa. 57:15 NKJV). God existed in eternity before He created the time-space universe. He has continued to exist in eternity since creation, and He will forever exist in eternity. However, He interacts with the time-space universe and especially with the beings he created within it.

In the eternal state believers will experience endless duration of time but not what might be called the "timeless" eternity that belongs only to God. He always will be the infinite Creator who exists in eternity, and all created beings, whether human or angelic will always be finite creatures who exist in a sphere of endless time.

The Bible sometimes expresses eternity by using the plural and by repetition of terms for temporal ages. This, however, does not mean eternity for God is an endless series of ages. How else could finite humans express eternity than through grammatically manipulating familiar terms? Such time terms are used of the believer, who "will live forever" (*zēsei eis ton aiōna*, John 6:58), but in Revelation 4:9 they are also used of God "who lives forever and ever" (*tō zōnti eis tous aiōnas tōn aiōnōn*). Since time terms are used of God, they must be able to express the kind of eternity that Scripture ascribes to God (Isa. 57:15).

Though God exists in another dimension than does His finite creation, He is still present in, and interacts with, His universe and people (Gen. 3:8; Isa. 57:15; Jer. 23:23-24; John 3:16; 2 Cor. 6:16; Gal. 4:4; Eph. 4:6; 2 Peter 3:3-13). This truth opposes deism, which teaches that God exists entirely separate from the world and does not intervene in the world or influence humans.

THE ETERNAL STATE

Biblical Concepts

"The day of God" (2 Peter 3:12) coincides with the eternal state and includes the "new heavens and a new earth, in which righteousness dwells" (3:13). The day of God begins after "the Day of the Lord" (1 Thess. 5:1-3; 2 Peter 3:10), or more specifically, after the millennial heavens and earth have passed away and the Great White Throne Judgment is completed (2 Peter 3:10-12; Rev. 20:11-21:1).[4]

A new heaven and a new earth come into existence only after the first heaven and the first earth pass away (Rev. 21:1). The commencement and continuance of the day of God seems to coincide with the new heavens and the new earth. The "Day of the Lord" concerns the present heavens and earth, which are reserved for fire (2 Peter 3:7, 10).

Christ will reign in the Millennium over the earthly, mediatorial kingdom, subject all things to Himself, and continue in subjection to the Father "so that God may be all in all" (1 Cor. 15:24-28). Thus "the day of God" refers to the eternal state in which God is "all in all."[5]

Inhabitants of the Eternal State

Human spirits and angels as spirits (Heb. 1:14) will exist forever though they have a temporal beginning as finite creations. And in the eternal state resurrected humans and angelic spirits will exist forever either in fiery punishment away from the Lord (Matt. 25:41, 46; Rev. 20:10-15) or in heavenly blessedness with the Lord (1 Thess. 4:17; Heb. 12:22-23; Rev. 21:1-3). Therefore angelic spirits and resurrected humans will never be destroyed in the sense of annihilation, but they can exist forever separate from God in the lake of fire (Rev. 20:14; 21:8).

Earthly human bodies obviously do not exist forever, but they deteriorate until they die (2 Cor. 4:16; Heb. 9:27). However, all human bodies will be raised (John 5:28-29; Acts 24:15). The bodies of dead unbelievers will be raised at the Great White Throne Judgment, and their resurrection bodies will suffer punishment forever in the lake of fire (Rev. 20:11-15). The bodies of dead believers will be raised and the bodies of living believers will be transformed at the return of Christ so that all believers will receive a glorified body conformed to Christ's perfect humanity (1 Cor. 15:51-53; Phil. 3:20-21; 1 Thess. 4:16-17). The glorified bodies of believers will enter God's eternal kingdom to experience eternity with the Lord in the new heavens and the new earth (1 Cor. 15:50; 2 Peter 1:11; Rev. 21:1-3).

God has made humans to exist forever, and He has set eternity in their hearts (Eccl. 3:11). At the core of their being, humans know that they will survive death in conscious existence. So people fear death unless they claim victory over death and freedom from fear through faith in Christ (John 11:25-26; 1 Cor. 15:26, 51-57; Heb. 2:14-15).

ETERNAL HEAVENS AND EARTH

The Need for Something New

The existing heavens and earth are not a fit habitation for the eternal state. The earth was cursed when Adam and Eve transgressed God's commandment (Gen. 3:17-19; Rom. 8:19-22; cf. Rev. 22:3). Even the heavens are no longer pure in God's sight, for they have become a spiritual battlefield (Job 1:6-12; 2:1-6; 15:15; Eph. 2:2; 6:10-12; Rev. 12:7-9). The heavens are contaminated by Satan and his demons.

Thus "the present heavens and earth by His word are being reserved for fire, kept for the day of judgment and destruction of ungodly men" (2 Peter 3:7). The present heavens and earth will pass away to make way for the new heavens and a new earth (2 Peter 3:10-13; Rev. 20:11). In Revelation 21:1, John noted this sequence: First heaven and first earth pass away; new heaven and new earth come into being. The first earth goes through four phases between creation and destruction:

- First, the original heavens and the earth and all that God made were "very good" (Gen. 1:31).
- Second, the earth entered its post-fall condition under the consequences of Adam and Eve's sin (Genesis 3; Romans 8). The effects of sin were so severe that God judged it by flood (Gen. 6:7, 17). All flesh was destroyed except for Noah's family and the animals aboard the ark (Genesis 6-8; 1 Peter 3:20; 2 Peter 3:6).
- Third, the fallen earth will continue in its fallen state in an evil age until Christ's return with His angels (Gal. 1:4). At his coming, Christ will judge the world and its inhabitants (Matt. 13:39-43, 49-50; 24:30-31; 25:31-46; 2 Thess. 1:5-10; Jude 14-15; Rev. 19:11-21).
- Fourth, Christ will establish His millennial reign on earth (Matt. 19:28; see also Acts 1:6-7; Rom. 8:19-23; 1 Cor. 15:23-26; Rev. 20:1-6).

After this final phase comes recreation (Rev. 21:1).

Permanence of the New

The present heavens and earth are temporary, at least in form, as the psalmist vividly explains: "Of old Thou didst found the earth, and the heavens are the work of Thy hands. Even they will perish, but Thou dost endure; and all of them will wear out like a garment; like clothing You will change them and they will be changed. But Thou art the same, and Thy years will not come to an end" (Ps. 102:25-27; cf. Isa. 66:22).

The earth is firmly established and the operation of earth's seasons and heaven's lights are fixed (e.g., Gen. 8:22; 1 Chron. 16:30; Ps. 93:1; 104:5; 119:90; Eccl. 1:4; Jer. 31:35–36) so long as God continues the present order of the physical universe. However, the present heavens and earth are temporary because they will be replaced by new heavens and a new earth (Ps. 102:25–26; Matt. 24:35; Heb. 12:26-27; 2 Peter 3:7, 10-11; Rev. 20:11; 21:1). Since the first heaven and first earth will pass away, some conclude with John Walvoord that "it is a totally new heaven and new earth, and not the present heaven and earth renovated."[6]

However, it is possible that the *substance* of the heaven and earth *continues*, while the *form* is drastically *changed* or renovated to create a new heaven and earth. The new heaven and earth are constituted from the dissolved elements of the old. For the present heaven and earth to "perish" does not necessarily mean annihilation. Rather it may mean transformation into "a new heaven and a new earth" that will endure (Rev. 21:1; cf. Isa. 66:22; 2 Peter 3:7-13).[7]

Purpose of the New

When God created the original heavens and earth He formed the earth into a suitable habitation for man (Genesis 1-2; Isa. 45:18). God will also "create new heavens and a new earth" as an ideal habitation where redeemed humans and the holy angels can dwell with Him forever (Isa. 65:17; Heb. 12:22-23; Rev. 21:1-3).

Preparation to Enter the New

Heaven is indeed a prepared place for a prepared people. Believers *can know* that they have eternal life (1 John 5:13) and that they will go to be with Christ when they die or when Christ returns (John 14:1-3; Acts 16:31; 2 Cor. 5:8; 1 Thess. 4:13-17; 1 Peter 1:2-5). Christ wants His people to rejoice that their names are recorded in the Lamb's Book of Life (Luke 10:20; Phil. 4:3; Heb. 12:23; Rev. 3:5; 17:8; 20:12, 15; 21:27; cf. Rev. 13:8). A believer's place in heaven is secure.

Significance of the New

God will complete His redemptive plan by conforming His people to Christ's glorified humanity (Phil. 3:20-21). Then they will be righteous like Christ and prepared to live with Him in the recreated heavens and earth (2 Peter 3:13). These truths about our future likeness to Christ and presence with Christ in the new heavens and earth should motivate us to practice three key principles.

1. *We are to be holy, godly, peaceful, pure, and heavenly minded.* The temporal order of things will be replaced by an eternal order of things. Cataclysmic

events will close out God's program for the present heavens and earth (2 Peter 3:7–12). His fiery destruction of the universe ought to motivate us to godliness. Since we seek a new place where righteousness dwells (3:13; cf. Rev. 21:1–4), we should focus on eternal things and follow His will instead of the world's ways (3:14; see 2 Cor. 4:18; Col. 3:1–4; 1 John 2:17, 28).

2. *While we live as strangers on earth, we are to fix our hope on Christ and the New Jerusalem* (John 14:2–3; 1 Peter 1:3–5; Rev. 21:3). Abraham ultimately desired a heavenly country (Heb. 11:13–16). God promises that all believers will reside in the city of the living God (Heb. 12:22).

3. *We are to rejoice in trials because they are temporary.* We will receive an inheritance when Christ comes. Peter teaches that we have been "born again to a living hope" through the resurrection (1 Peter 1:3). This is a certain hope (1:4; cf. Col. 1:5) for a glorified body, rewards, residence in the new heavens and the new earth, and participation with Christ in His glory (John 17:22, 24; Rev. 22:5).

THE ETERNAL, GLORIFIED BODY

God prepares His people to enter the new heavens and new earth by giving them an immortal, glorified body (1 Cor. 15:50–57; 2 Peter 1:11). The redemption of the believer's body (Rom. 8:23) is an essential part of God's plan of salvation (1 Thess. 5:23).

Significance of the New Body

God created the believer's body to attain glorified form. God created people physically and spiritually (Gen. 2:7; Num. 16:22; Pss. 100:3; 139:13–16). Christ died for the whole human being (Ps. 22:1–21; Isa. 53; 1 Peter 2:24–25; 3:18), and He will redeem our whole being (e.g., Rom. 8:23; Phil. 3:20–21; 1 Peter 1:9). The body is decaying, but the inner man is being renewed (2 Cor. 4:16). At glorification the believer's body is conformed to Christ's perfect humanity (1 Cor. 15:51–54; Phil. 3:20–21). Thus redemption includes the body.[8]

Between physical death and the bodily resurrection, the "inner man" (2 Cor. 4:16) does not exist in an unconscious or a semi-conscious, dream state. The body without the spirit is dead, but the soul is alive and alert in the presence of the Lord (2 Cor. 5:8; Phil. 1:23; James 2:26). The souls of believers martyred in the tribulation period are seen to have memory and awareness (Rev. 6:9–10). Abraham, Isaac, and Jacob were physically dead when Jesus spoke of them as "the living" (Matt. 22:32).

Therefore to go to Christ is better than to remain in the body (Phil. 1:23; cf. Luke 23:43, 46; Acts 7:59; 2 Cor. 5:8; Phil. 1:21). Ultimately, however, we will have a glorified body (2 Cor. 5:2).

Christ was raised in a permanent glorified body. Christ came in a human body (John 1:14), died in a body (Matt. 27:58-60; 1 Peter 2:24), rose from the dead in a body (Luke 24:39), ascended to heaven in a body, and will return in a body (Acts 1:9-11). Believers will receive glorified bodies to inhabit forever just as Christ will forever inhabit His glorified body (Rom. 8:11; Phil. 3:20-21).

Glorified believers will be able to walk, talk, and eat in their bodies, just as Christ did in His glorified body (e.g., Luke 24:36-43; John 20:19-20, 25, 27; Acts 10:41). Christ's permanent incarnate form shows God's plan for His unique Son and His spiritual sons to retain "flesh and bone" bodies throughout eternity (Luke 24:39; cf. 1 Cor. 15:50). The human body is not evil in itself, as the Gnostics taught. The body is consistent with perfected humanity because the divine Christ is perfected humanity. He retains His body through resurrection and forever (1 Cor. 15:20, 42-49). "Holy Scripture knows nothing of a spaceless, timeless, non-material heaven," observes Sauer.[9]

Forefathers to the Gnostics, Greek philosophers generally affirmed the immortality of the soul but denied the resurrection of the body. Plato taught that the body was the prison of the soul, so the doctrine of resurrection seemed repugnant to a Platonist. The Resurrection meant permanently imprisoning the soul in the body. Thus when Paul preached to Greek philosophers at Athens (Acts 17:16-34, esp. 22; cf. 1 Cor. 15:12-20), they jeered and sneered at His message of Christ's resurrection (Acts 17:18, 31-32). But Paul did not compromise the message of Christ's bodily resurrection and coming righteous judgment to accommodate the false beliefs of his audience. The Hellenistic background of Corinthian Christians made them liable to question the bodily resurrection, so in 1 Corinthians 15 Paul gave a strong defense for the resurrection of Christ and His people.

Thus, the believer's body will be raised in a glorified form. Scripture teaches that the believer's body is a temple of the Spirit (Rom. 8:11; 1 Cor. 6:19) and destined to become glorious and immortal (Phil. 3:20-21; 1 Cor. 15:51-54).

Need for the Glorified Body

Paul said that "flesh and blood cannot inherit the kingdom of God" (1 Cor. 15:50), but he did not say that a body cannot inherit the kingdom of God. A natural body (i.e., a "flesh and blood" body) cannot "inherit the kingdom of God" (1 Cor. 15:50) because it cannot enter "the eternal kingdom" and experience its blessings (2 Peter 1:11). People can experience only what they are equipped to experience. Properly functioning eyes and ears are essential to see and hear adequately. Even with perfect sight, we must use a telescope to see certain heavenly bodies and a powerful microscope to see very minute things. An astronaut requires a space suit in order to travel in a space ship. Likewise, the imperishable, immortal, glorified body (1 Cor. 15:51-54) we will receive at Christ's return will prepare us to "inherit the kingdom of God" (15:50).

Nature of the Glorified Body

Aspects of the glorified body may be beyond our comprehension now, but we can learn something about them from Scripture. The Bible records that others have been restored to life after they had experienced physical death (1 Kings 17:17-23; 2 Kings 4:32-37; 13:21; Matt. 9:24-25; Luke 7:11-15; John 11:43-44; Acts 9:36-41; 20:9-12).[10] Christ taught that all humans will be resurrected (John 5:28-29; cf. Dan. 12:2; Acts 24:15). Most significantly, He predicted and accomplished His own resurrection from the dead. Christ became "the first fruits of those who are asleep" (1 Cor. 15:20) and "the firstborn from the dead" (Col. 1:18; cf. Rev. 1:5). If his body was the firstfruit of the harvest, the rest of the bodies will be like his (see 1 Cor. 15:21-23). Here, then are some things we can say about the believer's future glorified body:

1. *It is a physical, material body.* Christ's resurrected body was not a spirit, a phantom, or emanation, but a genuine body to hear, see, and touch (John 20:20, 27; cf. Luke 24:39-40; 1 John 1:1-2).
2. *It is a transformed body.* We will be conformed to Christ's glory (Phil. 3:21).
3. *It is a recognizable body.* Still, the risen will retain identity and continuity (Luke 16:19-31; 1 Cor. 15:35-44, 51; cf. Luke 24:39-40; John 20:20, 25-29). Christ said, "It is I myself" (Gk., *egō eimi autos*), emphasizing that He was the same person who had been crucified. His resurrected, transformed body could be identified as the one that had hung on the cross. This accords with 1 Corinthians 15:35-41, which rejects two common errors: (1) that the resurrected body is just the original body reformed, or (2) that there is no connection between old and new bodies.[11] Sauer remarks, "We know each other here, and certainly we shall not be more foolish in heaven than we are now."[12] In their glorified bodies believers will recognize friends and family. In fact they will now know one another perfectly (1 Cor. 13:12).
3. *It is an imperishable body* (1 Cor. 15:42, 53-54). The glorified body is incorruptible and therefore free from decay and suffering that accompanies decay (Rev. 21:4; cf. 2 Cor. 4:16). It will never grow old or become weak or ill.[13] Our experience in the new heavens and earth will not involve hunger, thirst, or heat from the sun, or pain (Isa. 49:10; Rev. 7:16-17; 21:4).
4. *It is an immortal body* (1 Cor. 15:53-57; cf. Luke 20:35-36; Rom. 8:11; 1 Cor. 15:26; 2 Cor. 5:1, 4). Since the resurrection body is eternal and unlimited by time or change, it can never bring the sorrow and sense of loss associated with death (1 Thess. 4:13; Rev. 21:4).
5. *It is a body with many of the same abilities as now.* Jesus ate (Luke 24:41-

43) and walked (Luke 24:15). However, the glorified body apparently will not depend upon food for sustenance (1 Cor. 6:13). The glorified saints may be able to perceive thoughts (cf. 1 Cor. 13:12), but Scripture suggests that they will use verbal communication (Matt. 28:18-20; Luke 24:13-17; John 20:19; cf. Matt. 17:3).

6. *It has what we would call supernatural abilities.* To sight, Jesus could appear and disappear (Luke 24:31, 36).[14] Apparently the glorified body can move in space instantaneously. Still, it is localized, unlike God's omnipresent spirit (1 Kings 8:27; Ps. 139:7-12; Jer. 23:23-24; John 4:24). The glorified human body is not limited by matter generally. The risen Lord demonstrated this by passing unhindered through a door (John 20:19, 26).

7. *It is sinless.* Instead of a "body of sin" (Rom. 6:6), the glorified body like Christ's body will be free from the practice of sin (2 Peter 3:13; Rev. 21:27), from the principle of sin and even from the possibility of sin (1 John 3:2, 5). The body is not sinful in itself, but the sin principle uses the body and its members as instruments of sin (Rom. 6:13, 19). Glorified believers will not have any sin within them to operate through their bodies. That sinlessness will foster a perfect environment without need for armies, police, jails, doctors, hospitals, funeral homes, or cemeteries. There will be no natural or man-made disasters.

8. *It shares Christ's glory* (1 Cor. 15:43). At Christ's return the believer's humble body is conformed to "the body of His glory" (Phil. 3:21).

9. *It is an unfailing body* (1 Cor. 15:43). Our human bodies limit and cramp. The resurrection body will have no such limits (1 Cor. 15:42-53; Rev. 21:4). It will be free from frailty. As long as we are in our "earthen vessels," we "groan within ourselves, waiting eagerly for our adoption as sons, the redemption of our body" (Rom. 8:23; see 2 Cor. 4:7).

10. *It is a spiritual body.* The earthly body is "natural" (Gk., *psychikon*, "soulish"). It will be "spiritual" (Gk., *pneumatikon*; 1 Cor 15:44; cf. v. 51). Even godly human beings feel the conflict between their fleshly lusts and their indwelling Spirit (Gal. 5:16-18; cf. Matt. 26:41; 1 Peter 2:11). In our glorified bodies the Holy Spirit will perfectly dominate our natures without resistance. Glorified human nature will produce only the fruits of the Spirit; the sinful flesh will be gone (Gal. 5:16-23).[15]

11. *It is a heavenly body* (1 Cor. 15:47-49; cf. Gen. 2:7; 3:19; 2 Cor. 5:1-2). Our earthy body matches its temporary existence and moral imperfection (2 Cor. 4:16-18; Phil. 3:13-14; Heb. 9:27). The heavenly body will be suited to eternal, abundant life and moral perfection (1 Cor. 15:50-57; 2 Peter 1:11; 1 John 3:2; Rev. 21:1-3). All saints will enjoy

unhindered and unending fellowship with God the Father, the Son, and the Holy Spirit and with other believers.

12. *It is a body clothed in the brightness of heavenly glory* (Dan. 12:3; Matt. 13:43; 17:2). People on earth clothe themselves in perishable material (Gen. 3:21; 1 Tim. 6:8; cf. Ps. 102:25–26). The heavenly body may be attired only in God's enduring, radiant glory. We read of the saints in heaven clothed in white (Rev. 4:4; 6:11; 7:9, 13–14) and in "fine linen" (19:8). They are seen wearing golden crowns (4:4). The garments and crowns may be symbols of righteousness and rewards, rather than literal apparel. Or possibly they are literal adornments that have symbolic significance. In any case, our earthly body are a tent, compared to the imperishable, celestial palace of our heavenly bodies (2 Cor. 5:1, 4; 2 Peter 1:13–14).

13. *It is a body in which we will not be married* (Matt. 22:30). All bodies in the eternal state are immortal, so no need will exist for replacement of bodies through reproduction.

14. *It is a fully mature body.* God wants His people to grow to mental, physical, spiritual, and social maturity in this life (Luke 2:52; Heb. 6:1; 2 Peter 3:18; 1 John 3:2), so we can anticipate that a believer's resurrection body will be as mature as Christ's perfect humanity. The bodies likely will not appear to be the same age as at death. Those who die in infancy or with mental inability will be raised as perfected humanity, their bodies and faculties fully developed. We can expect to continue forever in the age God considers ideal, free from decay and aging (1 Cor. 15:52–54). [16]

15. *It is a body that will retain no negative effects of the earthly life.* God promises, "I create new heavens and a new earth; and the former things will not be remembered or come to mind" (Isa. 65:17). "The former things" will certainly include the old heavens and earth. God "will wipe away every tear from their eyes, and there will no longer be any death; there will no longer be any mourning, or crying, or pain, the first things have passed away." [17]

THE ETERNAL CITY OF GOD

The new Jerusalem will come down from heaven (Rev. 21:2). In the eternal state the New Jerusalem seems to rest on the new earth, which has no sea (21:1–2, 10). Four Bible texts most explicitly mention the new heavens and earth (Isa. 65:17; 66:22; 2 Peter 3:13; Rev. 21:1). However, far more in Scripture is said about the New Jerusalem (especially in Rev. 21:2–22:5).

Interpretation of the New Jerusalem

We can properly understand the biblical description of God's eternal city in a literal sense but also see symbolic significance beyond its literal meaning. As

Robert Thomas notes, "The details of the description show . . . that the bride-city (Rev. 21:2, 9) will be a real city with a material existence. The materialistic nature of the city has spiritual significance."[18] For example, the city is made of "pure gold, like clear glass" (21:18). Yet this precious metal also reflects and symbolizes the glory of God (21:10–11; cf. Ps. 26:8; 29:9).

Location of the New Jerusalem

Since John saw "the holy city, New Jerusalem, coming down out of heaven from God" (21:2, 10), some premillennialists believe that the New Jerusalem is suspended above the earth during the Millennium. This seems reasonable but has no direct biblical support. In any case, the New Jerusalem comes down after a new heaven and a new earth are in view.[19]

Titles of the New Jerusalem

The title *New Jerusalem* (21:2; cf. 3:12; 21:10) distinguishes it from the old city. It is also called *the heavenly Jerusalem* (Heb. 12:22) because it originates in heaven (Rev. 3:12; 21:2, 10; cf. John 18:36). As Hebrews 13:14 reminds believers, "We do not have a lasting city, but we are seeking the city which is to come."

It is called *the Jerusalem above* because it is spiritually free and properly claimed by all believers as "our mother" (Gal. 4:26; cf. v. 31b). In contrast, Jerusalem below was enslaved to the law with her unbelieving children (4:25; cf. v. 31a).

The title *the city of the living God* (Heb. 12:22; cf. Rev. 3:12) is appropriate because the city is God's creation, and it will be God's eternal residence with His people (Heb. 11:10).

As *the holy city* (Rev. 21:2, 10; 22:19) it contrasts with the earthly Jerusalem, which was "the holy city" in an ideal sense as God's chosen city (Neh. 1:9; Matt. 4:5; 27:53). However, Jerusalem is spiritually comparable to Sodom and Egypt (Rev. 11:8) and with other corrupt cities (cf. 17:1–18:24). The holy God with His holy people and holy angels will dwell in the true "holy city" (21:2, 10; cf. 21:27).

Purpose of the New Jerusalem

God designed the New Jerusalem to be His eternal dwelling place among His people (21:3). The throne of God and His Son will be on the new earth and in the New Jerusalem (Rev. 21:3, 5; 22:1). Thus the New Jerusalem is God-centered and particularly focused on Christ as the Lamb of God (7:17; 21:9, 14, 22, 23; 22:1, 3; cf. John 1:29; Rev. 5:12–13). The lamb is pictured as the shepherd of His redeemed people (7:17) and as the lamp of the city (21:23).

The presence of God within the New Jerusalem far exceeds the magnificence and significance of the city itself (21:3; 22:3), for the builder of the city is greater than the city (Heb. 3:3-4). Jesus evidently had the New Jerusalem in mind when He gave His followers this promise: "In My Father's house are many dwelling places; if it were not so, I would have told you; for I go to prepare a place for you" (John 14:2). The Greek noun for "dwelling places" (*monai*) here indicates "heavenly dwellings."[20] The Greek verb for "prepare" (*hetoimasai*) is the same basic word used to indicate that the new Jerusalem is "made ready" (*hētoimasmenēn;* Rev. 21:2). In Hebrews 11:16 God "has prepared [*hētoimasen*] a city" for His people.

Description of the New Jerusalem

The Dimensions

The New Jerusalem measures fifteen hundred miles in length, width, and height. As a perfect cube this would measure 3.375 million cubic miles in volume.[21] It would be less if the top is smaller than the base, and the general shape is that of a pyramid, as some scholars believe (see Rev. 21:16).[22]

The Materials

The city is "pure gold, like pure glass" (Rev. 21:18), and the other components of the city are made of precious stones (21:11, 18-21). That jasper (21:11) and gold (21:18, 21) are said to be translucent is uncharacteristic of these elements as they now are found.

The Lighting

Unlike the garden of Eden, this city has no need for light from the sun or moon (cf. Gen. 1:14-19; Isa. 60:19; Rev. 21:23; 22:5). God's glory illumines His dazzling city, so that it has no night darkness (Rev. 21:11, 18, 21, 23, 25; 22:5; cf. Isa. 60:19; 1 Tim. 6:16). The Lamb is its lamp, and the nations walk by its light (21:11, 23-24).

The Wall

"A great and high wall" made of jasper surrounds the city. The wall has "twelve foundation stones" which are "adorned with every kind of precious stone," and these bear the names of the Lamb's twelve apostles (Rev. 21:12-20; cf. Eph. 2:20). The wall is 216 feet thick (or high; Rev. 21:12, 17; cf. Ps. 125:2). This symbolizes the security of God's people there (cf. Isa. 26:1-4).

The Gates

The New Jerusalem has twelve gates, each attended by an angel, evidently like an honor guard. Each gate is a pearl (Rev. 21:12, 21). The twelve gates are inscribed with the names of the twelve tribes of Israel and positioned with three gates at each compass direction (vv. 12-13). Since the city has no night-time, the gates are never closed (v. 25).

The Street

Only one street is mentioned, a pavement of pure gold, like transparent glass (Rev. 21:21). A river flows down the middle of this street to form a boulevard (22:1-2).

The Temple

The city has no material temple for the Father and the Son are always present, whereas Israel's earthly temple was a material, earthly representation of God's presence (Rev. 21:22; see 1 Kings 8:10-11).

The River

There is no sea, but the "river of the water of life" flows "from the throne of God and of the Lamb in the middle of its street" (Rev. 22:1-2).

The Tree of Life

The city also has "the tree of life" on "either side of the river," and the tree bears "twelve kinds of fruit, yielding its fruit every month; and the leaves of the tree" are "for the healing of the nations" (Rev. 22:2; cf. Gen. 2:9; 3:22, 24; Rev. 2:7; 22:14, 19). Why should the nations require such healing in the eternal state? John Walvoord explains:

> Based on this statement some have referred this situation back to the millennial times when there will be sickness and healing. However, another meaning seems to be indicated. The word "healing" (*therapeian*) can be understood as "health-giving." The English word "therapeutic" is derived from this Greek word. Even though there is no sickness in the eternal state, the tree's fruit and leaves seem to contribute to the physical well-being of those in the eternal state.[23]

The Throne

The throne of God, once was only in heaven (Ps. 103:19; Matt. 5:34-35). Now it will be among God's people (Rev. 22:3). The response of all created inhabitants of the New Jerusalem will be, "To Him who sits on the throne, and to the Lamb, be blessing and honor and glory and dominion forever and ever" (5:13). The throne of God and the Lamb shows that the Father continues to reign through the Son, and God's people reign with them in an eternal kingdom where everything remains subject to the Father's rule (1 Cor. 15:28; 2 Peter 1:11; Rev. 11:15; 22:5).

The Glory and Honor

The nations of the earth will bring their glory and honor into the city (Rev. 21:24, 26).

The Prominent Number Twelve

The number twelve is a remarkably frequent figure in the description of the city. There are references to twelve gates (Rev. 21:12, 21), twelve angels and twelve tribes of Israel (21:12); twelve foundations and twelve apostles (21:14). The twelve gates are twelve pearls (21:21). In height or width the wall of twelve squared (or 144) cubits (21:17), and the city's total dimensions are twelve thousand *stadia* (about 1500 miles) in length, width, and height (21:16). The tree of life bears twelve fruits (22:2)

In summary, this city's precious minerals and metals, its beautiful colors, and its immense dimensions portray a superlative splendor. The New Jerusalem is God's future, permanent city, prepared for God's people and sought by God's people (Heb. 11:16; 13:14).

Blessings of the New Jerusalem

The permanence and other features of the heavenly Jerusalem (Rev. 21:1–22:5) far excel the earthly Eden:

1. *It is free from sin, Satan, demons, and temptation to sin.* Only righteousness dwells in the new heavens and new earth. None of God's enemies will intrude (2 Peter 3:13 cf. Matt. 25:41; Rev. 20:10).
2. *It abounds with life* (Rev. 21:6). The river of abundant life in the New Jerusalem contrasts with the lake of the second death (Rev. 20:14; 21:8). The tree of life on either side of the river in the new Jerusalem is always available to the redeemed (Rev. 22:2), whereas Adam and Eve forfeited the privilege to partake of the tree of life (Gen. 2:9; 3:22–24).
3. *All things are new there.* The inhabitants of the New Jerusalem have a new name (Rev. 2:17; 3:12), sing a new song (5:9; 14:3), and dwell in new heavens and a new earth. God has made all things new (21:5).
4. *There we will serve God without hindrance* (Rev. 22:3). The service of glorified believers will not involve any of the suffering, deprivation, or weariness that earthly believers experience (7:15–16).
5. *There we will see the Lord's face and have His name on our foreheads* (Rev. 22:4; cf. Job 19:26–27; Isa. 33:17; Matt. 5:8; 1 John 3:2). That the Lord's name will be on the foreheads of his people shows the intimate relationship between believers and God in the eternal state (Rev. 2:17; 3:12; 7:3; 14:1).
6. *It will be ruled by God and His people* (Rev. 22:5; cf. 2 Tim. 2:12; Rev. 5:10; 20:4–6). God commanded humankind to subdue and rule over the earth (Gen. 1:26–28; Ps. 8:3–8). But their transgression ended their

life in Eden and their ability to properly rule for God. They brought a curse upon the earth (Gen. 1:28; 2:17; 3:1-24). Consequently the earth groans and suffers under bondage to corruption, but it anticipates freedom when God will redeem creation (Rom. 8:19-23).[24]

Residents of the New Jerusalem

The most important residents of the New Jerusalem are God and the Lamb (Rev. 21:3, 5; 22:3). God will dwell among His holy people in the New Jerusalem (21:2-3). His omnipresence (or immensity) contrasts with humans and angels who are localized, finite beings. Even the new heavens and new earth cannot contain Him because they are still finite creation, and God is infinite in relation to space (2 Chron. 6:18; Jer. 23:24).

The city of God is also the home of three groups of redeemed humans who are pure, clean, and holy (Rev. 22:14, 17). First, there will be Israelites (Isa. 65:15-17; Rom. 11:1-5, 25-27; Gal. 3:9; Heb. 11:13, 16, 40; 12:23; 13:14; Rev. 7:3-8). Second, the church will be present (Acts 10:34-48; 11:11-18; 15:7-11, 14; Rom. 3:29-30; 1 Cor. 12:12-13; Gal. 3:14, 26; Eph. 3:4-7; Heb. 12:23). Third, there will be other redeemed gentiles saved outside the church age (Job 14:14-15; 19:25-27; Rev. 7:9, 14; 21:24, 26; 22:2).

Israel still will have a distinct name among God's people in the eternal state, according to Isaiah 66:22: "'For just as the new heavens and the new earth which I make will endure before Me,' declares the LORD, 'So your offspring and your name will endure'" (cf. Isa. 48:19; 56:5; Jer. 31:3, 36-37; Heb. 12:22-23; Rev. 21:12). God further assures elect Israel that they have "been saved by the LORD with an everlasting salvation; you will not be put to shame or humiliated to all eternity" (Isa. 45:17).

ETERNAL THINGS

Some eternal things from God are particularly significant in the new heavens and the new earth.

God's Eternal Things

His Glory

God's glory has attended Him from eternity past, and His glory shared with His Son and His Spirit will continue through eternity future (John 17:5; 1 Peter 5:10; 2 Peter 3:18). The Son has returned to His glory with the Father (Heb. 2:9). God now calls us to His eternal glory in Christ (1 Peter 5:10). Christ will bring "many sons to glory" (Heb. 2:10; cf. 2 Tim. 2:10). Then believers will forever be in glory and see the glory that the Father has given the Son (John 17:22, 24).

His Word

As God is eternal, so His word is eternal. The psalmist affirmed, "Forever, O LORD, Your word is settled [lit. "stands firm"] in heaven" (Ps. 119:89). The enduring word of God contrasts with the present temporal order as Isaiah notes: "The grass withers, the flower fades, but the word of our God stands forever" (Isa. 40:8). Jesus declared, "Heaven and earth will pass away, but My words will not pass away" (Matt. 24:35).

The present heavens and earth will be destroyed and replaced by new heavens and a new earth (2 Peter 3:7, 10-13; Rev. 20:11; 21:1), yet God's word will continue into the eternal state. The only thing that we can hold in our hands that lasts forever is God's truthful word (John 17:17).[25] And God wants us to treasure His eternal word in our hearts so that we can resist sin and be holy because He is holy (Ps. 119:9, 11, 60, 133; Luke 4:1-11; 1 Peter 1:15-16).

His Kingdom

God rules as King over everything (1 Chron. 29:12) in "an everlasting kingdom" (Ps. 145:13). We may call His comprehensive and absolute rule the universal kingdom. God also rules through human agents upon the earth, and we may call this temporal, earthly rule within the universal kingdom the mediatorial kingdom. The mediatorial kingdom is in view when Scripture teaches that Christ "hands over the kingdom to the God and Father, when He has abolished all rule and all authority and power" (1 Cor. 15:24). Christ reigns in the mediatorial kingdom until He has destroyed death, the last enemy (15:25-26; Rev. 20:1-15).

Our Eternal Things

Every believer in Christ receives the gift of eternal life (John 3:16; Rom. 6:23) and the promise of an eternal inheritance (Heb. 9:15; 1 Peter 1:3-4). God also enables believers to produce eternal spiritual fruit (John 15:16) and to earn eternal rewards (1 Cor. 3:11-15; 2 Cor. 5:10).

Spiritual Fruit

Christ taught His disciples, "You did not choose Me but I chose you, and appointed you that you would go and bear fruit, and that your fruit would remain" (John 15:16). Believers produce spiritual fruit by abiding in Christ and being filled with the Spirit (John 15:1-5; Gal. 5:22-23; Eph. 5:18). True spiritual fruit is only from the Lord (cf. Hos. 14:8b), and it is permanent.

Spiritual "fruit" (Gk., *karpos*) includes (1) manifestation of Christlike character (Gal. 5:22-23), (2) presentation of praise and thanks to God through Christ (Heb. 13:15), (3) contribution to the Lord for Christian works and workers (Phil. 4:14-19; esp. v. 17), (4) salvation of souls through evangelism (John 4:35-37; 15:16; 2 Tim. 4:5), (5) edification of other believers (Rom. 1:13), and (f) production of good works (Col. 1:10; e.g., 1 Tim. 5:9-10).[26]

Reward

The Lord will reward believers for their genuine spiritual fruit, which includes "good works" (Eph. 2:10; cf. Col. 1:10; Titus 2:14; 3:8). We receive our rewards at the judgment seat of Christ (2 Cor. 5:10; cf. 1 Cor. 3:11-15), which occurs when or soon after He comes for us (1 Cor. 4:5; Rev. 22:12).

Eternal Destiny of Unbelievers

In the new heavens and new earth, believers will dwell in perfect righteousness and eternal blessedness (2 Peter 3:13; Rev. 21:1-22:5). But outside the new heavens and new earth and in the lake of fire, unbelievers, Satan, and his angels (demons) will dwell in eternal punishment (Matt. 25:41, 46; 2 Thess. 1:9; Rev. 20:10, 14-15; 21:8; 22:15).

Punishment

When unbelievers die, they immediately begin conscious suffering in *Hades* (or *Sheol* in the Old Testament) until they are raised, judged at the Great White Throne, and thrown into the lake of fire (Luke 16:19-28; Heb. 9:27; Rev. 20:10-15). Death then is a trapdoor to *Hades* for unbelievers (Luke 16:22-23; Heb. 9:27) but a gateway to glory for believers (Phil. 1:23; 2 Cor. 5:8).

Scripture says that "death and *Hades* gave up the dead which were in them" and that "death and *Hades* were thrown into the lake of fire" (Rev. 20:13-14). Here death refers to the burial place of the unbeliever's body while Hades refers to the place of confinement of unbeliever's spirit or the soul.

Hell (*Gehenna*) is the precise term for the eternal place of eternal punishment (Matt. 5:22, 29-30; 10:28; 18:9; 23:33; Mark 9:43, 45, 47; Luke 12:5). It is distinct from Hades or Sheol, the place of conscious suffering between death and the resurrection (Luke 16:19-28), and is the same as the lake of fire (Rev. 20:14-15). All people who die in unbelief ultimately will "go into hell [*Gehenna*], into the unquenchable fire" (Mark 9:43; cf. Isa. 66:24), which is also "the eternal fire which has been prepared for the devil and his angels" (Matt. 25:41; cf. Jude 7).

We should not confuse the biblical doctrine of eternal punishment with the idea in Eastern religion of *karma*, that one's conduct determines the inevitable results one experiences in this life or in an endless series of reincarnations. The Bible absolutely opposes reincarnation. "It is appointed for men to die once and after this comes judgment" (Heb. 9:27; cf. Luke 16:22-23, 26).

Also, the biblical teaching of "eternal punishment" opposes *annihilationism* the view that God's punishment of unbelievers is temporary, because God will eventually annihilate them, or the related *conditional immortality*, which teaches that only believers have eternal existence and that unbelievers cease to exist at death or at the final judgment. The Bible teaches that all will be resurrected to eternal life or to eternal condemnation (Dan. 12:2; Matt. 25:46; John 5:28–29; Acts 24:15; Rev. 20:11–15).

Severe Punishment

Eternal punishment of unbelievers is unimaginably relentless and severe. They will be cast into "the outer darkness" (Matt. 8:12; 22:13; 25:30) in contrast to believers who will enter the eternal kingdom of light (2 Peter 1:11; Rev. 21:23–24; 22:5; cf. Col. 1:12–13). The appointment of unbelievers to "outer darkness" means permanent separation from God and from other humans. This will be final and complete social ostracism.

The isolation and loneliness of the eternally condemned will be more horrific than forever falling through outer space with no place to land. It is solitary confinement without release, relief, or light—ever. No earthly human can comprehend the awful destiny of being eternally alone in sorrowful, painful despair accompanied only by one's Christ-rejecting thoughts. No wonder those in "the outer darkness" will "weep and gnash their teeth" (Matt. 8:12; 13:42, 50; 22:13; 24:51; 25:30), so intense will be their emotional and physical pain.

Every deceased human will be resurrected in a body (Dan. 12:2; John 5:28–29; Acts 24:15; Rev. 20:1–6, 12–13) and will enter the eternal state in a body, whether they are believers who enter the new heavens and the new earth or unbelievers who are thrown into the lake of fire.[27] Human existence in the eternal state is *embodied existence.*

Scripture teaches that there will be degrees of punishment (Matt. 10:14–15; 11:20–24; Luke 12:47–48; John 19:11), as there will be degrees of reward for believers (1 Cor. 3:11–15; 2 Cor. 5:10). The degree of punishment in the lake of fire for individual unbelievers is based on the record of their deeds as it is recorded in the books (Rev. 20:12–13). These degrees of punishment will not alleviate the fact that all who die in unbelief will experience severe, eternal punishment.

Eternal Destiny of Believers

The fear of such torment brings oppressive bondage, but faith in Christ frees us from bondage to sin and fear (John 8:31–36; Rom. 6:14–22). Through Christ we are prepared to live abundantly now (John 10:10; 2 Peter 1:3) and to face death and the future fearlessly (Phil. 1:21; 2 Cor. 5:8; Heb. 2:14–15). We are destined to be like Christ and to be with Him forever in the new heavens and new earth (Rom. 8:29; 1 Thess. 4:17; Rev. 21:1–22:5).

Endnotes

Introduction

1. For a basic history, see Ed Dobson, Edward E. Hindson, and Jerry Falwell, *The Fundamentalist Phenomenon* (Garden City, N.Y.: Doubleday, 1981), 1-26; William G. McGloughlin, *The American Evangelicals, 1800-1900* (New York: Harper & Row, 1968); George Dollar, *A History of Fundamentalism in America* (Greenville, S.C.: Bob Jones University Press, 1973); David O. Beale, *In Pursuit of Purity: American Fundamentalism Since 1850* (Greenville, S.C.: Unusual Publications, 1986); and George Marsden, *Fundamentalism and American Culture* (New York: Oxford University Press, 1981).

2. G. K. Claybaugh, *Thunder on the Right: The Protestant Fundamentalists* (Chicago: Nelson-Hall, 1974), xvii. He labels the theological right wing as "Fundarists" and likens them to Hitler! Even Edward J. Carnell, the late president of Fuller Theological Seminary, criticized fundamentalists for a mentality that "holds with obscurantism to the verbal inspiration and inerrancy of the Holy Scriptures," in *The Case for Biblical Christianity* (Grand Rapids: Eerdmans, 1969), 40-47.

3. Ernest Sandeen, *The Roots of Fundamentalism: British and American Millenarianism 1800-1930* (Chicago: University of Chicago Press, 1970). Sandeen's reductionist reasoning, that fundamentalism can be explained in light of nineteenth-century millenarianism must be rejected as inadequate.

4. D. B. Stevick, *Beyond Fundamentalism* (Richmond: John Knox, 1964), 19.

5. Milton L. Rudnick, *Fundamentalism and the Missouri Synod* (St. Louis: Concordia, 1966), 40-41.

6. George Marsden, "Fundamentalism as an American Phenomenon: A Comparison with English Evangelicalism," *Church History* 46 (June 1977): 215-32.

7. Ibid., 215-16. His careful scholarship and incisive evaluations are indispensable to a proper understanding of American fundamentalism.

8. See the extensive evaluation by Cornelius Van Til, *The New Modernism* (Philadelphia: Presbyterian and Reformed, 1972). For original sources, see W. R. Hutchinson, ed., *American Protestant Thought* (New York: Harper & Row, 1968).

9. J. Gresham Machen, *Christianity and Liberalism* (New York: Macmillan, 1923). This book became the fundamentalist manifesto. It represents the best scholarship of the day against modernism, and the liberals never adequately answered Machen.

10. Ibid., 71. This statement appears in his defense of verbal inspiration in the light of historical verification.

11. On the rise of liberalism in America, see G. Atkins, *Religion in Our Times* (New York: Round Table, 1932); and W. R. Hutchinson, *The Modernist Impulse in American Protestantism* (Cambridge: Harvard University Press, 1976).

12. Charles C. Ryrie, *Neoorthodoxy* (Chicago: Moody, 1956), 14-15. For a detailed analysis, see Van Til, *The New Modernism*.

13. J. I. Packer, *"Fundamentalism" and the Word of God* (Grand Rapids: Eerdmans, 1958), 25-26.

14. See T. Altizer and W. Hamilton, *Radical Theology and the Death of God* (Indianapolis: Bobbs-Merrill, 1966); Bernard Ramm, *After Fundamentalism: The Future of Evangelical Theology* (San Francisco: Harper & Row, 1983).

15. See R. Webber and D. Bloesch, eds., *The Orthodox Evangelicals* (Nashville: Nelson, 1978); Rene Padilla, ed., *The New Face of Evangelicalism* (Downers Grove, Ill.: InterVarsity, 1976); J. D. Hunter, *American Evangelicalism* (New Brunswick, N.J.: Rutgers University Press, 1983); J. D. Hunter, *Evangelicalism: The Coming Generation* (Chicago: University of Chicago Press, 1987); Francis Schaeffer, *The Great Evangelical Disaster* (Westchester, Ill.: Crossway, 1984); Mark Noll, *The Scandal of the Evangelical Mind* (Grand Rapids: Eerdmans, 1994).

16. Carl F. H. Henry, "Evangelicals: Out of the Closet but Going Nowhere?" *Christianity Today*, 4 January 1980, 22.

17. See B. B. Warfield, *The Inspiration and Authority of the Bible* (repr. ed., Philadelphia: Presbyterian and Reformed, 1956). For a view a century later, see D. A. Carson, *The Gagging of God* (Grand Rapids: Zondervan, 1996).

18. Bruce Shelley, *Evangelicalism in America* (Grand Rapids: Eerdmans, 1967), 67.

19. John Woodbridge, Mark Noll, and Nathan Hatch, *The Gospel in America* (Grand Rapids: Zondervan, 1979), 59.

20. James Barr, *Fundamentalism* (Philadelphia: Westminster, 1977), vi, vii. See also pp. 1–11.

21. On the variations of the five to fourteen points of fundamentalism, see S. G. Cole, *The History of Fundamentalism* (New York: Richard Smith, 1931), 52-64; and Sandeen, *The Roots of Fundamentalism*, 52-64.

22. This argument is also developed by Harold Lindsell, *The Battle for the Bible* (Grand Rapids: Zondervan, 1976), 17-40. See also Norman Geisler, ed., *Inerrancy* (Grand Rapids: Zondervan, 1979); Carl F. H. Henry, ed., *God, Revelation, and Authority*, 4 vols. (Dallas: Word, 1976); and Earl Radmacher and Robert Preus, eds., *Hermeneutics, Inerrancy, and the Bible* (Grand Rapids: Zondervan, 1984).

23. Robert P. Lightner, *Neoevangelicalism Today* (Schaumburg, Ill.: Regular Baptist, 1978), 183. See also Lightner's *A Biblical Case for Total Inerrancy* (Grand Rapids: Kregel, 1978).

24. See the excellent defense of the deity of Christ from His sinless and supernatural life by Wilbur Smith, *The Supernaturalness of Christ* (Boston: W. A. Wilde, 1940). See also Richard Lee and Edward E. Hindson, *No Greater Savior* (Eugene, Ore.: Harvest House, 1995).

25. On the atonement, see Leon Morris, *The Apostolic Preaching of the Cross* (Grand Rapids: Eerdmans, 1960); idem, *The Cross in the New Testament* (Grand Rapids: Eerdmans, 1965); David Wells, *The Search for Salvation* (Downers Grove, Ill.: InterVarsity, 1978); John Stott, *The Cross of Christ* (Downers Grove, Ill.: InterVarsity, 1986); D. Martyn Lloyd-Jones, *The Heart of the Gospel* (Wheaton, Ill.: Crossway, 1991).

26. Cf. Edward E. Hindson, *Final Signs* (Eugene, Ore.: Harvest House, 1996); Paul N. Benware, *Understanding End Times Prophecy* (Chicago: Moody, 1995); Mal Couch, ed., *Dictionary of Premillennial Theology* (Grand Rapids: Kregel, 1996); Thomas D. Ice and Timothy J. Demy, eds., *When the Trumpet Sounds* (Eugene, Ore.: Harvest House, 1995); J. Dwight Pentecost, *Things to Come* (Grand Rapids: Zondervan, 1961); and John F. Walvoord, *Major Bible Prophecies* (Grand Rapids: Zondervan, 1991). Cf. R. C. Sproul, *The Last Days According to Jesus* (Grand Rapids: Baker, 1998).

27. Kirsopp Lake, *The Religion of Yesterday and Tomorrow* (Boston: Houghton-Mifflin, 1925), 61-62; quoted in Beale, *In Pursuit of Purity*, 4.

28. See Hank Hanegraaff, *Christianity in Crisis* (Eugene, Ore.: Harvest House, 1993); Richard

John Stott, *The Cross of Christ* (Downers Grove, Ill.: InterVarsity, 1986); D. Martyn Lloyd-Jones, *The Heart of the Gospel* (Wheaton, Ill.: Crossway, 1991).

26. Cf. Edward E. Hindson, *Final Signs* (Eugene, Ore.: Harvest House, 1996); Paul N. Benware, *Understanding End Times Prophecy* (Chicago: Moody, 1995); Mal Couch, ed., *Dictionary of Premillennial Theology* (Grand Rapids: Kregel, 1996); Thomas D. Ice and Timothy J. Demy, eds., *When the Trumpet Sounds* (Eugene, Ore.: Harvest House, 1995); J. Dwight Pentecost, *Things to Come* (Grand Rapids: Zondervan, 1961); and John F. Walvoord, *Major Bible Prophecies* (Grand Rapids: Zondervan, 1991). Cf. R. C. Sproul, *The Last Days According to Jesus* (Grand Rapids: Baker, 1998).

27. Kirsopp Lake, *The Religion of Yesterday and Tomorrow* (Boston: Houghton-Mifflin, 1925), 61–62; quoted in Beale, *In Pursuit of Purity,* 4.

28. See Hank Hanegraff, *Christianity in Crisis* (Eugene, Ore.: Harvest House, 1993); Richard Lee and Edward E. Hindson, *Angels of Deceit* (Eugene, Ore.: Harvest House, 1993); R. C. Sproul, *Lifeviews: Understanding the Ideas That Shape Society Today* (Old Tappan, N.J.: Revell, 1986); John Armstrong, ed., *The Coming Evangelical Crisis* (Chicago: Moody, 1996); Kenneth Boa and Robert Bowman, *An Unchanging Faith in a Changing World* (Nashville: Nelson, 1997).

Chapter 1

1. Unless otherwise noted, all Scripture references and quotations in this chapter are from the *New American Standard Bible.*

2. According to Mortimer J. Adler, the long history of religious and philosophical thinking contains "apparently unanimous agreement on the nature of truth." He explained, "just as everyone knows what a liar is, but not as readily whether someone is telling a lie, so the philosophers seem able to agree on what truth is, but not as readily on what is true." Whether the idea of truth is thought to correspond to reality, cohere with reality, or to participate in reality, Adler finds all thinkers concurring that the truth of ideas "depends on their conformity to reality." See Mortimer J. Adler, ed., *The Great Ideas: A Syntopicon of Great Books of the Western World,* vol. 2 (Chicago: William Benton, 1952), 916; cited in Gordon R. Lewis, *Testing Christianity's Truth Claims* (Chicago: Moody, 1976), 19. Adler wrote this nearly half a century ago. Whether one accepts his analysis or not, it may be said that there is no longer agreement as to what truth is. The critical issue today is not: What is true? but: What is *truth.*

3. Immanuel Kant was a German philosopher, "the embodiment of the Enlightenment" during "a time when thinkers were struggling to free themselves from what they perceived as the bondage of authoritarian thinking, especially ecclesiastical." His three great *Critiques* "were designed to destroy false dependence upon unknowable absolutes and force man back on himself as the source of authority. Metaphysical realities cannot be known; we have only our subjective apprehensions of things." J. D. Douglas, Walter A. Elwell, and Peter Toon, eds., *The Concise Dictionary of the Christian Tradition* (Grand Rapids: Zondervan, 1989), 214.

4. Dennis McCallum, ed., *The Death of Truth* (Minneapolis: Bethany, 1996), 24.

5. Ibid., 50–51.

6. Gene Edward Veith Jr., *Postmodern Times* (Wheaton: Crossway, 1994), 193.

7. Allan Bloom, *The Closing of the American Mind* (New York: Simon and Shuster, 1987), 25.

8. *The Barna Report: What Americans Believe* (Ventura: Regal, 1991), 83–85; cited by John D. Castelein, "Can the Restoration Movement Plea Survive If Belief in Objective Truth Is Abandoned?" *Stone-Campbell Journal* 1 (spring 1998): 27. Copan reads the

Barna Report a little differently: he says it found 66 percent of American adults didn't believe absolute truth exists. He also *quotes* the report differently saying, "Specifically, they agreed that there is 'no such thing as absolute truth; two people could define truth in totally conflicting ways, but both could still be correct.'" See Paul Copan, *True for You, But Not for Me*, (Minneapolis: Bethany, 1998), 11.

9. Copan, *True for You, But Not for Me*, 11.

10. Veith, *Postmodern Times*, 28–29.

11. Robert E. Fitch, "The Obsolescence of Ethics," *Christianity and Crisis: A Journal of Opinion* 19 (16 November 1959): 163–65; cited by Ravi Zacharias, "Being a Man of the Word," in Howard Hendricks, ed., *A Life of Integrity* (Sisters, Ore.: Multnomah, 1997), 60.

12. Carl F. H. Henry, *Carl Henry at His Best* (Portland: Multnomah), 203.

13. Andrew Delbanco, *The Death of Satan: How Americans Have Lost the Sense of Evil* (New York: Farrar, Straus, and Giroux, 1995), 107.

14. Leith Anderson, "Theological Issues of Twenty-First-Century Ministry," *Bibliotheca Sacra* 151 (April-June 1994): 138–39.

15. Ibid.

16. Scripture is clear. Paul gives thanks for the believers in Thessalonica (and by implication, all Christians) because God has chosen them "from the beginning for salvation through sanctification by the Spirit and *faith in the truth*" (2 Thess. 2:13). Whatever else this passage teaches, it tells us that truth is the object of saving faith. It is not faith alone (*sola fidei*) that saves; it is faith *in the truth* alone (*sola fidei vero*) that saves. Faith of the greatest kind, if placed in Buddha, will not save. "It won't be Oh Buddha that's sittin' on the throne; It won't be ol' Mohammed that's callin' us home; It won't be Hari Krishna that plays that trumpet tune; No, we're goin' to see the Son, not Reverend Moon." (from the song "Oh Buddha" sung by the Imperials, on the album *Heed the Call* published by Day Spring, a division of Word, 1979).

17. Major theories or concepts of the *nature* of truth include the traditionally held "correspondence view," the "pragmatic view," the "coherence view," and the "performative view." See Norman L. Geisler and Paul D. Feinberg, *Introduction to Philosophy* (Grand Rapids: Baker, 1980), 235–51. A more recent modification, which has received attention in the recent inerrancy debate, may be called the "intentionality" or "functional" view of truth. See Norman L. Geisler, "The Concept of Truth in the Inerrancy Debate," *Bibliotheca Sacra* 137 (October–December 1980): 328, 337; and John S. Feinberg, "Truth, Meaning, and Inerrancy in Contemporary Evangelical Thought," *Journal of the Evangelical Theological Society* 26 (March 1983): 17–30.

18. Winfried Corduan, *Handmaid to Theology* (Grand Rapids: Baker, 1981), 10.

19. D. A. Carson, *The Gagging of God* (Grand Rapids: Zondervan, 1996), 182. Carson argues "against Kant, who (as we have seen) insists that one cannot by reason move from the phenomenal realm to the noumenal realm, . . . the apostle Paul is entirely prepared to infer from the created order God's existence, power, and divine nature (Rom. 1:20). Nor is this merely a matter of abstract doctrine for him: it is also a matter of evangelistic strategy and apologetic. According to Luke's witness, Paul openly and repeatedly drew such connections when he was evangelizing gentiles (Acts 14:15–18; 17:24–29)."

20. John V. Dahms, "The Nature of Truth," *Journal of the Evangelical Theological Society* 28 (December 1985): 456. Dahms adds, "though the author of the Johannine gospel and epistles evinces such an interest in 'truth' and . . . such things to say about it that one may wonder whether he, at least, may not have had such an understanding."

21. Norman L. Geisler, "The Concept of Truth in the Inerrancy Debate," *Bibliotheca Sacra* 137 (October–December 1980): 331.

22. This of course is not to say that the Scriptures were inspired by "dictation."

23. Jack. B. Scott, *"Amēn," Theological Wordbook of the Old Testament,* ed. R. Laird Harris, Gleason L. Archer Jr., and Bruce K. Waltke (Chicago: Moody, 1990): 1: 52.

24. R. W. L. Moberly, *"Amēn,"* in William A. VanGemeren, ed., *New International Dictionary of Old Testament Theology and Exegesis* (Grand Rapids: Zondervan, 1997), 1: 429.

25. Jack B. Scott, 1:53.

26. A. C. Thiselton, "Truth," in Colin Brown, ed., *The New International Dictionary of New Testament Theology,* 3 vols. (Grand Rapids: Zondervan, 1978), 2:875.

27. Ibid.

28. Roger Nicole, "The Biblical Concept of Truth," in D. A. Carson and John D. Woodbridge, eds., *Scripture and Truth* (Grand Rapids: Zondervan, 1983), 293.

29. See for example, D. M. Crump, "Truth," in *Dictionary of Jesus and the Gospels,* ed. Joel B. Green, Scot McKnight, and I. Howard Marshall (Downers Grove, Ill.: InterVarsity, 1992), 860; A. C. Thiselton, "Truth," in Colin Brown, ed., *The New International Dictionary of New Testament Theology,* 3 vols. (Grand Rapids: Zondervan, 1971), 3:889–90; John Albert Bengel, *New Testament Word Studies,* 2 vols., trans. Charlton T. Lewis and Marvin R. Vincent (repr. ed. Grand Rapids: Kregel, 1971), 1:552; and E. W. Hengstenberg, *Commentary on the Gospel of St. John,* 2 vols. (Edinburgh: T & T Clark, 1865; repr. ed., Minneapolis: Klock & Klock, 1980), 1:47.

30. D. M. Crump, "Truth," in Joel B. Green, Scot McKnight, and I. Howard Marshall, eds., *Dictionary of Jesus and the Gospels* (Downers Grove, Ill.: InterVarsity, 1992), 861.

31. Henry Alford, *The Greek Testament,* 4 vols., rev. Everett F. Harrison (Chicago: Moody, 1958), 4:488; R. C. H. Lenski, *The Interpretation of the Epistles of St. Peter, St. John, and St. Jude* (Minneapolis: Augsburg, 1966), 493; Donald W. Burdick, *The Letters of John the Apostle* (Chicago: Moody, n.d.), 313; D. Edmond Hiebert, *The Epistles of John* (Greenville, S.C.: Bob Jones University Press, 1991), 192–93; and Stephen S. Smalley, *1, 2, 3 John,* Word Biblical Commentary (Waco, Tex.: Word, 1984), 231.

32. Besides those passages mentioned, Scripture gives numerous examples of the correspondence view of truth. Joshua's covenant with the Gibeonites was based on a falsehood, by which Joshua was deceived (Josh. 9:1–27). The Gibeonites claimed to be "from a far country," when in fact they were not. Jeremiah denounced the people of Jerusalem for swearing "falsely" (Jer. 4:2). God says of the people of Judah, "they bend their tongue like their bow; lies and not truth prevail in the land" (Jer. 9:3); "everyone deceives his neighbor, and does not speak the truth, they have set their tongue to speak lies" (Jer. 9:5); "through deceit they refuse to know Me" (Jer. 9:6). Ananias and Saphira learned the consequences of lying. Their report to the apostles did not correspond to the facts (Acts 5:1–11). Paul finds the whole world guilty because "they exchanged the truth of God for a lie" (Rom. 1:25). In worshiping the creature rather than the Creator, they denied reality. Their worship was not true. Examples could be multiplied, where truth is seen as the opposite of lies and falsehood (e.g., Rom. 9:1; 2 Cor. 4:2; 7:14; 11:10–13; 2 Thess. 2:11–12; 1 Tim. 2:7; 2 Tim. 3:13; 1 John 1:6–10). Passages also abound in which truth claims are shown to be true or false depending on their reflection of reality (e.g., Num. 11:23; Deut. 13:2–14; 18:22; 22:20; Josh. 9:15; Ruth 3:12; 1 Kings 22:16; Isa. 48:1–3; Dan. 3:14; 6:12; 9:12–13; 11:2; Mark 5:33; John 1:14; 19:35–36; 2 Cor. 7:14; Titus 1:13–14).

33. These implications are also *biblically* supported, either directly or indirectly.

34. Josh McDowell and Norm Geisler, *Love Is Always Right* (Dallas: Word, 1996), 22.

35. Norman L. Geisler and Ronald M. Brooks, *When Skeptics Ask* (Grand Rapids: Baker, 1990), 265.

36. Carl F. H. Henry, *Christian Countermoves in a Decadent Culture* (Portland, Ore.:

Multnomah, 1986), 110; cited in Erwin W. Lutzer, *Christ Among Other Gods* (Chicago: Moody, 1994), 54.

37. R. Scott Richards, *Myths the World Taught Me* (Nashville: Nelson, 1991), 67.

38. Augustine, *On Christian Doctrine,* trans. D. W. Robertson Jr. (Indianapolis: Bobbs-Merrill, 1958), 54; cited in D. Bruce Lockerbie, "A Call for Christian Humanism," *Bibliotheca Sacra* 143 (July–September 1986): 198.

39. Gordon R. Lewis, "Three Sides to Every Story," in R. Laird Harris, Swee-Hwa Quek, and J. Robert Vannoy, eds., *Interpretation and History* (Singapore: Christian Life, 1986), 209.

40. Frank E. Gaebelein, *The Pattern of God's Truth* (Chicago: Moody, 1968).

41. Norman L. Geisler and Paul D. Feinberg, *Introduction to Philosophy* (Grand Rapids: Baker, 1980), 247.

42. After many years of teaching in Bible college and seminary, Jim Andrews became senior pastor at Lake Bible Church, Lake Oswego, Oregon.

43. Dorothy L. Sayers, "Creed or Chaos?" in John Jefferson Davis, ed., *The Necessity of Systematic Theology,* 2d ed. (Grand Rapids: Baker, 1980), 30. The title of her article, from which the quote was taken, sums it up rather concisely: "Creed or Chaos?" The word "creed" derives from *credere* (Latin, "to believe"), and *credo* (Latin, "I believe"). If truth is not the object of our creed (i.e., what we believe), the alternative is chaos.

44. Josh McDowell and Bob Hostetler, *Right from Wrong* (Dallas: Word, 1994), 81.

45. R. Albert Mohler Jr., "'Evangelical': What's in a Name?" in John Armstrong, ed., *The Coming Evangelical Crisis* (Chicago: Moody, 1996), 39.

46. For a critique of this view see Norman L. Geisler, "The Concept of Truth in the Inerrancy Debate," *Bibliotheca Sacra* 137 (October–December 1980): 327–39.

47. James Oliver Buswell Jr., *A Systematic Theology of the Christian Religion* (repr. ed., Grand Rapids: Zondervan, 1962), 1:19.

48. Norman L. Geisler and Ronald M. Brooks, *When Skeptics Ask* (Grand Rapids: Baker, 1990), 264.

49. Geisler, "The Concept of Truth," 333.

50. Ravi Zacharias, *Can Man Live Without God?* (Dallas: Word, 1994), 11.

51. Norman L. Geisler and Ronald M. Brooks, *Come, Let Us Reason* (Grand Rapids: Baker, 1990), 7. See also J. P. Moreland, *Love Your God with All Your Mind: The Role of Reason in the Life of the Soul* (Colorado Springs: Navpress, 1997).

52. For discussions on this see Frederic R. Howe, *Challenge and Response* (Grand Rapids: Zondervan, 1982); and Ronald B. Mayers, *Both/And: A Balanced Apologetic* (Chicago: Moody, 1984). See also Ronald B. Mayers, "Both/And: A Biblical Alternative to the Presuppositional/Evidential Debate," in Michael Bauman, David W. Hall, and Robert C. Newman, eds., *Evangelical Apologetics* (Camp Hill: Pa.: Christian Publications, 1996).

53. It is not useful at this point to become side-tracked into all the issues involving the *imago Dei,* the *noetic* effects of sin, and the doctrine of revelation. *Imago Dei* is a Latin term meaning literally "image of God," sometimes *imago divina,* "divine image," and is used by theologians in reference to the likeness or resemblance to God in which man was originally created and which was lost, marred, or vitiated in the Fall; *noetic* (from the Greek *noetikos,* "intellectual," and *noein,* "to perceive") relates to the mind or intellect, and pertains to the view that knowledge comes through the intellect. See related articles in this volume by Thomas R. Edgar, Henry M. Morris, and L. Paige Patterson.

54. Much of this discussion is indebted to the thought of Norman Geisler and is adapted from a course on "Prolegomena" taught by Geisler in 1981.

55. Henry C. Thiessen, *Lectures in Systematic Theology,* rev. Vernon D. Doerksen (Grand

Rapids: Eerdmans, 1979), 8.

56. Thomas Aquinas, *The Summa Theolgica,* trans. Fathers of the English Dominican Province, rev. Daniel J. Sullivan, 2 vols. (Chicago: Encyclopedia Britannica, 1952): 1:11.

57. Thomas C. Oden, *The Living God, Systematic Theology,* vol. 1 (San Francisco: Harper, 1987), 6.

58. Charles Hodge, *Systematic Theology,* 3 vols. (repr. ed., Grand Rapids: Eerdmans, 1975), 1:49.

59. John H. Gerstner, "Reason and Revelation," *Tenth: An Evangelical Quarterly* 9 (October 1979): 8.

60. William G. T. Shedd, *Dogmatic Theology,* 3 vols. (New York: Charles Scribner's Sons, 1889; repr. ed., Minneapolis: Klock & Klock, 1979), 1:47.

61. Pascal quoted in Hank Hanegraff, *Counterfeit Revival* (Dallas: Word, 1997), 11; as cited by David J. MacLeod, "Counterfeit Revival: A Review Article," *The Emmaus Journal* 7 (summer 1998): 71.

62. Benjamin B. Warfield, "Christianity the Truth," in John E. Meeter, ed., *Selected Shorter Writings of Benjamin B. Warfield II* (Nutley, N.J.: Presbyterian and Reformed, 1973), 216.

63. John Charles Ryle, *Knots Untied* (repr. ed., Cambridge: James Clarke, 1977), 43.

64. Os Guiness, *No God but God* (Chicago: Moody, 1992), 169.

65. Alister E. McGrath, "Doctrine and Ethics," *Journal of the Evangelical Theological Society* 34 (June 1991): 150.

66. Ibid.

Chapter 2

1. See John D. Woodbridge, *Biblical Authority* (Grand Rapids: Zondervan, 1982), esp. 153–55; also John D. Woodbridge and Randall H. Balmer, "The Princetonians and Biblical Authority: An Assessment of the Ernest Sandeen Proposal," in D. A. Carson and John D. Woodbridge, eds., *Scripture and Truth* (Grand Rapids: Zondervan, 1983), 251–79.

2. Alan Richardson, "The Rise of Modern Biblical Scholarship and Recent Discussion of the Authority of the Bible," in *The Cambridge History of the Bible,* vol. 3, *The West from the Reformation to the Present Day* (Cambridge: Cambridge University Press, 1963), 298.

3. Ibid., 299, 305.

4. Ronald A. Nash, *The Word of God and the Mind of Man* (Phillipsburg, N.J.: Presbyterian and Reformed, 1982), 9–41, esp. 20, 28.

5. Richardson, "The Rise of Modern Biblical Scholarship," 308.

6. Ibid.

7. Ibid., 294–311. To hold the idea that belief in the literal truth of the Bible is due to a wrong adherence to the scientific spirit of the age and, at the same time, to use the scientific historical study of the Bible as evidence for this is a glaring inconsistency.

8. Ibid., 23. As Nash states, there is, "much evangelical disregard for the revealed truth of God," and an effort, "to substitute other concerns for that truth." Also, see Martin Marty's comment that, "evangelicalism is taking on and will increasingly take on the burdens of interpretation and accommodation that have created troubles for the mainstream groups," in "Tensions Within Contemporary Evangelicalism," in David F. Wells and John D. Woodbridge, eds., *The Evangelicals* (Nashville: Abingdon, 1975), 187.

9. David L. Smith, *A Handbook of Contemporary Theology* (Wheaton, Ill.: Victor, 1992), 288–89. Smith also states, "Contemporary sociological studies demonstrate that the

"twenty-plus" generation, as it is often called, is affective rather than cognitive in style. It responds much more deeply to emotion and feelings than to reasoned objectivity." He also adds "that society is gradually being directed toward New Age thinking is unquestionable" (289).

10. The three different Greek words used in these three verses have a specific and differing connotation. They all can be translated as "empty" or "in vain," depending on the context.

11. Although some interpret the words translated "assurance" and "conviction" as referring to the reality of the objects, this is in violation of the entire passage which refers to the individual's personal faith apart from actual sight, the same concept stated in verse 1.

12. Paul Helm, "Faith, Evidence, and the Scriptures," in Carson and Woodbridge, eds., *Scripture and Truth*, 303-20; R. C. Sproul, "The Internal Testimony of the Holy Spirit," in Norman L. Geisler, ed., *Inerrancy* (Grand Rapids: Zondervan, 1979), 336-54; and E. H. Bancroft, *Christian Theology*, rev. ed. (Grand Rapids: Zondervan, 1949), 344-51.

13. There is a long history of attempts to disclaim Mosaic authorship and place the writing of the Pentateuch in the times of the kingdom or later. Many in the academic world assume late authorship as a universal assertion, although no proofs have even been assembled. The most serious evidence has come in archaeological evidence for an exodus later than the fifteenth century B.C. (evidence that is open to differing interpretations) and comparative literary analysis (using methods that have been discredited). Even unbelieving archaeologists and textual historians have disproven the foundations of higher criticism. For a concise historical review by a former student of Rudolf Bultmann who came to reject higher criticism, see Eta Linnemann, *Historical Criticism of the Bible*, trans. R. Yarbrough (Grand Rapids: Baker, 1994).

14. See chapter 18 in this volume, "The Work of the Holy Spirit Today," by Paul N. Benware.

15. See chapter 4 in this volume, "The Revelation, Inspiration and Inerrancy of the Bible," by Harold D. Foos and L. Paige Patterson.

16. Ibid.

17. The words used here can be translated in more than one way. The emphasis in any case is on teaching and imparting information.

18. The word translated, "discern," *anakrinō,* means to examine in order to make a correct judgment, to judge, or evaluate. A good example is 1 Cor. 4:1-4, where Paul says that he is not really concerned with human evaluations or judgment. This inability to evaluate spiritual truth properly is the reason the unbeliever cannot "know" (*ginoskō*). This does not necessarily rule out a cognitive knowledge (*oida*) but a personal grasp or understanding, particularly the ability to understand the "deep things" of God, the things He has prepared for the believer (1 Cor. 2:10-12).

19. Vern S. Poythress, "Language and Accommodation," in E. D. Radmacher and R. D. Preus, eds., *Hermeneutics, Inerrancy, and the Bible* (Grand Rapids: Zondervan, 1984), 351-76, especially 366.

20. The "modern" hermeneutical concept that the meaning of a text must include what the reader thinks is not really new. It is merely using the term, "meaning," in the same contexts as before but with a changed meaning, so that, in effect, it does not refer to the meaning of the text but the meaning to "me."

21. For a fuller treatment see Wayne A. Grudem, "Scripture's Self-Attestation and the Problem of Formulating a Doctrine of Scripture," in Carson and Woodbridge, eds., *Scripture and Truth*, 19-59.

22. Peter does not say that Joel 2 is fulfilled in Acts 2. Joel refers to a time when heavenly signs will abound and the sons and daughters of Israel (generally) will see visions and dreams.

23. Thomas R. Edgar, *Miraculous Gifts* (Neptune, N.J.: Loizeaux Brothers, 1983), 46-85,

260-78; and Thomas R. Edgar, *Satisfied by the Promise of the Spirit* (Grand Rapids: Kregel, 1996), 52-88, 231-50.

24. Wayne Grudem, *The Gift of Prophecy in the New Testament and Today* (Westchester, Ill.: Crossway, 1988), 109-12. See also Edgar, *Satisfied*, 72-85, 100-18.

25. Jack Deere, *Surprised by the Voice of God: How God Speaks Today Through Prophecies, Dreams, and Visions* (Grand Rapids: Zondervan, 1998). In this volume, Deere includes many events that can hardly be classified as "communications." Miracles, healing, and physical deliverance by angels are historical events, not "communications" or revelations. Preaching under the influence of the Holy Spirit does not imply special revelation. The incident in Acts 14:9-10 says only that "Paul saw." It says nothing about "supernaturally saw," as Deere argues (p. 55).

25. Henry I. Lederle, *Treasures Old and New: Interpretations of "Spirit Baptism" in the Charismatic Renewal Movement* (Peabody, Mass: Hendrickson, 1988), 37.

Chapter 3

1. Bernard Ramm, *Protestant Biblical Interpretation*, 3d rev. ed. (Grand Rapids: Baker, 1976), 1.

2. Gordon D. Fee and Douglas Stewart, *How to Read the Bible for All It's Worth: A Guide to Understanding the Bible* (Grand Rapids: Zondervan, 1993), 16.

3. John Stewart, "Interpretive Listening: An Alternative to Empathy," *Communication Education*, October 1983, 381.

4. Ibid., 382.

5. Friedrich Nietzsche, *The Will to Power, A New Translation*, trans. Walter Kaufmann and R. J. Hollingdale (New York: Random House, 1967), section 481.

6. Immanuel Kant, "What Is Enlightenment?" in *Critique of Practical Reason* (New York: Macmillan, 1993), 286.

7. A. Berkeley Mickelsen, *Interpreting the Bible* (Grand Rapids: Eerdmans, 1982), 5.

Chapter 4

1. In the second century Marcion challenged the validity of some New Testament books on gnostic theological grounds, and Porphyry attacked the trustworthiness of Daniel on neo-Platonist philosophical grounds. Both formed groups that lasted in one form or another for a few centuries, but neither gathered much of a following.

2. Stanley Hauerwas, *Unleashing the Scripture* (Nashville: Abingdon, 1993), 20.

3. Nowhere are these terms more lucidly defined than in a short monograph by the early Clark Pinnock titled, *A Defense of Biblical Infallibility* (Philadelphia: Presbyterian and Reformed, 1967). See especially this succinct definition on p. 1: "The Bible in its entirety is God's written Word to man, free of error in its original autographs, wholly reliable in history and doctrine. Its divine inspiration has rendered the Book "infallible" (incapable of teaching deception) and "inerrant" (not liable to prove false or mistaken). Its inspiration is "plenary" (extending to all parts alike), "verbal" (including the actual language form), and "confluent" (product of two free agents, human and divine). *Inspiration* involves *infallibility* as an essential property, and infallibility in turn implies *inerrancy*. This threefold designation of Scripture is implicit in the basic thesis of Biblical authority." Pinnock also wrote on p. 5, "The theology which delights in the absence of final truth is nonsense."

4. Karl Barth, *The Epistle to the Romans*, ET (New York: Oxford University Press, 1933). Barth wrote this commentary in 1919.

5. Karl Barth, *Church Dogmatics*, 2 vols., ET (Edinburgh: T & T Clark, 1963), 1.463.
6. Ibid., 507.
7. Ibid., 509.
8. Emil Brunner, *Our Faith* (New York: Charles Scribner's Sons, n.d.), 6.
9. In language, semantics is the study or science of meaning in language forms; in logic, it is the study of relationships between signs and symbols and what they represent.
10. Kirsopp Lake, *The Religion of Yesterday and Tomorrow* (Boston: Houghton, 1926), 61. For a brief but immensely helpful historical survey see R. Laird Harris, "Verbal Inspiration in Church History," in R. Laird Harris, ed., *Inspiration and Canonicity of the Bible* (Grand Rapids: Zondervan, 1957), 72-84.
11. Harold Lindsell, *The Battle for the Bible* (Grand Rapids: Zondervan, 1976), 132. Lindsell documents the movement of individuals and institutions away from inerrancy.
12. For an example see *The Authority of Scripture at Fuller*, a special issue of *Theology News and Notes* published for Fuller Seminary Alumni in 1976.
13. *The Other Side*, May-June 1976, 9.
14. Ibid., 10-11.
15. For example see Carl F. H. Henry, "Conflict over Biblical Inerrancy," *Christianity Today*, 7 May 1976, 23-25.
16. Clark Pinnock, "Inspiration and Authority: A Truce Proposal," *The Other Side*, May-June 1976, 61-65.
17. Robert P. Lightner, *Handbook of Evangelical Theology* (Grand Rapids: Kregel, 1995), 26. For a discussion of the limited inerrancy view by those who embrace it, see Jack Rogers, ed., *Biblical Authority* (Waco, Tex.: Word, 1977). For a critique from those who oppose it, see Norman L. Geisler, ed., *Inerrancy* (Grand Rapids: Zondervan, 1980); Harold Lindsell, *The Battle for the Bible* (Grand Rapids: Zondervan, 1976); and Harold Lindsell, *The Bible in the Balance* (Grand Rapids: Zondervan, 1979). For a brief historical discussion noting significant representatives in the debate (for example Lindsell, Henry, Rogers, G. C. Berkouwer, Dewey Beegle, and Donald McKim) see John Hannah, ed., *Inerrancy and the Church* (Chicago: Moody, 1984), esp. 144-48, 381ff.
18. J. I. Packer, "Encountering Present Day Views of Scripture," in James Montgomery Boice, ed., *The Foundation of Biblical Authority* (Grand Rapids: Zondervan, 1978), 65-66.
19. Charles C. Ryrie, *Basic Theology* (Wheaton, Ill.: Victor, 1986), 77.
20. John Warwick Montgomery, "Inspiration and Inerrancy: A New Departure," in *Bulletin of the Evangelical Theological Society* 8.2 (spring 1965).
21. J. I. Packer, "Encountering Present Day Views," 61.
22. Ibid., 63.
23. Pinnock, *Defense of Biblical Infallibility*, 18.
24. John Wesley, *The Works of Rev. John Wesley* (London: Wesleyan Methodist Book Room, n.d.), 9.150; see also John Wesley, *The Journal of Rev. John Wesley*, ed. N. Curnock (London: C. H. Kelly, n.d.), entry, 24 August 1776.
25. Boice, *Foundation of Biblical Authority*, 9. See the preface for a brief statement of the Council's purpose, objectives, and major participants.
26. See n. 17.
27. The Chicago Statement on Biblical Inerrancy has appeared in various publications. For example, see it as an appendix to J. I. Packer, *God Has Spoken* (Grand Rapids: Baker, 1979), 139-55.
28. Boice, *Foundation of Biblical Authority*, 11.
29. Charles C. Ryrie, "The Importance of Inerrancy," *Bibliotheca Sacra* 120 (April-June 1963): 140.
30. Lightner, *Handbook of Evangelical Theology*, 28. To see how one who believes in the total

inerrancy of Scripture approaches the problems, see Gleason L. Archer, "Alleged Errors and Discrepancies in the Original Manuscripts of the Bible," in Geisler, ed., *Inerrancy,* 55-82.

31. Clark Pinnock, "Three Views of the Bible in Contemporary Theology," in Jack Rogers, *Biblical Authority* (Waco, Tex.: Word, 1977), 49.

32. J. I. Packer, *Fundamentalism and the Word of God* (Grand Rapids: Eerdmans, 1959), 140.

33. Edward J. Young, "Are the Scriptures Inerrant?" in Merrill C. Tenney, ed., *The Bible: The Living Word of Revelation* (Grand Rapids: Zondervan, 1968), 103-4, 208.

34. Edward J. Young, *Thy Word Is Truth* (Grand Rapids: Eerdmans, 1960), 139.

35. Ibid., 113.

36. See Pinnock, "Three Views," 63-68. The author asks seven questions of those who embrace a total inerrancy.

37. Ray Summers, "How God Said It," *Baptist Standard,* 4 February 1970, 12.

38. For more on Christ's view of Scripture, see below.

39. For an excellent summary of issues related to the New Testament's use of Old Testament passages see Young, *Thy Word Is Truth,* 149-50.

40. Lightner, *Evangelical Theology,* 29.

41. Pinnock, *Defense of Biblical Infallibility,* 10. There follows a summarization of textual support.

42. Ibid., 12.

43. Young, *Thy Word Is Truth,* 165-66.

44. Lindsell, *Battle for the Bible,* 17-18.

45. Young, "Are the Scriptures Inerrant," 118.

46. B. B. Warfield, *The Inspiration and Authority of the Bible* (Philadelphia: Presbyterian and Reformed, 1948), 162-63. For further discussion of this analogy see Packer, *Fundamentalism and the Word of God,* 82-84.

47. Young, "Are the Scriptures Inerrant?", 125.

48. B. B. Warfield, Ibid., 124-25.

49. Ibid., 165.

50. Pinnock, *Defense of Biblical Infallibility,* 13.

51. Young, *Thy Word Is Truth,* 166.

52. Young, "Are the Scriptures Inerrant?" 104.

53. Packer, *Fundamentalism and the Word of God,* 61-62.

54. Ibid., 141.

55. Lightner, *Handbook of Evangelical Theology,* 30.

56. Ibid.

57. Young, *Thy Word Is Truth,* 44.

58. Everett F. Harrison, "The Phenomena of Scripture," in Carl F. H. Henry, ed., *Revelation and the Bible* (Grand Rapids: Baker, 1958), 250.

59. Robert P. Lightner, *A Biblical Case for Total Inerrancy* (Grand Rapids: Kregel, 1978), 74.

60. Pinnock, *Defense of Biblical Infallibility,* 16.

61. Harold John Okenga, foreword to Lindsell, *Battle for the Bible.*

62. G. Aiken Taylor "Doing Battle for the Bible," *Presbyterian Journal,* (6 October 1976): 8.

63. Lindsell, *Battle for the Bible,* 26.

Chapter 5

1. All Scripture references and quotations in this chapter are from the King James Version of the Bible.

2. Stephen Jay Gould, "Nonoverlapping Magisteria," *Natural History* 106 (March 1997): 61.

3. Ernst Mayr, *Omni,* February 1983, 74.

4. Richard E. Leakey, "Hominids in Africa," *American Scientist* 64 (March–April 1976): 176.
5. David Berlinski, "Was There a Big Bang?" *Commentary,* February 1998, 37.
6. Phillip E. Johnson, *Defeating Darwinism by Opening Minds* (Downers Grove, Ill.: InterVarsity, 1997), 66.
7. Ibid., 67.
8. Romans 1, Psalm 19.
9. Michael J. Behe, *Darwin's Black Box* (New York: Free Press, 1996), 130–31.
10. Natalie Angier, reported by Rick Thompson/San Francisco, *Time Magazine,* 25 February 1985, 70.
11. Duane Gish, *Dinosaurs, Those Terrible Lizards* (San Diego: Creation Life, 1989), 50–55. Also see Jobe R. Martin, *The Evolution of a Creationist* (Rockwall, Tex.: Biblical Discipleship, 1994), 29–31.
12. Psalm 19.
13. Stephen Jay Gould, "Is a New and General Theory of Evolution Emerging?" *Paleobiology* 6 (January 1980): 127.
14. Mark Ridley "Who Doubts Evolution?" *New Scientist* 90 (25 June 1981): 830–31.
15. Hugh Ross, "Facts and Faith," *Reasons to Believe* 12.3 (3d Quarter 1998): 3.
16. Gen. 1:11–12, 21, 24–25.
17. Ross, "Facts and Faith," 6.
18. Indefinite, long periods of time might be suggested with the use of the Hebrew words *ribbow* or *ohlam,* or even *yom* without the numerical qualifier.
19. Gen. 5:5
20. Exod. 20:9–10, 11.
21. Gen. 1:16.
22. Rom. 5:12.
23. Job 38:7.
24. Gen. 1:31.
25. Gen. 1:28.
26. Gen. 2:22.
27. John 2:10.
28. John 18:10; Luke 22:51.
29. Lyall Watson, "The Water People," *Science Digest* 90 (May 1982): 44.
30. Richard Milton, *Shattering the Myths of Darwinism* (Rochester, Vt.: Park Street, 1997), 208; see his self-described atheism on p. 269.
31. Ibid., 195.
32. "Anthropological Art," in *Science Digest* 89.3 (April 1981): 44.
33. Mark 10:6.
34. Gen. 9:3.
35. Gen. 1:30.
36. For a documented study of the mammoth remains and other animal finds that relate to the flood, see Joseph Dillow, *The Waters Above: Earth's Pre-Flood Vapor Canopy* (Chicago: Moody, 1982).
37. G. Richard Lydekker, "Mammoth Ivory," *Smithsonian Reports,* 1899, 363.
38. M. L. Ryder, "Hair of the Mammoth," *Nature* 249 (10 May 1974): 190–91.
39. Gen. 7:11.
40. Anthony J. Gow, "Glaciological Investigations in Antarctica," *Antarctic Journal of the United States* 7.4 (1972): 100–1. Also Frank C. Hibben, *The Lost Americans* (New York: Crowell, 1946), 176–78.
41. Gen. 2:5–6.

42. Gen. 9:13. For more information about the flood and its ramifications, see John C. Whitcomb Jr. and Henry M. Morris, *The Genesis Flood: The Biblical Record and Its Scientific Implications* (Philadelphia: Presbyterian and Reformed, 1961).

43. Ken Ham, Andrew Snelling, and Carl Wieland, *The Answers Book* (Green Forest, Ark.: Master Books, 1996), 123–24.

44. "That Choking Feeling . . . An Astonishingly Fast Growth of Solid Rock in a Man-Made Pipe," *Creation ex Nihilo* 20.4 (September–November 1998): 6.

45. Dennis R. Petersen, *Unlocking the Mysteries of Creation*, vol. 1 (El Cajon, Calif.: Master Books, 1988), 35.

46. For more information about the Poynting-Robertson effect, see R. L. Wysong, *The Creation-Evolution Controversy* (Midland, Mich.: Inquiry, 1981), 454ff. See also Scott Huse, *The Collapse of Evolution* (Grand Rapids: Baker, 1983), 29.

47. Petersen, *Unlocking the Mysteries of Creation*, 38.

48. Louis B. Slichter, "Secular Effects of Tidal Friction upon the Earth's Rotation," *Journal of Geophysical Research* 8.14 (1964): 4281–88.

49. Huse, *The Collapse of Evolution*, 28–29.

50. Thomas Barnes, "Earth's Magnetic Age: The Achilles Heel of Evolution," *I. C. R. Impact* 122 (August 1983). See also T. G. Barnes, "Origin and Destiny of Earth's Magnetic Field," *I. C. R. Technical Monograph*, no. 4 (1973); *I. C. R. Impact* 100 (October, 1981).

51. Robert V. Gentry, et al., "Radiohalos in Coalified Wood: New Evidence Relating to the Time of Uranium Introduction and Coalification," *Science* 194 (15 October 1976): 315–17.

52. Walter T. Brown, *In the Beginning* (Phoenix: Center for Scientific Creation, 1989), 18.

53. Steven A. Austin, "Mount St. Helens and Catastrophism," *I. C. R. Impact* 157 (July 1986): 1–2. Dr. Austin has an excellent video presentation, *Mount St. Helens: Explosive Evidence for Creation*, produced by the Institute for Creation Research, El Cajon, Calif., 1992. Also see Greg J. Beasley, "Long-Lived Trees: Their Possible Testimony to a Global Flood and Recent Creation," *Creation Ex Nihilo Technical Journal* 7, part 1 (1993): 43–67.

54. John D. Morris, *The Young Earth* (Colorado Springs: Creation-Life, 1994), 109–12.

55. Ibid., 85.

56. Ibid., 88.

57. Ibid., 90.

58. Jobe R. Martin, *The Evolution of a Creationist* (Rockwall, Tex.: Biblical Discipleship, 1994), 189.

59. Gen. 5:21.

Chapter 6

1. All Scripture references and quotations in this chapter are from the King James Version of the Bible.

2. Michael Ruse, "From Belief to Unbelief—and Halfway Back," *Zygon* 29 (March 1994): 31. Ruse is professor of Philosophy and Zoology at Guelph University in Canada.

3. Richard Dawkins, "God's Utility Function," *Scientific American* 273 (November 1995): 85.

4. Stephen Jay Gould, "The Power of This View of Life," *Natural History* 103 (June 1994): 6.

5. Arthur Falk, "Reflections on Huxley's Evolution and Ethics," *The Humanist* 55 (November–December 1995): 23–24.

6. Bertrand Russell, *Religion and Science* (London: Oxford University Press, 1961), 73

7. Charles Darwin, *Origin of Species by Natural Selection* or *The Preservation of Favored Races in the Struggle for Life* (various eds.). The quote is from the final paragraph.

8. David L. Hull, "The God of the Galapagos," review of *Darwin on Trial* by Philip Johnson, *Nature* 352 (August 8, 1991): 486. Hull is professor of Philosophy at Northwestern University.

9. Carl Sagan, *Cosmos* (New York: Random House, 1980), 30.

10. Pattle P. T. Pun, "A Theory of Progressive Creationism," *Journal of the American Scientific Affiliation* 39 (March 1987): 14.

11. G. Richard Bozarth, "The Meaning of Evolution," *American Atheist*, February 1978, 19.

12. A. J. Mattill Jr., "Three Cheers for the Creationists," *Free Inquiry* 2 (spring 1982): 17–18.

13. Michael Ruse, "A Few Last Words—Until the Next Time," *Zygon* 29 (March 1994): 78. *Zygon* calls itself "a journal of science and religion."

14. Ruse, "From Belief to Unbelief," 31.

15. Isaac Asimov, "In the Game of Energy and Thermodynamics You Can't Even Break Even," *Smithsonian*, June 1970, 10. Asimov, reputedly author of about five hundred books on science, was president of the American Humanist Association.

16. Roger Lewin, "A Downward Slope to Greater Diversity," *Science* 217 (24 September 1982): 1239.

17. John Ross, letter to the editor, *Chemical and Engineering News*, 7 July 1980, 40.

18. Asimov, "In the Game of Energy and Thermodynamics You Can't Even Break Even," 6.

19. Derek V. Ager "Fossil Frustrations" *New Scientist* 100 (10 November 1983): 425. Ager was president of the British Geological Association.

20. Niles Eldredge, *Time Frames: The Rethinking of Darwinian Evolution and the Theory of Punctuated Equilibria* (New York: Simon and Schuster, 1985), 51–52. Eldredge, a leading paleontologist, works at the American Museum of Natural History.

21. Samuel Paul Welles, "Fossils," *World Book Encyclopedia* 7 (1978): 364. Welles was a research paleontologist at the Museum of Paleontology of the University of California, Berkeley.

22. Samuel Paul Welles, "Paleontology," in *World Book Encyclopedia* (1978).

23. See Henry M. Morris, *The Long War Against God* (Grand Rapids: Baker, 1989), 189–95, for a discussion of this remarkable development.

24. W. B. N. Berry, *Growth of a Prehistoric Time Scale* (San Francisco: W. H. Freeman, 1968), iii–iv.

25. Hollis D. Hedberg, "The Stratigraphic Panorama," *Bulletin, Geological Society of America* 72 (April 1961): 503.

26. J. E. O'Rourke, "Pragmatism Versus Materialism in Stratigraphy," *American Journal of Science* 276 (January 1976): 53.

27. Ibid., 54. Emphasis O'Rourke's.

28. O. H. Schindewolf, "Comments on Some Stratigraphic Terms," *American Journal of Science* 255 (June 1957): 395.

29. O. D. von Engeln and K. C. Caster, *Geology* (New York: McGraw Hill, 1952), 423.

30. Derek V. Ager, *The New Catastrophism* (Cambridge: Cambridge University Press, 1993), xii.

31. Derek V. Ager, "The Stratigraphic Code and What It Implies," in W. A. Berggren and J. A. Van Couvering, eds., *Catastrophes and Earth History* (Princeton, N.J.: Princeton University Press, 1984), 93.

32. Derek V. Ager, *The Nature of the Stratigraphical Record*, 3d ed. (New York: John Wiley, 1993), 141.

33. Warren D. Allmon, "Post Gradualism," review of *The New Catastrophism*, by Derek V. Ager, *Science* 262 (1 October 1993): 122–23.
34. Gordon L. H. Davies, "Bangs Replace Whimpers," *Nature* 365 (9 September 1993): 115.
35. Robert H. Dott, "Episodic View Now Replacing Catastrophism," *Geotimes* 27 (November 1982): 16.
36. Ibid.
37. Ager, *Nature of the Stratigraphical Record*, 132.
38. This brief discussion cannot deal with all the geological and other aspects of the flood. See John C. Whitcomb and Henry M. Morris, *The Genesis Flood: The Biblical Record and Its Scientific Implications* (Philadelphia: Presbyterian and Reformed, 1961) for a fairly comprehensive discussion. Numerous aspects of the flood are discussed in pages of *Creation Research Society Quarterly*.
39. See John Woodmorappe, *Noah's Ark: A Feasibility Study* (San Diego: Institute for Creation Research, 1996), for detailed resolution of all problems raised about the ark.
40. Henry M. Morris, *The Genesis Record* (Grand Rapids: Baker, 1976), 683–86, lists one hundred evidences—some biblical and some scientific—for a world flood.

Chapter 7

1. For a fuller discussion of points summarized in this chapter, see Robert P. Lightner, *Angels, Satan, and Demons* (Dallas: Word, 1998).
2. The term *gnostic* is derived from the Greek word *gnosis*, "knowledge." Salvation was attained by spiritual knowledge, said the Gnostics. They believed and embraced a dualistic philosophy, arguing that matter was evil and spirit was good. Therefore, one foundational belief was in a good god and a bad god, both possessing about the same level of power.
3. See Duane Garrett, *Angels and the New Spirituality* (Nashville: Broadman & Holman, 1995), 88–89, for evaluation of Thomas Aquinas's contribution regarding angels.
4. A. C. Coleridge, ed., "The Belgic Confession of Faith," *Reformed Confessions of the 16th Century* (Philadelphia: Westminster, 1966), 196.
5. Garrett, *Angels and the New Spirituality*, 93.
6. Charles C. Ryrie, *Neo-Orthodoxy: What It Is and What It Does* (Chicago: Moody, 1956), 37.
7. Philip Lochhaas, "The New Age Movement: Dancing in the Dark," *Lutheran Witness* April 1987, 80–82.
8. Just a few of these are Joan Webster Anderson, *Where Angels Walk* (New York: Ballantine, 1993); Alma Daniel, Timothy Wyllie, and Andrew Ramer, *Ask Your Angels* (New York: Ballantine, 1992); Sophy Burnham, *A Book of Angels* (New York: Ballantine, 1990); and John Randolph Price, *The Angels Within Us* (New York: Fawcett, 1993).
9. Not all evangelicals agree that Satan is involved at all in Ezekiel 28. See for example Garrett, *Angels and the New Spirituality*, 39–42. In defense of the view presented in this chapter, see Lightner, *Angels, Satan, and Demons*, 67–73.
10. Garrett, *Angels and the New Spirituality*, 36–39. Garrett argues that Satan is not in view in Isaiah 14:12-19. For a contrary view see Lightner, *Angels, Satan, and Demons*, 70–73.
11. See John Davis, *Demons, Exorcism and the Evangelical* (Winona Lake, Ind.: BMH, 1977), 8–10, for a fuller discussion on demon exorcism.
12. See Robert P. Lightner, *Speaking in Tongues and Divine Healing* (Schaumburg, Ill.: Regular Baptist, 1984), for a defense of the cessation of the temporary gifts.
13. All Scripture references and quotations in this chapter are from the *New American Standard Bible*.

Chapter 8

1. All Scripture references and quotations in this chapter are from the King James Version of the Holy Bible.

Chapter 9

1. Cited by Joel F. Drinkard Jr., in Drinkard, ed., *Benchmarks in Time and Culture: An Introduction to the History and Methodology of Syro-Palestinian Archaeology* (Atlanta: Scholars, 1988).
2. Neil Asher Silberman, "Digging in the Land of the Bible," *Archaeology* 51.5 (September–October 1998): 36.
3. Frank Moore Cross in a letter to the editor, "Queries & Comments," *Biblical Archaeology Review* 24. 6 (November–December 1998): 68; cf. March-April 1996 issue.
4. All Scripture references and quotations in this chapter are from the *New American Standard Bible*.
5. Amihai Mazar, in an interview at the Institute of Archaeology, Jerusalem, October 1996.
6. Cf. Shemaryahu Talmon, "Was the Book of Esther Known at Qumran?" *Dead Sea Discoveries* 2.3 (November 1995): 1–11. Talmon discusses eighteen phrases in Qumran texts that are similar to, or identical with, expressions in the book of Esther. Eight of these are based on *hapax legomena* (words occurring once in Scripture) in Esther. This indicates that the authors of these texts were familiar with the biblical book. There is also additional support in Aramaic fragments from Cave 4, which are enough like the text that they are called "Proto-Esther" (4Q550). Talmon proposes that Esther was not included, because it had not yet achieved canonical status in the Qumran community. He finds some support for this in the Talmud account of a third-century A.D. debate over the status of Esther (b. Meg. 7a). Also, there is no mention of the festival of Purim among the Qumran texts.
7. Gonzalo Báez-Camargo, *Archaeological Commentary on the Bible* (New York: Doubleday, 1984), xxii.
8. D. Winton Thomas, ed., *Archaeology and Old Testament Study* (Oxford: Clarendon, 1967), xxiii.
9. Mazar interview.
10. For recent comprehensive surveys of Old Testament archaeological data, see J. Randall Price, *The Stones Cry Out: What Archaeology Reveals About the Truth of the Bible* (Eugene, Ore.: Harvest House, 1997). For individual site reports and publications, see the bibliographies in the survey books.
11. See M. J. Selman, "The Social Environment of the Patriarchs," *Tyndale Bulletin* 27 (1976): 114–36; "Comparative Customs and the Patriarchal Narratives," *Themelios* 3 (1962): 239–48.
12. Kathleen Kenyon, *The Bible and Recent Archaeology*, rev. ed. (Philadelphia: Westminster, 1987), 107.
13. See Volkmar Fritz, "Temple Architecture: What Can Archaeology Tell Us About Solomon's Temple?" *Biblical Archaeology Review* 13.4 (July–August 1987): 38–49.
14. See "In the Name of the King," *Eretz* 48 (September–October 1996): 66.
15. For details of the discovery see Zvi Greenhut, "Burial Cave of the Caiaphas Family," *Biblical Archaeology Review* 18.5 (September–October 1992): 28–44, 76; Greenhut, "Caiaphas' Final Resting Place," *Israel Hilton Magazine*, spring 1993, 16.
16. The two-foot by three-foot slab known as the Pilate Inscription, was found reused as a building block in a fourth-century remodeling project, but it was originally written to commemorate Pilate's erection and dedication of a Tiberium, a temple for the worship

of Tiberias Caesar, the Roman emperor during Pilate's term over Judea. The Latin inscription of four lines gives his title as "Pontius Pilate, Prefect of Judea," a title very similar to that used of him in the Gospels (see Luke 3:1).

17. See V. Tzaferis, "Jewish Tombs at and near Giv'at ha-Mivtar, Jerusalem," *Israel Exploration Journal* 20.1-2 (1970): 18–32.

18. As deciphered by the epigraphist Joseph Naveh, "The Ossuary Inscriptions from Giv'at ha-Mivtar," *Israel Exploration Journal* 20.1 (1970): 33–37.

19. For complete details see V. Tzaferis, "Crucifixion—The Archaeological Evidence," *Biblical Archaeology Review* 11.1 (January–February 1985): 44–53; and Joe Zias and E. Sekeles, "The Crucified Man from Giv'at ha-Mivtar: A Reappraisal," *Israel Exploration Journal* 35.1 (1985): 22–27.

Chapter 10

1. All Scripture references and quotations in this chapter are from the King James Version of the Bible.

2. James Luther Mays, ed., *Harper's Bible Commentary* (New York: Harper and Row, 1988).

3. This remains the great chasm between law and gospel. As Matthew Henry observes:

> The Law did not and could not of itself provide righteousness before God for individuals (cf. Rom. 3:20; 7:7). But Christ fulfilled the Law (Matt. 5:17-18) by keeping it perfectly during His sinless life (cf. John 8:46) and then gave His life in payment for the penalty of sin and the broken Law (cf. Eph. 2:15; Col. 2:13-14). The Law then pointed to Him as the Source of the God-provided righteousness it could not supply (Gal. 3:24).
> —Matthew Henry, *Matthew Henry's Commentary on the Bible* (Peabody, Mass.: Hendrickson, 1997).

Such faith was too easy and was a stumbling block to Israel. The preaching of the Cross is meaningless and an abhorrence to unsaved Israel.

4. John A. Witmer, *The Bible Knowledge Commentary, New Testament,* ed. John F. Walvoord and Roy B. Zuck (Wheaton, Ill.: Victor Books, 1983), 448.

5. Henry, *Matthew Henry's Commentary.*

6. Ibid.

7. Witmer, *The Bible Knowledge Commentary, New Testament,* 486.

8. Henry, *Matthew Henry's Commentary.*

Chapter 11

1. R. C. Sproul, *Essential Truths of the Christian Faith* (Wheaton, Ill.: Tyndale, 1992), 36.

2. Wayne Grudem, *Systematic Theology* (Grand Rapids: Zondervan, 1994), 250.

3. Lewis Sperry Chafer, *Systematic Theology,* 8 vols. (Dallas: Dallas Seminary Press, 1947), 1:313-15.

4. All Scripture references and quotations in this chapter are from the King James Version of the Bible.

5. Robert K. Brown and Mark R. Norton, eds., *The One-Year Book of Hymns* (Wheaton, Ill.: Tyndale, 1995).

Chapter 12

1. See John Hick, "A Pluralist View," in Dennis L. Okholm and Timothy R. Phillips, eds., *More Than One Way?* (Grand Rapids: Zondervan, 1995).

2. Ibid., 35, 53.

3. John Dominic Crossan, *Jesus: A Revolutionary Biography* (San Francisco: Harper, 1994).

4. John P. Meier, *A Marginal Jew* (New York: Doubleday, 1992).

5. "Church Split by Leader's Doubts About Christ," *St. Petersburg Times*, 19 December 1997, 23A.

6. John A. T. Robinson, *Redating the New Testament* (Philadelphia: Westminster, 1976).

7. Millard J. Erickson, *Where Is Theology Going? Issues and Perspectives on the Future of Theology* (Grand Rapids: Baker, 1994), 170.

8. Ibid.

9. Ibid., 171.

10. *Maranatha! Music Praise Chorus Book* (Costa Mesa, Calif.: Maranatha! Music, 1983).

11. Erickson, *Where Is Theology Going*, 171–72.

12. Louis Berkhof, *The History of Christian Doctrines* (Edinburgh: Banner of Truth, 1937), 110–11.

13. *New Heavens and a New Earth* (Brooklyn, N.Y.: Watchtower, n.d.), 27.

14. *The Kingdom Is at Hand* (Brooklyn, N.Y.: Watchtower, n.d.), 46–49.

15. Kenneth Copeland, *Now Are We in Christ Jesus* (Fort Worth: KCP, 1980), 16–17, 20–24.

16. Kenneth E. Hagin, *The Name of Jesus* (Tulsa: Kenneth Hagin Ministries, 1979), 29–32.

17. For a capable analysis and refutation of the false teachings of the prosperity movement, see Michael Horton, ed., *The Agony of Deceit* (Chicago: Moody, 1990) and Bruce Barron, *The Health and Wealth Gospel* (Downers Grove, Ill: InterVarsity, 1987).

18. C. S. Lewis, *Mere Christianity* (New York: Macmillan, 1952), 40–41.

19. All Scripture references and quotations in this chapter are from the *New American Standard Bible*.

20. Homer A Kent Jr., *The Epistle to the Hebrews* (Grand Rapids: Baker, 1972), 44.

21. Leon Morris, *The Gospel According to John*, in The New International Commentary (Grand Rapids: Eerdmans, 1971), 853–54.

22. A. T. Robertson, *A Grammar of the Greek New Testament in the Light of Historical Research* (Nashville: Broadman, 1934), 786.

23. The reading *monogenēs theos* ("only begotten God") has strong textual support, being found in *p66*, (c. A.D. 200 manuscript) and *p75*, an early third-century manuscript. In addition, this reading is found in *Aleph, B, C* and other early manuscripts.

24. BAGD, 459.

25. Wayne Grudem, *Systematic Theology* (Grand Rapids: Zondervan, 1994), 544.

26. Morris, *The Gospel According to John*, 251.

27. Benjamin Breckinridge Warfield, *The Person and Work of Christ* (reprint, Philadelphia: Presbyterian and Reformed, 1950), 39.

28. Fritz Rienecker, *A Linguistic Key to the Greek New Testament*, ed. Cleon L. Rogers Jr. (Grand Rapids: Zondervan, 1982), 550.

29. There is a play on words in the Greek text: "many believed [*episteusan*] in His name. . . . But Jesus, on His part, was not entrusting [*episteuen*] Himself to them, for He knew all men" (John 2:23–24). They believed (superficially) in Jesus but He did not believe in them because He knew their fickle hearts.

30. Merrill C. Tenney, *John: The Gospel of Belief* (Grand Rapids: Eerdmans, 1948), 311–13.

31. Ibid., 313.

32. Morris, *The Gospel According to John*, 82–83.

33. A. T. Robertson comments: "Second aorist middle indicative of *ginomai*, the constative aorist covering the creative activity looked at as one event in contrast with the continuous existence of *hen* in verses 1 and 2" (*Word Pictures in the New Testament*, 5 vols., [Nashville: Broadman, 1932], 5:5).

34. BAGD, 791.

35. J. B. Lightfoot, *Saint Paul's Epistles to the Colossians and to Philemon* (repr. ed., Grand Rapids: Zondervan, 1959), 156.

36. Raymond E. Brown, *The Gospel According to John 1–12,* in The Anchor Bible, 2d ed. (Garden City, N.Y.: Doubleday, 1966), 376.

37. Ibid., 237.

38. Morris, *The Gospel According to John,* 73.

39. Christian Lore Weber, *WomanChrist* (San Francisco: Harper & Row, 1987), 43.

40. Morris has a helpful discussion stating that this form was not used in ordinary speech. In using it, Jesus adopted "the divine style." Morris argues strongly for Christ's eternality and deity (*The Gospel According to John,* 473–74).

41. J. B. Lightfoot, *St. Paul's Epistle to the Philippians* (repr. ed., Grand Rapids: Zondervan, 1953), 132. See pp. 127–33, in which Lightfoot compares *morphē* (that which is inward and essential) with *schēma* (that which is "accidental and outward").

42. B. F. Westcott, *The Epistle to the Hebrews* (repr. ed., Grand Rapids: Eerdmans, 1965), 24.

43. Henry Barclay Swete, *The Apocalypse of St. John* (repr. ed., Grand Rapids: Eerdmans, 1968), 307.

44. Carl Friedrich Keil, *Biblical Commentary on the Old Testament: The Twelve Minor Prophets* (repr. ed., Grand Rapids: Eerdmans, 1949), 1:480.

Chapter 13

1. John M. Frame, "Virgin Birth of Jesus," in Walter A. Elwell, ed., *Evangelical Dictionary of Theology* (Grand Rapids: Baker, 1984), 1143.

2. A. N. S. Lane, "Virgin Birth," in Sinclair Ferguson and David Wright, eds., *New Dictionary of Theology* (Downers Grove, Ill.: InterVarsity, 1988), 708–9.

3. F. F. Bruce, "The Person of Christ: Incarnation and Virgin Birth," in Carl F. H. Henry, ed., *Basic Christian Doctrines* (New York: Holt, Rinehart & Winston, 1962), 128.

4. BAGD, 632.

5. Frame, "Virgin Birth of Jesus," 1143–44.

6. James Orr, "The Virgin Birth of Christ," in *The Fundamentals* (Los Angeles: Biola, 1917), 258–59.

7. See details in Robert G. Gromacki, *The Virgin Birth* (Nashville: Nelson, 1974), 83–85; H. A. Hanke, *Validity of the Virgin Birth* (Grand Rapids: Zondervan, 1963), 45–49; and Raymond Brown, *The Virginal Conception and the Bodily Resurrection of Jesus* (New York: Paulist, 1973), 47–52.

8. Brown, *The Virginal Conception,* 47.

9. J. Gresham Machen, *The Virgin Birth of Christ* (New York: Harper & Row, 1930), 7.

10. Edward E. Hindson, "The 'Bruiser' and the 'Crusher' in Genesis 3," in E. J. Mayhew, ed., *Shalom* (Farmington Hills, Mich.: William Tyndale College Press, 1983), 11–22.

11. Charles L. Feinberg, *The Minor Prophets* (Chicago: Moody, 1976), 173.

12. For survey of the historical development of the interpretation of Isaiah 7:14, see Edward E. Hindson, *Isaiah's Immanuel* (Philadelphia: Presbyterian and Reformed, 1978), 15–24.

13. Cyrus Gordon, " *'Almâh,* in Isaiah 7:14," *Journal of Bible and Religion* 21 (1953): 106.

14. Edward J. Young, *Studies in Isaiah* (Grand Rapids: Eerdmans, 1954), 143–98; cf.,

Edward E. Hindson, "Immanuel Prophecy," *Mid-America Theological Journal* 15.1 (1991): 79–85.

15. G. A. F. Knight, *A Christian Theology of the Old Testament* (London: SCM, 1964), 310

16. See George A. Buttrick, ed., *Intrepreter's Bible* (New York: Abingdon, 1956), 5:218. It is interesting to note that the exegetical and homiletical sections of this work were done by different authors. On the same page the exegete denies Isaiah is predicting the virgin birth of Christ, and the expositor claims that he *is* predicting the virgin birth.

17. J. Greenstone, *The Messianic Idea in Jewish History* (Philadelphia: Jewish Publication Society of America, 1943), 109–35.

18. J. Broadus, *Commentary on the Gospel of Matthew* (Valley Forge: American Baptist Publication Society, 1886), 11.

19. R. Lenski, *Interpretation of St. Matthew's Gospel* (Columbus, Ohio: Wartburg, 1943), 52.

20. BAGD, 677.

21. Lenski, *Interpretation of St. Matthew's Gospel* 53.

22. Bruce, "The Person of Christ: Incarnation and Virgin Birth," 124–25.

23. Frame, "Virgin Birth of Jesus," 1145.

24. James Orr, "The Virgin Birth of Christ," *The Fundamentals* (Grand Rapids: Kregel, 1980), 2:247.

25. Ibid., 2:249.

26. Cf. H. D. McDonald, "The Kerygmatic Christology of Rudolf Bultmann," in H. H. Rowdon, ed., *Christ the Lord* (London: InterVarsity, 1982), 311–25; and R. P. Martin, "The New Quest for the Historical Jesus," in Carl F. H. Henry, ed., *Jesus of Nazareth: Savior and Lord* (Grand Rapids: Eerdmans, 1966), 23–45.

27. For a general survey of twentieth-century Christology, see Klaas Runia, *The Present-Day Christological Debate* (London: InterVarsity, 1984); and J. D. G. Dunn, *Christology in the Making* (London: SCM, 1980).

28. Brown, *Virginal Conception*, 41.

29. T. W. Manson, "Quest for the Historical Jesus," *Church Quarterly Review* 1 (1933): 12, quoted in Hugh Anderson, *Jews and Christian Origins* (New York: Oxford University Press, 1964), 88.

30. Kenneth Kantzer, "The Christ Revelation as Act and Interpretation," in Henry, ed., *Basic Christian Doctrines*, 248.

31. John Stott, *Authentic Christianity* (Downers Grove, Ill.: InterVarsity, 1995), 35.

32. Ibid., 36.

Chapter 14

1. Unless otherwise noted, all Scripture references and quotations in this chapter are from the *New American Standard Bible*.

2. Henry C. Thiessen, *Lectures in Systematic Theology* (Grand Rapids: Eerdmans, 1979), 84.

3. Ibid., 85.

4. Walter A. Elwell, ed., *Evangelical Dictionary of Theology* (Grand Rapids: Baker, 1989), 312.

5. Ewald M. Plass, *What Luther Says* (St. Louis: Concordia, 1972), 1299.

6. Benjamin B. Warfield, *The Person and Work of Christ* (repr. ed., Philadelphia: Presbyterian and Reformed, 1950), 422.

7. Ibid., 422–23.

8. A. H. Strong, *Systematic Theology* (Old Tappan, N.J.: Revell, 1969), 297.

9. Charles Ryrie, *Basic Theology*, Wheaton: Victor Books, 1987, 294-95.
10. There is a difference of opinion among conservative scholars as to whether Paul's meaning in Rom. 3:25 referred to Christ as becoming *the place of propitiation* (i.e., our "mercy seat") or whether He *was the propitiation*. John Walvoord writes, "The ultimate meaning, however, is not too different as in either case it is a direct statement not only that God requires satisfaction for sin, but that such satisfaction was provided in the propitiation of Christ in His death." (*Jesus Christ Our Lord* [Chicago: Moody, 1969], 173-74).
11. Quoted in ibid., 172.
12. Paul P. Enns, *Moody Handbook of Theology* (Chicago: Moody, 1989), 325.
13. BAGD, 95.
14. Walvoord, *Jesus Christ Our Lord* , 169.
15. Fritz Reinecker, *Linguistic Key to the Greek New Testament,* ed. Cleon Rogers (Grand Rapids: Zondervan, 1980), 214.
16. Walvoord, *Jesus Christ Our Lord* , 168.
17. Charles C. Ryrie, *Basic Theology* (Chicago: Victor, 1986), 291-92.
18. Walvoord, *Jesus Christ Our Lord* , 177.
19. R. C. H. Lenski, *The Interpretation of 1 and 2 Corinthians* (1937, repr. ed., Minneapolis, Minn.: Augsburg, 1963), 1045.
20. H. Vorländer and Colin Brown, "Reconciliation," in Colin Brown, ed., *The New International Dictionary of New Testament Theology* (Grand Rapids: Zondervan, 1986).
21. Murry J. Harris, "2 Corinthians," in Frank E. Gaebelien, ed., *The Expositor's Bible Commentary* (Grand Rapids: Zondervan, 1976), 354.
22. Walvoord, *Jesus Christ Our Lord* , 189.
23. Enns, *Moody Handbook of Theology*, 324.
24. Ibid., quoting Edwin H. Palmer, *The Five Points of Calvinism* (Grand Rapids: Guardian, 1972), 44.
25. Ibid., quoting "Atonement, Extent of," in Elwell, ed., *Evangelical Dictionary of Theology.*
26. Lewis S. Chafer, *Systematic Theology,* 8 vols. (Dallas: Dallas Seminary, 1947), 3:204.
27. Enns, *Moody Handbook of Theology*, 325.
28. BAGD, 125.
29. Enns, *Moody Handbook of Theology*, 326.
30. Robert P. Lightner, *Sin, the Savior, and Salvation* (Grand Rapids: Kregel, 1991), 222.

Chapter 15

1. In my publications on Jesus' resurrection, I have used the "minimal facts method," which builds on data that are heavily supported by evidence, and that both believers and unbelievers generally hold in common. This way, an apologetic case for the Resurrection is broad-based and convincing. For further discussion of some of these facts, see Gary R. Habermas, *The Historical Jesus: Ancient Evidence for the Life of Christ* (Joplin, Mo.: College Press, 1996), 158-67.
2. We will discuss in the next section some of the evidences for the empty tomb.
3. For a discussion of other theories and some of the problems involved, see Gary R. Habermas and J. P. Moreland, *Beyond Death: Exploring the Evidence for Immortality* (Wheaton: Crossway, 1998), 115-26.
4. Reginald H. Fuller, *The Foundations of New Testament Christology* (New York: Charles Scribner's Sons, 1965), 142.
5. James D. G. Dunn, *The Evidence for Jesus* (Louisville: Westminster, 1985), 75-76.
6. On the strength of the appearance data alone, see Gary R. Habermas, "The Resurrection

Appearances of Jesus," in R. Douglas Geivett and Gary R. Habermas, eds., *Defense of Miracles: A Comprehensive Case for God's Action in History* (Downers Grove, Ill.: InterVarsity, 1997), 262-75.

7. Michael Grant, *Jesus: An Historian's Review of the Gospels* (New York: Charles Scribner's Sons, 1976), 176.

8. For an in-depth discussion, with citations and examples of these critical studies, see Grant, *Jesus,* 128-33; cf. Habermas, *The Historical Jesus,* 152-57.

9. Unfortunately, this attitude may be changing. I have catalogued the reappearance of some of the older sorts of critical theories and a number of scholars who favor them. See Gary R. Habermas, "The Recent Renaissance of Naturalistic Responses to the Resurrection," lecture to the *Evangelical Philosophical Society,* 19 November 1998. The lecture is available on cassette from ACTS, 14153 Clayton Road, Town and Country, MO, 63017, 1-800-642-2287.

10. For published debates with critics who hold this view, see William Lane Craig and John Dominic Crossan, *Will the Real Jesus Please Stand Up?* ed. Paul Copan (Grand Rapids: Baker, 1998); Gary R. Habermas and Antony Flew, *Did Jesus Rise from the Dead? The Resurrection Debate,* ed. Terry L. Miethe (San Francisco: Harper and Row, 1987).

11. For an overview of current positions on the nature of Jesus' appearances after His resurrection, see Gary R. Habermas, "Jesus's Resurrection and Contemporary Criticism: An Apologetic," part 1, in *Criswell Theological Review* 4.1 (fall 1989): 59-174; part 2, in *Criswell Theological Review* 4.2 (spring 1990): 373-85.

12. For a scholarly treatment of a related topic, see Caroline Walker Bynum, *The Resurrection of the Body in Western Christianity, 200–1336* (New York: Columbia University Press, 1995). Bynum concludes that bodily continuity remained the predominant view during this time period, while noting varying concepts regarding the form of the resurrection body (pp. 5-6, 11, 24-25, 341-43).

13. There is some overlap between these points. For details concerning each, see Gary R. Habermas, "The Early Christian Belief in the Resurrection of Jesus: A Response to Thomas Sheehan," *Michigan Theological Journal* 3.2 (fall 1992), particularly 115-20.

14. Robert H. Gundry, *Soma in Biblical Theology: With Emphasis on Pauline Anthropology* (Cambridge: Cambridge University Press, 1976; Grand Rapids: Zondervan, 1987), 165-66.

15. Ibid., 182.

16. John A. T. Robinson, "Resurrection in the NT," in George Buttrick, ed., *The Interpreter's Dictionary of the Bible* (Nashville: Abingdon, 1962), 4:48.

17. A. N. Sherwin-White, *Roman Society and Roman Law in the New Testament* (1963; repr. ed., Grand Rapids: Baker, 1978), 190.

18. C. H. Dodd, "The Appearances of the Risen Christ: An Essay in the Form Criticism of the Gospels," in *More New Testament Essays* (Grand Rapids: Eerdmans, 1968).

19. Grant R. Osborne, *The Resurrection Narratives: A Redactional Study* (Grand Rapids: Baker, 1984), esp. 10-11, 43-192.

20. For strong discussions of the empty tomb, see William Lane Craig, "The Empty Tomb of Jesus," in R. T. France and David Wenham, eds., *Gospel Perspectives: Studies of History and Tradition in the Four Gospels* (Sheffield: JSOT, 1981), 2:173-200; Edward Bode, "The First Easter Morning," in *Analecta Biblica* 45 (Rome: Biblical Institute, 1970), esp. 155-75; and Robert H. Stein, "Was the Tomb Really Empty?" *Journal of the Evangelical Theological Society* 20 (1977): 23-29.

21. See Gary R. Habermas, "Resurrection of Christ," in Walter A. Elwell, ed., *Evangelical Dictionary of Theology* (Grand Rapids: Baker, 1984).

22. For more thorough discussion of these connections, see the author's *The Centrality of*

the Resurrection: Theology and the Centrality of the Resurrection (Joplin, Mo.: College Press, forthcoming; title tentative).

23. Quotations in this section are from J. B. Lightfoot, ed. and trans., *The Apostolic Fathers,* ed. J. R. Harmer (repr. ed., Grand Rapids: Baker, 1956).

24. Tertullian, *De Resurrectione Mortuorum* 53:8, 12; *De Anima* 5-9.

25. Origen, *Contra Celsus* 7:32.

26. For other questions and challenges, especially on the objectivity-subjectivity issue, see Gary R. Habermas, "Philosophy of History, Historical Relativism and History as Evidence," in Michael Bauman, David W. Hall and Robert C. Newman, eds., *Evangelical Apologetics* (Camp Hill, Pa.: Christian Publications, 1996), 91-118.

27. On the uniqueness of Jesus's claims, see Norman Anderson, *Christianity and World Religions: The Challenge of Pluralism* (Downers Grove, Ill.: InterVarsity, 1984); Stephen Neill, *Christian Faith and Other Faiths* (London: Oxford University Press, 1970; Downers Grove, Ill.: InterVarsity, 1984); Stephen Neill, *The Supremacy of Jesus* (Downers Grove, Ill.: InterVarsity, 1984); and Gary R. Habermas, "The Uniqueness of Jesus," in Terry L. Miethe and Gary R. Habermas, eds., *Why Believe? God Exists! Rethinking the Case for God and Christianity* (Joplin: College Press, 1993).

28. Christopher Tuckett, *Nag Hammadi and the Gospel Tradition* (Edinburgh: T & T Clark, 1986). For a more accessible, although brief, treatment, see Craig Blomberg's overview *In the Historical Reliability of the Gospels* (Downers Grove, Ill.: InterVarsity, 1987), 208-19.

29. On the Gnostic understanding of the Resurrection, see Gerald O'Collins, "Luminous Appearances of the Risen Christ," *The Catholic Biblical Quarterly* 46 (1984): 247-54; Daniel Kendall and Gerald O'Collins, "The Uniqueness of the Easter Appearances," *The Catholic Biblical Quarterly* 54 (1992): 287-307; and Habermas, *The Historical Jesus,* chap. 5.

30. Besides Blomberg's *The Historical Reliability of the Gospels,* other volumes that have made a start in this direction include the older but still helpful volume by F. F. Bruce, *The New Testament Documents: Are They Reliable?* rev. ed. (Grand Rapids: Eerdmans, 1960). See also: Robert P. Lightner, *A Biblical Case for Total Inerrancy* (Grand Rapids: Kregel, 1978); John Wenham, *Christ and the Bible* (Grand Rapids: Baker, 1984); and Paul Barnett, *Is the New Testament Reliable? A Look at the Historical Evidence* (Downers Grove, Ill.: InterVarsity, 1986).

31. For details, see Gary R. Habermas, "Resurrection Claims in Non-Christian Religions," *Religious Studies* 25 (1989): 167-177.

32. For details of the lengthy written debate between Norman Geisler and Murray Harris, see Murray Harris, *Raised Immortal: Resurrection and Immortality in the New Testament* (Grand Rapids: Eerdmans, 1985); Norman L. Geisler, *The Battle for the Resurrection* (Nashville: Nelson, 1989); Murray Harris, *From Grave to Glory* (Grand Rapids: Zondervan, 1990); Norman L. Geisler, *In Defense of the Resurrection,* rev. ed. (Clayton: Witness, 1993); and Robert D. Culver, *A Wake-Up Call* (Clayton, Mo.: Witness, 1993).

Chapter 16

1. Peter exhorts his readers concerning "the true grace in which you stand" (2 Peter 5:12). The implication is that some promote a grace that is not genuine.

2. "If [God's election through faith is] by grace, then it is no longer of works; otherwise grace is no longer grace. But if it is of works, it is no longer grace; otherwise work is no longer work" (Rom. 11:6).

3. *Knowledge That Leads to Everlasting Life* (Brooklyn, N.Y.: Watchtower Bible and Tract Society, 1995), 173.

4. Ibid., 178.
5. Rex E. Lee, *What Do Mormons Believe?* (Salt Lake City: Deseret, 1992), 39, 42.
6. LeGrande Richards, *A Marvelous Work and a Wonder* (Salt Lake City: Deseret, 1976), 266.
7. Lee, *What Do Mormons Believe?* 38.
8. Ibid., 42.
9. John F. MacArthur Jr., *The Gospel According to Jesus* (Grand Rapids: Zondervan, 1988), 207.
10. John F. MacArthur, *Faith Works: The Gospel According to the Apostles* (Dallas: Word, 1993), 211-12, quoting MacArthur, *Gospel According to Jesus,* 210.
11. John Gerstner, *Wrongly Dividing the Word of Truth: A Critique of Dispensationalism* (Brentwood, Tenn.: Wolgemuth and Hyatt, 1991), 210.
12. Ibid., 225-27.
13. Samuel Logan, "The Doctrine of Justification in the Theology of Jonathan Edwards," *Westminster Theological Journal* 46 (1984), CD-ROM.
14. Unless otherwise noted, all Scripture references and quotations in this chapter are from *The New King James Version* of the Bible.
15. C. E. B. Cranfield, "The Epistle to the Romans," in *The International Critical Commentary* (Edinburgh: T & T Clark, 1990), 1:224.
16. William F. Arndt and F. Wilbur Gingrich, *A Greek-English Lexicon of the New Testament* (Chicago: University of Chicago Press, 1974), 325 n 3, offer *find (for oneself), obtain,* giving Matt. 10:39; 11:29; Heb. 4:16; 12:17, among other texts, as references.
17. H. C. G. Moule, "Justification by Faith," *The Fundamentals: A Testimony to the Truth,* vol. 3 (repr. ed., Grand Rapids: Baker, 1998), 142.
18. Ibid., 143.
19. Ibid., 144.
20. Ibid.
21. The same preposition showing purpose, εισ, "as, for," can be translated in Hebrews 1:15, "I will be to him *for* a Father, and He will be to me *for* a Son." See also Mark 10:8.
22. The verb λογίζεται ("is accounted") must signify a counting that does not reward merit. It is free and unmerited divine grace. Luther said, "He who works properly receives a reward; but he receives the reward of debt, and not of grace. On the other hand, to him who does not rely on his works nor regards them as (necessary for salvation), righteousness is given freely by faith, which relies on God." Martin Luther, *Commentary on Romans* (Grand Rapids: Kregel, 1976), 82.
23. By means of this relative clause Paul gathers up and connects the thought of verses 4 and 5, making the connection between Ps. 32:1-2 and Gen. 15:6, identifying the forgiving of sins with the reckoning of righteousness apart from works (Cranfield, "Epistle to the Romans," 1:233).
24. Luther, *Commentary on Romans,* 83.
25. F. F. Bruce, *The Epistle of Paul to the Romans* (Grand Rapids: Eerdmans, 1983), 111.
26. Daniel B. Wallace, *Greek Grammar Beyond the Basics* (Grand Rapids: Zondervan, 1996), 33; A. T. Robertson, *A Grammar of the Greek New Testament in Light of Historical Research* (Nashville: Broadman, 1934), 498; and Cranfield, "The Epistle to the Romans," 1:236. Bruce calls it a "genitive of definition" in Bruce, *The Epistle of Paul to the Romans,* 116.
27. Cranfield, "The Epistle to the Romans," 1:236.
28. Ibid.
29. Bruce, *The Epistle of Paul to the Romans,* 116; Johannes P. Louw, and Eugene A. Nida, *Greek-English Lexicon of the New Testament Based on Semantic Domains* (New York: United Bible Societies, 1989), s.v. "δωρεάν."

30. Louw and Nida, *Greek English Lexicon of the New Testament*.
31. Charles Hodge, *Systematic Theology* (repr. ed., CD-ROM, Oak Harbor, Wash.: Logos Research Systems, 1997).
32. The expression "save your souls" does not mean to save one's soul from hell, but to save one's life from present trials, temptations, and the death-dealing power of sin. See Zane Hodges, *The Gospel Under Siege*, 2d ed. (Redencion Viva, 1992), 26–28.
33. This is theological eisegesis—a reading of one's theological system into James's text.
34. Louw and Nida, *Greek English Lexicon of the New Testament*.
35. Hodge, *Systematic Theology*.
36. *Greek Grammar Beyond the Basics*, 335. That this is the referent is further supported by the repetition of the phrase *by grace you are saved*. The first time Paul uses the phrase, in Eph. 2:5–6, it is a parenthetic explanation of complete salvation. God "made us alive together with Christ, raised us together [with Christ], and seated us together [with Christ]." Accordingly, *that* in verse 8 denotes not grace or faith, but our grace-given salvation that one receives by faith.
37. Moule, "Justification by Faith," 150. The reference is to the first Aswan Dam, which was completed in 1902. The Nile project continued until the final dam was completed in 1960.
38. Ibid., 154.
39. Paul likewise does not mention repentance in Galatians, which is noteworthy, because he defends the gospel of grace vigorously against legalists who seek to pervert the free grace nature of the gospel of Christ (Gal. 1:6–9). If repentance were a necessary component of receiving eternal life, it seems reasonable that he would have mentioned it.
40. See Zane Hodges, "Arguments from Silence, and All of That: Repentance Reconsidered," *Grace in Focus* 13.3 (May–June 1998): 1–4.
41. For a significant step toward interpreting passages that include the notion of repentance, see chapter 12 of Zane Hodges, *Absolutely Free!* (Grand Rapids: Zondervan, 1989).

Chapter 17

1. Unless otherwise noted, all Scripture references and quotations in this chapter are from *The New King James Version* of the Bible.
2. The indicators for plurality within unity are so subtle in the Old Testament that they are open to differing interpretations, even among conservative Old Testament scholars. Most of the singular/plural distinctions can be subsumed under the Hebrew linguistic concept of a plural of heaviness or majesty. This chapter argues that plurality in unity is so powerfully demonstrated in these constructions that its trinitarian connection seems probable. Whatever the grammatical reasons, in God's superintending of the Hebrew language the Jewish mind was opened to thinking in terms of divine plurality, without being drawn toward idolatrous polytheism.
3. The *Shema* is Israel's confession throughout history, and many Jewish martyrs went to their deaths with these words on their lips rather than give even token worship to pagan gods. It is found in Deut. 6:4–5: "Hear, O Israel: The LORD our God, the LORD is one! You shall love the LORD your God with all your heart, with all your soul, and with all your might."
4. The Athanasian Creed is of unknown origin and was written following the death of Athanasius (c.296–373). It builds on the Nicene Creed against heresies regarding the persons of the Trinity. It was written in Latin and is most accurately called the *Quicunque Vult*.
5. "Very God of very God" is used in the Nicene Creed to powerfully confess the deity of Christ. The same words apply to the Holy Spirit.

Chapter 18

1. James Montgomery Boice, *Foundations of the Christian Faith* (Downers Grove, Ill.: InterVarsity, 1993), 381.
2. Joseph R. Chambers, *The Holy Ghost in the Believer* (Charlotte: Paw Creek Ministries, n.d.), 1.
3. Charles C. Ryrie, *The Holy Spirit,* rev. ed. (Chicago: Moody, 1997), 54–58.
4. Ibid., 86.
5. Charles Hodge, *Systematic Theology,* 3 vols. (repr. ed., Grand Rapids: Eerdmans, 1995), 3:35.
6. Charles C. Ryrie, *Basic Theology* (Wheaton: Victor, 1988), 358.
7. Ibid., 107.
8. John R. W. Stott, *The Baptism and Fullness of the Holy Spirit* (Downers Grove, Ill.: InterVarsity, 1964), 4.
9. Ibid., 17–22.
10. Ryrie, *Basic Theology,* 358.
11. W. E. Vine, *Vine's Complete Expository Dictionary of Old and New Testament Words* (various editions), s.v. "Comfort, Comforter, Comfortless."
12. Acts 1:24–26; 2:2–4, 6–12, 33, 43; 3:1–10, 16; 4:7–8, 10, 16, 30–31, 33; 5:3–10, 12, 15–16, 19; 6:8, 10; 7:55–56; 8:6–7, 13–17, 19, 29, 39; 9:3–18, 34, 40; 10:3–6, 10–16, 19–21, 22, 30–33, 38, 44–47; 11:4–10, 12–17, 24, 28; 12:7–11, 23; 13:2, 4, 9–11, 52; 14:3, 10; 15:8, 12; 16:6–7, 9–10, 18, 26; 18:9–10; 19:6, 11–12; 20:9–12, 23; 21:4, 11; 22:17–21; 23:11; 27:23–24; 28:3–6, 8–9.

Chapter 19

1. Some Baptist groups in the Southern part of the United States do not believe in the universal church. They view all references in the New Testament to church as referring to the local church.
2. Scripture references and quotations in this chapter are from the *New American Standard Bible.*
3. Lewis Sperry Chafer, *Systematic Theology,* 8 vols. (Grand Rapids: Kregel, 1993), 4:47–53.
4. Ibid., 53.
5. David L. Smith argues to the contrary: "The church was the continuation of spiritual Israel, not of ethnic Israel." See David L. Smith, *All God's People: A Theology of the Church* (Wheaton, Ill.: Victor Books, 1996), 324.
6. J. B. Lightfoot, *Saint Paul's Epistles to the Colossians and to Philemon* (London: Macmillan, 1927), 166.
7. Louis Berkhof, *Systematic Theology* (Grand Rapids: Eerdmans, 1968), 577–78.
8. John Eadie, *Commentary on the Epistle to the Ephesians* (Grand Rapids: Zondervan, n.d.), 220.
9. Ibid.
10. G. Abbott-Smith, *A Manual Greek Lexicon of the New Testament* (Edinburgh: T & T Clark, 1937), 431.
11. Robert L. Saucy, "The Church as the Mystery of God," in Craig A. Blaising and Darrell L. Bock, eds., *Dispensationalism, Israel, and the Church* (Grand Rapids: Zondervan, 1992), 144.
12. A. T. Robertson, *A Grammar of the Greek New Testament in Light of Historical Research* (Nashville: Broadman, 1934), 967–69.
13. James M. Stifler, *The Epistle to the Romans: A Commentary, Logical and Historical* (London: Revell, 1897), 254.

14. See Earl D. Radmacher, *What the Church Is All About* (Chicago: Moody, 1978), 298–301.
15. C. W. Slemming, *Echoes from the Hills of Bethlehem* (London: Henry E. Walter, 1949), 17–36.
16. A minority view among evangelicals is that Christ was addressing both believers and nonbelievers. See related view in Frederick Louis Godet, *Commentary on the Gospel of John* (Grand Rapids: Zondervan, 1969); and James E. Rosscup, *Abiding in Christ* (Grand Rapids: Zondervan, 1973).
17. See Radmacher, *What the Church Is All About*, 266–67.
18. Chafer, *Systematic Theology*, 2:67–68; see 2:64–68.
19. Ibid., 79.
20. Ibid., 81–92. Chafer defends standard proofs of Christ's resurrection.
21. Ibid., 99.
22. Benajah Harvey Carroll, *An Interpretation of the English Bible*, ed. J. B. Cranfill and J. W. Crowder (New York: Revell, 1913), 15:102.
23. Ethelbert W. Bullinger, *How to Enjoy the Bible* (Grand Rapids: Kregel, 1990), 94–96, 145–49.
24. Alfred Edersheim, *Sketches of Jewish Social Life in the Days of Christ* (Grand Rapids: Eerdmans, 1957), 148.
25. Augustus Hopkins Strong, *Systematic Theology* (Philadelphia: Griffith & Rowland, 1909), 3:899.
26. John Calvin, *Institutes of the Christian Religion* (Grand Rapids: Eerdmans, 1962), 4.1.7.
27. Berkhof, *Systematic Theology*, 577–78.
28. Smith, *All God's People*, 341.

Chapter 20

1. Josh McDowell, broadcast, KCBI-Radio, Dallas, Texas, 7 October 1998.
2. David J. Bosch, *Believing in the Future* (Valley Forge, Pa.: Trinity, 1995), 1. Bosch cites Hans Küng's description of the contemporary world "as post-Eurocentric, post-colonial, post-imperial, post-socialist, post-industrial, post-patriarchal, post-ideological, and post-confessional."
3. Larry Dixon, *The Other Side of the Good News* (Wheaton: BridgePoint, 1992), 11.
4. D. Martyn Lloyd-Jones, *Authority* (London: Inter-Varsity, 1964), 30.
5. One who speaks for those who do not accept such an analysis is David Bosch (see above). Bosch sees a far different role for the church. He believes the words of the New Testament are largely irrelevant until today's church radiates new relevance for them. He would reject any concept of timeless authority contained in propositional truth. He believes it will not do to directly apply the words of biblical authors to our situation. We should, rather, with creative, responsible freedom, extend the logic of the ministry of Jesus and the early church to a new context. God communicates his revelation through human beings and events, not by abstract propositions. Biblical faith is "incarnational" as God enters human affairs. See David D. Bosch, *Transforming Mission* (Maryknoll: Orbis, 1991), 181.
6. John W. Wenham, in Norman L. Geisler, ed., *Inerrancy* (Grand Rapids: Zondervan, 1980), 17.
7. A. W. Tozer, *The Knowledge of the Holy* (New York: Harper and Row, 1961), 9.
8. Charles C. Ryrie, *Basic Theology* (Wheaton: Victor, 1986), 39.
9. Ibid., 59.
10. Ibid., 40–41. "The picture of a nervous, ingratiating God fawning over men to win their

favor is not a pleasant one; yet if we look at the popular conception of God that is precisely what we see. Twentieth-century Christianity has put God on charity. So lofty is our opinion of ourselves that we find it quite easy, not to say enjoyable, to believe that we are necessary to God. But the truth is that God is not greater for our being, nor would He be less if we did not exist. That we do exist is altogether of God's free determination, not our desert nor by divine necessity. Probably the hardest thought of all for our natural egotism to entertain is that God does not need our help. We commonly represent Him as a busy, eager, somewhat frustrated Father, hurrying about seeking help to carry out His benevolent plan to bring peace and salvation to the world; . . . The God who worketh all things surely needs no help and no helpers."

11. Ibid., 6.
12. Tozer, *The Knowledge of the Holy*, 16.
13. Unless otherwise noted, Scripture references and quotations in this chapter are from the King James Version of the Bible.
14. J. Ronald Blue, "Untold Billions: Are They Really Lost," in Roy B. Zuck, ed., *Vital Theological Issues* (Grand Rapids: Kregel, 1994), 73.
15. Dixon, *The Other Side of the Good News*, 145.
16. Ibid., 9.
17. David Hesselgrave, *Scripture and Strategy* (Pasadena: William Carey Library, 1994), 140.
18. Allan Tippet defines missiology as "the academic discipline or science which researches, records, and applies data relating to the biblical origin, the history, . . . the anthropological principles and techniques, and the theological base of the Christian mission." Allan R. Tippet, *Introduction to Missiology* (Pasadena: William Carey Library, 1987), xiii. See also Norman E. Allison, "The Contribution of Cultural Anthropology to Missiology," in Edward Rommen and Gary Corwin, eds., *Missiology and the Social Sciences* (Pasadena: William Carey Library, 1996), esp. p. 31.
19. See K. A. McElhanon, "Prototype Semantics: Insights for Intercultural Communication," in Rommen and Corwin, *Missiology and the Social Sciences*, 48.
20. James Davison Hunter, *Evangelicalism: The Coming Generation* (Chicago: University of Chicago Press, 1987), 38. Hunter says, "Evangelicals generally and the coming generation particularly have adopted to various degrees an ethical code of political civility. This compels them not only to be *tolerant of others'* beliefs, opinions and lifestyles, but more importantly, to be *tolerable to others*. The critical dogma is not to offend but to be genteel and civil in social relations. . . . [Such] a religious style . . . entails a de-emphasis of Evangelicalism's more offensive aspects, such as accusations of heresy, sin, immorality and paganism, and themes of judgment, divine wrath, damnation and hell."
21. Michelle Phillips, "Dropping the Ball," in *The Gospel Message* 106.3.
22. George W. Peters, *A Biblical Theology of Missions* (Chicago: Moody, 1972), 170.
23. Bosch, *Believing in the Future*, 29.
24. W. E. Vine, Merrill F. Unger, and William White Jr., *An Expository Dictionary of Biblical Words* (Nashville: Nelson, 1984), 1237.
25. Hesselgrave, *Scripture and Strategy*, 137.
26. Woodrow Kroll, *The Vanishing Ministry* (Grand Rapids: Kregel, 1991), 95.
27. Robert J. Priest, Thomas Campbell, and Bradford A. Mullen, "Missiological Syncretism," in Edward Rommen, ed., *Spiritual Power and Missions*, The Evangelical Missiological Society Series, no. 3 (Pasadena, Calif.: William Carey Library, 1995), 10–11.

Chapter 21

1. Scripture references and quotations in this chapter are from the *New American Standard Bible*.
2. "Faces of the Dalai Lama," *Quest,* autumn 1993, 80.
3. Antony Flew, "Theology and Falsification," in *New Essays in Philosophical Theology* (New York: Macmillan, 1955), 96.

Chapter 22

1. The challenge of pluralism has been experienced by the author for over twelve years of military chaplaincy. I have labored to provide faithful ministry in an institutional environment, remaining faithful to my ecclesiastical endorsement, ordination, and evangelical theology. Yet my friends and colleagues are certainly diverse religiously and politically. They include Episcopal, Orthodox, and Roman Catholic priests, a Jewish rabbi, and Protestant ministers from across the theological spectrum. The officer and enlisted communities in military life cover an even broader religious spectrum.
2. E. D. Cook, "Pluralism," in David J. Atkinson, David Field, Arthur Holmes, and Oliver O'Donovan, eds., *The New Dictionary of Christian Ethics and Pastoral Theology* (Downers Grove, Ill.: InterVarsity, 1995), 666.
3. Examples abound of confusion regarding the meaning and application of *pluralism.* In discussing the moral dilemma America confronts because of its pluralistic makeup, James Davison Hunter asks, "Are there any limits to pluralism? Is there anything, in other words, that we will not view as acceptable behavior or lifestyle? Should there be any such limits? And on what grounds can a community justify the imposition of limits to pluralism? What compelling reasons, acceptable to all, are there for establishing boundaries between what is acceptable and what is not?" (p. 308) The issue is not pluralism itself, but the moral and theological dilemma pluralism creates. Different philosophies spawn different ethics with different morals. Are there limits to our tolerance of these philosophies? Should some values or morals be tolerated while others are not? Pluralistic societies need practical ways to discern what is good for the society as a whole and what is detrimental. For the full discussion, see James Davison Hunter, *Culture Wars: The Struggle to Define America, Making Sense of the Battles over the Family, Art, Education, Law, and Politics* (New York: Basic, 1991), 308–12.
4. D. A. Carson, *The Gagging of God: Christianity Confronts Pluralism* (Grand Rapids: Zondervan, 1996), 13–18. Carson's concept of *cherished pluralism* is "an additional ingredient to empirical pluralism." It identifies gains from living in a society that assimilates the views of others into its infrastructure. Again, this term adds to the confusion of the meaning of pluralism—*cherished pluralism* describes more of what people are willing or not willing to tolerate within a pluralistic setting.
5. Gene Edward Veith Jr., *Postmodern Times: A Christian Guide to Contemporary Thought and Culture* (Wheaton: Crossway, 1994), 152. See also, Paul C. Vitz, *Psychology As Religion: The Cult of Self-Worship,* 2d ed. (Grand Rapids: Eerdmans, 1994), 166–68. Vitz argues that "separatist and secessionist movements are surfacing around the globe. Here in America the question of what can hold us together is on the minds of most thoughtful observers of the social and political scene" (166).
6. Samuel P. Huntington, *The Clash of Civilizations and the Remaking of World Order* (New York: Simon and Schuster, 1996), 21.
7. Ibid., 28.
8. Nina Shea, "Atrocities Not Fit to Print," *First Things,* November 1997, 33.
9. Ibid.

10. Huntington, *Clash of Civilizations,* 217.
11. Don E. Eberly, *Restoring the Good Society: A New Vision for Politics and Culture* (Grand Rapids: Baker, 1994), 78.
12. Hunter, *Culture Wars,* 41.
13. S. D. Gaede, *When Tolerance Is No Virtue: Political Correctness, Multiculturalism and the Future of Truth and Justice* (Downers Grove, Ill.: InterVarsity, 1993), 49.
14. Ibid., 60.
15. Ibid., 74.
16. Hunter, *Culture Wars,* 325.
17. James F. Childress and John C. Fletcher, "Respect for Autonomy," *Hastings Center Report* (May–June 1994): 35.
18. Margaret Norden, "Whose Life Is It Anyway? A Study in Respect for Autonomy," *Journal of Medical Ethics* 21 (1995): 182.
19. Thomas H. Murray, "Individualism and Community: The Contested Terrain of Autonomy," *Hastings Center Report* (May–June 1994): 33.
20. William D Watkins, *The New Absolutes: How They Are Being Imposed on Us and How They Are Eroding Our Moral Landscape* (Minneapolis: Bethany House, 1996), 29.
21. John Hick, "A Pluralist View," in Dennis L. Okholm and Timothy R. Phillips, eds., *Four Views on Salvation in a Pluralistic World* (Grand Rapids: Zondervan, 1995), 38.
22. Ibid., 39, 45.
23. W. Gary Phillips, "Evangelical Pluralism: A Singular Problem," *Bibliotheca Sacra* 151 (April–June 1994): 141–42.
24. Carson, *The Gagging of God,* 19–26.
25. James D. Chancellor, "Christ and Religious Pluralism," *Review and Expositor* 91 (1994): 542. Chancellor remarks that Muslims and Buddhists understand that religious pluralism is inconsistent with their own practices.
26. Carl F. H. Henry, *Carl Henry at His Best: A Lifetime of Quotable Quotes* (Portland, Ore.: Multnomah, 1989), 209–10.
27. Carson, *The Gagging of God,* 27.
28. For examples of religious pluralists who understand the exclusivist message of the Scripture, yet adjust its application and meaning to fit their pluralist agenda, see Paul Schrotenboer, "Varieties of Pluralism," *Evangelical Review of Theology* 13.2 (1989): 117.

Chapter 23

1. R. J. Rummel, *Death by Government* (New Brunswick, N.J.: Transaction, 1994), 9. See Tim LaHaye's chapter, "The Spiritual War for the Soul of the West" for a similar assessment by former U.S. foreign policy advisor Zbigniew Brzezinski.
2. Ibid., 13.
3. David Horowitz, *Radical Son: A Journey Through Our Times* (New York: Free Press, 1997), 405. For those interested in further study in this area see Martin Jay, *The Dialectical Imagination: A History of the Frankfurt School and the Institute of Social Research, 1923–1950* (Berkeley, Calif.: University of California Press, 1973). See Ludwig von Mises, *Socialism* (Indianapolis, Ind.: Liberty Classics, 1981), esp. p. 523 for background on Critical Theory. The socialist tactic of painting enemies as fascists or Nazis is readily seen in the influential work by Marxist Theodor W. Adorno, *The Authoritarian Personality* (New York: Norton, 1983).
4. James C. Dobson and Gary L. Bauer, *Children at Risk* (Dallas, Tex.: Word, 1990), 22.
5. Richard John Neuhaus, *The Naked Public Square: Religion and Democracy in America* (Grand Rapids: Eerdmans, 1984,1986). Nancy R. Pearcey and Charles B. Thaxton, *The*

Soul of Science: Christian Faith and Natural Philosophy (Wheaton, Ill.: Crossway, 1994), 19, "In the late nineteenth-century [ca 1893] England, several small groups of scientists and scholars organized under the leadership of Thomas H. Huxley to overthrow the cultural dominance of Christianity—particularly the intellectual dominance of the Anglican church. Their goal was to secularize society, replacing the Christian worldview with scientific naturalism, a worldview that recognizes the existence of nature alone." The British Fabian Society was also heavily involved in replacing Christianity with socialism. "Socialism was demonstrably conceived as an universal 'religion' and 'faith' . . . based on the religion of scientific humanism." M. Margaret McCarran, *Fabianism in the Political Life of Britain, 1919–1931* (Chicago: Heritage Foundation, 1954), 50.

6. David C. Large, *Where Ghosts Walked: Munich's Road to the Third Reich* (New York: Norton, 1997), 245–46.

7. Ibid., 76f.

8. Mises, *Socialism*, 530.

9. Ibid., 190.

10. Phillip E. Johnson, *Reason in the Balance: The Case Against Naturalism in Science, Law and Education* (Downers Grove, Ill.: InterVarsity, 1995).

11. Ian T. Taylor, *In the Minds of Men: Darwin and the New World Order* (Toronto: TFE, 1984), 409.

12. For a complete understanding of socialism we recommend Ludwig von Mises, *Socialism*.

13. Friedrich A. Hayek, *The Road to Serfdom* (Chicago: University of Chicago Press, 1944), 28.

14. Hans Kohn, *The Mind of Germany* (New York: Harper and Row, 1960); quoted in Richard Vetterli and William E. Fort Jr., *The Socialist Revolution* (Los Angeles: Clute International, 1968), 88.

15. Ibid., 87.

16. John Robbins, *The Trinity Review* (February 1998).

17. Ibid.

18. Ibid.

19. See Gene Edward Veith Jr., *Modern Fascism: Liquidating the Judeo-Christian Worldview* (St. Louis: Concordia, 1993), 53–54. Veith discusses the role of the theologians in the rise of Hitler's National Socialism.

20. Ibid., 61f.

21. Jay, *Dialectical Imagination*, 24–25. For an insightful look at Tillich, see Hannah Tillich, *From Time to Time* (New York: Scarborough, 1973). Tillich was a radical Marxist theologian and a libertine.

22. Franklin H. Littell and Hubert G. Locke, ed., *The German Church Struggle and the Holocaust* (Detroit: Wayne State University Press, 1974), 24, quoted in Veith, *Modern Fascism*, 71.

23. Michael J. Wilkins and J. P. Moreland, *Jesus Under Fire: Modern Scholarship Reinvents the Historical Jesus* (Grand Rapids: Zondervan, 1995), 145.

24. Stanley G. Payne, *A History of Fascism, 1914–1945* (Madison, Wis.: University of Wisconsin Press, 1995), 485–86.

25. A. E. Wilder-Smith, *Man's Origin, Man's Destiny: A Critical Survey of the Principles of Evolution and Christianity* (repr. ed. E.T., San Diego: CLP 1975), 191.

26. Ibid., 186.

27. Z. Dobbs, *The Great Deceit: Social Pseudo-Sciences and Keynes at Harvard* (West Sayville, N.Y.: Veritas Foundation, 1964), 143.

28. Ibid., 144.

29. Veith, *Modern Fascism*, 26. Veith says, "The influence of Marxist scholarship has severely

distorted our understanding of fascism. Communism and fascism were rival brands of socialism." Mises (*Socialism*, 523) adds,

> It is of much greater consequence that the communists have succeeded in changing the semantic connotation of the term Fascism. Fascism, as will be shown later, was a variety of Italian socialism. If one wants to assign Fascism and Nazism to the same class of political systems, one must call this class dictatorial regime and one must not neglect to assign the Soviets to the same class. In recent years the communists' semantic innovations have gone even further. They call everybody whom they dislike, every advocate of the free enterprise system, a Fascist.

30. Fort, *Socialist Revolution*, 57.
31. Mises, *Socialism*, 525.
32. Fort, *Socialist Revolution*, 68.
33. Gene Edward Veith Jr., *Postmodern Times: A Christian Guide to Contemporary Thought and Culture* (Wheaton, Ill.: Crossway, 1994); Dennis McCallum, ed., *The Death of Truth* (Minneapolis: Bethany House, 1996); Lawrence Cahoone, *From Modernism to Postmodernism: An Anthology* (Cambridge: Blackwell, 1996); and Thomas C. Oden, *After Modernity . . . What?* (Grand Rapids: Zondervan, 1990).
34. For a more in-depth analysis of communism, see David A. Noebel, *Understanding the Times: The Religious Worldviews of Our Day and the Search for Truth* (Colorado Springs,: Christian Schools International, 1995).
35. Rummel, *Death by Government*, 8.
36. Josef Stalin, *Works* (Moscow and London: International, 1952–53), 1:304. Cited in Gustav A. Wetter, *Dialectical Materialism: A Historical and Systematic Survey of Philosophy in the Soviet Union* (Westport, Conn.: Greenwood, 1973), 325.
37. Karl Marx, *The Communist Manifesto* (Chicago: Henry Regnery, 1954), 30.
38. Ibid., 53–54.
39. For further discussion by the author of dialectical materialism, see David A. Noebel, *Understanding the Times: The Religious Worldviews of Our Day and the Search for Truth* (Eugene, Ore.: Harvest House, 1991), ch. 7.
40. V. I. Lenin, *Materialism and Empirio-Criticism* (New York: International Publishers, 1927), 34.
41. Marx, *The Communist Manifesto*, 54.
42. Ibid., 33.
43. Karl Marx and Frederick Engels, *Collected Works*, 40 vols. (New York: International Publishers, 1976), 6:494–95.
44. Malachi Martin, *The Keys of This Blood* (New York: Simon and Schuster, 1990), 177.
45. John Dewey, *A Common Faith* (New Haven, Conn.: Yale University Press, 1934), 87. For proof that secular humanism is a religion, see David A. Noebel, *Clergy in the Classroom* (Manitou Springs, Colo.: Summit, 1995).
46. Elasah Drogin, *Margaret Sanger: Father of Modern Society* (New Hope, Ky: CUL, 1986), 9.
47. Ibid., 38.
48. Ibid., 87.
49. Lena Levine, *Planned Parenthood News* (summer 1953): 10.
50. Sherri Tepper, *You've Changed the Combination* (Denver: Rocky Mountain Planned Parenthood, 1974).
51. George Grant, *Grand Illusions* (Brentwood, Tenn.: Wolgemuth and Hyatt, 1988), 49.
52. Ibid., 96.

53. Charles Francis Potter, *Humanism: A New Religion* (New York: Simon and Schuster, 1930), 128.
54. *Torcaso v. Watkins* (19 June 1961): "Among religions in this country which do not teach what would generally be considered a belief in the existence of God are Buddhism, Taoism, Ethical Culture, Secular Humanism and others." How this situation came about is told in Dobbs, *The Great Deceit: Social Pseudo-Sciences and Keynes at Harvard.* This study traces how a loose coalition of political and social humanist liberals slowly captured U.S. institutions by dominating social science education. They came to influence even teaching from pulpits. This study was conducted by the Veritas Foundation. For additional information on America's educational leftward slant from Dewey through George Counts, Harold Rugg, Benjamin Bloom, Brock Chisholm, and Chester Pierce, see John A. Stormer, *None Dare Call It Education* (Florissant, Mo.: Liberty Bell, 1998).
55. Paul Kurtz, *The Humanist Alternative* (Buffalo, N.Y.: Prometheus, 1973), 177.
56. Corliss Lamont; cited in Roger E. Greeley, ed., *The Best of Humanism* (Buffalo, N.Y.: Prometheus, 1988), 149.
57. William Provine, *The Scientist*, 5 September 5 1988, 10.
58. Carl Sagan, *The Dragons of Eden* (New York: Random House, 1977), 6.
59. Carl Rogers, *Journal of Humanistic Psychology*, summer 1982, 8.
60. Lawrence Casler, *The Humanist*, March–April 1974, 4.
61. Delos B. McKown, *The Humanist*, May–June 1989, 24.
62. Julian Huxley, *The Humanist*, March–April 1979, 35.
63. Paul Kurtz, ed., *Humanist Manifesto I* (Buffalo, N.Y.: Prometheus Books, 1980), 10.
64. Will and Ariel Durant, *The Lessons of History* (New York: Simon and Schuster, 1968), 18.
65. Ibid., 81.
66. Erwin W. Lutzer, *Hitler's Cross* (Chicago: Moody, 1995), 205.
67. Ibid., 201.
68. Ibid., 173-74.
69. A defense of the Christian worldview can be found in such volumes as Carl F. H. Henry, *God, Revelation, and Authority*, 6 vol. (Dallas, Tex.: Word, 1976-1983); J. P. Moreland, *Love Your God with All Your Mind* (Colorado Springs: NavPress, 1997); Ronald H. Nash, *Worldviews in Conflict: Choosing Christianity in a World of Ideas* (Grand Rapids: Zondervan, 1992); David A. Noebel, *Understanding the Times;* W. Gary Phillips and William E. Brown, *Making Sense of Your World* (Chicago: Moody, 1991); and Michael J. Wilkins and J. P. Moreland, eds., *Jesus Under Fire: Modern Scholarship Reinvents the Historical Jesus* (Grand Rapids: Zondervan, 1995). One author who has specialized in apologetics and worldview philosophy is Norman L. Geisler. See his *Baker Encyclopedia of Christian Apologetics* (Grand Rapids: Baker, 1997) and *Christian Ethics: Options and Issues* (Grand Rapids: Baker, 1990). See also Geisler and Thomas Howe, *When Critics Ask* (Grand Rapids: Baker, 1992); Geisler and Ron Brooks, *When Skeptics Ask: A Handbook on Christian Evidences* (Grand Rapids: Baker, 1996); and Geisler and Frank Turek, *Legislating Morality* (Minneapolis: Bethany House, 1998).
70. Lutzer, *Hitler's Cross,* 204.

Chapter 24

1. This essay comments most directly on the cultural situation in the United States and Canada and to some extent the U.K. and the spiritual devastation of northern Europe. Christians in other areas of the globe will, however, see helpful principles in this analysis and the same challenges to heed within their own cultural warfare.

2. Unless otherwise noted, Scripture references and quotations in this chapter are from *The New King James Version* of the Bible.
3. George Washington, "Address to Congress," 17 September 1796.
4. Quoted in David Barton, *America: To Pray or Not to Pray?* (Aledo, Tex.: WallBuilder, 1991), 9.
5. Alexis de Tocqueville, *Democracy in America* (repr. ed. E.T., New York: Vintage, 1945), 1:23, 314–15, 319.
6. Tim LaHaye, *The Battle for the Mind* (Sisters, Ore.: Multnomah, 1997); idem., *A Nation Without a Conscience* (Sisters, Ore.: Multnomah, 1997).
7. For further analysis of the reasons for the bloodbath of the twentieth century, see David A. Noebel's chapter in this volume, "The Worldviews of Destruction in the Twentieth Century." Noebel quotes R. J. Rummel, *Death by Government* (New Brunswick, N.J.: Transaction, 1994), who estimated that by 1988 the number killed by governments during the twentieth century had been no fewer than 180 million and possibly many more.
8. Augustine developed the metaphor of the two cities in *The City of God*.
9. The uniqueness of Christ's actions and power are one proof that he was not just a man. He was literally what he said he was and what the prophets had said he would be—"the Son of God." For other proofs see Tim LaHaye, *Jesus: Who Is He?* (Sisters, Ore.: Multnomah, 1997).

Chapter 25

1. D. A. Lyon, "Technology," in David J. Atkinson and David Field, eds., *The New Dictionary of Christian Ethics and Pastoral Theology* (Downers Grove, Ill.: InterVarsity, 1995).
2. David C. Lindberg, *The Beginnings of Western Science: The European Scientific Tradition in Philosophical, Religious, and Institutional Context, 600 b.c. to a.d. 1450* (Chicago: University of Chicago Press, 1992), 149–52.
3. Georges Duby, *The Age of the Cathedrals: Art and Society, 980–1420*, trans. Eleanor Levieux and Barbara Thompson (Chicago: University of Chicago Press, 1981), 146–65.
4. For much of the framework and thought of this essay, I am indebted to Stephen V. Monsma et al., *Responsible Technology: A Christian Perspective* (Grand Rapids: Eerdmans, 1986).
5. Jeremy Rifkin, *The End of Work* (New York: G. P. Putnam's Sons, 1995), 42. Rifkin offers a critique from the perspective that technology tends to be harmful to the global economy. For another evaluation of technology's unintended consequences in society, see Edward Tenner, *Why Things Bite Back* (New York: Vintage, 1996).
6. Rifkin, *The End of Work*, 42
7. Ibid., 44. Rifkin further argues that during the last half of the nineteenth century there was an ideological shift due to technology. As a result, "the technological vision had succeeded in converting the American masses from foot soldiers for the Lord to factors of production and from sentient beings created in the likeness of God to tools fashioned in the image of machines" (44–45).
8. Notable exceptions to this trend are Monsma, *Responsible Technology*, and Egbert Schuurman, *Technology and the Future: A Philosophical Challenge* (Toronto: Wedge, 1980). From a broader Christian perspective, two excellent works are Carl Mitcham and Jim Grote, eds., *Theology and Technology: Essays in Christian Analysis and Exegesis* (Lanham, Md.: University Press, 1984) and David H. Hopper, *Technology, Theology, and the Idea of Progress* (Louisville: Westminster/John Knox, 1991).
9. Monsma, *Responsible Technology*, 43–44.

10. Carl F. H. Henry, *New Strides of Faith* (Chicago: Moody, 1972), 129, 132.

11. Issues related to high technology warfare and the ethics of warfare, especially the Christian just war theory, are beyond the scope of this essay but should not be overlooked. Technology is once again transforming the battlefield and raises crucial questions that need a biblical response.

12. Ian Barbour, *Ethics in an Age of Technology* (San Francisco: HarperCollins, 1993), 3.

13. Charles Susskind, *Understanding Technology* (Baltimore: Johns Hopkins University Press, 1973), 132.

14. John Zerman and Alice Carnes, eds., *Questioning Technology* (Santa Cruz, Calif.: New Society Publishers, 1991), 217.

15. C. S. Lewis, *The Abolition of Man* (New York: Macmillan, 1965), 69.

16. Barbour, *Ethics in an Age of Technology*, 4–8.

17. Ibid., 8–10.

18. Ibid., 10–12.

19. Ibid., 12–15.

20. Ibid., 15.

21. Ibid.

22. Ibid., 18.

23. For consideration of how technology relates to justice, see George P. Grant, *Technology and Justice*, (Notre Dame, Ind.: University of Notre Dame Press, 1986).

24. David W. Gill, "Technology," in Robert Banks and R. Paul Stevens, eds., *The Complete Book of Everyday Christianity* (Downers Grove, Ill.: InterVarsity, 1997), 1017.

25. Lyon, "Technology," 833.

26. Ibid., 834.

27. Monsma, *Responsible Technology*, 49.

28. Lyon, "Technology," 834.

29. Monsma, *Responsible Technology*, 50, 58.

30. Ibid., 162. On a similar note, Dutch philosopher Schuurman writes of the Reformation perspective: "What one finds in the Reformation is an effort to return to the original command given humanity to dress and keep the creation. The Reformation views nature as *created* nature and has once and for all rejected any deified nature that might be reckoned untouchable. From a Christian standpoint, then, all technology, including modern technology, pertains to the service and glory of God. In modern humanism, however, this view has been secularized so that technology exists for and around humankind. Is it not precisely this that has proven so disruptive, that as autonomous humanity progressively set its stamp upon technological development, technology became an autonomous power set against humanity?" (354).

31. Monsma, *Responsible Technology*, 200.

32. Ibid., 59–68.

33. Ibid., 62–64.

34. Ibid., 62.

35. Ibid., 65–66.

36. Ibid., 66.

37. Ibid., 67.

38. Ibid., 68–69. Monsma writes: Thus a starting point is to ask—whether as a researcher, designer, fabricator, distributor, purchaser, or user of a technological object—if that object uses entities from God's creation in a manner that respects their God-given nature and purposes, and if it increases human beings' opportunities to be the joyful, loving, creative beings God intends them to be. Technological activities that are in keeping with the command to love and attempt to meet these two criteria help make possible

humanity's search for God's kingdom of shalom, a kingdom of activity, dynamism, and vibrancy, but also a kingdom of peace, harmony, and joy" (69).

39. These seven principles incorporate Monsma's eight principles, combining information and communication. See Monsma, *Responsible Technology*, 71–76, 170–77. For another perspective that upholds many of the same concerns, see Barbour, *Ethics in an Age of Technology*, 41–46.

40. Robert A. Wauzzinski, "Technological Optimism," *Perspectives on Science and Christian Faith* 48, no. 3 (September 1996): 150.

41. This is not condemn the accomplishments or motives of those working in the sciences nor denigrate their work. Scientists Enzo Russo and David Cove write: "The moral obligation of scientists is to inform the general public of the possible ways that scientific knowledge can be used and misused. Decisions over how scientific knowledge is used are independent of the knowledge and should be taken independently. Each of us has the moral obligation to understand more about what scientists are learning, how this scientific knowledge can be transformed into technology, how these new technologies could be misused and what could be done to avoid this potential misuse. This is the price we have to pay for having eaten from the tree of knowledge, as we are reminded in Genesis. To stop scientific research is both impossible and unwise. To slow down technological 'progress', may be very wise." *Genetic Engineering: Dreams and Nightmares* (Oxford: W. H. Freeman, 1995), 207.

42. Craig M. Gay, *The Way of the (Modern) World* (Grand Rapids: Eerdmans, 1998), 81.

43. Ibid., 82.

44. For a compact survey of bioethical issues from a Christian perspective, see volumes in the Bio Basics series, ed. Gary P. Stewart (Grand Rapids: Kregel, 1998). See also Timothy J. Demy and Gary P. Stewart, eds., *Genetic Engineering: A Christian Response* (Grand Rapids: Kregel, 1999).

45. John Polkinghorne, "Cloning and the Moral Imperative," in Ronald Cole-Turner, ed., *Human Cloning: Religious Responses* (Louisville: Westminster-John Knox, 1997), 42.

46. R. Albert Mohler Jr., "The Brave New World of Cloning: A Christian Worldview Perspective," in Ronald Cole-Turner, ed., *Human Cloning: Religious Responses* (Louisville: Westminster John Knox Press, 1997), 103.

47. Ibid.

48. Leo Alexander, "Medical Science under Dictatorship," *New England Journal of Medicine* 241.2 (July 1947): 39–47.

49. Rifkin, *The End of Work*, 5.

50. Thomas D. Ice and Timothy J. Demy, *The Coming Cashless Society* (Eugene, Ore.: Harvest House, 1996), 152–53.

51. Alvin Toffler, *Powershift: Knowledge, Wealth, and Violence at the Edge of the Twenty-First Century* (New York: Bantam, 1990), 20.

52. "The Wired World Atlas," *Wired*, November 1996, 162.

53. The propensity of some interpreters of prophecy, often within pretribulationism (which is the view this author holds), to seek to identify current technologies and weapons with the vocabulary of the biblical text is misguided and an aberration of consistent hermeneutical principles. At whatever point in human history the final events of Revelation transpire, the technology available at that time will be used. The preoccupation of many prophecy students with technology and the tribulation has unintentionally undermined premillennialism.

54. Roger L. Shinn, "Between Eden and Babel," in *Human Cloning*, 117.

55. Gill, "Technology," 1017.

56. Carl F. H. Henry, *Carl Henry at His Best* (Portland, Ore.: Multnomah, 1989), 28.

57. Carl Mitchum, "Technology and Ethics: From Expertise to Public Participation," *The World and I*, March 1996, 329.
58. Barbour, *Ethics in an Age of Technology*, 223.
59. Monsma, *Responsible Technology*, 209–17.
60. Ibid., 217.
61. Gay, *The Way of the (Modern) World*, 129.
62. Daniel J. Boorstin, *The Discoverers* (New York: Random House, 1983), 36.

Chapter 26

1. Lewis Sperry Chafer, *Systematic Theology*, 8 vols. (Dallas: Dallas Seminary Press, 1948), 2:77.
2. Unless otherwise noted, all Scripture references and quotations in this chapter are from the *New American Standard Bible*.
3. David F. Wells, *No Place for Truth: Or Whatever Happened to Evangelical Theology?* (Grand Rapids: Eerdmans, 1993), 135–36.
4. Ibid., 7.
5. Ibid., 95.
6. Rousas John Rushdoony, *Revolt Against Maturity* (Fairfax, Va.: Thoburn, 1977), 335.
7. Samuel J. Andrews, *Christianity and Anti-Christianity in Their Final Conflict* (Chicago: Bible Institute Colportage, 1898), 253–57.
8. Arthur L. Johnson, *Faith Misguided: Exposing the Dangers of Mysticism* (Chicago: Moody, 1988), 26.
9. Timothy Crater, "The Filling of the Spirit in the New Testament," (unpub. Th.M. thesis, Dallas Theological Seminary, 1971), 45.
10. Ibid., 46.
11. Some of the above material on the filling of the Holy Spirit was gleaned from Dwight Allen Ekholm, "The Doctrine of the Christian's Walk in the Spirit" (unpub. Th.M. thesis, Dallas Theological Seminary, 1973).

Chapter 27

1. Kerby Anderson, *Probe Perspectives* (Richardson, Tex.: Probe Ministries, 1996), 3.
2. Quoted in ibid., 3–4.
3. Raymond C. Ortlund Jr., "Male-Female Equality and Male Headship," in John Piper and Wayne Grudem, eds., *Recovering Biblical Manhood and Womanhood: A Response to Evangelical Feminism* (Wheaton, Ill.: Crossway, 1991), 95.
4. Ibid.
5. Ibid.
6. Ibid., 98.
7. Ibid., 99.
8. Carl Schultz, "ʿēzer," in *TWOT*.
9. Unless otherwise noted, Scripture references and quotations in this chapter are from the *New American Standard Bible*.
10. Ortlund, "Male-Female Equality and Male Headship," 101–2.
11. H. C. Leupold, *Exposition of Genesis*, 2 vols. (repr. ed., Grand Rapids: Baker, 1949), 1:172.
12. Robert D. Culver, "māshal," in *TWOT*.
13. Leupold, *Exposition of Genesis*, 175.
14. R. Kent Hughes, *Disciplines of a Godly Man* (Wheaton, Ill.: Crossway, 1991), 36.

15. Fritz Rienecker, *Linguistic Key to the Greek New Testament* (Grand Rapids: Zondervan, 1976, 1980), 622, quoting G. Abbott-Smith, *A Manual Greek Lexicon of the New Testament* (Edinburgh: T & T Clark, 1936); James Hope Moulton and George Milligan, *The Vocabulary of the Greek New Testament* (London: Hodder & Stoughton, 1952); and Friedrich Priesigke, *Wörterbuch der griechischen Papyrus-surkunden* (Heidelberg-Berlin, 1924–31).

16. Some have found it hard to reconcile Paul's statement of mutual submission in verse 21 with the following discussion of submission by wives to husbands (vv. 22–23). They find it contradictory. George W. Knight III gives a helpful explanation in his article, "Husbands and Wives as Analogues of Christ and the Church," in Piper and Gruden, eds., *Recovering Biblical Manhood & Womanhood*, 167. He writes:

> Verse 21 states a general and comprehensive principle before Paul moves to the specific roles of husbands and wives, parents and children, and masters and slaves, so that the specific is considered in the light of the general. . . . Paul reminds all in the congregation of their need for mutual submission in the Body of Christ before writing of the specific duties each has in his particular situation. This seems to do . . . justice to the reciprocal pronoun used, "one another" (*allēlon*). Furthermore, it is in line with the contextual understanding found elsewhere in Paul and Peter where a similar exhortation is given [Phil. 2:3; 1 Peter 5:5].

17. C. F. Keil and F. Delitzsch, *Commentary on the Old Testament*, 10 vols. (Peabody, Mass.: Hendrickson, 1989), 1:90–91.

18. Leupold, *Exposition of Genesis*, 1:137.

19. Ortlund, "Male-Female Equality and Male Headship," 95.

20. John F. MacArthur Jr., *The Family* (Chicago: Moody, 1982), 57–58.

21. Ibid., 59.

22. Ibid., 66.

23. Hughes, *Disciplines of a Godly Man*, 40.

24. MacArthur, *Family*, 68.

25. George W. Knight III, "The Family and the Church: How Should Biblical Manhood and Womanhood Work Out in Practice," in Piper and Grudem, eds., *Recovering Biblical Manhood and Womanhood*, 349.

26. MacArthur, *Family*, 100–102.

27. Rienecker, *Linguistic Key*, quoting R. C. Trench, ed., *Synonyms of the New Testament* (Grand Rapids: Eerdmans, 1953).

28. Ibid., 756.

29. A. T. Robertson, *Word Pictures in the New Testament* (Nashville, Tenn.: Broadman, 1930), 1:41.

30. R. C. H. Lenski, *The Interpretation of 1 and 2 Epistles of Peter, the Three Epistles of John, and the Epistle of Jude* (Minneapolis: Augsburg, 1966), 132–33.

31. Rienecker, *Linguistic Key*, 538, quoting A. T. Robertson, *Word Pictures in the New Testament* (repr. ed., Grand Rapids: Baker, 1982) *TDNT;* and Marcus Barth, *Ephesians,* in The Anchor Bible (Garden City, N.Y.: Doubleday, 1974).

32. Mary Kassian, *Women, Creation, and the Fall* (Westchester, Ill.: Good News, 1990), 74.

33. R. C. H. Lenski, *The Interpretation of St. Paul's Epistles to the Colossians, to the Thessalonians, to Timothy, to Titus, and to Philemon* (Minneapolis: Augsburg, 1966), 573.

34. BAGD, 561.

35. MacArthur, *Family*, 83.

36. Ibid., 82–83.
37. Ibid., 87.
38. Ibid., 88.
39. Joyce Brothers, *Washington Times,* 23 June 1988, E-1.

Chapter 28

1. All Scripture references and quotations are from the King James Version of the Bible.
2. Franz Delitzsch, *Biblical Commentary on the Psalms,* trans. Francis Bolton, 2 vols. (Grand Rapids: Eerdmans, 1959), 2:137.

Chapter 29

1. Joseph Story, *Familiar Exposition of the Constitution* (New York: Harper, 1862).
2. Joseph Story, *Commentaries on the Constitution of the United States,* 2d ed. (Boston: Little and Brown, 1851), vol. 2, sec. 1874, p. 593; cited in Robert L. Cord, *The Separation of Church and State* (Grand Rapids: Baker, 1988), 13.
3. The meaning of "religion" in the establishment clause is viewed as absolute by the courts, whereas "religion" in free exercise is limited. The right to believe is absolute, but the right to practice one's belief is necessarily limited. The Court enunciated this free exercise belief-action dichotomy in the *Cantwell* decision, in which Justice Roberts explained, "The amendment raises two concepts—freedom to believe and freedom to act. The first is absolute, but, in the nature of things, the second cannot be. Conduct remains subject to regulation for the protection of society. The freedom to act must have appropriate definition to preserve the enforcement of that protection. In every case the power to regulate must be so exercised as not, in attaining a permissible end, unduly to infringe the protected freedom." *Cantwell v. Connecticut,* 310 U.S. 296, 303-4 (1940).
4. Those unfamiliar with the U.S. government system should understand that the national constitution originally invested most governing responsibility in the states. The first ten amendments to the Constitution, called the Bill of Rights, were added immediately to further limit the power of national government over individuals. The American Civil War (1861-65) shifted most power from state to federal government. From its *Everson* decision on, the U.S. Supreme Court has held that the establishment clause, as incorporated through the Fourteenth Amendment, gave dominant authority over religious liberty to the national government. The difficulty with applying this clause against the states is that some states had established churches when the Constitution was written. This has been answered by Brennan in *Schempp,* "It has been suggested, with some support in history, that [incorporation of the establishment clause] is conceptually impossible because the Framers meant the [clause] also to foreclose any attempt by Congress to disestablish the existing official state churches. [But] the last of the formal state establishments was dissolved more than three decades before the Fourteenth Amendment was ratified, and thus the problem of protecting official state churches from federal encroachments could hardly have been any concern of those who framed the post-Civil War Amendments." Quoted in Gerald Gunther and K. Sullivan, *Constitutional Law,* University Casebook Series, 13th ed. (Mineola, N.Y.: Foundation, 1997), 1466-67.
5. See Presser, "Some Realism About Atheism: Responses to the Godless Constitution" *Texas Review of Law and Politics* (1997): 87, 121 (interacting with the perspectives of Kramnick and Moore regarding whether the Framers intended a purely secular Constitution and government).

6. The term "separation of church and state" is not found in the First Amendment, but if read literally would more accurately reflect the meaning of the First Amendment, that is, the separation of the institution of the church from the institution of the state. The term does not speak to the matter of religious influences on governmental views and functions, nor to accommodations or benefits that the government may give to religious citizens and causes that are religious in nature.

7. Robert Bork, *Slouching Towards Gomorrah: Modern Liberalism and American Decline* (New York: HarperCollins, 1996), 277.

8. Ibid., 174.

9. I. Kramnick and Robert Laurence Moore, *The Godless Constitution: The Case Against Religious Correctness* (New York, W. W. Norton, 1996).

10. See Presser "Some Realism About Atheism," 91, (interacting with the perspectives of Kramnick and Moore). Also see the interaction between Kramnick and Moore and Dreisbach: I. Kramnick and R. L. Moore, "Our Godless Constitution," *Liberty* (May–June 1996): 12; D. L. Dreisbach, "A Godless Constitution," *Liberty* (November–December 1996): 11; and D. L. Dreisbach, *Liberty* (March–April 1996): 11. See also by Dreisbach, "In Search of a Christian Commonwealth: An Examination of Selected Nineteenth-Century Commentaries on References to God and the Christian Religion in the United States Constitution," *Baylor Law Review* (1996): 48.

11. Quoted in Robert D. Linder, "Civil Religion in Historical Perspective: The Reality That Underlies the Concept," *Journal of Church and State* (1975): 399, 403.

12. Socrates was condemned to death by an Athenian jury in 399 B.C. on a charge of "introducing strange gods and corrupting the youth of the city-state. Whether these were trumped-up charges against a man who professed reverence for the laws of Athens, there is no doubt that he had attacked the religio-political order of the day." Ibid., 406.

13. See Everett Ferguson, *Backgrounds of Early Christianity* (Grand Rapids: Eerdmans, 1987) 153–65, for a good description of the "ruler cult" in the Hellenistic world, culminating in the Roman emperor cult. See also Harold O. J. Brown, "Civil Authority and the Bible," in H. Wayne House, ed., *The Christian and American Law* (Grand Rapids: Kregel, 1998), 112.

14. Walter Ullmann, *Law and Jurisprudence in the Middle Ages* (repr. ed., London: Gower, 1988), 32.

15. This is not to deny that other influences were at work. The argument is that these were the major sources of influence on the issue of law and religion.

16. John C. H. Wu, quoted in David Armstrong, "Law, Politics & the Social Sciences—A Troubled Trinity," *Simon Greenleaf Law Review* 131 (1984–1985): "The common law has one advantage over the legal system of any country: it was Christian from the very beginning of its history." See William Banner, "When Christianity Was Part of the Common Law," *Law and History Review* (1998): 27n. Banner argues that there was a connection between Christianity and common law, but Christian ideology was not a controlling influence on legislative development.

17. John Witte and John Arthur, "The Three Uses of the Law: A Protestant Source of the Purposes of Criminal Law?" *Journal of Law and Religion*: 433. Witte and Arthur argue that the third (restraining) use of the law in Reformation theology, provided the basis for criminal punishment.

18. Special Committee on the Tort Liability System, *Towards a Jurisprudence of Injury: The Continuing Creation of a System of Substantive Justice in American Tort Law*, Committee Preface (1984), quoted in Cook, "Negligence or Strict Liability? A Study in Biblical Tort Law," *Whittier Law Review* 1 (1992): 13: "So far as we know, there is no word in the Bible for 'torts.' Yet the 'norms' which the Creator told Moses to set before the Israelites, in the chapter of Exodus following the Ten Commandments, are filled with

what we think of as 'tort' rules. . . . We have indicated the depth of the roots of tort law in the Judeo-Christian tradition."

19. John Locke, *Of Civil Government*, quoted in John Eidsmoe, *Christianity and the Constitution: The Faith of Our Founding Fathers* (Grand Rapids: Baker, 1987), 39.

20. Ibid., at 11–33.

21. John C. H. Wu, *Fountain of Justice: A Study in the Natural Law* 65 (1955), quoted in Herbert W. Titus, *Revelation: Foundation for the Common Law, Regent University Law Review* 1 (1994): 4. See Banner, "When Christianity Was Part of the Common Law," *Law and History Review* (1998): 27, who argues that there was no uniform opinion at the beginning of the nineteenth century as to whether the common law embodied Christianity. Thomas Jefferson resisted the Christianity-law connection, but a cadre of legal scholars contradicted him. See discussion of this controversy in Dreisbach, 988–92.

22. Donald S Lutz and Charles S. Hyneman reviewed fifteen thousand items in the political writings between 1760–1805, reading closely twenty-two hundred with explicitly political content. Included were books, pamphlets, newspaper articles, and monographs printed for public consumption. Lutz, 191n; also see Charles S. Hyneman and Donald S. Lutz, eds., *American Political Writing During the Founding Era 1760–1805*, 2 vols. (Indianapolis: Liberty Fund, 1983).

23. The Enlightenment may be divided into at least three periods: the first represented by such men as Montesquieu, Locke, and Pufendorf; the second by Voltaire, Diderot, and Helvetius; and the third by Beccaria, Rousseau, Mably, and Raynal. Donald S. Lutz, "The Relative Influence of European Writers on Late Eighteenth-Century American Political Thought," *American Political Science Review* (1984): 289–90.

24. This idea was held by Augustine, Thomas Aquinas, and Samuel Rutherford in *Lex Rex*. Martin Luther King Jr. adopted it, citing Aquinas that "an unjust law is a human law that is not rooted in eternal law and natural law." Martin Luther King Jr., *Why We Can't Wait* (1964), 85. King writes, "All segregation statutes are unjust because segregation distorts the soul and damages the personality. It gives the segregator a false sense of inferiority. . . . Segregation is not only politically, economically, and sociologically unsound, it is morally wrong and sinful." Ironically, Austrian legal theorist Hans Kelsen stated that an unjust law is a contradiction in terms, because it is law that sets the standard for what is just. Indeed, the anti-Semite Adolf Hitler built his totalitarian philosophy around the Jewish Kelsen's arguments. Brown, "Civil Authority," 123.

25. Paul L. Hamlin, *Legal Education in Colonial New York* (1939; repr. ed., New York: Da Capo, 1970), 64–65. Lincoln said, "I never read anything which so profoundly interested and thrilled me." James M. Ogden, "Lincoln's Early Impressions of the Law in Indiana," *Notre Dame Law Review* (1932): 325–29.

26. The Bible's influence on law continued. For example, René Cassian and Charles Malik, leaders in developing the Universal Declaration of Human Rights, based these rights on the Ten Commandments. John W. Montgomery and Steven W. Webb, *Human Rights and Human Dignity* (New York: Probe, 1986), 275. This was confirmed when I attended the International Institute of Human Rights at the University of Strasbourg in July 1998. Two speakers—Boyle of the University of Essex and M. Camille Kuyu Mwissa of the Catholic University of Central Africa and University of Paris—specifically acknowledged the dependence of the Declaration on Christian views, though Boyle explained that resistance from Marxist countries caused the framers to make the language ambiguous. For other examples in the development of criminal law see Witte and Arthur, "Three Uses of the Law," 433. For examples in tort law see Cook, "Negligence or Strict Liability?" and for contract law see Harold J. Berman, "The Religious Sources of General Contract Law: An Historical Perspective," *Journal of Law and Religion* (1986): 103.

27. Hyneman and Lutz, eds., *American Political Writing*, 37. See also Dennis J. Mahoney, "The Declaration of Independence as a Constitutional Document," in Leonard W. Levy and Dennis J. Mahoney, eds., *The Framing and Ratification of the Constitution* (New York: Macmillan, 1987), 54, 65. Mahoney argues strongly that The Declaration of Independence is the preamble to the Constitution.

28. Approximately half of the delegates to the U.S. Constitutional Convention of 1787 had been representatives at their own state conventions. In these conventions the documents were replete with religious references. In the federal (not national) constitution, such references are largely omitted, since none really believed that the federal government should be involved in furthering religion. David E. Maas, "The Philosophical and Theological Roots of the Religious Roots of the Religious Clause," in Ronald A. Wells and Thomas A. Askew, eds., *Liberty and Law: American Life and Thought* (Grand Rapids: Eerdmans, 1987), 1, 7.

29. For reasons why some believe statements regarding God and the Christian religion are omitted from the Constitution, see *In Search of a Christian Commonwealth*, 955-64. Dreisbach examines the explicit and implicit references to God and the Christian religion in the Constitution on pages 964-94. For the meaning of the oath and religious test in the Constitution see "Philosophical and Theological Roots," 1-23.

30. McConnell, "The Origins and Historical Understanding of Free Exercise of Religion," *Harvard Law Review* (1990): 1409, 1473, quoted in *In Search of a Christian Commonwealth*, 983.

31. Ibid., 974-75.

32. R. C. Sproul, "The Biblical View of Submission to Constituted Authority," in H. Wayne House, ed., *The Christian and American Law*, 126-38. See also H. Wayne House, "The Christian's Duty of Civil Disobedience to the Government: Contemporary Struggles Between Christians and the State," in ibid., 139-74.

33. Pope Boniface VIII, *Unam Sanctum*, (1302), translated in Ernest F. Henderson, *Select Historical Documents of the Middle Ages* (repr. ed., New York: AMS, 1965), 435-37. Quoted in Eidsmoe, *Christianity and the Constitution*, 112.

34. Luther has often been viewed as placing reason and faith at opposite poles. See House, for a discussion of how Luther used the term *ratio*. H. Wayne House, "Luther's View of Apologetics," in *Concordia Theological Journal*.

35. John Calvin, *Institutes of the Christian Religion*, 1:116, quoted in Philip B. Kurland and Ralph Lerner, eds., *The Founders' Constitution*, 5 vols. (Chicago: University of Chicago Press, 1987), 44.

36. Calvin, quoted in Kurland and Lerner, eds., *Founders' Constitution*, 44.

37. King James II, instructions to Governor Thomas Dungan, quoted in *Founders' Constitution*, 52.

38. 330 U.S. (1947), 1.

39. *Separation of Church and State*, 9.

40. John Eidsmoe, *The Christian Legal Advisor* (Milford, Mich.: Mott Media, 1984), 151-52.

41. 330 U.S. (1947), 15-16.

42. Ibid., 18.

43. See 330 U.S. 26-27, 31-42.

44. 333 U.S. 203.

45. Ibid., 212.

46. Ibid., 211.

47. 370 U.S. 421.

48. Ibid., 428.

49. Ibid., 444.
50. 374 US. 203.
51. Ibid., 222.
52. *Lemon v. Kurtzman*, 403 U.S. (1971), 602, 612-13.
53. Ibid., 612-13.
54. See Bird, "Freedom From Establishment and Unneutrality in Public School Instruction and Religious School Regulation, 1979," *Harvard Journal of Law and Public Policy* (June 1979): 143-54.
55. 413 U.S. 756.
56. Ibid., 798.
57. 105 U.S. 2479.
58. Ibid., 2489. The *Agostini* decision uses the phrase "primary secular purpose."
59. 343 U.S. at 312, 314.
60. 473 U.S. 402, 413.
61. 473 U.S. 373.
62. *Meek v. Pittenger* (421 U.S. 329, 372).
63. Ibid., 391 (quoting *Zorach* v. *Clauson* [343 U.S. 306, 312]).
64. Ibid., 390.
65. Ibid., 389.
66. Ibid., 385.
67. Ibid., 393 (internal quotation marks omitted).
68. 473 U. S. 409.
69. *Agostini* (117 U.S. 2015). See, e.g., *Bowan v. Kendrick* (487 U.S. 615-17).
70. Ibid.

Chapter 30

1. Unless otherwise noted, Scripture references and quotations in this chapter are from the King James Version of the Bible.
2. In this construction the word for servant literally means "a liturgist." Use of this religious, priestly term, stresses the ministerial, worshipful aspect of government.
3. Παση/ ἀνθρωπίνη/ κτίσει, "every human institution or social institution," i.e., the state, the household, the family.
4. Διὰ τόν κύριον, "because of the Lord's example or because of the Lord's cause," i.e., the Christian cause.
5. Edward Gordon Selwyn, *The First Epistle of St. Peter,* Thornapple Commentaries, 2d ed. (Grand Rapids: Baker, 1981), 174.

Chapter 32

1. BAGD, 98.
2. Henry George Liddell and Robert Scott, comps., *A Greek-English Lexicon,* rev., H. S. Jones, 9th ed. (1940; repr. ed., London: Oxford University Press, 1990), 218-19.
3. George Gunn and Edward E. Hindson, "Apostasy," in Mal Couch, ed., *The Dictionary of Premillennial Theology* (Grand Rapids: Kregel, 1996).
4. Charles C. Ryrie, *Dispensationalism,* rev. ed. (Chicago: Moody, 1995), 140.
5. Ibid.
6. Ibid.
7. Jaca Book, *The Church in the Age of Humanism* (Minneapolis: Winston, 1981), 43b.
8. John Horsch, *Modern Religious Liberalism* (Chicago: Bible Institute Colportage, 1938), 9.

9. Ibid., 26.

10. Ibid., 28.

11. Ibid.

12. Arthur Pink, *The Sovereignty of God* (Grand Rapids: Baker, 1992), foreword.

13. Horsch, *Modern Religious Liberalism,* 220.

14. B. R. Hergenhahn and Matthew H. Olsen, *An Introduction to Theories of Personality,* 5th ed. (Upper Saddle River, N.J.: Prentice Hall, 1999), 473.

15. Mark Bleiweiss, *Jewish Spectator* 63.2 (fall 1998).

16. Ibid., 12.

17. Ibid., 14.

18. Edward E. Hindson, *Final Signs* (Eugene, Ore.: Harvest House, 1996), 189.

19. Faith Cook, *Grace in Winter* (Carlisle, Pa.: Banner of Truth, 1989), 75-76.

Chapter 33

1. Floyd Elmore, "Darby, John Nelson," in Mal Couch, ed., *The Dictionary of Premillennial Theology* (Grand Rapids: Kregel, 1996).

2. Mal Couch, "Rapture, Biblical Study of the," in *Dictionary of Premillennial Theology.*

3. For more on the following points, see Ibid.

4. John F. Walvoord, *The Rapture Question* (Grand Rapids: Zondervan, 1979), 73.

5. George Milligan, *St. Paul's Epistles to the Thessalonians* (Minneapolis, Minn.: Klock & Klock, 1980), 56.

6. Renald E. Showers, *Maranatha Our Lord, Come!* (Bellmawr, N.J.: Friends of Israel Gospel Ministry, Inc., 1995), 169.

7. Douglas Moo, *The Wycliffe Exegetical Commentary, Romans 1-8* (Chicago: Moody, 1991), 504.

8. Charles John Ellicott, ed., *Commentary on the Whole Bible* (Grand Rapids: Zondervan, 1959), 8:84.

Chapter 34

1. The specific form of premillennial teaching defended in this chapter, as throughout this volume, is traditional dispensational premillennialism.

2. Unless otherwise noted, Scripture references and quotations in this chapter are from the King James Version of the Bible.

3. Lewis Sperry Chafer, *Systematic Theology* (Grand Rapids: Kregel, 1993), 7:233.

4. J. Dwight Pentecost, *Things to Come* (Findlay, Ohio: Dunham, 1958), 507.

5. For extensive discussion of the glory of Christ in the millennium see Hoyt Chester Woodring Jr., "The Millennial Glory of Christ" (unpub. thesis, Dallas Theological Seminary), 62-134.

6. Cf. Merrill F. Unger, *Great Neglected Bible Prophecies* (Chicago: Scripture Press, 1955), 55-95; A. C. Gaebelein, *The Prophet Ezekiel* (New York: Our Hope, 1955), 271-73; and James M. Gray, *Christian Workers' Commentary* (New York: Revell, 1915), 265-66.

7. See John L. Mitchell, "The Question of Millennial Sacrifices," *Bibliotheca Sacra* (July 1953): 248-67; (October 1953): 342-61.

8. Gaebelein, *Prophet Ezekiel,* 312-13.

9. Gray, *Christian Workers' Commentary,* 268.

10. Cf. William Kelly, *Lectures of the Book of Revelation* (London: G. Morrish, n.d.), 459-90.

11. Chafer, *Systematic Theology,* 4:418-20, 427; 5:365-68.
12. Ibid., 5:360-61.

Chapter 35

1. Unless otherwise noted, Scripture references and quotations in this chapter are from the *New American Standard* version of the Bible.
2. A. H. Strong, *Systematic Theology* (Old Tappan, N.J.: Revell, 1969), 291.
3. James Montgomery Boice, *Foundations of the Christian Faith* (Downers Grove, Ill.: InterVarsity, 1986), 128.
4. Strong, *Systematic Theology,* 294.
5. Ibid., 297.
6. Charles Hodge, *Systematic Theology,* 3 vols. (repr. ed., Grand Rapids: Eerdmans, 1975), 1:417.
7. Louis Berkhof, *Systematic Theology* (London: Banner of Truth Trust, 1941), 731-32.
8. J. Dwight Pentecost, *Things to Come* (Grand Rapids: Dunham, 1964), 417.
9. John F. Walvoord, *Major Bible Prophecies* (Grand Rapids: Zondervan, 1991), 386.
10. Joseph Dillow, *The Reign of the Servant Kings* (Hayesville, N.C.: Schoettle, 1993), 73-82.
11. S. Lewis Johnson Jr., *A Case for Premillennialism: Evidence from Romans 9-11* (Chicago: Moody, 1992), 215.
12. Charles C. Ryrie, *Basic Theology* (Wheaton: Victor, 1988), 491.
13. Ibid., 514.
14. Robert Thomas, *Revelation 8-22: An Exegetical Commentary* (Chicago: Moody, 1995), 429.
15. Ibid., 430.
16. Pentecost, *Things to Come,* 424.
17. For more on this distinction, see Paul Benware, *Understanding End Times Prophecy* (Chicago: Moody, 1995), 306.

Chapter 36

1. Unless otherwise noted, Scripture references and quotations in this chapter are from the *New American Standard* version of the Bible.
2. Erich Sauer, *The Triumph of the Crucified* (Grand Rapids: Eerdmans, 1953), 181.
3. For a helpful discussion of the concept of eternity in philosophy and theology and a repudiation of Oscar Cullman's view that timeless eternity is unbiblical, see Carl F. H. Henry, "Eternity," in Walter A. Elwell, ed., *Evangelical Dictionary of Theology* (Grand Rapids: Baker, 1984).
4. In this view then the day of God begins (2 Peter 3:12) only after the day of the Lord ends (3:10). Buist M. Fanning believes that the day of the Lord and the day of God are identical. See Fanning's essay, "A Theology of Peter and Jude," in Roy B. Zuck, ed., *A Biblical Theology of the New Testament* (Chicago: Moody, 1994), 470. It is questionable that the "day of God" in its sole biblical occurrence (2 Peter 3:12) can be equated with the "day of the Lord" (cf. 2 Peter 3:10). The expressions "day of the Lord" and "that day" occur often. In its eschatological sense, the "day of the Lord" includes judgment associated with the return of Christ (e.g., Isa. 13:6-11; Joel 2:30-31; 3:14-16; Amos 5:18-20; Zeph. 1:14-18; Zech. 14:1; Mal. 4:5; Acts 2:20; 1 Thess. 5:1-3; 2 Thess. 2:1-4; Rev. 6:1-19:21). It also is used in reference to the blessing of Christ's millennial rule (e.g., Isa. 26:1-2; 29:18-24; Hosea 2:18-23; Joel 3:17-18; Micah 4:6-8; Zeph. 3:14-20; Zech. 2:11; 9:16; Rev. 20:1-6), and destruction of the millennial heavens and earth through fire (2 Peter 3:10; cf. Rev. 20:11; 21:1). Accordingly, Peter indicated that

"the day of the Lord will come like a thief [cf. 1 Thess. 5:2], in which the heavens will pass away with a roar and the elements will be destroyed with intense heat, and the earth and its works will be burned up" (2 Peter 3:10). The fiery destruction of the millennial heavens and earth occurs because of the advent of "the day of God" as 2 Peter 3:12 teaches: "Looking for and hastening the coming of the day of God, on account of which the heavens will be destroyed by burning, and the elements will melt with intense heat." Comments Charles Ryrie, "The destruction is in the Day of the Lord and as a preparation for the Day of God, which follows." Charles C. Ryrie, *Biblical Theology of the New Testament* (Chicago: Moody, 1959), 288.

5. David K. Lowery refers to "the eternal state that Paul cryptically described as God being 'all in all' (1 Cor. 15:28)." See Lowery's "A Theology of Paul's Missionary Epistles," in ibid., 297.

6. John F. Walvoord, "Revelation," in John F. Walvoord and Roy B. Zuck, eds., *The Bible Knowledge Commentary, New Testament* (Wheaton, Ill.: Victor, 1983), 983. God's promise in Haggai 2:6 is quoted in Hebrews 12:26, "Yet once more I will shake not only the earth, but also the heaven." According to the author of Hebrews, this quote "denotes the removing of those things which can be shaken, as of created things [i.e., this present temporal order of creation, including the present heavens and earth], so that those things which cannot be shaken [i.e., God's eternal kingdom in the new heavens and new earth] may remain" (12:27; cf. 1 Cor. 15:24-28; 2 Peter 1:11; Rev. 11:15).

7. The basic Greek word for "new" used in Rev. 21:1 of the "new [*kainon*] heaven and a new [*kainēn*] earth," is used to describe the Christian as a "new [Gk., *kainē*] creation" (2 Cor. 5:17). Moreover, 21:1 says that "the first heaven and the first earth passed away," and 2 Cor. 5:17 says the same of the Christian. Just as the Christian continues the pre-Christian self, so the new heaven and earth will have continuity with the first. For support of the view that the new heaven and new earth are a renovation, see Gale Z. Heide, "What Is New About the New Heaven and the New Earth? A Theology of Creation from Revelation 21 and 2 Peter 3," *Journal of the Evangelical Theological Society* 40 (March 1997): 38-56. See also Alva J. McClain, *The Greatness of the Kingdom* (Grand Rapids: Zondervan, 1959), 510; and Sauer, *Triumph of the Crucified*, 178-79. The plural form in "present heavens" (2 Peter 3:7; cf. Gen. 1:1; 2 Peter 3:10, 12) and the singular form in "the first heaven" (Rev. 21:1) encompass the whole physical universe besides the earth. The plural "heavens" (Heb., *shāmayim;* Gk., *ouranoi*) refers to the physical heavens. These are the *first heaven*, the atmosphere surrounding the earth (Gen. 1:20; Ps. 147:8; Matt. 26:64; Rev. 19:17) and the *second heaven*, the universe (Gen. 1:14-18; Deut. 4:19; Heb. 11:12). Both the plural form in Isaiah 65:17; 66:22 and 2 Peter 3:13 and the singular form in Revelation 21:1 refer to the physical universe. However, Scripture does not describe the new heavens.

8. Sauer, *Triumph of the Crucified*, 106.

9. Ibid., 181.

10. Matthew alone of the Gospels records that after Christ was raised from the dead, some Old Testament saints also were resurrected and appeared to many (27:52-53). One view is that these saints rose to natural life and would die again. According to this view, only Christ has been raised with a glorified body; the next people to be raised in glorified bodies will be at His coming (1 Cor. 15:23). Wayne Grudem expresses the alternative view, that the resurrected saints were raised to life after Christ and so received glorified bodies "as a kind of foretaste of the final day of glorification when Christ returns." See Wayne Grudem, *Systematic Theology* (Grand Rapids: Zondervan, 1994), 834-35. See also D. A. Carson, *Matthew,* in Frank E. Gaebelein, gen. ed., Expositor's Bible Commentary (Grand Rapids: Zondervan, 1984), 8:581-82.

11. S. Lewis Johnson Jr., "The First Epistle to the Corinthians," in Charles F. Pfeiffer and Everett F. Harrison, eds., *The Wycliffe Bible Commentary* (Chicago: Moody, 1962), 1257-58.

12. Sauer, *Triumph of the Crucified,* 192.

13. Grudem, *Systematic Theology,* 1161.

14. Ibid. Grudem theorizes that "to a glorified body the spiritual body will be 'visible.'"

15. Christ taught that the Spirit would dwell in New Covenant believers permanently (John 14:16-17), and God commands believers to "be filled with [i.e., controlled by] the Spirit" (Eph. 5:18). Surely with glorified, spiritual bodies the Spirit will completely fill or control us.

16. Here we are assuming that persons who die in infancy or with inability to respond to God's message are saved through God's mercy (e.g., 2 Sam. 12:23; Jonah 4:11; Matt. 18:10). The doctrine of infant salvation is debated because Scripture gives so little information.

17. The expression, "He will wipe away every tear from their eyes" (Rev. 21:4), is sometimes understood to mean that, at the judgment seat of Christ, God will wipe away the tears as believers recognize their own failures (2 Cor. 5:10; cf. Rom. 14:10; 1 Cor. 3:11-15). But in the context of verses 1-3, this expression refers to conditions in the eternal state after the first things have passed away. The judgment seat of Christ occurs at or shortly after the Rapture of the church, before the millennium. Since believers appear before the judgment seat of Christ in glorified form, it is unlikely that they will experience negative emotions (cf. Heb. 10:17; 1 Peter 2:24; 3:18). The judgment seat of Christ shows the accountability involved in serving Christ, but the result of a believer's failure in service is apparently limited to loss of reward (1 Cor. 3:11-15).

18. Robert L. Thomas, "New Heaven and New Earth" in Mal Couch, ed., *Dictionary of Premillennial Theology* (Grand Rapids: Kregel, 1996), 283. Walvoord argues for a literal interpretation of the New Jerusalem: "Since it is reasonable to assume that the saints will dwell in the city, it is best to take the city as a literal future dwelling place of the saints and angels" (Walvoord, "Revelation," 986).

19. John does not mention creation of the New Jerusalem at the time it descends, so it could already have been in existence and suspended over the earth. Second, the dimensions of the New Jerusalem prohibit its location on the millennial earth. Also, an earthly Jerusalem and temple exist during the Millennium (Ezek. 40-48). Third, the New Jerusalem could be the visible residence of the glorified saints who reign with Christ, while people in natural bodies are earthbound (Rev. 5:10; 20:4). Fourth, according to Revelation 21:24 and 22:2, "the nations" sustain a relationship to the New Jerusalem, and the mention of nations assumes a millennial setting. However, these references to "the nations" are best understood in the context of the eternal state (21:1-22:5) since the Millennium does not seem to be in view after Revelation 20:11. For further discussion of these issues, see J. Dwight Pentecost, *Things to Come* (Grand Rapids: Zondervan, 1958), 577-79; and John F. Walvoord, *The Revelation of Jesus Christ* (Chicago: Moody, 1966), 312-13, 319.

20. BAGD, 527. Luke 16:9 mentions "eternal dwellings" (Gk., *aiōnious skēnas*), but the terminology differs from that of John 14:2. Some teach that John 14:2-3 does not refer to Christ's literal return for believers. For instance, Robert Gundry thinks that the context of John 14:1-3 is "indicative of a spiritual relationship to the Father through union with Christ" (Robert H. Gundry, *The Church and the Tribulation* [Grand Rapids: Zondervan, 1973], 155). However, the striking parallel between the order of events in John 14:1-3 and those in 1 Thessalonians 4:16-17 and other considerations favor the view that this passage refers to Christ's literal return for believers (Stanley Ellisen, *Biography of a Great Planet* [Wheaton, Ill.: Tyndale, 1975], 112-13). See a thorough discussion of

John 14:2-3 by George R. Beasley-Murray in his *John,* Word Biblical Commentary (Waco, Tex.: Word, 1987), 248–51. Beasley-Murray supports the traditional view that the passage is an eschatological reference to Christ's *parousia.*

21. Sauer believes that the figures for the dimensions of the New Jerusalem indicate a cubical shape and that they should be taken symbolically rather than literally (*Triumph of the Crucified,* 193). He writes, "What matters is the colossal vastness and the symbolic meaning of the sacred number twelve."

22. Again, Walvoord interprets the dimensions and other descriptions of the city in a literal sense (Walvoord, *Revelation,* 319–24), and he suggests that the shape could be the form of a pyramid (ibid., 323).

23. Walvoord, "Revelation," 987.

24. The earth's regenerate state during the Millennium counters but does not remove the curse upon the earth (Isa. 65:20; Matt. 19:28; cf. Gen. 3:17-18; Rom. 8:19-23). There will be no curse in the eternal state (Rev. 22:3). The Millennium will be glorious. Christ will rule in righteousness (Isa. 11:1-5). The Spirit will minister abundantly (Isa. 32:15; Ezek 36:27). People will know the Lord (Isa. 11:9). Satan will be bound (Rev. 20:1-3). World peace will prevail (Isa. 2:4; Micah 5:4-5; Zech. 9:10). Israel will be restored to her land (Amos 9:14-15). The Gentiles will be blessed through Israel (Micah 5:7). Glorified saints will reign with Christ (Rev. 5:10; 20:6). People will live long, healthy lives (Isa. 35:5-6; 65:20-23). There will be plenty of food (Amos 9:13). Nature itself will be at peace (Isa. 11:6-9). On the dark side, sin and death will still occur (11:4; 65:20; Rev. 20:7-10; cf. Gen. 3:17, 19). God's promise to end the curse (Rev. 22:3) will be fulfilled only in the new order, after death, the last enemy, has been abolished (1 Cor. 15:26).

25. In a precise sense God's word is identifiable only with the original manuscripts of Scripture. However, we can properly speak of our present Bible translations as God's inspired word in a derivative and virtual sense in so far as they faithfully represent the original.

26. For further discussion of the biblical concept of spiritual "fruit," see James E. Rosscup, *Abiding in Christ* (Grand Rapids: Zondervan, 1973), 78–90.

27. Believers living at the time of the Rapture will receive glorified bodies equipping them to enter God's eternal kingdom (1 Cor. 15:50-54; 1 Thess. 4:13-17). Unbelievers living at the time of the great white throne judgment apparently will receive bodies suitable to experience eternal punishment in the lake of fire (Rev. 20:11-15).

Name Index

Subject Index

abortion 32, 376, 382, 459-66, 504-6
Abrahamic covenant 157-67, 187, 239, 349, 402, 534, 547, 559, 561
absolute authority 19, 20, 372, 465; God 341-43, 554; morality 388, 402, 501-2; truth 29-33, 39-48, 587
abyss 192, 384, 562
accommodation to culture 24, 66, 95, 371
Adam, covenant with 158, 187, 488; creation and 123, 288, 460, 488-89, 539, 580; death in 143-44, 344, 462-63, 544-45; fallen nature of 122, 130, 133, 143, 232, 237-39, 340-41; genealogy of 127, 464; headship of 440-43, 447; historicity of 24, 87, 134; second 333-34; sin of 121, 137, 142, 375, 451, 570
Africa 188, 372
Agostini decision 485
Aguilar v. Felton 484-85
AIDS 382, 387
Alexandria 174, 225, 227, 399
Alexandrine School 263
Allah 362, 377
American culture. *See* culture, Western.
American Revolution 402, 471-72
amillennialism 21, 26, 192, 324, 328-29
Amish 409
ancient evidence 170-82, 605
Ancient of Days 205
angels 64, 68, 145-55, 204, 212, 231, 301, 318, 357-58, 517, 538, 578; fallen 152-55, 276, 283, 322, 350, 352, 562
angel of light, Satan as 13
Anglican. *See* Church of England.
anthropology 49, 259-60, 340, 343-44, 347, 376, 428, 430, 462
Antichrist 155, 312, 360, 436, 510-13, 528, 536, 558, 561-62, 564
Antioch 225, 232, 291, 293
antirationalism. *See* postmodernism; rationalism.
antisupernaturalism 18

Apollinarians 212
apologetics 16, 52, 92, 211, 256, 261, 264-66, 588, 590, 605
apostasy, coming 14, 192, 509-520, 531; Jewish 188-90; of Western church 13, 337, 429-36
Apostles' Creed 225
appearances, postresurrection 253-55, 258, 260, 266, 606
Arabic 172
Arabs 159, 163, 174
Aramaic 172-73, 179, 181, 257, 600
Ararat 142
archaeology 16, 20, 102, 169-71, 173-75, 77-180, 182, 260, 592, 600-601
archangels 147, 334, 526, 535
Arians 212
Aristides 225
Aristotle 44, 399
Arius 219
ark. *See* flood. 241, 401
Armageddon 420, 558
Arminian theology 81
Articles of Confederation, U.S. 473
arts, creative 73-74, 78, 161, 173, 198-99, 204, 345, 392, 408, 514, 570
Aryans 386
Ashurbanipal 176
Asia 123, 291, 293, 427, 449, 513
astrology 146
Athanasian Creed 308, 609
Athanasius 609
atheism 19, 382, 387-88, 416
atonement 16, 18, 24-25, 93, 217, 223, 239-42; extent of 184, 247-49, satisfaction of God in 205, 243, 554 605; sufficiency of 23, 232, 250-51
Atrahasis Epic 176-77
attributes of God 36-37
Augsburg Confession 308, 589, 605, 622
Augustine 624
authorial-intended hermeneutics 77
authority 45, 47-48, 57, 59, 63, 66, 70, 74, 77, 83-84, 86, 93-99, 102, 104-8, 146-47, 150, 154, 182,

203, 212, 217-18, 251, 268, 270, 282, 290, 296; escape from 377, 426-29, 516-17, 587; of church 396, 470; of Father 300, 343, 466; of government 475-80, 487-508, 622-25; of propositional truth 611; of Scripture 18, 24, 58, 71, 90, 95-96, 312, 340-41, 346-47, 465, 515, 591, 593; of Son 321, 336, 539, 582
autographs 20, 23-24, 593
autonomy 45, 370, 375-77, 412, 415, 487

Baal 83, 189
Babel 369-70, 411, 420-21
baby-boomers 346
baby-busters 346
Babylon 174, 176-77, 188, 226, 397-99
Bahai 360
Bahaullah 388, 516
Baptist 9-10, 16-17, 21, 152, 197, 218, 306, 316, 324, 337
Barna research 31, 356, 587
Barnabas 291, 293, 432-33
Basilides 513
Beast 120, 124, 133, 420, 461, 489, 491
Beelzebub 153, 294
behaviorism 388, 516
Belgic Confession 147
Bhagavad Gita 86
Bible as human document 19; authority of 18, 21, 24, 58, 71, 90, 95-96, 340, 346, 465, 591, 593; conference movement 20-22; English 400; evidence supporting 153, 174, 213, 600-601; fundamentalism and 161; inerrancy of 21, 90-91, 94, 104, 108, 594; infallibility of 16, 23, 26, 66, 88-91, 94-96, 98-101, 103-5, 107-8, 119, 303, 513, 515, 593; inspiration of 16, 18, 20-21, 23-24, 34-35, 66, 85, 87-93, 95, 97, 99, 101, 103-7, 109, 211, 236, 254-55, 284, 290, 303, 399, 592-93
Bible Institute of Los Angeles 16

638

Scripture Index